Derek Walcott & West Indian Drama

Also by Bruce King

V. S. Naipaul
*Three Indian Poets: Ezekiel, Ramanujan and Moraes
Coriolanus
*Modern Indian Poetry in English
The New English Literatures: Cultural Nationalism in a Changing World
History of Seventeenth-Century English Literature
Marvell's Allegorical Poetry
Dryden's Major Plays

Books edited by Bruce King

The Later Fiction of Nadine Gordimer
Post-Colonial English Drama: Commonwealth Drama since 1960
The Commonwealth Novel since 1960
Contemporary American Theatre
West Indian Literature
*A Celebration of Black and African Writing
Literatures of the World in English
Introduction to Nigerian Literature
Dryden's Mind and Art
Twentieth Century Interpretations of 'All for Love'

Series edited by Bruce King

Modern Dramatists
English Dramatists

*Also published by Oxford University Press

Derek Walcott & West Indian Drama

'Not Only a Playwright But a Company'
The Trinidad Theatre Workshop
1959–1993

'I am not only a playwright but a company'
Derek Walcott to Gordon Davidson
13 May 1970

BRUCE KING

Clarendon Press · Oxford
1995

Oxford University Press, Walton Street, Oxford OX2 6DP
Oxford New York
Athens Auckland Bangkok Bombay
Calcutta Cape Town Dar es Salaam Delhi
Florence Hong Kong Istanbul Karachi
Kuala Lumpur Madras Madrid Melbourne
Mexico City Nairobi Paris Singapore
Taipei Tokyo Toronto
and associated companies in
Berlin Ibadan

Oxford is a trade mark of Oxford University Press

Published in the United States
by Oxford University Press Inc., New York

British Library Cataloguing in Publication Data
Data available

Library of Congress Cataloging in Publication Data
King, Bruce Alvin.
Derek Walcott and West Indian drama : not only a playwright but a
company, the Trinidad Theatre Workshop 1959–1993 / Bruce King.
'I am not only a playwright but a company, Derek Walcott to Gordon
Davidson, 13 May 1970.'
Includes bibliographical references.
1. Trinidad Theatre Workshop. 2. Theatre—Trinidad and Tobago—
History—20th century. 3. Walcott, Derek—Criticism and
interpretation. I. Title.
PN2440.T7K56 1995 792'.0972983—dc20 94–33837 CIP
ISBN 0–19–818258–9

1 3 5 7 9 10 8 6 4 2

Typeset by Graphicraft Typesetters Ltd., Hong Kong
Printed in Great Britain
on acid-free paper by
Biddles Ltd., Guildford and King's Lynn

This book is dedicated to
Adele King
and in memory of
Nicole King
(1966–1990)

Preface

ONE of the best poets writing in English, Derek Walcott is also a major dramatist, certainly the most important West Indian dramatist. When he began he saw himself as the heir of such poet dramatists as Marlowe and Shakespeare; as, however, there was little amateur West Indian theatre, and no professional theatre, Walcott at first thought he would need to leave the Caribbean to see his plays properly performed. Instead he decided to stay and create a world-class theatre company which he would lead and direct, and for which he would write. It would be a West Indian equivalent of Brecht's Berlin Ensemble. He would somehow find ways to earn his living from the theatre in the West Indies. He would also create a specifically West Indian style of acting, as distinctive and recognizable as Noh or Kabuki theatre. To do this Walcott had to find the actors, dancers, technicians, and stage hands; he had to produce, design, find theatres for, direct, and stage his plays; he needed to create his audience, raise local critical standards, and shape the debate about the nature and future of Caribbean culture. He would show by doing that the creation of great theatre by a great drama company was the true West Indian revolution, the true liberation from the burden and shame of history, in contrast to tyrannical post-colonial governments that falsely claimed to speak for the people. This is a book about that vision, what was required to transform such a vision into reality, the harsh actualities, and the results in productions of such plays as *Ti-Jean and his Brothers*, *Dream on Monkey Mountain*, *The Joker of Seville* and *O Babylon!*.

This is also a book about Walcott's love of his creation, the Trinidad Theatre Workshop, and the Workshop's love of Walcott through its dedication to his vision of what his actors could achieve. Like most true romances it consists of many details of its heroic struggle to survive, of great accomplishments, disappointments, bitter quarrels, a long separation, and a happy ending. Great lovers and visionaries have obsessions, rages, troubled lives, but unless we see them close up, giving attention to the realities of their lives, we cannot know why they are really great; we will instead be left with a sentimental mythology. Such mythologies about post-colonial arts are dangerous as they mislead us into thinking that culture is somehow created by skin colour, nations, politicians or the folk, or by such abstractions as 'resistance' or 'opposition'. To understand the great outburst of creative energy in the new nations during the second half of the twentieth century we need to pay attention to what the artists were actually doing and why, how they developed their arts, and the problems they faced.

Derek Walcott's creation of and relationship to the Trinidad Theatre Workshop is a great story of our time, as well as an instructive example of how a modern culture was built over the decades from the final years of colonialism to what is currently termed post-colonialism. The story about Walcott and West Indian drama, especially his long struggle to build and develop an actors' studio into a world-class theatre company, has not been told before. It is only known to the participants and a few others who became aware that Walcott's Trinidad Theatre Workshop had become part of theatre and West Indian history, a part that still awaited recognition. I think it is a heroic story.

This book is a detailed history of the Trinidad Theatre Workshop and of Walcott's role in the development of modern West Indian drama. It shows the problems Walcott and the Workshop faced and what they accomplished. It discusses Walcott as a theatre director, the influence of dance on the kind of total theatre he wanted, the relationships between his paintings and plays, and the unique acting style he created. I think that the future will want to know how Walcott's plays were acted and staged. Dates of productions of plays and tours, and information about casts and similar matters are based on programmes, advertisements, various internal TTW documents, and newspaper reviews. Where possible published announcements have been checked against several sources for changes from what was planned. From reviews, articles, and interviews it is possible to establish a detailed chronology of performances and other events. Because of the lack of documentation a few performances during tours in Trinidad and on West Indian islands are not included in the Theatre Calendar. All of this is new to literary criticism of Walcott's work, and I believe that the way I have integrated the study of practical theatre with theatre history and literary criticism is one of the ways cultural history should be written.

I quote from many reviews of plays because, besides their value as history and in showing the contexts of Walcott's plays, West Indian theatre reviews are often of a higher standard than academic literary interpretations of Walcott's plays. Walcott has a first-rate mind and is unusually articulate in explaining in his many articles, letters, and interviews his ideas, goals, and the problems he faced in creating a West Indian theatre; the views he expresses about theatre and drama are also relevant to his poetry. Where possible I offer a précis of what Walcott wrote rather than superfluous commentary of my own. I have no doubt that the story of Walcott and the Trinidad Theatre Workshop will eventually become a recognized part of theatre history as well as illuminating areas of modern culture that have previously been ignored. The relationship of the Rockefeller Foundation to West Indian theatre, for example, is part of a much larger story about foundation patronage of modern culture that needs to be told.

Many topics touched upon in the following chapters are new to scholarship and themselves deserve the attention of literary, dance, theatre, and cultural historians. The Walcott Collection at the University of the West Indies, St Augustine, was still uncatalogued during the time I was using it. The wealth of materials concerning the arts and humanities at the Rockefeller Archives in Tarrytown, New York, has seldom interested scholars. Presumably other foundations have similar gold mines of material. Without basic research, how is it possible to generalize about post-colonialism or anything else? Ethnomusicology is far in advance of literary and cultural studies in its formal analysis, sociology, and awareness that culture is always intercultural and transnational.

B. K.

Acknowledgements

THE idea of writing a history of the Trinidad Theatre Workshop was suggested to me by Derek Walcott who wanted to celebrate the Workshop's thirtieth anniversary. At the time, from the perspective of literary and theatre history, this was mostly unmapped territory. There was no detailed record or chronology of modern West Indian drama or of the Trinidad Theatre Workshop. A National Endowment for the Humanities: Interpretive Research Division grant made the research, travel, and writing possible, for which I am deeply grateful. A grant-in-aid from the Rockefeller Archives allowed me to consult and photocopy its files. Robert Hamner provided me with a preliminary bibliography. My research was made easier by the generous help of Judy Stone, a former TTW actress, theatre producer, arts reviewer and independent scholar who made her files available, even photocopying for me hundreds of documents. Various articles by Victor Questel, along with Irma Goldstraw's *Derek Walcott: An Annotated Bibliography of His Works*, were extremely helpful.

As my work progressed I came to think of it as a community project in which members of the Trinidad Theatre Workshop and others recalled their part in making recent cultural history. There were over eighty hours of recorded interviews, many more hours of discussion; dusty trunks were opened and photographs found; theatre programmes, Workshop rehearsal and tour schedules, reviews, autograph albums, and other documents were made available for photocopying. While much of the material to which I refer is not available in libraries, there are photocopies in my own files. Margaret Walcott and Judy Stone read part of the manuscript for possible errors. Those that remain are my own.

The following list of acknowledgements is poor repayment for all the help I received:

Trinidad Eunice Alleyne, John Andrews, Charles Applewhaite, Michael Beaubrun, Andrew Beddeau, Arthur Bentley, Leonore Bishop, Maurice Brasch, Adele Bynoe, Leone Campbell, Helen Camps, LeRoy Clarke, Clara Rosa de Lima, Noble Douglas, Irma Billie Goldstraw, Laurence Goldstraw, Benny Gomes, Anson Gonzalez, Tony Hall, Wilma Hoyte, Brenda Hughes, John Isaacs, Horace James, Geddes Jennings, Barbara Jenson, Corinne Jones, Errol Jones, Greer Jones, Terry Joseph, Vere Knight, Carol La Chapelle, Albert Laveau, Christopher Laird, Colin Laird, Stanley Marshall, Beryl McBurnie, Norline Metivier, Sonya Moze, Dr Ogundipe, Hamilton Parris, Bruce Pattison, Errol Pilgrim, Claude Reid, Marcia Reilly Slaney, Gordon Rohlehr, Nigel Scott, Eintou Pearl Springer, Sally Stollmeyer, Peter Stollmeyer, Judy Stone, André Tanker, James Lee Wah, Margaret Walcott, George Williams.

St Lucia Father Anthony, Charles Cadet, Pat Charles, Robert Devaux, McDonald Dixon, Mrs Vincent Floissac, Kendel Hippolyte, Arthur Jacobs, Robert Lee, Kenneth Monplaisir, George Odlum, Dunstan St Omer, Margot Thomas, Derek Walcott.

St Thomas Gilbert Sprauve, Mary Alexander.

Grenada Hilda Bynoe, Gloria Payne, Francis Urias Peters, Wilfred Redhead.

Guyana Ian McDonald.

Barbados Kevyn Arthur, Ken Corsbie, Cecily Spenser Cross, Thom Cross, Kathleen Drayton, Andrea Gollop, Oliver Jackman, Alfred Pragnell, Leonard St Hill, Pamela Walcott St Hill, Wendel Smith, John Wickham.

Jamaica Eddie Baugh, Cheryl Dash, Michael Dash, John Hearne, Archie Hudson-Philips, Mary Brathwaite Morgan, Mervyn Morris, Rex Nettleford, Trevor Rhone, Franklyn St Juste, Ralph Thompson, Noel Vaz, Hardclyde Walcott.

Canada Ronald Bryden, Jeff Henry, Slade Hopkinson, Chelva Kanaganayakam, Patrick Taylor, Roderick Walcott.

England Yvonne Brewster, John Figueroa, Bridget Jones, Zack Matalon, Norman Rae.

USA Robert Hamner, Errol Hill, Lynette Laveau, Elena James, Galt MacDermot, Richard Montgomery, Sally Montgomery, Sigrid Nama, Arnold Rampersad, Ken Rose, Tom Rosenbaum, Rhonda Cobham Sander.

Libraries Banyan Company Video Archives; University of the West Indies, St Augustine (West Indian Library, Continuing Education Library and Derek Walcott Collection); National West Indian Reference Library (Trinidad); National Trust (Archaeological & Historical Society, St Lucia); Arthur Lewis Community College (St Lucia); Folklore Research Institute (St Lucia); St Lucia *Voice* files; University Centre (Continuing Studies, St Lucia); National Library (Grenada); University of the West Indies Continuing Education Library (Grenada); Archives of *The Nation* and *The Barbados Advocate* (Barbados); University of the West Indies, Mona (West Indian Collection, Creative Arts Centre, School of Continuing Education); Jamaican Institute and National Library;

Media Center, University of Toronto; Rockefeller Archive Center (Tarrytown, New York); Ball State University.

I assume that this book is only the beginning of detailed research into an important part of Walcott's life. The Walcott Archives at the University of the West Indies, St Augustine, include drafts of his plays, production notes, drawings for productions, and other materials that should interest scholars. I would like to think that many of the artists mentioned in this book will themselves become the subject of study. We need less careless vapourizing about 'race', 'class', and 'gender', and more research into and analysis of the life and work of Roderick Walcott, Dennis Scott, André Tanker, Carol La Chapelle, George Williams, Andrew Beddeau, Lennox Brown, Trevor Rhone, Errol Jones, Albert Laveau, Helen Camps, Michael Gilkes and others who shaped modern West Indian culture.

Contents

List of Illustrations   xv

Part I Roots 1948–1965

1. 1948–1959 Forming a Vision   3
2. 1959–1965 The Little Carib Theatre Workshop   30

Part II The Great Years (West Indian Style) 1966–1976

3. 1966 The Basement Theatre The First Season   55
4. 1967 *Dream on Monkey Mountain* in Canada
         The First Tours   75
5. 1968 *Dream on Monkey Mountain* *Henri Christophe*
         Homeless Again The Five-Island Tour   87
6. 1969 *Dream* in Connecticut and for NBC   107
7. 1970 A New *Ti-Jean* Black Power Aquarius IV   122
8. 1971 *Ti-Jean* and *Dream* in Jamaica *In A Fine Castle*   147
9. 1972 *Ti-Jean* in Central Park Astor Johnson
         Theatre Fifteen *Pieces One*   162
10. 1973 The Second Season *Franklin* *The Charlatan*   178
11. 1974 An American *Charlatan* A New *Dream*
          A West Indian *The Joker of Seville*   196
12. 1975 *The Joker* Revised and on Tour   220
13. 1976 *O Babylon!* Carifesta TTW Dance Company
          Walcott's Resignation   242

Part III Separation and Reconciliation 1977–1993

14. 1977–1983 The Trinidad Theatre Workshop and
               Dance Company   269
15. Walcott 1977–1981 *Pantomime* *Remembrance*
                       Marie Laveau   288

xiv   **Contents**

16. Walcott 1982–1983   *The Last Carnival   A Branch of the
                         Blue Nile*   310
17. Walcott 1984–1990   *Haytian Earth*   Another New
                         Dream   Another *Branch*
                         Another *Franklin*   324
18. 1984–1993   The Trinidad Theatre Workshop   'Let
                Resurrection Come!'   341

        Theatre Calendar   363

        Select Bibliography   374

        Index   395

List of Illustrations

Between pages 208–209

1a Albert Laveau and Derek Walcott, 1966, Little Basement Theatre.
1b *The Blacks*, Basement Theatre, 1966.
1c *The Sea at Dauphin*, Basement Theatre, 1966. Photo: Hollister Chong.
2a *Dream on Monkey Mountain*. Rehearsal, Basement theatre, 1967. Photo: Hollister Chong.
2b *Dream on Monkey Mountain*. Queen's Hall, 1968. Photo: Hollister Chong.
3a *Henri Christophe*, 1968.
3b *Dream on Monkey Mountain*. From television production, 1969.
4a *Ti-Jean and His Brothers*, 1970. Photo: Hollister Chong.
4b *The Charlatan*, 1973.
5a *The Joker of Seville*. Little Carib Theatre, 1974. Photo: Albert Laveau (?)
5b *The Joker of Seville*. Little Carib Theatre, 1974. Photo: Albert Laveau (?)
6a *O Babylon!* Little Theatre, Kingston, Jamaica, 1976.
6b *O Babylon!*, 1976.
7a *Pantomime*. The Boston Playwrights' Theatre, 1993. Photo: Joshua Lavine.
7b Albert Laveau and Derek Walcott, backstage at the Boston Playwrights' Theatre, 1993. Photo: Bill Grant.
8a *Ti-Jean and His Brothers* and *Nobel Celebration*. Rehearsal, Boston, 1993. Photo: Bill Grant.
8b *Nobel Celebration*, Boston, 1993. Photo: Bill Grant.

PART I

Roots

1948–1965

1948–1959

Forming a Vision

AFTER Derek Walcott was awarded the 1992 Nobel Prize in Literature *A Nobel Celebration* was staged in Boston during April 1993 with scenes from his plays performed by the Trinidad Theatre Workshop which he founded in 1959 and led until late 1976. Among the performers were many of the actors and dancers around whom Walcott had built his theatre company, held weekly workshops, premièred his plays, and toured through the West Indies. Errol Jones had first acted in a Walcott play during 1954, joined Walcott's Theatre Workshop when it began and remained one of its leading actors. After Walcott resigned as Artistic Director of the Trinidad Theatre Workshop, Jones along with Stanley Marshall, Claude Reid, Albert Laveau, and Nigel Scott kept the Workshop going, sometimes as barely more than a production company; in recent years they acquired a theatre of their own, Albert Laveau became Artistic Director and the Trinidad Theatre Workshop began again having regular productions and teaching the performing arts.

Others in the Boston *Celebration* who were at times important Trinidad Theatre Workshop regulars included the dancers Adele Bynoe and Carol La Chapelle and the musical director André Tanker. Jones has become probably the most famous and respected West Indian actor, while La Chapelle as a choreographer has a significant place in the development of modern dance in Trinidad. Tanker, who came to Boston directly from the Lincoln Center in New York where he provided music for a play by Mustapha Matura, is regarded in Trinidad as a composer, musician, and leader of world-class ability who shies away from international recognition. Asked by several companies to remain in the United States so he could record, he said that he was not ready yet and returned to Trinidad.

Walcott had devoted many years of his life to make the Trinidad Theatre Workshop into the equivalent of a national theatre company, an ensemble of international ability, which he hoped would perform his plays on Broadway and in the West End, proving to the world that West Indian drama, theatre, dance, and music were of the highest standards. The few foreign theatre directors who saw the Trinidad Theatre Workshop in performance agreed with Walcott's estimation, but American union rules, the expense of taking the Trinidad Theatre Workshop abroad, and other problems limited the company to tours of the West Indies, and a few short appearances in North America, often without making any profit.

There was the inherent irrationality of the situation in terms of commercial American and British theatre. Where would paying audiences be found for plays written in complex verse, having Caribbean subject matter and themes, filled with West Indian idioms and allusions, and acted in a West Indian gestural manner with Trinidadian pronunciation? Joseph Papp had produced Walcott's *Ti-Jean and his Brothers* in New York and sent it on tour of the Boroughs only to be faced by the incomprehension of young African Americans to its Caribbean folk-tale. A shortened version of *Dream on Monkey Mountain* was filmed for American television and a production by the Negro Ensemble Company was awarded an Obie, but Equity had prevented Walcott from using his Trinidad actors in American productions. Since then Walcott's plays had become more complex, more expensive to stage. The Royal Shakespeare Company commissioned Walcott's *The Joker of Seville*, but after Terry Hands saw the wildly successful Trinidad Theatre Workshop production in Port of Spain he realized that there was no way an English company could create a comparable theatre experience in London. The more successful Walcott was, the more strain there was on his actors. Eventually there was a quarrel, Walcott resigned from the Trinidad Theatre Workshop and a few years later he began teaching at universities in the United States. He, however, was never satisfied with non-West Indian productions of his plays, and he remained in contact with the Trinidad Theatre Workshop, usually premièred his plays in the West Indies, and, after his Nobel award, began once more working with the Trinidad Theatre Workshop, which he still considered his company, the one theatre company that knew how his plays should be acted.

During conversations between rehearsals and at a farewell dinner after the Boston *Celebration*, Walcott talked to his company about his vision of their future as if nothing had intervened between 1976 and

1993 and he was picking up from yesterday. There were possibilities of American performances and tours abroad to Europe and Asia. Theatre people who had seen them in Boston would tell others. Walcott and the Trinidad Theatre Workshop were active once more. There were further productions of *Celebration* in the West Indies and a dramatized reading of Walcott's play *The Odyssey* in Port of Spain during August 1993. Eunice Alleyne, one of the original Workshop actors, came to the United States for a reading of *The Odyssey* in New York during September. Meanwhile the Workshop was performing *Dream on Monkey Mountain* in the Netherlands, followed by performances in Trinidad. There were many of the same problems as in the past— union regulations, finances, amateur actors with regular day-time jobs that would not allow time off for tours abroad—but Walcott was again in his visionary mode, the same mode that shaped his poetry and which made him the natural leader of the Trinidad Theatre Workshop and West Indian drama for many decades. It was a vision that required immense faith, dedication, discipline, and hard work from everyone. His own talent, faith, dedication, and discipline had taken him from the self-publication of his first volumes of poetry in St Lucia and Jamaica to the Nobel Prize. As much spirit and effort had gone into the Trinidad Theatre Workshop. Walcott was determined that his achievement in the theatre and that of his theatre company should be recognized. In his sixties Walcott took up again what he had begun in 1959 and which had its origins in the late 1940s when he began writing plays and when modern West Indian drama started.[1]

There had of course been theatre in the West Indies for centuries. The islands had wealthy white settlers at a time when most of North America was still frontier. When George Washington visited Barbados in 1751 he hoped to attend a performance at the Garrison Theatre. A touring circuit for European artists that included North America, the Caribbean, and South America still functioned until the 1950s. There were sporadic attempts to create local, racially mixed, or non-white, theatre, such as the Georgetown Dramatic Club, founded in 1891 for coloured people, or the British Guyana Dramatic Society, which existed between 1936 and 1948, to promote the Indian plays of Tagore and Kalidasa (and which excluded 'coloured'). Such groups, usually no more than social clubs, produced no dramatists, actors, or productions of note and are obscure footnotes in West Indian theatre and cultural history.[2]

Throughout the twentieth century West Indian intellectuals and men of letters wrote plays and a few were performed. C. L. R. James's pageant *The Black Jacobins* is sometimes republished. The novelist Roger Mais wrote many plays, but he had no ability to turn ideas into theatrical images, and his scripts can read like pastiches of the verse plays of Byron and other nineteenth-century poets. Norman Cameron tried to make British Guyana aware of the possibilities of local theatre, but his plays were not produced when the new West Indian drama groups began looking for local material to perform. Similar to many other modern artistic movements that developed during the late colonial and early independence period, modern West Indian drama has no direct links to earlier colonial arts. West Indian novelists working within conventions of realism might build on earlier fiction, but for the modern West Indian dramatist, like the modern Indian poet writing in English, there were no useful models to use. Colonial culture is usually out of date, provincial, and imitative. Colonial societies modernize as they develop towards independence, even modernizing various cultural traditions of the past into a usable national history. So the new national arts find ways of blending representative aspects of local culture with the models and attitudes of the modern international culture.[3]

Before 1948 most high culture was imported and there was little in the way of indigenous theatre. The few local amateur theatre groups were white, with some light-skinned non-whites, and performed European or American plays. The British West Indies consisted of colonies governed by the British and most of its literary culture was British. There were few secondary schools, no local universities; training in the professions and performing arts had to be acquired abroad. The best earlier West Indian writers, such as Jean Rhys or Claude McKay, left and lived abroad. West Indian literature as we know it now began in the 1940s and 1950s with Edgar Mittelholzer, Samuel Selvon, John Hearne, V. S. Naipaul, and Derek Walcott. Theatre is a communal activity requiring producers, directors, actors, dramatists, performance spaces, rehearsals, lighting, scenic designers, money, and an audience. In the West Indies, as in most of the former British Empire, the conditions were not right for local serious theatre until after the Second World War.[4]

During the Second World War the political and cultural climate began to change. The war isolated the colonies from England, led to the development of local industries, created new sources of wealth, increased the value of exports, and resulted in the liberalizing presence of American soldiers with their money and less rigid class and cultural prejudices. Immediately after the war there was talk of independence, the return from London of students inspired by Indian and African ideas of political freedom, and the arrival of a new generation of white immigrants with more liberal racial and social ideals. Throughout the former colonies political and cultural decolonization had begun; to prepare the colonies for independence there were local elections and the development of local political parties, more advanced jobs available for non-whites, an increasing interest in local culture, more scholarships to study abroad, and the building of new universities. Versions of what happened in the West Indies occurred elsewhere. India became independent and Pakistan was created in 1947. Ghana became independent in 1957, Nigeria in 1960. The West Indian Federation, which lasted from 1958 until 1962, was part of the withdrawal of the British Empire, and an attempt to create a modern state, a governing elite, and a local high culture to replace what was being taken away. The sun of the Empire was setting. The mixture of suspicion, scorn, enthusiasm, and support which West Indian drama received at the time was echoed by the reception of the new drama companies and dramatists in Canada, New Zealand, and Nigeria for over a decade.

There is an unfortunate tendency to regard the West Indies in simplistic polarities derived from North American history and social prejudices whereas the eastern Caribbean islands have had an especially complex history. St Lucian history and culture cannot be reduced to the simplicities of black versus white. For most of its history the island where Derek Walcott was born was either governed by the French or when under British rule continued to speak French and be influenced by French customs and law. Because the French and English, who fought over the magnificent harbour at Castries, enlisted black support for their cause, and because of French attitudes towards blacks, many St Lucians, like many Trinidadians, regard their island as having had only fifty years of slavery, the period of British rule before emancipation.

Green, mountainous, heavily forested, with dirt roads often unusable during heavy rains, St Lucia is still not an easy place in which to travel and many villages were until recent times largely isolated; travel to the French-speaking island of Martinique is easier and there is a constant flow of people, goods, and culture between the two islands. While St Lucia's original Amerindian culture is extinct, the island has villages in which African culture in the form of music, dance, and customs still survives and is passed on from generation to generation as a consciously African heritage. There is also a rich national folk culture of partly French, partly African origins. Although St Lucians have become bilingual, patois is still the language most people speak among themselves and until recently most education was controlled by the French Catholic church. In such a context the overwhelming majority of the population regard themselves as black French-Catholic Creoles and the social composition of the island in the 1940s would have ranged from white British administrators, a few older white French settlers, expatriate French and Irish priests, to a black patois-speaking Catholic majority and to isolated villages still retaining African customs. A local patois folk culture had centuries earlier developed with its own annual festivals organized by various 'societies' of probably mixed French and African origins. British rule created further levels in the social spectrum. Besides the expatriate officials, and the occasional English settler, lighter-skinned English-speaking West Indians immigrated to St Lucia. As elsewhere in the West Indies, shades of skin colour in the past were and still may be the basis of social distinctions, but, beyond the poverty that characterized so many colonies, St Lucia does not have the bitter racial history of Jamaica or Cuba.

Derek Walcott and his twin brother Roderick were born in Castries, St Lucia, 23 January 1930. Their father, Warwick, died the next year and they were raised by their mother, Alix, a headmistress of the local Methodist Infant school. Derek has light skin and, like many St Lucians, green eyes. In the West Indies, where 'Negro' is still often used to describe people of African and part African descent, Derek's place on the colour spectrum is 'red', someone more negroid in features than a 'near white', but lighter than most middle-class 'browns' and 'coloureds'. Derek Walcott was born into a small but important social class of English speakers, mostly Methodists, who had their own school that produced many of the island's leading politicians, professionals, and intellectuals. Within St Lucia the Methodists were a minority, energetic, progressive, and, being at home in English culture, close to the governing elite. Like many of the West Indian islands, in St Lucia education was of extremely high standard and limited to those who could attend the few church schools. The West Indian school teachers of previous generations remain justifiable legends celebrated by many West Indian writers including Walcott. Strict disciplinarians with an excellent command of Latin and Greek, at home in European and classical literature, the teachers had large libraries, subscribed to the latest British literary and political journals, and provided those who could attend their classes with an education far superior to that available in most North American or European schools. Those students who managed to go abroad for further education usually excelled. The 1979 Nobel prize-winning St Lucian economist Arthur Lewis is probably the best-known product of St Lucia's educational system before Derek Walcott; both Lewis and Walcott attended St Mary's College.[5]

Derek Walcott's father was a civil servant, a Deputy Registrar, with a broad interest in the arts. Although self-educated, he was part of a group that held play readings and he was an amateur painter. Although Warwick died before he could directly influence his two sons, his reputation for learning and interest in the arts was passed on by his wife and friends and became a model for his children.[6]

In St Lucia Derek received an excellent education both in school and outside. After the Methodist primary school he moved to St Mary's College, 1941–7, where, besides following a syllabus that included Latin, there were young Irish teachers who talked about Yeats, Synge, the Abbey Theatre, and Irish nationalism. Outside school Derek's father's friends lent him books and discussed literature and culture. His mother early had ambitions for him and encouraged his writing. Walcott learned at an early age to stand up to those in authority; by the time he was fourteen he had already become a local celebrity by publishing a poem in the *Voice of St Lucia* which a local priest denounced as blasphemous. Later attacks on him by politicians and intellectuals seemed a natural part of what an artist in small West Indian communities had to face. He began writing poetry while still a child and from the age of sixteen he was writing verse plays. His interest in the theatre was supported by the Methodist school which gave 'concerts'. Soon a group of friends was formed to read and perform the plays Walcott wrote while still in school.[7]

An important influence was Harold Simmons, a local painter with an unlimited interest in local arts, customs, music, and folklore. Simmons and Walcott travelled by boat to otherwise inaccessible villages to study local folk-ways; Simmons also encouraged Walcott as a painter, lending him his studio. This period, when Derek Walcott, Dunstan St Omer and Simmons felt they were the Van Goghs and Impressionists of a new St Lucian culture, has been written about in Walcott's autobiographical poem *Another Life*. Simmons was from a distinguished family; St Omer was darker-skinned, green-eyed, and from a poor Catholic family. Simmons painted water-colours, St Omer was to become the first eminent St Lucian modernist painter and famous for his church murals. Irving Stone's *Dear Theo: The Autobiography of Vincent Van Gogh* was probably more influential on Walcott and many other West Indian artists of this period than any immediate concern with the politics of decolonization. Rather their aim was to live fully, to create, to break through the confines of stuffy provincial colonial culture with its social distinctions, inhibiting manners and values, and old-fashioned tastes. They wanted to paint and write about the world around them; they wanted to discover and make use of the world's culture, especially modern European art. After graduating from St Mary's Walcott stayed on at the college for a time as a tutor. While in St Lucia he published his first books of poems (*25 Poems*, 1948; *Epitaph for the Young*, 1949) and wrote plays including *Harry Dernier* (1946), *Another World for the Lost* (1947) and *Henri Christophe* (1949). His *Senza Alcun Sospetto* (also known as *Paolo and Francesca*) was broadcast by the BBC Caribbean Voices programme in London on 28 May 1950. The same year he co-founded with Maurice Mason the St Lucia Arts Guild. On 9 September 1950, Walcott directed his *Henri Christophe* at St Joseph's Convent, the first full-length play performed by the Arts Guild.[8]

When Derek left for University College of the West Indies, Jamaica, later in September 1950, his brother Roderick became the leader of the Arts Guild and began directing plays. The Arts Guild presented Derek's *Paolo and Francesca* and *Three Assassins* along with scenes from Shakespeare at the St Joseph's Convent 28 March 1951. Roderick directed productions of Marlowe's *Doctor Faustus* (1951), *Richard II* (1952), Tennessee Williams's *I Rise in Flames* and Christopher Fry's *A Phoenix Too Frequent* (1953), Derek's *The Sea at Dauphin* (1954), three one-act plays by Anton Chekhov (1955) and then himself became a dramatist. He directed his three one-act plays, *The Harrowing of Benjy*, *Shrove Tuesday March* and *The One Eye is King* (1956) and Derek's *Ti-Jean and his Brothers* (1957).

The early formative period of modern West Indian drama lasted for two decades from, say, 1947 until 1966 when the Trinidad Theatre Workshop began regularly performing as a company. After the war the British Council began actively promoting British literature, especially British drama, throughout the colonies; often this led to the formation of local drama groups, the writing of plays, and a few scholarships to England for training in the performing arts. There were annual competitions for the best poems, short stories, and plays. The BBC Overseas Services also broadcast to India and the Caribbean the newly discovered writers. (Like many other topics touched upon in the following pages, a book needs to be written on the subject; George Orwell was involved with the broadcasts to India.) Around 1947 Errol Hill started, with British Council support, the Whitehall Players in Port of Spain, Trinidad, which was the first predominantly non-white, interracial theatre group on the island. He was soon followed by his brother Sydney Hill, Horace James, the playwright actor Freddie Kissoon, and others.

Trinidad soon had a small but developing local theatre movement. Errol Hill left for professional theatre training in London on a British Council scholarship and was subsequently appointed, along with Noel Vaz (a Jamaican who had trained at the Old Vic), as a tutor in Drama in the Extra-Mural Department at the new University College of the West Indies. They advised the University Drama Society and travelled to other islands giving drama workshops. Grenada for a short time had a small but interesting dramatic movement, but when Wilfred Redhead, the only dramatist of importance, left for Barbados, activity became intermittent. Barbados, British Guyana and other places had white expatriate theatre groups and school plays. By 1956 Guyana had an interracial Theatre Guild with good actors, but without notable local dramatists. For over a decade the new West Indian drama was mostly to be found in Trinidad, St Lucia and Jamaica.

In the early period modern West Indian drama depended on the presence of a creative dramatist who was usually also a director and producer of plays. There was no canon of local plays, no theatre companies, performance spaces, or a pool of trained non-white actors upon which a director could draw to stage productions. There was no audience used to paying to attend serious theatre and it was thought that audiences needed a variety of entertainment during an evening including skits, one-act plays, poetry reading, and music. The move from such 'concerts' to theatre began with evenings devoted to several one-act plays. Productions were for only one or two performances, usually in the auditorium of a school as no other suitable space existed.

The St Lucia Arts Guild under Roderick's leadership became one of the leading new drama companies in the West Indies and Roderick Walcott was himself considered a significant dramatist whose plays some critics at the time preferred to those of his brother. His *Harrowing of Benjy* won the Best West Indian Comedy award at the Adults Drama Festival in Jamaica in 1957. The Arts Guild was the first of the new West Indian drama companies to tour the islands, premièred some of Derek's early plays, and continued to develop until 1968 when Roderick moved to Canada, after which it would annually be resurrected for 'national' productions sponsored by the St Lucia government.

Along with Derek Walcott a group of dramatists, actors and directors came together at the University College of the West Indies, Jamaica, between 1950 and 1957. These were the golden years of Jamaican theatre when many talented young people from the region were in

Jamaica forming small theatre companies and performing the first modern West Indian plays by Derek Walcott, Roderick Walcott, Errol Hill, Slade Hopkinson, and others. This was slightly earlier than but similar to the outburst of good writing in Nigeria during the late 1950s and early 1960s when Wole Soyinka, Chinua Achebe, Christopher Okigbo, and J. P. Clark were at the University College Ibadan and part of the Mbari Club.

The University College of the West Indies was founded in 1948 with a Medical School and in 1950 had its first intake of General Degree Arts students, including Walcott, to prepare school teachers. Walcott, who studied French, Spanish, and English, rapidly started two student magazines, *The Barb* and *The Pelican*, was a leader of the literary society and a writers' workshop, gave lessons in painting, played drums, became President of the University Drama Society, directed plays, and was recognized, even while an undergraduate, as a significant writer and creative intellectual, besides being known for his dirty blue jeans, haughty manner, and witty barbed tongue. He painted a mural on the walls of the Student Union building. The Drama Society had readings of one-act plays and G. B. Shaw's *Saint Joan* (1950); Walcott directed his own *Harry Dernier* (1952) aided by Slade Hopkinson, and graduated the next year.[9]

Walcott was already becoming famous among his generation and those involved with developing West Indian literature and theatre. His plays were being performed by the new amateur groups throughout the region and even in London. *Henri Christophe* was produced in London 25–27 January 1952, at the Hans Crescent House, Colonial Students' Residence by the West Indian Student Association with a cast that included many names that would soon become famous in Caribbean literature, culture, and politics. Those involved in the production were Errol Hill, the novelist George Lamming, the dramatist Frank Pilgrim, Maurice Mason and Kenneth Monplaisir from the St Lucia Arts Guild, the future Prime Minister of Trinidad A. N. R. Robinson, the dramatist Errol John, Roy Augier, Noel Vaz, and the Trinidadian artist Carlisle Chang. The group, with V. S. Naipaul taking the part of Hounakin, performed Walcott's *Sea at Dauphin*. It also read *Henri Christophe* (1951), *Harry Dernier* (1952), and other plays on the BBC Caribbean Voices programme.[10]

The cultural and political significance of the new West Indian drama groups, theatre, and especially Walcott's plays can be seen from a review of the 1952 London production of *Henri Christophe*:

In the development of an indigenous culture in the Caribbean (and no West Indian Federation can be really without it) no element is of greater potential importance than a West Indian theatre, for the theatre is the meeting place and the nursery of the arts. At the same time the initial obstacles are formidable. The three essential elements in the theatre—the playwright, the actor and the audience—must exist together if the theatre is to be a living reality in the life of the people. This condition has not hitherto existed in the West Indies. . . . There have certainly been writers, actors and audiences in the West Indies in the past, but not West Indian writers of West Indian plays for West Indian actors to perform to West Indian audiences. . . . In this critical stage of development of a West Indian theatre, the recent production of *Henri Christophe* . . . is an event of the first importance. It was in every way a West Indian production.[11]

Walcott stayed on at UCWI for a year avoiding his courses in Education, then taught in a secondary school for six months in Grenada, returned to Jamaica as a teacher in Jamaica College and quit to join the staff of the journal *Public Opinion*. Walcott's reputation as a dramatist continued to develop. *Henri Christophe*, directed by Walcott, was performed by the University Players, March 1954, with a cast that included Slade Hopkinson and the soon-to-be-famous dancer and choreographer Rex Nettleford. The stage manager was James Lee Wah from Trinidad who would return to form his own theatre group in San Fernando; Mary Brathwaite, sister of the now famous poet Edward Kamau Brathwaite, was Walcott's assistant and in charge of properties.

A few months later, Walcott's *The Sea at Dauphin* was among the first plays that Errol Hill published in the Extra-Mural Department's *Caribbean Plays* series, a series which for many years provided the only available texts of West Indian drama for the new acting groups. At first the *Caribbean Plays* were cyclostyled like acting scripts, later they were printed. Hill produced *Sea at Dauphin* in August 1954, in Port of Spain, Trinidad, with Errol Jones taking the role of Afa. This was the first time Jones, who was to become a foundation member of the Trinidad Theatre Workshop, heard of Walcott. (Walcott has said that what he originally assumed was the African-sounding name of a St Lucian fisherman, 'Afa', was probably his own mishearing of 'Arthur'.) In November Hill directed *Henri Christophe* in Port of Spain, again with Errol Jones. Eric Williams, the future Trinidadian prime minister, wrote the prologue for this production. Many of the people whom Walcott would soon be working with in Trinidad were in the cast and production crew. In December 1954 Roderick Walcott directed *The*

Sea at Dauphin with the Arts Guild in St Lucia. Around this time an early version of Walcott's *The Charlatan* was performed by the University Players with Walcott directing. Late in 1955 Walcott spoke to the University Drama Society about 'Poetic Drama in the Twentieth Century'. During 1956 *The Pelican* announced that Walcott's *Countess of Quinine* 'is unfortunately not yet available', but promised a production of *The Sea at Dauphin*, which was directed by Slade Hopkinson in April. It included Rex Nettleford as Augustin, and was taken on tour around Jamaica by Mary Brathwaite. It was awarded the prize for the 'Best West Indian Tragedy' in that year's Jamaica Adult Drama Festival.

Apparently Walcott and others in his circle had already been thinking about the problems of writing plays in West Indian forms of English. Slade Hopkinson, writing in *The Daily Gleaner* about *The Sea at Dauphin*, mentions that while the idiom is 'a little difficult to the non-St Lucian' the play 'is clarified for the spectator through dramatisation'; the meaning can be found in the action, gestures, facial expression, and intonations of the actors. During August 1956, Slade Hopkinson produced and Walcott directed Walcott's new play *The Wine of the Country* on campus and then moved it to the Ward Theatre in Kingston. During March 1957 the Federal Theatre Company, recently formed by Errol Hill, Slade Hopkinson, Ronnie Llanos, and Carmen Manley, presented Walcott's *Ione* at the Ward Theatre with Errol Hill and Ronnie Llanos as co-directors. In December Slade Hopkinson directed three one-act plays in Montego Bay; they included Derek Walcott's *Cross Roads* (an early version of *Malcochon*) and Roderick's *A Flight of Sparrows*, along with a play by Hopkinson.[12]

The plays that Walcott wrote were often controversial with critics polarized for and against. As during the mid- and late-1950s Errol Hill, the Reckord brothers and others were also gaining attention as up-and-coming West Indian dramatists, some West Indian critics appeared confused by the way Walcott's plays were rapidly becoming the staple diet of the new theatre groups and were being played abroad in art theatres and by West Indian companies in England. As Walcott restlessly experimented with different kinds of plays each play brought about a minor explosion from some critic. The headline of a review of *The Sea at Dauphin* was 'Not the Stuff for a West Indian Theatre', of *Malcochon* 'Arts Guild Play Objectionable', and of *Ione* 'Colourful but Academic'. Walcott replied to the latter review by objecting to closed minds concerning the form and subject-matter of West Indian theatre. The stage will be as violent or crude as the life it represents.

The critic 'cannot foresee what form our tragic theatre will take'. 'Those people who are seeking for myths in the arts are wasting their faith. There has only been one myth, in several disguises, and that is the pride of man and the pride of God, depending on the kind of pessimism of your own time.' This seems to me as good an interpretation of *The Sea at Dauphin* and other Walcott plays of this period as any I have read, and it might be kept in mind when reading his later plays.[13]

Walcott was dissatisfied with his life in the West Indies. He had married early to Faye Moyston (1954; they were divorced in 1959), had a son, Peter, but there were no obvious opportunities for Walcott to use his talents as a serious writer. The first West Indian novelists after the war had emigrated to England and were now beginning to be published. There were no local publishing houses for serious literature, and few theatres beyond the recently established Little Theatre of Jamaica, with its still largely British outlook and where creativity meant the West Indianization of the Christmas pantomime. Walcott's likely future was that of an alienated teacher or newspaper writer living on a poor salary, complaining about provincial, colonial life, and corrupt local politicians. His disaffection was no different from that, say, of V. S. Naipaul or of other West Indian writers of the time. Emigration to England seemed likely. Only outside the West Indies, in exile, could you be a West Indian writer. The modernist classics, and the lives of writers such as James Joyce and T. S. Eliot, seemed to point towards expatriation and alienation, an attitude reinforced by a view, common in the West Indies at the time, of the artist as a bohemian, a Van Gogh living for his art. Even the novelists Roger Mais and John Hearne, both of whom are now thought to be 'political', regarded themselves as free spirits and lived for a time as impoverished romantics in southern France. John Hearne, whom he knew in Jamaica, told Walcott that it was necessary to meet international standards; Hearne was published by Faber. Praise came too easily in the West Indies, but seldom led to the artist's development.[14]

It was in the hope of keeping Walcott and other talented artists in the West Indies that the Rockefeller Foundation soon became involved in plans for creating a regional 'national' theatre centred on the Little Carib Theatre in Port of Spain, Trinidad. The Rockefeller Foundation since the 1930s had aided some university drama groups and community theatres in the United States. After the Second World War the Foundation's interests began to turn abroad. It rather cautiously provided grants to enable a few theatre departments to get off the ground, especially the new School of Drama at the University of Ibadan, Nigeria, and the Extra Mural Department of the University College of the West Indies, which was created to develop the Performing Arts in the region. Philip Sherlock, Director of the Extra Mural Department, acting Vice Principal and future Vice Chancellor, believed that the performing arts were the cement that might bring the various peoples, religions, and places of the West Indies together into a shared culture. His first two appointments as Extra-Mural tutors were Errol Hill and Noel Vaz. Through the University College of the West Indies Extra-Mural Department the Rockefeller Foundation reluctantly became involved with a proposed Arts Festival which would celebrate the inauguration of the West Indian Federation in 1958 and for which Walcott was commissioned by the University to write a pageant play.[15]

In 1956 Philip Sherlock wrote to Thomas Patterson of the Stratford Shakespeare Festival Foundation of Canada asking for help with a proposed Caribbean Arts festival. Patterson was the moving force behind the Stratford Festival, had persuaded Tyrone Guthrie to leave stardom in London for then provincial Ontario, and between Patterson and Guthrie the Festival quickly became an international attraction, a model for other new drama groups in the British colonies and dominions that were trying to establish their own theatres. Until then theatre in the British Empire consisted largely of touring professional productions imported from London and New York or sporadic, very amateurish, untrained, local drama groups with genteel and arty pretensions. Anyone seriously interested in theatre had to leave the colonies for professional training and a career.[16]

Patterson, who previously had help from the Foundation, discussed with J. P. Harrison of the Rockefeller Foundation the need to give professional advice, perhaps sending Guthrie to be Festival Director. With the Stratford model of attracting tourists in mind, Guthrie was thinking of premiering at the Festival, and then transferring to Broadway, a musical play that Duke Ellington had written. As the Caribbean Festival was planned to coincide with the opening of the West Indian Federation in 1958, the West Indians, especially Errol Hill, wanted a West Indian to write a play as the centre piece of the occasion. In Jamaica, Robert Verity, who was Chairman of Jamaica's contribution to the West Indies Festival of the Arts, mentioned to Walcott during the summer of 1957 that he would be commissioned to write an epic pageant as the centre piece of the Festival as the University College's contribution to the Festival.[17]

In June 1957, during a trip to South America, Harrison visited

Trinidad and met Noel Vaz and Beryl McBurnie. Vaz claimed that drama was the most significant art form in the region and would have the most impact on local thought. The Festival would influence how West Indian drama developed as previously local talents had fled the islands for careers in the arts abroad. The only outstanding artist who had remained was Beryl McBurnie, who returned from a successful career as a dancer abroad to create her own dance company and train local dancers at her Little Carib Theatre. Derek Walcott was clearly the best dramatist and poet to appear in many generations, but wanted to go to England so that his plays could be performed and he could gain recognition. McBurnie pointed out that such dancers as Bosco Holder and Percy Borde (whom she had developed) and the actor-dramatist Errol John had left Trinidad because of the lack of opportunities. Harrison also met with various local politicians including the Acting Chief Minister Patrick Solomon who wanted Rockefeller Foundation co-operation in producing the Festival as the cost would cause local criticism. He and his political party wanted to encourage the Arts but they did not have the resources, support, or talents to do the Festival on their own. They would at least need technical assistance from outside. If Guthrie would not visit Trinidad, could a group including Vaz and Derek Walcott visit Guthrie and ask him to give advice and perhaps be Director?[18]

The Rockefeller Humanities Drama programme awarded $2,000 to the University College of the West Indies for Vaz, Errol Hill, and Walcott to travel in September 1957 to Stratford, Ontario, and New York to consult with Guthrie and others. The trip proved unexpectedly productive to Walcott. Besides hearing Guthrie's advice about the pageant, Walcott met the actress Siobhán McKenna with whom he discussed the Abbey Theatre and W. B. Yeats. In New York, feeling lost and frightened in his hotel, in three days he rapidly wrote Ti-Jean and his Brothers, based on St Lucia's folk lore. Derek sent the handwritten manuscript with drawings showing how he imagined the play should be staged to his brother Roderick, who produced Ti-Jean with the St Lucia Arts Guild during December 1957. It was through the proposed Arts Festival that Walcott was brought to the attention of the Rockefeller Foundation, which was to have a helpful role in his career as a West Indian dramatist until 1970. Harrison was sent copies of Walcott's plays and poems and his advisors were impressed by what they read.[19]

As Walcott travelled back and forth between Jamaica, St Lucia and Trinidad to research and work on preparing the staging of his pageant for the Arts Festival, his views about living in the West Indies began to change. He fell in love with Trinidad and saw in its many cultures and peoples and small theatre and dance groups a vitality that appeared to be missing elsewhere in the region. Port of Spain was to be the capital of the new West Indian Federation and many of his friends from St Lucia and Jamaica were moving there or, like Ronnie Llanos, returning home.

Port of Spain had old wooden French and Spanish architecture, it had a wide variety of music ranging from Spanish to African including its own calypso and steel bands, it was multiracial, multiethnic and multicultural with British, French, Spanish, Portuguese, Chinese, Latin Americans, Syrians, Asian Indians, Negroes (the then current and still a common West Indian term for those primarily of African descent), and many people of mixed parentage. There were artists such as McBurnie and J. D. Elder who were actively studying and renewing local cultures. Trinidad might be described as a young society. V. S. Naipaul has called it half-formed. Over the decades its society tended to divide along class and ethnic lines, in which money, education, or some affiliation with Europe was significant. There were not the sharp racial divisions then existing in North America, although there were strong political tensions between Hindu Indians and the black community. There was a racially mixed upper bohemia of talented people who read books, played musical instruments, acted in plays, and drank and talked late into the night. There were even local theatre companies, including some predominantly black companies since 1947 when Errol Hill and others founded the Whitehall Players, the New Company and the Company of Players (which incorporated the two). While Errol Hill and his brother Sydney (who formed the Company of Five) were creating black-led theatre companies in Port of Spain there were other amateur theatre groups which made Trinidad, along with Jamaica, the centre of West Indian theatrical activity at the time. There was the Trinidad Dramatic Club which although white and British-oriented had begun to accept a few local actors, such as Errol Jones, as guests for plays. There was the Trinidad Light Operatic Society and, outside of Port of Spain, the St Augustine Players and the San Fernando Drama Guild (formed by Horace James in 1955) and the San Fernando Carnegie Players. It was from such groups that Walcott would eventually form the Little Carib Theatre Workshop. Walcott decided to stay. For the next twenty years Port of Spain would be his home.[20]

Walcott directed his own *Ione* in Port of Spain, 7–9 November 1957, for the Company of Players with Eunice Bruno (later Alleyne) and

Jean Herbert in the cast and with Colin Laird in charge of the setting. Eunice Bruno was later to become one of the main actors in the Trinidad Theatre Workshop. The play used the Folk Singers of Trinidad under the direction of the musicologist J. D. Elder.[21]

When Walcott arrived in Trinidad he first stayed with Bruce Procope, a prominent barrister who was co-Chairman of the Music and Dance Subcommittee of the West Indies Festival of the Arts. Procope was on the 'pageant' committee responsible for the 'Epic', which was the working name for Walcott's *Drums and Colours*. Walcott then moved to a house at 6 Bengal Street, St James, that was co-rented by Veronica Jenkin, a school teacher with an active interest in the arts who had acted in his plays, and Irma 'Billie' Pilgrim (later Goldstraw), a British-born West Indian who had lived in Guyana and who came from a family involved with the arts. Walcott had been given the names of Jenkin and Pilgrim by John Hearne. The house in Bengal Street was a meeting place for the Port of Spain upper bohemia and intellectuals of the period, a generation of Trinidadians of various colours, classes, and expatriates who shared a concern for progressive causes, local culture, and the arts, especially music, literature, and theatre. Through Jenkin and Pilgrim he met the lawyers, politicians, artists, and patrons, who would be useful to his taking root in Port of Spain and becoming a Trinidadian dramatist. Veronica Jenkin would eventually return to England. Billie Pilgrim was then being courted by a British naval officer, Laurence Goldstraw, whom she married. She would later work for the library at the University of the West Indies, St Augustine, and research and write the standard bibliography of Walcott's works. Laurence Goldstraw, who had acted in school in England and in shows in the navy, later became a member of the Trinidad Theatre Workshop and often was a leading actor, especially in plays where Walcott needed a white male.[22]

As West Indian history was not taught in St Lucian schools, Walcott's sense of its chronology was spotty. Although he had read into Haitian history for *Henri Christophe* his formal education was in the history of the British Empire and its heroes. As the commissioned author of an epic pageant celebrating the opening of the West Indian Federation he had rapidly to fill in his knowledge and find incidents and issues of dramatic interest. In the article he contributed to the official souvenir programme for the Festival he mentions having chosen 'to begin with a school boy's view of the past, remembering certain pictures in primary school books, such as Columbus in chains, Raleigh and Gilbert at the foot of the old Sailor in the Millais painting, the portraits of

Toussaint'. The French Revolution and the Haitian rebellion were 'an organic insight into the changing world thought and the emergence of an enslaved Indies'. He wanted his play to have 'active tableaux, such as the paintings of Columbus and Raleigh and the boy Gilbert to remind the imagination of the audience'. Walcott was already seeing his plays as scenes in paintings, a characteristic of his drama and of how he directs productions. (Paradoxically, because he is a verse dramatist who uses words to set a scene and because of the conditions in which he had to work, his *mise en scène* is more a theatre of poverty without elaborate sets, props and equipment.) As he continued to read into history and his central figures—Columbus, Raleigh, Toussaint, and Gordon—came alive to his imagination, he became 'aware of the repetition of human effort and conflict'. From the issues he began creating other characters, giving them names, mixing real names with fiction, making the main figures recede, and grafting the four main stories into one.[23]

His imaginative instincts, the way the pictorial may be charged with varied symbolic significances, can be seen from the story of the death of Raleigh's son which appeared to summarize the 'misdirection of a great but often callous man' and 'the passing of the Elizabethan spirit'. The visit to Stratford Festival Theatre strengthened his convictions about the continuing possibilities of Shakespearean epic drama written in verse rather than prose, but he had also developed an awareness of the stage as a space in which actors create art and communicate by using their bodies. Commenting upon the open-air stage used for the West Indies Festival, Walcott says it calls upon the actor to do what the modern theatre has taught actors to forget, 'using his entire body, revolving it, using his voice'. Walcott concludes his short essay with sentiments which might be said to anticipate his work with the Trinidad Theatre Workshop.

On a stage such as this, actor and writer and director must work together constantly, and this means more freedom of conception, more flexibility of direction and more spontaneous joy from the actors. . . . I hope that our poets will be tempted to write great plays for a great stage. As for our actors I have complete confidence that they can be among the best in the world.

Walcott was learning about the full use of the stage. Tom Brown of the Stratford Shakespeare Festival came to Trinidad to help him with the stageability of his script. The Rockefeller Foundation provided grants so that stage and lighting directors from Stratford could help with the actual production of the Festival.

Walcott's pageant play *Drums and Colours* was performed, 25 April–1 May 1958, at the Royal Botanical Gardens, for the West Indian Festival of the Arts, to inaugurate the West Indian Federation. This was a lavish event involving talents from all the islands and brought him into contact with most of the significant theatre people in Trinidad. *Drums and Colours* was very much an official production. Besides being commissioned by University College of the West Indies, and receiving technical assistance from the Rockefeller Foundation, the many kinds of wood for the attractive stage were a gift to the Festival from the government of British Guiana (which had decided against entering the Federation). The actors, producers, and others were from various islands, often with each island rehearsing some section as its own, as a primary goal of the Festival was to show that the many local governments and peoples of the Federation could work together. The text with illustrations was published as a special issue of *Caribbean Quarterly*: when Walcott asked for royalties from sales he was told that his original fee from the University College was all he could expect.[24]

While *Drums and Colours* and Beryl McBurnie's Little Carib dance company were the main attractions of the Arts Festival, there were also presentations of plays, music, and dance by various performing arts groups from throughout the region. A theatre group from San Fernando, led by James Lee Wah, included in its cast Mavis Lee Wah, Albert Laveau, and Stanley Marshall. Laveau and Marshall would become two pillars of the Trinidad Theatre Workshop. The St Lucia Arts Guild planned to present Roderick Walcott's *Banjo Man*, but stayed at home after local Catholic priests condemned the play for portraying life in St Lucia as sexually immoral. *Banjo Man* would not be performed again until 1971 when, under Roderick Walcott's direction, it would be a 'national production' sponsored by the government of St Lucia, which also would send it to the first Carifesta, held in Guyana in 1972.[25]

Drums and Colours might be regarded as a nationalist work. It provides a 'usable' past, or history, in an epic manner, about the various 'races' and nationalities that had been at the forefront of Caribbean politics. Colin Laird described it as a 'symbol . . . a culmination of the political ambitions of the West Indian as exemplified in the Federation'. Unlike West Africa where the colonizer and colonized were distinct, the West Indies, except for the now almost extinct original Amerindians, consisted of those who were once alien and who would need to live together in the near future with the coming departure of imperial power. The occasion of the play is sufficient evidence of its politics, the new professional élite which expected to rule the English-speaking islands of the region through a federal bureaucracy. The mixture of carnival with which it begins and concludes and its Shakespearean sweep and manner attempt to bridge the distance between high and popular culture. The Haitian scenes use a recurrent Walcott theme, the disillusioning similarities between whites and blacks in power. Both races share human faults. This might be contrasted to Caribbean literary texts which see life through the perspective of the history of slavery and its effects. Walcott had already written on the Haitian revolution in *Henri Christophe* and would return to it again in *Haytian Earth*.[26]

Drums and Colours was widely reviewed in the West Indies. Anyone in West Indian literary circles who had not known Walcott's name now did. In *Bim*, Barbados, Veronica Jenkin offers what might be thought to be an inside view of its themes and structure. Using the personal tragedies of five 'heroes'—Columbus, Raleigh, Toussaint L'Ouverture, George, William Gordon, and a shoemaker named Pompey—the play shows the destructive, corrupting greed for gold and the tolerance men learn through strife and suffering. (The latter would remain an important Walcott theme as can be seen in *Pantomime*.) While finding the verse and characterization good with many changes in mood, scene, and pace, Jenkin felt there was too much richness in the play despite Walcott's cutting during rehearsals. The production was confused, there was too much to digest, and while it was never boring, there was a lack of balance that made it difficult to follow. Walcott's blank verse is much less imitative of Eliot, Auden, and Fry than previously and ranges from moving simplicity to sonorous nobility and broken despair, but it lacks the speech rhythms of conversation except in prose scenes where Jenkin is reminded of Synge's use of dialect.[27]

Walcott had already met the dancer Beryl McBurnie, at a summer school at the University College of the West Indies in Jamaica during 1957. *Drums and Colours* introduced him to many other Trinidadian actors and artists. Those who participated included the actors Eunice Bruno, Errol Jones, Freddie Kissoon, Horace James, the now famous artist Peter Minshall, and the lighting technician George Williams. Colin Laird (an English architect who married a Trinidadian during the war and settled in Port of Spain) was in charge of the stage design as was the well-known painter Carlisle Chang. Veronica Jenkin was a prompter and Claire Creteau, a librarian, was House Manager. Margaret Maillard, who was to become his second wife in 1960 and an invaluable support in future, helped with sound. The Hill family (Errol Hill,

Sydney Hill, and Jean Hill Herbert), which had until then dominated the new Trinidadian theatre scene, were prominently involved with the pageant as actors. Walcott's role in *Drums and Colours* gave him a place within local society. Most serious artists need to find or create a supportive environment. For all his bohemianism, moodiness, and gruffness, Walcott attracted useful friends and inherited his mother's sense of priorities and leadership. Many of the artists Walcott worked with on *Drums and Colours* were involved in his 27–29 June 1958 production of *Ti-Jean and his Brothers* at the Little Carib, followed by a performance at San Fernando, 2 July. A note in the *Trinidad Guardian* said that four of Trinidad's best-known actors were involved—'Errol Jones, who has won his reputation with memorable performances in plays like *The Sea at Dauphin*', Freddie Kissoon, Horace James, and Jean Herbert. Walcott was producer and director. Veronica Jenkin prompted. Colin Laird did the setting and played clarinet in the small orchestra directed by John Henderson who also played quatro. (The quatro is a small banjo-like Spanish string instrument found throughout the Eastern Caribbean and Latin America. It is especially associated with parang, traditional Spanish music sung at Christmas in Trinidad, but is also used by folk musicians in St Lucia.) Horace James played Mi-Jean, Freddie Kissoon played Ti-Jean and Jean (Hill) Herbert and Veronica Jenkin alternated as the Mother. Bertrand Henry played the Frog and Marilyn Clarke played Cricket. Errol Jones, who was to become the personification of the Trinidad Theatre Workshop actors, was invited to play the triple part Devil, Planter, and Old Man of the Forest, after Ronald Williams discovered he would be tied up in government business. Jeff Henry, then a leading dancer with Beryl McBurnie, supervised the dancers from the Little Carib company. The programme describes the six scenes; in Scene iv 'Ti-Jean learns the value of fear, and that there is something to be said for anarchy'. The music was based on Creole folk melodies. There was a poor audience on opening night probably because of the competition of a Miss Trinidad contest.[28]

The *Trinidad Guardian* reviewer thoroughly disliked the play. He thought Walcott garrulous, prolific, untidy, and capable of outrageous nonsense. 'The friendliest thing that can be said of *Ti-Jean* is that it is a slight play which begins by being entertaining and ends.' Walcott was in 'an existentialist mood, pleading the virtues of humility, mediocrity and humour, in a world where strength of any kind is a presumption'. The acting was undistinguished. While Walcott in *Drums and Colours* and *Ti-Jean* attempts to incorporate indigenous forms such as dance and music into West Indian theatre, whenever a character burst into song or dance it appeared gratuitous. Walcott is an experimenter, obsessed with non-naturalist staging. A single symbolic set is successfully used throughout the production, although the stage at the Little Carib was too small.[29]

Although UCWI and Federation politicians saw the Arts Festival as contributing to the development of a regional culture and political unity, Harrison of the Rockefeller Foundation had a different interest. Aid in staging the Festival was part of the Foundation's long-established policy of helping promising young dramatists and the development of community Little Theatre groups; Harrison hoped that a national, regional theatre company would emerge from the Festival. His own and the Stratford drama advisors were impressed by the plays Walcott had sent to them. Here was someone with unusual promise.

For nine months beginning September 1958 Walcott was in New York on a Rockefeller Foundation fellowship to study drama, theatre design, directing, and acting. Walcott primarily studied with Jose Quintero at the Circle in the Square Theatre where he was interested in the three-dimensional staging. Walcott began classes in scenic design with Lester Polakov, but thinking that they were too much aimed at Broadway and unsuitable for the West Indies he instead studied scene construction with Stuart Vaughan at the Phoenix Theatre. He attended plays where he would constantly draw what he had seen as a way of learning about scenic design. At the Phoenix he followed the creation of productions from the reading for parts, rehearsals, blocking, staging, and lighting rehearsals to the striking of the sets. He went to opera and dance recitals as well as theatre. While in New York he saw Kurosawa's film *Rashomon*, and discovered Noh and Kabuki drama with their stylized acting and conventionalized theatre (as can be seen from his *Malcochon*). Using his observations of the New York theatre scene Walcott began revising his own play scripts to make them more stageable. He also became aware that in the United States he would be expected to be 'black' and write protest plays and comedies on racial themes. The problems of black America were not his own. He saw himself using Western artistic forms to give expression to the local lives and experiences of the West Indies, to create a West Indian art that could stand equal to the art of Europe and which would share in his own dual heritage.[30]

Walcott left New York in June 1959, three months before his fellowship ended, to help with the Trinidadian tour of the St Lucia Arts Guild during July when they presented Derek's *Journard* and *Malcochon* and four of Roderick's plays. Beryl McBurnie rather uncertainly recalls that it was the difficulties that Derek and Roderick faced with this tour that led her to invite Derek to form a Theatre Workshop as part of the Little Carib.[31]

Walcott was no longer a beginning colonial dramatist who knew theatre through books and local amateur productions. He had seen what New York had to offer on and off Broadway; he had come into contact with many first-rate talents in Jamaica, in Canada, in Trinidad through the Festival, and in New York. He returned to the West Indies with a vision of creating his own theatre company of international standards, with its own West Indian acting style, which he would lead and direct and which would perform his plays and those of classical and contemporary world theatre. He had in mind a director's theatre in which he would shape every visual detail, gesture, movement, or spoken phrase. It would be a highly visual as well as textual theatre. Walcott originally thought of himself as a painter and still continues to paint, exhibit, and sell his paintings. His plays often start with drawings, sketches, the visualization of scenes, or by having in mind a famous painting or the characteristics of a period of art. While he knew he could not support himself as a painter in the West Indies, he would somehow find a way to live as a professional director and playwright in the West Indies. This would take years of creating a theatre ensemble, training the actors, building an audience, setting standards for reviews, finding ways to support himself and his theatre company, finding theatres, generating publicity, ghosting articles in local newspapers, arranging tours, and much else.[32]

Walcott has given two explanations of the origins of the idea of the Trinidad Theatre Workshop. Both concern the period 1957–8. During the 1957 Summer School for Dance and Drama at the UCWI, Jamaica, Derek Walcott, Roderick Walcott, Slade Hopkinson, and others met Beryl McBurnie, Jeff Henry, and other Trinidadian dancers. According to Roderick Walcott and others it was at the summer school, which McBurnie dominated with her energy and personality, that Derek saw the possibilities of using the West Indian body rhythms, movements, and gestures that the dancers had developed as the basis for an acting style. Until then he had been a poet-dramatist largely influenced by Marlowe, Shakespeare, Dylan Thomas, and the model of the 'national' theatre that Yeats, Lady Gregory, and others had formed in the Abbey Theatre at the turn of the century in Dublin. Now for the first time there was a way to go beyond folk themes, settings, and dialect to an acting style which would be West Indian.[33]

McBurnie is a modern folk dancer who had studied and worked with Martha Graham, influenced Katherine Dunham, and performed in the United States before returning to Trinidad. She researched folk-dances and music of the eastern Caribbean, including the African survivals or Nation dances on Carriacou, an island off Grenada, and tried to create a modern folk style bringing together folk traditions with the principles of Graham and Dunham. She had an immense influence on Caribbean culture by showing local dancers, including Ivy Baxter and Rex Nettleford, how they could create an alternative tradition to the British–European ballet that was taught locally. She took West Indian dance beyond the exotic tropical nights Caribbean shows offered tourists in nightclubs. She saw that it was necessary to have a theatre devoted to dance and in 1948 established her Little Carib Theatre for her dance company. Although originally little more than a shed behind a house, the Little Carib became a place where every night there was drumming and dancing, a centre for those interested in creating a new West Indian culture during the twilight of colonialism.[34]

McBurnie was part of the first postwar phase of cultural decoloniza-tion, which found expression in music and dance. She, Elder, Simmons, and others were assembling and partly modernizing a 'usable' past from folk culture. Walcott's *Ti-Jean and his Brothers*, with its use of St Lucian dialect and folklore, and its model in Synge's Irish nationalist peasant drama, brought such cultural nationalism into the West Indian theatre. Walcott was also drawn to the energy, dynamism, and phys-icality of McBurnie's dancing and personality. It corresponded to his own lust for life and idea of vital theatre.

Walcott, being younger than McBurnie, was part of the second wave of cultural decolonization. Like other colonial writers born around 1930, including Wole Soyinka, he wanted to go beyond the romanticization of the 'primitive' and join the modern world while creating his own 'national' and personal identity from many sources. There were the Shakespeare and John Webster influences on *Henri Christophe*, the Dylan Thomas late modernism of *Harry Dernier*, the Oriental stylization of *Malcochon*, and the classical mythological foun-dations of *Ione*.

If Walcott's meeting with Beryl McBurnie during July 1957 gave him a vision of what a West Indian acting style might be like, it was during his period in New York, on a Rockefeller Fellowship during 1958–9, that Walcott formed the notion of creating a West Indian drama company equal to the great drama ensembles elsewhere. It would be stylized and use dance and music like Japanese Kabuki and Noh theatre; it would be a company with an ensemble style, led by a director-dramatist, like Brecht's Berlin Ensemble. American method acting techniques would enable his actors to go beyond British acting and training methods. It would be serious 'little theatre', aware of the avant-garde, but without the ephemeral fringe attitudes of off-off Broadway. He would commit his life to creating such a theatre company and raise West Indian drama to international professional standards.

Notes

1. *A Nobel Celebration*, 26 Apr. 1993, Charles Playhouse, Boston; *Pantomime*, 29 Apr.–2 May 1993, Boston Playwrights' Theatre, Boston; *The Odyssey: A Stage Version*, 20 Sept. 1993, Unterberg Poetry Center, New York; *Dream on Monkey Mountain*, 21–2 Sept., and *Celebration*, 23–4 Sept. 1993, Shouwburg, Rotterdam; *Dream on Monkey Mountain*, 20–5 Oct. 1993, Little Carib Theatre, Port of Spain.

2. Errol Hill, *The Jamaican Stage 1655–1900: Profile of a Colonial Theatre*, Amherst, University of Massachusetts Press, 1992; Errol Hill, 'The West Indian Theatre (1)', *Public Opinion* (31 May 1958), 9; Joel Benjamin, 'The Early Theatre in Guyana', *Kyk-over-al*, 37 (Dec. 1987), 24–44.

3. Errol Hill, 'The West Indian Theatre (2–4)', *Public Opinion* (7 June 1958), 7; (14 June 1958), 7; (21 June 1958), 9; Errol Hill, 'The Emergence of a National Drama in the West Indies', *Caribbean Quarterly*, 18/4 (December 1972), 9 40; articles on theatre in Guyana by Joel Benjamin, Jeremy Poynting, Frank Thomason and Ron Robinson in *Kyk-over-al*, 37 (Dec. 1987), 24–58; some of Roger Mais's play scripts were published in various issues of *Focus* (Jamaica); Bruce King, *New English Literatures: Cultural Nationalism in a Changing World* (London: Macmillan, 1980); Bruce King, *Modern Indian Poetry in English* (Delhi: Oxford University Press, 1987, revised 1989, 1994).

4. Bruce King (ed.), *West Indian Literature* (London: Macmillan, 1979).

5. 'Tiny School Produces Two Nobel Winners', *Trinidad Guardian* (9 Oct. 1992), 6.

6. Derek Walcott, 'Meanings', *Savacou*, 2 (1970), 45–51.

7. Derek Walcott, 'Leaving School', *London Magazine*, 5/6 (1965), 1–14; interviews with Derek Walcott, Pamela Walcott St Hill and Leonard St Hill (summer 1991) in St Lucia and Barbados; Derek Walcott, '1944', *The Voice of St Lucia* (2 Aug. 1944), 3; C. Jesse FMI, 'Reflections on Reading the Poem "1944" ', *The Voice of St Lucia* (5 Aug. 1944), 4; [A. Seeker], 'The Offending Poem', *The Voice of St Lucia* (9 Aug. 1944), 3.

8. Derek Walcott, *Another Life* (New York: Farrar, Straus & Giroux, 1973); Edward Baugh, *Derek Walcott: Memory as Vision: Another Life* (London: Longman, 1978); *Dear Theo: The Autobiography of Vincent Van Gogh*, ed. by Irving and Jean Stone (Garden City, NY: Doubleday, 1937). John Hearne also told me about the

influence of Irving Stone's books about Van Gogh on his generation of West Indian writers.

9. Copies of the *The Barb* and *The Pelican* are in the West Indian Collection of the University of the West Indies, Mona; Samuel O. Asein, 'Walcott's Jamaica Years', *The Literary Half-Yearly*, 21/2 (July 1980), 23–41; Samuel O. Asein, 'Walcott and the Great Tradition', *The Literary Criterion*, 16/2 (1981), 18–30. Also see Harry Milner's review of Walcott's *The Dying Gods*, in the *Sunday Gleaner* (15 Feb. 1953), 4.

10. Kenneth Monplaisir (July 1991, Castries) acted in the London West Indian student production of *The Sea at Dauphin* with V. S. Naipaul.

11. 'A special correspondent', *West India Committee Circular* (Feb. 1952), 38, quoted from Rhonda Cobham, 'The Background', in King, *West Indian Literature*, 21–2.

12. The cast of the joint New Company and Whitehall Players *The Sea at Dauphin*, 13–15 Aug. 1954, included Horace James, Errol Jones, Freddie Kissoon and Colin Laird; others involved were Jean Herbert, George Williams, Jean Hill and Selby Wooding. The production of 'Three West Indian Plays' was at the Government Training College; *Henri Christophe* by the 'A New Company & Whitehall Players' (27 Nov.–1 Dec.) included Errol Jones, Horace James, Jeff Henry, Neville La Bastide and Sydney Hill in the cast, while Selby Wooding read Eric Williams' prologue. (Many of those who helped Walcott when he moved to Trinidad and who first joined Walcott's Little Carib Theatre Workshop had already acted in his plays.) Slade Hopkinson, 'So the Sun Went Down', *The Daily Gleaner* (15 Apr. 1956), 17; ' "Wine of the country" Walcott's New Play at UCWI Friday', *The Daily Gleaner* (14 Aug. 1956), 14; 'Drama Festival Awards', *Public Opinion* (28 July 1956), 7; 'Next Production', *The Pelican*, 3/4 (Jan. 1956), 9; 'West Indian Plays', *The Pelican*, 3/5 (Feb. 1956): 6; 'Strong cast for "Ione" ', *The Daily Gleaner* (14 Mar. 1957), 18.

13. For the reception of Walcott's plays see J. S. Barker, 'Not the Stuff for a West Indian Theatre', *Trinidad Guardian* (15 Aug. 1954), 4; ' "Wine of the Country" Stark, bold and ruthless', *The Daily Gleaner* (20 Aug. 1956), 16–17; 'Violent Walcott Verse Play', *Public Opinion* (18 Aug. 1956), 8; Michael Manley, 'Root of the Matter', *Public Opinion* (23 Mar. 1957), 4; ' "Ione" Opens New Era in Jamaican Theatre', *Sunday Gleaner* (10 May 1957), 12; John Figueroa, ' "Ione": A Stimulating Play', *Public Opinion* (23 Mar. 1957), 6; Norman Rae, ' "Ione" Colourful but Academic', *The Daily Gleaner* (18 Mar. 1957), 18–19; Derek Walcott, 'A Modern Theatre', *The Daily Gleaner* (25 Mar. 1957) [Walcott's reply to Rae's review]; 'Place of Drama in the New West Indian World', *Sunday Guardian* (1 Dec. 1957), 8; Fr. C. Jesse, 'Arts Guild Play Objectionable', *The Voice of St Lucia* (7 Mar. 1959), 8.

14. Interview with John Hearne, Jamaica (Aug. 1991).

15. The correspondence between Harrison, Patterson, Hill, Walcott, Sherlock and others is cross-filed in the Rockefeller Archives, Tarrytown, NY, under the names of the individuals and further cross-filed under the University of the West Indies Extra-Mural Department, the Little Carib, etc.

16. Bruce King, 'Introduction' to *Post-Colonial English Drama: Commonwealth Drama since 1960* (London: Macmillan, 1992), 1–16.

17. Rockefeller Archives, Tom Patterson to John Harrison (29 Nov. 1956; 17 Apr. 1957).

18. Rockefeller Archives, John P. Harrison, South Africa Trip (24–25 June 1957); for Siobhan McKenna and Ti-Jean see Noel Vaz to John Harrison (31 July 1957) in the Rockefeller Archives.

19. Rockefeller Archives Grant in Aid, GA HUM 57117 (approved 23 Aug. 1957); Noel Vaz to John Harrison (19 June 1958).

20. Interview with Derek Walcott, Boston (Sept. 1989); Derek Walcott, 'On Choosing Port of Spain', in David Frost Introduces Trinidad and Tobago (London: André Deutsch, 1975); 14–23.

21. 'Company of Players Try A Walcott Opus', Sunday Guardian (13 Oct. 1957), 7; 'Trinidad to See A Walcott Play Again', Trinidad Guardian (30 Oct. 1957); John Grimes, '"Company of Players" Win Praise For "Ione"', Trinidad Guardian (9 Nov. 1957), 5.

22. Interview with Walcott, Boston, 1989; Irma Goldstraw, Trinidad, July 1990.

23. Derek Walcott, 'Drums and Colours', West Indies Festival of Arts Trinidad April 1958, 8–9.

24. Derek Walcott, Drums and Colours, Caribbean Quarterly, 7/1–2 (Mar.–June 1961); repub. Caribbean Quarterly, 30/4 (Dec. 1992), 22–135.

25. Samuel O. Asein, 'Drama, The Church and The Nation in the Caribbean', The Literary Half-Yearly, 26/1 (Jan. 1985), 149–62.

26. Colin Laird, 'The Arts in the West Indies', Shell Trinidad (Sept. 1958), 8.

27. Veronica Jenkin, 'Drums and Colours', Bim, 7/27 (July–Dec. 1958), 183–4; Tony Swann, 'Drums and Colours—Guts at Least', Public Opinion (10 May 1958), 7; Adrian Espinet, '"Drums and Colours" Seeks to Trace Evolution of West Indian Consciousness', Sunday Guardian (27 Apr. 1958), 7.

28. 'Top Actors for Roles in "Ti-Jean"', Trinidad Guardian (June 1958), 5; 'Poor audience saw "Ti-Jean"', Chronicle ([June] 1958).

29. Adrian Espinet, 'Undistinguished—That's The Word for "Ti-Jean"', Trinidad Guardian (1 July 1958), 4.

30. Rockefeller Fellowship Recorder for Derek Walcott (14 June 1959) W-RWJ (Walcott-Robert July).

31. Rockefeller Fellowship Recorder for Derek Walcott (14 June 1959) W-RWJ; interview with Beryl McBurnie (June 1991). According to Richard Montgomery, that Walcott was mugged in New York encouraged the decision to return to Trinidad.

32. Clara Rosa de Lima, 'Walcott: Painting and the Shadow of Van Gogh' in Stewart Brown (ed.), The Art of Derek Walcott (Wales: Sren Books, 1991), 171–92. For Walcott and painting, see her end notes.

33. 'Drama in the Idiom at Guild', Guyana Graphic (17 Aug. 1967), 6; Norman Rae, 'Fine Productions—But Where were the Audiences?', The Daily Gleaner (20 Dec. 1957), 28; Roderick Walcott, interview, Toronto (Nov. 1991).

34. Victor D. Questel, 'The Little Carib Theatre (1948–1976)', Caribbean Contact, 4 (Dec. 1976), 22; Molly Ahye, Cradle of Caribbean Dance: Beryl McBurnie and the Little Carib Theatre (Trinidad: Heritage Cultures, 1983).

1959–1965

2

The Little Carib Theatre Workshop

DURING July 1959 Walcott invited some of the better actors in Trinidad to a weekly theatre workshop at the Little Carib on Fridays after their normal working day. The actors were from San Fernando as well as Port of Spain and were expected to pay a small fee as dues, although they seldom did. Until then, training of actors was mostly through British Council courses in movement, mime, and voice rather than in the interpretation of parts. Some companies, such as the primarily white Trinidad Dramatic Club, held workshops for their members, but the approach was similar to British Royal Academy of Dramatic Arts methods. Trinidadian actors usually began by memorizing their lines; Walcott thought this resulted in repeating mistakes throughout rehearsals. A role should slowly be developed during workshops with attention to psychology and interpretation of possible subtexts. Even today some of the actors who were trained in Walcott's workshops will learn their lines during rehearsals. Walcott's approach emphasized memory, improvisation, and the sensory. Scenes and characters evolved from workshop exercises; each gesture should be part of the interpretation. Although he drew upon various sources one model was the Actors' Studio—the modified Stanislavskian technique that developed in the United States. In such a model understanding and interpretation of a part, often drawing upon the actor's own interior experience, is more important than emphasis on exteriorized skills. Improvisation and group criticism are used to create the techniques needed for interpretation.

Walcott wanted to combine dance with acting using the rich West Indian movements and gestures that McBurnie had achieved with her dancers; he wanted detailed psychology of character, in the Method tradition, and a mimetic power such as that found in dance. The visual difference between the kind of acting style Walcott was creating and what is common to British theatre might be compared to the kind of revolution that Elvis Presley brought to the singing of popular music. Whereas serious European acting might be described as vertical and restrained, West Indians are more expansive in their movements, more gestural, more likely to move from the hip and pelvis. West Indians acting in serious plays felt constrained, uptight, and thought their natural style only correct for popular comedy. Walcott wanted the actors to learn how to use their movements and gestures for serious plays; he aimed eventually to create a West Indian ensemble style. He was especially concerned with developing a stage language of West Indian body movements. Actors would be asked to improvise a story using facial and body gestures without speaking a word. Sometimes one actor would narrate a story and the other actors would be expected to improvise accompanying movements and gestures.[1]

All aspects of performance had to be reconsidered. There were some well-educated Workshop members who had acted in Shakespeare's plays, came from educated families, and could easily speak British English; others, especially those who joined later, were raised by parents with little schooling, themselves had little education, and had difficulty reading and pronouncing their lines. Walcott decided that the actors must concentrate on speaking clearly the words and rhythms of the lines, but that the audience would need to accept serious drama in Trinidadian pronunciation. Later, even on tours abroad, Walcott told his actors that just as American and British actors had their own national accents, so Trinidadians should not be ashamed of sounding like Trinidadians; the audience would need to make the effort to listen carefully and watch the action on stage.

One of the problems Walcott faced was the apparent distance between verse drama and Trinidadian speech. Iambics were in themselves not necessarily un-West Indian; calypso lyrics often fall into iambic pentameters. Rather the question involved decorum, the authenticity of the poetic in the modern world, and training his actors to speak verse with a natural rhythm, neither stiltedly nor sloppily. Too often the actors would forget a line and improvise something that might make sense but was certainly not verse. This was not a question of metrics. Years later Walcott gave Webster's 'Cover her face. Mine eyes dazzle. She died young' as an example of the dramatic possibilities of verse: each of the three divisions of the line is filled with 'room

enough and depth enough for an actor to pace, reflect'. The problem was that some of his actors were too self-conscious of being West Indian, of not having the right education, social background, or pronunciation, to act in serious theatre: 'An Actor rises to a text and his tongue stumbles on words that have less immediacy than his dialect and he collapses, or fakes difficulty, abashed. He confronts proper speech as his body once confronted certain "inflexible" classic gestures. He stands torn between the wish to amuse or to illuminate his people.'[2]

While Walcott had to work with little and poor lighting equipment, he was aware that lighting effects on the modern stage are used to create the changing colours and shifting moods that were in the past part of verse. Off-Broadway productions showed that while limitations of playing space could be overcome with ingenuity in staging and blocking, there needed to be additional attention to lighting. 'The area lighting off-Broadway is supremely professional, related to the infinitesimal relationship of actor and his immediate area . . . there is an expertise of lighting the play to the nearest half-inch of spill from a spotlight that helps to make the sense of movement possible . . . In a small theatre, illusion is possible not by less, but by more light.' His drawings for his plays sometimes include detailed illustrations of how and where he wanted lights and tones. Both George Williams and John Andrews became skilled at improvising lighting effects from coloured cellophane, milk cartons, bits of tin foil; theatre professionals who have seen Andrews' lighting designs for TTW productions have described him as a genius.[3]

The Little Carib Theatre Workshop was intended for directors and writers as well as actors. The members would form small groups which would, often at random, study, perform, and produce short extracts from various kinds of plays. Scripts were often exchanged so that each of the actors would read all the roles during a workshop. Each performance would be followed by critical discussion. Walcott felt that

every speech or gesture must be interpreted not in the light of its surface content or its immediate effect, but as a product of the psychological and physical forces that go to make up the humanity of the character at that moment . . . not one word should be spoken or one finger moved without consciousness on the part of the actor of how the word or gesture fits in with his conception of the character . . . underneath to be brought to light.

To keep the focus on acting the performances would be arena style, with as few artificial aids as possible. Make-up was kept to a minimum. Workshops were spent on eye contact to create an ensemble style on stage. In the early days Walcott saw himself primarily as a chairman who, although he would direct one of the scenes, wanted to encourage an analytical approach to the theatre and sharpen the sensitivity of actors and directors towards the dramatic presentation. A few pages of a script or a few lines would be discussed or rehearsed with an emphasis on minute detail. How did the scene reflect or sensitively observe humanity? What could be extracted from it? What could be further revealed by more workshops, discussion, and rehearsals? What other possibilities, or variety, could be found in the scene or character? How did such a detailed analytical approach contrast to the actor's normal way of acting a part?[4]

The building of a part through detailed analysis, discussion, introspection, and criticism was then foreign to Trinidadian theatre where the usual method was to be given a script and read it. Although Walcott brought new techniques to West Indian acting, his main contribution was to require intelligence from his actors. Performers had to develop a concept of character and the play. Walcott did not say what interpretation he wanted; he would question the actors about how they understood their role, some lines, or what they felt the play was about. Scenes were gone through carefully. His actors were expected to become serious artists by researching, innovating, and intellectualizing their art. Walcott's actors were told to observe people on the street, follow them, imagine their lives, research characterization. They were made to do physical exercises, to spend hours reading a few lines in a variety of ways, told of recent theories of acting and performance, told to find sources for the emotion in their own lives. They were not to fall into stereotypes of characterization; instead they were to recall times when they were in love, felt loss, or had other deep emotions, and draw upon such feelings in building the part. Similarly Walcott did not want stereotypical gestures that had been seen on stage or in movies as that would inhibit the actor's own West Indian body language. Walcott was the actor's channel of information from the contemporary theatre world while he attempted to drill them into a style capable of performing Shakespearean verse, the theatre of the absurd, and West Indian dialect. The exercises varied from such common techniques as feeling and describing a ball when blindfolded, acting as objects and animals, and reading two lines from *Macbeth* in endlessly different ways and tones, to improvisations in dialect on Little Red Riding Hood. He wanted complete actors who could mime, dance, sing, and play comedy and tragedy, European and West Indian plays. Eventually the weekly workshops were scheduled for twice each week.

While Walcott had in mind the eventual creation of a company with its own distinctive style to perform his plays, those of other West Indians, and of world theatre, that was not the initial declared objective of the Theatre Workshop and would have been premature. Years would be needed to raise local standards of acting, to make local actors aware of contemporary methods of developing their skills, and to create a style. Walcott had no intention of beginning with productions and, even after a group of actors had been trained and the basis of a company existed, he resisted his actors' wish to perform publicly. Some actors objected to Walcott's leadership, others wanted regular productions, attendance at workshops was sporadic (one night only one actor came), dues were not paid, meeting every Friday after work conflicted with family life and other engagements; it was not clear what Walcott intended and it took several years before the basis for a regular company was established. Somehow aspiring actors heard about the Workshop and became members while those unwilling to follow Walcott's leadership drifted away. Claude Reid, who was to become one of the 'foundation' members, turned up on two Friday nights before finding Walcott on the third.

The first, private performance of the Theatre Workshop took place at the Little Carib Theatre on 11 December 1959 at 8.30 p.m. with J. P. Harrison of the Rockefeller Foundation in the audience. The programme was a cyclostyled sheet folded in thirds and cost twenty cents. Walcott's 'Note to Audience' for *Showcase I* said that the Workshop was 'simply a studio' where actors from various companies were invited to expand their knowledge in the 'practice' of theatre. The actors were dedicated amateurs who wanted to improve their technique. During its six-month existence sessions had been devoted to understanding the problems of actors with attention to verisimilitude and detail. The *Showcase*, in which they would present six short scenes, was intended to invite scrutiny and comments; the audience would be asked for their views during the interval and after the second half. The *Showcase* was not a full-dress production and the emphasis would be on acting, the actor as interpreter, without make-up, music, costume, or any necessary scenery in an intimate arena setting.[5]

Showcase I consisted of six scenes from four plays—Errol John's *Moon on a Rainbow Shawl*, Tennessee Williams's *This Property Condemned*, Shaw's *Saint Joan*, Arthur Miller's *The Crucible*—and an adaptation of a story by the Trinidadian Samuel Selvon. Walcott directed four of the scenes (Selvon, John and Williams); Veronica Jenkin and Anthony Selman were the other directors. Except for Errol Jones and the St

Lucian Joel St Helene, few of the original Workshop members would be found in later productions. James Lee Wah, who had studied at the University College of the West Indies (UCWI) in Jamaica, had his own theatre company in San Fernando. Freddie Kissoon also had a theatre company specializing in dialect 'back yard' comedy, although it actually consisted of a few actors who came together to perform in his productions. Many of those involved in *Showcase* already had local reputations in theatre. Some were well connected socially and politically. Vicki Rambert, from Belmont, who performed in a scene from *Moon on a Rainbow Shawl*, was light-skinned and acted locally as a romantic lead; she had performed in a production of *Twelfth Night*. Russell Winston was a radio announcer who worked in the Prime Minister's Office. Denis Solomon, who performed in the scene from *St Joan*, was the son of Pat Solomon, then second to Eric Williams in the government. Denis was a Cambridge University graduate and later a diplomat. Within a year Walcott's Little Carib Workshop had generated interest. During April 1960 Bruce Procope reported to the Rockefeller Foundation that the response to Walcott's theatre workshop was enthusiastic, had attracted people from all sections of society, and two other local playwrights were attending as well as actors and dancers.[6]

Margaret Maillard was in charge of properties and 'front of house'. She became Walcott's second wife. She is from an important black French Creole Trinidadian family, had taken a university degree in England, and shocked her conservative family when she married Walcott in 1960. A trained social worker, she at times had the only steady income in the family. During 1960 Walcott became a regular book, theatre, and arts reviewer for the *Trinidad Guardian*. His work as a journalist, the small royalties he would later receive from his publications, and some literary awards were the source of his income. As an all-purpose reviewer of the arts he attended plays, concerts, dance recitals, calypso performances, films, and exhibitions of paintings and also wrote book reviews. His columns discussed such practical problems as stage make-up for dark-skinned actors, ticket prices, and why Thomas à Becket's spiritual conversion in T. S. Eliot's *Murder in the Cathedral* was difficult to communicate on stage. He was also scouting talented local actors and dancers for his Workshop.

Walcott had already formed many of his ideas about theatre and the role of the arts in the West Indies; constant reviewing of theatre productions, dance recitals, and films sharpened his awareness of the problems of performance, the need for professional skills, and the kinds of adaptations necessary to work in Trinidadian conditions. In his reviews and articles he was often indirectly writing about his own plans and vision. Just as Walcott's poetry often moves rapidly between his own life and that of his generation and the West Indies, so Walcott the dramatist, his hopes, and the new movement in West Indian theatre appear the same.[7]

Walcott wrote on the need for a Little Theatre in Port of Spain. Productions of two recent plays showed the need for 'a small, well-equipped theatre with a seating capability of about three hundred'. There was now a small body of locally written plays of interest to Trinidadians. Possibly plays will need 'first to meet with the seal of foreign approval' before the West Indian middle class will accept them, but Errol John, Errol Hill, William Archibald and Douglas Archibald have already had successes abroad. Each year new plays are added to the new repertoire. Walcott suggests that a company of actors could be established to perform Douglas Archibald's *Anne Marie* and *Junction Village*, William Archibald's *The Innocents* (an adaptation of a Henry James novel), Errol John's *Moon on a Rainbow Shawl*, Errol Hill's *Man Better Man* and such one-act scripts as Hill's *Ping Pong*, John's *The Tout*, Barker's *Bond of Matrimony* and Naipaul's *B. Wordsworth* (an adaptation of the short story). In reply to those who feel that Trinidadians only want comedy, Walcott argues that audiences are only being offered 'thin, imported farce' with no relationship to their own society. Even productions of Shakespeare and classical English drama are damaging in a community with no theatrical tradition, where it is foolishly necessary to claim Shakespeare can be fun to attract an audience.

What Port of Spain needs is a small, modestly equipped theatre, with raked seating and a cheap enough rental to encourage small groups, in contrast to the recently built all-purpose Queen's Hall where the cost of production is likely to exceed receipts and where the stage is too large for plays with a small cast and simple settings. The little theatre should have facilities for rehearsals and be a centre for serious theatre. Those who claim there is no audience for serious theatre in Port of Spain should be aware that until 'a true theatre is built we have no reason to expect packed houses'.[8]

In Port of Spain there were basically three unsatisfactory performance spaces in addition to the assembly halls of schools and colleges. There was the new Queen's Hall, the new Town Hall auditorium, and the Little Carib. Each had severe disadvantages. Queen's Hall, designed by Colin Laird, was intended as a multipurpose community centre; it is too large for most productions, has several areas in which the sound is dead, and is located on a busy thoroughfare with noise from the streets as well as noise from its two bars where people often gather during performances. The Town Hall auditorium and the Little Carib were not built for staging plays and lacked everything needed for theatre from proper lighting to changing rooms.

The Rockefeller Foundation kept its eye on how the Little Carib was developing as John Harrison hoped it could be developed into a national theatre for the West Indian Federation. During September 1960 Patterson reported to Harrison that the Little Carib dancer Jeff Henry after a year of studying dance in England was coming to Stratford, Ontario, on a Canada Council Fellowship to study theatre management, which the Little Carib badly needed. Sherlock was appointed Vice-Principal of the UCWI and was in charge of its new Trinidad campus, which Harrison and Patterson felt would be helpful to the Little Carib Theatre. A few months later Patterson and Harrison again spoke about the Little Carib. Patterson thought the quality of the Little Carib dancers and performances was superior to the national African dance companies that were then touring abroad, but it lacked responsible management and organization.[9]

During the first week of June 1961, Harrison visited Trinidad to see what was taking place at the Little Carib Theatre and performing arts in general. He spoke with Sherlock who said he hoped to appoint Errol Hill, then on a Rockefeller fellowship at Yale University, as head of a Faculty of Fine Arts. While the teaching and training of the performing arts would be part of the university's mission, it would evolve directly from the Little Carib. The government would support the salaries of teachers; the community, through patronage and ticket sales, would support the costs of Little Carib productions. Harrison also spoke with Bruce Procope who told Harrison of plans to build a new 500-seat Little Carib designed for both dance and drama, which they wanted to have ready by February 1962.[10]

Harrison also met Colin Laird, the architect of the proposed new Little Carib. Harrison thought that Laird needed contact with theatre designers elsewhere to understand the differences between building and its function as theatre. He spoke with Walcott and others about the usefulness of Laird meeting George Izenour, whose advanced technical work on the scenery and lighting of small theatres the Rockefeller Foundation had supported for some years at Yale University. Laird was awarded a three-week travelling grant to visit theatres in Florida, Boston, New York, and Stratford, Ontario, and to consult with Izenour. Izenour and Laird drafted a new plan for the theatre, which was approved on his return to Trinidad. The Rockefeller Foundation was willing to equip the New Carib with an up-to-date pushbutton system of stage machinery and lighting designed by Izenour. The theatre was to seat 480, be used for experimental theatre and dance, and be rapidly rearranged to allow for 'fetes' and 'jump-ups', the parties in which the cast danced with the audience after Little Carib productions. The theatre was also meant to be a centre for a school, for ethnographic and folklore research, and for a semi-professional drama company. It was to cost $250,000 and there were hopes to have it near completion by Independence day.[11]

The Little Carib Theatre (LCT) was legally formed as a limited company on 17 October 1961 by seven 'Associates' including McBurnie ('Physical Education and Dance' instructor), Procope and H. O. B. Wooding (both 'Barrister at Law'). Its first fifteen members of Council, or directors, included Walcott and Sherlock.

Herbert Machiz, who had directed on- and off-Broadway, was asked by the Rockefeller Foundation to stop off in Trinidad on his return from Brazil. During October 1961 Walcott wrote to Harrison to say that Machiz talked to Workshop members and met John Hearne and Errol John who were visiting. Machiz and Walcott got along well and Machiz said he might be able to help Walcott towards a grant of $3,000 so that he could be freed from writing for the newspaper for a year. (This was Walcott's 1962 Ingram Merrill Foundation award.) They also discussed Machiz's giving a six-weeks intensive summer course, an idea that Harrison thought a logical next step if the Little Carib were to make effective use of the proposed new theatre. Machiz drew up a proposal to return to Trinidad to help formulate plans for a national theatre and for a summer seminar in drama which would include teachers of acting, directing, playwriting, movement, and voice.[12]

A colonial society is usually an underdeveloped society in which there are few professionals or specialists and in which amateurs are required to be jacks-of-all-trades. As Walcott and others tried to move the performing arts in a more professional direction, there was the continuing problem of who could teach the skills needed for further development. The task of developing an actors' studio and drama group within the Little Carib took much of Walcott's time and meant that he was responsible for kinds of training with which he was himself unfamiliar. The proposed linkage between the Little Carib and the UCWI was rapidly moving towards plans for a summer school in the performing arts in which McBurnie and Walcott would be tutors, but other tutors were needed. Procope wrote to Harrison to say that the

LCT's board was asking for advanced training fellowships for a number of people who would be offered scholarships and expected on their return to join the LCT and teach others.[13]

By December 1961 the idea that Machiz would direct a six-week seminar in theatre the next summer had taken shape. Machiz wanted professionals to teach directing, acting, script analysis, management, production, voice, and movement. Harrison wrote to Walcott saying he was prepared to discuss this, but he wanted to know whether there were sufficient talented people seriously interested in theatre and dance to justify such an expenditure of funds. Could the Little Carib be transformed into a national theatre company? Harrison proposed Machiz's return to Trinidad for ten days to develop plans for the summer school and discuss how a national company might be formed.[14]

The long correspondence between Walcott and Harrison concerning the rapid development of the Little Carib is rather tricky to read. Harrison obviously relied on Walcott's judgement of the local situation and kept pressing him for opinions about the plans of McBurnie, Procope, and others. Walcott seldom offered a discouraging opinion, but was careful to distance himself from ambitious claims about the Little Carib raising the necessary local funds and rapidly building a new theatre. Instead his letters detail what his Theatre Workshop needed and what it could do. This was wise as Trinidadian money for a new Little Carib was never found and the whole project collapsed. Walcott replied to Harrison that he needed a director who could analyse scripts, teach acting, and produce a play during the six-week course. He also needed someone who was a producer, stage manager, and administrator who could teach everything about mounting productions. There was a need for teachers of speech and voice and of movement, especially of mime, who could also teach dancers. Both the acting and production–stage management classes would be of benefit to the dancers who were by then starting to attend his Drama Workshop. While Walcott was certain that at least thirty of his Workshop members would attend, he wanted the summer school courses open to other theatre and dance companies and hoped that in future students would be attracted from other islands, especially from the St Lucia Arts Guild.[15]

In June 1962, Harrison left the Rockefeller Foundation and his responsibilities were taken on by Gerald Freund. At first Freund was unhappy with the lack of clear planning between the Little Carib and the university concerning teaching. There appeared a duplication of plans and requests for assistance with no demarcation of what each institution was doing, but Freund continued Rockefeller support for the Little Carib and became a strong supporter of Walcott and the Workshop. During 1962 Rockefeller fellowships were granted to George Williams to study theatre lighting at Yale and to Errol Jones to study acting in New York. Jones studied with Herbert Berghoff and Gene Frankel and had 'observer' status at Actors' Studio. After his return to Trinidad he became a leader of the Theatre Workshop's acting sessions.

Errol Jones was born in San Fernando in 1923. His father, an Anglican, was a seaman, with primary-school education, who had an interest in music. His mother, also Anglican, attended secondary school and had an interest in music, theatre, and dance. As a result of often being taken by his mother to the movies, Errol became interested in acting. He attended the élite Queen's Royal College in Port of Spain and became an immigration officer in 1942, a position in which he continued until 1977 when he took early retirement from being chief immigration officer.

After seeing Errol John acting in a Whitehall Players' production of *An Inspector Calls*, Jones asked a friend in the Customs Department who was a member of the Whitehall Players how he could join. He first performed in 1949 in the Whitehall Players' production of Peter Ustinov's *The Different Shepherd* directed by Winnifred Dunn. He had roles in their *Juno and the Paycock*, *An Enemy of the People* and Walcott's *Henri Christophe* as well as the Trinidad Dramatic Club's *Othello*, in which he played the title role, and the Company of Players' production of Capek's *The Insects*, in which Arnold Rampersad also participated. He met Walcott during rehearsals of *Drums and Colours* and he was in Walcott's 1958 production of *Ti-Jean*. Walcott invited him the next year to join the Theatre Workshop he was starting. Jones soon became the most important member of the Workshop after Walcott. He already had a reputation as one of the best Trinidadian actors, brought other good actors into the Workshop, and became part of the small inner circle upon whom Walcott relied. After Walcott resigned from the Workshop in 1976, Jones kept it going. Jones has an unusually large presence on stage and a loud, clear voice. A rather still actor on stage, who normally interiorizes emotions, he developed great command of his facial features and his body movements, which he uses economically to dramatize changes of emotion. He was one of the first Theatre Workshop actors to gain attention abroad. During 1965, Jones was a member of the *Man, Better Man* company formed for the first Commonwealth Arts Festival in England and Scotland. He was

Actor in Residence at Grinnell College, Iowa, during 1970. Besides Trinidad Theatre Workshop tours he has acted outside Trinidad in a production of Errol John's *Moon on a Rainbow Shawl* at Theatre Royal, Stratford East in London, Rawle Gibbons's *I, Lawah* at Caribbean Focus '86 in London, and various productions in Barbados and Jamaica. His awards include the National Cultural Council Award for Acting (1981), the first person honoured by National Drama Association of Trinidad and Tobago (1984), the Hummingbird Medal—National Independence Anniversary Award, President's 25th Anniversary Award (1987) and the McBurnie Foundation Award (1987).[16]

George Williams worked with Walcott's first productions in Port of Spain and the early Theatre Workshop shows. He was the only one at the time doing lighting and he taught it to John Andrews and others. Originally an electrician he was sent by his company to help with a show and he developed into a lighting technician at a time when there were few materials available in Trinidad for stage productions. Everything had to be improvised. Recognizing his unusual abilities the Rockefeller Foundation sent him to Yale University to study technical design and lighting.

Williams was born (1930) in a village near Tunapuna. His parents were Anglican. His father, an agricultural field assistant, was half-Negro, half-Scots Barbadian, with an interest in music; his mother was Negro and a housewife with primary school education. After Williams did the lighting of a 1949 production of *Romeo and Juliet* for the Company of Five at the Public Library, he was used by most of the local drama and dance groups including the Whitehall Players, Company of Players and the Little Carib Theatre. He worked on the lighting for the West Indies Festival of the Arts and designed for the 1963 Carnival the lights for the parallel stage in the Savannah. The only other person with knowledge of stage lighting was an Englishman who returned to England in 1963. Since then Williams has done the lighting for each Carnival as well as the lighting for most big Port of Spain events such as operas and many concerts at Queen's Hall. Starting in 1966 he began teaching lighting at the extra-mural summer school at the University of the West Indies, St Augustine. He is often sent overseas by the Trinidadian government to do lighting for Carifesta and other shows in England, Canada, Grenada, Switzerland, Cuba, Guyana, and Barbados. Essentially self-trained except for the year at Yale he keeps up with the latest lighting techniques through subscribing to magazines, obtaining catalogues of equipment, and reading plays and books on lighting. Most people now doing theatre lighting in the eastern

Caribbean were taught by Williams. While Walcott was clearly the leader of the Little Carib Theatre Workshop, the members were teaching each other as they learned about professional theatre. Williams remembers having shown Walcott the necessity of carefully marking the script to produce a cue sheet for the lighting.

It was understood that the University of the West Indies would eventually create a Creative Arts Centre with teaching functions, and that there would be co-operation between the University and the Little Carib which, besides having its own dance and theatre company, would be used as a place for teaching and developing the performing arts in the region to professional standards. The integration of teaching and performance between university and a national theatre proved impossible if only because with the collapse of the West Indian Federation there was no longer a financial source for a national West Indian theatre company. The university survived as a regional institution, although local politics required it to spread its resources more thinly and duplicate degree programmes throughout the region. Each micronation approached culture in its own way. Jamaica continued to support élite culture with its base in the university. In St Lucia the Arts Guild and the Extra-Mural Department worked together towards a yearly Arts Festival. Grenada would be affected by its political situation. In Trinidad the government decided to put its money into the villages and folk traditions.

Although Eric Williams, leader of the People's National Movement (PNM), at first appeared favourable towards new West Indian writers, his view of the arts was political. He appointed a Minister of Culture, talked of building a grandiose Soviet-style national hall for the arts and gave government support to village dramatic skits and folk-dances. As happened elsewhere in many new nations, soon after independence a split developed between the writers, with their concern for artistic standards and free speech, and the politicians, with their official state culture and desire for control. Within a decade Walcott would regard Williams as a tyrant, another example of how the failure of the Haitian revolution would be repeated throughout Caribbean history.

While the Workshop remained a workshop, by 1962 the actors were becoming impatient to perform in public. This coincided with Walcott's interest in the theatre of the absurd. The first public production of the Little Carib Theatre Workshop, 11–13 May 1962, consisted of a double bill of Samuel Beckett's *Krapp's Last Tape* and *The Caged*, a symbolic play by the talented West Indian Dennis Scott. Walcott's preface to the programme mentions that the two plays are of 'the avant-garde school' and that the Workshop hopes to bring about the same 'interest in drama as there is in dance at this theatre, and is experimenting with the possibilities of fusing the two into an indigenous West Indian form'. Slade Hopkinson, a brilliant actor from Guyana and Barbados, who had been at the UCWI, Jamaica, with Walcott, performed the solo part of Krapp. Hopkinson was already an actor with great stage presence who moved with authority, spoke clearly, and was used to acting in productions of Shakespeare's plays. His voice could range from middle tenor to bass profundo. Actors and reviewers have said that Hopkinson, along with Errol Jones, was the finest actor in the West Indies. His performance of King Lear at the University College is still remembered by those who were present. Small, balding, he somehow seemed large, powerful, and intense on stage, and had an unusual command of inflections and nuances of speech. Trained as a classical actor, Hopkinson, however, did not use his body as the West Indian actors did. Karl Douglas in the *Trinidad Guardian* praised Hopkinson's ability to mime and establish character as a tour de force. Unfortunately Beryl McBurnie and Walcott were quarrelling then, as often; McBurnie purposefully flushed the toilet of the Little Carib in the middle of *Krapp's Last Tape*.[17]

During December the Little Carib Theatre Workshop again appeared in public, this time with *The Charlatan*, a play that Walcott has revised over the years from the time when it was first performed after winning a Jamaican Adults Drama Festival. In December 1962 it was performed for two nights for the opening of the Naparima Bowl in San Fernando, and then moved to the Little Carib Theatre, where it ran 7–10 December. Co-directed by Slade Hopkinson and Walcott, who also wrote the lyrics, *The Charlatan* had sets based on a design by Peter Minshall. The cast included Johnny Cayonne, Fred Hope, Ronald Llanos, Lima Hill, Arnold Rampersad, Slade Hopkinson, Ralph Campbell, Mavis Lee Wah, Judy Miles, Leo Rufino, Geddes Jennings, and Stanley Marshall. Claude Reid was in charge of stage management. Errol Jones was then in the United States.[18]

Hopkinson, Llanos and Mavis Lee Wah had been at UCWI with Walcott. Mavis Lee Wah, a Jamaican, had married James Lee Wah and performed in his San Fernando Drama Guild. Marshall and Reid also came from San Fernando theatre groups. Stanley Marshall, one of the foundation members of the Trinidad Theatre Workshop, was born (1924) in San Fernando into a 'black Negro' Methodist family. His father was a tailor with an elementary school education and an interest in reading and singing. His mother had an elementary school education.

Stanley attended a Methodist school where he became involved with theatre, and a government training school also in San Fernando. He was a foundation member of Horace James's San Fernando Drama Guild which began with studio sessions and moved on to productions. His stage debut was in the Drama Guild's production of Chekhov's *The Marriage Proposal* (1956) followed by Synge's *The Shadow of the Glen* (1956) and *Playboy of the Western World* (1957). Invited to be a member of Walcott's Little Carib Theatre Workshop, Marshall, a geological draughtsman, moved to Port of Spain in 1959 where he found employment in the Civil Service. Marshall regularly attended workshops finding them lively, sometimes fiery. He was in almost every production of the Trinidad Theatre Workshop, if not on stage then backstage. He is perhaps the most underrated of the Trinidad Theatre Workshop actors with an ability to draw comedy from minor, even silent walk-on roles. His gestures and facial expressions can be larger than life, and he can hold his body in awkward, uncomfortable postures for long periods without showing signs of discomfort. The National Drama Association of Trinidad and Tobago honoured him in 1989.

Arnold Rampersad, the now well-known scholar of American literature, was for a time involved with the Workshop. Although his name is Indian, from an Indian Christian grandfather, he is 'black'. His grandmother was a black Protestant. He was born in Port of Spain (1941) to a Roman Catholic mother and father. His mother had minimal education and worked as a telephone operator at the American naval base. His father was from Barbados and worked as a primary school teacher and as a reporter for the *Guardian*. The family was poor and Rampersad's parents divorced when he was young. He attended Belmont Intermediate Roman Catholic school and then St Mary's College, 1959–60, after which he taught at Fatima College for a year, then worked for Radio 610 as an announcer before obtaining a job in the Prime Minister's office at Whitehall. Interested in drama, he met Freddie Kissoon and Sydney Hill through the British Council and performed in Errol Hill's companies before the Theatre Workshop.

As the Theatre Workshop changed from the 1959 *Showcase* towards a more stable company its complexion became darker and its membership less part of an already existing artistic and social élite. Many of the male members were from artisan and lower-middle-class backgrounds; they were part a new black middle and upper-middle class in the making. Somewhat better educated than their parents, their interest in theatre was part of the opportunities that were beginning to develop in the last years of colonialism. Many moved from the provinces to Port of Spain; Jones, Reid, Marshall, and Albert Laveau, who were over the years to become the core members of the Workshop, were from San Fernando. During a time when there were few chances for the less wealthy Trinidadian to make a mark on society as an artist or in other careers, acting offered an opening to those with larger interests and a desire for mobility. It was 'something to do' for those wanting more from life. Many members of the Theatre Workshop are now prominent in Trinidad both as artists and in their careers. No doubt being on stage contributed to their prominence, but at the time they were often told that they would move no higher in their careers if they continued to devote so much time to acting. Those who continued to act had strong wills and much energy as well as being dedicated to the theatre.

Many members of the Trinidad Theatre Workshop came from families headed by preachers, nurses, school teachers, mechanics, and carpenters, careers in which it was possible to be trained locally. This was a time when such careers were the upper limit available to those without the financial means to go to élite schools and abroad for further education. Secondary schooling in Trinidad was limited to a few select institutions which required the passing of entrance examinations and there was no local university. To pass the entrance examinations it was usually necessary to have attended one of the better primary schools in Port of Spain and to have tutoring. Social divisions were now more economic in terms of educational qualifications than by colour, although those too impoverished to be able to afford better schools were more likely to be non-white. To be a preacher or school teacher was to be respectable, if poorly paid. The opening of public service jobs to non-whites after the Second World War provided an opportunity for the children of the previous lower middle class to move to secure, pensionable, government positions with the possibility of promotion up the administrative ladder. While their families cannot be said to be cultured, in the way that Derek Walcott's father was familiar with the literary classics and art, they were raised during a time when in the West Indies there did not exist the sharp division that had already occurred elsewhere between modern high culture and popular culture. Their parents listened to opera recordings, and expected their children to participate in family evenings when each person would recite poetry, act in a skit, sing, dance, or contribute in some way to the entertainment. At school there were public-speaking contests, performances of scenes from plays, 'concerts' with singing, dancing, and recitations. This common culture disappeared as the result of changes, including the mass entertainment industry, television, and the acceptance of a youth culture, after the Second World War, but not before it formed several generations of non-white West Indians with the desire somehow to participate in a more interesting creative world that had been previously denied them and to which they felt they had a right. In this they were no different, if more disadvantaged, than many whites at the time who were brought up to enjoy the arts, but who saw no way to go further with them in the then still isolated, provincial, colonies. Those with ambitions who could went abroad: Walcott and McBurnie decided to stay and lead those who had to remain and build their own theatre and dance companies.

Writing regularly for the *Trinidad Guardian* and *Sunday Guardian* Walcott could publicize and discuss theatre beyond reviewing performances. Reading through the reviews, news articles, and columns he wrote, it is possible to see him thinking through the practical problems of establishing a solidly based West Indian theatre and trying to influence public opinion, including the local arts community. A column headed 'A Need For Supporters' begins 'If there were a theatre season here, where would you fit it in?' Trinidad before and after Christmas is obsessed by preparing for Carnival and for many people it would be sacrilege to have theatre during Lent. Walcott's article announces that the Little Carib Theatre Workshop ('a suicide squad of which I confess membership') will perform Ionesco's *The Lesson* during January 1964, and makes a somewhat tongue-in-cheek comparison of the play to Calypso, 'The Mighty Ionesco, king of Caiso.' He also plugs the forthcoming annual Dimanche Gras Carnival show by Errol Hill. Jeff Henry, the former Little Carib dancer, would return to do the choreography. As usual there were problems over the Dimanche Gras show with its immense cast and large expectations. As the 1963 show was thought to have too much talk, the 1964 show would be more like mime. Another theme of the article is the need for local patronage of the arts. Walcott asks why local businessmen and the financially well-off do not directly finance a little theatre, a chamber orchestra, an art gallery, and scholarships and grants for local artists to raise the standard of local arts including radio and television productions. Local businesses should make a policy of purchasing the work of at least one artist each year.[19]

The Theatre Workshop's double bill of *The Lesson* and Walcott's *Malcochon* was acted at the Little Carib Theatre 22–24 January 1964. *The Lesson* was directed by Walcott with Eunice Alleyne, Slade Hopkinson and Bernardine Moore. The cast of *Malcochon* (which had already been produced by the St Lucia Arts Guild, the Royal Court Theatre in London and off-Broadway at the Judson Theatre) included Claude Reid, Johnny Cayonne, Fred Hope, Lima Hill, Errol Jones, Ralph Campbell, and Geddes Jennings, along with a small orchestra in which Stanley Marshall played maracas and Leo Rufino played flute. Lighting was by George Williams; Walcott directed. This production was repeated at the Guild Hall of the University and at San Fernando's Naparima Bowl. At both later performances Joy Ryan replaced Eunice Alleyne who was away on study leave. Mae Frazer took the part of the Maid in *The Lesson* at San Fernando. The ability to replace other actors, change, share roles, or help back stage or in the orchestra was part of what Walcott wanted. The Trinidad Theatre Workshop was to be a company in which each individual would have many skills and responsibilities.[20]

By 1964 Walcott's plans to build a theatre company was becoming more than a dream; five years of weekly workshops had produced a core of trained actors with shared ambitions, used to working together, and following his leadership. His ensemble consisted mostly of 'blacks' with a few whites in supporting roles. Occasionally someone of Asian Indian descent would belong. The core of the company included Eunice Alleyne and Joy Ryan along with Leone Campbell; the male actors were Slade Hopkinson, Errol Jones, Stanley Marshall, Claude Reid, Fred Hope, Ralph Campbell, Geddes Jennings, Leo Rufino. George Williams was still in charge of lighting. Albert Laveau had met Walcott in 1961, joined the Workshop in 1962, was often busy with his job, but would begin participating regularly from 1965.

The women in the Trinidad Theatre Workshop have usually had strong personalities; they needed it to survive Walcott's own dominant personality and strong tongue. They have been hard working and ambitious, either from important families or determined to make a place for themselves in society. Eunice Bruno Alleyne, like Errol Jones, began in the lower-middle class and moved to the top of Public Service. Eunice Bruno was born (1936) in Caracas, Venezuela, into a Roman Catholic Negro family. While her father was a mechanic with no cultural interests, her mother was a school teacher with many cultural interests. Eunice Bruno attended St Joseph's Convent in Port of Spain where she gave the valedictory speech; the clarity of her articulation is often mentioned by actors. At school she became interested in theatre and participated in the Catholic Youth Organization. In 1957 she won the prose and verse competition in the National Arts Festival. She went directly from school into the Public Service. After working for the Central Water Distribution Authority and the Registrar's General Office she applied to the Government Broadcasting Unit and moved up from Broadcasting Officer to Programme Director and then to the Public Relations Office for the Prime Minister, where she is Director of Information. In the late 1950s she became a member of the Company of Players, acted first in Wilfred Redhead's *Goose and Gander*, then in a production of Walcott's *Ione* (1957). She was a 'female slave' in *Drums and Colours* and was invited by Walcott to join the Theatre Workshop at its inception. She usually managed to combine her career with theatre and attended Trinidad Theatre Workshop rehearsals regularly after work and on weekends. She participated in workshops given by any visiting foreign directors and when the Trinidad Theatre Workshop was on tour. She was impressed by Walcott's total commitment and thought of him as an excellent teacher who 'expects no compromise'. Alleyne likes to be challenged to expand her acting and dancing skills and is conscious that each character requires a change in attitude and posture from your finger tips to your eye brows. She is praised for her nuances of tone and sensitivity of features, especially the eyes, when acting.[21]

Leone Campbell was born (1932) in St Kitts. Her parents were Anglican. Her father was brown; her mother, who was light brown, graduated from secondary school and played piano. Leone attended Westminister College of Commerce in London and the Trinidad and Tobago Hotel School. While in London she became interested in theatre through the British Council and joined a small drama group formed by a British Council tutor. When she returned from London her husband introduced her to Walcott, whom her husband had known from the UCWI, Jamaica. Walcott was then forming the Theatre Workshop and invited her to join. She attended every workshop. Later she often went abroad on diplomatic missions and then became self-employed. Ralph Campbell is her brother-in-law.

The company participated in the 28 February 1965 Dimanche Gras production of Walcott's *Batai* by the Carnival Development Committee at the Savannah. Although this was not an official Workshop production, the programme listed the director as 'Derek Walcott of the Theatre Workshop' and gave the Workshop credit for providing the main actors. Of the perhaps two hundred people involved in the production the cast included Albert Laveau, Johnny Cayonne, Geddes Jennings, Ralph Campbell, Fred Hope, Eunice Alleyne, Errol Jones, and Slade Hopkinson. This was an evening Walcott tried to forget.[22]

Walcott had early developed a theory about the relationship of folk culture to high art. While all arts begin in the folk, folk culture is limited as a model for the serious artist who is likely to invest it with false complexities. The natural, primitive, or ethnic artist will fail to develop without studying art itself. Theatre is a profession with a hierarchy 'based at its simplest on writer, director, actor and builder. Its composition implies rule, obedience, dedication. Its enactment requires sequence.' Attempts to reproduce folk culture in the theatre are likely to result in sentimentalized naturalism.[23]

Walcott had criticized Errol Hill's attempts to unify the carnival show with a central story. They had quarrelled publicly over whether Carnival itself had a theatrical form (Hill's argument) or whether West Indian theatre would need to use Western dramatic forms (Walcott's view). Now this was Walcott's chance to show what might be done with a Carnival show. The Dimanche Gras play is an important event in Trinidad and the Governor-General was to be present as patron. Over two hundred people were involved in the production and everything went wrong. The police band, which was to play the national anthem and overture, lacked transportation and arrived more than a half-hour late. This was the first time they used transistor microphones at Carnival and after five minutes the sound failed, leaving the actors gesturing inaudibly in front of the large, boisterous carnival crowd. Some new lighting equipment, including a strobe light, also failed at key moments. Walcott, who was standing at the back of the Carnival crowd, watched his play collapse and became so angry that he fractured his fist by smashing it through a window. He afterwards collected all copies of the play and would never mention it again, resisting attempts by Workshop members to perform *Batai* in more suitable circumstances.[24]

The exact cause of the Theatre Workshop's rupture with the Little Carib is not clear. McBurnie and Walcott have dominating, larger-than-life personalities; they at times strongly disagreed with each other and McBurnie was unhappy with the kinds of experimental plays Walcott was producing. The actors were taking more and more Little Carib time for rehearsals, using the Little Carib for drama, whereas McBurnie saw her theatre as primarily for dance. As the Theatre Workshop planned to move beyond a small actors' studio towards a production and repertory company there were bound to be problems over conflicting rehearsals. A dispute about when the Theatre Workshop could rehearse is said to have become a heated argument about Walcott and the actors not paying their dues or some rental to the

Little Carib, after which the actors arrived one evening and the door of the Little Carib was locked; they had to find a new home. At the time they were rehearsing Slade Hopkinson's *Fall of a Chief*, which included Errol Jones, Albert Laveau, Ralph Campbell, and Fred Hope. This play, under various titles, would be rehearsed over the years without being produced by the Workshop.[25]

After the break with the Little Carib the Theatre Workshop met once a week at the Government Training College. Spirits were low, members dropped out, until only a small core, then only Errol Jones, remained. In October a new home was found. An unused bar in the basement of Bretton Hall Hotel could be converted into a small inti- mate theatre which if limited would put emphasis on acting rather than scenery. Some architect friends helped Walcott with the transfor- mation. There was a need for lights, painting, a canvas backdrop, but at the end of the conversion they had a theatre which at first seated about 60 people. The exact number varied with each production and ways were found later to add tiers for additional space so that up to 90 could be seated. The Little Carib Theatre Workshop now became the Trinidad Theatre Workshop, although it was also referred to as the Basement Theatre. After Walcott was locked out from the Little Carib, McBurnie's career stalled. The Little Carib was often closed and she was at times without a regular dance company. Local sponsorship for a new Little Carib had not been found and the building deterio- rated until two decades later a government grant helped to build a new, still unsatisfactory, theatre for her. The responsibility for creating a 'national' theatre for the region was now Walcott's and those who had followed him this far.[26]

Notes

1. Walcott's 'Meanings', *Savacou*, 2 (Sept. 1970), 45–51: 46. My discussion of such matters as gestures and pronunciation is based on comments Walcott, Laveau, and others have made at various times, including rehearsals (Apr. 1993) for the Boston tour. Richard Montgomery and Walcott have mentioned to me changes in acting style according to the kind of play. Also see Derek Walcott, 'Interview with an Actor', *Trinidad Guardian* (13 Oct. 1965), 5.

2. Derek Walcott, 'The Poet in the Theatre', *Poetry Review*, 80/4 (winter 1990– 91), 4–8; Derek Walcott, 'What the Twilight Says: An Overture', in *Dream on Monkey Mountain and Other Plays* (New York: Farrar, Straus and Giroux, 1970), 3–40: 25.

3. Derek Walcott, 'Derek Walcott Looks At Off-Broadway Theatre', *Trinidad Guardian* (20 Oct. 1963), 15.

4. 'The Little Carib Theatre Workshop', *Opus*, 1/1 (Feb. 1960): 31–2. *Opus* was published by Irma Goldstraw; the article is possibly by Walcott.

5. Victor Questel's 'Trinidad Theatre Workshop: A Bibliography', *Kairi 76* (1976), 53–9 includes a useful rudimentary chronology of productions. Questel was preparing a book on the Trinidad Theatre Workshop before his death; a rough draft exists in the University of the West Indies, St Augustine, West Indian Collection. App. III (pp. 559–625) of Questel's Ph.D. thesis (1979), 'Derek Walcott: Contradiction and Resolution' concerns 'The Trinidad Theatre Workshop 1959–76'.

6. Bruce Procope to John P. Harrison (4 Apr. 1960). Most of the correspondence for 1960–63 concerning The Little Carib Theatre, Derek Walcott, fellowships for Errol Jones and others, can be found in the Rockefeller Archives under 'Little Carib Theatre'.

7. For Walcott's journalism see Irma Goldstraw, *Derek Walcott: An Annotated Bibliography of His Works* (New York: Garland, 1984); and Robert D. Hamner, 'Bibliography' in id. (ed.), *Critical Perspectives on Derek Walcott* (Washington, DC: Three Continents Press, 1993), 410–30.

8. Derek Walcott, 'Need for a Little Theatre in POS', *Sunday Guardian* (10 July 1960), 22.

9. Thomas Patterson—John P. Harrison (8 Sept. 1960; 7 Dec. 1960), Rockefeller Archives.

10. John P. Harrison, 'telephone call' to George Izenour (9 June 1961); Harrison to Walcott (14 June 1961); Harrison to Walcott (26 June 1961); Harrison memo, 'Synthesis of Trinidad Diary'(13 July 1961), Rockefeller Archives.

11. Derek Walcott, 'Unique Lighting Equipment Offered New Little Carib', *Sunday Guardian* (20 Aug. 1961), 7.

12. Herbert Machiz, Rockefeller Archive file (2 May 1961; 16 Sept. 1961; 3 Dec. 1961; 5 Dec. 1961; 13 Feb. 1962; 20 Feb. 1962; 21 Feb. 1962); Harrison to Walcott (5 Oct. 1961); Walcott to Harrison (16 Oct. 1961), Rockefeller Archives; and Derek Walcott, 'US Stage Director Takes A Look At Queen's Hall', *Trinidad Guardian* (30 Aug. 1961), 5; Derek Walcott, 'US Stage Director on Observation Trip', *Trinidad Guardian* (4 Mar. 1962), 5.

13. Bruce Procope to John P. Harrison (25 Nov. 1961), Rockefeller Archives.

14. John P. Harrison to Derek Walcott (20 Dec. 1961), Rockefeller Archives.

15. Derek Walcott to John P. Harrison (11 Jan. 1962), Rockefeller Archives. John Harrison's letter to Bruce Procope (23 Feb. 1962) makes clear that the Rockefeller Foundation would only help to develop a summer school in dance and drama if the purpose of the Little Carib is to develop into something like a national repertory group for the West Indies. Several members of the St Lucia Arts Guild did attend.

16. Information about Errol Jones, George Williams, and others from interviews, a questionnaire, and résumés. Arnold Rampersad was interviewed by telephone during 1993.

17. Derek Walcott, 'Public Debut for Theatre Workshop', *Sunday Guardian* (25 Mar. 1962), 7; 'Workshop Makes Debut', *Trinidad Guardian* (1 May 1962); 'Little Carib Turns Now to Drama', *Trinidad Guardian* (6 May 1962), 6; Karl Douglas, 'Requiem on Tape for a Lost Soul', *Trinidad Guardian* (13 May 1962),

13; Derek Walcott, 'Actor Slade Hopkinson Gives a Farewell Interview', *Trinidad Guardian* (14 July 1965), 6.

18. 'P. O. S. to See "Charlatan" ', *Trinidad Guardian* (4 Dec. 1962), 6; Karl Douglas, ' "Charlatan" Scores—Comedy Wise', *Trinidad Guardian* (10 Dec. 1962), 5; ' "The Charlatan" Gets 5 Calls', *Evening News* (11 Dec. 1962).

19. Derek Walcott, 'A Need for Supporters', *Trinidad Guardian* (25 Dec. 1963), 5.

20. L. C., 'Actors Score with Comedy and Drama', *Trinidad Guardian* (24 Jan. 1964), 7.

21. Lesley Ackrill, 'For Eunice Alleyne's . . .', *People* (Sept. 1980), 41–2.

22. 'Batai—Battle of the Cannes Brules', *Daily Mirror* (23 Jan. 1965). *Batai* was thought to be a 'lost' Walcott play, but there are two copies among George Williams's blueprints for the lighting of Carnival shows, one as originally written, the other adapted for performance.

23. Derek Walcott, 'West Indian Dance, Dancers', *Sunday Guardian* (28 July 1963), 14.

24. For Walcott and Hill on Carnival see Derek Walcott, 'National Theatre is the Answer', *Trinidad Guardian* (12 Aug. 1964), Derek Walcott, 'S. Grande Tonight; Broadway Next', *Trinidad Guardian* (27 Jan. 1965), 5; Errol Hill, 'No Tears for Narcissus', *Sunday Guardian* (7 Mar. 1965), 7; Errol Hill, *The Trinidad Carnival, Mandate for a National Theatre* (Austin: University of Texas Press, 1972).

25. Derek Walcott, 'Energetic Guild Comes to Town', *Trinidad Guardian* (19 May 1965), 5.

26. For McBurnie's later career see Ahye, *Cradle of Caribbean Dance*.

PART II

The Great Years
(West Indian Style)
1966–1976

1966

3

The Basement Theatre
The First Season

THE loss of the use of the Little Carib and the building of a small theatre in the basement of Hotel Bretton Hall led to the first repertory season, the renaming and transformation of the Little Carib Theatre Workshop into the Trinidad Theatre Workshop, and a theatre company that would regularly perform publicly, would need to support itself financially, and which became the most important theatre company in the West Indies. Actors could no longer be off-and-on members although some continued to perform with other companies. Workshops would be more geared towards productions and when there were no rehearsals there were two workshops a week, on Tuesday and Friday evenings. The Basement Theatre was for two years a place where the actors could meet to discuss plays and their parts, rehearse together, and feel at home. It was their territory, a small intimate theatre offering immediate rapport with the audience.

The older members of the Workshop say that it was in the Basement Theatre that the company formed its ensemble style. The variety of plays they performed, ranging from the naturalistic to Genet and Soyinka, was demanding and required a greater understanding of acting. While the Workshop's style was more broadly gestural than British acting, it varied according to the kind of play, and changed over the years as the actors matured in their art. During the 1973 Jamaica tour, for example, *Franklin* was performed in a naturalistic, almost Chekhovian manner while *The Charlatan* used extremely suggestive body movements to emphasize the text in the manner of Calypso tent performances. In workshops Walcott made the actors rapidly change from emotion to emotion doing an improvisation, sometimes treating each line in a radically different mood. To develop a consistency of intensity he would interrupt actors, tell a joke, and expect them immediately to return to the previous emotion as if there had been no interruption. Errol Jones was famous in the West Indies for how in *Dream on Monkey Mountain* he performed Makak in an ape-like manner and then suddenly transformed himself into an erect, proud, haughty monarch; decades later in Boston he relied more on the interiorization of mood and less on contrasting extremes of visual appearance. Walcott himself would change, wanting to try new acting techniques and interpretations of a role, and often being annoyed with younger actors who performed with exaggerated gestures and postures that distracted from the mood of a scene or were likely to obscure the meaning of the words.

While each of the actors developed a personal way of learning lines and preparing a role, they learned to work as an ensemble in a style which might be approximately described as a blend of Stanislavski, the Method, and West Indian body movements and gestures. Their style was further modified by Walcott's own directorial instincts for the visual and pictorial, his concern for the interpretation and phrasing of each word and line, his desire for a total theatre of music, dance, and mime, and his interest in the methods of such directors as Brecht, Grotowski, and Artaud. Even when actors had developed an interpretation of character, their movements were shaped by Walcott's painterly sense for the visual.[1]

The Basement Theatre was 50ft × 25ft × 10ft with a stage 18ft × 8ft about 6 inches off the floor. To get maximum seating and visibility the stage was centred against one long wall, which allowed viewing from three sides, and permitted up to ninety-five seats. Such a small theatre was demanding on the actors; similar to performances of southern Indian plays in temples, the closeness of actors to audience meant that every gesture counted, the eyes, the facial muscles, the lips all were interpreted by the audience. Even today Workshop actors have an unusual completeness of detail in their performances. The Workshop was from the first trained to be closely observed. The Basement Theatre was painted black, which extremely concentrated the mood and effect. Walcott wanted silence before performances so that actors could meditate, mentally rehearse their lines, and get into their roles. While the small theatre allowed intimacy there was the danger that the actors would lose their sense of projection and movement.[2]

Although now sentimentalized as home, the Basement Theatre was a terrible place in which to work. Actors needed to enter and exit through the side stairs, there was no place for the technicians and those in charge of the lighting hid under the stairs or were on the staircase. The lights were fixed into the ceiling; because of the heat the cellophane had to be changed each night after every performance. The stage was small and could hold perhaps six actors comfortably, although it was used for larger casts. Staging had to be simple, with a scene painted on the walls and a few simple props. By necessity this was both an intimate theatre and a theatre of poverty. The actors were literally performing at the feet of those in the first row. Such a theatre was fine for poetic plays with small casts and allowed appreciation of facial gestures, but Walcott, influenced by the theatre of violence, wanted a highly physical theatre and produced such works as *The Blacks*, which required space and which brought physical action and harsh emotions close to the audience. The small stage was inappropriate for 'lateral' plays, like Soyinka's *The Road*, where spatial symbolism is significant. The small seating area also limited what could be earned from admissions. No sooner had Walcott found a home for his company than its limitations became evident. Yet it was the only home they would have. (If this sounds somewhat like the story of Naipaul's Mr Biswas . . . well, it's Trinidad.)

In Port of Spain where serious plays until then had one or two performances by groups that were organized for productions, the Basement Theatre gave the Workshop a chance to build an audience and a 'season' without the embarrassment of empty seats. Five packed nights at the Basement Theatre felt more like real theatre than playing before the same number of people on one night in Queen's Hall and seeing unfilled chairs. It would take time before the Workshop could build an audience of thousands for a longer run.

Conversion of the former Paddock Bar in the basement of Hotel Bretton Hall started in October 1965 and by 7–12 January 1966 the company performed a double bill of Derek Walcott's *The Sea at Dauphin* and Edward Albee's *Zoo Story*. The casts included Albert Laveau as Jerry, Errol Jones as Peter (*Zoo Story*) and Ralph Campbell, Claude Reid, Geddes Jennings, Peter Bruce, Inniss Vincent, Constance Allsop, Grace Walke, Leone Campbell, Janet Stanley, and Lucita Baptiste. Several of the cast (Peter Bruce, Inniss Vincent, Grace Walke, Janet Stanley, and Lucita Baptiste) were not mentioned among the twenty-six Workshop members listed later in year.

Until the expansion of Walcott's plays to include significant amounts of dance, the female membership of the Workshop was small and changing. The Workshop in origins was primarily male and Walcott's principal roles are for male actors. His plays concern the male world and Walcott wanted a very physical company of a kind he thought could only be built with male actors. In his early plays, except for *Ione*, women are usually market women or have small parts. Women were sometimes uncomfortable with Walcott's rough language and the way the Workshop members would gather for late-night drinking after workshops and rehearsals. Some of the drinking sessions erupted into fights. Then there were the usual problems women face—husbands and children who wanted their meals, husbands and fathers who did not want their women out at night in the company of other men. The role of women in the Workshop was often a problem. As the Workshop was thought of as an ensemble, a family, all members had to be present throughout all the rehearsals and performances, although workshops and rehearsals could last until 2 or 3 a.m. Later, on tours, the men felt it was their duty to protect the younger women and treat them as daughters, but this meant that when strong-willed women became Workshop members their leadership was resented; and as the Workshop grew and further members were added there were the usual seductions and love affairs.

Karen Phelps in the *Trinidad Guardian* offered some favourable comments on the acting in *The Sea at Dauphin* and *Zoo Story*, but her main concern was the hope that having found a place of its own the Workshop would perform several productions a year and inspire local writing for the theatre. Her article was accompanied by a photograph of the British author J. B. Priestly and the local British Council representative attending a performance. Priestly left before *Zoo Story*.[3]

Another reviewer, possibly Walcott himself, in 'Two Plays that Lifted the Basement Theatre', called the double bill an instant success, said the language of *Sea* offered word pictures with graphic detail, commented on the use of St Lucian patois—which the audience might not understand—criticized Peter Bruce's acting of the priest and the 'women' of Dauphin as too mechanical, and praised Jennings's 'naturalness' and Laveau as 'convincing'. In *Zoo Story* Laveau's 'phoney yankee accent' was too much and sometimes broke, while Jones 'with hardly a word registers a gamut of reactions that clearly reflect his feelings'.[4]

In the early years of the Workshop's productions, especially on tours, such unsigned reviews were common and were probably written directly from publicity material that Walcott supplied. It is impossible to be certain of their authorship. Such reviews and announcements of productions often turn up in photocopies of photocopies, with no indicated source, date, or pagination, in files—many times literally bags—of 'cuttings' preserved in West Indian libraries. Even some news-paper files consist of cuttings without dates or pagination.

In February Gerald Freund of the Rockefeller Foundation, who had been following the development of the Little Carib, received a long letter from Walcott explaining what had happened since his break with McBurnie. Since acquiring their own theatre the company was now having a second night of workshops each week for beginners. Numbers were up to thirty to thirty-five. Walcott said that they could have continued for a long time with their first production except that Errol Jones had to go to the United States and England as part of the training for his present job. Walcott thought they now had a potential paying audience of 700. He had organized a committee to keep the Workshop going; it included the architect John Gillespie, the lawyer Selby Wooding, Errol Jones, Fred Thomas, Margaret, and himself. Thomas, a businessman, had managed to raise $500; others contributed $300. Walcott hoped that they could get patronage from some banks or Radio Trinidad. Although they had to pay Albee what for them was a large fee, Walcott thought that they could be self-supporting with-out needing large sums from the Rockefeller Foundation. They had even managed to pay the actors an honorarium. He was anxious for Errol Jones to return from abroad so that they could continue. Walcott was at the theatre at least three nights a week. Four of their actors left Trinidad last year, but others were joining.

Walcott was, however, concerned that he would lose his job with the *Trinidad Guardian* as their regular drama, music, art, book, and film critic. He was thought obscure and not needed. Instead he had been offered a monthly retainer plus payment for articles accepted. Walcott wanted to stay in Trinidad holding workshops, building a company, and not go abroad in anger the way other West Indian writers had. He had created a 'monster', a theatre company, and wanted it to continue. Could the Rockefeller Foundation come up with money for six to twelve months so Walcott could continue with his work? Walcott would do so whether or not he received the money. He felt embarrassed to be asking for money for himself instead of for the four or five actors whom he wanted especially to help develop. He did not want a scholarship to go overseas; he wanted to stay in Trinidad where he belonged. He was also writing to the Farfield Foundation.[5]

Freund perceptively replied that in the future many Ph.D. candidates would be searching the *Trinidad Guardian's* files for Walcott's articles. At present the Rockefeller Foundation was only concerned with the arts in the United States, but he would sound out his colleagues. Later in February the Farfield Foundation granted Walcott $1,500 as a temporary measure and recommended that the Rockefeller Foundation make an exception to its policies.[6]

The failure of the West Indian Federation, 1958–62, remained a concern to Walcott and other West Indian writers. To be West Indian was a source of identity and the Federation might provide an economic basis to support a culture; micronationalism could do neither. When two more islands became independent, Walcott complained that such micronationalism was inhospitable to the arts as it divided West Indians into small ethnic groups, fragmenting their diversity of cultures, and would result in artificial national cultures and lower standards. At present south of Jamaica only Trinidad could provide a place for an artist to work. Other islands were too small to support professional artists and writers.[7]

The second production of 1966 was of Eric Roach's *Belle Fanto*, performed 14–27 April; its nine nights were then the longest run for any play in Trinidad and surprised the Workshop which had not planned for performances beyond the first week. The cast included Eunice Bruno Alleyne as Tan, Sydney Best as Noah, Stanley Marshall as Uncle Willie, Claude Reid as Frank, Lynette Laveau as Feo, Lucita Baptiste as Esther, and Constance Allsop as Belle. Walcott directed, Lionel Kearns was in charge of sound, the set construction was by Geddes Jennings, and Peter Bruce was stage manager.

Belle Fanto was Lynette Laveau's first appearance with the Workshop. The youngest of a family of eleven brothers and sisters, she, like her older brother Albert, had acted in the Carnegie Players, a drama group in San Fernando. She had taken some extra-mural drama courses at the University of the West Indies, studying with Freddie Kissoon, and had been persuaded by her brother to join the Workshop, although she still lived in San Fernando and found transportation a problem. Lucita Baptiste joined the Workshop the previous year. The programme mentioned that this was Stanley Marshall's 'first major appearance with the Theatre Workshop', although he was one of the early foundation members from the Little Carib Theatre.

Walcott's 'prologue' to the programme spoke of the Workshop now entering a new phase, attempting to provide continuous theatre with an established company of over twenty actors. Until now the company limited themselves to one production a year of 'original works by West Indian playwrights along with plays by Beckett, Ionesco and Albee . . . preferring to concentrate on developing technique and an ensemble style at Friday workshops'.

An article in the *Sunday Mirror* by 'a Correspondent' says that Roach's poetry is rooted in the peasantry and that *Belle Fanto* is his first full-length play to give physical expression to the folk. It has the simple poetic directness of 'a peasant tragedy by Lorca'. Karen Phelps's vague review in the *Trinidad Guardian* objects that *Belle Fanto* portrayed a village and was written for a large stage not for the confined space of the Basement Theatre with its single backdrop. She praises the actresses, mentions that Walcott painted the sets, and wishes the Workshop well.[8]

Various short reviews mention that the play was well applauded, that Roach came on stage afterwards, and that the audience was packed with VIPs. Some of the short newspaper articles read as if theatre performances were social events with every 'Dr' in the audience deserving a mention. Yet it was Walcott's ability to attract such an audience through his personal friendships and reputation and through Margaret's social position that initially allowed the Workshop to survive. Many in Trinidadian society were willing to help sell tickets, bring friends, even work in the box office. At first the audience was élite, a coterie of local artists (such as the dramatists Marina Maxwell and Douglas Archibald, the painter Carlisle Chang), old friends from Jamaica (such as James and Mavis Lee Wah), various professionals, especially medical doctors, and some people from the embassies with an interest in local arts. It would take the Workshop time to extend its audience to other segments of the population.[9]

The Workshop had become Walcott's creation. Without the actors there would be no Workshop, but Walcott was not only its founder, leader, publicity department, set designer, and audience creator, he was also responsible for advertising and the programmes. Small advertisements for the plays published in the local newspapers include his drawings of the cast. As Walcott is himself a poet and painter it was natural to regard the Basement Theatre as an arts centre which in sponsoring non-theatrical events would help build an audience for plays and create a local arts scene. There is a bit of confusion about who read and when at the Basement Theatre; often the only surviving records are comments in the newspapers long after the events, but poetry readings began 24 and 25 March with Walcott, E. M. Roach, and Lionel Kearns (a Canadian who was involved with the Workshop). On 1 May a group from *Voices*, a literary magazine edited by Clifford Sealy, gave readings. On 2 and 3 June (the dates may not be exact) there were readings by the well-known West Indian novelists John Hearne and George Lamming. The Workshop also helped sponsor an exhibition of paintings by Naomi Mandel, an Israeli. A reviewer of the Lamming–Hearne reading said that the Basement Theatre has 'come to be looked upon as the "in" thing—a sort of status symbol'.[10]

In 'West Indian Art Today' Walcott surveyed the situation of the West Indian artist and claimed that humanism is central to the region's arts. 'The little art we produce asserts the integrity of the individual, however tragic.' There is a separation between public and artist partly because of illiteracy, partly from indifference. Those dramatists who have tried to cross the gap between popular and formal theatre have failed because their approach is academic. So far the public has shown a preference for the comic; burlesque in action or language is close to the common experience. Both V. S. Naipaul and C. L. R. James make use of nineteenth-century comedy. West Indian art is old-fashioned if seen from London or New York where the arts are restless. West Indians who complain that the public is uninterested in the avant-garde do not realize how much media publicity goes into promoting the metropolitan avant-garde artist. The West Indies lacks the dealers, millionaires, critics, cultists, magazines, and galleries. The West Indian artist also lacks knowledge of the artists of Central and South America, such as Wilfredo Lam, Orozco, Borges, and Neruda, who have more to offer than recent American and British culture. The theatre still lags behind the West Indian novel. Errol Hill's collection of West Indian plays barely scrapes the surface of what is available. 'It is hard to have to say this, but racial alienation still exists in theatre companies, involuntarily or not.' Local plays will remain nineteenth-century in mould unless the dramatists see that this can be changed, accept the need for greater experimentation, and risk failure. First there is the need to establish a classically composed tradition without folk gimmickry, while a more daring experimental drama is being created in smaller theatres. The West Indian artist will remain schizophrenic, having two languages, imitating the stylistic and technical advances of the European tradition while developing his own self-expression. Such contradictions can be hammered out, but the artist must remain a humanist concerned with love of his characters and their landscape.[11]

While Walcott's newspaper articles are focused on the direction theatre and other arts should take in Trinidad, the actual week-by-week workshops reflected his changing ideas, excitements, and the limitations of his actors. An article by Ulric Mentus begins with a description of a rehearsal of *Waiting for Godot* in which the actors say they do not understand what they are portraying. There was also a rehearsal of the *B. Wordsworth* script that had been made from Naipaul's short story. At the time Walcott was thinking of alternating, for a week each, *Godot* and *Basement Lullabies*, the acting scripts that had been made from Sam Selvon's fiction. *B. Wordsworth* was to be part of a bill with *Jourmard*. Walcott was hoping to take the Workshop to Queen's Hall at least once a year so that the actors could learn how to move on a larger stage, and was thinking of Errol John's *Moon on a Rainbow Shawl*.[12]

Robert Lowell wrote in May urging Rockefeller support of Walcott. Lowell called Walcott the most promising Negro poet, brilliant by any standards, with an outlook unlike other writers. His presence in Trinidad 'alters the scene' as much as any individual could, yet it is impossible for him to earn a living as a writer there. The Rockefeller Foundation should consider Walcott as contributing to American letters. Freund urged his fellow directors at the Rockefeller Foundation that a grant for $10,000 be awarded Walcott over two or three years. Others liked the idea but there was a continuing discussion of how to justify it and obtain approval. There was also a concern about the exact nature of Walcott's personal finances. In June it was decided to ask him for a budget statement of needs broken down into living expenses and 'work-cost', along with a statement of what Walcott would be doing over the next two or three years.[13]

The Trinidad Theatre Workshop was rebuilding rapidly after being evicted by McBurnie; in January 1966, it had fifteen members, by the end of the year it had twenty-six, then thirty-five members. Walcott often tried out the potential of an aspiring actor by creating an uncomfortable situation where he could see how that person would react. In 1966, Brenda Hughes, while still a schoolgirl, was dared by her friend Sonya Moze to 'go in' to the Workshop. When she said she wanted to be an actor Walcott gave her a broom and told her to sweep the floor. She still does not know if he was mocking her or trying her as an actor; most likely he wanted to see what she would do in such an embarrassing, humiliating situation. Would she walk out, become angry, docilely sweep, or 'act' a woman sweeping the floor? Judy Stone remembers being told to stand on one foot and recite a nursery rhyme. The only one she could remember was 'Ba Ba Black Sheep', which she was made to repeat over and over with increasing embarrassment. Walcott still often tests people in similar ways.[14]

In June Walcott's 'Focus on the Arts' column mentioned several local productions including future performances by the Guardian Players of Roderick Walcott's *A Flight of Sparrows* and Errol Hill's *A Square Peg* at the Guardian Sports Club. The trouble with these and all productions is the lack of a suitable modest-sized theatre with flexible possibilities. It is, however, pointless to keep hoping for an ideal theatre in Trinidad where all such plans evaporate. Theatre must adapt to necessities; production costs abroad have led to the off-Broadway and off-off-Broadway performing small avant-garde plays, mimes, even using coffee houses for one-act plays. Commercial plays now have small limited casts. The necessity of working locally with small, inappropriate stages may have the advantage of more truthfulness, more intimacy, economy, and power. The limited number of genuine local actors need a 'more concentrated experience, to widen their range'. There are good dialect actors and good 'imitators of West End mannerisms'. (Readers might like to keep this in mind in regard to Walcott's later play, *A Branch of the Blue Nile*.) While only a national theatre company could overcome such schizophrenic division, the Extra-Mural Department summer school has a communal theatre feeling. There is a need for 'dispassionate, uninvolved' foreign instructors who can see 'problems coldly' and state the obvious that 'this city needs a new theatre and a national company'.[15]

During August Walcott taught in the University of the West Indies, St Augustine campus, summer school in creative arts. Several new female members of the TTW were found through Walcott's summer school courses which usually included a reading or production of a play. Elena James, one of the few Indian members of the TTW at this time, was one of his students; some Workshop actors attended his course for further training.

In September Walcott published in the *Sunday Guardian* an article announcing the opening of Trinidad's first 'repertory theatre'. This is probably the first time 'in the history of local theatre' that actors would be expected to play three different roles in one season. Walcott announced that there would be play readings to find actors for the next year and a play-writing contest open to all West Indians. Two one-act plays would be selected for performance next season and the prizes would be $150 and $100. (The winning play was not produced.) The repertory season would be a test of the public's interest in continuous theatre. Walcott then discussed Genet's *The Blacks* and Soyinka's *The Road*. 'If the Basement Theatre's plan meets with good public response, something like a semi-professional theatre will begin to work in this city.'[16]

The first repertory season opened at the Basement Theatre on 6 October and ran for a month, twenty-six nights, until 5 November. There was, 6–15 October, a recent French avant-garde play, Jean

Genet's *The Blacks*, which in its violent aggression towards whites might be seen as appropriate to the West Indians. *Belle Fanto*, 20–22 October, was a naturalistic folk-play in the 'yard' tradition, written by a contemporary Trinidadian poet. It was published the next year by the Extra-Mural Department in the Caribbean Plays series. And then there was Wole Soyinka's *The Road*, 26 October–5 November, a contemporary Nigerian play that might be described as avant-garde and ritualistic.

The actors were Leone Campbell, Sydney Best, Geddes Jennings, Errol Jones, Stanley Marshall, Ralph Campbell, Albert Laveau, Lynette Laveau, Claude Reid, Constance Allsop, Esther Bailey, Marilyn Clarke, Hamilton Parris, Elena James, Eunice Alleyne, Joel St Helene, and Lennox Grey. Backstage there were George Williams and John Andrews (lighting), Ken Morris (masks), LeRoy Clarke (sets and stage management), and Derek Walcott (director and designer). Williams was teaching Andrews to take over from him so that the Workshop would have its own lighting designer.

John P. Andrews (b. 1936) operated the lights for the Workshop's first 1962 production and since 1966 has been considered their lighting designer. Born into a rising working-class black family, in his case Roman Catholic, in which both parents only had primary school education, Andrews has become a top-level civil servant. Educated at the Progressive Educational Institute, he later studied taxes at the Harvard Law School, became Permanent Secretary in the Ministry of Finance and Head of the Public Service. His father worked on the railways first as a brakesman, then as a supervisor. His mother was a seamstress. Although there were no cultural interests in the family, Andrews became a folk-dancer at school, then danced between 1953 and 1958 at clubs for tourists. The dance group wanted to get out of Trinidad where they saw no future, and toured Brazil for a month and a half in 1958. When the others decided to go on to the United States, Andrews, their lead dancer, returned to Trinidad. He was a lighting operator at the Little Carib and was introduced to Walcott by George Williams as a lighting technician. Working with little equipment, needing inexpensively to create the visual effects Walcott wanted, Andrews has impressed professional theatre people from abroad with his lighting designs. Rather than lighting the entire stage he created tones and moods. He would focus on specific actors, but otherwise the lighting changed and flowed with the feeling of the play.

A new member of the Workshop was Hamilton Parris, one of its best actors until he gave up theatre as it was taking too much time from his family. An Anglican 'Negro' born in San Fernando, 1921, he was educated to seventh standard in school followed by a certificate in Boiler Engineering and a career as a mechanical supervisor. He played in musical comedy and operettas before joining the Workshop. Reviewers often commented favourably on his singing and his natural ability to appear and sound 'folk'. His inflections sounded genuine. His presence on stage made even the allegorical seem like realism. Audiences were always sympathetic to him. Parris developed unusual control of his body and facial features on stage. As the Frog in *Ti-Jean and his Brothers* he performed while squatting like a frog and contorted his facial features to resemble a frog. While Walcott liked to cite Parris and later Beddeau as examples of how the Workshop drew its membership from a wide social range, including those with little formal education, Parris was notorious for forgetting or misunderstanding lines.

Jean Waggoner, visiting Trinidad, was impressed by a rehearsal of *The Blacks*, calling it 'amongst the most stimulating I have attended'. She commented on the ambition and energy of the actors, noting that during her stay one actor had an art exhibition, another was rehearsing with a steel band, another was teaching a drama course at the university, while a fourth was dancing with the Little Carib company.[17]

The season started well with full houses, about seventy-five seats a night, and there were soon plans to revive *The Blacks*, 10–12 November. The *Trinidad Guardian* even featured the Basement Theatre in an editorial contrasting the power of drama with politics; 'the world of drama, a world within which names linger longer than those of politicians' and in which 'issues transcend centuries'. The Basement Theatre might make use of 'our inexhaustible predilection for intrigue, for the ridiculing of others . . . in time, there may well emerge a school of dramatists more truly nationalist than the flag itself'. The editorial urged readers to attend the 'stagings' to encourage 'local talent' and viewed the struggle to create theatre in Trinidad as similar to the earlier pioneers of the steel band. Praising V. S. Naipaul's *Suffrage of Elvira* for its treatment of politics, the editorial concludes by hoping that the Basement Theatre will be similarly 'daring'.[18]

The notion of continuous serious theatre was new to Port of Spain, and there was a need to create an audience. The West Indies always had its intellectuals and aspiring writers, always had its well-read school teachers, lawyers, and other professionals, but they were a small percentage of the population, spread thinly among the islands, and were not necessarily going to turn up on a specific night to pay to see a contemporary play by a Frenchman, Nigerian, or even a Tobagean. Those to whom Soyinka or Genet were familiar names were likely to have seen theatre in London and New York and would be sceptical of local amateur productions. Walcott had to create his audiences.

One way was by writing articles in advance of productions explaining the significance of the plays. In 'The Great Irony' Walcott discussed the writing of Genet and especially *The Blacks*. For Genet God is not dead, He is guilty, guilty of white Christian civilization. While it seems necessary to kill such a God, Genet is writing in the tradition of such poets as Rimbaud and Baudelaire who raged against French bourgeois values. His aim is to attack cultural smugness by ridiculing the 'idea of a God who has allowed the crimes of civilization to be committed in His name'. While some directors have approached *The Blacks* as a tireless diatribe against whites, the play is a comedy of human behaviour, of pride and prejudice. For the West Indian the history of slave trade has long passed. West Indians will be attracted to such theatrical elements as masking, ceremonial costumes, and ritual. The Court is like a Carnival band or like the elaborate mock battles that are part of the Rose and Marguerite Festivals in St Lucia. Yes, the play is about Negroes, but it is about what is a Negro? 'The mask we wear is a mask that burns and disfigures.' A Negro supposedly asked Genet to write a play for Negro actors and Genet had to ask himself what is a Negro, what is his colour? If the greatest play so far written about Negroes is by a white man it is because the poet is 'an outlaw, a comedian, a black farceur, one who could therefore understand the sufferings of the race'.[19]

Walcott had long been interested in Genet and *The Blacks*. Early in 1965 he had discussed the use of vituperation and hatred in recent literature, especially the theatre, where the prose-poetry of Genet is 'charged with a lyrical power that transcends its coarseness'. In the theatre 'no emotion is ugly' if well expressed. In *The Blacks* 'what is exciting and true is not the language that is used, but the subtlety and force of certain emotions and reactions'. Scatology is employed less to shock than as part of self-discovery. Genet 'is a poet' and his 'use of language is itself a progress of exploration'. His crudities are satiric, self-mocking, beautiful rhetoric, inflated beyond normal language. He 'sees a play as a metaphor'.[20] Theatre in Port of Spain was still a social event for which the audience dressed up and expected bourgeois standards of propriety. Walcott wore jeans and the plays he chose represented the current avant-garde. Stanley Marshall remembers the first act of *The Blacks* ending with abrasive sexual language. When the lights came up for the intermission he became aware of two priests in the front row. Would they leave? They stayed on, told the actors afterwards that the show was better than a production they had seen abroad. On subsequent nights nuns and other priests came to the show.

Eric Roach's review was headlined 'This fierce satire is wildly amusing' and began by calling the play witty, poetic, poignant, profane, and blasphemous, and described it as a mockery of the conceptions whites hold about blacks. The blacks mount a performance in mockery of their own condition. The key figures of imperialism are in the court, and wear white masks, such as a decadent monarch and the Governor.

> The trouble with this kind of play is that the Trinidad audience of all complexions of thought is not really part of this confrontation of Africa and Europe . . . Producing a play like this in the cosmopolitan twilight world of Port-of-Spain is deliberately to stick one's neck out . . . Mr Walcott has performed another miracle of production in his limited basement space, and the actors have set themselves high standards.[21]

As Walcott was still the primary theatre reviewer for the *Trinidad Guardian* and *Sunday Guardian* and as other newspapers did not yet take local theatre seriously enough to have reviewers, there was at first little informed comment on the Basement productions. Often Walcott wrote pieces for the newspapers about the Workshop's plans or provided promotional material. The situation would soon change in Trinidad as the Workshop gained attention and as others replaced Walcott as theatre critic; on other islands, however, except for Jamaica, which had a long established tradition of theatre criticism, and Barbados, where reviewing was erratic, reviewing was often little more than puffery or reports of future events.

'L.C.', attending the Basement Theatre for the first time, was 'enthusiastic, evangelistic' and suggested that the Workshop should tour the island with *Belle Fanto*. 'The language is vigorous, witty' and the play 'attempts passionate statements about race, about roots in a proud tribal past and degeneration'. The actors make good use of gesture and Eunice Alleyne's timing and tone of voice are especially good.[22]

The Road was the most difficult of the plays the Workshop performed during its first season. It has a complex time scheme, uses many rapid flashbacks, makes numerous unexplained allusions to contemporary Nigerian politics, and the narrative can be difficult to follow as, with many of Soyinka's plays, its inner coherence depends on Soyinka's own interpretation of Yoruba mythology and ritual. Particularly difficult is Soyinka's assumption that the actor undergoes a state of possession that is similar to that of the ritual masquerader—who while masked is possessed by the god—and which shares in Ogun's journey through the abyss of unformed nothingness and death that divides the spiritual world from the human. To prepare his actors for their roles Walcott circulated among them books and articles on African culture and Nigerian ritual. While possession is known in local Caribbean cults, the inability of the actors to feel what Soyinka wanted was evidence to Walcott that the links between Africa and the Afro-Caribbean had been broken by the middle passage. His actors could act, but they were not possessed. They did not become Ogun in his drunkenness killing his own followers. They did not enter the abyss of unformed nothingness. Part of the later attraction of Andrew Beddeau to Walcott was that Beddeau was a Shango priest who had experienced possession.[23]

Walcott introduced the forthcoming Workshop play to his potential audience through a newspaper article. 'Opening the Road' begins with a spatial analysis of The Road contrasting the Church from which the Professor has been expelled with the 'haven, or heaven' where the Professor is a kind of parody God of his own new religion; the third area is the 'Aksident' store of spare parts and truck drivers. As it is impossible to portray all three areas within the limited space of the Basement stage it has been necessary to concentrate, simplify, and 'essentialise' the action. (The production had to cram thirteen actors onto a space that was comfortable for only six.) In the play 'language is action' and the 'Word is what matters'. The Professor's visionary language contrasts to the lack of understanding of his followers and the physical violence outside where 'accident is the god'. But the world outside is also theatre with the touts acting like 'carnival barkers' pleading, cajoling, and entertaining potential customers. This is a poet's play in which the characters speak prose-poetry regardless of their social origins. The Professor's speeches are like sermons and have great power and symbolism. Kotonu is a Hamlet-like figure who comes closest to resolving tradition with invention. 'What links Commonwealth writers and poets is this exciting combination of the old and the new tongues, of ancient myths and contemporary problems.'[24]

An unsigned article, probably influenced by Walcott, seems to have been the only review of The Road. Noting Walcott's need to pinch and pare to fit the play onto the Basement stage, the critic says Walcott depended on the interplay of character and mentions outstanding scenes by Ralph Campbell, Sydney Best, and Stanley Marshall. The article continues by offering a complex interpretation of the play's symbolism and characters which seems more like Walcott's own vision than the mythology behind Soyinka's play.[25]

'A Special Correspondent' observed that 'By now Mr Derek Walcott's Basement Theatre group has become part of our cultural landscape.' Walcott had discovered people 'among us' anxious 'to put their creative energy and imagination to the test in a theatre workshop'. The Basement Theatre has opened a way for 'untried talent to prove itself', but the theatre is much too small. Intimate, yes, but too much so. It is stuffy and there is not enough distance between the actors and the audience. In *The Blacks* the lack of distance prevents detachment. Should we expect metropolitan theatre standards in Trinidad? Walcott aims for such standards in his poetry and his book reviews. Because of the immaturity of local audiences 'mediocre performances by inexperienced players are being hailed' as great achievements; such uncritical praise will doom genuine talent to stagnation. The truth is that *The Blacks* failed. The audiences were embarrassed and did not understand it, nor did the actors who hurried over the language and garbled it. *Belle Fanto* succeeded because it was easier. While it offered something familiar, part of its beauty was sacrificed by the actors for 'skit'. *The Road* was the most successful of the three, perhaps because 'there were no women'.[26]

I imagine that this reflects Walcott's personal summary of the first season of the Workshop as a repertory company. After seven years of preparation the company could now appear in public and aim at international standards, but their local success was dangerous, too easily achieved, and might cause the actors to stop working for the highest standards that Walcott was himself aiming towards. The local audiences were uncritical and the actors unused to the intellectual demands of great and modern theatre. A small intimate theatre was good in principle; in practice it had many disadvantages including the difficulty of producing dramatic illusion.

It was not until 10 October that Walcott wrote to Joseph Black, Director of the Humanities and Social Sciences, of the Rockefeller Foundation, about his needs for the forthcoming years. Walcott sent Black two acts of *In A Fine Castle*, a play he was writing which is related to his earlier *The Wine of the Country*. He said that whether or not he was given a grant he intended to stay in Trinidad developing a repertory company and writing. Except for occasional pieces, he wanted to stop writing journalism. He offered, as an example of how his time was divided, the tasks facing him that day: (1) he had to block a play in rehearsal and design advertising; (2) he wanted to work on a long poem that he had been writing for the past year; (3) priority, however, had to be given to writing his newspaper column as that was how he earned his money. He often missed deadlines because of his creative work. The company was now averaging three meetings a week, but as long as they remained in the Basement Theatre the top salary for the season would be $100. They needed more training, refresher courses, and an outside summer director who could prepare for the second season. They needed lighting equipment and a theatre library. There should be short visits abroad of perhaps two actors at a time to see off-Broadway theatre and take professional acting courses. The Workshop could also use a camera to make short movies and television shows. Walcott wanted help with tutoring the actors, as that was not his area of expertise. It was necessary for the Workshop to acquire a new theatre space as soon as possible. They could earn for each performance a maximum of $180 at $2 a seat. They had to pay each night $40 rent, $10 to the lighting assistant, and an average of $25 royalties. They also had to pay $5 rental for each rehearsal.[27]

Walcott earned WI $400 monthly as a journalist and his wife earned about the same. He then earned about WI $250 royalties and sometimes was given grants or won prizes. Rent was $168. To devote himself entirely to writing and the theatre, along with a little freelance journalism, he would need a minimum of US $300 a month, say, $10,800 over three years. He would be satisfied with a 12- or 18-month grant. Walcott knew he was 'casual' about accounts and sometimes confused production costs, taxi fares to and from the theatre, and the cost of entertaining visitors to the theatre and actors after rehearsals.

Now that the Workshop had moved from the Little Carib to its own theatre its finances were more precarious. Walcott received an anonymous donation of $1,200 towards building the Basement Theatre. The Rockefeller Foundation discussed the possibility of a special $10,000 grant and the attitude was favourable, but there were questions about Walcott's actual needs, probably because his letter was not detailed in an expected way.

The programme for the next 'season' announced 'two new plays by Theatre Workshop playwrights', a music and poetry evening, courses in playwriting, scenic design, and short story. Membership in the Workshop was $2.00 monthly.

Two plays were rehearsed during 1966 which were never performed by the Workshop, Song of a Goat by the Nigerian J. P. Clark and Beckett's Waiting for Godot. Godot would remain a possible Workshop production for many years as the actors struggled with it before deciding that it was beyond them. In a Trinidad where secondary-school education remained rare, most Workshop actors were still unfamiliar with contemporary dramatic literature and the unusual acting problems that Walcott was bringing to them. How do you achieve possession in *The Road*? How do you act in *Godot*? *Belle Fanto* was more like what Trinidadian theatre had known; it was a naturalistic play about local society. Walcott was not only dramatist, director, teacher of acting, he was also the one who was bringing local theatre into contact with African drama, the theatre of the absurd, the contemporary avant-garde, new styles of acting. The Workshop had made a step towards professionalism. Although the actors were only being paid five or ten dollars, this was the first time in Trinidad that actors earned money from serious plays.

Slade Hopkinson, who had been working towards a doctorate at Yale University on a Rockefeller Foundation fellowship, would soon rejoin the Workshop. In July he gave up his scholarship and returned to the West Indies to be in charge of the drama section of the 'Caribbean Text Book Project'. He was against rote learning and wanted children taught by improvisations as a way to encourage imaginative participation and avoid the anxieties of speaking poor English. While Walcott was favourable to the West Indianization of the syllabus and agreed that it was necessary to allow children to express themselves in local English, he warned against the chauvinism that would teach 'the most luridly sentimental verse' in preference to Wordsworth's 'Daffodils'. 'It is better to learn a good poem about daffodils than a bad one about West Indian sunsets.'[28]

Walcott was against the sentimentalizing of the culture of the poor. In 'Beyond the Backyard' he discusses some of the problems in portraying the West Indian middle class in the theatre. Significantly he is not concerned with arguments about their untypicality, but rather that European theatrical and language conventions are not appropriate in a society where houses are built differently and where finding the right level of speech is difficult. In Errol Hill's early plays 'actresses tend to go hard after diction', which for most of them is accent not clarity. 'There are few plays about the middle class because the playwrights cannot believe what they make their characters recite.' Dramatists want to get beyond the 'peasant and backyard dramas, the holding your headtie and bawling stuff'. While Walcott was thinking of a kind of theatre which had been common in the West Indies, the most likely dramatist he had in mind was Freddie Kissoon, director of the Strolling Players, a group that features backyard comedy. He thought Kissoon and others had wasted their talents on dialect farces.[29]

NOTES

1. Ronald John, 'Errol Jones remembers', *Trinidad Guardian* (29 July 1987), 28 ['The basement was where the original acting style of the Workshop evolved . . . our exercises comprised of character development and ensemble playing, which is something we arrived at by the late 60s.']; various remarks about Workshop actors by Mervyn Morris, Derek Walcott, and Richard Montgomery.

2. Different sources give slightly different dimensions for the stage. The Little Basement Theatre is discussed by Victor D. Questel, 'The Trinidad Theatre Workshop 1966–1967', *The Literary Half-Yearly*, 26/1 (Jan. 1985), 163–79.

3. Karen Phelps, 'Where Actors and Audience Share Same Level', *Trinidad Guardian* (12 Jan. 1966), 3; 'Mr. Priestly Sees for Himself', *Daily Mirror* (12 Jan. 1966), 14; Eric Roach, 'It must Be an Agonising Place to Act', *Evening News* (17 Jan. 1966).

4. 'Two Plays that Lifted the Basement Theatre', *Trinidad Guardian* (11 Jan. 1966), 5.

5. Derek Walcott to Gerald Freund (31 Jan. 1966), Rockefeller Archives.

6. Gerald Freund to Derek Walcott (10 Feb. 1966), Rockefeller Archives.

7. Derek Walcott, 'The Prospects of a National Theatre', *Sunday Guardian* (6 Mar. 1966).

8. [A Correspondent], 'When Belle Says "No!"', *Sunday Mirror* (3 Apr. 1966), 7; Karen Phelps, ' "Belle Fanto" Much Too Confined', *Sunday Guardian* (17 Apr. 1966), 6.

9. An unidentified newspaper clipping mentions three Dr's, four dramatists, several theatre producers, Carlisle Chang and someone from the Netherlands Embassy among those in the audience and backstage for performances of *Belle Fanto*; Sally Stollmeyer and others have mentioned that Walcott was given moral and practical, rather than financial, support with productions by his friends.

10. Ulric Mentus, 'Reading', *Daily Mirror* (7 June 1966), 9.

11. Derek Walcott, 'West Indian Art Today', *Sunday Guardian* (8 May 1966), 8.

12. Ulric Mentus, 'The Little Workshop's Mammoth Task of 5 Plays a Year', *Sunday Mirror* (8 May 1966), 19.

13. Robert Lowell to Gerald Freund (21 May 1966), Rockefeller Archives.

14. Interviews with Sonya Moze and Brenda Hughes (July 1990).

15. Derek Walcott, 'Writer's Cramp on a Stage', *Trinidad Guardian* (8 June 1966), 5.

16. Derek Walcott, 'Trinidad's 1st Repertory Season Opens Next Month', *Sunday Guardian* (11 Sept. 1966), 6.

17. Jean Waggoner, 'Independence Dance and Drama', *DJ Weekly Magazine* (July/ Aug. 1966), 3, 6.

18. ' "The Road" Starts Scheduled Run Tonight', *Trinidad Guardian* (26 Oct. 1966), 5; 'Kicking Off with The Blacks', *Trinidad Guardian* (6 Oct. 1966), 10.

19. Derek Walcott, 'The Great Irony', *Sunday Guardian* (25 Sept. 1966), 6.

20. Derek Walcott, 'The Theatre of Abuse', *Sunday Guardian* (3 Jan. 1965), 4.

21. Eric Roach, 'This Fierce Satire is Wildly Amusing', *Sunday Guardian* (6 Oct. 1966), 10.

22. L.C., 'Basement Develops Sure Touch!', *Trinidad Guardian* (22 Oct. 1966), 5.
23. Walcott's comments on *The Road* and his later disillusionment with Andrew Beddeau in 'What the Twilight Says: An Overture', in *Dream on Monkey Mountain and Other Plays* (1970), 3–40: 8, 27.
24. Derek Walcott, 'Opening the Road', *Sunday Guardian* (23 Oct. 1966), 6.
25. 'Walcott Loads his Tiny Basement Bus', *Trinidad Guardian* (1 Nov. 1966), 16.
26. [Special Correspondent], 'Derek Walcott's Basement Theatre', *Trinidad Guardian* (4 Nov. 1966), 12.
27. Derek Walcott to Joseph Black (10 Oct. 1966), Rockefeller Archives.
28. Derek Walcott, 'Writing for Children Pt. III', *Sunday Guardian* (13 Feb. 1966), 3.
29. Derek Walcott, 'Beyond the Backyard', *Sunday Guardian* (11 Dec. 1966), 10, 27.

1967

4

Dream on Monkey Mountain
in Canada
The First Tours

MANY of Walcott's concerns for the next decade and a half were already defined. An article he published in January makes a clear distinction between the situation of the black American and that of the black West Indian. While African Americans had a genuine tradition of protest literature, a self-critical, satiric literature is more suitable for the West Indian. Walcott was distrustful of intellectuals and politicians who offered quick cures by reverse racism or suppressing freedom The region needed creative energy not rhetoric and self-pity. In 'Fellowships' he claimed that there really was no tradition of protest poetry in the West Indies because there was nothing to protest against that was similar to the condition of black Americans. Nor was there a history of cultural suppression. Independence has been 'placidly' bestowed. The West Indies have not had the horrors and grandeurs of the revolts in Haiti, Algeria, and Cuba; instead there is the petulance of economic dependency on British goodwill and American largess. Because of this there is self-abhorrence, social disgust, and escape into such 'visionary rhetoric' as imagining an African black Atlantis or the annihilation of history through Marxism. The New World writer often merely changes masters, surrendering art for politics. Even West Indian militancy is dated and imitative, it is the rage of an irritated bourgeoisie after the withdrawal of a generous 'enemy'. 'The West Indian environment is smug and barren. So is our protest poetry.'

We must be sincere enough to refute a past that never was grand but debased, not to divide our history into pogroms. . . . From there it is an easy stcp to that aggressive self-pity . . . that makes so much of our literature specious. The present is boring, ironic, banal. We need to be lacerated by the kind of satire that shows us how dull we have become, or illumined by the gift that can make our banalities shine.[1]

There remained the problem of how Walcott was to survive as a professional dramatist and director in the West Indies and how he could train and support his company. For the present the Rockefeller Foundation seemed the only probable source of funds. The Rockefeller Foundation grant to Walcott took much consultation. Although those concerned with the grant were highly favourable, there was no current policy under which it could be considered, no money budgeted for such a purpose. Joseph Black, Director for the Humanities, decided that as the Foundation had a previous interest in Walcott and West Indian cultural development it would be possible to make a special grant of $10,000 to Walcott which would enable him to give up his time-consuming work as reporter and devote himself to creative activities for three years. The Rockefeller Foundation, however, put off deciding what to do about the Trinidad Theatre Workshop. Shortly after being informed of the award Walcott attempted to receive half of it immediately to purchase a 16 mm camera to use for film and television, but the request was denied. The lack of suitable camera and video equipment remained a problem over the years; hardly any filmed examples exist of the TTW in action. In March Walcott announced that he would no longer be regular drama reviewer for the *Trinidad Guardian* as he found it increasingly difficult to be objective about the work of other companies.[2]

While the Basement Theatre was useful in many ways—in January the Trinidad Dramatic Club used it to hold readings for casting *Othello*—it required a steady source of income. The rent itself was $3,000 a year. In April the Workshop ventured outside its new theatre to perform Errol John's *Moon on a Rainbow Shawl* at Queen's Hall, from 14–19 April. The production was a popular success. Although the Workshop had only rented 400 chairs the production averaged 350 in the audience each night and could have continued longer except that the Hall was already booked. The response was important as it proved that the Workshop could build enough of an audience to rent such a large hall and pay the actors a salary after expenses and royalties. When Walcott wrote to Freund about the Workshop he had in mind a potential audience of around 700, but over 2,000 people attended *Moon* and there was a profit of $2,000. This was the Workshop's first use of a full three-dimensional set in contrast to the bare stage of previous productions. They also performed for one night in San Fernando to 500 people. The Workshop now had saved $2,400 which could be used to cover expenses of tours.[3]

Errol John, originally from Tobago, along with Errol Hill was one of those who began modern West Indian drama in Trinidad; he was a member of the Company of Five (with Barbara Assoon and Errol Hill), Hill's Whitehall Players, then emigrated to England where he wrote some television plays. His *Moon on a Rainbow Shawl* won the *Observer's* playwriting competition in 1957, was produced professionally in 1958 (when he was given a Guggenheim award), and for a time brought John to international attention. Both Faber and Grove Press published *Moon*. He never had another major success and remained in England, acting professionally on stage, including the Old Vic, and in films when a West Indian or 'black' was needed. *Moon*, however, was until Walcott's *Dream on Monkey Mountain* the best-known West Indian play, remained central to the West Indian theatre repertory, and is still performed. John had used *Moon* for workshop exercises with the Little Carib Theatre Workshop on visits to Trinidad and for a time, around 1962, was listed as a Workshop dramatist when the Rockefeller Foundation awarded him a grant to be a writer in residence at the Little Carib. *Moon* is an older kind of play than Walcott wrote, in the earlier 'yard' tradition, which both portrays and sentimentalizes the life and problems of the poor, especially the women. While it uses the West Indian stereotypes of strong women and weak men, there is some strength of will when the young man, Ephraim, escapes by rejecting promotion to a better job and leaving Rosa, the girl he made pregnant.[4]

The cast of *Moon* included Albert Laveau, Terrence Joseph, Roger Dean, Lynette Laveau, Constance Allsop, Leone Campbell, Elena James, Stanley Marshall, Brenda Hughes, Ralph Campbell, Hamilton Parris, Leo Rufino, and Sydney Best. Walcott was director and John Andrews did the stage lighting. The set was by Colin Laird and LeRoy Clarke.

Therese Mills in the *Sunday Guardian* thought *Moon* was a good choice, although dated and less urgent than when it was written a decade previously. She was bothered by the audience reaction. Trinidad had become richer and comfortable; the poverty and problems of the past were now considered hilarious and a serious play was viewed as amusing. 'Too many of us still think of the backyard as a place of sheer comedy' in which the poor are incapable of such emotions as love, hate, and despair. There is a new theatre audience, attracted to the Workshop's activities, 'who are yet unaccustomed to the idea of a home theatre of us and about us'. For the Workshop to fill 400 seats for each of five nights was an accomplishment, but only further exposure to serious theatre could teach the new audience to be less 'leather-skinned' about the poor.[5]

Eric Roach favourably commented upon the 'shoddy clapboard set', broken iron bed, dirty washtub, battered pots and pans, and harlot's red door as capturing the hell of a slum backyard. 'What came forth was the stench of broken hopes, dreams, loves . . . the cesspool of shame and distress.' Walcott and Leone Campbell 'knew Mrs. Adams to the marrow'; Leone Campbell played her convincingly 'to the full, earthy, tender, tough, malleable, enduring'. Constance Allsop, however, seemed to play the prostitute without conviction. Elena James lacked skill, but this fitted the role of Rosa, abandoned by Ephraim. If the women in the play were strong, the men were weak and Ephraim an escapist. The production was slow, the scene changes took too long, and the audience often laughed in the wrong places, mistaking pathos for comedy. Several of the entrances and exits were disconcertingly short. Although it had faults the production should be taken on tour around the villages to show what folk theatre might be like. Ulric Mentus in the *Evening News* thought that the production's success belonged to the actors as the play was concerned with the now threadbare theme of barrack-yard life during the 1940s.[6]

Gerald Freund, Rockefeller Associate Director, wrote saying that while the Foundation could help Walcott as an individual, its policies did not allow it to assist an overseas theatre and it was doubtful that any American foundation could. While Freund had earlier invited Walcott to the Rockefeller's Bellagio, Italy, Centre, only to be told that 'Rome is for Romans', he had recently suggested to Asa Briggs that Walcott be invited to the University of Sussex as an artist in residence for a year. Walcott replied that he was working on a full-length play which he had started in 1958 (presumably *Dream on Monkey Mountain*), that the company was invited to Canada and Guyana, and there were possibilities of being invited to Venezuela. The Toronto trip would be paid for by the Centennial Committee, and Walcott was wondering if on the way to Guyana, they could perform for a few nights in New York, off-off-Broadway, perhaps at the Judson Theatre and see some plays. Could the Foundation pay for their New York hotel expenses? Could the Foundation send a second director to help Walcott as he was feeling his limitations especially about physical movement and the rhythm of productions. Walcott had already heard that he would be invited as a visiting professor of Commonwealth

Literature at Leeds University, England, but if he accepted he would need a director to keep the theatre company going until his return. Walcott's landlord was selling their house and Walcott wanted to buy it. To take out a bank loan he would need to do some freelance writing and had agreed to stay on with the *Guardian* on a retainer of $70 a month as this would enable him to keep his pension alive. This would not affect his agreement with the Foundation to devote himself full time to his creative writing.[7]

Activity continued into June with a performance on the 21st of *Zoo Story* and *Jourmard* at the University's Guild Hall in St Augustine as part of Festival Week. *Jourmard*, which was written when Walcott was in New York on a Rockefeller Fellowship in 1958, is, like *Zoo Story*, set in a park, this time West Indian. Three vagrants acquire a coffin and have trouble disposing of it until Jourmard, a poet, shocks everyone with a satirical West Indian version of the Resurrection. The play's subtitle is 'A comedy till the last minute'. It was performed at Judson Hall in New York and was among the early plays cyclostyled by the Extra-Mural Department, University of the West Indies. This was the first time it was performed by the Workshop.[8]

No sooner had Walcott established a little theatre and had a first season than he began to set his sights on international recognition. Touring enabled the Workshop to perform more often, was expected to be financially profitable, and Walcott felt it would help toughen the company, making it more of an ensemble. Except for a few earlier tours by the St Lucia Arts Guild, the Trinidad Theatre Workshop was the first theatre company regularly to perform throughout the region. On 29 June, Walcott, John Andrews, LeRoy Clarke, Errol Jones, Errol Pilgrim, and Terrence Joseph flew to Barbados. Six of the seven, excluding Jones, might be described as technical and stage crew. The next day the rest of the Workshop arrived.

The Workshop's short Barbadian tour lasted 30 June–2 July. They were invited by Caribbeat Enterprises and the Barbados Arts Council; performances were at St Winifred's School. On 30 June they performed Walcott's *Jourmard* and Edward Albee's *Zoo Story*. Although the plays were at a higher level and more serious, such a double bill might be said to continue the assumption that West Indian audiences were only prepared to accept an evening of one-act comedies. For *Zoo Story* Walcott used Albert Laveau as Jerry and Errol Jones for Peter. *Jourmard* had a larger cast including Stanley Marshall, Ralph Campbell, Hamilton Parris, Claude Reid, Albert Laveau, Lynette Laveau, Elena James, Eunice Alleyne, and Brenda Hughes. On 1 July they twice performed

Belle Fanto, gave a matinee performance the next day, followed by the double bill that evening.

The Barbadian tour set a model for the many tours that followed. Walcott and a few technicians would arrive a day or so before the performance to oversee problems, hastily build a set, and produce lighting from bits of equipment they carried with them. As they had no professional lighting equipment and many of the lighting effects were home-made or modified from simple store-bought electrical parts, and as they had no money for professional packing and shipping, parts were carried by the company on their laps on the airplanes. Few places in which they performed would have theatre lighting; so the lighting system, including wiring, needed to be improvised on the spot. The tours were strenuous. No sooner did the actors arrive in Barbados than they were expected to perform that evening. If possible there would be a rehearsal on the local stage earlier in the day, soon after arrival. As many performances as possible would be fitted in and often there were requests for additional shows to meet audience demand. In Barbados there were five performances in three days. Publicity was usually done by the local sponsoring groups through advertising on radio and newspaper and with newspaper articles based on publicity material Walcott had sent ahead. The local sponsors were people whom Walcott had known in Jamaica or St Lucia and who kept up an interest in the arts, sometimes being part of local dance or theatre groups.

While tours were important to the Workshop in establishing a reputation and because there was insufficient audience in Trinidad to keep a serious theatre group occupied, there was also the continuing ideal of the West Indian Federation. Walcott regarded the TTW as a regional as well as Trinidadian theatre. Although the Federation only lasted from 1958 to 1962, the artists, intellectuals, and many of the professional class still thought of themselves within terms of the Federation. For someone with education, cultural awareness, artistic abilities, professional training, or money, to have given up access to the British Empire for the micronationalism of Grenada or Guyana was still an unacceptable shock. A multiracial Federation, giving the English-speaking nation the status of Canada or Australia, led by a 'brown' (culturally and often socially) middle class was what independence was supposedly about before it had been hijacked by local nationalists.

Implicit in TTW tours, with their regional and international ambitions, were assumptions clearly not held by those who wanted the Workshop to tour the villages and put on less complex, popular plays about folk life. Even if Walcott and his actors wanted to perform village plays—and their ambition was instead to raise West Indian arts to international professional standards—such tours would have been almost physically and financially impossible. Such touring companies in Africa have either been university- or government-financed or have grown as commercial enterprises within the local culture. When popular village drama did develop in the West Indies it had local roots; it is performed in dialect or patois, is mostly unintelligible to outsiders, and whatever its other merits it has not been of outstanding artistic accomplishment to date, although that might change.

The Workshop was radical in being a Negro and Brown company, in performing many West Indian plays, and in its élite, avant-garde ambitions in contrast to the white, British, middle-class culture that had dominated colonial life. Its founder, leader, artistic director, and dramatist had led the breakthrough to modernist art in the West Indies and was taking his Workshop in that direction. The Green Room Players, the best theatre group in Barbados at the time, was white or light-skinned and almost totally non-West Indian in its cultural orientation. During April, for example, they had performed Arthur Miller's *Crucible* and Agatha Christie's *Rats*. They did perform their first West Indian play, *Seance* by George Graves, but Barbados lagged behind Trinidad, St Lucia, and Jamaica. *The Crucible*, *Rats*, and *Seance* were not *The Blacks*, *The Road*, and *The Sea at Dauphin*.

In an interview Walcott commented that Barbados was not as theatrically active as Trinidad and Bajans seemed unaware that there were a number of West Indian plays available. They were requested to perform *Blacks* in Barbados, but Walcott was sceptical of the likely response there. Barbados seemed 'prejudiced and insular'; it needed a bold theatre that could tackle 'their particular problems'. The TTW could have extended their tour to Grenada and St Lucia had they not already been invited to Canada. There was a large potential audience throughout the region. They were already the first Trinidadian drama group to tour in the region; now they would be the first West Indian drama company to perform outside the region. Walcott was concerned with the Workshop's reputation of being élitist. They had attracted a larger audience than anyone thought possible, and had tried to mix their plays, from the theatre of the absurd to naturalism and farce. It was demanding on the actors to have to play such a variety of roles in one year. The money made on *Moon* would help finance the Guyana tour. A 'friend of the company' had given them $1,200 last year, India Overseas had let them use the Astor Cinema on Sunday mornings for rehearsals, and recently they had been given $500 when the

St Augustine Players disbanded. Perhaps when the company was better established they might apply to the Government for grants for the actors to study abroad and for a grant towards a theatre.[9]

After returning to Trinidad Walcott worked on a script of V. S. Naipaul's *A Flag on the Island*, a story Naipaul was commissioned to write for a film and which, after withdrawing from the project, he published as a book along with some short stories. The Workshop gave some performances outside of Port of Spain including at Mausica Teacher Training College. On 14–16 July the Workshop presented a double bill of *Jourmard* and *Zoo Story* at the Basement Theatre to overflowing audiences. Then on 23 July *Belle Fanto* was presented in the afternoon and evening at Bishop Anstey High School, Scarborough, Tobago; on 28 July it was offered again at Naparima Bowl, San Fernando. Therese Mills commented after the Basement Theatre double bill that the company had learned that theatre consists of more hard work than glamour, that there is no short cut to professional standards, and that talent is not enough. The Workshop had wisely built on solid foundations, using the same actors, rather than building on stars and a variety of performers.[10]

The most important event of 1967 was the invitation to Walcott to bring the Workshop to the first Caribana Festival, as part of Canada's Centennial Celebrations, in Toronto, 5–13 August. This was to include the first performance of *Dream on Monkey Mountain*, a play Walcott had been writing for the past decade. Most of the play had been workshopped in bits and pieces as Walcott tried out lines and scenes with the actors during weekly workshop sessions. Although the idea for the play had been in Walcott's mind since Jamaica, the actual script and even the characters were prepared with specific actors in mind. Makak was based on Errol Jones's physique, facial appearance, and abilities as an actor. In workshops Walcott would give the actors bits and pieces, sometimes a line, sometimes a scene to improvise, and the play that eventually resulted grew from his work with the company. When the Workshop left for Toronto the play still had not been rehearsed beyond the first act. Walcott's plays at this time still used animal symbolism. In *Ti-Jean and his Brothers* some of the stage characters are animals. In *Dream* the animalization is in the symbolism and workshops were devoted to doing animal mannerisms which were later incorporated into the characterization. Errol Jones, for example, did workshop exercises with his body and voice imitating apes and lions, while Stanley Marshall tried to be a mosquito. The actual rehearsals for the play lasted three months.

The trip to Canada and their first days there were chaotic. They had to fly island by island to Puerto Rico, then to the American mainland, then to Canada, often spending long hours in airport transit rooms, with their box of props and scenery, including a large painted canvas backdrop, causing innumerable problems, especially with customs officials. The Workshop had no 'roadies', no official status, no international artists' agency to meet them, handle local problems, or obtain permits. All was done by Walcott on a shoe-string budget and required patience from the cast.

Caribana itself immediately presented problems. The Festival was conceived as an open-air West Indian carnival with dancing, twelve bands, continuous live music, 'fire and bottle eating', water ski shows, a 'floating night club', food stalls, folk-dancing, fashion shows, parades, and wandering noisy crowds. The Workshop was to perform on an open stage on Centre Island each night at 9 p.m. but the wind and noise soon proved more difficult than was anticipated. No detailed written record exists of what happened, and the only published records I have found of the start of the Caribana '67 are contradictory. A Caribana programme claims that there would be a play every night at 9 p.m. A Caribana advertisement in the *Toronto Daily Star* refers to 'Drama Festival—The Derek Walcott Players' beginning on Monday, 7 August. On the basis of extensive interviews and comparing intentions with memories, it seems that there were two performances of *Belle Fanto* on Centre Island and one evening of *Jourmard* (without the *Zoo Story*). The stage was a metal caravan and the audience could come on stage. The general mood was of carnival and the sustained seriousness of theatre was impossible. The TTW had to find another location. On 9 August rehearsals of *Dream on Monkey Mountain* started at St Mary's College Dormitory, where the Workshop was accommodated. The next day they began rehearsing the play at the Central Library theatre. *Dream on Monkey Mountain* was first performed at the Central Library on 12 August (the second act still had not been completely run through in a rehearsal!), followed by *Zoo Story* and *Jourmard* at the library on 13 August. Both nights they had full audiences for the 209 seats.[11]

The cast included Joel St Helene as the dancer, Albert Laveau as Basil (a part that did not exist in earlier versions of the play and which was written to give Laveau something to do), Sydney Best as Tigre, Hamilton Parris as Souris, Ralph Campbell as Lestrade, Claude Reid as Pamphilion, Errol Jones as Makak and Stanley Marshall as Moustique. Other actors were Eunice Alleyne, Brenda Hughes, Elena James (as the Apparition), Marcia Slaney and Terrence Joseph. As Constance Allsop was marrying Roger McTair, she was replaced on the tour by Lynette Laveau. 'Decor' was by Walcott and LeRoy Clarke.[12]

Because the Workshop had contracted to appear in Guyana at the invitation of the Guyana Theatre Guild, it could not accept invitations to stay on in Canada to appear at the Trinidad and Tobago Pavilion at Expo 67 in Montreal and two theatres in Montreal. The details of the remaining days of the Workshop in Canada are as hazy as the details of the first days. Between 5 August and 14 August recordings were made for the Canadian Broadcasting Company of Lennox Brown's play *Fog Drifts in the Spring* (Brown was a Trinidadian who had migrated to Canada in the 1950s) and *Crew from Sorrow Hill*, an adaptation of Wilson Harris's Guyanese novel *Palace of the Peacock*. The Workshop left Canada for the long journey back on the morning of 14 August, stayed overnight in Trinidad on 15 August, and arrived in Guyana on 16 August.

They performed *Zoo Story* and *Jourmard* on 17–19 August, *Belle Fanto* on 21–23 August, and *Dream on Monkey Mountain* on 24–26 August at the Guyana Theatre Guild's Playhouse in Kingston. The casts were the same as in Canada with such changes as the fifteen-member Guyana Police Male Voice Choir supplying the singing for *Dream*. Marcia Slaney stayed on in Canada for the Allsop–McTair wedding, but arrived in time for the performances of *Dream*. Although audiences were small the reviews praised the performances. 'This is probably the first opportunity that Guyanese have had to see a season of West Indian drama of such caliber.' One reviewer criticized Elena James for laughing at her own lines and averting her head from the audience in *Belle Fanto* and thought Claude Reid unaware of stage mechanics as he stood too close to others, blocking the sight line. Eunice Alleyne had an electric vibrancy, evoking a range of soul-searching cadences 'hardly ever equalled on the Theatre Guild stage'. Stanley Marshall was 'stellar' as Uncle Willie. Brenda Hughes and Lynette Laveau were 'mischievous, but heart-warmingly funny'. The play was 'hauntingly alive'.

The critics in Guyana were surprised at the quality of the plays and the productions. *Dream on Monkey Mountain* was called the 'finest West Indian play ever written', 'a traumatic dramatic experience of tremendous intensity' and 'a triumph for Errol Jones'. An editorial ('What we Think') said that the local audience was confused, expecting the TTW to do the same kind of plays as the Theatre Guild. The Workshop so stunned the local audiences in presenting three West Indian plays that people were seldom aware the 'outstanding dramatic performances were situations which they themselves had experienced'. 'It is time the leading dramatic group in this country established a programme of plays which reflect West Indian backgrounds.' It was shameful for the Workshop to have played to such small audiences; but with such short runs there had been no forewarning what to expect and for word to get around of such worthwhile drama. Slade Hopkinson complained in the *Sunday Graphic* that Guyanese were willing to pay more to attend a British touring company's production of *She Stoops to Conquer* than the TTW shows, although the work 'displayed a level of technical expertise and a quality of coherent ensemble playing unknown in Guyana'. 'To the coarse intelligences of the pseudo-sophisticates, an automatic prestige attached' to the British company, 'since they were English and sponsored by the British Council'.[13]

Walcott wrote to Freund about the tour to Canada and Guyana that although their passage and accommodation in Canada was subsidized the actors lost money as they had to pay for food and transportation within Toronto. The company lost the money they had earned from *Moon on a Rainbow Shawl* on the Guyana tour as they had to pay their own air fare and subsistence and audiences were poor. In Guyana there was still no notion of professional theatre; producing plays was still seen as amateur and a civic duty. John Hearne had invited the company to Jamaica for the coming year and Walcott hoped that the Foundation might provide a travel grant and send an American director. He felt that the Workshop was at last becoming the good, semi-professional company they had worked towards.[14]

Freund suggested that he look into sending André Gregory, of the Los Angeles Inner City Repertory Company, as a visiting director. Walcott liked the idea, said Gregory could stay with him, and mentioned that the company had received an invitation from the Barbados Arts Council and that they were rehearsing four plays, his *Henri Christophe*, Pinter's *The Lover*, and J. P. Clark's *The Raft* and *Song of a Bird* [sic; *Goat*]. Walcott was hoping someone would co-direct the coming season with him as in the past year and a half he had directed eight plays and felt the company needed a fresh approach.[15]

NOTES

1. Derek Walcott, 'Fellowships', *Sunday Guardian* (15 Jan. 1967), 8.
2. Derek Walcott to The Rockefeller Foundation (4 Mar. 1967), Rockefeller Archives; Derek Walcott, 'Looking on In Comfort', *Trinidad Guardian* (14 Mar. 1967), 7.

3. Derek Walcott, 'On the Theatre', *Trinidad Guardian* (30 Jan. 1967), 8; John Carib, 'From All Quarters', *Sunday Guardian* (7 May 1967).

4. Derek Walcott, 'Othello Off and On', *Sunday Guardian* (7 May 1967), 6. 'Errol John's Prized Play at Queen's Hall', *Trinidad Guardian* (17 Apr. 1967), 4.

5. Therese Mills, 'The Theatre Workshop', *Sunday Guardian* (23 Apr. 1967), 1.

6. Eric Roach, 'Mrs. Adams—The Heroine', *Trinidad Guardian* (19 Apr. 1967), 7; Ulric Mentus, '10 Years Old—But Still Going Strong', *Evening News* [1969].

7. Gerald Freund to Derek Walcott (2 May 1967); Derek Walcott to Gerald Freund (28 May 1967), Rockefeller Archives.

8. 'Double bill at UWI', *Trinidad Guardian* (21 June 1967), 5; Derek Walcott, *Journard or A Comedy Till the Last Minute* (Extra-Mural Department, University of the West Indies), cyclostyled, undated, fourteen pages.

9. Derek Walcott, 'Bajans Are Still Very Insular and Prejudiced', *Sunday Guardian* (23 July 1967), 5.

10. 'From all Quarters', *Sunday Guardian* (2 July 1967), 6; 'Players Return to Base', *Trinidad Guardian* (11 July 1967), 5; 'Theatre Group for Canada', *Express* (15 July 1967), 9; ' "Belle Fanto" Goes to its "Birthplace" ', *Trinidad Guardian* (27 July 1967), 4; Therese Mills, 'No "Stardust," Just the Polish of Hard Work', *Sunday Guardian* (23 July 1967), 5.

11. *Toronto Daily Star* (5 Aug. 1967), 32.

12. Terry Joseph, 'Derek's Forgotten Friends', *Sunday Mirror* (18 Oct. 1992), 30.

13. 'Drama in the Idiom at Guild', *Guyana Graphic* (17 Aug. 1967), 6, 7; 'Small Audiences at T.G.', *Guyana Graphic* (25 Aug. 1967). Unidentified review, 'The Wandering T'dad Theatre' by Mary Nunes, ' "Belle Fanto"—A Review', and editorial ('What we Think') 'Theatre Guild'; Slade Hopkinson, 'Poor Response to Quality WI Plays', *Sunday Graphic* (10 Sept. 1967). The reviews of *Dream* are from unidentified issues of *Guyana Graphic*, *Guyana Sunday Mirror* and *Guyana Sunday Chronicle*.

14. Derek Walcott to Gerald Freund (7 Sept. 1967), Rockefeller Archives.

15. Gerald Freund to Derek Walcott (20 Oct. 1967); Derek Walcott to Gerald Freund (6 Nov. 1967), Rockefeller Archives.

1968

Dream on Monkey Mountain
Henri Christophe
Homeless Again
The Five-Island Tour

DURING 1968 the Trinidad Theatre Workshop performed *Dream on Monkey Mountain* and *Henri Christophe* in Trinidad and had an extremely successful second 'annual' international tour—this time to Antigua, St Lucia, Barbados, St Vincent, and Grenada. Plans fell through for tours to Jamaica and Canada. The Workshop was evicted from its Basement Theatre and for the next two decades would be homeless, needing to rent rooms for workshops and rehearsals, lacking even storage space. It had, however, passed its first test of survival during 1965–66, when it lost the use of the Little Carib, and it now continued to grow under Walcott's leadership, on regional tours, and performing his plays.

In contrast to the little attention and support that the Workshop had received so far in Trinidad, the few visiting American theatre directors who saw the Workshop understood, and reported to others, that here was a unique example of true theatre, of what the theatre should be. Here was a potentially great theatre company working directly with a serious dramatist, with the dedication and energy of obsessed artists. Here was the true theatre of poverty that metropolitan intellectuals were seeking during the 1960s as more authentic than their own involvement in the 'system'. Unlike those fattened by the system, Walcott and his Workshop were already lean, did not have resources of the New York and London publicity network, had already managed to survive for ten years, and were just at the beginning of what was to become a decade of brilliant accomplishments. Its one real sponsor was the Rockefeller Foundation whose aid was mostly to Walcott as a poet and dramatist, although it did find ways from time to time to send visiting directors to train the Workshop for short periods.

Meanwhile the company increased. Andrew Beddeau (1920–91), the Shango priest, drummer, and singer, officially joined in December 1967; he was already well known, having worked with McBurnie and recorded for American musicologists. His records were available in local shops. Slade Hopkinson, who was to have an important role both as one of the Workshop's best actors and as someone whom Walcott respected, returned to Trinidad from Guyana, where he was teaching at the university. As Walcott's productions started to become grander, he added for a time the Hiland Park Entertainers, a folk-song group, to provide music. At this point the Workshop's repertory consisted of Soyinka's *The Road*, Genet's *The Blacks*, Roach's *Belle Fanto*, John's *Moon on a Rainbow Shawl*, Albee's *Zoo Story*, *Dream on Monkey Mountain* and two one-act Walcott plays, *Jourmard* and *The Sea at Dauphin*. Reviews of Workshop productions were beginning to be longer and more thoughtful. The company was already tending to become a vehicle for performing Walcott's plays as there was no other West Indian dramatist who created the same interest.[1]

The production of *Dream on Monkey Mountain* at Queen's Hall, 26–29 January, was the first Trinidadian performance of the play. As many new Workshop members were added, especially as the Market Women, the cast of twelve actors expanded to about thirty performers. Walcott wrote in one extra line to give Leone Campbell a speaking role for this performance.[2]

Dream on Monkey Mountain is dedicated 'To Errol Jones and the Trinidad Theatre Workshop' and for many of the older members this is remembered as the classic Workshop production in its cast and roles which included Errol Jones (Makak), Albert Laveau (Basil), Hamilton Parris (Souris and peasant), Stanley Marshall (Moustique), Andrew Beddeau (conteur and drummer), Sydney Best (Tigre and litter bearer), Ralph Campbell (Corporal Lestrade), Christopher Jordan (dancer and Watusi warrior), Helen Camps (Apparition, white goddess), Claude Reid (Pamphilion and litter bearer), Eunice Alleyne and Lynette Laveau (Sisters of Revelation), Leone Campbell and Gloria Mark (Market Women), Avis Greenidge, Pamela Franco, Marylin Clarke, Esther Bailey, Lynette Wilson and Shirley Atherly (Wives of Makak), George

Corbie, Terrence Joseph, Hurley Blackman, John Daniel (peasants), the Hiland Park Entertainers (choir), John Andrews (lighting designer), Errol Pilgrim (stage manager), Felice Lashley and Elena James (wardrobe), Anne Hilton (properties), Terry Chandler, Ken Alleyne, Ewart Giuseppi, Walter Edinborough and Stuart Hahn (stage crew) and Derek Walcott (playwright, director, designer).

Although the Workshop was still primarily non-white and male, the cast now included Helen Camps as the white Apparition, a role that had been previously played by Elena James, an Indian. This visually strengthened the symbolism. Camps, an Irish woman married to a West Indian, would soon emerge as a strong personality within the company. The continuing relationship of Walcott's theatre to Beryl McBurnie's role in developing West Indian dance can be seen in the programme note that 'scene III, the "healing scene" owes an obvious debt to Miss Beryl McBurnie's "Spirit"'.

John Melser wrote of *Dream* as a personal triumph for Walcott who had a hand in all parts of the play, including rehearsals, the drumming, and building the Workshop. Total theatre, *Dream* uses such current theatre idioms as the theatre of the absurd in its abrupt changes of pace and mood and use of deflating incongruities; Brecht in its use of dance, colour, and visual impact. It treats of 'colour, colonialism, poverty versus privilege, black power, the rule of law, and the search for identity through social or racial "causes"'. The audience enjoyed itself, laughed, and was excited by the variety of the action, surprises, and reversals of mood. The production was highly successful with excellent choreography and sets. The Workshop reached a standard of professionalism unlike the bumbling amateur shows common to Trinidad. Judged by the highest standards the actors would need to work on their voices; the poetry was spoiled by swallowing words or bad inflections. Melser thought the central theme was that the dreams and hunger for identity drive both the black and mulatto to violence 'which stultifies both the vision and the person unless they are resolved in a common humanity'. Home is not Africa or Europe; it is the 'secure possession of one's native place'. Past visions are not, however, easily put aside. The attempt to return to Africa and put aside 'whiteness' is a necessary step, but only a step, in coming to terms with the truth.[3]

Melser found the 'magic' of the poetic and dramatic imagery and tone well sustained, but felt that the transitions and contrasts were not clearly enough marked (a common criticism of most productions of the play). Jones gave a beautifully sustained performance, bringing out the pathos of Makak, but his inflections were weak. He needed more power and command to be convincing. Laveau has an impressive stage presence but a bland voice. Both actors moved well. Ralph Campbell was energetic and possessed the stage but swallowed his words. Marshall had excellent timing and sharp delivery. Reid, Best, Parris, and Alleyne gave first-rate performances with an exact sense of how far they could go with comedy. They played broadly but with sufficient restraint to keep within the mood. Honours should go to the chorus, drummers, and dancers which set the mood and created the magic. Walcott's movement and groupings were pleasing, but some characters gestured too much. It was curious that Walcott concentrated so much on the visual, dance, and song, allowing his actors to get away with weak delivery of his poetry. The play could be cut by fifteen minutes to create a sharper impression, but deserved a long run and frequent revivals.

Ulric Mentus thought *Dream* a protest play against white injustice. It had a deep buried warhead that has 'not yet exploded', but the dream-like structure, in which the play is a projection of Makak's psychoses, was bewildering, although the 'dream' is common to 'poverty-ridden black men in the Caribbean' as shown by the Rastafarian movement. While most of Mentus's review consists of plot summary and quotation, he praises the acting and observes that the 'stage setting epitomises the hopelessness of the situation—a towering dark mountain flanked on either side by giant spider webs. The only escape in the mind.'⁴

Earl Lovelace in the *Sunday Express* claimed that Walcott's 'Dream exposes truths we try to suppress', took a 'frontal approach to the race issue' and set out to 'provoke' with truths and contradictions that cannot be ignored. The play might free 'ourselves of colonial neurosis'. Both the negro and mulatto are 'caged' in their responses to the white world. Makak, the negro, is caged in self-hatred and imagined ugliness in relation to whiteness. Lust of the white woman represents 'all that he finds inaccessible'. Colonel Lestrade is the 'native intellectual' who upholds the white man's law which gives him power over his black half-brother. Makak attempts to break from his cage by an imagined return to Africa which the play explores. The rich symbolism makes the emotions realistic, but the language is at times indulgent and requires 'strenuous' mental effort. Perhaps Walcott wanted to shock people into an awakening. Walcott's reputation as 'perhaps the best director in theatre in the West Indies was enhanced' by this production. The handling of the crowd scenes was especially good. 'One could see every gesture of the actors weaving the atmosphere.'

The excellent sets and lighting also contributed to the atmosphere. Ralph Campbell as Lestrade was credible while creating a range of emotions. Claude Reid as Inspector Pamphilion was sparkling. Walcott, however, did not create sympathy or polarization of emotions for his characters, which made identification difficult. (Lovelace was probably objecting to the alienation or distancing effect Walcott had learned from Brecht and others.)[5]

By now many of the actors learned how to tap their emotions for powerful performances. Brando was often the model. Walcott would push Jones further and further to let it all out. Therese Mills was impressed by Ralph Campbell's portrait of the mulatto Corporal Lestrade, which she compared in style with that of Marlon Brando. She interviewed Campbell for the *Sunday Guardian* a week after the opening of *Dream*. Campbell, from Morvant, attended St George's College and Government Training College, was then twenty-six years old, a bachelor, and a secondary school teacher in love with the theatre. He had been with the Workshop since 1961 after having started in other drama groups. Walcott 'drives you like hell, but what he is asking for cannot be denied'. You rehearse and rehearse 'striving for perfection'. The Workshop does not aim at producing stars. 'We go after concentration and refinement.' As soon as Campbell read the script he wanted the role of the corporal. Campbell felt he needed further training, especially in voice control; he was hoarse the second and third evenings. He wanted to go abroad for further training as an actor and become a professional; he would soon go to Nigeria, Canada, and the United States.[6]

As with many of Walcott's plays before *The Joker of Seville*, the basic idea of *Dream on Monkey Mountain* has its origins in the St Lucia of his youth. In St Lucia, as in Port of Spain, there were impoverished peasants who lived in the hills and came to the towns to sell charcoal. One man who was often drunk, uncouth, and terrifying, in particular fascinated Walcott. The infusion of such a character with dreams of returning to Africa, discovery of royal African origins, and revenge on whites were not only commonplaces of black West Indian thought for the past century but had their attraction to Walcott himself with his concern with his dual heritage. The quotation from Frantz Fanon which prefaces the printed version of the play points to another thematic dimension; Fanon's criticism of the black bourgeoisie which wears the face of white culture while because of skin colour feeling inferior to the whites is followed by Fanon's criticism of the new nationalist order which inherits the state from the colonizers. This neocolonialism pays homage to the African past while remaining an appendage of the European colonizer. Authentic psychological freedom and renewal only comes from an act of violence against the white oppressor, an act which destroys dependency and enables the colonized to create a genuine modern culture based on the people. Walcott uses this model but treats it critically in *Dream*.

While the play itself, in its present published form, is a product of the 1960s and influenced by the violent, possessive, and complex narrative structures of Genet's *The Blacks* and Soyinka's *The Road*, as well as by such literary classics as *Don Quixote* and *Waiting for Godot*, the essential problem Walcott faced was how to avoid the feeling of stasis found in such interiorized dramas as *Samson Agonistes* and *Murder in the Cathedral*, where the main conflicts are psychological and subjective. How to represent Fanonian psychology on stage? Here Walcott externalizes it as action. The dream, with all the shifting and jumping, fragmentation, and dislocations common to dreams, becomes stage action, visual stage images. The reader of the play and some in the audience will follow the complex movement with its layering of many themes and general drift of an argument about desire, rebellion, violence, and acceptance of the self and reality; many in the audience are, however, likely to focus on only a few threads of the play and either simplify the significance or become lost. To communicate visually the acting is often done in broad gestures echoing words in the text. Some scenes—the 'healing' or 'resurrection' scene, for example—are extremely interiorized in the demands they make on the actors and require genuine understanding of Method acting. Errol Jones was already well known in Trinidad as a good actor, but his concentration and the range and depth of changes in the role of Makak rapidly made him famous throughout the West Indies. In this, perhaps Walcott's most complex analysis of the 'black' mind, there is an abundance and richness of theme, irony, and character. *Dream* is a sympathetic but critical reading of Fanon by someone who is the heir of Shakespeare and Ibsen and of the modern tradition of literature and criticism which has valued complexity.

In March Walcott was invited to the Creative Arts Centre, University of the West Indies, Jamaica, where he, John Figueroa, and Dennis Scott read from his poetry. There were plans to invite the Workshop to the Centre in October; as preparation Walcott gave a lecture on the 'Origins and Operations of the Basement Theatre, Trinidad'. While he was in Jamaica, the Barbados Arts Council announced that Walcott had won $200 for the best three-act play in its play-writing competition, for his revised, enlarged *Franklin*, another play begun in his Jamaica days.

In March there was also a production in Jamaica by the National Theatre Trust of Walcott's early *Malcochon* as part of a double bill with Marina Maxwell's *Play Mas*. Maxwell, a Trinidadian who at times was involved with the Little Carib and the Trinidad Dramatic Club, wanted a consciously black, 'revolutionary' theatre. *Play Mas* was an experiment in free form, late 1960s-style, mixing surrealism with Carnival to offer a revolutionary political statement. The programme note is filled with such 1968 comments as 'Where do we stand?', 'Where do you belong?' Similarly Michael Reckord's 'The Artist in Our New Society', which prefaces the programme, uses such clichés as 'the Third World's search for identity' and the need to 'break away from the traditions of Old World Theatre'. Dennis Scott, himself a dramatist, cuts through such babble in the rest of the printed programme by discussing Walcott's plays in rather different terms; 'the French-Creole language of his characters attains a rhythm and vibrancy rich in metaphor and magic. . . . Dance, music, song, mime—he makes use of the many devices by which the theatre lifts the imagination towards the extraordinary. A Walcott play is an intensely theatrical experience . . .'. After mentioning Walcott's debts to the Kabuki and Noh theatre for his techniques, and the use of character types found in myths, rituals, and folklore, Scott concludes that Walcott's success as a dramatist owes as much 'to his compassion, his control of language, his tremendous respect and affection for the people he re-creates'. He finds in their tragedies a dignity not always granted them 'by others'.[7]

The March–June issue of *Caribbean Quarterly* carried Scott's interview with Walcott and a shortened version of *Dream* with photographs of scenes. During the interview Walcott speaks of a play as poetry, poetry resulting more from lighting and structure than conscious metaphor or symbolism. Indeed he distinguished between writing plays in verse and the poetry that they might become on stage. The poetic then is the visual, the sound, the presentation, not the words on paper. The poetry is what theatre becomes at its best and not the text itself. Walcott mentions that his own poetry is becoming much plainer, less obscure than in the past, and speaks of his interest in post-impressionist painters who treated of domestic scenes and objects. While such a change in direction will not be immediately obvious, the plays which follow *Dream* are less troubled, less obscure, more physically imagined.[8]

During mid-April the Management Committee of the Workshop

met at Walcott's home with Walcott, Jones, Marshall, Albert Laveau, John Melser, Errol Pilgrim, John Andrews, Margaret Walcott, and Eunice Alleyne attending. They decided to sponsor and share profits for the forthcoming Brian Barnes one-man show in June, 60 per cent for Barnes, 40 per cent for the Workshop. A brochure would be prepared for the tenth anniversary. Walcott discussed his ideas of a board of management and trusteeship council which would acquire $25,000 for the publication of local TTW plays, offer short-term scholarships, pay for travelling expenses, and remunerate the Workshop members for their performances.[9]

André Gregory, the American theatre director, now perhaps best known for the co-scripting of and his central role in Louis Malle's film *My Dinner with André*, arrived 12 April, his air fare paid by the Rockefeller Foundation. He and Walcott got along well and he suggested that Walcott ask the Rockefeller Foundation to send him a professional designer for costumes and lighting and someone who could help redesign the sets for touring as the sets were too cumbersome and amateurish. The company would need to learn such skills from a professional and Walcott thought classes might be given to other Trinidadian theatre companies at the same time. Walcott had been thinking of touring in rural areas where they would need portable sets.[10]

As part of the Trinidad and Tobago Festival, 26–28 April, the Workshop presented *Henri Christophe* at Queen's Hall and later, on 11 May, at Naparima Bowl in San Fernando. This was the fourth time *Henri Christophe* had been performed outside St Lucia where Walcott had written it at his brother Roderick's suggestion during the late 1940s. The new Workshop production cost TT $4,800 and was sponsored by Angostura Bitters and R. J. Shannon. The first night was attended by André Gregory. *Henri Christophe* required a large cast that included Wilbert Holder as Vastey, Ralph Campbell as Jean Jacques Dessalines, John Melser as Brelle, Albert Laveau as Henri Christophe, and Stanley Marshall as Sylla. Errol Jones, Geddes Jennings, Claude Reid, and others doubled or tripled many minor parts. This was the first time that Holder, who had immigrated from Guyana, and Melser, a New Zealander, performed with the Workshop. Holder was later to become one of its main attractions.[11]

Henri Christophe is less a celebration of the Haitian revolt against France than a study in why it went wrong, why its black heroes and the first black anti-colonial revolt produced tyranny and even greater hardship for the blacks. It covers thirteen years, from 1807 until 1820, and follows the fortunes of the revolt through Jean Jacques Dessalines' proclamation of himself as king, his murder, the civil war, and Henri Christophe's assumption of kingship. What begins as a revolt against oppression and racism becomes a quest for personal power and results in tyranny to keep power. Black is no different from white. In the play there are whites who are favourable to the black cause and blacks willing to betray other blacks to whites or blacks for advancement. Power corrupts, noble ideals cover base motives; those who have paid for their freedom want revenge and privilege. The complexity of behaviour is Shakespearean, the disillusionment Websterian. Although written when Walcott was in his teens, *Henri Christophe* anticipated the wry view he often had of black nationalist movements in the Caribbean. An Eric Williams, a Papa Doc, was likely to follow in the steps of Dessalines and turn a people's revolt into a personal tyranny.

Earl Lovelace's review was headed 'Christophe—Image Packed Essay Mouthed by Actors'. Walcott focuses on 'the intrigues' with which the two black generals were involved and 'their personal dilemmas' as ex-slaves attempting to reconcile their past to kingship. The play is wordy, and draws upon a 'universal vocabulary' often inappropriate to the characters. Three hours of verbal gymnastics is too much. Wilbert Holder and Stanley Marshall were outstandingly convincing. Ralph Campbell, however, moved over too many tonal ranges without control of his voice. Brunell Jones called the play a success but also complained that three hours was too much. While the acting was good there was a tendency for voices to become lost in the poor acoustics and for actors to speak away from the audience.[12]

A letter to the *Guardian* was less favourably inclined. Winston Smart, of Belmont, objected that the national anthem was not played, that the show did not start on time, and that there were too many Shakespearean similes, personifications, and metaphors. There was no justification to put such elevated and verbose speech into the mouths of some rough, uneducated ex-slaves, who never had even the rudiments of formal education. The letter writer had been bored by three almost uninterrupted hours of 'revolution, murder, politics, intrigue, ambition, jealousy, devices, and factors as wit, satire, humour, irony, dramatic irony, innuendo, euphemism, etc.' and warned that if Mr. Walcott did not avoid such faults in his next play the Workshop would soon need to return to the Basement. Was the letter a parody?[13]

André Gregory returned to the United States full of enthusiasm for Walcott and the Workshop. Reporting to the Rockefeller Foundation in June he admitted that he had gone to Trinidad with much scepticism, expecting to find little of interest in the way of theatre. Instead he found a brilliant playwright with a vision of the theatre and a 'theatre phenomenon' in the tradition of Shakespeare and Molière. As with such writers, Walcott's plays develop from his relationship to his actors.[14]

Walcott is comparable, Gregory said, to Joan Littlewood, Roger Planchon, or Brecht in his devotion to the theatre and concern with modernizing traditional theatre. As Walcott is a playwright it is possible that his company if properly nurtured will develop into a theatre of world renown. At present the Workshop is impoverished, stumbling and not yet professional, but it is worth more than all Broadway combined in its love of theatre. A true company, together for over ten years, working in harmony and dedicated to Walcott, it is more permanent than any regional American company. Walcott demands total devotion to the theatre. The members come to the theatre directly from their jobs and often do not know how they will get home at night. Of the thirty actors about fifteen are the core. 'The talent is tremendous.' Through the experience Walcott and Jones had in the United States they developed techniques of improvisation and sensory exercises to improve their talent and find a common language. American repertory companies may be more facile and appear more professional, but do not concern themselves with the heart of the craft and do not have the same abilities. The company still cannot relate their exercises to productions and tend to overact, but because of their years of improvisation and sensory exercises, a director could solve such problems within a year. About six of the actors are potentially very good. That is as much as any company in the world. Surprisingly Gregory had especial praise for the younger women. Brecht's Berlin Ensemble is of a much higher standard, but does not have as many actors who are really top calibre. The Workshop actors sing well, play musical instruments, but have little sense of stage movement or voice techniques. They cannot project well in large auditoriums.

Walcott had developed his own studio practices. He would have three improvisations on a theme going on at the same time, yet they would be connected with a play he was writing. Gregory continued by comparing Walcott and the Workshop with Herbert Blau, Jules Irving, and the San Francisco Actors Workshop. It would need help to move on to the next phase of its development if it were to have a similar influence.[15]

The Workshop needed everything, Gregory wrote, 'since they have so little'. They needed a real theatre of their own as the Basement was the smallest of off-off-Broadway theatres without room for make-up or storage. The stage was only 27ft × 13ft. Besides paying rent for the theatre the company had to rent a room in the hotel for making up and storage. Although a board of trustees was being formed to build a theatre, that, Gregory felt, was a probable dead end. The government had no interest in it and no one in Trinidad had any notion of the real importance of the Workshop or of Walcott. While Walcott was a director, writer, teacher, designer, he was also responsible for the business side, which was absurd as Walcott was 'completely impractical' about anything outside his work and had not the least notion of how to raise funds. The company needed an administrator and business manager, and none were in sight.

Walcott also needed a director to work with the company to bring some outside discipline and take the actors further in their development. No director should direct all the plays of a company. They needed someone to help with the visual side so that the costumes and sets would have more impact. Audiences are not aware of acting technique; they judge by visual appearance and by such standards the Workshop will seem amateur to those who have seen theatre abroad. Walcott needed help from a set and costume designer transforming his own painterly vision into practical stage realities. Their present sets needed redesigning for tours. They also needed basic tools and equipment for construction. They needed a voice teacher for three or four months and someone to help with organic movement in relation to emotion and acting. After the company had been given such training, the core should be put on permanent salaries so that they could devote themselves full time to the theatre. Most of the company were government officials or teachers earning perhaps $75 a week, so it would not be expensive to subsidize them. Gregory wanted to return to Trinidad to work with the company and bring some designers with him.

Gregory's report was discussed within the Rockefeller Foundation. Because of past interest in Walcott and West Indian performing arts, and because of the merits of the case, the feeling was that the Foundation should help; this, however, would be an exception for the Arts Program to assist a company outside the United States. Various sums were discussed internally as an exceptional grant. Freund was willing to consider a grant of $25,000 if the Trustees would approve. Another official was willing to recommend $15,000 as an exception. Generally it was felt that here was one of the few theatre groups genuinely intertwining music, song, dance, and movement with acting, unlike the mixed media circuses of the time. So a grant might be seen as supporting new directions in theatre that were meant to have a wider impact outside the West Indies.

Meanwhile John Hearne had been attempting to raise some funds from the Rockefeller Foundation to bring the Theatre Workshop on tour to Jamaica. Estimated costs were $7,500 of which the university could cover a third. Walcott also wrote asking Freund for two visiting designers, and funds to purchase materials and to print a booklet publicizing the company so that he could gain the attention of Edinburgh and other international festivals. Walcott apparently already had a sense that he was making theatre history, although few had yet noticed, and mentioned that he was writing an essay on the history of the TTW and the problems it faced. I imagine that this eventually became 'What the Twilight Says', the essay that prefaces the *Dream on Monkey Mountain* volume of plays, although Walcott at various times thought of writing a book about the Workshop. Freund replied that the Foundation could not help with the tour and that any decision concerning the Workshop would take time.[16]

In June the Workshop sponsored Brian Barnes's version of Dylan Thomas's *Under Milkwood*. One month later the Workshop was forced to leave the Basement Theatre it occupied at the Bretton Hall Hotel since 1966. Although the exact reasons for the eviction of the theatre group are unclear, they may have been the result of Walcott's relationship with the hotel owner's wife. In the Basement Theatre the Workshop had offered its first season, which ran for twenty-six nights, six full-length plays, and various cultural events. It was a place where the actors could meet and rehearse or workshop outside scheduled hours, and a space for poetry readings. After late July 1968, the Workshop would have no regular home until it leased the Old Fire Station in 1989. It would be forced to move from rented space to rented space using, at various times, an annex to the Zoo Pavilion off Queen's Park, the Catholic Youth League (near the Pelican Inn) and Bishop's High School auditorium. From now on the company would no longer be the Basement Theatre and the title Theatre Workshop would stick with it until the present.[17]

In August Walcott taught drama at the University of the West Indies Creative Arts summer school at St Augustine. This was the third such summer school; the instructors included Beryl McBurnie and Alexander McDougall (from the Winnipeg Ballet) in dance. As usual there were a number of young women in the summer courses. Recent Workshop members Esther Bailey and Pamela Franco were in Walcott's summer school production of Aristophanes' *Lysistrata*. During September plans were in progress for the coming year. Plays by Harold Pinter, Frank O'Hara, and Samuel Beckett were in rehearsal. There was talk of adding to the company's repertoire a play by Chekhov, Miller's *Death of a Salesman*, Brecht's *Threepenny Opera*, and some West Indian plays. Lighting at the various venues, especially on tour and at the Little Carib, remained a problem and Walcott asked Barclays Bank to contribute $1,000 towards purchasing lighting equipment. The bank donated $200.[18]

Walcott wrote in the *Sunday Guardian Magazine* 'the burden of the West Indian Playwright is that he must create not only a theatre but its environment'. He can destroy his creative impulses building an audience. The dramatist needs to be a director, form an acting company, manage, and find a theatre. Most dramatists will not be able to do this and West Indian play scripts will remain on the shelves. The Workshop began with the notion of finding an honest, powerful performing style. Now the task is to create a body of West Indian plays equal in power to foreign plays. Too much West Indian theatre is limited, provincial, inferior to the West Indian novel. The Workshop is not a provincial company, it aims at international standards and responses to the modern language of theatre. This has been achieved in poverty and deprivation. It is necessary to convince society that theatre is needed and within 'the emotional response' of the average person, 'however obscure' the text may appear. The Workshop is an interracial company which will perform the great plays of the world along with West Indian plays. It is necessary to get beyond the village attitude that you put on a play for one night and then forget it. It is necessary to get beyond the self-hate that assumes that a semi-professional company is impossible in Port of Spain. The Workshop has already reached the point that it can pay principal actors $100 a night for large productions and still clear expenses such as renting Queen's Hall. They filled Queen's Hall for five nights for *Moon on a Rainbow Shawl* and could have had a longer run except that the Hall was already taken. They have done this without a government subsidy. They will probably in future often tour overseas as that will temper and polish them through abrasion. The company does not exist to offer 'racial plays', but in choosing great plays, like *The Blacks*, they are interested in works that say something 'about race and posturing about race'. That the *The Blacks* was performed in the small Basement Theatre trapped spectators into confronting 'racial and sexual virulence' unlike that previously seen in Trinidad. *Belle Fanto* has already had twenty-six performances and will have another seven nights on the forthcoming tour. The Workshop now has an audience that guarantees sell outs for two nights, but the actors are already getting restless and five or six have emigrated in the hope of becoming professionals abroad. 'A Workshop actor surrenders all of his time to his art', but the rewards are small. The Workshop needs a home where it can build a larger audience for the arts as well as providing the actor with employment. The Workshop is a 'real West Indian company'.[19]

The high point of the year was a five-island tour, 10–27 October, performing Roach's *Belle Fanto* and Walcott's *Dream*. As with many Workshop events some details are a bit uncertain as extra shows were performed without advance notice or because of late changes in plan. The tour started in Grenada with a 'command performance' of *Belle Fanto* on 10 October at Government House for Her Excellency Hilda Bynoe (aunt of Workshop actor and dancer Adele Bynoe), followed by performances of *Dream* at Grenada Boys' Secondary School, 11 October, and *Belle Fanto*, 12 October. Publicity was done mostly over the local radio. On 15–16 October there were performances of *Belle Fanto* and *Dream* at the Town Hall, Castries, St Lucia, hosted by the University of the West Indies Extra-Mural Department. *Dream* was acted in Barbados, 18–19 October, at Combermere High School, hosted by the Barbados Arts Council. In Antigua, 22–23 October, and St Vincent, 25–26 October, *Belle Fanto* and *Dream* were performed. The company included Slade Hopkinson, Geddes Jennings, Claude Reid, Hamilton Parris, Errol Jones, Elena James, Stanley Marshall, Eunice Alleyne, Pamela Franco, Esther Bailey, Avis Wilson, Errol Pilgrim, and Terrence Chandler. This was Avis Wilson's first stage appearance. Walcott left the company in Barbados to fly to Washington, DC, for a poetry reading. For the performances in Antigua another actor was flown in to replace Slade Hopkinson who had to return to his job as a school teacher in Trinidad.

The arrangements and publicity for the tour were done by Walcott's friends, who usually were also developing the arts on their islands; they often were from the St Lucia Arts Guild or his time in Jamaica. The Barbados Arts Council was a group of individuals granted an official title without much government support. Sometimes local groups sponsored the Workshop, but usually their role was limited to publicity, finding playing sites, and arranging for housing. Walcott was really the entrepreneuring producer whose money financed the tour and who would make a profit or loss. The publicity and many reviews sound as if they were based on Walcott's advance publicity releases.

The coming appearance of the Workshop in St Lucia was heralded by several articles in the *Voice of St Lucia* such as 'Errol Jones—T'dad's No. 1 Actor Soon to Appear Here', 'The Belle of "Belle Fanto"' (about Eunice Alleyne), 'Walcott And Group Arrive on Monday' and 'Rave Notices for Theatre Workshop', written by members of the St Lucia Arts Guild. A somewhat negative review by the St Lucian novelist Garth St Omer (a relative of Walcott's close friend, the painter Dunstan St Omer) was titled 'Dream, But Not, Please, on Monkey Mountain'. While praising the quality of the performances of both plays, St Omer objected to élite theatre which would not be seen or read by most of the population of the island. Roach's play communicated to the audience in a way that Walcott's sophisticated writing never could. The audience undoubtedly did not understand the message of *Dream* and was entertained by the spectacle. The theatre needed to establish real contact with the audience using oral, not European models.[20]

Various readers of *The Voice of St Lucia*, including some who had not seen *Dream*, joined in the subsequent fray. The most important reply to St Omer was a letter from Stanley Reid the next Saturday. St Omer's comments are typical of the 'crass artistic idealism' of the West Indian intellectual in assuming that drama must have 'some sort of meaning for the masses'. In the arts there are many levels of perception; *Belle Fanto* is escapist entertainment for the middle class and hardly touches on the issues raised by Walcott's play. *Dream* was intimate, you laughed at yourself. 'It is the first time I have observed subliminal techniques used in the theatre.' The audience knew they were Lestrades; their secrets were betrayed. Reid also objected to St Omer's interpretation which confused Moustique with Makak as representative of the truth. Walcott had established the contact with the audience St Omer wanted; St Omer in his assumed role as cultural physician minimized the effect.[21]

Faith Marshall's review, headlined 'Such Brilliance Seldom Seen on Barbadian Stage', claimed that *Dream* blended the 'primitive poetry' of the Rastafarians, piquant St Lucian patois, and racy scintillating Trinidadian picong into a powerful, frightening, document of the inner conflicts of the Negro. It is 'a stage show brilliant in conception and execution, design and movement'. The 'throb of the drums', the vitality of the singing, the music and the dance are part of 'a flawless production'. Scene changes are fast, the play has a flow in its transitions from reality to dream and back. Slade Hopkinson, as Lestrade, shows the Negro's desire to create a dream kingdom, to establish his own milieu, but, betrayed by his internalized craving for whiteness, the dream kingdom becomes a reign of terror, destruction, and, in the form of Basil, death, the ultimate reaper of all races. Hopkinson's interpretation is convincing and 'flawless to the last detail' in conveying the various ideas and contrasts through tone and movement while remaining attractive and humorous. Each character is a set of contrasts, conflicts, and contradictions. Errol Jones as Makak is at the same time strong and weak, 'princely and impractical'. He is apelike yet at times rises to poetic heights by an intuitive sense of beauty. Jones brings out the subtleties and interplay of light and shade in Walcott's play. Stanley Marshall's role as Moustique is less complex, but also is based on contradictions; he is the materialist who knows 'that this cannot be all' and who will be destroyed by love of gain. The play offers contrary currents, but no solutions. We want to go home, but to where or what? 'One noted the positive reaction of some of the elements of the audience when the white devil appeared and one was struck by the irony. There were we looking and laughing with Walcott, laughing at ourselves and hardly aware of it.'[22]

John Wickham wrote in *Bim*, the influential West Indian literary review published in Barbados, of his 'pure delight' in Walcott's language, comic twists, and ability to transform a human situation into a fable. He commented on the symbolic names (rat, tiger, mosquito) and the superb staging of controlled acting, saying it was among the best Barbados had ever seen. There was a power and intensity in the acting. Wickham especially praised Eunice Alleyne's ability to convey a scene through words as she describes it to others. Wickham hoped that the Barbados Theatre Workshop would be encouraged by having seen what can be done by an 'indigenous theatre' through hard work, dedication, and intellectual honesty.[23]

Mary E. Morgan's review in *The Vincentian* spoke of the physical poetry of the production of *Dream*. The basic set, with two black cages on either side of a dim prison, and the animal symbolism of the characters' names, were part of the confident, controlled gestures and dance sequences. The production had superb team work. Hopkinson brought to Lestrade a mixture of bravado and courage, comic fantasy, and stature. He was swift, business-like, cunning, and dominant. Jones's voice ranged from the whimpering of an old man though the lyrical crooning of a man in love to the commanding tone of a natural leader. As his dream disappears his voice became a whisper. His movements expressed his changes in personality. *Belle Fanto* began with drumming, the drummers' red head-bands expressive of tragedy.[24]

In 1980 reviewing a local production of *Dream* John Wickham wrote that the 1968 production included two of the most moving 'bits' of theatre he had ever seen and called Slade Hopkinson probably the finest actor, with perfect timing and vocal authority, that the West Indies produced. The two scenes the reviewer remembered so well were when Makak, with hot fiery coal in his hands, makes the snake-bitten man sweat and heal; and the scene where Lestrade commands Makak to kill the white witch or Muse. The reviewer also mentioned Albert Laveau's 'menace' as Basil. By 1980 *Dream* no longer seemed an obscure, difficult play. Kathleen Drayton, reviewing the local production, spoke of *Dream*'s simple structure and could refer to its sources in Carnival robbers' speech, and ultimately Kalinda and mumming plays. 'The mimicry of "robber talk" and the stick-fighting songs are apotheosed into the universal myth of death and resurrection.'[25]

After Walcott returned to Trinidad he said the tour was fantastic. 'We never thought we would draw such houses.' They had given fifteen performances in seventeen days. In St Vincent they had been asked to give a matinee at 10 a.m. *Belle Fanto* and *Dream* were plays with which the common person identified. The Workshop probably could have toured for six months playing to villages throughout the Caribbean. They had been offered free accommodation for future tours; now all they would need to do would be to arrange for leave from their jobs. He compared the company to the African Ballet (of Mali). The box office could pay the actors subsistence and salaries. 'I believe there are few directors with a company like mine.' In St Vincent they had to build a complete set in two hours after the set did not arrive from Antigua; they had in a few hours to teach local singers. In Barbados they arrived at 4 p.m. for an 8.30 p.m. show. There would be an additional performance of *Dream on Monkey Mountain* at Queen's Hall on 9 December.[26]

Seven years later Slade Hopkinson recalled the 1968 tour as one of the most inspiring experiences in his life. Hopkinson flew back and forth between the islands where the Workshop was playing and Trinidad where he was teaching. When he arrived in St Lucia there was a meeting of the Workshop as the two scheduled performances had been sold out and they were asked to give an additional matinee. They would need to act from 4 p.m. until 7 p.m., somehow eat during the next hour, and do an evening show between 8 p.m. and 11 p.m. The company agreed. The extra matinee played to an overflowing crowd. The people who went to *Dream*, despite Walcott's reputation as an élite, highbrow writer, were the same people who would otherwise have gone to a cowboy film. Hopkinson heard people in St Lucia discussing which to attend, the play or the cinema. The people who came to the plays were mostly not intellectuals; the halls in St Lucia, St Vincent and Grenada were never large enough to take all who wanted to attend. Such people might not have intellectually understood *Dream*, but they could recognize that it was about the life they knew. By contrast in Barbados where the audience was more educated, there were claims that although the play was impressive it was inaccessible. Other productions of *Dream* have shown a similar pattern—the more developed the country the more pallid the approval. '*Dream* is, in part, about West Indian man's rejection of his home, and therefore of himself.' It is about mental and psychological migration to Europe or Africa. Walcott and Brathwaite maintain that it is impossible to find fulfilment until we accept the place we live in as home.[27]

Although the Jamaican part of the tour was cancelled when the university was unwilling to underwrite a bank loan, the five-island tour was a financial success. Walcott had taken a loan of three thousand West Indian dollars, but managed by the tour's end to cover costs of the fares, pay the actors a subsistence of sixty dollars and up to one hundred dollars each, and still made a profit of a thousand dollars. The company could now expect at least to recoup its expenses in tours throughout the region. Walcott hoped that such tours would become annual fixtures of the Workshop and had his eyes set in future on Miami, Puerto Rico, Caracas, and maybe New York, hoping that his company could travel perhaps three months each year. He worried that the Workshop was becoming too much his own, too much mannered by his ideas; he still wanted the Rockefeller Foundation to send him a visiting co-director.

NOTES

1. 'Dream on monkey mountain called the best in W. I.', *Sunday Guardian* (14 Jan. 1968), 6.
2. 'Two Expo Dancers Added to Cast of "Monkey Mountain"', *Trinidad Guardian* (25 Jan. 1968), 5; Leone Campbell's copy and interview (1990).
3. John Melser, 'Landmark for Local Drama and Triumph for Workshop', *Trinidad Guardian* (29 Jan. 1968), 11.
4. Ulric Mentus, 'Warhead in "Dream" Has Not Yet Exploded', *Evening News* (31 Jan. 1968).
5. Earl Lovelace, '"Dream" exposes truths we try to suppress', *Sunday Express* (1968).

6. Therese Mills, 'All the Time I am Bursting to be On Stage', *Sunday Guardian* (1968).

7. See Marina Maxwell, 'Towards a Revolution in the Arts', *Savacou*, 2 (Sept. 1970), 19–32.

8. Dennis Scott, 'Walcott on Walcott', *Caribbean Quarterly*, 14/1–2 (Mar./June 1968), 77–82, 120–6.

9. Management Committee, Trinidad Theatre Workshop (15 Apr. 1968), Walcott Collection, University of the West Indies, St Augustine.

10. Gerald Freund to Derek Walcott (31 May 1968), Rockefeller Archives.

11. 'Tonight: Walcott's "Henri Christophe"', *Trinidad Guardian* (26 Apr. 1968), 6; Agnes Sydney-Smith, '"Henri Christophe" Poet Walcott's First Major Play on Haitian Revolution', *Evening News* (21 Apr. 1968).

12. Earl Lovelace, 'Christophe—Image Packed Essay Mouthed by Actors', *Express* (30 Apr. 1968), 12; Brunell Jones, 'Walcott's Play—A Success at Festival', *Evening News* (3 May 1968).

13. Winston Smart, 'There were More Faults than Virtues', *Trinidad Guardian* (14 May 1968).

14. André Gregory's proposal and Gerald Freund's recommendation are contained in Inter-Office Correspondence from Freund to others (23 May 1968). There are also several notes between Freund and other Rockefeller directors during June in the Rockefeller Archives.

15. 'Six or seven different improvisations, all of which seemed to be in some way related to each other.' Wallace Shawn and André Gregory, *My Dinner with André* (New York: Grove Press, 1981), 32.

16. Derek Walcott—Gerald Freund (20 May 1968); Gerald Freund—Derek Walcott (31 May 1968). The various documents can be found in the Rockefeller Walcott files.

17. 'The Lights in the Basement Dim Out', *Sunday Express* (6 Oct. 1968), 5.

18. Therese Mills, 'A Taste of Honey on the Campus', *Sunday Guardian* (Aug. 1968).

19. Derek Walcott, 'The Theatre Workshop at the Crossroads', *Sunday Guardian*, (29 Sept. 1968), 4, 11.

20. C. A. P. St Hill, 'Errol Jones—T'dad's No. 1 Actor Soon to Appear Here', *Voice of St Lucia* (9 Oct. 1968), 3; 'Walcott And Group Arrive on Monday' and George Odlum, 'Rave Notices for Theatre Workshop', *Voice of St Lucia* (12 Oct. 1968), 2, 3; C. A. P. St Hill, 'The Belle of "Belle Fanto"', *Voice of St Lucia* (16 Oct. 1968), 7; Garth St Omer, 'Dream, But Not Please, on Monkey Mountain', *Voice of St Lucia* (2 Nov. 1968), 3, 6.

21. Stanley Reid, 'St Omer Has Made Several Mistakes', *Voice of St Lucia* (9 Nov. 1968), 6.

22. Faith Marshall, 'Such Brilliance Seldom Seen on Barbadian Stage', *Advocate News* (22 Oct. 1968), 4.

23. John Wickham, 'Theatre: "Dream on Monkey Mountain"', *Bim*, 12/48 (Jan.–June 1969), 267–8.

24. Mary E. Morgan, 'Trinidad Theatre Workshop in St Vincent', *The Vincentian* (9 Nov. 1968), 6, 12.

25. John Wickham, 'A Tale of Two Dreams', *Sunday Sun* (3 Feb. 1980), 27; Kathleen

Drayton, 'A Dream to Change the World', *Caribbean Contact*, 7/11 (Mar. 1980), 15.

26. 'Five-Island Tour', *Sunday Guardian* (3 Nov. 1968), 11.

27. Slade Hopkinson, 'Dream on Monkey Mountain and the Popular Response', *Arts Review*, Jamaican Creative Arts Centre, 1/1 (Jan. 1976), 3–7; repub. in *Caribbean Quarterly*, 23/2–3 (June–Sept. 1977), 77–9.

6

Dream in Connecticut and for NBC

As the Trinidad Theatre Workshop still remained an extension of Walcott as director-producer, with no legal existence, he proposed that it should be incorporated as a limited liability company with a nominal capital of $1,000. Wanting the company to keep to its original objectives and stay out of the hands of others, he proposed that the Workshop would have two director-shareholders who would have full control. Registration would cost $50 and legal fees and would make clear the distinction between the liabilities of the company and 'owners' in case productions lost money. Once the Theatre Workshop was registered it could apply to the government to lease Crown Lands near the Zoo Pavilion and build a theatre. It would be necessary to make a public appeal for funds. Versions of this plan kept appearing for the next two decades.

In February the Workshop announced that its new season would begin with dramatized readings from the works of the Trinidadian fiction writer Samuel Selvon, continue with a double bill of Oliver Jackman's *Stepchild, Stepchild* and Harold Pinter's *The Lover*, followed by J. P. Clark's *Song of a Goat*, Brecht's *Threepenny Opera* and revivals of *Dream* and Genet's *The Blacks*. Plans were made later for an open-air street presentation of Tennessee Williams' *Camino Real*. As usual many of the projects did not materialize and remained ideas on which Walcott continued to work over the years. And as usual unexpected opportunities were presented which furthered the reputation of Walcott and the Workshop abroad.[1]

The World of Sam Selvon offered readings by Selvon from *A Brighter Sun, I Hear Thunder*, and *The Housing Lark*, along with six dramatizations of short stories and episodes from Selvon's novels. Selvon had lived in England for the past sixteen years and returned to Trinidad on a Guggenheim Fellowship. The formula gave the company many roles. Claude Reid performed 'The Seagull' from *The Lonely Londoners* as a monologue; Hamilton Parris and Geddes Jennings shared 'Basement Lullaby' from *Ways of Sunlight*; 'The Calypsonian' and 'The Village Washer' from *Ways* each required nine actors. The cast included Esther Bailey, Ewart Giuseppi, Pamela Franco, Avis Wilson, Ermine Wright, Stanley Marshall, and Helen Camps. John Andrews was lighting designer. This was the first appearance of Ermine Wright, a school teacher who joined the Workshop in 1968 and who was to become their leading actress of mature, down-to-earth, commonsensical women of the people.

The Theatre Workshop opened *The World of Sam Selvon* with two shows at Naparima Bowl, San Fernando, on 6 March, moved to Town Hall, Port of Spain, for two performances each day on 7 March and 15 March. The Extra-Mural Department, UWI, was co-sponsor and the programmes carried an advertisement for the Summer School in Creative Arts. The productions were simple, using a bare stage with changes of mood suggested by area lighting and the rearrangement of some coloured boxes on stage. The script of 'The Calypsonian' has Walcott's drawings showing how the actors should use the boxes, sometimes sitting, sometimes gesturing over them, sometimes resting a leg or posturing on them. Three episodes—'Brackley and the Bed', 'Waiting for Aunty to Cough' and 'Basement Lullaby'—were filmed by Trinidad and Tobago Television, under Walcott's direction, and shown as a half-hour programme on 30 April.[2]

In the *Trinidad Guardian* Eric Roach wrote that the Selvon pieces worked best when the author was reading them or when he was reading them along with mime and dramatizations. When Selvon was not on stage, the lack of depth of the material showed, especially as without a narrator they were rather hard to follow if you did not know them already. Although the audience enjoyed themselves, Roach felt this was not much of a test for the Workshop. He wrote favourably of Claude Reid's mime and of Hamilton Parris. John Melser's 'Focus on the Arts' described *The World of Sam Selvon* as 'a cheerfully light-hearted series of virtuoso performances' and spoke of the high standard of acting as a sign of the maturity and assurance of the Workshop. The playlets were so recognizably Trinidadian that Melser wondered why it had not been done before. 'The program underlined yet again what a genius Basement Theatre has for comedy.' Hamilton

Parris was singled out for the way in which with an economy of means he created a moving portrait of compassion and strength 'in the face of alienation'. The television production of three episodes from *The World of Sam Selvon* was warmly received and described by reviewers as one of the best surprises to come from Television House. 'Argus' even claimed that it had the professionalism 'that one normally associates' with foreign shows and which is seldom seen in local productions.[3]

The Workshop and Walcott were not universally accepted as bringing new standards to Trinidad. Some of the other dramatists were angry with the attention Walcott was getting and with his claims. Those who had started modern Trinidad theatre were being pushed to the side, ignored, or criticized. Although Walcott has written favourably of Douglas Archibald, and told me that he thinks *The Rose Slip* a good play, Archibald refused to let me interview him concerning Walcott and the Workshop. He claimed Walcott had used his name in promoting the Workshop. The Trinidadian popular dramatist Freddie Kissoon, leader of the Strolling Players, lashed out at Walcott in the *Trinidad Guardian* and called the language of *Dream on Monkey Mountain* 'confused, far fetched and far removed from reality'. 'People yawned with boredom.' Back in the 1930s Mr Roberts, a local school teacher, wrote plays about the life of the people. Afterwards Kissoon, Errol John, Errol Hill, Douglas Archibald, and others worked in 'our beautiful and picturesque creolese'. Since then Walcott 'the poet laureate, left Mt. Olympus and formed a group to perform mainly for the intelligentsia'. Walcott has failed 'to use the direct and communicative language of the people'. Although some of the complaints were sour grapes at the Workshop's success it is true that Walcott had shown a remarkable ability to publicize and promote his theatre company and plays. Even before his arrival in Trinidad he was the darling of the intelligentsia and the media, someone who won prizes, gained international attention, and claimed to be moving West Indian culture towards new standards. Even negative reviews caused controversy and brought publicity. Increasingly his productions were reviewed by Earl Lovelace, Eric Roach, and Victor Questel, creative writers with their own claim to attention by critics of West Indian literature. An analogous situation in which good writers reviewed each other's plays occurred in the late nineteenth and early twentieth century when G. B. Shaw and others were establishing the 'New Drama'.[4]

During March George White of the O'Neill Memorial Theatre Foundation of Waterford, Connecticut, visited Port of Spain at the suggestion of the Rockefeller Foundation. After a private performance of scenes from *Dream on Monkey Mountain* and Genet's *The Blacks*, he invited Walcott and the Workshop to Connecticut for five weeks during July–August. He was especially impressed by the 'intense and intimate relationship between playwright and ensemble' and the Workshop's 'ensemble style'. At the O'Neill Playwrights' Conference they could do workshops in dance, theatre, directing, and criticism with American professional actors, technicians, and critics including Lloyd Richards, a leading black director and teacher of acting. This would be a temporary solution to the various problems raised by Gregory and Walcott about needing outside professional help. At the end of the conference they could present *Dream on Monkey Mountain* for a week. There were, however, problems. Who would pay? Walcott would also need to fly to England during that time to read at Poetry International before returning to Connecticut.[5]

Although his plays and theatre were at least as significant to Walcott, his poetry was gaining international recognition, especially in England and the Commonwealth: in June the Society of Authors in England gave him their Cholmondeley Award, worth £650. Walcott had originally decided to remain in the West Indies to create a theatre and make that his profession, but he was increasingly supporting himself with his poetry and creative writing on foreign grants and awards. The Trinidad Theatre Workshop was still unprofitable, and, while gaining a reputation in the region as a serious theatre company of a kind previously unknown to West Indian theatre, it too required foreign support, although mostly in the way of advanced training and the experience of working alongside professionals. Serious modern arts usually require patrons, but government and foundation patronage was not available in Trinidad where there was no tradition of supporting theatre and writing. Walcott understood that if a West Indian theatre of international standing were to develop and expand, it needed to be plugged into the international circuit and required foreign help. The large American foundations, however, after the disillusionment of the war in Vietnam were now turning towards their own national problems. The active encouragement of the arts abroad would increasingly be seen as imperialistic intervention in other lands at the expense of American minorities. Gerald Freund and others continued to try to help Walcott and the Trinidad Theatre Workshop, but this became more difficult, and, as so often happens, official America lost interest in what it helped start abroad. Individuals and theatre people, however, were becoming interested.

To understand some of the tensions and quarrels that later developed between Walcott and some leading members of the Workshop, it is useful to remember that not only did Walcott want a national theatre company and international recognition and standards, but that the Workshop's foundation and development were intertwined with foreign support. There was insufficient demand in Trinidad for such a company or for Walcott's career as a dramatist. Even later with the tremendous success of *The Joker of Seville* there were few profits and the original impulse came from abroad when the Royal Shakespeare Company commissioned Walcott to translate a sixteenth-century Spanish play. The rapid 'take-off' of the Trinidad Theatre Workshop and Walcott's career as a dramatist after 1969 was partly the result of George White and the Workshop's production of *Dream on Monkey Mountain* at the O'Neill Foundation theatre in Waterford, Connecticut.

George White wrote to the Rockefeller Foundation requesting $9,500 to bring Walcott and twelve members of the company to Connecticut for a month. White hoped that the Workshop could afterwards work for a week with Michael Schultz and the Negro Ensemble Company and perhaps with Charles Reinhart at the American Dance Festival. White proposed to use box office revenue from *Dream* to pay for sending further assistance to Trinidad as he felt Walcott had done excellent work against incredible odds in creating an exciting ensemble of disciplined performers, making them a de facto National Theatre of Trinidad. Although the company needed polish it was 'one of the most stimulating theatrical enterprises anywhere in the world'. There was, however, a need for training in technical direction, lighting, and stage design. At the O'Neill the company would have a concentrated period of work with many professionals including four directors— Michael Schultz, Glenn Jordan, Jay Ranelli, and Melvin Bernhardt. Later, in May, André Gregory telephoned the Rockefeller Foundation to say that he would like to work with the company while it was in the United States.[6]

Walcott wrote enthusiastically to Freund about White's proposal. He and his company needed all the help they could get in terms of exposure to all aspects of theatre, such as dance, production, and even scheduling. They risked repeating themselves without further input from outside. The company had to move from their rehearsal hut at the Zoo Pavilion and were still looking for a theatre they could use. If Walcott accepted a six-month appointment at Leeds University the coming year, he would need a visiting director and designer for that period.[7]

Within the Rockefeller Foundation there were objections raised to bringing a theatre company from Trinidad to the United States for study and performance; it was suggested by Norman Lloyd, Freund's superior, that this might be the proper point for the Foundation to end its long interest in Walcott. Freund wrote to tell Walcott the bad news.[8]

During 12–15 June the Workshop presented a double bill of Oliver Jackman's *Stepchild, Stepchild* and Harold Pinter's *The Lover* at Town Hall. Both plays require three characters and are about middle-class adultery. In Jackman's play the skin colours of the characters range from black to white; in Pinter's they are white. Jackman is a Barbadian diplomat and writer; *Stepchild* is his only play that has been performed. The cast included Susan Reynolds, Slade Hopkinson, and Helen Camps. The cast of the Pinter play was Judy Stone, John Melser, and Nigel Scott. Walcott directed both plays, Andrews was in charge of the lighting, but this time Stanley Marshall was stage manager. Susan Reynolds was a New Zealander who had lived in Trinidad for the past two years. Melser previously acted with the Trinidad Dramatic Club and in the Trinidad Theatre Workshop's *Henri Christophe* and in New Zealand. This was Nigel Scott's first appearance with the Workshop; previously he had performed with the Trinidad Dramatic Club. Walcott would come to regard him along with Laveau, Jones, and Marshall as a potentially world-class actor. Judy Stone had also worked with the Trinidad Dramatic Club after she came to Trinidad. The TDC was a well-established, older, primarily white, amateur company; that the Workshop was attracting its actors was significant. Where formerly a few talented blacks were allowed to perform in a white theatre company, now talented whites were joining a predominantly black company. This raised the problem of how to make use of the white actors. Walcott thought of the Workshop as reflecting multiracial Trinidad, but not all the actors agreed and some felt that he was obsessed with the white side of his heritage.

Nigel Scott (b. 1947) comes from a family that has been in Trinidad since the late eighteenth century. His great-grandfather was the Mayor of Port of Spain. Raised in Port of Spain Scott is at ease in its ethnic cultures, both sharing the aspirations of the Workshop and knowing that as a white in a predominantly black group there are times he will be marginal. Because of his colour his roles are also limited. At St Mary's School he became interested in theatre and acted in plays by Shakespeare and Goldsmith. He joined the Trinidad Dramatic Club and performed in its 1967 *Othello*. He was Cassio, John Melser played

Iago, and Errol Jones played Othello. Many in the cast soon joined the Workshop. Scott's membership in a largely black group raised eyebrows and caused comments at the still mostly white country club to which he belonged.[9]

Judy Stone (b. 1939) considers herself a Trinidadian as her family first came to the island in 1851. A product of a broken marriage, her education was erratic: she attended thirteen primary schools. She always had an interest in the arts, learned violin and piano, and had tuition in speech and drama. Born in England, she came to Trinidad on holiday to visit her father and decided to stay. She began acting in Trinidad in 1962 and soon was playing pantomime with the Trinidad Dramatic Club. In 1968 she joined the Workshop and remained a member until 1973. A freelance writer who contributes regularly on the arts, especially theatre, to the *Trinidad Guardian*, she has written a thousand articles on theatre in Trinidad and the first critical survey of West Indian theatre.[10]

Although Walcott felt it was time to look at middle-class anxieties, the private complexities of sex and marriage, and get away from a steady diet of plays about nationalist and racial concerns, there was some discontent with the Workshop taking this direction, as there would be in future when the Workshop moved into what were thought to be themes of white theatre. Lovelace complained that *The Lovers* treated of a vegetable middle-class liberal white existence. Lovelace praised Judy Stone as achieving a tonal range of a standard unusual in local theatre and the production as succeeding in conveying boredom and anxieties, but otherwise he seemed uncomfortable with the play without clearly saying why. *Stepchild*, a play about interracial marriage, Lovelace clearly found disappointing; it was humourless, too short, and at times incoherent. The actors could not do anything with it.[11]

Eric Roach called the double bill an evening of mere frustrations as he wanted a 'native theatre' unlike the exotic foreign images on television and cinema. He described Jackman's *Stepchild* as the 'rainbow fantasy of West Indian middle class Negrodom . . . reaching for the white and alien sky'. While the play touches on white prejudice it is too short to treat the problem seriously. Except that both plays are set in suburbia, have balding males and similar cluttered ornate middle-class sets (to suggest that the middle class is the same on both sides of the Atlantic) they are dissimilar. While *The Lovers* is a brilliant subdued comedy it failed to work in this production as Melser looked too villainous and gave the wrong emphasis, often treating lightly what should have been serious. Roach's main complaint, however, was that in the West Indies a play about black characters should naturally be the main concern and here the white play had the main billing; the black play was little more than a skit.[12]

Plans to bring the Workshop to the O'Neill Memorial Theatre appeared defeated after the Rockefeller Foundation decided for policy reasons that it could not pay for sponsorship and transportation of the company to the USA. Dale Wasserman, author of the very successful *Man of La Mancha*, came to the rescue by paying for travelling expenses; the total cost was $9,000.[13]

A group of fourteen, including actors and technicians, from the Workshop left for the United States on 6 July to attend forums and give presentations. The Workshop stayed part of the time at Connecticut College for Women where Walcott and Hopkinson gave readings and lectures, Beddeau demonstrated his drumming, and scenes from *Dream* and Errol John's *Moon on a Rainbow Shawl* were performed for the Black Studies programme. At Waterford some of the actors were chosen to perform in Leon Gillen's play *Rose Man*. During 1–9 August the Workshop presented *Dream* in an outdoor amphitheatre at the O'Neill Memorial Theatre at Waterford, Connecticut. The cast included Wilbert Holder as Basil, Claude Reid as Tigre, Parris as Souris, Hopkinson as Lestrade, Jones as Makak, and Marshall as Moustique. Others who had roles were Eunice Alleyne, Ralph Campbell (who came from Toronto where he was studying), Errol Pilgrim, Pamela Franco, and Terrence Chandler. The Trinidadian dancer Percival Borde from the Negro Ensemble Company did the choreography although partly based on Beryl McBurnie's work.

The social range and the way many members of the Workshop had become important members of Trinidadian society can be seen from the Company list in 'The Scene' distributed to the participants. Eunice Alleyne was then Director of Government Broadcasting in Trinidad, John Andrews was a field officer with the Inland Revenue Department, Holder was a radio and TV announcer and producer, Errol Jones was an immigration officer, Claude Reid was an internal auditor in the Ministry of Housing, Stanley Marshall a geological draftsman. Terrence Chandler, Suzanne Nunez, and Errol Pilgrim were school teachers. Elena James was an agricultural clerk. Both Hopkinson and Ralph Campbell were then planning to study drama in the USA during the coming year. Two important members were not middle class—Andrew Beddeau was a mason, Parris was a boiler operator.[14]

Reviews were very good although, as often in the United States at this time, the Workshop actors were more highly praised than Walcott's script. In New London, Connecticut, *The Day* described *Dream* as 'an auspicious beginning' of the season, claimed the play was a folk allegory written in free verse and poetic prose, and said the company 'is amazingly good', especially as the actors are not full-time professionals.[15]

Variety wrote that although *Dream* was of 'considerable quality' it would need cutting and clarification to play commercially in New York. A 'rambling folk drama' with 'a potentially fascinating theme', it needs to be more sharply focused. The production is lively, colourful, but slow-paced.[16]

Joyce Tretick in *Show Business* praised the play as 'filled with imagery, suspense, elements of the macabre, and possibly the dream of many black men'. Jones is a strong actor with an ability to change character. 'It is exciting just to watch him twisting his body in an ape-like manner, or crying just to be free. His performance is a towering achievement.' Slade Hopkinson is 'excellent'. Reid and Parris play their roles to the fullest. Tretick praised Beddeau's singing and drumming and the women singing calypso hymns. More people should be able to see the play which would make 'a marvelous property for some producer'.[17]

Samuel Hirsch in the *Herald Tribune*'s Show Guide described the Workshop as 'a disciplined, remarkably supple and resonant group of talents, men and women able to speak like classical actors and move like dancers'. They have a radiant colourful ensemble unity. Although the play is rambling, Walcott's images disturb. 'His poetic concept captures the music and movement of a primitive people, but, curiously, there is a sophistication in his language and style that suggests a complex world of ideas inside the primeval jungle.' Although his staging is simple he uses the energy and eloquence of his players with 'remarkable results'. Jones as Makak 'gives a towering performance'. He has an 'inner volcanic power'. All the performances are controlled, articulated, and deeply felt. Slade Hopkinson is superb 'with a style and speech reminiscent of Sir Laurence Olivier'. The Trinidad Theatre Workshop is 'an ensemble of extraordinary power' whose style has grown out of West Indian culture. Under Walcott's leadership they are 'building a folk theatre of international importance'.[18]

The American reviewers were aware of a unique, strong ensemble style of acting and the abilities of Errol Jones, Hamilton Parris, and Slade Hopkinson, but *Dream on Monkey Mountain* confused them, and seemed to lack commercial possibilities, although they recognized that it was an unusually powerful play packed with verbal and visual images. As would often happen, the American critics felt that Walcott's play lacked a tight plot, was too long, and the production slow. Many in the audience who saw the performances were more impressed by the play than were the reviewers.

Because of the success of the *Dream* at the O'Neill, the Mark Taper Forum took an option to bring a nucleus of the Workshop to Los Angeles in 1970 for a long run of *Dream*. George White also recommended to NBC in July that *Dream* be recorded for presentation on their Experiment in Television series. The Audrey Wood Foundation presented Walcott with $3,500 American dollars to continue his work on theatre in Trinidad. Walcott's letter thanking Audrey Wood mentioned that for the past five years he had lived mostly from foundation money and various prizes in pursuing his calling as a poet and playwright.[19]

Walcott was also offered a one-year Audrey Wood Fellowship in Playwriting tenable at Wesleyan University, which he decided not to take. Percival Borde, Director of the Primus-Borde Dance School, wanted to work with Beddeau in future. Esther Bailey accepted a scholarship to the Primus-Borde Dance School. Errol Jones was offered a residency at Grinnell College. Terrence Chandler was likely to have his art exhibited in New York.[20]

After returning from the five weeks in Connecticut, Walcott, in an article in the *Trinidad Guardian*, said he was excited by the notion of Arena Theatre and wanted to work on the idea of a mobile instant theatre which could perform any place, such as a car park or an empty site. Mocking the government's vague promises of some day building a National Theatre, Walcott said that his mobile theatre would not require $750,000. It would be possible to offer a play reading every month and then go on to produce some of the offerings. He wanted to bring two directors to Trinidad to work with the Workshop. Walcott thought the Workshop would soon be ready to start a second company. In a private letter to Freund, Walcott was, however, depressed on his return by the consciousness of how far from local realities were his hopes of building a permanent theatre in Trinidad, a 'launching site for stars'. Instead the government was squandering a large amount of money investigating discrimination at the Country Club, an exercise as valuable as trying to prove 'that the moon is a dead stone'.[21]

Freund's 'trip diary' concerning the O'Neill mentions that while Walcott was lionized in Connecticut, the Workshop could not perform at La Mama in New York during August as the actors had to return to their jobs. George White wanted a nucleus of the Workshop to return to work with American directors—this would expand the O'Neill conference each year. Freund had to tell Schultz that there was no chance of the Foundation bringing Workshop actors to Los Angeles for the production of *Dream* at the Mark Taper Forum. Audrey Wood, impressed by *Dream,* had asked Tennessee Williams to travel with her to Trinidad to help the Workshop stage a revival of *Camino Real.* The American National Theatre (ANTA) had asked about performing *Dream.*[22]

In a memo circulated within the Rockefeller Foundation, Freund mentioned that the Workshop had no theatre of its own, no equipment, or costuming. Walcott was going to Leeds University for six months and both Errol Jones and Hopkinson were invited to Grinnell for a semester. Freund wanted the Rockefeller Foundation to fund George White and the O'Neill Foundation to build a small portable theatre which could be used on the Savannah in Port of Spain and elsewhere in the Caribbean. As the lumber would probably be donated in Trinidad the cost would be $2,500. Another $1,000 would be needed for tools which could be used later to build scenery. $2,500 was needed for lighting equipment. There was also a need for short visits, two months each, for two directors and a designer. Jay Ranelli and Robert Steinberg, both of whom had been at Waterford, were possibilities. This might cost $4,500. Freund wanted John Andrews to be sent to Yale Drama School or New York to learn more about lighting and administration. The total cost would be $12,000. The grant could be administered by the O'Neill Memorial Foundation. Howard Klein, Assistant Director of the Humanities Arts Program, was stunned that Trinidad had not done more for Walcott and the Workshop; he agreed that the Foundation should try to do something in co-operation with the O'Neill Foundation and he wrote to Stephen Benedict of the Rockefeller Brothers Fund's Music Program asking if he could think of a way around policy limitations.[23]

Walcott recommended to Gordon Davidson, of the Mark Taper, that Michael Schultz direct *Dream,* as Schultz would not bowdlerize or emasculate its primitivism or turn Makak into an Uncle Tom. The problem was how to make black America understand the play and not Americanize it. Schultz was worried about using Workshop actors but Walcott was certain that they would respond to Schultz's direction and conception. Walcott was hoping that Jay Ranelli and André Gregory might come to Trinidad to direct during January–June when he would be in England. If Schultz did not direct the play Walcott could do it, but he preferred that it were someone else. Walcott especially wanted

Errol Jones for Makak as 'The play was written with him in mind, or rather, grew around him.' Jones is capable of greater complexities and subtleties than he has shown so far. He is aware of his weaknesses—excess of pathos, inhibition towards the grotesque, a 'pretty magnificence', even modesty. No one could come closer to giving what Walcott wants from the part. While Jones would surrender the part if Davidson needed a star, Walcott would be disappointed. It was essential that the Los Angeles production have Jones as Makak, Stanley Marshall as Moustique, Andrew Beddeau and Esther Bailey (as dancer and for the communication between drummer and dancer). Marshall was needed because of the dialect and the close relationship between Makak and Moustique. Others he would like to see in the production are Slade Hopkinson, Hamilton Parris, and Claude Reid, although Reid was slightly wrong for his part as Tigre. Laveau was the original Basil, but the part is 'neutral' and Laveau would have problems getting leave for a long trip to the United States. While Walcott was grateful to George White and others in the United States, acknowledgment should be made to the Workshop as to the play's origin.[24]

The Trinidad Theatre Workshop had during the year added a new member in Suzanne Nunez, from Port of Spain, the wife of the black American, Hugh Robertson, who was to produce the National Broadcasting Company version of *Dream on Monkey Mountain*. During the next few years a curious relationship developed between Robertson and Walcott. Robertson, who was at the time successful in Hollywood and American television circles, dressed like a black hippie (as did Walcott at times) and spoke excitedly of dropping out of the rat race and settling in Trinidad. He was, however, Walcott's seeming entry into American big money, films, and television; both men kept throwing ideas for productions at each other and stimulating each other with plans for projects that seldom materialized. Walcott appears to have been privately sceptical of Robertson after the problems that would develop with the television production of *Dream*, but Robertson worked with people who were at the time beyond Walcott's reach and seemed to be a very useful contact.

There was much confusion about the NBC filming of *Dream*. In the fifty-two minutes available Walcott wanted a history of the Workshop with selected scenes, a film which would be focused on the problems of creating a serious indigenous theatre of world class in Trinidad and what had been accomplished. In a nine-page document he submitted to NBC, Walcott wanted to concentrate on the task of building a theatre company in adverse conditions, the conflict the actors faced between their jobs and vocation, their dedication, and the lack of a theatre building. He wanted to show Beddeau as a construction worker and as a Shango priest, Parris as a boiler operator, Laveau as a factory supervisor, Alleyne as a public relations officer and Hopkinson as a school teacher. The film would then shift to Walcott as director, struggling for ten years to build a professional company in such conditions. While in New York on his first Rockefeller grant Walcott wanted to return home to form a company equal to the great ensembles anywhere, an ensemble based on collaboration between the playwright and the actors, between literature and a physical style. While in New York he had his first notion of *Dream*, although it took him ten years to finish it. The play was formed about his company. While the part of Basil had to be written because they were going to Canada and there was no role for Albert Laveau, Basil became central to the pivotal theme of the play, man's confrontation with death and the meaning of his life. Dancing was important to the company's style along with dialect and heightened language. Walcott mentioned some of the folk elements in *Dream*; he added some notes on the symbolism and how selected scenes might be filmed.[25]

After Robertson arrived in Trinidad Walcott had to abandon his script; Robertson wanted a shortened version of the three-hour play. They used most of the original cast of *Dream* with Jones as Makak, Marshall as Moustique, Laveau as Basil, Parris as Souris, Reid as Tigre, and Hopkinson as Lestrade. Rehearsals began 3 November. Filming started 10 November and continued at various locations in Trinidad until 10 December. Leave arrangements for Jones and others had to be made through the Minister of Home Affairs and the Ministry of Education. Almost immediately a conflict developed between Stanley Marshall and the film makers. Marshall had developed a technique of twisting his toes over each other to create an illusion of a deformed leg. At Waterford two members of the audience were so convinced that his leg was misshapen that they came back stage afterwards to see if they were correct. The film makers, however, were afraid that he could not hold his leg consistently in the same way for the many takes and demanded that he act with a cast on it. Marshall tried it for one day, told Walcott it was too uncomfortable, and quietly got rid of the cast without the film makers realizing that he had returned to twisting his toes. The original budget of $100,000 expanded to Trinidadian $160,000. Afterwards NBC sent Walcott a gift of $10,000 Trinidadian dollars as a contribution towards the 'establishment of a professional theatre'. Although Walcott was glad that his play and company would appear on American television, he was unhappy with the film, while dissatisfaction by some over what they had been paid for their acting contributed to a bitter quarrel concerning Walcott's leadership of the Workshop.[26]

NOTES

1. '"The World of Selvon"—that's the Workshop's big anniversary opener', *Express* (25 Feb. 1969), 10; '"Workshop" starts anniversary with readings by Selvon', *Trinidad Guardian* (26 Feb. 1969), 5; 'Double-bill by Theatre Workshop next month', *Sunday Guardian* (25 May 1969); 'The Nervous Strain of an Inter-Racial Marriage', *Express* (25 May 1969), 15; Judy Stone, 'Street Theatre Could be Winner', *Trinidad Guardian* (19 Feb. 1985), 6; *Camino Real* was announced in *Voices*, 2/1 (1969), 30.
2. '"The World of Selvon"' op. cit.; '"Selvon's England" for TTT', *Trinidad Guardian* (29 Apr. 1969), 4.
3. Eric Roach, 'Theatre Workshop Season off to Breezy Start Return to Sanity', *Trinidad Guardian* (1969); John Melser, 'Basement Proves a Genius for comedy', *Trinidad Guardian* (21 Mar. 1969), 6; 'Televiewing with Argus/"Selvon's England"—a nice surprise', *Evening News* (1969).
4. Freddie Kissoon, 'Playwright: Let Me Do My Thing', *Trinidad Guardian* (29 May 1969), 40. Except for Douglas Archibald's name appearing on some early Little Carib Theatre Workshop lists, I found no evidence he was ever 'used' by Walcott.
5. 'Trinidad's Foremost Dramatic Group's Visit Sponsored by Eugene O'Neil [sic] Memorial Theatre Foundation', *Trinidad Guardian* (10 June 1969), 7; 'Theatre Workshop to Perform in the U. S.', *Trinidad Guardian* (10 June 1969), 7; 'Theatre Workshop to perform WI plays in US next month', *Express* (10 June 1969), 13.
6. George White to Gerald Freund (23 Apr. 1969), Rockefeller Archives.
7. Derek Walcott to Gerald Freund (27 May 1969), Rockefeller Archives.
8. Norman Lloyd to Gerald Freund (25 May 1969), Rockefeller Archives.
9. Lesley Acrill, 'Because of his Good Looks and Acting Skill', *People* (Apr. 1980), 41–2. Interview (July 1990).
10. Lesley Acrill, 'Her Writing is Mostly a Labour of Love', *People* (Apr. 1980), 42–3; Judy Stone, *Studies in West Indian Literature: Theatre* (London: Macmillan Caribbean, 1994). Interviews (July 1990).
11. Earl Lovelace, 'Derek's "Stepchild" was Nothing but a Big Disappointment', *Express* (16 June 1969), 9, 15.
12. Eric Roach, 'Double-Bill of Mere Frustrations', *Trinidad Guardian* (17 June 1969), 7.
13. Rockefeller Foundation internal memo by Gerald Freund (Aug. 1969).
14. 'The Company', *The Scene*, special edn., 'Theatre Workshop of Trinidad', 1/10 (29 July 1969).

15. Raymond K. Bordner, 'Allegorical Folk Play Produced in Waterford', *The Day* [New London, Conn.] (2 Aug. 1969), 15.

16. 'Trinidad Group Does Folk Play At O'Neill Meet', *Variety* (13 Aug. 1969), 57.

17. Joyce Tretick, 'Dream on Monkey Mountain', *Show Business* (5 Aug. 1969), 13, 17.

18. Samuel Hirsch, 'Ensemble of Extraordinary Power', *Sunday Herald Tribune*, S Travel sect., Show Guide (10 Aug. 1969), 1, 9.

19. Derek Walcott to 'Ralph' [Audrey Wood Foundation] (14 Aug. 1969), Walcott Collection, University of the West Indies, St Augustine.

20. William Doyle-Marshall, 'Bouquets Thrown in the US at the Theatre Workshop', *Express* (22 Sept. 1969), 4.

21. 'Walcott Plans "Instant Theatre!"' *Trinidad Guardian* (20 Aug. 1969), 8; Derek Walcott to Gerald Freund (15 Aug. 1969), Rockefeller Archives.

22. Gerald Freund diary (Aug. 1969), Rockefeller Archives.

23. Gerald Freund 'Visit' to Kenneth W. Thompson and Joseph E. Black (Aug. 1969); Howard Klein (15 Sept. 1969); Howard Klein to Stephen Benedict of the Rockefeller Brothers Fund (24 Sept. 1969), Rockefeller Archives.

24. Derek Walcott to Gordon Davidson (14 Aug. 1969), copies in Rockefeller Archives and in Walcott Collection, St Augustine.

25. Undated single-spaced nine-page typed document by Walcott about NBC one-hour special on Trinidad Theatre Workshop, Walcott Collection, University of the West Indies, St Augustine.

26. 'NBC Crew Due Next Week to Film Play by Derek Walcott', *Evening News* (24 Oct. 1969); the Walcott Collection also has a 'Bulletin' for Workshop members involved in the filming which explains the schedule, locations, transportation, and such matters as salary scales; 'Theatre Workshop gets $10,000' and '$10,000 Grant from NBC for Workshop', *Trinidad Guardian* (Dec. 1969), 1 and unidentified press clipping (Dec. 1969).

1970

7

A new *Ti-Jean*
Black Power
Aquarius IV

WALCOTT decided not to accept the visiting professorship at Leeds University; too much was happening with the Workshop including rehearsals for a new musical version of *Ti-Jean and his Brothers* and there was no other director whom Walcott trusted. Slade Hopkinson, one of Walcott's close friends and supporters from the University College of the West Indies days, was one of the best actors in the region, but never fulfilled his promise as a dramatist or director. A poet, intellectual, well read, one of the founders of modern West Indian drama, a brilliant teacher, Hopkinson as a theatre director was lax and unable to command obedience. After Walcott returned from abroad and found that Hopkinson's rehearsals were in shambles with few actors attending, a heated argument followed which foreshadowed further disagreements.[1]

Hugh Robertson's film of *Dream on Monkey Mountain* was featured in February on NBC's 'Experiment in Television'; it was shown in black and white (although shot in colour) on Trinidad and Tobago Television and at the library of the United States Information Services with A. N. R. Robinson, the Minister of External Affairs, attending. *Ti-Jean and his Brothers* was also taped for the Canadian Broadcasting Company by the Workshop with Peter Donkin producing, on a budget of $13,000. In March the Workshop, in keeping with a policy of fostering cultural events, sponsored at Town Hall a school matinee and evening performance of *The Pickwickians at Manor Farm* by Brian Barnes, a British actor.[2]

Clyde Hosein, writing before *Dream* was shown on TTT and possibly acting as Walcott's mouthpiece, said that because of the need to reduce the play to fifty minutes the television version was difficult to follow. The story line was broken as was the visual logic of the scenes which appear jumpy. The sound track is also poor. Some letters to local newspapers complained that it was incomprehensible or that it lampooned blacks by not showing them as heroic. One letter suggested that Walcott should read Nigerian Amos Tutuola's *The Palmwine Drinkard* to understand the black mind! Another objected to the word 'nigger', to the suggestion that God first made man as an ape rather than in His own image, and claimed that the characters belong to the Caribbean past. Hosein returned to the subject arguing that Walcott should have refused such a hastily put together version and that Robertson could not have been alert to what he was doing since there were such basic production flaws as the mole on an actor's face being on opposite sides in different shots. The long shots were held too long and Robertson did not use such techniques as wipes, fast pans, and other common effects to suggest the passing of time. Slade Hopkinson's lines were inaudible.[3]

The fading copy I viewed at the Media Center at the University of Toronto is interesting as a historical document as it is the only extended example of the Workshop on film: I can, however, imagine it disappointing someone unfamiliar with the play and the conflicting aims behind the script. In the *Express* Benedict Wight saw the NBC filming of *Dream* as evidence of the failure of the Ministry of Culture which had devoted its attention to calypso and carnival while ignoring creative writing and theatre. Although Douglas Archibald had said that the theatre audience in Port of Spain numbered at most 1,200 people, Wight asked how this should be when the West Indies were no longer the brutish philistine society of plantation days. Since 1945 some forty-seven writers had produced at least 160 plays and yet perhaps only one-third had been performed on stage. As a consequence only half the dramatists were still productive. Walcott had survived because of his strong will, incorruptible dedication, and energy. Walcott had made a conscious choice to stay in the West Indies; the foreign success of *Dream* is his own in the face of a lack of local support. The government's Hummingbird award to Walcott is tokenism at best, even farce, when the Cultural Advisor to the Prime Minister is notorious for his 'sordid achievements'.[4]

Denis Solomon tried to review the television version of *Dream* as a complete artistic statement and found it had 'considerable power in its own right'. He thought the cinematic elements, such as the use of close-ups and dream effects, powerful, although the reduction of the long scenes and speeches lost some of the tragic grandeur. Solomon's complex, thoughtful review is difficult to summarize as it rapidly touches on many issues and in passing throws light on Walcott's influences and allusions. Solomon was concerned with the place of *Dream* in the then current debate about art as social protest, the supposed alienation of the West Indian artist from the folk, and claims that Walcott's world was inside his own head and lacked affirmation. While *Dream* ends with an affirmation of a West Indian identity for blacks this would be a simplification of what the play is about. It is 'a metaphysical hall of mirrors' which offers no blueprint for action. All action seems corrupt. Although a play about blacks *Dream* elevates the problem of identity to the universal human plane. Is man an ape or a god, is he a mimic, does he have an essence or is he an existentialist making existence as he goes along? This duality is presented in racial terms of white and black. Alluding to the Platonic allegory of the cave and Walcott's possible use of *The Republic*, Solomon says that if the notion of a racial war to destroy the shadows of the white man's vision within the black man's mind is a false illusion, the dream of it is a cleansing liberation, a necessary stage before any real liberation. In this sense the play itself, as dream, is part of the liberation. If the play offers no formula for political action, it is sensitive to the private drama and individual consciousness of the people. As art it offers a synthesis of public and private suffering to create the people's dream.[5]

On 24 February Walcott wrote flatteringly to Hugh Robertson about the televised *Dream*, saying that any success was due to the editing and camera work. There were too many faults in the performance. Jones had a habit of dropping his endings into a self-pitying fall which they should have noticed and corrected. The African scene was too much a static school pageant lacking anger, frustration, and explosion. The departure of the dream was not clear. And the transformation of character did not work as narrative. These were problems in Walcott's own style. Walcott lists a number of other faults, but says that his pride remains in the company's level of acting, especially Hamilton Parris, Claude Reid, Albert Laveau, and Wilbert Holder. The problem of cutting a three-hour play to fifty-three minutes was too much. He hoped that he could work with Robertson on *In A Fine Castle*, a play he had been writing for the past seven years; he had stills, tapes, and some photographs he could send along with a documentary about the Calypsonian Mighty Sparrow. He thought the government might provide camera equipment and there would be local investors. Walcott was also hoping to make a television production of Michael Anthony's novel *Green Days by the River* and his own *Franklin*.[6]

Such buttering up of foreign correspondents sometimes appears in Walcott's letters of the 1970s when he was trying to make his way into the North American theatre and television market. In other letters, such as to Gordon Davidson, who ran the Mark Taper Forum Theatre, Walcott complained bitterly about the NBC Robertson production of *Dream* as a hasty, badly photographed emasculation of his play. The original idea of a documentary about the Theatre Workshop was jettisoned by Robertson who decided instead on using the play to exhibit the talents of Walcott and the actors. There was no opportunity to think about the revised project; even the time allowed for filming was shortened by five days of rain.[7]

Although Errol Jones and Albert Laveau helped run sections of the Workshop, especially on acting, Walcott felt that the company needed the experience of professional teachers and directors. He managed to convince an American foundation to pay for the expenses of Jay Ranelli, an American who was impressed by the Workshop during the O'Neill visit, to come to Trinidad to give workshops and direct a play. This took much correspondence and use of Rockefeller contacts. Although the Rockefeller Foundation could not help directly, Ranelli's visit was indirectly sponsored through a grant made to Wesleyan University and the O'Neill Foundation. On 3 February Walcott wrote to Ranelli that a visit of five weeks to put together a production from late March on would be a strain on the actors who also had daytime jobs. They should find a play with a small cast that would be easy to design and mount so it could become part of their touring repertory. Ranelli suggested Albert Camus's *Caligula*, which Walcott had not read, or an adaptation of Molière, which interested Walcott more. Walcott was still hoping that part of the company could be in the Los Angeles production of *Dream* at the Mark Taper Forum and that others might take a play to Canada, in which case only a reduced company would be available to Ranelli. Walcott was having trouble with *Camino Real*, especially problems about finding proper furniture, backcloths, and platforms, and was thinking about a 'Haitian' *Macbeth* or *Godot*.[8]

Walcott next wrote that he had found a house, Judy Stone's, where Ranelli and his family could stay from 1 April. He had now read *Caligula* and thought it was not Workshop material: there were not enough parts for women and many of his actresses had been without parts in recent plays; he could not see his black cast in Roman togas. Marlowe's

Faustus would be too expensive in terms of costumes; rereading it the comedy seemed banal and not worth the elaborate staging it required. While the verse was magnificent the play was static and there were few parts for women. *Macbeth* would be too hard to do in the short time available for rehearsal and a Haitian *Macbeth* would be 'forced'. Walcott was interested in doing a Brecht play, perhaps *Baal*, *Mother Courage* or *Threepenny Opera*. They had worked on the latter but were stumped by the songs. Walcott, however, had done the drawings, costumes, and set designs and there were parts for women in it. Maybe they could use one organ and a local rhythm for the music while travelling and a steel band when in Port of Spain. Eventually Walcott and Ranelli settled on Genet's *The Balcony*.[9]

In March both the *Express* and *Evening News* carried articles asking whether anyone knew of a possible 'home' for the TTW. Since being forced from the Basement Theatre the actors had rehearsed at the Zoo Pavilion, a school, and other places as they became available and according to their ability to pay the rent. Now with Ranelli coming from the United States and with some Workshop members complaining that Walcott was putting too much money into salaries and fees, including his own, rather than acquiring a permanent building, the problem of housing became even more important. The $10,000 grant from the National Broadcasting Company made it possible to negotiate a long lease if a proper building for conversion could be found. Walcott wanted premises that could be converted into a studio capable of seating one hundred to one hundred and fifty, air-conditioning, and parking space. There would also need to be space for a dressing room, bar, lounge, and box office. If such a place could be found the Workshop could show films and have poetry readings along with plays. The Workshop currently assumed an audience of one thousand and hoped to expand that number if they could perform regularly.[10]

The season was planned as a week's run, 10–17 May, at Queen's Hall. This was the first time the Workshop had booked Queen's Hall for a week and would be a test of how far they had progressed in creating an audience for serious theatre. Two plays were planned: a new, expanded version of *Ti-Jean* with folk-songs and André Tanker's music, and *The Balcony*, the latter directed by Ranelli. Because of Black Power demonstrations and the declaration of a national emergency both plays were cancelled, and Ranelli returned to the United States.

The post-colonial is as subject to cultural lag as the colonial. May 1968 reached Trinidad during 1970 in the form of Black Power demonstrations that nearly toppled the government. The Black Power demonstrations began during the February Carnival after Stokely Carmichael was banned from returning to Trinidad and continued into March with student protests, street marches of up to 10,000 people, and much violence including the use of incendiary bombs against banks and shops. In April the funeral of one of the demonstrators, who had been shot by the police, turned into a mass procession, the resignation of the Minister of External Affairs, and on 21 April the declaration of a State of Emergency and the imposition of a curfew. As parts of Port of Spain were burned and looted, a section of the Trinidad Defence Force revolted and was only prevented from joining the demonstrators by some warning shots from the Coast Guard which remained loyal. During May order was restored by the police, who also remained loyal, after the Venezuelan air force and American navy began patrolling the coast. While the demonstrations were clearly influenced by events in the United States and Paris during the late 1960s, they were expressions of discontent within the black community and by the young towards Eric Williams's government. After two decades of black rule there was still massive unemployment, extreme class divisions, a growing division between the new bourgeoisie and the poor, and much political corruption and tyranny. For many black people nothing had changed since independence except increased disillusionment and alienation. Unfortunately the demonstrations soon took on a racial aspect, thus alienating the Indians who were already victims of Williams's racial policies, many of the sympathetic brown liberals, and many of the Marxist intellectuals. Although Williams retained power the legacy of the demonstrations would influence cultural attitudes in Trinidad for the next five years with intellectuals and theatre critics judging art by 'revolutionary' political standards.[11]

If Williams, who saw himself as a black nationalist socialist and the father of Trinidad independence, was confused by the eruption of Black Power protests against his government, Walcott, who saw himself bridging the gulf between white and black culture, and who had shown in *Dream* the impossibility of a cultural return to Africa, was to find himself often under attack in Trinidad for not being sufficiently radical or black. Walcott's response to the demonstrations was a mixture of sympathy with those who wanted to overthrow the corrupt Eric Williams's regime and distrust of racial slogans imported from the United States into multiracial, black-ruled Trinidad. The controversies that surrounded the Black Power rebellion continued to haunt Trinidadian politics for several years and to influence criticism of Walcott and the Workshop.

Slade Hopkinson had trouble with the police during the Emergency and became influenced by black nationalist thought. He felt that the Workshop was not producing enough plays by West Indian dramatists and that Walcott's plays were insufficiently radical. These feelings boiled over during the Black Power demonstrations which Hopkinson and others in the Workshop joined. Walcott had mixed feelings. He was upset by cancellations of Workshop productions and by his actors demonstrating in the streets instead of continuing with workshops and rehearsals. Walcott felt that the Workshop was creating a revolutionary West Indian culture and the radical political rhetoric was just another imported fashion, another West Indian mimicry, this time of black urban America. While he understood the rage and demands for social justice that had brought the young and unemployed into the streets, he saw the Black Power slogans in black-governed Trinidad as absurd and likely to lead to increased racial strife and political repression by either the government or the radicals if they won.

As part of discontent in the air, there had been complaints about the Workshop having changed from a group of actors to a company increasingly devoted to producing Walcott's plays. Although that had always been part of Walcott's intention in starting the Theatre Workshop, his aims were not clear to others and would not have mattered to most foundation members. They were drawn to the Workshop because of Walcott's reputation as dramatist and director. After Walcott's success with *Dream on Monkey Mountain*, plans for a new version of *Ti-Jean*, and the arrival of an American director for *The Balcony*, the Workshop was rapidly becoming Walcott's company. Errol Jones and some others enjoyed being directed by Ranelli who gave them more freedom in deciding how a part should be interpreted than would Walcott; it was a new, broadening experience. The Workshop, however, had a number of newer members who were conscious that productions directed by others in the company never seemed to get off the ground. Although the membership was asked its views, decisions were taken by Walcott and finances were obscure. The Workshop seemingly had no legal status, no bank account of its own, no budget, and payment was at Walcott's will. Walcott openly said he believed theatre was an undemocratic dictatorship in which the talented ruled and others followed. Not having access to financial information, most members did not know much about the Rockefeller subsidies or that Walcott was using money from his various grants and awards to support productions.

The finances of the Workshop were always messy, improbable,

chaotic, a production-by-production assemblage of money and support from here and there. Walcott would take from one pocket to invest in a production or tour, put money into another pocket in the form of royalties and director fees, put money into a bank account as Workshop profits, lose money on a production, return money earned as royalties, accept a donation. In the early days this did not matter, but with increased touring, longer runs of productions, and money earned through television and radio, the Workshop had stopped being a group of amateurs. The Workshop needed a bookkeeper and manager, but then it needed everything else so much more. At this time Walcott was often drinking heavily and becoming argumentative during and after workshops; he was also so completely involved in his work that he was distracted and forgetful about practical matters. When not at the theatre he would stay at home in his pyjamas writing and thinking. A secretary he often used recalls going to the bank to withdraw several hundred dollars and giving the money to Walcott in an envelope which he distractedly put into his pyjama pocket while reciting lines from a poem he was writing. The pyjamas had no pockets and the envelope dropped to the ground where the secretary found it. Amused by Walcott's absent-mindedness she waited to see what would happen. A few hours later Walcott had forgotten about the money and once more asked her to go to the bank.[12]

As the Rockefeller and other grants were paid directly to Walcott to support his own creative work, there was no clear line between personal and Workshop expenses. There were accounts of costs, lines of scripts were carefully counted to determine fees and the actors asked to agree, but in practice Walcott was his own judge of what was appropriate. On 3 May Slade Hopkinson led an attack on Walcott at a General Meeting of the Workshop, accusing him of dictatorial leadership, not allowing others to direct, not performing plays by other West Indians, and financial mismanagement. Walcott was accused of having mismanaged the fees paid to the actors for performing for foreign television and radio companies and of being mysterious about the money given by NBC. Walcott angrily resigned and wrote an official letter of resignation on 10 May to the management committee of the Workshop. Especially angered at Slade Hopkinson's complaints of financial mismanagement, Walcott said that he would be available to discuss the financial dissolution of the company, but he gave notice that if such an implication continued to be made he would take legal action of defamation of character and of his professional standing as a writer, director, and stage designer.[13]

As in most quarrels there were various issues involved, but at the heart of the matter was the conflict between Walcott's view of himself as a full-time professional in the theatre, someone to be paid royalties and a salary for directing plays, someone who devoted his time to finding theatres, publicity, advertising, arranging tours, and preparing scripts, in contrast to those, such as Hopkinson, who still saw West Indian theatre as amateur, something to be done outside one's normal job, in which everyone should be given a chance. Walcott's success and the money being earned from foreign television and radio was bound to sharpen this conflict, especially as Walcott was earning more than his actors from productions. Hopkinson, although a brilliant actor and one of the original band who started modern West Indian theatre in the 1950s, was being left behind as Walcott pushed local theatre towards professional standards. Moreover, as would soon become clear, the cultural and political fashions of the 1960s had differently affected Walcott and Hopkinson. Walcott saw himself perhaps more like one of the flower-power, hippie gurus, a leader of an alternative theatre, like the Becks' Living Theatre. Hopkinson was becoming more influenced by the political, Third Worldism and notions of leaderless collectives.[14]

Having withdrawn from the Workshop Walcott immediately planned his own theatre company, Group III, and Aquarius Productions to put on Ti-Jean in June and to tour Tobago, Grenada, Barbados, and St Lucia in July. He budgeted $1,000 for the adaptation of a play for Trinidad and Tobago Television in June. He hoped to negotiate the video filming of Ti-Jean in Barbados, produce a second play for the tour, work on the film script for In A Fine Castle, and contract for Dream on Monkey Mountain with the Mark Taper Forum using Trinidadian actors. In other words Walcott was planning to continue with his projects, using most of the Workshop actors, but for his own production company without the burden of a management committee and criticism within the group.[15]

Walcott made a list of the Theatre Workshop's current assets, such as canvas, frames, costumes, polaroid cameras, make-up kit, and other properties, noting that the films of Dream and Ti-Jean were his own possessions. He also on 10 May drafted a letter to proposed members of Group III saying that he was legally establishing a company with a lawyer and if they joined he would serve as their agent and negotiator. They would have individual contracts and could invest in the company which would have audited accounts. This group would be a business company, not a theatre club, Walcott would have sole discretion to hire actors on contract. The actors or investors should be represented by lawyers. He also drafted a poster for *Ti-Jean* which was to be presented by Group IV (he erased III from the poster) and Aquarius on 25–28 June at Town Hall. The actors would include Parris, Reid, Marshall, Ermine Wright, Belinda Barnes, Albert Laveau, and Desmond Parker. John Andrews would do the lighting and Tanker the music. Errol Jones was still out of the country. He also drew up a draft of an advertising campaign that included the *Guardian* and *Express*, several television previews and 'spots', and 'beautiful art posters' and handbills. He planned to record *Ti-Jean* for Barbados TV that week using a similar cast including Neville La Bastide and John Henderson.[16]

Despite the Black Power demonstrations and state of emergency there was furious activity by Walcott and members of the Workshop. John Andrews 'as an ordinary member of the Workshop' called a general meeting of the membership on 13 May at Bishop Anstey High School to discuss the situation in the light of recent conversations he had with Walcott, Walcott's resignation, and the need to reconstruct the Workshop. Twenty-two members attended. After a prolonged discussion at which every member could speak, a majority voted that the Workshop should continue and that it should produce plays, sponsor other theatrical groups, and be involved in radio, screen, and television productions. The Workshop should be registered or incorporated, which it was not until then. A management committee should be appointed to nominate an Artistic Director, create a panel of directors, ascertain the assets and liabilities of the Workshop, and make recommendations about the future. A management committee was formed consisting of Eunice Alleyne, John Andrews, Judy Stone, Wilbert Holder, John Hilton, and Pamela Franco, which was to report to the membership within a month.[17]

The committee met on 19 May and drafted a letter to Walcott suggesting that his position as Artistic Director be changed to Artistic Advisor which would give him full authority to 'advise' on plays, tours, and schedules; ultimate authority would be with the management committee consisting of three persons, including a treasurer, to work with the Artistic Advisor. There would be a production assistant for liaison between the Artistic Director and management committee for each production. 'Every effort' would be made to have a budget for each production. There would be 'Directors workshops' for those interested in trying to become directors of plays and there would be closed productions to give them experience. The committee wanted to know whether Walcott would be willing to work in such conditions;

if so they would propose them to the membership at a general meeting before 12 June.[18]

A brief outline was also drawn up concerning legal status. The Trinidad Theatre Workshop would be a non-profit organization with a management committee, an Artistic Director and members. Membership would be open to actors, directors, dancers, musicians, singers, writers, and technicians. The Workshop aimed to promote and develop theatre throughout the region, develop an indigenous acting style, and work towards professional theatre in the West Indies. It would be financed by membership dues, productions, annual subscriptions, and donations. Being non-profit it should be exempt from taxes, and liability would be the company's not individuals'. Performers and others would be paid for their work.[19]

Meanwhile Walcott was busy planning for his Derek Walcott Group IV Aquarius Productions. The Governor General of Grenada had been contacted and expressed interest in having the tour come there. Accommodation in Barbados was confirmed. Maybe André Tanker's band could get nightclub bookings during the tour? The actors could be contracted to be paid a percentage of the profits of productions.[20]

Walcott replied to 'The Committee' on 30 May with a seven-page single-spaced letter which began by saying he would try to keep it short! The tone of the committee's letter showed the same dissatisfaction with him as the meeting of 3 May and made an implicit criticism of him, not of certain members of the company. Having like Moses a vision and having led his company for ten years through the desert, now that the promised land is in sight he is being asked to abandon the Law and serve as advisor to his own vision. You offer the old burden but with new ropes. Has the committee offered to expel those who torment and humiliate him? What the Workshop needs is not a committee but a spiritual conversion that makes them conscious of malice and envy. They can have another leader, but no matter what they do they need a leader and only one pair of eyes to tell them what to do. Walcott suggested that they appoint Errol Jones as their leader. Walcott would serve under Jones, Andrews, or Stanley Marshall. The others are mere opportunists, not leaders.[21]

Walcott, however, proposed that he 'seem' to continue to be Director until after the *Ti-Jean* tour is over to avoid their mutual embarrassment. Walcott will leave Trinidad if they mistreat Jones and, in future, work abroad for white men and white money. Walcott continued by announcing his Group IV in which he would bring together the best of the Workshop actors including members of the committee, leaving the Workshop a 'shell' with 4,000 dollars. Walcott was willing to have Group IV co-operate with the Workshop on productions which he would finance through his Aquarius Productions, and which might be seen as a company of the pure in contrast to the irresponsible and disaffected. He would choose his actors, expel them, canonize them as sacred as actors, the way Artaud, Brecht, Grotowski, the Becks, or other theatre visionaries would do. If others call him a puppet master it is because he directs puppets. He has created a style which twenty million North Americans have seen on television. The committee should realize that Walcott intended to keep to the vision with which he started the TTW and that legally he and Errol Jones along with Stanley Marshall were the founding members of the TTW and 'own' the Workshop, as can be seen by asking for its bank account at Barclays Bank.

The letter continues with Walcott saying that the foreign cheques were naturally made out to him, that only he and Jones could legally use the account, and that complaints about salaries were absurd as the actors had been consulted and some were present during negotiations with the foreign companies. Basically all was done according to Equity scales and practice. He proposed that *Ti-Jean* be advertised as *Group IV Trinidad Theatre Workshop* and wanted a reply immediately. He will not accept the designation of Artistic Advisor as it is humiliating, but they can discuss this after the tour. In any case he will be busy from July until October and by then the Workshop might produce some absurd farce. The Workshop may feel that he is abandoning them to go to Los Angeles for the production of *Dream*, but they must realize that the enemy is amateurism. The Workshop died on 3 May. He would resurrect it with Group IV.

Walcott rejected the notion of making the TTW more democratic; he saw demarcations of duties as criticism of himself and as a falling away from the ideals he had set the Workshop of reaching the highest professional standards. He wanted to purify the Workshop of his critics whom he regarded as malcontents without ideals and dedication and he intended to tighten his control of the artistic side by limiting membership in Group IV to those who were willing to accept his leadership unquestioningly. Although he did not spell out who would or would not be accepted, it appears that he intended to exclude over one-fifth of the TTW from Group IV. If the letter of 30 May appears to make the Workshop into his personal property, or the property of himself and two or three foundation members, it also concludes by suggesting a meeting to discuss matters in light of the forthcoming tour. So in fact Walcott was already moving towards reconciliation while retaining his dignity and leadership. The essential point was that the Workshop meant little without Walcott, but Walcott needed the Workshop actors for the productions of his plays. And there were enough of the best actors loyal to Walcott that he could go his own way if necessary; he could even perhaps make a career in American theatre if he wanted.

Except for Hopkinson, his most important actors, Jones and Marshall, stood behind him. But it was true that Walcott had no talent for handling finances and that as the Workshop moved towards professionalism he needed to delegate non-artistic areas of theatre management to others. This would remain a continuing problem. Unfortunately the issues were raised in the worst way possible to allow Walcott to accept a delegation of responsibility, and later events, in 1976, were to suggest that Walcott was temperamentally unable to work with the committees that the Workshop would form. He is like his apparent opposite, V. S. Naipaul, in having an obsessive sense of a vocation as an artist, a vocation which overrides all other concerns. Such idealism does not make someone willing to accept the restraints of a committee or the views of others. The arts are highly competitive; there can only be one King of the Cats. Among those who began modern West Indian drama, Walcott and Errol Hill had quarrelled, Walcott and McBurnie had quarrelled, and now Walcott and Hopkinson quarrelled. Such quarrels were never really reconciled. Each would go his or her own way. In the realm of dance a similar break occurred between McBurnie, Jeff Henry, and others.

Walcott was divided between his desire to create a West Indian literature and theatre of international standards and his ambition to make a name and money for himself abroad. The West Indies was his subject matter, his culture, what he wrote about, and provided the only actors, critics, and audiences that understood his plays and what he had achieved with the Workshop. He wanted to show that the West Indies could be as good as Europe or North America, but the West Indies could not provide the material conditions for a professional theatre and, as Naipaul had argued, was a place that denied itself heroes, preferring to humiliate its larger talents than accept their uniqueness. The islands were small communities in which everyone knew everyone else too well. A pattern can be observed throughout the history of the Theatre Workshop. After each notable success a movement would start to make the company more democratic, to give ultimate power to an elected management committee, to perform the plays of others, to let others direct and in general to make Walcott an equal rather than leader. That reforms were needed in the management of the Workshop is clear, but even without the problem that any such change would threaten Walcott's own driven vision which was the sole basis of the company's existence, there was really no one else to do what had to be done. There was no one else devoting him- or herself full time to the theatre.

Hopkinson, now radicalized and ill from a kidney ailment, had joined the demonstrations, quit the Workshop and on 1 June formed the Caribbean Theatre Guild to promote West Indian and Third World plays. Unlike the Walcott-founded and led TTW, the Caribbean Theatre Guild, of which Hopkinson was artistic director, actor, and dramatist, was meant to be different, without a 'dictator', and to be 'something vibrant that penetrated into the community and into which the community penetrated'. In several interviews Hopkinson criticized Walcott's theatre as the art of a 'coterie' and the performance of a dramatist's own plays 'in various capital cities in the West Indies in front of small audiences, to friends and acquaintances, in short runs'. He wanted something more concerned with the 'working and peasant class'. He accused Walcott of having an Olympian detachment from the arts-and-crafts street culture that was part of the period and cited the way Errol Hill in the 1950s would refer to the political turmoil in Ireland as the basis of the art of Yeats, Synge, and O'Casey. The Caribbean Theatre Guild partly consisted of students and graduates whom Hopkinson taught at St George's College, along with an actor or two who had worked with the TTW. The CTG was to have an unusual history, at one point turning to radical street theatre, disappearing from sight for years, before eventually becoming an established theatre group with good young actors. During its first fifteen years it produced a few of Hopkinson's plays, some of the early Caribbean Plays scripts, *Moon on a Rainbow Shawl*, Douglas Archibald's *The Rose Slip*, and Wole Soyinka's *The Lion and the Jewel*; it never did perform the French and Spanish Caribbean and Latin American plays Hopkinson had said were among his aims and it discovered no significant new West Indian dramatist.[22]

Problems had arisen about plans to produce *Dream on Monkey Mountain* at the Mark Taper Forum in Los Angeles. Although *Dream* had opened in Toronto and been performed in Trinidad before being taken to Connecticut, the O'Neill Foundation was claiming credit for premièring the play. This was part of a general tendency by Americans to devalue the West Indianness of the play. Walcott had planned that it would be acted by members of the Workshop, but transportation costs and American union regulations resulted in it being done with black American actors, although Walcott would be brought to Los Angeles to assist with the production. Increasingly Walcott was being faced by a choice between success in America and keeping to his ideal of creating a West Indian theatre. Walcott felt that if he established an American reputation he could expand the opportunities for the Workshop to perform abroad and receive American financial support. He had managed to do something similar with his own career as a poet and dramatist and in setting up the Workshop, but as American producers wanted Walcott's plays performed according to American standards and tastes Walcott was, and would continue to be, faced by an insoluble problem. His own career as an artist would conflict with his ideals.

A long letter that he wrote to Gordon Davidson on 13 May reveals the background to his ideas, Walcott's conflicts about the turn of events regarding *Dream*, and what he saw himself as doing in the West Indian theatre. The play was 'the work of an ensemble', written with specific actors in mind; it is 'total' theatre of an indigenous kind, its poetry is indigenous.[23]

By this Walcott did not mean the Calypso speech that he often cited when he defended the use of the iambic; rather he meant that for twenty years he had been evolving a stage speech that ranged from the subtle to the coarse, based on local rhythms and vocabulary which would be universal, capable of intellectual complexities and the subtle apprehension of experience through metaphor, 'folk homily', and prov-erb. Such speech should dance in its movement and the dances on stage should reflect the movement of the speech, being raw and rig-orous, patterned on the various sources of West Indian culture rang-ing from the bongo or wake dance, the donkey dance, the baptist and revivalist, Shango rites and African dances. In *Dream* all this is expressed on stage in the songs ('sung by a narrator-dancer, the well spring of the vision, the interior track of the dream') and the drummer who is the high priest. Walcott wanted Mike Schultz to understand what he was aiming at—a 'rigidity, this classic petrification of our footloose forms' using the discipline and 'tight articulation of the Kabuki Theatre'. Walcott had studied the 'simplicities' of Hokusai's drawings and local Caribbean rites and rituals, such as 'the burroquite dance'.

Walcott's letter to Davidson continues, 'I am not only a playwright but a company, and not only a company but also a form.' When he lived in Greenwich Village during 1958–59 he had a vision of a company and style that would be 'true as the earth from which I prayed that form would spring'. While writing conventionally structured plays he sought a discipline through spiritual coherence that expressed a 'depressed but creatively powerful people'.

Walcott felt that his plays had never been realized in productions abroad; he cited some of the absurdities of American productions. *Malcochon* takes place in a forest near a waterfall, but at the Judson Theatre they used a piano and American music. Another production of *Malcochon* emasculated it by using 'calypso style straw hats' and having a beautiful female narrator speaking in 'beautiful black Afro-style' although it is a play 'of masculine violence'. American aesthetics, black or white, are contrary to the West Indian. 'To be black does not mean that one can speak for all black people.' Such productions harm Walcott's reputation. America is an imperial power and treats the language of colonials as gibberish. This is not a question of accents. The genius of the colonial comes from the economic deprivation that makes an amateur. The 'spirit' of *Dream* is the soul of its characters and requires Americans, whether black or white, to have 'a humility of interpretation'; otherwise it will become part of American imperialism, 'redirecting its force inward towards America itself'. In other words, Walcott was warning against transforming the cultural complexities and Caribbean affirmation of *Dream* into another American black-protest text. He wanted the play to express the spirit of 'a people' and not to have the polish of professionalism.

Walcott wanted his 'own acting company' performing the play. That is part of his vision, part of his Dream. Now he was, as he would so often be, forced to choose between not having his play performed or having it performed and directed by Americans. Equity would not let the Mark Taper use TTW actors. Walcott felt the United States was often the serpent offering him a tempting apple, indeed the Big Apple of New York and Los Angeles. He knew this problem would continue. He also knew that after devoting so much of his life to the Workshop he had become obsessed by it and was being carried away by unrealistic notions and blinded to its weaknesses. But he still felt that at the core of the play its inner radiance came from its relationship to the Workshop actors.

The vision of a West Indian theatre that had sustained Walcott since New York on his Rockefeller Fellowship during 1958–9, was still being proclaimed during a time when he had resigned from the Workshop and was telling its members that the Workshop no longer existed. Clearly Walcott intended to reform it or continue with it; he saw himself as a prophet with a mission who had been betrayed by a few of his disciples, but this would eventually strengthen his cult by eliminating the unfaithful, corrupt, and weak-willed. Only in the Caribbean, and only with the actors of the TTW, could he fully realize his vision of his plays and his dream of the kind of theatre and place in history that he wanted.

The new musical version of *Ti-Jean* after three postponements opened at Town Hall for three days, 25–27 June; there were also performances 29–30 June. Because of the curfew the curtain time was 6 p.m. and the show ended at 7.30 p.m. This was the February production, which Peter Donkin had recorded for CBC radio, with Parris as the Frog, Reid as Gros Jean, Marshall as Mi-Jean, Laveau as Devil-Planter, Ermine Wright as the Mother and Belinda Barnes as the Bolom. An important change was that a young boy, Ellsworth Primus, would perform the role of Ti-Jean, providing a natural innocence, cheerfulness, and spontaneity to the symbolism. Besides the overture and finale there were now eleven songs, some of which were St Lucian, some Trinidadian, some composed by Tanker, some composed by Tanker in collaboration with Walcott.[24]

Drawings for this *Ti-Jean* show Walcott's detailed involvement with all aspects of the production. A drawing of the logs, dated 22 June 1970, indicates such details about their construction as the colour of the jute, the need for 1/2-inch rope for loops, the need for heavy scissors to cut the bag and canvas, two pots of 'Jamaican hard, quick sticking glue'. Twine in red paint glued to bits of polythene was to be used for Bolom's costume. The illustrations show exactly how Walcott wanted the logs to appear both from a distance and how they were to be constructed. Scribbled at the top is a note 'for Margaret' listing six tickets at $3 each to be collected at the door on Thursday reserved for someone. The costumes were 'executed' by Malcolm Chandler and Helen Camps, the masks and accessories by Ken Morris, and the lighting designed by John Andrews. Pamela Franco was in charge of properties and stage management. The play was 'Designed and Directed by Derek Walcott'.[25]

In the *Sunday Guardian* Walcott wrote about the origins of *Ti-Jean and his Brothers*; written in New York during 1957 it was the most spontaneous of his plays in terms of rhythm and concept, being a product of exile and loneliness. He wanted to write 'a softly measured metre whose breathing was formally articulated yet held the lyrical stress of dialect speech'. The breakthrough was to divide the iambic line in half, into three feet that provided lilt capable of oral delivery

which seemed to capture the sound of the quatro, flute, and oral story
telling. It now seems simple, but it created its own instinctual rhythm,
fusing metre with the folk. It had behind it Lorca's swift self-arresting
metre, Brecht's distancing of character, and through Brecht 'the Noh
Theatre with its use of masks, musicians and the mimetic indications
of scenery'. There was also the voice of a friend in St Lucia, St Lucian
folk-tales and rituals and masks, the African tradition of story telling,
and the mythology of the peasant world. Now *Ti-Jean* 'has found an
acting company that is able, with hard study and technical skill, to
communicate its primal sincerities and grotesqueries without affecta-
tion'. And now in Tanker, Walcott has found a composer 'disciplined
enough to be simple'.[26]

In the 'Prologue' to the programme for the 1970 *Ti-Jean* Walcott
drew parallels between the use of fable as a form, the simple presentation and meaning of his play. Grotowski's 'Poor Theatre' was applicable to West Indian theatre where artists need to work under
'embittering conditions'. Local culture needs 'both preservation and
resurgence'. 'We present to others a deceptive simplicity that they
may dismiss as provincial, primitive, childish, but which is in truth a
radical innocence. That is what our fable is about.' The Workshop
was aiming for a style that could be performed 'under some backyard
tree', yet which would have the devices of 'the rich theatre'.

While *Ti-Jean* was reviewed twice in the *Trinidad Guardian* under
the headlines 'A Most Significant Musical Contribution' and 'Stormy
Applause Well Deserved', the reviewers seemed confused by the form
of the play and by the ready response of the audience. Clyde Hosein
said the play wrestles with the clash of good and evil but thought the
ending unconvincing. He saw the play as a version of the 'nancy'
stories, noted how the audience responded readily to remarks like
'This is a state of emergency', but felt it deserved its 'stormy applause'.
Brian Dockray, who was assigned to review the music, objected that
only one member of the cast can sing, Ellsworth Primus. Laveau is a
star actor but should take singing lessons. Dockray seemed confused
by the unusual nature of the play, a folk-musical. While he felt that he
could not separate the music from the drama, he objected that the
musical numbers were too scrappy and that Tanker had not synthe-
sized folk-music and calypso into a personal form. Dockray concluded,
however, that Walcott and the Workshop had 'made a grand show'.[27]

Other reviewers were more sure-footed. Eric Roach mentioned some
universal characteristics of folk-tales which he found in *Ti-Jean* and
went on to interpret the play in terms of Caribbean black history.

Gros-Jean is 'of the brawny post-slave generation' which easily succumbs to the wiles of the white man, Mi-Jean is infused with middle-class values. Ti-Jean is 'of today's generation'. Roach praised Belinda Barnes's Bolom, Tanker's music and the 'sleek, well-oiled' direction. He asked what is going to become of Laveau, 'who appears to be nearing the peak of his application in part time amateur drama' and what will become of the Theatre Workshop? 'Walcott has forged an instrument for the country, but one fears that the country . . . doesn't have the foggiest notion what Theatre Workshop is about. It is almost impossible to see "Ti-Jean," to hear Walcott's poetry, wit and humour, and realise his talent at directing and the talent of his cast, without asking oneself these difficult questions.'[28]

Syl Lowhar called Ti-Jean a folk-musical of 'powerful beauty'. He thought it treated of 'the development of national identity' and of the struggle of the poor to improve 'their lot in life'. The unborn nation is represented by the Bolom, a foetus that was strangled by its mother. Barnes's 'unfolding' from the deformed, twisted creature into a full moral being is one of 'the most dramatic moments of the production'. Lowhar interpreted the plot as showing that 'in the rise of nationhood Africa must remain a memory and not a living force'. The three sons represent different generations and social movements. Gros-Jean is like Butler and the rise of the labour movement during the late 1930s. Mi-Jean is an intellectual, a 'typical Afro-Saxon', a prisoner of modern education. Ti-Jean is the up-and-coming generation which does not follow the rules or pretend to be powerful or intelligent in asserting its identity.[29]

The Workshop toured with Ti-Jean to Grenada, St Lucia and Barbados, 3–20 July. The tour opened in Grenada with a special performance on 3 July at Government House before Her Excellency Dame Hilda Bynoe, which was followed by a dance at Islander Hotel, supposedly to André Tanker. As Tanker's quartet for Ti-Jean was not a dance orchestra, and had no repertoire for the purpose, there was a local group for dancing. On 5 July the Workshop performed Ti-Jean twice at a school auditorium. The performances were sponsored by the Grenada Amateur Athletic and Cycling Association in aid of sending the Grenada team to the 1970 Commonwealth Games. Tickets were three and two Grenadian dollars, one dollar for children.

From Grenada the Workshop moved north to St Lucia arriving on 6 July. In Grenada the Workshop stayed at the Carifta Cottages; in St Lucia to save money the Workshop would stay with Walcott's friends. Besides rehearsals there were rehearsals of a TV script (adapted by

Helen Camps) of *Ti-Jean* which was to be shot in Barbados. They would rehearse from 10 a.m. until 1 p.m., have the afternoon off, unless there was a 4 p.m. matinee, eat at 7 p.m., and perform at 8.30 p.m. at Castries Town Hall. On the 9 July they toured St Lucia and on Sunday, 12 July, they went to Marigot Bay after rehearsing in the morning and lunch. There were four performances of *Ti-Jean* in St Lucia. On 13 July they flew to Barbados, where they stayed at Paradise Beach, performed from 16 July until 18 July, with two performances on 18 July, at Combermere School Hall, and returned to Trinidad on 20 July.

Stanley Reid in *The Voice of St Lucia* praised Laveau's 'flawless performance' and saw the play as about recognizable phases of black West Indian history, with Mi-Jean as the petit bourgeois pseudo-intellectual. A revised version of this review appeared in the *Barbados Nation* where Reid also praised the music behind the Bolom's dance, Parris's cool sustained performance as the Frog, Ermine Wright's tortured performance as the Mother, and the surprising assurance of young Ellsworth Primus along with the discipline of the Workshop. A still slightly different version of Reid's review and ten photographs of *Ti-Jean* by Gregory Regis, were later published as a 'Photo-Review' in Barbados. While *Ti-Jean* was usually interpreted politically or in terms of its universal themes, the St Lucian press made a point of seeing it in terms of preserving and renewing local folk tradition. C. A. P. St Hill complained about the agony of the metal seats used at Castries Town Hall, but said the play explored the archaeology of local beliefs; *Ti-Jean* was a tale told to children at night in rural areas.[30]

After returning from the tour the Workshop performed *Ti-Jean* in San Fernando, 6 August, at a matinee and in the evening; then in Tobago, 15 August, gave a special performance on 2 September for Hugh Robertson and Lloyd Reckord (director of the Jamaica National Theatre) and at Town Hall on 18–19 September. 'Humming Bird' in the 'Talk of Trinidad' called *Ti-Jean* the Workshop's 'most successful' production. The success of *Ti-Jean* brought the Workshop together again. Although a few members were lost, others were added. Charles Applewhaite, who had been invited to be part of the backstage crew for the *Ti-Jean* cancelled because of the Black Power demonstrations, joined the Workshop and, like others, began to work his way from backstage to becoming an actor. He attended the September meeting at which the Trinidad Theatre Workshop officially asked Walcott to return as its leader. In 1993 Applewhaite was still part of the company, acting in the Boston *Nobel Celebration*.[31]

Walcott's discomfort with events in Trinidad coincided with a period of travel beginning with the August Los Angeles production of *Dream* by American actors. An undated memorandum that he wrote to Michael Schultz during Los Angeles rehearsals of *Dream* pointed to some of the problems in using American rather than Workshop actors. Rather than being a West Indian play it has become an American production of a play by a West Indian performed in a mixture of American-Method Naturalism, Kabuki, and Martha Graham with an imitation of dialect rhythms and ethnic music. If the play is not made West Indian it will fail, as it will not represent 'the triangular passage of the colonial victim in its quest backwards to its roots'. Walcott then gives Schultz many examples from the text and visual symbols of the quest being blocked by amnesia (the black West Indian's loss of any tribal or African cultural identity).

Significantly the main examples Walcott gives are visual, both pictorial and symbolic actions; the visual images are as important as the language. The crossroads are forked with indecision and Makak is led and abandoned by his friend. When Moustique moves by instinct towards the Market (symbol of the degradation of the black race by the profit motive and materialism) he pauses because he feels that he too has lost his way. The actors must learn to arrest the act for moments; as in Kabuki there are moments of non-movement when the audience should feel that is not the way to go. Lestrade's amnesia is shown by the blank signs. Makak is the focus of the play; he is the body as it discovers its origins and evolution from Ape to Adam and the discovery of a New World. He is Adam awakening in the morning. The actors must seek these blank signposts that should paralyse them, shatter their characterizations; the revealing loss is a moment of illumination. The passage of the moon through the night and its obscuring by a cloud is an example of a symbol of the journey that the play and its characters undertake.

There also is the underlying religious symbolism. When Moustique betrays Makak at the crossroads he is like Judas. The murder of Tigre should be made unbearable; he is like Cain who although not God's favourite contains the 'criminal majesty, tragedy of man'. Walcott constantly refers to the Garden of Eden, the Fall. The Forest is a magic enchanted circle, a 'ring whitened by the moon', an Eden surrounded by madness and horror. When Lestrade goes mad he is lost, but finds himself; he re-enacts the death that the race must undergo to find itself again, like Adam or Crusoe, to discover the wonder of the New World. The actors should think of a forest in the morning, the stillness and vigour of grass. They should be still like animals. Instead they drift, they try to speak like poets; scenes seem long because they lack wonder. The actors are not mesmerized by the elemental.

Walcott wanted Schultz to keep to a totality of concept in which the search for African roots is found impossible and leads to the rediscovery of the New World which is seen as an Adamic discovery, a new beginning, and in which biblical analogies are the main metaphors. He also wanted an acting style that would be more Japanese, less American. This was the opposite of what the Americans wanted. They wanted a less static production than what Walcott would direct, something more rapid, naturalistic, with a simple reduction of the story to a racial–political allegory, whereas Walcott saw his play as similar to his poetry in its complex affirmation of the West Indies as an Eden in which all things await naming and identity. Whereas the Americans wanted a play about the burden of history, Walcott's play said the opposite; there is no way back to origins except by accepting the present as an innocence, a new Eden, a new world.[32]

Late in 1970 Walcott was invited to the Creative Arts Centre of the University of the West Indies, Jamaica. There was talk of performing *Macbeth* and even Tennessee Williams's *Camino Real* (Williams and Walcott had the same agent and Williams visited Jamaica to attend rehearsals) but as mostly women came to the tryouts Walcott decided to première his new two-act version of *In A Fine Castle*, a play which, although begun years before, in themes and subject matter could be seen as a comment on the Trinidad Black Power demonstrations. It opened at the end of October with a set by Richard Montgomery, costumes by Sally Thompson (later Montgomery) and lighting by Franklyn St Juste, one of the original members of the St Lucia Arts Guild.[33]

Montgomery, a well-known English costume and set designer, had been invited to Jamaica for part of the year to teach and do a production. A professional with many credits on his résumé, quiet, soft spoken, and talented, Montgomery got on well with Walcott and would in future be involved with some of his most important productions. He has an unusual ability to understand what Walcott wants, and can turn Walcott's drawings into sets, as well as designing sets and costumes that Walcott likes. They would soon team up with Galt MacDermot.

Walcott's 'Author's Note' in the programme of the Jamaican production of *In A Fine Castle* mentions that the play began in a television outline 'proposed by an actor who worked with Bergman', became a full-length three-act play, which was interrupted by 'the world without the Castle', then was reworked as a possible film script, and now has become a play again. In each version he tried to keep in its style the 'fluent impartiality' of a camera. Only after facing the madness of the world and accepting his own flaws can a person find 'true peace, which is separate, personal'.

Harry Milner thought *In A Fine Castle* 'a beguiling, gripping, beautiful and professional piece of theatre'. At the same time he found it complex, baffling, and taxing especially in its mixture of glib satire on West Indian Black Power and the more interesting study of Caribbean European decadence which, Milner thought, transposed a Bergman cinema subject to the theatre. As often in reviewing Walcott, Milner was disturbed by what he thought was a lack of a clear message, but he saw that the love between Brown and Clodia signified the need for personal love if the destructive public hatred between the races is to be ended. Although Milner wrote that any thinking Jamaican should see the play, he did not like Montgomery's 'Brechtian slides' and 'cinemascope-Kabuki stage' and he thought that the direction tended to drag in the second act (a common fault of Walcott's productions due to lengthy, careful rehearsing of the first act). Milner praised the visual beauty of Sally Thompson's costumes in scenes based on Watteau's painting of the 'Embarkation'.[34]

NOTES

1. Information from Stanley Marshall (July 1990). Apparently problems began with the June 1969 production of Oliver Jackman's *Stepchild, Stepchild*.
2. 'Walcott's 'Dream on TTT', *Trinidad Guardian* (12 Feb. 1970), 4.
3. Clyde Hosein, 'See Walcott's "Dream" on Television Tonight', *Trinidad Guardian* (14 Feb. 1970), 2; George Allan, 'Dream on Monkey Mountain', *Trinidad Guardian* (20 Feb. 1970), 8; Clyde Hosein, 'Focus on the Arts: No Beating About the Bush', *Trinidad Guardian* (4 Mar. 1970), 4.
4. Benedict Wight, 'The success of Derek Walcott', *Express* (16 Feb. 1970), 9.
5. Denis Solomon, 'Ape and Essence', *Tapia* 7 (19 Apr. 1970), 6.
6. Derek Walcott to Hugh Robertson (24 Feb. 1970), Walcott Collection, University of the West Indies, St Augustine.
7. Derek Walcott to Gordon Davidson (13 May 1970), Walcott Collection, University of the West Indies, St Augustine.
8. Derek Walcott to Jay Ranelli (3 Feb. 1970), Walcott Collection, University of the West Indies, St Augustine.
9. Derek Walcott to Jay Ranelli (3 Mar. 1970), Walcott Collection, University of the West Indies, St Augustine.

10. 'Has Anyone A Suitable Site for the Theatre?', *Express* (24 Mar. 1970), 12; 'Workshop looking for a new home', *Evening News* (20 Mar. 1970).
11. See Ivar Oxaal, *Race and Revolutionary Consciousness: A Documentary Interpretation of the 1970 Black Power Revolt in Trinidad* (Cambridge, Mass.: Schenkman, 1971).
12. Interview with Leonore Bishop, Port of Spain (4 July 1970).
13. Derek Walcott to Management Committee (10 May 1970); this and other documents mentioned are in the Walcott Collection or in Judy Stone's personal files.
14. When I interviewed Hopkinson (Toronto, Nov. 1991 and several earlier telephone conversations) I was struck by the discrepancy between what he felt he had accomplished and how few of his works had been produced, published, or finished. Admittedly he had long been ill and was near death.
15. Group III, Aquarius Productions (10 May 1970). The Walcott Collection has the various documents and notes concerning Group III, Aquarius, etc.
16. The various items mentioned are in the Walcott Collection.
17. 'Minutes of a general meeting held at Bishop Anstey High School on Wednesday 13th May 1970 at 6:00 p.m.'
18. Management Committee to Derek Walcott (19 May 1970). In the Walcott Collection there is a document from an undated committee meeting, signed by John Andrews, spelling out functions in more detail.
19. 'Trinidad Theatre Workshop. Legal Status' (undated).
20. Derek Walcott's plans for Aquarius Production's presentation of *Ti-Jean* dated 20 May 1970 and undated typed notes about Barbados and Grenada, Walcott Collection.
21. Derek Walcott to 'The Committee' (30 May 1970), Walcott Collection. While Walcott may well have had a 'Messiah-complex', such religious figures of speech, especially the analogy to Moses and the Promised Land, were commonplace to West Indian black politics at the time, were frequently used by supporters of Eric Williams, and were part of the rhetoric of persuasion.
22. Michael Anthony, 'Conversation with Slade Hopkinson', *Sunday Guardian* (8 Sept. 1970), [?], 16; Fred Hope and Slade Hopkinson, 'The Changing Needs of our Theatre', *Sunday Guardian* (4 July 1971), 5; Edgar White, 'Caribbean Theatre Guild', unidentified magazine article (1984 or 1985); interview with Eintou Springer (July 1990).
23. Derek Walcott to Gordon Davidson (13 May 1970), Walcott Collection and Rockefeller Archive.
24. 'Theatre Workshop Revives a Musical', *Express* (11 June 1970), 2; 'Theatre Workshop to Tour Caribbean Islands', *Trinidad Guardian* (13 June 1970).
25. The drawing (dated 22 June 1970) is in the Walcott Collection.
26. Derek Walcott, 'Derek's Most West Indian Play', *Sunday Guardian Magazine* (21 June 1970), 7.
27. Clyde Hosein, 'Stormy Applause Well Deserved', and Brian Dockray, 'A Most Significant Musical Contribution', both *Trinidad Guardian* (27 June 1970), 4.
28. Eric Roach, 'This Musical Fuses both Traditions of Folk Legend', *Sunday Guardian* (28 June 1970).

29. Syl Lowhar, 'Ti-Jean—A Mom and Son's Battle for a Better Life', *Express* (14 July 1970), 13 and 'A Struggle for Freedom', *Tapia*, 8 (9 Aug. 1970), 6.

30. Stanley Reid, 'Ti Jean And His Brothers', *The Voice of St Lucia* (11 July 1970), 9; Stanley Reid, 'A Moving Interpretation of Local Tradition', *Advocate News* (20 Aug. 1970), 1 [This review also introduces 'Photo-Review Ti Jean and his Brothers' with ten photographs by Gregory Regis]; Earl Huntley, 'Dr Figueroa So Right', *Voice of St Lucia* (11 July 1970), 10 and C. A. P. St Hill, ' "Psyche derek"[sic] Folk Opera', *The Crusader* (12 July 1970), 11–12.

31. 'Hummingbird', 'Talk of Trinidad', *Trinidad Guardian* (17 Sept. 1970), 5; interview with Charles Applewhaite (July 1990) and letters.

32. Derek Walcott to Michael Schultz (undated, 1970), Walcott Collection.

33. Information from Richard Montgomery, Boston (Apr. 1993).

34. Harry Milner, 'The beauty of decadence', *The Sunday Gleaner* (1 Nov. 1970), 5, 9. In the revised version, *The Last Carnival*, there is an unfinished copy of Watteau's 'Embarkation' on the wall, Act II, Scene i.

1971
Ti-Jean and Dream in Jamaica
In A Fine Castle

DURING November 1970 an ambitious 'members' directory and schedule' was circulated for the coming year. Walcott hoped for official state recognition of the Theatre Workshop to make foreign tours easier; he expected that a forthcoming tour to Jamaica would include Bahamas and Guyana, and he intended to rehearse five plays so that the company could have several 'seasons' a year. Max Frisch's *Fire-Raisers* (directed by Judy Stone) was in rehearsal for February, *Ti-Jean* was scheduled for April, rehearsals of *In A Fine Castle* were to begin in February, *Dream on Monkey Mountain* was to be revived in April, and rehearsals of *Macbeth* were planned for August. Roles were distributed among the twenty actors and three musicians in the Workshop. The production and management staff now added up to eight, but consisted mostly of Walcott and John Andrews, their wives, Albert Laveau's wife and the less important actors. Holly Chong was the official photographer for the company. Four names were listed as members abroad—Ralph Campbell, LeRoy Clarke, Sydney Best, Lynette Laveau.[1]

There were now about twenty-five active members—Claude Reid, Errol Jones, Hamilton Parris, Stanley Marshall, Helen Camps, Judy Stone, Albert Laveau, Nigel Scott, Rowena Scott, Ermine Wright, Adele Bynoe, Michael Coryat, Andrew Beddeau, Charles Applewhaite, Noreen Bradford, Ellsworth Primus, Eunice Alleyne, and Avis Martin along with André Tanker and the guitarist Peter Shim. Michael Coryat was an actor and musician. Three of the main members were white— Helen Camps, Judy Stone and Nigel Scott. Stone is listed as directing *Fire-Raisers*, as assistant to the director in *Ti-Jean*, Elizabeth in *Castle* and as Lady Macduff. Scott was scheduled for the Fire Chief in *Fire-Raisers*, an alternative to Laveau's tri-part devil role in *Ti-Jean* and Antoine in *Castle*, had no part in *Dream* and nothing in *Macbeth*.

The Negro Ensemble Company's production of *Dream on Monkey Mountain*, with Roscoe Lee Browne, opened off-Broadway during March 1971, was awarded an Obie by the New York critics, and taken to Munich for the Olympics. Meanwhile preparations were going ahead for the Workshop's Jamaican tour of *Dream on Monkey Mountain* and *Ti-Jean*. Plans to do two shows in Trinidad before the Jamaican tour were abandoned as they could not be prepared in time; *The Fire-Raisers* and *Macbeth* were not produced.[2]

Walcott's rehearsal notes for *Ti-Jean* on 23 March 1971 include fifty-five comments ranging from the weakness of Noreen Bradford's voice and the slowness of the production to such details as the musicians should come in earlier after the devil has eaten Gros-Jean. There are notes to shorten several songs, many comments about facial expressions, the need for characters to pay more attention to each other, musical balance, use of hands, body and stage movements, blocking, characterization, exits, even suggestions about using different voice registers at various points to bring out the situation. Such total shaping of both the visual picture and of the actor's tones phrase by phrase had become characteristic of his directing of plays. Besides voice, blocking, speed, and visual matters, Walcott was especially sensitive to the integration of music and song to the action, with comments on the use of the flute, musical keys, and the transitions between songs and speaking.[3]

The Jamaican tour was sponsored by Pan-Jamaica Investments, led by Walcott's friend Ralph Thompson; Pan-Jamaica covered costs and paid the actors' salaries, in fact subsidizing the tour, but kept the gate receipts. Walcott's memo to the Workshop said that the tour should be viewed as rather an opportunity to break into the Jamaican market than financially profitable. The Workshop could not afford the costs of such tours (about $350 for each person in air fare and $240 in hotel expenses) and it would be necessary afterwards to have performances in Trinidad to recover costs of costumes and props. Everyone would need to pay a two-dollar exit tax from Trinidad and contribute a dollar and fifty cents towards the three Old Oak cases used for packing purchased from Angostura Bitters. No advances could be paid.[4]

As usual the schedule was hectic. Although both plays were in repertory there were rehearsals beginning at 6.30 p.m. of *Ti-Jean* on 5 April to 7 April, followed by a rehearsal of *Dream* on 8 April, followed by a break for Easter and a rehearsal of *Ti-Jean* on 13 April, after which there was packing of materials. The next day at 5 p.m. there was a compulsory meeting and on 15 April at 5.45 a.m. the company flew to Jamaica and rehearsed that night. The actors stayed two to a room and ate at the Sandhurst Guest House. A bus picked them up at 7 p.m. for 8.30 p.m. curtain time. Rehearsals of *Ti-Jean* on the mornings of 16 and 17 April were followed by performances at the University of West Indies Creative Arts Centre both evenings and the evening of Sunday, 18 April. Monday was a day off, although with a cocktail party that evening. Tuesday's 'touch up' rehearsal was followed by *Ti-Jean* which continued through Sunday, 25 April. Meanwhile rehearsals for *Dream* started on the morning of the 22 April and continued until the 27 April, although the play began on the night of the 26 April and ran until 1 May. On Saturday, 24 April there were two shows of *Ti-Jean*; there were two shows of *Dream* on Saturday, 1 May. The final performance of *Dream* was attended by the leaders of the two main political parties, Michael Manley and Edward Seaga. The next day, 2 May, the Workshop returned to Trinidad.[5]

Eighteen actors travelled to Jamaica and there were changes from the original casts. In *Ti-Jean* Adele Bynoe replaced Belinda Barnes as Bolom; Helen Camps played the Bird and Noreen Bradford was the Cricket. In *Dream* Helen Camps was the Apparition, Albert Laveau was Lestrade, Claude Reid played Tigre, Charles Applewhaite took over Basil, and Ellsworth Primus had a part as a boy. Albert Laveau removed all his clothing and played the 'Too late have I loved thee, Africa of my mind' scene in the nude, as the script demands of Corporal Lestrade, which he had not done before; in Trinidad he played it in trunks and singlet: 'I kiss your foot, O Monkey Mountain. [*He removes his clothes*] I return to this earth, my mother. Naked, trying very hard not to weep in the dust.' It was not until 1983 that any actor appeared nude on stage in Trinidad; even in the seduction scene of *The Joker of Seville* Nigel Scott performed in boxer shorts.[6]

If in Trinidad the 1974 production of *The Joker of Seville* at the Little Carib is usually thought the highest achievement of the Theatre Workshop and of West Indian theatre, in Jamaica the 1971 tour has a similar reputation. Mervyn Morris warned readers that they could not afford to miss either play. Morris, a poet, scholar, and actor, noted that the text of this production of *Ti-Jean* differed considerably from the recently published American edition which has less material concerning the relationship of black labour to white masters. *Ti-Jean* is an example of what folk theatre can achieve and is the opposite of

Walcott's *In A Fine Castle*. The meaning of the play is complex and cannot be expressed so simply as the potentiality and phases of black rebellion and choice of life; perhaps it is as much about common sense equipping people better to survive as book learning or brute force; and it is about God, the changing nature of evil and love.[7]

Morris describes the production as opening with the house lights on as the musicians enter, go to a bench towards the back of centre stage, and begin to tune up. The actors amble on, pick up bits of costumes as the lights dim and the music starts. Hamilton Parris, as Frog and story teller, has a beautifully controlled slow delivery which hypnotically holds attention without concern for time. The effect of magic and illusion is reversed at the end when the musicians take off their masks and the lights turn up to return the audience to reality. The company plays well especially in relation to each other. Gros-Jean's stupidity is expressed through Claude Reid's body as anger and frustration mounts beyond his control. Ellsworth Primus as Ti-Jean is assured and subtle in inflection. Adele Bynoe's speech is remarkably clear despite the contorted position required by her part as Foetus. The finest performance is by Albert Laveau in the varying voices, transformations and postures, yet always remaining the Devil. Tanker's music is well integrated into the wonderful performance.

Harry Milner called the production of *Ti-Jean* magical. The Workshop may at times lack professional polish, but it is a fine instrument through which Walcott can express his feelings and conception. Jamaican theatre can be more professional, but lacks such a company with its relationship to a writer-director. While *Ti-Jean* is simple enough to be followed by children, it has a deep wisdom and beauty. Although Ellsworth Primus, the young boy who played Ti-Jean, was naturally engaging, his naturalness was out of key with the more stylized acting of the rest of the cast. It could be argued, however, that such essential humanity and cheekiness represents the cheerful indomitability of the human race.[8]

In his 'Merry-Go-Round' column R.R. praised *Ti-Jean* for being both entertaining and related to the social and political problems of the 'black man living in a white dominated society'. Walcott uses the language and music of the region to show a universal situation. 'I felt proud knowing that I was able to live in the time of Derek Walcott and to view one of his plays, directed by the playwright.' In her gossip column 'Stella' remarked that Walcott is 'sensitive, a little puzzling sometimes but capable of inspiring the most fanatic loyalty from his fans'.[9]

Morris wrote that *Dream* deserves the highest acclaim as a complex drama and poetic statement about the psyche of West Indian colonized blacks. It is resourceful in theatrical means, its verbal and visual images form a complex network of references. He mentions that the songs often offer an ironic commentary, that there is an interplay between visual and verbal images, that textual images are picked up in body movements and mime (possibly referring to a performance style in which each word may be accompanied or underlined by a gesture). While the language was magnificent the production of *Dream*, unlike *Ti-Jean*, had some weak spots. The crowd scenes felt underpopulated, and Charles Applewhaite as Basil has a weak stage presence in contrast to the shrewdness and affectionate tenderness projected by Stanley Marshall as Moustique and Errol Jones's overwhelming Makak, especially in the latter's transformation from a whimpering ape-like peasant to a majestic African king. 'His body spoke dignity when Jones told it to, and it always seemed to contain a power which might break loose. The voice, a booming baritone sounded at times (as it was supposed to) like something from some dark primeval cave. His grunts and his cries of anguish had an animal force.' Jones could, however, 'modulate into the gentlest lyric poetry' and delicate tenderness. Morris felt that the play was about the multiple betrayal of a vision of racial and personal dignity—a vision given by the white apparition—by those who use the vision for their own aims such as power, money, or revenge.[10]

Harry Milner questioned the *New York Times* description of *Dream* as bewildering. It is a dream play in the tradition of later Strindberg or the films of Fellini. Actually there are two dreams. There is Makak's Judaic-Christian inspired dream, given by the white apparition, of faith healing and peacefully leading his people back to Africa. The second dream is of militancy and revenge. This becomes a nightmare which destroys everything Makak loves about Western civilization. The play seems to say that rather than expecting a revolution it is best to cultivate one's own garden and trust in God. Makak is Walcott's Lear, and Jones wisely did not reduce the character to pathos. Although Laveau showed confidence and versatility, combining both comedy and feeling and convincingly changing character, some of the lines of his role are weak. *Dream* could use revision and cutting. Basil was miscast and two actors were not word perfect. The music was distracting. Milner admitted that others whose opinion he respected thought the play the most exciting they had seen.[11]

Lloyd Coke called the two productions 'unforgettable' and wrote of the deceptive casualness of Walcott's craftsmanship, professionalism, and expression of a Caribbean ethos. Jamaicans have rarely seen a company effortlessly combine body movement, dialect, and poetry with such virtuosity. As Makak—'holy man, epileptic hermit and charcoal burner' who fills 'an ecological niche in the West Indian psyche'—Errol Jones has a tremendous vocal range and 'massive gorilla-like dignity'. Albert Laveau was polished and assured. 'Theater makes possible the wedding of oral and dance traditions with literature' and reaches a wider public than the printed page.[12]

The Prime Minister of Jamaica, Michael Manley, wrote to Walcott on 12 May saying that he found both plays and performances among the 'truly memorable experiences' of his life. As theatre *Dream on Monkey Mountain* is as arresting as Genet's *The Blacks* in its psychological insights. The relationship between Makak and Moustique is superb contrapuntal writing. The two evenings were rare watersheds of artistic experience. Perhaps, Manley suggested, in future the TTW might return under more official sponsorship.[13]

Radio and television work offered a possible additional source of income if the actors were to make the transition to professionals. There had already been the occasional radio or television recording of plays for the Canadians, NBC, and in the West Indies, and some of the actors were being paid to appear in television commercials and on some radio and television series. The problem was how to establish such work on a regular basis and earn repeat fees for rebroadcasts. Walcott wanted the Workshop to contract radio and television work as a group; he would be the agent as he thought the actors were not earning enough for appearances in advertising commercials, and he hoped to establish a regular series of broadcasts of serious plays. He felt that as agent he could raise the level of payment; in return 10 per cent of contractual earnings would be put into the Workshop's bank account.

In January Peter Donkin's production of *Ti-Jean* was broadcast across Canada on the Canadian Broadcasting Corporation; on 24 May Walcott signed a contract at the Canadian High Commission in Port of Spain for the Workshop to record for CBC an adaptation of Wilson Harris's novel *Palace of the Peacock*, which would be called *The Crew from Sorrow Hill*, and Lennox Brown's *The Throne in an Autumn Room*. Peter Donkin was again producer. *Throne* would be made into a record to be distributed through the CBC's International Service. Recording would start on 27 May and last about ten days. In June a ten-minute segment of *Ti-Jean*, with Hamilton Parris, Ermine Wright, Ellsworth Primus, and

Stanley Marshall, was filmed for National Educational Television to be shown on 'Black Journal' in the United States. The film version of *Dream*, which had not previously been shown publicly in Trinidad, was projected at Tapia House for one night in June. There were also plans to produce *Ti-Jean* at Tapia House, which was now sometimes used for workshops, but nothing came of it.[14]

During April and June Clyde Hosein published in his 'Focus on the Arts' in the *Trinidad Guardian* articles about and interviews with Walcott and the Workshop actors. Hosein was sceptical of Walcott's desire for a theatre which would extend from Calypso to a 'black Hamlet'. Where Walcott saw a local 'exuberance' of desire for the arts, Hosein only found apathy. Hosein was also sceptical of talk about an island condition; people live first in the world and on an island only secondarily. Walcott was most valuable in informing the State of our true condition and showing us what we are. Hosein thought Trinidad had some of the finest actors in the world and praised Eunice Alleyne for her natural flow of hand movements and use of eyes and voice.

During an interview Albert Laveau remarked that a basic problem of Trinidadian theatre is the lack of a history of theatre. Jones spoke of the lack of freedom as a problem. The allusions to the state of emergency in their Queen's Hall performance had created a strong reaction. Marshall and the others spoke of the lack of finance which caused dependency on other countries and fear of losing 'our bread-and-butter' jobs. Whenever they have to tour their applications for leave are treated with disrespect; others do not understand how hard they work to perfect their art and assume that if they were any good they would go away to work elsewhere. People regard the arts as spare-time activity like collecting stamps or drinking rum. Other islands have national theatres and the national political leaders go to the theatre; in Trinidad only A. N. R. Robinson has come to a performance. People have talked for years about an open-air theatre without anyone offering a design; money for it will probably need to come from abroad. Too often the young think talent is inherent and that all you need to do is express yourself. That is a West Indian attitude. People do not realize the work that goes into a single gesture or the development of a manner for a part. Trinidad has been rich in theatrical talents, but most of its theatre groups have failed from lack of leadership.[15]

During June Therese Mills also interviewed Walcott for the *Sunday Guardian*. In reply to Mills's comment that in Trinidad the theatre was seen as political and the politicians as actors, Walcott said that while the 1970 demonstrations were genuine protests many of the leading demonstrators played theatrical roles. Even more theatrical is Eric Williams's recent call for the decolonization of the arts, as Williams always has been against black radical thought and art forms. The Trinidadian political system is inherited from the British and is based on Western liberal notions of freedom of expression and individual liberties. Now with cultural decolonization these values are being attacked and there is a desire for a monolithic culture paying homage to the political. But real cultural change will come through revolutionaries and artists critical of this cultural fascism, which is similar to the Nazi concept of Aryanism. Both the Nazis and the black extremists want to 'cleanse' society of supposed foreign impurities. Such views are often found among cultural nationalists but also appear among Communists with their notion of bourgeois enemies of the State. Trinidad is rapidly moving in that direction. Besides preventing free expression there is intimidation. Walcott told Mills that his actors who work for the government know that they may be risking their careers by not being aligned with the government.

If there were real decolonization the government would rid themselves of the nineteenth-century notion of the artist as someone born to suffer. Both the government and radicals are afraid to see the reality of West Indian culture as it has developed. Ten years ago they were proud to be British; now they are proud to be African. There is a refusal to be Trinidadian or St Lucian. Everyone talks about decolonization, but that is fakery; the West Indies will always be a colony, whether the colonialism is American, Latin American or African. Within three generations the model has changed from English to African to black American. Economically we are colonies of America. There are those who would make us Cubans. We waste energy picking out symbols. West Indian culture is a fusion which makes the slogans of 'decolonization' meaningless. Writers are daily going through decolonization, but writers do not use such stupid words because they are receptive to all that is of value including Europe, Africa, and America.

One of the more dangerous signs of fascism, Walcott said, is the assimilation of folk culture to the state and the manifestation of the state's image through folk-costumes, folk-parades, and folk-circuses. The people, not the state, will need to choose their image. The young radical's image of urban revolt was a romantic restatement of the state's image of a folk culture rooted in Africa. Such programmes for a folk culture destroy its freshness and vitality and create the illusion that people can be artists without the discipline of art. A scholarship for further training of a real artist has more value than any Best Village programme. The arts are hierarchical, based on an inequality of talent. Folk-arts can shut off growth especially if folk-arts are seen as mass arts which do not allow for individual talents. Culture is created by individuals. Each great calypso artist is different. We do not see the artist as a citizen who contributes to society.[16]

On 30 July Walcott was appointed to Trinidad's Cultural Council and on the same day signed a contract for the Workshop to record a series of plays for 610 Radio. 'Theatre Ten' was sponsored by Texaco. Every Sunday, from 8 August until 10 October, at 5.30 p.m. 610 Radio would broadcast thirty-minute programmes of West Indian plays adapted and acted by the Workshop. The series, in a similar form, was expanded during 1972 and an even larger series of such broadcasts was planned for 1973, but did not take place.[17]

The plays recorded for the 1971 season included Douglas Archibald's *Anne-Marie*, directed by Stanley Marshall, adapted by Judy Stone; Walcott's *Sea at Dauphin* and *Henri Christophe*, directed and adapted by Walcott; Roderick Walcott's *The Harrowing of Benjy*, directed by Helen Camps; Lennox Brown's *Fog Drifts in the Spring*, directed by Derek Walcott; E. Kamau Brathwaite's *Odale's Choice*, adapted by Ken Corsbie; and Eric Roach's *Belle Fanto*. *Anne-Marie* and *Belle Fanto* were in two half-hour segments; *Henri Christophe* in two forty-five minute segments. The actors were mostly such TTW regulars as Brenda Hughes, Ermine Wright, Judy Stone, Hamilton Parris, Errol Pilgrim, Stanley Marshall, Albert Laveau, Errol Jones, and Nigel Scott. Along with those recorded in 1972 the Workshop would eventually have sixteen plays, or over eight hours of broadcast time for possible sale to radio stations in the Caribbean.[18]

The after-effects of the 1970 Black Power demonstrations influenced the Trinidadian cultural scene for a few years, providing a ready-made, unthinking political correctness. In August Walcott defended Rex Nettleford's Jamaica National Dance Company's recent performance at Queen's Hall against Trinidadian charges that it was insufficiently Black. Now that the danger of revolution has passed, anything 'which is not young, black and belligerent' is being questioned by the bourgeois intellectuals and officialdom, the very people whom the demonstrations were against. Fury has become the fashion of the establishment. Trinidadians have not only imported revolutions and their language, they have also imported the masochism of the white liberal middle-class dilettante. Nothing could be more black or beautiful than Nettleford himself, but his company is accused of mimicry and assimilation. 'Revolutionary culture produces enthusiasm, and because such enthusiasm relates to spasms of power and is subject to disenchantment, it is short-lived and antagonistic to disciplines.' 'In the colonial consciousness definitions of soul have become as intricate as medieval heresies.' Nettleford is the true revolutionary in his revolutionary techniques which work against the abstractions of their mould.[19]

Ti-Jean was revived for a performance, 13 October, at Town Hall, and for two nights, 23–24 October, at Queen's Hall, with the same cast as during the tour. The Queen's Hall performances were not well attended.[20]

In A Fine Castle was awaited with expectation; it concerned the conflict between the European colonial heritage and the black consciousness that only a year before had almost overthrown the Trinidadian government. While the play was being performed a Sedition Bill was proposed which defined sedition as creating ill-will between classes and races. Several newspaper articles and reviews used Walcott's new play to make a contrast between Eric Williams's claim that only government power could keep the country from racial civil war and Walcott's message of interracial love and understanding.

On 28 October Walcott's *In A Fine Castle* opened for a three-night run at Queen's Hall and had a second run of two nights, 28–29 November, at Town Hall. This was the first Trinidadian performance of the play which had been premiered in Jamaica during 1971 and which was under option in the United States by the Mark Taper Forum. Richard Montgomery's original Jamaican stage design was slightly modified for Queen's Hall. The cast included Albert Laveau as Brown, Vanessa Gilder—a young black American actress—as Shelley, Helen Ross, Bernard Rothwell, Stanley Marshall, Helen Camps, Nigel Scott, Errol Jones, Judy Stone, and Ermine Wright. Ellsworth Primus played Brown as a child; Wilbert Holder and Claude Reid alternated the role of Michael. The crowd scenes included Charles Applewhaite, Christopher Piniero, Adele Bynoe, Avis Martin, Noreen Bradford, and Hamilton Parris. The play had a larger cast than usual for Walcott and was unexpectedly naturalistic. *In A Fine Castle* was bound to be controversial. Advance publicity claimed that the play was written for Helen Camps and 'focusses on the domestic complexities of a French Creole family during Carnival and on the eve of the February Revolution last year'. Walcott even published a condensed version in *Express* under the title 'Conscience of a Revolutionary'. Some newspaper articles warned that the play could be banned under the new Sedition Bill.[21]

Eric Roach saw the play as about a racially divided society. The old white French ruling order is that of Tennessee Williams's degenerates and is afraid of blacks; the blacks, screaming for revolution are 'trapped in their own abomination of fear and folly, colour and hatred'. Both sides will come to a bad end unless there is love. Brown, Walcott's central character, is a black Hamlet who is too disillusioned, intelligent, and indolent for a black revolution, but sleeps with a white woman from the old order. Roach thought the play satirizes the young black revolutionaries' search for identity and especially in Shelley the importation of black American rhetoric and fashions; it was much more sympathetic to the whites than to the blacks. 'Only the expatriate will find full pleasure in the cleverly worded satire and the ignorant North American lap it up for the West Indian gospel.' It is for the 'champagne and brandy drinker' who speaks 'the Queen's English', 'not for the Carib beer and Caroni rum people'.

Those reviewers who disliked the compassion Walcott had for Brown and his French Creole characters tried themselves to sound like 'Caroni rum people' to the point of near unintelligibility. Earl Augustus's attempt at Calypsonian punning wit and sexual innuendo resulted in a poorly written review which confused actors with characters and the play with the author. While he claims that Walcott is making the 'Negro-Saxon plea for special privilege' left over from the colonial period of those who imitated the whites, Augustus also says that Walcott 'asserts the inevitable tragic emptiness of the Negro-Saxon conscience'. If Augustus had no sympathy for the story and characters he had seen on stage, and kept arguing with the play, he was aware of some of Walcott's own ambivalence towards the passivity of Brown and those who did not take sides, although for Walcott the issue was less political commitment than living fully, actively, a commitment towards life and the West Indies. Brown lacks such vitality and commitment.[22]

The poet Anson Gonzalez was more sympathetic and analytical; he thought *In A Fine Castle* examines the future of the French-Creole plantocracy and the future roles of whites in Trinidad while looking critically on revolutionary rhetoric as futile carnival that will change nothing for the better. The play shows the effects of militancy on social institutions and the need for protest to be more subtle. It is a well-knit, finely constructed play that makes good use of space and movement. While the design and direction were superb, the poor lighting equipment resulted in some areas of the stage being insufficiently dark. Both Gonzalez and Roach praised the way Stanley

Marshall, as George, dominated the scenes he was in, although he had a minor part with few lines. The audience applauded him continuously at the curtain call. Nigel Scott was also spontaneously applauded by the audience. Gonzalez praised Albert Laveau's skilful and sensitive portrayal of Brown's hurt, displacement, and alienation.[23]

In *Tapia* Syl Lowhar began his review by saying the venomous attacks on *In A Fine Castle* proved Walcott's point. In *Henri Christophe* he showed that black leaders who have an intense hatred of whites end up dictators enslaving blacks. The attacks on the former political leader Albert Gomes and the violent ejection of whites from political meetings are part of the same antipathy that develops from the pain of falling out of love. Those who have been liberated for a long time are not as furious or resentful. The play's title comes from a slave song:

> In a fine castle, do you hear my sisi-O
> Which one do you want do you hear my sisi-O
> The one with the golden hair . . .

In the play black Shelley is contrasted to white Clodia La Fontaine in the castles of their skin, but the play rejects such skin polarities to ask which one do you want in terms of humanity. If the carnival is revolution, then one by one the La Fontaines leave their castle to join the Carnival. Walcott warns against excessive sympathy with the whites. By yielding to Clodia the black reporter becomes a house slave. But the play is boring because of its quandaries, complexities, and inconclusiveness. Brown, the reporter, sickens of the black radicals' inhumanity and unthinking creation of new injustices, but he feels he lacks the rage and hatred necessary for the revolution that he desires.[24]

Denis Solomon's two-part review appeared several months later in *Express* as an answer to the demands by Roach and Augustus for radical political correctness. Solomon thought *In A Fine Castle* one of the best Caribbean plays and felt that Roach's attack on Walcott's language was the jealousy of someone who wrote English poorly. Similarly Roach's attack on Walcott as an outsider was absurd as the concerns of the play are not just local or racial. If *Dream* concerned the problems of ridding oneself of the roles imposed by others, here Walcott shows two groups supported in their attitudes by the other as they 'pivot about the central emptiness of Carnival'. Like many West Indians, Walcott is 'Brown' for whom Blake is more part of his inheritance than Eldridge Cleaver is for the black revolutionaries. But whereas Makak can return to his 'green beginnings' such comfort is not allowed in *Castle*. While it is possible to see hope in a message of interracial love, that may not be the message of the play as Brown is left confused and isolated. Must we demand that Walcott always write *Ti-Jean* and not a play of metaphysical despair? Cannot a play be honest to itself and its vision? Is a play to be enjoyed as a sermon? The reviewers seem to judge the play only in terms of its possible political symbolism. It is always possible to discover content, no matter how inept the work, instead of considering form and skill.[25]

Solomon comments that Walcott is a West Indian, but also an English poet. The play concerns this cleavage, a cleavage reflected in the Workshop itself where some of the actors are excellent in creole prose parts but make a hash of the English poetry—Slade Hopkinson and Albert Laveau are the obvious exceptions. Of the four principal white actors in *Castle* two are English and one Irish. Thus the cleavage in the play's themes, the cast, and Walcott's poetry. It is with this in mind one should examine the interplay between form and content in *Castle*.

Solomon says that except for *Franklin* this is Walcott's first naturalistic play and is remarkable for the pace and interest of the dialogue. The early scenes especially build up and resolve tensions. Using a conventional form Walcott is naturally directed to the drawing room of the educated and literary and to dwell on the psychological and sexual conflicts within 'the castle'. The revolutionary blacks are not important; Walcott's concern is the literary attraction of the white drawing room and what it represents. Is it possible to write naturalistic plays about the poor black? G. B. Shaw argued that a completely realistic play about the poor, uneducated labourer is impossible and there is reason to think that is true of the poor black. Those who have tried, such as Douglas Archibald, Errol John, or Errol Hill, have sentimentalized. Walcott refuses to fall into this trap and has instead poeticized the peasant through verse and fable. Walcott's critics demand, however, that he write sentimental plays and they judge him accordingly.

The writing of *In A Fine Castle* began long before 1970 and the play is part of Walcott's continuing concern with his divided white and black heritage and the multiracial, multicultural composition of the West Indies. It is as much an exploration of himself and his world as *Dream on Monkey Mountain*. That *In A Fine Castle* provided principal parts for the Workshop's white members and required additional whites translated its themes into theatre politics. Although the Workshop began as multiracial it had been predominantly a black company. *In A*

Fine Castle, Franklin and *The Charlatan*, the main plays with which Walcott and the Workshop were to be involved for the next few years, have principal white characters and are concerned with the place of whites in the West Indies. This was not a new concern to Walcott. Draft versions of *The Charlatan* and *Franklin* were first written in the early 1950s when Walcott was at the University College of the West Indies and probably are based on whites he had known or observed. The rise of the Black Power movement during the late 1960s and early 1970s had made their themes timely, especially as some of the more active members of the Workshop—Nigel Scott, Judy Stone and Helen Camps—were white. That Walcott himself is a painter in the French tradition means that he is culturally part de la Fontaine as well as Brown.

After *Castle* Walcott left for the United States to direct *Ti-Jean* at the New York University Drama School. Tanker went with him to help with the music. Although some Americans thought Walcott's direction too static, the NYU production caught Joseph Papp's attention and led to Papp's own production of *Ti-Jean* with Walcott directing and Hamilton Parris and Albert Laveau being highly praised by the New York critics. It also led to Laveau giving up a brilliant career with Lever Brothers to become, for a few years, a professional actor in the United States.

NOTES

1. 'Members' Directory & Schedule Trinidad Theatre Workshop', two pages, 'Weekly Rehearsal Schedule', one page. Judy Stone's files.
2. 'Dream Gets Top U.S. Award', *Trinidad Guardian* (29 May 1971), 9; information from Judy Stone.
3. The notes of 23 Mar. 1971 are in the Walcott Collection, University of the West Indies, St Augustine.
4. 'Trinidad Theatre Workshop Jamaica Tour 1971', three pages. Ralph Thompson's files.
5. 'Theatre Workshop Leaves', *The Daily Gleaner* (3 May 1971), 22.
6. 'Walcott Records Success in Jamaica and New York', *Trinidad Guardian* (29 Apr. 1971), 7; Walcott, *Dream on Monkey Mountain* (1970), 299; Judy Stone, 'Highway Drama of Cops and Naked Actors', *Trinidad Guardian* (26 July 1983), 21.
7. Mervyn Morris, 'Folk Theatre as Fine Art', *The Daily Gleaner* (20 Apr. 1971), 24.
8. Harry Milner, 'Two Theatrical Treats', *The Sunday Gleaner* (25 Apr. 1971), 5, 8. Milner had surveyed Walcott's plays in 'Masterly Work', *The Daily Gleaner* (2 Apr. 1971), 6.

9. R. R., 'Merry-Go-Round', *The Daily Gleaner* (27 Apr. 1971); Stella, 'Partyline', *The Star* (24 Apr. 1971), 10.

10. Mervyn Morris, 'A vision betrayed', *The Daily Gleaner* (28 Apr. 1971), 22.

11. Harry Milner, 'Makak's Nightmare', *The Sunday Gleaner* (2 May 1971), 4.

12. Lloyd Coke, 'Walcott's Mad Innocents', *Savacou*, 5 (June 1971), 121–24.

13. Michael Manley to Derek Walcott (12 May 1971), Walcott Collection, University of the West Indies, St Augustine.

14. 'Behind-the-Bridge Play to Get World Audience', *Trinidad Guardian* (26 May 1971); '"Dream" at Tapia House Moonlight Theatre', *Tapia*, 17 (27 June 1971). On the same page is Walcott's uncollected 'Poem' ('Why do I Imagine the Death of Mandelstam').

15. Clyde Hosein, 'The Creative Man's Two Worlds', *Trinidad Guardian* (21 Apr. 1971), 6; Clyde Hosein, 'Actors Define Theatre Problems', *Trinidad Guardian* (9 June 1971), 6; Clyde Hosein, 'Lack of Appreciation Drives One to Madness', *Trinidad Guardian* (10 June 1971), 6; Clyde Hosein, 'Stepping-up the Creative Drive', *Trinidad Guardian* (23 June 1971), 6, 8.

16. Therese Mills, 'Conversation with Derek Walcott', *Sunday Guardian* (20 June 1971), 10, 17.

17. 'Caribbean Works for Radio Series', *Trinidad Guardian* (31 July 1971), 9; 'Texaco Sponsors Radio Theatre' and 'The Plays and the Playwrights', *The Texaco Star* (13 Aug. 1971), 1.

18. Lists of Theatre Ten recordings for 1971 and 1972 and various newspaper advertisements and publicity releases from Judy Stone's files.

19. Derek Walcott, 'Superfluous Defence of a Revolutionary', *Express* (20 Aug. 1971), 4.

20. 'Weekend billing Start of New Lease for "Ti Jean"', *Trinidad Guardian* (21 Oct. 1971), 7; Dalton James, 'Ti-Jean and his Brothers: A Brilliant Effort But Why was Queen's Hall Half-filled?', *Express* (7 Nov. 1971), 16.

21. 'Hit Play Comes to Queen's Hall', *Express* (13 Oct. 1971), 13; Derek Walcott, 'Conscience of a Revolutionary', *Express* (24 Oct. 1971), 22–4; '"In A Fine Castle" may be in for it', *Express* (30 Oct. 1971).

22. Eric Roach, 'Walcott Makes Fine Castle of Hate, Fear', *Trinidad Guardian* (1 Nov. 1971), 6; Earl Augustus, 'In A Fine Castle', *Express* (7 Nov. 1971), 17, 30.

23. Anson Gonzalez, 'In A Fine Castle', *Embryo*, 4/4, 2–3.

24. Syl Lowhar, 'Another Station of the Cross', *Tapia*, 23 (26 Dec. 1971), 19. Albert Gomes was a leading trade unionist activist of the late 1930s who by the 1950s became Minister of Labour and then Chief Minister. Brutally attacked by Eric Williams' followers he fled to England in 1962 after the failure of the West Indian Federation. His creative writing is discussed in Reinhard Sander's *The Trinidad Awakening: West Indian Literature of the Nineteen-Thirties* (New York: Greenwood Press, 1988), 71–89.

25. Denis Solomon, 'Can Walcott Deal with the Poor of our Society?', *Express* (4 Jan. 1972), 9, 12; (5 Jan. 1972), 9.

1972

Ti-Jean in Central Park
Astor Johnson
Theatre Fifteen
Pieces One

9

WHILE the controversy concerning *In A Fine Castle*, like most disputes which claim to represent an authentic popularist nativism against an alien sophistication, was misleading, there was the underlying problem that Walcott's plays, the Trinidad Theatre Workshop, and many Caribbean artists and arts were larger than the local cultural marketplace. Anyone familiar with the history and economics of modern Caribbean popular music will recognize the problem. A musician or group will create a new musical style by fusing various local and contemporary foreign characteristics, lack good local recording studios and places in which to play, go abroad to record and work, have an international hit, and then become popular at home; as the group tries to remain interesting and moves on to new instrumentation, harmonies, and more contemporary rhythms, it will be accused of selling out to foreign tastes. This happens with each generation. All art is transnational: today's traditions were yesterday's intercultural fusions.[1]

Although Walcott had avoided refocusing of his plays and drama company on the American and British theatre market, there was still a necessary dependency on recognition and financial support from abroad. Only the West Indies, as a region (the abandoned West Indian Federation), provided a large enough audience and economic basis for his equivalent of a national theatre company. Like popular reggae and zouk groups Walcott wanted international professional standards of performance and production. Unlike such groups his material and the style he created remained uncompromisingly rooted in the Caribbean, while theatre, unlike music and dance, is limited by its language to a more narrow audience. Thus there was often a contradiction, with resulting disappointments, when his plays were produced or his actors worked in the United States.

The 1969 O'Neill production of *Dream on Monkey Mountain* brought Walcott into contact with Lloyd Richards, head of Drama at New York University, who asked him to produce a version of *Ti-Jean* for the School of Drama. Richards in turn brought Walcott to the attention of Joseph Papp who wanted Walcott to direct *Ti-Jean* at the Delacorte Theater in Central Park. With the Negro Ensemble Company's production of *Dream on Monkey Mountain* already a success and with the publicity from the NBC television version, it appeared that Walcott's personal dream of gaining international recognition for his theatre company was becoming a real possibility. Albert Laveau had already signed a contract with a New York agency to represent him as an actor and director in the United States and on 29 February Walcott discussed *Dream* and introduced excerpts from *Ti-Jean* on 'Black Journal' on WNET-13 in New York. So, while workshops and rehearsals continued in Port of Spain, there was excitement about the forthcoming New York production which would include two of the Workshop's actors and which might lead to further work in the United States for the company.[2]

Early in May Joseph Papp wrote to Laveau and Hamilton Parris saying that Actors' Equity Association had agreed that they could be hired to perform in his production of *Ti-Jean* at the Delacorte Theater in Central Park to be directed by Walcott. Rehearsals for the New York Shakespeare Company production of *Ti-Jean* began on 15 June with Albert Laveau in the triple role of Devil, Papa Bois and Planter and with Hamilton Parris as Frog. Joseph Papp also brought André Tanker to New York although as the music for *Ti-Jean* was Tanker's first attempt at composition and at that time he could not orchestrate, an American-based West Indian was hired to provide musical charts and make the idiom more American. *Ti-Jean* was performed at the Delacorte Theater, Central Park, 11–30 July and then toured the five boroughs 2–30 August. This was Papp's first production of a contemporary play and was probably the wrong choice for New York. Although textually sophisticated and suggestive of a rich variety of significances, its folk elements, dialect words and folk speech, French patois pronunciations, and the kind of children's story acting it in places requires, can make the play appear the opposite of urban sophistication, especially to the large 'mass' audience Papp was trying to reach.[3]

The Obie award to *Dream on Monkey Mountain* led to hopes that Walcott might be an outstanding black dramatist capable of appealing to American audiences. There are, however, great differences between West Indian and African-American culture; American theatre audiences and critics also are less habituated to complex dramatic language and non-linear narrative than audiences in London or, since the Theatre Workshop, Port of Spain. The minority youth in the five boroughs, who it was assumed were starved for black theatre, were especially puzzled by a densely written poetic play with its West Indian dialect, eastern Caribbean folklore, and an apparently non-revolutionary message.

The New York critics seemed baffled by Walcott's *Ti-Jean*, but were impressed by the two Trinidadian actors. Clive Barnes called Laveau a 'fine actor' but claimed that Walcott had not yet found himself as a dramatist. Barnes's review is an extremely convoluted example of an American theatre critic faced by the need to write about serious poetic drama from another culture and knowing that what he is seeing is somehow important, but hardly understanding any of it, making contradictory statements, and getting his facts wrong. Barnes's assumptions about the level of his own readership can be seen from such remarks as 'it is a fantasy with music rather than a musical' and Walcott writes plays 'full of hints and imagery'. That such an influential critic could make or break a play in New York, rather than leading theatre-goers to an understanding of what is significant, remains a crime against the arts in America. Barnes did, however, say Walcott had staged his play 'with finesse and imagination'.[4]

John Simon appears to have seen a radically different play from Barnes. He condescendingly wrote of its 'plain but good English' and absurdly of its relevant black parable 'inciting anti-white revolution' which is 'muddied by metaphysical speculations about the nature of evil and assorted literary allusions'. 'The writing is prosy in verse and prosaic even in prose: lacking in poetic imagination.' 'No symbol goes unexplained or, indeed, unre-explained.' Maybe Simon should have explained the play to Barnes who could in return have mentioned some of its complexities? Simon did say that Laveau and Parris were excellent actors, favourably contrasting their discipline and accomplishment to the 'non-Trinidadians'.[5]

Douglas Watt of the *Daily News* noted the colour, humour, and use of music and dance but found the play shapeless, annoyingly pathetic, and pretentious, and thought Walcott's staging indulgent. Laveau and Parris, however, were praised as superb actors. John Beaufort in *The Christian Science Monitor* praised 'the superb performance of Albert Laveau' for his ability to range from the 'satanically crafty' through the 'colonially haughty' to 'terrifying magnificence' in the three roles required of his part. While finding the play static and wordy, he called it musically and visually a 'treat'. Beaufort was also favourably impressed by the play for its 'special brand of poetry, wisdom, and humour', the blend of music and dance, and Walcott's 'sensitive ear for words and zest for irony'.[6]

William Raidy in the *Long Island Press* sang the praises of *Ti-Jean* as 'a folk fable set to fabulous, authentic music by André Tanker . . . a political parable . . . about the colonial sun setting reluctantly in the Caribbean skies'. Where Barnes and Simon seemed irritated by the verse and allegory, Raidy found 'magic', 'humour', 'warmth and whimsy', 'mysticism and carnival' in the combination of animals, people, and 'a strange borrowed eloquence that is right out of Shakespeare, Marlowe and Byron'. Albert Laveau 'is a brilliant performer'; Hamilton Parris is 'simply beautiful'.[7]

It is not surprising Walcott has commented that theatre criticism in the West Indies is often of a higher level and more serious as well as being better informed than in the United States. Barnes, for example, calls Walcott a native Trinidadian rather than St Lucian (the other reviewers got this right so there is no reason for Barnes to get it wrong), assumes that the play takes place in Haiti, and that voodoo is limited to Haiti. Barnes assumes that there is a complex message which Walcott has failed to make clear; Simon finds a message that is too simple for his taste. And, God forbid!, that anyone should write plays in verse with images and symbols and a non-linear narrative. I wonder what the London audiences of the verse plays of Tony Harrison and Steven Berkoff would make of such critics?

Walcott thought Albert Laveau an actor of international potential who should leave Trinidad to become a professional in the United States. Laveau (Walcott insisted on using the French La Veau as he did with Beddeau in place of Beddoe) was born in Trinidad in 1935 into a Roman Catholic family although his part French, part Negro father was an atheist who once kicked a priest out of the house. Albert's father was a machinist-seaman and machine-shop foreman who had only attended primary school but was a voracious reader. Albert's mother, who died when he was thirteen, was from a black Anglo-Saxon family from Tobago. They had a large family in which the children became interested in acting. Albert's sister Lynette now teaches theatre in Boston.

Laveau was one of the non-white actors who began to appear in the new theatre groups during the 1950s. Beginning in his teens in San Fernando he acted for ten years with the Carnegie Players. Moving to Port of Spain he performed with the Company of Players, where he met Errol Jones who introduced Laveau to Walcott. Although not one of the earliest Little Carib Theatre Workshop members, he, along with Jones, Marshall, and Reid, became one of the foundation members of the Trinidad Theatre Workshop who remained with it until the present. In 1961 he joined Lever Brothers West Indies, was sent by them to Zaire for eight months in 1969 to gain international management experience, returned as Production Manager, and by the early 1970s was being groomed to be the first black Trinidadian of Lever Brothers Board of Directors. Laveau had always studied as much as he could about acting, reading whatever he could find on the subject, practising at home and with others, trying to become complete, totally skilled, in the art. The temptation of becoming a professional actor was stronger than a career in business and Laveau abandoned a secure position to follow Walcott's vision of total commitment to the arts. He resigned from Lever Brothers to become a full-time actor and theatre director. Laveau is light-skinned, handsome, and a highly skilled actor, familiar with the various ways of creating a character. His stage presence is perhaps less characteristic of a Workshop actor than of a classical actor. In avoiding excess and perhaps aiming for understatement, he can at times appear too laid back and unengaged in a role, but, when he is inspired or the part requires it, can reach those heights of performance that other actors speak of as greatness.

When *Ti-Jean* was performed in New York, Laveau's acting impressed Joseph Papp who said that he could become a great black actor, a star, and offered to help him. Laveau returned to the United States, worked as a consultant to Papp and the Public Theatre, obtained an Equity card, but was only given permission to be a resident alien for each contract. He worked professionally with the Negro Ensemble Company, touring with the Broadway hit *River Niger*. He appeared in two television soap operas, taught at New York University and at the National Centre for Afro-American Artists, and directed at the Public Theatre and at the National Centre for Afro-American Artists annual show, *Boston Black Preacher*. He earned a living, sent money to his family, but he did not become suddenly famous and missed his wife in Trinidad. In the United States he was only considered for black roles and there were many good black actors available with whom he was competing. The jobs that he wanted did not necessarily go to the best actor; although some of the famous actors with whom he worked behaved unprofessionally they had the contacts, friends, and lovers necessary for a career. When Papp did audition him for a part in *Coriolanus* there was a feeling that his style did not mesh with the African-American actors: Laveau was lonely, regularly wrote to his wife, and looked forward to being able to resettle his family in New York. Judged by most standards he was a successful actor, and he could support himself; he had the looks, skills, and work in the theatre, but he lacked the driving ambition and toughness needed in America where acting was a profession not necessarily aimed at creating culturally significant drama.[8]

Laveau returned to Trinidad in late 1974, knowing he was of professional standard as an actor. He had worked alongside famous African-American actors and knew that he was more professional in his approach to the stage. But he had not acted on Broadway, and no longer believed he would become famous. He felt he was a professional actor, but in Trinidad there was still no full-time work in local theatre and wages with Walcott were erratic. After Walcott's resignation from the Theatre Workshop in 1976 Laveau began to lose interest in acting. He occasionally directed for others, taught drama for the Extra-Mural Department of the university, built sets, and worked as a master carpenter. When the TTW eventually did obtain a theatre much of the reconversion work was Laveau's and the first classes were offered by him.

While Walcott's attempt to make North Americans aware of his plays and of the Workshop was making progress, there was still the problem of how to translate the drama company he had built from part-time amateurs into paid professionals. During the spring the Workshop recorded for Radio Canada International *The Throne in an Autumn Room*, by the Trinidadian writer Lennox Brown. The cast included Errol Jones, Albert Laveau, Eunice Alleyne, Wilbert Holder, Judy Stone, and Nigel Scott. Radio Canada International, which is located in Montreal, made available to educational and religious radio stations a one-hour long playing disc (E 1024) of the play for non-commercial use. During May and early June when Walcott began workshopping *The Charlatan* without Albert Laveau and Errol Jones, Laveau started rehearsals of a possible stage production of *The Throne in an Autumn Room* with Errol Jones and Holder. The New York production of *Ti-Jean* brought both projects to a halt.[9]

The *Trinidad Guardian* announced in August that Derek Walcott's Theatre Workshop would present a series of plays sponsored by Trinidad-Tesoro in association with 610 Radio as part of the celebration of Trinidad's tenth year of independence and 610 Radio's fifteenth birthday. 'Theatre Fifteen' would consist of plays by 'local writers' and was part of Trinidad-Tesoro's support of the arts, which included sponsoring a drama group, the Trinidad-Tesoro Players, which normally participated in Carnival and Folk festivals. 'Theatre Fifteen' would consist of fifteen thirty-minute dramatic presentations to be heard on Sundays. Some of the plays would be performed in two or more segments over several weeks, The first would be *B. Wordsworth*; Ken Corsbie directed Judy Stone's adaptation of V. S. Naipaul's short story. This was Stone's own adaptation, although an earlier one-act version of *B. Wordsworth* had become a staple of West Indian drama.[10]

Other 'Theatre Fifteen' plays included an adaptation of Samuel Selvon's *Basement Lullaby*, a story about two Trinidadian musicians in London, which was performed along with Daniel Samaroo's *Taxi, Mister*, in which a taxi-driver tells his passengers how he fell for a confidence trick; Lennox Brown's *Wine in Winter* (directed by Laveau with Jones, Holder, and Noreen Bradford), concerning the conflicting emotions of a black American prisoner and a Barbadian police sergeant in a London prison; *My Brother's Keeper* (adapted by Judy Stone from a television script by Carmen Manley, daughter of the Jamaican Prime Minister), about the conflict between a college boy and his uneducated brother in a Jamaican village; Eric Roach's *Calabash of Blood* (directed by Claude Reid with Arnold Rampersad, Errol Jones, Ermine Wright, Stanley Marshall, and Judy Stone), a rather violent mixture of slavery, lust, voodoo, injustice, and deaths set before emancipation; E. K. Brathwaite's *Odale's Choice* (directed by Ken Corsbie); Walcott's *Henri Christophe*; Walcott's *Jourmard*; Mustapha Matura's *As Time Goes By*; and *The Rape of Fair Helen* by the St Lucian dramatist Stanley French.

After discussing the series with Walcott, Judy Stone was in charge of liaison with the studio, selection of the scripts, adapters, directors, casts, and payments and royalties. She adapted five of the scripts for radio, and Helen Camps adapted three. Stone was also the typist, kept records of who should be paid, and directed two of the plays. Walcott, Holder, Marshall, Nigel Scott, and Ken Corsbie, the Guyanese director and actor who lived in Barbados, directed the other plays.

Twenty-four members of the TTW participated in the series along with five outsiders. All members of the Workshop, except Walcott and Helen Camps, had acting roles. Errol Jones was a principal actor in seven half-hour segments, followed by three each for Albert Laveau and Arnold Rampersad. Jerline Quamina twice had principal roles and four supporting parts. Ermine Wright had two principal roles and three supporting parts as did Stanley Marshall, Nigel Scott, and Judy Stone. Claude Reid was paid for two-and-a-half principal roles and two supporting roles. Recording and broadcasting started late July.

Each thirty-minute segment had a total budget of $500 for royalties, adapters' fees, actors, director, and cost of typing. Workshop members were required to pay ten per cent of their earnings to the Workshop which acted as their agent. The money was used for further productions and in the hope of some day obtaining a theatre for the Workshop. Usually the author was paid a royalty of $120 for the half-hour segment, which included the right to one optional rebroadcast. The director earned seventy dollars and, depending upon the size of the cast, the principal actors would earn about seventy dollars. When two plays were performed in one night, such as Selvon's *Basement Lullaby* and Samaroo's *Taxi, Mister,* the payments were halved. While the sums were small they could add up; for the half programme that used *Taxi, Mister,* Holder earned thirty dollars as adapter, thirty-five dollars as director, another thirty-five dollars as the sole actor, and was paid $5.60 for providing scripts. He earned a further thirty-five dollars for directing the Selvon story which made up the other half of the thirty-minute segment. So he earned in all about one hundred and forty dollars for the show.[11]

As so often in Trinidad there were various problems ranging from bad studio conditions, and undelivered and unanswered letters, to late payment. Judy Stone failing to reply to Lennox Brown's agent later apologized to Brown that their Treasurer had still not paid fees; 'It's my British up-bringing, West Indians always say English girls say nothing but "I'm so sorry", even in bed.' She also had to reject some of Brown's plays and ideas for plays by Africans and African Americans. Plays had to have West Indian subject matter. The sponsor would not accept plays written by a West Indian with 'universal' themes unless the Workshop could disguise them by 'localising' the dialogue. For the next season they were hoping to use one of Brown's plays with a Belmont setting. Would Brown be willing to write a play on a $120 commission if it could be arranged? Brown replied by sending some of the scripts he had been writing since 1966. Commenting upon

Albert Laveau's success in New York, Brown felt that West Indian actors would only get the exposure they deserved if black drama got beyond 'Hate Whitey' themes. Universal themes were necessary as there is more to life than hate. Brown liked the idea of 'localising' his plays. He felt frustrated as a West Indian that his plays were produced in Canada and the United States but not in the Caribbean. Too much was lost in 'translation'. He needed the response more than the money. He also thought that the Canadian plays would provide roles for Judy and Nigel Scott. Knowing what it is like to be denied a chance to act because of skin colour in North America, he wanted to offer the white members of the Workshop more than bit parts; Trinidad is a multiracial society and while blacks are still culturally discriminated against the theatre should transcend such stupidities.[12]

By October Selvon had not yet been paid his sixty Trinidadian dollars (about US $30 at the time) and wrote an amusing letter in dialect grumbling about the small fee and wanting to be paid up front before 'funds run low' or people forget to pay.[13]

The Trinidad Theatre Workshop was not invited to Carifesta in Guyana, 25 August–15 September, but Lennox Brown was; he wrote to Stone that he was given a half-day's notice to prepare for a six-week trip. The Workshop had a new project to record six plays for stereo radio and had already recorded an act and a half of Brown's *Song of a Spear*, but the stereo facilities at Radio 610 were proving to be too primitive and limited for recording a series for international use. The studio was also seldom free when the actors were. There was talk of recording twenty plays on non-stereo along with six plays on stereo the coming season, but Judy Stone thought that stereo would be impossible unless they could use another studio.

As usual Walcott and the Workshop seemed bigger than what Trinidad and the West Indies could offer in the way of opportunities. The arts in Trinidad were modernizing themselves much more rapidly than the commercial side of society that might have made the arts economically profitable. The neocolonial is when a society depends on jobs with the government and local branches of foreign corporations rather than producing its own entrepreneurial class. At the time Walcott was the only significant entrepreneur in the arts. Too much money was going into such events as Carifesta and Best Village competitions rather than helping artists become professionals and creating the conditions from which they might become economically independent. A similar pattern would be observable later when Trinidadian Soca became a Caribbean and worldwide dance fashion, but there were no good recording studios for the purpose in Trinidad, as there were in Barbados and Jamaica, and success meant recording abroad and usually went to non-Trinidadian bands.

An attempt was made to sell the various 610 Radio transcriptions to other radio stations in the West Indies and in parts of the Commonwealth. In all there were twenty plays available, but nothing much came of it as Caribbean radio and television stations are usually short of money and reluctant to pay for local arts. Lennox Brown thought they might sell to Canada. Writing to Judy Stone about the possibility of selling the Theatre Fifteen series to Canadian Radio, or preparing new programmes, Brown pointed out that a North American budget for an hour show was about $5,000, not TT $500. The TTW should ask a minimum of TT $7,000 (US $3,500); otherwise its programmes would not be taken seriously and it would be underselling itself. Several of the plays were rebroadcast during 1974–6 on Radio 610 as part of 'Sunday Theatre'. My own attempt to trace the subsequent history of the series ended with the attempted Jasmaat-al-Muslimeen *coup d'état* during July 1990, when the radio station, which kept broadcasting in defiance of the coup, was set afire. I never returned to see whether any files or recordings concerning the Trinidad Theatre Workshop were saved.[14]

While Walcott's original problem of how to earn a living as a professional from West Indian theatre had become more complicated with the development of the Workshop into a semi-professional acting company and his responsibility towards others, radio and television were not a solution. There were odd jobs, but no way of regularly supporting Walcott and a core of actors. About once a year Trinidad and Tobago Television produced a Walcott play. On 12 December TTT taped a forty-minute version of *Malcochon* with Hamilton Parris as Chantal, Errol Jones as the Old Man, and Stanley Marshall as the Mute. Walcott worked closely with the production, advising on every shot. Radio and television gave the Workshop actors some money and a feeling of making progress in their attempt to shape careers from the theatre, but local conditions could not support the serious art theatre they wanted. Trinidad was too small for what Walcott had created.[15]

During August the *Express* republished an interview from the New York *Daily News* which quoted Walcott as presently revising *Franklin* and *The Charlatan* and working on a film script of *In A Fine Castle*. Walcott had for some time been wanting to write for cinema. He had worked on a script for *A Flag on the Island*, and, according to friends, often had a film script in his pocket. Apparently towards the end of 1972, Walcott was commissioned by Dino De Laurentiis to write a script for a proposed film about the life of Jesus Christ. Over the years there would be a number of such projects, including a few television films that were made by Walcott's friends, but none of the major film projects got beyond scripts.[16]

Besides the New York *Ti-Jean* and the attempt to find means of supporting the Workshop actors through radio and television, the other main event of 1972 was the relationship that developed between the Workshop and the dancer choreographer Astor Johnson. This rapidly made a substantial contribution to how the Workshop and Walcott's plays developed during the next five years. Johnson, who had joined the Workshop during the Basement Theatre period, was the original Basil in *Dream on Monkey Mountain* before the role was enlarged for Albert Laveau. Although Johnson appeared to lack energy, Walcott encouraged him to form his own dance company. During April 1972 Astor Johnson's Repertory Dance Theatre began with workshops at Government Training College and a lecture demonstration at Town Hall. Ever since Walcott's first meeting with Beryl McBurnie at Arts Workshop at the University College of the West Indies, Jamaica, he had been influenced in his concept of a West Indian acting style by West Indian dance; he saw dance as part of the total theatre he wanted. Astor Johnson was in terms of dance style the next phase beyond McBurnie's modernization of folk-dance. If Katherine Dunham's 'primitive' style was part of the 1940 reassertion of cultural folk roots which McBurnie developed in her own way in Trinidad, Johnson integrated the Trinidadian heritage, especially the black heritage, into more recent developments in modern dance. Although his emphasis was on black culture he also drew on other parts of the Trinidadian dance heritage such as Spanish dances and British ballet.

Johnson's aims were similar to Walcott's. Both wanted to bring Trinidadian arts up to international standards of performance and create a contemporary idiom for local culture. Although Johnson's achievement was less seminal than McBurnie's and less full than Walcott's, he remains a lasting influence on Trinidadian modern dance. Many of those who worked with him are now well-known dancers; there is usually an annual performance of his dances at Queen's Hall. Despite their shortness by modern standards and some period clichés of supposedly African-influenced dance, his work remains powerful. Like Walcott, Johnson assumed that the folk traditions would ossify unless infused with contemporary idioms. In terms of Trinidadian dance styles his works had more narrative than McBurnie's, and were not as abstract as those later developed by Noble Douglas and Carol La Chapelle.[17]

During August Astor Johnson's Repertory Dance Theatre staged an experimental programme at Town Hall and then in November presented *Da'aga* in San Fernando. This was its first season. *Da'aga* included 'Spanish Trio', 'Victim', 'House of the Lord' and such Johnson classics as 'For Better or for Worse', 'Defiant Era' and 'Fusion', which are still performed in Trinidad. Walcott had been following the progress of the company and his notes include the remark that 'Repertory' and 'Theatre' were ambiguous and off-putting. A simpler more appealing name was needed.[18]

Walcott's role in the recognition of Johnson and the RDT is clearly expressed in Johnson's article 'Two Years of Steady Progress' :

it was at the last performance of our season in November 1972 that our luck turned. After playing to empty halls for six consecutive performances, we were performing our seventh performance at the UWI hall St Augustine to about forty people, when Derek Walcott saw us and generously decided to do a joint production, 'Pieces 1' at Bishop Anstey, in December that same year. Since then the Company has not looked back. As a matter of fact 'Pieces 1' has been a milestone in Trinidad theatre since it was a glowing demonstration of how badly our artistes need each other that we are all seeking the same ideals only through varying modes of expression.[19]

On 8 and 9 December the Trinidad Theatre Workshop joined forces with the Repertory Dance Theatre in *Pieces One*. The event was sponsored by the TTW and performed in the auditorium of Bishop Anstey school. The idea was to combine the two companies for an evening of theatre and dance with some of the actors and dancers appearing in both. Adele Bynoe was already a member of both companies. The programme also allowed the TTW to present some shorter non-Walcottian plays. This was intended as a future regular event, hence the *One* in the title. The main dramatic work was Neville de La Bastide's short play *One for the Road*, directed by Walcott. There were also two dramatic sketches. De La Bastide is a Trinidadian school teacher and his play had been around for a while in the Caribbean Plays series. He was paid a thirty dollar royalty fee for the two evenings.

Walcott introduced *Pieces One* to the public with an article in the *Trinidad Guardian* calling Astor Johnson the 'most imaginative' Trinidadian choreographer since McBurnie. As he concentrates on dancing and not on promotion, Johnson has, however, had poor audiences of less than a hundred. He will need to 'hustle and hard-sell

like everybody else'. The arts in Trinidad require advertising, interviewing, and 'begging'. This is a young, fresh company both in age
and in having been trained elsewhere. Johnson blends modern American with ethnic dance and uses 'intricacies of pattern and statement'.
He also has brought his dancers close to acting. He shows how
Trinidadians can fuse dance and drama without using the American
musical as a model. Johnson's pursuit of his private vision may antago-
nize those followers of folk-dance, but folk forms 'freeze and become
repetitive'. Audiences are jaded with the monotony of folk-dance.
Johnson brings a new approach to the folk tradition. As the Repertory Dance Theatre has been neglected so far by the public, the
TTW, for whom Johnson teaches movement, will present a joint
programme.[20]

Jeremy Taylor described the evening as a perfect blend of music
and dance. Both companies have a similar seriousness of purpose,
similar aims including high standards. 'Dance melted into drama and
word into movement' naturally. The programme was carefully constructed, varied, and moved forward rapidly. The Repertory Dance
Company fitted better onto the small stage of Bishop Anstey school,
on which they could establish the right atmosphere, than the large
stage of Queen's Hall. The dances now had a firmer shape than before
and were precise and energetic with a controlled tension. The TTW
was good to watch with an ability to tread the line between reality and
absurdity.[21]

The poet-dramatist Eric Roach, who often appeared to be carrying
on an argument with Walcott about the aesthetics of West Indian art,
liked *Pieces* for its folk and African qualities and recommended that it
be taken on tour of the villages. *Pieces* was 'creole marrow' mixing
laughter with the tears of frustration and despair. *One for the Road*
treats of the real world of small wasted lives in slums. Johnson's amusing
dance-mime comedy 'For Better or for Worse' has been lengthened
and deepened by folk-dancing. His dancers are better trained than
others in Port of Spain and he is intelligent. He feels like the 'man we
have been waiting for since Beryl McBurnie'. 'Fusion' strikes fire with
its superimposition of jazz styles on African movements. It is physically exhilarating. But he should have put the drummer on stage as in
Africa the drummer is part of the dance.[22]

Walcott and Johnson might be said to have progressed beyond the
cultural nationalist's creative use of the past to a more complex view
in which local culture is treated in modernist forms. Both McBurnie
and Johnson (like Walcott) can be seen as phases of cultural nationalism

and modernization, but in the second phase the folk and primitive elements have already become assimilated (as in Walcott's *Sea at Dauphin*), now seem dated, and there is a need once more to modernize (as in *Dream*), with more attention to contemporary fashions, forms, and standards. This is possible because a local tradition of modern art has already been established. Basically all culture is transnational, cross-cultural, partaking of 'here' in all its variety, and 'there' in its many aspects. McBurnie's modern folk-dance would have been impossible without the many kinds of dancing she found in the West Indies, and without kinds of modern dance she found abroad. Johnson was remixing the elements, bringing them up to date, working towards more sustained forms. To understand the continual arguments between Walcott and his nationalist or 'black' critics, we need to see that his own work thrived on the tensions between 'here' and 'there', and that his development as a dramatist, leader of the TTW, and even theatre director, is parallel to the three periods of Trinidadian dance represented by McBurnie, Johnson, and soon by La Chapelle-Douglas. Having taken a dance company under the wings of the Theatre Workshop, Walcott would increasingly make use of dance in his plays, train dancers to act, and eventually form the Trinidad Theatre Workshop Dance Company, making the TTW into an equivalent of a national theatre with its own theatre and dance companies. This could be seen as healing the fracture between theatre and dance which occurred when McBurnie banned the Theatre Workshop from using the Little Carib Theatre in 1965.

Considering Astor Johnson's reputation in Trinidad since his death in 1985 it is shocking to realize that he might have sunk without a trace in 1972 if Walcott had not recognized his talents, seen similar aesthetic aims, and used his own reputation and that of the TTW to give Johnson's Repertory Dance Theatre a boost in public. Without the publicity of *Pieces One* Johnson might have remained largely ignored.

Dream on Monkey Mountain made Walcott one of the better-known 'black' dramatists, but as can be seen by the New York reviews of *Ti-Jean*, by Eric Roach's attitudes towards Astor Johnson's Repertory Dance Theatre, and by some of the remarks I have cited from Lennox Brown's letters to Judy Stone, 'blackness' and 'folk' were limiting the development of modern West Indian culture. Walcott had known that from the start. Being half white, being a modernist and someone with respect for the techniques and standards of great art, his desire to put Caribbean society on the world's cultural map using a blend of European and local art forms kept running into opposition by those, white and black, Americans and Trinidadians, who knew what 'blacks' or 'West Indians' should be writing and thinking. Walcott's view of the West Indies as a multiracial-multicultural society was soon tested in productions of *The Charlatan* and *Franklin*, two plays with central roles for white members of the Workshop.

Meanwhile, the Royal Shakespeare Company had been thinking about producing Tirso de Molina's *El Burlado de Sevilla* and commissioned Walcott to translate the play into modern verse. The commission had an unexpected effect on the Workshop's future and Walcott's life.

NOTES

1. The problems and contradictions of 'identity' within Caribbean popular music are discussed by Jocelyne Guilbaut, *Zouk: World Music in the West Indies* (Chicago: University of Chicago Press, 1993). The artificiality of such distinctions as authentically traditional versus the alien modern are shown in Akin Euba, *Essays on Music in Africa 2: Intercultural Perspectives* (Bayreuth African Studies 16, 1989), and Akin Euba, *Yoruba Drumming: The Dundun Tradition* (Bayreuth African Studies 21/22, 1990).

2. Sidney Fields, 'A Gift for Words', *Daily News* [New York] (20 Jane 1972), 68, repub. as '"Another Life" coming', *Express* (22 Aug. 1972), 24; Letter by Bruce Savan of the Agency for the Performing Arts (11 Jan. 1972), concerning Albert Laveau's request for resident alien status; 'Future Fan?', *The New York Times* (27 Feb. 1972), D 17.

3. Joseph Papp's letter (2 May 1972) to 'Albert LaVeau c/o Walcott' on New York Shakespeare Festival stationery is in Laveau's files.

4. Clive Barnes, 'Walcott's "Ti-Jean" Opens in Park', *The New York Times* (28 July 1972), 20.

5. John Simon, 'Theatre: Debilitated Debbil', *New York Magazine* (14 Aug. 1972), 69.

6. Douglas Watt, '"Ti-Jean & Brothers" Comes to Central Park', *Daily News* (28 July 1972), 57; John Beaufort, ' "Ti-Jean" as told by Frog; Trinidad Play in Central Park', *The Christian Science Monitor* (31 July 1972), 7.

7. William A. Raidy, 'Exhilarating and Free!', *Long Island Press*, (27 July 1972), 16.

8. William Doyle-Marshall, 'Albert Le Veau Still Dreams of Pro Theatre', *People* (Oct. 1978), 49–51; Judy Stone, 'Albert Laveau: One of the Finest TT Actors', *Trinidad Guardian* (1 May 1989), 11; Laveau's answers to a questionnaire, his résumé, his trunk of personal letters, pay slips, various interviews with Laveau, Lynette Laveau, and other Workshop actors.

9. Information about plans to stage Brown's *Throne* and Walcott's *The Charlatan* is in a letter from Judy Stone to Lennox Brown (7 Aug. 1972).

10. 'Workshop to present Theatre 15', *Trinidad Guardian* (1 Aug. 1972), 4; 'Local writers featured on the air', *Express* (27 July 1972), 12. A newspaper

advertisement incorrectly describes the director of *B. Wordsworth* as Stanley Marshall. Judy Stone informs me that Corsbie was the director (letter, Feb. 1994).

11. Documents in Judy Stone's files and the Walcott Collection, University of the West Indies, St Augustine.

12. Judy Stone to Lennox Brown (7 Aug. 1972); Lennox Brown (Toronto) to Judy Stone (21 Aug. 1972).

13. Samuel Selvon (c/o Ismith Khan, Del Mar, California) to Judy Stone (1 Oct. 1972).

14. Lennox Brown (Toronto) to Judy Stone (2 Oct. 1972); Lennox Brown (Toronto) to Judy Stone (21 Oct. 1972). Some rebroadcasts are mentioned in Irma Goldstraw's *Bibliography* under 'Published Plays by Derek Walcott', 55–72.

15. Information about TTT filming of *Malcochon* from Judy Stone (Feb. 1994).

16. Sidney Fields, op. cit.; Judy Stone, 'Walcott's "Joker" returns after 12 years', *Trinidad Guardian* (30 Dec. 1987), 10. Information about Walcott's film scripts comes from remarks made by friends, brief comments in published interviews and newspaper reviews, and other sources which while reliable may be inaccurate as to the precise year, especially as some of the scripts were worked on over several years.

17. Comments on modern West Indian dance are based on discussions with Noble Douglas, Norline Metivier and, especially, Carol La Chapelle.

18. Walcott's notes on the RDT are in the Walcott Collection, University of the West Indies, St Augustine.

19. Astor Johnson, 'Two Years of Steady Progress', *The Repertory Dance Theatre*, 8–page publicity programme printed for the August 1974 season, p. 7.

20. Derek Walcott, 'Mixing the Dance and Drama', *Trinidad Guardian* (6 Dec. 1972), 4.

21. Jeremy Taylor, 'Perfect Blend of Music and Dance', *Express* (16 Dec. 1972), 9, 10.

22. Eric Roach, '. . . of Creole T'dad's Dance and Drama', *Trinidad Guardian* (12 Dec. 1972), 3.

10

The Second Season

Franklin

The Charlatan

WHEREAS a decade, or even five years, earlier the story of Walcott's attempt to build a national theatre company was straightforward, by 1973 trying to follow Walcott, the Trinidad Theatre Workshop, its actors, and its relationship to Johnson's Repertory Dance Theatre is rather like keeping track of a many-ringed circus. At one point, during May, Walcott was in Jamaica arranging for a forthcoming tour of the Workshop, trying to plan an adaptation of Daniel Berrigan's poems into a musical show, telephoning London about his translation, and flying between North America and the islands, so that long letters in the Walcott archives at the University of the West Indies were written on 8 May in the morning in Jamaica and in the evening in Trinidad. His translation of Tirso de Molina's *El Burlador de Sevilla* was rapidly turning into a completely different play, the first important new play he had written in years.

During January a casting sheet and rehearsal schedule gave each member assignments for the year. Four plays were listed—Walcott's *Franklin*, *The Charlatan* and *Malcochon* (which was not performed) and Edward Kamau Brathwaite's *Odale's Choice*. Errol Jones was cast as Charbon in *Franklin*, Elias in *Charlatan* and alternating Chantal in *Malcochon*. Hamilton Parris would be Fagette in *Franklin*, Dr Voltaire in *Charlatan* and part of the crew for *Odale's Choice*. Claude Reid was Morris in *Franklin*, Cobo in *Charlatan*, on the crew of *Odale's Choice* and alternated Chantal and the Nephew in *Malcochon*.

There had not been another fully planned 'season' since the

Workshop lost the Basement Theatre. It was hoped to have a second season which would include the Repertory Dance Theatre and a summer tour. Rehearsals would be held either at Bishop Anstey High School or Walcott's house and would begin on Tuesday, 9 January, with at one end of the hall a run-through of Act I of *Franklin* while at the other end of the hall there would be readings from and casting of *Odale's Choice*. The next night there would be readings from and blocking of Act II of *Franklin*. Thursday the first act and prologue of *The Charlatan* would be read. On Friday parts of *The Charlatan* would be read and blocked, while there would be blocking for *Odale's Choice* at the other end of the hall. Saturday should be used for learning lines. Sunday would be a complete run-through of Act I of *Franklin*. Monday should be used for learning scripts with Tuesday devoted to a run through of Act I of *Charlatan* and blocking of *Odale's Choice*. Weekly schedules were given out; scripts were bound with the opposite side of each page blank for re-rewrites, inserts, and blocking.[1]

Trinidad, like most of the the West Indies, had experienced continuing political unrest. The 1970 model was American Black Power, the model was now Castro and Che. In the hills beyond Port of Spain there was a guerrilla movement linked with the university. The details are unclear, except that a war between the police and the guerrillas took place without much publicity beyond the occasional report of a death. V. S. Naipaul's novel *Guerrillas* combines the 1970 riots with the 1973 situation in his allusions to mysterious guerrillas in the hills. Many of the guerrillas were students, children of the well-off; some among the university and arts community, including at least one member of the TTW, provided 'safe' houses and other support. Theatre criticism was often political and radicalized, with reviewers likely to lecture a dramatist. Victor Questel, who later became one of the best critics of Walcott's work, attacked Walcott in *Tapia* as elitist, having a martyr complex, pretending to be a poor black, unwilling to make use of the African past and, as a consequence, not being the kind of director that Trinidad needed. While Questel avoids the simplicities of people's revolution, back-to-Africanism, and Black Power, it is clear that he feels they are closer to what is needed than Walcott's complexities, heightened sense of individualism, and dedication to his art. Walcott had recently been awarded a D. Litt. from the University of the West Indies, Mona, for his contribution to poetry, drama, and criticism; and the manuscripts and sketchbooks for his plays were displayed at branches of the University's library. Allusions in the essay to Walcott's honorary doctorate suggest that this may have been the irritant that occasioned Questel's remarks. Many similar articles appeared during 1973.[2]

While the Workshop recorded in March a two-hour version of *In A Fine Castle* for the Canadian Broadcasting Corporation, which Peter Donkin produced with Judy Stone replacing Helen Camps as Clodia, the 610 Radio series ran into problems as it proved too expensive to find sponsors, and sales to the other islands were not successful. Plans by Radio 610 to build a drama studio were abandoned. Fees and royalties were not paid to the TTW and no one was certain what they would earn. Lennox Brown wrote from Canada asking for the royalties for *Song of a Spear* only to be told that the show not yet been aired and no one knew when it would be.[3]

April saw the second 'season', an attempt to have several weeks of continuous planned theatrical productions. Therese Mills described the new attempt to have a season as 'an experiment in courage'. No Trinidadian company had attempted such a long run. Until now four nights were thought the most possible for the potential audience which had been calculated as a maximum of two thousand. *Dream* and *Moon on a Rainbow Shawl* had run for four nights. *Franklin* would run for eight nights. Walcott felt the Workshop could perform for three or four months if it had a theatre. The company already had a repertory of six plays which could be staged if it had a permanent theatre instead of having to build new sets every time. The Workshop needed a subsidy of $5,000 as working capital for a season. There should be support from both the state and the business community.[4]

The second season ran from 14 April to 29 April at Bishop Anstey High School Auditorium and consisted of Walcott's new script for *Franklin, A Tale from the Islands*, 14–21 April, and *Pieces Two*, 25–29 April, a follow-up of the Astor Johnson–TTW *Pieces One* of 1972. Advertisements said that the TTW and the Repertory Dance Theatre 'fuse again' and Eric Roach is quoted as saying that Johnson 'is the man we have been waiting for since Beryl McBurnie'. While Walcott's short 'Overture' in the programme speaks of a crew of over fifty being combined from the two companies for the second season, he also says 'the Trinidadian artist continues to mine one resource, himself'.

Franklin began as a one-act play during Walcott's undergraduate days at UCWI and had been staged in Guyana. Set in St Lucia in the late 1940s, *Franklin*, along with *The Charlatan*, requires some white actors and is concerned with the multiracial and multicultural composition of the West Indies. Some themes and incidents in *Franklin* recur in *Pantomime*. Franklin is a retired English schooner captain who struggles to become accepted by the villagers on a small island. Walcott had predicted that there would be a reaction to any West Indian play with a central white character. He defended his subject by saying that whites are a minority in the Caribbean and writers concern themselves with minorities. A man who earns his right to settle in a place has earned it regardless of his colour. But 'the price that he pays to possess the place he lives in, is too often a total one—that of dispossession'.[5]

Walcott composed a paragraph introduction to *Franklin*, 'The Lengthened Shadow of a Man', which appears in the programme and was later used elsewhere. Franklin is seen as man alone, stripped, a Crusoe facing a new beginning, someone who turns his back on Europe and the Empire and casts his lot with the Fridays of the village. The use of Crusoe as a figure for the possibilities of the New World is often found in Walcott's poetry at this time. The cast included Christen Krogh as Franklin and Laurence Goldstraw as Major Willoughby, along with Hamilton Parris, Noreen Bradford, Claude Reid, Ermine Wright, Errol Jones, and Stanley Marshall. This was Krogh's first performance with the Workshop, although he often performed with the Point à Pierre Players in the south. Krogh is sometimes said to be an example of Walcott's seeing an actor's potential and bringing it to a much higher level than others expected. This was also the first time Goldstraw, who was married to Billie Pilgrim, appeared with the TTW. The others were TTW regulars, Bradford, one of the few Asian Indians, having been on the Jamaica tour two years previously. She would eventually emigrate to England where she is active in women's theatre.

The dramatist Eric Roach negatively reviewed *Franklin* in a barely disguised attack on Walcott. Like other attacks during this period, usually coming from a black nationalist or 'people' position, Roach's writing is difficult to précis as there are more attitudes than linked thoughts. Roach says that Walcott's plays are more appreciated abroad than at home because of 'their peculiar pitch in today's frantic orchestration of race and colour'. If Walcott has not 'managed to strike a very responsive chord from native and home audiences' he has received 'kudos' in the 'off beat theatre of "experimentalism" in North America' where the mixture of West Indian situations, language, and music is exotic to 'the North American theatre avant garde'. *Franklin* is about the dissolution of Empire and the groundswell of the subject races. Franklin's dispossession of Charbon is 'symbolic of the whole African uprooting, abandonment and disgrace on the islands and the conflict between the two men is personal, racial and historical'. Walcott concludes the play by giving the white man hope. While the actors do not disappoint, they are flat as if they had not 'realised' the characters. 'Race' may be the source of this lack of realization.[6]

Walcott replied to Roach with 'Why This Astigmatism towards the Workshop's White Actors?' in which he pointed out that Roach had previously reviewed *In A Fine Castle* without mentioning one of its principal actors, Nigel Scott. Now Roach reviewed *Franklin* without mentioning Christen Krogh, the actor playing the central character. This is like reviewing *Belle Fanto* or *Hamlet* without commenting upon the performance of the person playing Belle or Hamlet. In reply to Roach's remarks about 'off-beat' theatres, Walcott cites a list of productions ranging from the Shakespeare Festival in Central Park to the Canadian Broadcasting Corporation and expresses amazement that they are regarded as 'off beat'. 'I don't know what is Mr. Roach's beat, but if it's native, thank God, I don't dance to it.'[7]

In *Tapia* Denis Solomon's review of *Franklin* began by pointing out that Walcott is a university-educated mulatto and that is part of being West Indian. Critics are absurd to regret that he writes plays out of his own experience instead of what they say society 'needs'. *Franklin* courts the ire of racially militant critics by being about racial conflict and refusing 'to assign blame unequivocally'. The motives in the play are complex. Does Maria, the Indian girl Franklin marries, kill herself because she is being used or because she is pregnant with the child of a black man? There is a parallel to the drowning of Franklin's first, white, wife. Walcott is using the manner of a naturalistic play, but his means of expression is poetic. In *Dream*, *Ti-Jean*, *Castle*, and *Franklin* Walcott has created 'a body of work as complete and as immediately related to our contemporary situation as any society could hope to have. The virulence of the critical commentary they have aroused is alone a sufficient testimony to this.'[8]

The second season ended with *Pieces Two*, consisting of Edward Kamau Brathwaite's *Odale's Choice* (a short play based on the Antigone story), dramatized readings of passages from Brathwaite's long poem *Rights of Passage* and three numbers by the Repertory Dance Theatre. In the *Trinidad Guardian* Walcott explained the theatrical possibilities of *Rights of Passage*, and commented on its many voices, its musicality, and the way the music comes out of the speech itself. Besides 'Fusion', Johnson's most exciting work which is still being performed in Trinidad, his dance company again offered 'Defiant Era', a longer work, based on the Haitian revolution. *Odale's Choice* was directed by Malcolm

Jones and featured younger members of the Workshop. Eric Roach's review grudgingly praised the drumming and the African links in the dancing and choreography, but otherwise was reserved. In *Rights of Passage* the speakers were said to lack competence in oratory, and to be ill at ease with the Barbadian dialect; Holder was too fastidious and precious in his reading of Rasta passages.[9]

In *Tapia* Syl Lowhar commented upon the sparse audiences which he blamed on lack of advertising. He found the Repertory Dance Theatre's *Streets*, with its calypso influences, 'real cool . . . well improvised', praised the drumming and Astor Johnson's performance in *The Defiant Era* and found the message of *Odale's Choice* so 'relevant to our time [that] it more than compensates for the deficiencies of the performance'. The fusion of the TTW with the Repertory is what Walcott needs, but some of the new actors need more grooming and are uncertain in their roles.[10]

Walcott participated in the University of Miami American Assembly's four-day discussion of 'The United States and the Caribbean'. The *Sunday Guardian* quotes him as rejecting V. S. Naipaul's pessimism about the West Indian as a Mimic Man. He spoke favourably of Carnival, calypso, the steel-drums, and contrasted the temporary nature of West Indian art forms with the built-in obsolescence of manufactured objects in richer lands. The talk was later published as 'The Caribbean: Culture or Mimicry?' Walcott's essay has a complicated movement, seeing the Americas as one and finding much of its creative vitality in black America, but a principal theme is 'Nothing will . . . be created in the West Indies, for quite a long time, because what will come out of there is like nothing one has ever seen before.' Cultures originate in their surroundings, and given the choice between revenge for the past and nothing, it is better to choose nothing and begin again with a renewed vision of the American archipelago.[11]

Walcott then went to Jamaica in early May to discuss with Ralph Thompson plans for the forthcoming July tour of the TTW; they discussed such matters as the setting up of the sets at the Little Theatre, lighting, publicity, and costs. Because the Little Theatre was already booked Walcott would not be able to move the set in until a day before opening. Ronald Bryden wanted Walcott to fly to London immediately to discuss with Terry Hands the translation of *The Joker of Seville*. Walcott begged off as he had to return to Trinidad two days later; a three-day trip Jamaica–London–Trinidad, two of which would be spent flying, seemed too hectic. Walcott unsuccessfully tried to telephone Hands at the Aldwych Theatre in London and left a message. A problem was the form into which to translate the Spanish play. Walcott was using Roy Campbell's octosyllabic rhymed version as an aid, but Campbell's translation was too slow-paced and Walcott was then thinking of a fast-paced, highly rhetorical prose rather than pentameter and a clear style. His free adaptation, more an original play than a translation, was rather different from what the Royal Shakespeare Company had in mind. Rather than translating a sixteenth-century Spanish play into modern English poetry, Walcott was using the original as his model, much the way (to borrow a comparison from his letter to Bryden) Picasso had used Manet's *Déjeuner sur l'herbe*. While recognizably using the structure and paying homage to the original, Walcott was transforming his model into an 'existential' play in which, rather than glorifying hedonism outside morality, Juan challenges the silence of a possibly non-existent God. Juan will have the underlying sadness that is part of living without limits, an awareness of the decay and mortality of the flesh found in the exercise of freedom. Juan's world both shimmers and is hallucinatory as it is unstable. While in Jamaica Walcott discussed with the composer Gary Friedman the possibility of doing the score for *Joker*; Friedman was writing music for *Heavenly Silence*, a play based on Berrigan's poems that Walcott had been working on since the past November. Friedman declined as *The Joker* was not, then, a musical. Walcott planned to use Workshop actors to record a demonstration tape of *Heavenly Silence* for foreign producers, but nothing came of the project.[12]

A new version of *The Charlatan*, with many new songs, was directed by Walcott at Town Hall from 29 June until 3 July, before being taken to Jamaica. Productions of *The Charlatan* are of interest because they show another side of the Workshop's acting style. *Franklin* was performed in a subdued, naturalist, rather introverted manner, the way Chekhov's plays are sometimes performed. *The Charlatan* was treated as broad comedy and the acting style was consciously Calypsonian. Walcott had long been aware of the unique performance style used in the Calypso tents, with often obscene gestures accompanying each word, but *The Charlatan* appears to have been the only play in which such acting was fully developed (although some of the comic scenes in *Joker* use such illustrative gestures). The cast included Marshall, Holder, Judy Stone, Goldstraw, Ermine Wright, Errol Pilgrim, Noreen Bradford, Scott, Helen Camps, Parris, and Jones.

Although Walcott had been revising *The Charlatan* since his University College of West Indies days, Denis Solomon thought this Walcott's first specifically Trinidadian play. Besides the Carnival setting and music there was a special understanding between author, actors, and audience. The comedy was like Calypso in being slightly wild and unreal, which blunts the cutting cruelty. 'This is achieved in a most professional way by the company, all of whom display . . . a versatility that fully entitles them to the name of a theatre company.' With other Walcott plays one remembers the dialogue; here memories are visual. 'Stanley Marshall torn between responses of lechery and caution' to Helen Camps' advances; 'Goldstraw again, weighed down and almost invisible under the ample thighs of Judy Stone, paddling his canoe on an imaginary lake as they sing a love duet'. The play shows, as one of its songs has it, a nation 'divided by class, united by bacchanal'. A quarrel, however, had developed between Walcott and Stone over Walcott's rehearsal practices. Insecure about her abilities as a singer, Stone wanted first to learn her songs in private, whereas Walcott insisted she learn them with the group at rehearsals. While this was part of Walcott's method of building an ensemble, the effect was emotionally devastating upon Stone.[13]

Before leaving for the Jamaican tour Walcott circulated a four-page memo to the Workshop. *The Charlatan* in Trinidad made less money than expected because of the transfer from Bishop's to Town Hall with its high rental and other costs. Musicals cost more because of the need to hire musicians and they had to save money on costumes. John Andrews economizes wonderfully on lighting, but they must get better equipment, especially a dimmer board. Town Hall caused aesthetic compromises, such as its awful curtains. At Town Hall the ceiling was too high for intimacy. Walcott's set design was too conservative and stolid. The backstage crew did an inestimable job, especially Winston Goddard who had to travel every day from San Fernando; it was painful not to be able to pay them more; others should help them. Too many actors think of themselves as stars and will not move furniture or sweep. The company is playing in front of friends, family, and well-wishers; they must keep to the highest standards, and it is Walcott's responsibility as director to insist on such standards.

While Walcott would always discuss his decisions, a play is a metaphor, a concept, as whole as a painting or a poem. He learned from the past [Walcott probably meant 1970] that to retreat before criticism within the company is a weakness that only confuses issues. If they are being called Walcott's puppets and slaves, then they need to remember that it is his company: he formed it, created it with his own sweat, and it will remain his even if most of the actors leave. He, however, treats everyone in the company as equals, as his peers. Everyone is harmed if an actor throws rehearsals into chaos by arriving late. The company must remember that they are becoming known internationally, if only slightly. If they were professionals they would be working harder and not sulking. Walcott will not write down to his audiences, nor does he consider himself above them. Acting is a divine calling and it does not matter whether or not the Workshop likes Walcott. Jamaica takes greater pride in the TTW than does Trinidad. Two local papers still have not reviewed *The Charlatan* a week after its opening. So in local journalistic history the play was never performed. In Jamaica they will be treated with the highest courtesy because of the reputation they achieved with *Dream* and *Ti-Jean*. 'It's up to you to drive yourself to that illumination of your own souls that makes your vocation worthwhile.'

The Jamaican tour lasted from 8 July until 22 July. Judy Stone had resigned from the Workshop and was replaced on the tour by Mavis Lee Wah from San Fernando. As usual letters had to be written requesting employers to give leaves of absence to the actors and stage crew; the time was taken from annual leave so that salary would continue to be paid. Then there was the need for travel arrangements, income tax exit permits, visas, and other problems arising from moving a theatre company from one island to another.

The company would check in together along with their costumes at Piarco airport at 6 a.m. on Sunday, 8 July, for a 7.30 a.m departure. To cut down on expenses and because several actors worked in the private sector where it was more difficult to get leave, some of the cast who performed only in *The Charlatan* followed later. In Jamaica their host would be Ralph Thompson, director of Pan-Jamaican Investments, who arranged the tour. They shared rooms and took meals at the Sandhurst Hotel. They had to pay bar bills and were warned to avoid drugs and carrying contraband. If the group accepted an invitation to a party, then everyone was expected to attend. The tour managers were John Andrews, Stanley Marshall, and Errol Jones. Charles Applewhaite was stage manager.

On Sunday night they would meet the press and there would be a party at Ralph Thompson's. On Monday, 9 July, at 10 a.m., the crew would set up the props at the Little Theatre and meet with the set designer, Richard Montgomery. Additional assistance was voluntary. Between 11 a.m. and 1.30 p.m. they would rehearse the first act of *Franklin*. After a one-hour lunch break, probably on sandwiches, Act II would be rehearsed until 5.30 p.m. On Tuesday they would rehearse Act III of *Franklin*. Wednesday (Krogh's birthday) there was a

run-through of *Franklin* in the morning and afternoon along with setting up of the sets and lighting. Everyone was expected to help. Errol
Pilgrim would arrive during the day. That night they would open at
the Little Theatre, so everyone must be on the bus from the hotel in
time. It would all be very rushed with the half-hour call at 7.30 p.m.
and opening at 8 p.m. The Prime Minister of Jamaica would be at the
performance and after the show there would be a reception at the
Prime Minister's residence. Thursday was a day off except for work on
the props for *Charlatan*. On Friday, 13 July, there would be rehearsal
of music and rearrangement of movement for the play. Rehearsals
would be held at the hotel if the Little Theatre was not available.
Mavis Lee Wah and Nigel Scott would arrive.

On Saturday Michael Boothman would arrive and there would be
two performances of *Franklin*. On Sunday, 16 July, there would be a
rehearsal of the first act of *The Charlatan* in the morning and a performance of *Franklin* in the evening. After the performance everyone
would be required to pack up the set of *Franklin* and move in the set
for *The Charlatan*. Beginning at 8.30 a.m. on Monday the set and props
for *The Charlatan* must be arranged, followed by a run through from
11.30 a.m. to 3.30 p.m. They would open that night; the half-hour call
would be at 7.30 p.m. 'Company is advised to rest before opening.
Energy is crucial.' The last two performances of *Charlatan* would be
Saturday, 21 July. Bags had to be packed for the next day's departure.

They played at the Little Theatre, Crossroads. Richard Montgomery,
their set designer, was born in England, studied at the Birmingham
College of Art and Design before training at the Old Vic Theatre
School, worked for the Birmingham Repertory Theatre and was hired
by the Royal Court, London, as a costume designer. While expecting
a position with the Royal Shakespeare Company, he decided to spend
time working in the West Indies. Over the years Montgomery had
come to know Peter Minshall, Noel Vaz, and other West Indian theatre people and was appointed Resident Designer and Tutor at the
Creative Arts Centre, Mona, 1970–2. He stayed on in Jamaica until
1979 before moving to the United States. He met Walcott in Jamaica
in 1970; *Franklin* and *Charlatan* were his first designs for the TTW, and
he would become Walcott's regular designer, especially for costumes.[14]

Walcott publicized the opening of his plays with various interviews
and announcements in the Jamaican press. The *Sunday Gleaner* carried
an interview in which Walcott contrasted the lack of playing sites
in Trinidad with Jamaica's comparative wealth in the Little Theatre,
the Ward, the Barn, and the Creative Arts Centre. In Jamaica the

government supported the arts through grants and financial help, while in Trinidad only the village groups and steel bands were supported. Whereas Jamaican businessmen were willing to sponsor *The Joker of Seville*, it appeared that a production of Trevor Rhone's *Smile Orange* in Trinidad might be cancelled as Trinidadian businesses were unwilling to support a Jamaican play. West Indian culture was not 'exotic' or the expression of a self-contained subgroup, such as African-American writing, but has its origins in many cultures and cultural forms including Europe, Asia, and Africa. The West Indian artist has to examine and make use of his multicultural environment rather than assume that some forms are indigenous to the exclusion of others.[15]

In Jamaica, with its more developed theatre scene than Trinidad, reviews tend to be less about culture and politics and more focused on theatre craft and details of performance. Archie Lindo called *Franklin* a very good, well-written, well-produced play, but felt that the pace was slow, too much took place off stage, and the actors were not up to the long speeches in Act I. Beginning in Act II the performers came to life as events speeded up. He praised Errol Jones's strong personality and voice, and the sensitivity and sincerity of Ermine Wright.[16]

Harry Milner thought *Franklin* intentionally derivative of Joseph Conrad's 'A Tale of the Islands' and deliberately evocative of all the clichés about the exotic tropics; yet by orchestration Walcott had created a 'genuine, moving, intelligent and relevant play that is both West Indian and universal'. In a time when West Indian whites are regarded as subhuman it is courageous to have written a play showing understanding for the British-born islander. Franklin is a kind of Lord Jim, someone who lost his nerve during the Second World War and became dependent on a black youth who saved him. Originally a misfit in white clubs he begins to 'go native' as he feels part of the people on the island after the war. After his romance with an Indian woman ends disastrously, he is told that he is disliked by everyone and plans to leave the island, but discovers that in fact he is respected and remains to face the future with the other islanders. Milner comments that Franklins are more common on the smaller islands than Jamaica. Unfortunately Krogh as Franklin was not always audible, but Goldstraw as the Major was both touching and authentic. Noreen Bradford needs voice training, but sensitively offered a gamut of emotions. Claude Reid had good stage presence, and moved and spoke well. Stanley Marshall was outstanding in his portrayal of the Indian woman's father, bringing out the dignity of his character and smoothly switching from comedy to tragedy.[17]

Dennis Scott in the *Daily Gleaner* recommended *Franklin* as 'theatre-worthy' and commented that Walcott had taken a risk in building the language and action from a minimal level in Act I towards a powerful conclusion, which meant that the first act was flat and only in the second and third acts did the play catch fire. There are few poetic lines that stand out; the language is easier to follow. The play 'makes its points clearly through the delineation of character in action, and through its visual images'. *Franklin*, like many of Walcott's poems, is concerned with belonging to a place. Does Franklin have a right to be on the island? Does his personal tragedy expiate the crimes of history? 'Walcott's answer is yes . . . in the generosity with which Walcott rounds out his characters and refuses to stereotype them, and the subtlety of their relationships, he constructs a political metaphor in which polarisations of Black and White, native and expatriate, guilty and innocent, find no place.' Now that exclusion seems to be the common basis of building West Indian society, Walcott proposes for-giveness both for the oppressor and the oppressed. Scott also men-tioned that the air-conditioning in the newly roofed theatre made some of the actors inaudible.[18]

Jean Lowrie called *Franklin* 'a must for lovers of good theatre'. The direction was skilled, the performance polished, the audience appre-ciative. *Franklin* explores racial and class conflict in a way that causes tears and laughter. Noreen Bradford is passionate, wilful, and childlike as Maria. Jones as Charbon is powerful, thundering out his lines. His gruff tenderness at the end of the play is moving. Parris's creole accent and mouth-organ music relieved the tension of the play. Lowrie also comments on the setting, especially on such visual symbolism as the changing colours and kinds of clothing Maria wears.[19]

The next week Lowrie wrote that *The Charlatan* is lively entertain-ment with racy calypsos and eccentric colourful characters which the audience enjoyed. Holder's calypsos are well performed and his move-ments brought laughter from the audience. Stanley Marshall's guitar-playing mime was timed well. Although many West Indian problems are touched upon by the play, Walcott keeps the mood light. There are visual contrasts and the transitions to various locations are cleverly arranged.[20]

Dennis Scott saw in the symbolism of illusion, charlatans, and mas-querade an image of the West Indies where people survive by guile and artists turn away from the problems of society. The gusto, timing, and infectious warmth of Stanley Marshall and Wilbert Holder kept the play moving. Goldstraw is consistent and makes much use of gesture, but does not play as closely to the style of the others as he should. Helen Camps, as Heloise Upshot, is light and intelligent; she slips in and out of parody without a conflict in styles. Ivor Picou is witty and excellently timed in his movements. Ermine Wright uses her body well. Richard Montgomery's economical set is interesting to look at. Walcott uses song to move the action forward and the music permeates the action.[21]

During August the TTW began discussing plans for a West Indian Playwrights' Conference. The aim was once again to discover new plays for performance. Walcott and Holder and the critic Raoul Pantin were involved with the planning. The committee met in early October with Walcott in the chair, along with Errol Jones, Holder, Horace James, and John Andrews. They decided that the conference would stage previously unacted plays by dramatists who attended the conference. Those who would be invited included the Jamaicans Barry Reckord, Dennis Scott, Trevor Rhone, and Samuel Hillary; Roderick Walcott from St Lucia; and the 'Trinidadians' Errol Hill, Derek Walcott, Errol John, Freddie Kissoon, Douglas Archibald, Lennox Brown, and Mustapha Matura. Many of the playwrights lived abroad. Brown and Roderick Walcott now resided in Canada; Hill was in the United States. Possible directors were discussed including the Walcotts, Errol Hill, James Lee Wah, Dennis Scott, Noel Vaz, Lloyd Reckord, Ken Corsbie, and Carol Dawes. Possible actors included Eunice Alleyne, Laveau, Reid, Lynette Laveau, Judy Stone, Ralph Maraj (an up-and-coming dramatist from San Fernando), Mavis Lee Wah, and twelve from the the TTW. The lists are noticeable for their emphasis on Trinidadian talents along with a core of people who were at the University of the West Indies, Kingston, in the early 1950s. As usual when such conferences were discussed, there was the problem of finances. The Workshop hoped to provide board and lodgings, would ask the actors, directors, and playwrights to donate their talents, and sought aid from Canadian External Affairs to bring West Indians from Canada. Despite all the theatre now being produced in the West Indies, the financial situation had not changed much since the mid-1950s when Tom Patterson of the Ontario Stratford Shakespeare Festival was asked to come to Jamaica as advisor for the West Indian Arts Festival and offered board and lodgings as payment.

Walcott's plea for a multicultural, multiracial West Indies, his argument against both black nationalists and the state-sponsored Best Village culture of Trinidad, and his claim that theatre was cultural and political engagement, found expression in a long two-part interview with Raoul Pantin. Replying to criticism that the language of TTW productions is too complex for ordinary people, Walcott claims that it is the duty of the theatre to reach the people through intensity and clarity of performance, not by lowering standards. After fifteen years persistence the TTW now has an audience of people from all walks of life. Walcott has learned to use the language, racial complexity, culture, and history of his society. Such a wealth of material would not be available for him if he lived in London. Many of Naipaul's criticisms of Trinidad are correct, but Walcott is the polar opposite of Naipaul in seeing the possibilities of such folk arts as calypso and in his commitment to the society. Commitment, however, does not mean dashing off bad verse about fashionable political subjects to get applause. It does not mean inverting racial prejudices so that instead of whiteness, blackness becomes the standard of goodness and people are judged by how black they are. Both the black radicals and the politicians lie in claiming that the West Indians can become powerful by adopting correct attitudes. The West Indies are poor and will never be powerful. Slavery and poverty have made people aware of the truth; they do not need political lies. The 1970 demonstrations began as a genuine revolt of the young, poor, and unemployed against the politicians, but it was hijacked and transformed into an attempted racial revolution which turned people against each other. All revolutions based on race or forms of exclusiveness are suicidal as the rhetoric takes over and slogans deflect people from the objective to internal quarrels.[22]

Walcott argued that the Trinidad Theatre Workshop is genuinely revolutionary. Some of its members were virtually illiterate, they had little education and could not read well, yet they have found fulfilment as actors and craftsman. Rather than being outside society the TTW and Walcott are very much inside it; he has to work continually to get advertisements and other things to keep the theatre going. He felt that the Trinidadian government is totally indifferent to the arts except for the public amateurism of the Best Village shows which draws tourism and instils pride but which works against the development of individual talents and leaves the talented frustrated. The government's assumptions are those of the welfare period and community workers, when culture meant learning basket weaving and when everyone should be part of a community and not an individual. Trinidad is rich by West Indian standards, yet for fifteen years it has not provided training and places for its potential artists. People should be able to study the craft of theatre. The West Indian is naturally theatrical. That is part of the culture in Carnival: masquerade, public display, and gestures. The ruling party considers itself the entire country and expects everyone to toe the party line. It tries to censor opposing ideas. It dislikes theatre which offers criticism in public. Theatre reaches many people and affects opinions. If someone brings Walcott a play, Walcott has to create a theatre each time, find a place, wire it, find chairs for the performance, build the sets. It takes an immense amount of work that needs to be repeated for each production. Port of Spain needs a building for theatre, teaching, and workshops; if such a place existed Walcott said he would spend his life there teaching as he comes from a family of teachers.

Ralph Campbell, one of the early Workshop actors, returned from several years of study, travel, and work abroad and wrote a series of articles discussing theatre in Trinidad. Campbell attacked Walcott for following foreign idols, for using only middle-class actors from Port of Spain and for elitism. Why was Walcott writing about whites? Why wasn't he training the uneducated in the villages? As far as Campbell was concerned Americans wanted black theatre, real black theatre, not Trinidadian black theatre. Black is where the money is. 'Once more black is a priceless commodity for everyone but himself. But our local black themes are somewhat ridiculous, if handled the way the white, jewish manipulators of American theatre are doing.' Campbell was against 'all this professional Trinidad Theatre Stuff'. Trying to write 'like Shakespeare is a waste of time'. Make money by being black was his message. Americans would buy it.[23]

An attempt at wit appeared in *Tapia* with Victor Questel pretending he was a tipster giving inside information about the local theatre. Reviews included '*In A Fine Castle* was hastily conceived, ill-trained and carelessly ridden'. Many of the remarks are racial. *Franklin* 'was doped in Jamaica and ran quite well, but you know how the bookies in Jamaica love a white horse, especially if ridden by D. W.'. About *The Charlatan* Questel comments 'D. W.'s weakness is that he is owner, trainer and jockey. D. W. don't even have a stable of his own. Is a hustle here and a rent there. But it is symbolic somebody tells me. The literary top jockey of no fixed place of abode . . . D. W. has a weakness for piebald mounts. He gets this bias from his grandfather.' In other words Walcott runs the Workshop as his own show, is not black enough, is not from Trinidad, and desires mixed-blood actresses. Questel's picong is the stuff of calypsos and shows some of the animosity in the air during 1973.[24]

The Royal Shakespeare Company, hampered by its own budget problems and puzzled by what Walcott was making of his translation, decided that the Trinidad Theatre Workshop could premiere *The Joker of Seville*. Walcott had sent a complete first draft to Ronald Bryden who replied that Terry Hands was thinking of visiting Trinidad. During September Walcott wrote to Bryden from Port of Spain that he was excited about the possibility of Hands working with the TTW for a few weeks on *Joker*, which by now had become a rhymed play. Besides the experience of working with Hands in Trinidad, Walcott obviously wanted to show him how the theatrical forms, such as stick-fighting, picong, and folk-songs, were natural to Trinidad whereas they might seem artificial in London. Walcott wanted community participation from the audience, with the stage used as a ring that could equally serve as a cockpit, stick-fight area, or bull ring in which the actors could dance, duel, or leap. He was now working closer to Tirso's model while keeping to a correspondence between Trinidad and Tirso's Spain. He wanted pace, panache, rhythm, bareness—the elemental and the organic feel of a poem in a pliant but rapid diction. Walcott was sending Hands a montage of TTW faces so he would know what he is working with. Walcott did not want to come to London to meet Hands as the next months in Trinidad were when the costumes were being prepared for the parang bands and Carnival. If Hands and a designer came in November there would be an immense amount of materials useful for staging *Joker* in England. The actors had done a complete reading, although final casting was not settled. Walcott was confident that he was on the right track in giving emphasis to ebullience, vigour, and bareness as these were West Indian qualities growing out of the poverty of the society. The play had become a West Indian play, a TTW play, like *Dream* and *Ti-Jean*. He would like it to be a mobile play that could be staged with a small orchestra in an open space anywhere. He had been rereading T. S. Eliot on the Elizabethan dramatists and was convinced that great drama was poetry. Bryden in commissioning *Joker* for the Royal Shakespeare Company had done more for Trinidadian culture than all the years of the Trinidadian National Council for Culture.[25]

From 14 November until 19 November Walcott and six others toured St Croix University and the College of the Virgin Islands, St Thomas, as part of West Indian Student week. They stayed at the dormitories on campus. The two-hour programme was arranged as an introduction to the company and Walcott's plays. It began with Walcott reading from 'What the Twilight Says' (his introduction to the 1970 *Dream on Monkey Mountain and Other Plays*), followed by extracts and songs from *Dream*, *Franklin* and *The Charlatan*. Besides Walcott those on the tour were Stanley Marshall, Wilbert Holder, Nigel Scott, Ermine Wright, Noreen Bradford, and the musician Michael Boothman.

During November the *Sunday Guardian* published an interview with

Walcott by Therese Mills titled 'Don Juan was a Stickman!' The pun between a Trinidadian stick fighter and the male sexual organ is typically Walcottian, a pun he often uses in the play. After mentioning that Ronald Bryden invited him to do a translation, which is expected to be performed at the Aldwych Theatre in London, Walcott says 'when I came to adapt the play I did not want to produce a play purely for the Shakespeare Company or English actors and audiences. I wanted to write a play that could also be produced in the West Indies.' The basic concept was clear. The play would open with a stick fight with 'Gayelle and Parang and Burroquettes' and Calypsos, then the action would move to Seville. Don Juan would be treated as a Caribbean. At this point Walcott was thinking of using André Tanker for the score. He planned on a March opening with the TTW and some rehearsals were under way.[26]

The Workshop sponsored a performance of Ken Corsbie and Mark Matthews' *Dem Two*, 30 November–1 December, at Bishop's Auditorium. This consisted of Corsbie and Matthews from Barbados doing dramatizations and songs about the Caribbean by West Indian poets. By December Walcott's plans for a musical adaptation of Daniel Berrigan's *Heavenly Peace* included music by Gary Friedman and the Family Tree and choreography by Astor Johnson. This was another play that did not get beyond rehearsals. The same week Walcott signed a contract with Horace James of the Trinidad and Tobago Television for TV rights to *Sea at Dauphin* and the supply of Workshop actors for another television production. At that point the Trinidad Theatre Workshop had a credit of $1,300 in the bank of which Walcott would be paid $300 for the TV rights to *Sea* and Holder and Wright would each get $150. The TTW would get $100 as the 'agent' and a further 10 per cent ($55) 'dues' on what was paid Walcott, Holder, and Ermine Wright.[27]

NOTES

1. Most of the internal Workshop letters, schedules, and other documents are in the Walcott Collection, University of the West Indies, St Augustine.
2. Victor Questel, 'The Horns of Derek's Dilemma', *Tapia*, 3/12 (25 Mar. 1973), 4–5.
3. 'Picking Up Where "Pieces" Left Off', *Express* (20 Mar. 1973), 7; Lennox Brown to Judy Stone (19 Mar. 1973); Stone to Brown (19 Mar. 1973).
4. Therese Mills, 'This Is an Experiment in Courage', *Sunday Guardian* (15 Apr. 1973), 8.

5. The quotation from Walcott is from Mills' article above (see n. 4).

6. Eric Roach, 'Experiment in Establishing the West Indian Theatre', *Trinidad Guardian* (18 Apr. 1973), 4.

7. Derek Walcott, 'Why This Astigmatism toward the Workshop's White Actors?', *Trinidad Guardian* (19 Apr. 1973), 5.

8. Denis Solomon, 'Beginning or End?' *Tapia*, 3/16 (22 Apr. 1973), 2–3.

9. 'Second Season Ends with Dance, Drama', *Trinidad Guardian* (25 Apr. 1973), 5; Derek Walcott, '"Rights of Passage" drama in itself', *Trinidad Guardian* (25 Apr. 1973), 5; Eric Roach, '"Pieces Two" Is an Experiment in Progress', *Trinidad Guardian* (28 Apr. 1973), 7.

10. Syl Lowhar, 'Drums and Colours', *Tapia* 3/18 (6 May 1973), 9–10.

11. 'Mimic Men? Absurd', *Sunday Guardian* (29 Apr. 1973), 1; Derek Walcott, 'The Caribbean: Culture or Mimicry?', *Journal of Interamerican Studies and World Affairs*, 16/1 (Feb. 1974), 3–13: 9.

12. Derek Walcott to Ronald Bryden, Kingston (8 May 1973); Derek Walcott to Ronald Bryden, Port Of Spain (8–9 May 1973), Walcott Collection, University of the West Indies, St Augustine.

13. Denis Solomon, 'Divided by Class, United by Bacchanal', *Tapia*, 3/27 (8 July 1973), 6. Interview with Judy Stone (July 1990), and a note from her (Feb. 1994).

14. Judy Stone, 'Just Who is this Richard Montgomery?', *Trinidad Guardian* (8 Jan. 1988), 5.

15. Derek Walcott, 'Walcott on the Theatre in Trinidad and Jamaica', *The Sunday Gleaner* (15 July 1973), 5.

16. Archie Lindo, 'Two Plays—Both Interesting', *The Star* (19 July 1973), 18.

17. Harry Milner, 'Courage of the Classical', *The Sunday Gleaner* (22 July 1973), 14.

18. Dennis Scott, 'The Man who Belonged', *The Daily Gleaner* (13 July 1973), 30.

19. Jean Lowrie, 'Tears, Laughter in Walcott Play', *Jamaica Daily News* (13 July 1973), 18.

20. Jean Lowrie, 'Carnival Comes to Little Theatre', *Jamaica Daily News* (18 July 1973), 20.

21. Dennis Scott, 'An Ending in Carnival', *The Daily Gleaner* (18 July 1973), 27.

22. Raoul Pantin [interview with Derek Walcott], 'We are Still Being Betrayed', *Caribbean Contact*, 1/7 (July 1973), 14–16; 'Any Revolution Based on Race is Suicidal', *Caribbean Contact*, 1/8 (Aug. 1973), 14–16.

23. Ralph Campbell, 'The Birth of Professional Theatre in Trinidad', *Sunday Guardian* (22 July 1973), 4; 'To Whom can the Playwright Turn?', *Trinidad Guardian* (5 July 1973), 11.

24. Victor Questel, 'From the horses mouth', *Tapia*, 3/31 (5 Aug. 1973).

25. Derek Walcott to Ronald Bryden (10 Sept. 1973), Walcott Collection, University of the West Indies, St Augustine.

26. Therese Mills, 'Don Juan was a Stickman!', *Sunday Guardian* (18 Nov. 1973), 5.

27. Various documents in University of the West Indies, St Augustine, Walcott Collection.

11

1974

An American *Charlatan*

A New *Dream*

A West Indian *The Joker of Seville*

BETWEEN 1974 and 1976 the TTW reached the highest peak of its achievement; like earlier peaks (the 1966 'season' and the 1970 *Ti-Jean*) such moments resulted from productions and plays that made new demands, required new approaches to the theatre. This one evolved from Walcott's commission to prepare a translation of a sixteenth-century Spanish play and from the Los Angeles production of *The Charlatan*, which resulted in his collaborating with Galt MacDermot, already famous for the music for *Hair*. The promised land was no longer just a national theatre company, it now had its own imperial Faustian dimensions—success on Broadway, the West End, and in Hollywood. Walcott and several of his actors were now almost always on tour from production to production. A two-week engagement by the Trinidad Theatre Workshop at a famous theatre festival in Connecticut, which would previously have been the big event of the year, is now part of a hectic non-stop schedule.

The Joker of Seville and *O Babylon!* are examples of Walcott's interest in the American musical as a form which integrates the performing arts into a total theatre; because of its music and dance, the musical could enable Caribbean drama to reach a larger audience, thus bridging the gap between popular and élite culture. Although Walcott never mentions such an analogy, the musical has many of the stylized elements and conventions of classical Greek theatre; its emphasis on dance and song might provide the Caribbean with a New World alternative to the conventions of Oriental theatre. Later Walcott rejected the

Broadway musical as without content and observed that African-Americans were limited to being entertainers, but for a time the musical was an interesting form to master while offering the possibilities of international success. During the years of slogging to create West Indian theatre he had a trifocal perspective, seeing himself as a West Indian artist, potentially a classic within the British tradition, and as someone from the New World to whom the United States offered opportunities and models not to be found elsewhere. The counter-culture of the 1960s, the success on Broadway of such musicals as *Hair*, the interest taken in his plays by Joseph Papp and others, made such ambitions seem possible. The integration of West Indian dance and music with serious theatre would prove V. S. Naipaul was wrong in saying the West Indies had created nothing.

After being commissioned to write *The Joker of Seville* for the Royal Shakespeare Company, Walcott wrote a letter to the TTW saying that the company had helped him to whatever foreign success he had achieved or would achieve. The best TTW actors were as good as those abroad; there were very few permanent acting companies in the world and even fewer playwrights who had such companies. The plays belong as much to the TTW as to Walcott. They could only have been produced in an atmosphere of love.

Such a letter shows Walcott's leadership, his close identification with his company, and his recognition of how over the years the Workshop had contributed to his growing international reputation as a dramatist; it might also be seen as a sign that Walcott's desire for international success would put increasing strains on his actors who were perpetually busy with new demands on top of their jobs and personal lives. When the company was not performing, touring, or rehearsing, there were workshops two nights each week. Soon a dance company would be formed which would also hold workshops twice a week, which meant that the dancers were attending workshops four nights a week when they were not rehearsing or performing.

Walcott was in St Croix during January 1974 as part of his continuing involvement with the Courtyard Players, the theatre at Frederiksted, and the University of the Virgin Islands in St Croix and St Thomas. Ruth Moore, an American married to a Crucian, was a force within the Courtyard Players and saw that Walcott offered a way to develop local interest and talent, as he already had experience building theatre groups in St Lucia, Jamaica, and Trinidad. The usual arrangement was for Walcott with some members of the TTW to hold workshops while rehearsing a production using local actors. Most workshop expenses would be paid, but the theatre production was at Walcott's own financial risk. Walcott returned to St Croix with Holder early in March and in April *Ti-Jean* was performed in the two principal cities.[1]

Walcott returned to the United States for the 27 May opening of the revised musical version of *The Charlatan* at the Mark Taper Forum in Los Angeles with Mel Shapiro directing. In New York he briefly met a young dancer, Noble Douglas, who was returning to Trinidad and soon would have a significant role in the TTW. Noble Douglas began studying dance in Trinidad, then in Canada where she studied both ballet and modern dance. She, like Carol La Chapelle, went to the London College of Dance and Drama, followed by the London School of Contemporary Dance and the Martha Graham School of Contemporary Dance. She appeared in various Canadian and American musicals and was in the Martha Graham Apprentice Company. Albert Laveau was now a member of Equity, and from April to November was in the Negro Ensemble Company's tour of Joseph Walker's *The River Niger* which opened in Detroit and then moved to Chicago, Cleveland, Baltimore, Washington, and Philadelphia. Walcott and the Workshop were spreading their wings, and Walcott's vision of remaking the map of Western culture seemed within reach.

The Mark Taper production of *The Charlatan* had favourable if mixed reviews. As often with North American productions of his plays, Walcott's reviewers and audiences found the complex society and culture of the West Indies beyond their experience. Henry Goodman wrote in the *Wall Street Journal* that *The Charlatan* is lively and charming, lyrical and mythical and said that it illustrated the conquest of Death by Love. While showing the amusing revelry and confusion of Carnival, the play, Goodman felt, was difficult, partly because he could not follow the 'Calypso enunciation', partly because he could not enter into the bewildering mixture of cultural assumptions. He would have liked the play to be more explicit.[2]

Regardless of any of its faults, or failure to make the production clear to the audience, the play has a complexity uncommon to American musicals. Walcott was attempting in the musical a transformation similar to that which T. S. Eliot had tried in his later dramatic works, where the well-made West End drawing-room comedy became a vehicle for serious verse drama with ritualist, mythic, and religious foundations. Walcott was attempting something even more complex with the American form, as on such mythic foundations there was also the psychological, symbolic, musical, and cultural world of Carnival, itself a ritualized disorder of liberation and rebirth. With hindsight it is possible to see Walcott's debate with Errol Hill over the potentials of using Carnival for a West Indian theatre was misleading. In many plays Walcott uses Carnival as a central symbol, and explores its significance more deeply than Hill, but, as Walcott warned, and as Goodman's review shows, there is the problem of finding a theatrical form to embody the seeming disorder of the event.

Walcott's notes to Mel Shapiro show some of the problems with North American productions of his plays, why Walcott needed West Indian actors, and why it became important for him to create an exchange of American and Trinidadian actors. The Americans had acting technique and a sense of production values, but they lacked the specific cultural awareness and concern with theatre as art that a West Indian could give. One actor kept changing his role into that of a Southern preacher, pausing, mugging, losing the precision of the verbal exchanges, losing the speech rhythms of Walcott's text. Another actor had no understanding of the magnificence of the great English eccentrics, the English madman in the tradition of Blake; this actor instead was playing the part as a charming boulevardier without any of its manic vision similar to that of a poet-creator. Walcott found the actors too busy, neglecting the words and even the music.[3]

American producers and directors have sometimes commented that Walcott's directing and actors are static. While the difference might be explained in terms of the American passion for action and Walcott's concern with the text and visual images, there is also the complex acting style which he had developed with the TTW and which was attentive to the interpretive possibilities of each detail. Walcott had in mind a director's theatre, of the kind more often found in Europe than the United States, with an ensemble style, a serious theatre of great power, intensity and energy, in which the visual would carry the 'story' even if the audience missed the words. By contrast American theatre is stripped down, explicit, avoids complexities, and panders to the audience's limited attention span and distrust of irony and high culture. As Walcott found ways to make his theatre more attentive to American demands, he had to learn how he could achieve what he wanted by other means. The Los Angeles production of *The Charlatan* is an interesting example of Walcott rethinking his plays.

The new *Charlatan* was revised from suggestions by the Director Mel Shapiro and was closer to a musical than earlier versions of Walcott's play. This was the first time Walcott collaborated with the composer Galt MacDermot. MacDermot had worked with serious dramatic scripts, provided music for versions of *Hamlet* and *Troilus and*

Cressida and for films; he had composed a *Mass in F*, which was presented at St John's the Divine at Easter, 1973, and he was commissioned to write an oratorio for the new Canadian Cultural Centre for the Performing Arts. He had worked with Joseph Papp's New York Shakespeare Festival. He had both élite cultural and Broadway credentials, someone who could write the musical hits in *Hair* and work with theatre classics for the contemporary stage. Just what Walcott himself was aiming at. He would become Walcott's composer for his next two big plays and they would continue to collaborate on various projects including *The Joker of Seville*, *Marie Laveau*, *Haytian Earth*, and a long-playing record of *The Joker of Seville*. MacDermot was someone who could introduce Walcott to Broadway producers, would come to Trinidad for rehearsals, and write new music whenever it was needed by Walcott or his dancers.

There were aesthetic reasons for working with MacDermot. Walcott's notes for the Los Angeles *Charlatan* show that he was conscious of developing a new form and he saw MacDermot as someone who had preceded him in that direction. There is a page of single-spaced notes discussing form, in which Walcott mentions his reservations as a poet with MacDermot's treatment of the text in Joseph Papp's production of *Two Gentlemen of Verona*, but he also felt that MacDermot had created a form different from the American musical, a form which he thinks Shakespeare himself might have approved provided that he could have written the lyrics as well as the text. The parallel to Walcott is obvious.

Walcott's notes include the most complete description of what he was aiming at in the theatre at this time and of the ways in which the acting style for *The Charlatan* was influenced by the performance of Calypso in Trinidad. Walcott insists that the words of his lyrics must be delivered precisely with the care given verse; if poetic qualities are deleted from speeches and dialogue for the sake of narrative, they must be compensated for in songs which themselves must contribute to the narrative progression. Walcott sees the play as a collaboration in which Shapiro and MacDermot are editing and reforming his text into a production with its own structure, to which he writes new sections as needed. While Walcott is pleased by the attention being given to reshaping his play for the American stage, he insists on the importance of the words over the fake excitement of movement and on the need to communicate the songs through visual gesture. A calypsonian's words may often be lost to the audience, but the meaning is conveyed verse by verse, even line by line through body language

201 Charlatan, Dream, and The Joker

and mime. (Anyone who has seen the later *Celebration* will recognize that just such a visual style is used in the sections performed from *The Joker of Seville*.) He wants such a mime dance as well as song; American actors are scared of using such vulgar body language. There is more need for participation in the words and less modesty.

Walcott saw song as part of story telling and the lyrics as a means of advancing the plot. Verbal significance is complemented by gesture the way it is in Calypso. Speeches can be cut, deleted, or rewritten, but what is left in the script has to be spoken clearly and with attention to West Indian speech rhythms, so it does not sound unnatural like 'poetry'. While being conscious that his original script lacked a clear, tight, narrative progression, he was also conscious that its verse qualities and complexities were being sacrificed to the American taste for movement; he suggests that by making the songs more tightly integrated into the narrative and making their meaning more explicit through gesture, some of what was being lost could be regained. Body language replaces the textual as communication and as symbolism. He accepts that his plays need to be speeded up, with fewer long speeches and without the still points towards which he had previously worked; instead there would be a more complete integration of text, song, dance, and gesture as a means of advancing the story and its symbolism.

Walcott returned to Port of Spain for the May 1974 TTW-sponsored readings by Carolyn Reid-Wallace of African-American poetry at the Little Carib. Workshop involvement included Stanley Marshall as Stage Manager, John Andrews in charge of lighting, Wilbert Holder partly responsible for publicity, and André Tanker leading the musicians. In June *Sea at Dauphin* was filmed for Trinidad and Tobago Television. A Caribbean Playwrights' Conference again was planned by the TTW for the three weeks 29 July-19 August and a circular printed and distributed. The Workshop was hoping to hold its own version of the O'Neill Playwrights' Conference, but once more funding did not materialize, nor did the conference.

During July the Repertory Dance Theatre performed with new dances by Noble Douglas and Carol La Chapelle, who had also recently returned to Trinidad. The Astor Johnson classic *Defiant Era* used Wilbert Holder as a speaker 'Courtesy Trinidad Theatre Workshop'. André Tanker was in charge of the music, John Andrews in charge of lighting, and Walcott and Beryl McBurnie were artistic advisors.

Carol La Chapelle was the first Trinidadian who having earned one of the four-year government scholarships to go abroad insisted that she be allowed to study dance and drama instead of one of the usual professions. When the committee considering scholarships interviewed her and saw that she would not change her mind, they agreed if she would also study education to prepare herself as a teacher. She went, in 1969, to the London College of Dance and Drama and simultaneously attended the Dartford College of Education. When she returned to Trinidad in 1973 she joined the Repertory Dance Theatre as a teacher, choreographer, and dancer. Her idea of dance is similar to Walcott's notion of theatre and poetry. She wants to take the 'raw, rustic folk dances . . . and combine them with . . . foreign elements or ballet' to create 'a national dance style'. She wants the arts of Trinidad to become totally professional. She reached the highest standards that anyone in Trinidad has attained in British ballet and is a member of the Royal Academy of Dance and an Associate of the Imperial Society of Teachers of Dancing.[4]

Although Douglas and La Chapelle have both studied classical and modern dance, they are physically opposites. Douglas has broad hips and works more in the 'black' tradition of strong pelvic movements. La Chapelle has the long, thin physique typical of English ballerinas, and her work is based more on classical ballet. Although reviews contrast their dancing by describing Douglas as warm and sexual and La Chapelle as refined and intellectual, both Douglas and La Chapelle are Trinidadian in their blend of foreign and local dance; they represent the different possibilities and tendencies that make West Indian art interesting. They contributed towards the diversity within Astor Johnson's RDT and would soon enable Walcott to make full use of dance in his productions.

There was an important revival of *Dream on Monkey Mountain* at the Little Carib, 1–6 August, directed by Walcott, for the Trinidad Theatre Workshop's Fifteenth Anniversary production. Since its 1967 première in Toronto there had been productions by the TTW at Queen's Hall twice in 1968 and various tours including the 1969 production at the O'Neill Foundation, but no further performances in Trinidad. There were several changes in the cast since the earlier productions. Errol Jones still acted Makak, Stanley Marshall continued as Moustique and Beddeau was principal drummer and singer, but Albert Laveau was in the United States and was replaced by the dancer Astor Johnson as Basil. Winston Goddard replaced Sydney Best as Tigre. Errol Pilgrim replaced Hamilton Parris as Souris. Anthony Hall replaced Ralph Campbell as Corporal Lestrade and Astor Picou replaced Claude Reid as Inspector Pamphilion. None of the original women were involved in this production. Ermine Wright played the Market

Woman and the dancers Noble Douglas and Adele Bynoe, Jerline Quamina, Avis Martin, and Stephanie King played the Sisters of the Revelation and Market Women. There was now choreography by Astor Johnson and masks by Ken Morris. Stage construction was by Errol Pilgrim and music by Michael Boothman.

While some of the changes can be accounted for by members being overseas, personal problems, arguments, or by plans to take *Dream* to the United States, Tony Hall and Noble Douglas were among a new group of younger actors and dancers, trained abroad, who were changing the balance of the Workshop. Hall, from Tobago, had studied theatre for four years at the University of Alberta, Edmonton. The older generation of Jones, Marshall, Laveau, and Reid were brought up during a time when even secondary education was scarce and highly competitive and there was no chance of being trained in the performing arts overseas. They had to learn what they could from the Workshop and from the opportunities the Workshop provided by way of the Rockefeller Foundation or the O'Neill Conference. The years of working together provided a camaraderie, a similarity of outlook and purpose. Since then Trinidad had discovered oil wealth, a new middle class developed, and a new generation was studying dance and theatre in Canada, England, and the United States. They would have a broader education in theatre, but would not necessarily have the same close relationship to Walcott's aims.

Walcott's 'Personal Note' prefacing the programme recalled that fifteen years ago at the old Carib he began what became the Trinidad Theatre Workshop. Although they were promised endowments, subsidies, scholarships, state support, and a building, the company was still homeless and promises of patronage were not kept. In recent years everyone talks for or against revolution, but no one has a programme concerning the culture of the people and training and development of artists. *Dream* is 'the problem of emigration, visionary or nostalgic' that remains the basic problem of the West Indies. The status quo is like the Corporal who models himself on whites. The revolutionary playing at being black is also absurd. Makak, the fool, embodies the artist and artisans who remain rooted. After all the promises of Euro-centred conservatives and Afro-centred radicals, the lies about cultural excitement, the Trinidad Theatre Workshop remains, like Makak, rooted 'here' despite its homelessness and poverty. It is history whereas Roman law and ghetto anarchy have been mostly theatre.

John Falcon's review mentions the Spiritual Baptist songs in this production which is also the debut of Astor Johnson and some members of the Repertory Dance Theatre. Falcon comments that the various characters are aspects of human weakness. Lestrade ruthlessly upholds any system regardless of which side he is on since all sides must have systems upheld by ruthlessness. The play is filled with ambivalence, irony, self-mockery and suggests futility and despair about the condition of the black man.[5]

Bruce Paddington thought the revival a triumph. Walcott has rejected naturalism and used such Brechtian devices as the actors speaking directly to the audience. The various characters are aspects of Makak's imagination. Like Africa Makak is continually being exploited. Lestrade follows Fanon's advice and puts on a new black mask; no longer an imitation white he becomes a fanatic so that he can maintain a high position in the new order. There are many rapid changes of mood and allusions to radical nationalism, Shakespeare's *The Tempest*, Martin Luther King, Kenyatta, and the Nigerian–Biafran civil war. The presentation, sets and dancing are excellent.[6]

An unusually thorough review by Victor D. Questel appeared under the title '"Dream on Monkey Mountain" in Perspective' over four issues of *Tapia*. Questel notes that Walcott has been working on the play at least since 1962. *Dream* contains most of Walcott's themes and personal concerns along with his views on the chief topics of West Indian intellectuals. Makak accommodates the 'split' in Walcott, between the desire to return to the bush and to accept reality. The bush is Africa, the past, the folk, the primitive, the non-white, origins; it is also other traditions of narrative, dance, and the mimetic in contrast to the European, the literary, and the classical. The play argues that spiritual wholeness for the Caribbean is possible only by ridding the individual's fear and desire for whiteness rather than in political or physical terms of revenge, violence, revolution, and destruction. *Dream* is a Strindbergian dream play in which anything can happen, but it is about individuals not society as community. Makak is used to being by himself and is isolated until he recently became a seller of coal and began a friendship with Moustique. It is Lestrade, the upholder of Law, who turns Makak into a political monkey. Much of the play is about manipulation of Makak and others, about the master/slave relationship. The master depends on having a slave, the slave on the master. They need each other. As soon as Makak stops accepting the view of others about himself, he is free to live in reality.

Makak is Walcott's second Adam, the Adam of the New World who can name the world, create his identity, and reintegrate with the natural world. But there is the danger of wanting to become a Negritude black Adam, of wanting to return to a pre-European past. Part of Makak's desire to return to the past is the lust for power, the desire to rule and avenge the past. He is a potential bloody tyrant. The answer then is not political, it is spiritual, within the self. There is no way you can revise history and return to a pre-European Africa, nor would it be peaceful and innocent if you could. Besides the need for self-acceptance there is man's relationship to Death (Basil in the play) and God. Questel examines Walcott's remarks about God to show that there is both bleak existential despair that outside this world there is 'nothing', and also a deep faith in God. God seems to be within the self, an inner spiritual force. People must believe in themselves, otherwise they will be misled by the Messianic notions of others. Makak is Adam alone, the artist alone, in solitude at one with the forest and God.

Some characteristics of the play include Walcott's use of symbols and his treatment of duologues. The central symbols are the circle and the moon. The play begins and ends with the drawing of a circle, which marks the area in which the players perform like animals in time. It is the circle of history, a limited, recurring history of political, social man in motion that goes no place. The moon of lunacy and art is the mirror. The duologues consist of one character undercutting another and are based on the reductive sense of humour common to Trinidad which brings a direct, often cruel, earthiness and common sense to dreams and fantasies.

The various influences on Walcott's writing have all come together in the latest *Dream* with its balance between song, dance, and verbal literariness. The play shows Walcott's admiration of Oriental theatre's combination of bareness and spectacle, the impact of costume, gesture, mime, dance, and song against a bare stage. This is his version of the epic theatre, his Brechtian smashing of the illusion of reality. Unlike the 1968 production with its towering mountain and spider webs suggesting that the only escape is through the mind, in the new production the stage is bare, the backdrop is a few dry pieces of bamboo, like the pine tree of the Kabuki.

Questel says of the acting that Jones understands Makak intimately and is a moving figure of incoherence and lucidity, apehood and kingliness; Beddeau gives the rhythmic control and vocal presence that the play requires; Marshall captures the earthiness and directness of Moustique; but Ivor Picou as Pamphilion did not understand his role and his acting was below Workshop standards. Hall plays up the loud angry side of Lestrade in contrast to Slade Hopkinson's menacing contemptuous dignity. In the NBC film version with Hopkinson, Lestrade was ludicrous when he breaks down. The fluid role-changing by the Sisters of Revelation from chorus to giggling court women to market women and wives of Makak is effective. Questel complains, however, that while the Workshop has remarkably achieved a professional standard of acting for the West Indies, it lacks a style of its own and he blames this on Walcott. Citing Ralph Campbell's articles in the *Sunday Guardian* Questel claims that Walcott is a director not a serious teacher and that his actors are so awed by and obedient to him that they have never developed.[7]

Shortly after the Little Carib revival of *Dream* the company left for the United States. An invitation to perform *Dream on Monkey Mountain* and *Ti-Jean* later in August at the White Barn, Connecticut, was the result of Ralph Alswang, the White Barn's Artistic Director, hearing enthusiastic stories about the Walcott–Holder *Ti-Jean* in Frederiksted, St Croix. Three other companies would perform at the White Barn's theatre Festival—the famous La Mama troupe from New York, the well-known Campesino Players, and the Trinity Players from Philadelphia.[8]

Walcott circulated a letter within the company concerning the forthcoming tour to Connecticut. The letter is a remarkable mixture of practical detail, including advice to diet and rest, extremely unrestful schedules, pride in what the TTW had accomplished as a theatre company, hopes for professional recognition, confidence in the company's contribution to West Indian culture, and annoyance with indiscipline. Often the distinction between Walcott and the Workshop is not clear; he seems the leader of a community. He describes *Dream* and *Ti-Jean* as the spiritual property of the TTW, complains that voices and diction need to be developed and made more crisp. More work has to be done on the singing, dances, costumes, make-up, and beards. The singing should be more accurate, the dances more precise and powerful. The actors are responsible for their props and costumes. They should rebead their costumes, silently rehearse their lines, and work while on the airplane, as many lines have been dropped from *Dream* for this production. Walcott hopes that the Connecticut Festival might lead to a two-week professional booking next year. Five actors still have not picked up their passports and tickets; this is the worst indiscipline for a long time. Saturday, 10 August, there will be rehearsals from 10 a.m. until 6 p.m. On Sunday, 11 August, at 10 a.m., *Ti-Jean* will be performed before an invited audience. On Monday at 7.30 a.m. they will leave for the United States.[9]

The TTW performed at the White Barn Festival in Westport,

Connecticut from 15 August until 27 August. Walcott conducted public seminars on the philosophy and techniques of the company on 16
and 17 August. Twenty-one actors and musicians came with the company. *Dream* had the same cast as at the Little Carib, but *Ti-Jean* was
performed with a rather different cast from in the past. Errol Pilgrim
replaced Hamilton Parris as Frog, Adele Bynoe returned from Bolom
to her old role as Cricket, Noble Douglas was now Bolom, Stanley
Marshall replaced Laveau as Devil–Planter–Papa Bois, Anthony Hall
took over Marshall's Mi-Jean, Ivor Picou instead of Ellsworth Primus
played Ti-Jean, Winston Goddard replaced Claude Reid as Gros-Jean,
Ermine Wright remained the Mother; Stephanie King was now the
Bird whereas in 1970 it was Roslyn Rappaport. The music was still
André Tanker's, but only bass guitarist Wayne Bonaparte remained of
the original 1970 musicians.

Such changes are natural in any theatre company, but the TTW
had been going through rapid changes in recent years. While Walcott
always trained his actors so that they could play any part in a production, he, in practice, tended to associate individuals with certain types
of characters, based on their physical presence on stage. Now that the
company was often touring, there were many changes in roles and the
new actors did not have the long training of the older members. This
resulted in a change in Walcott's directing methods. Instead of the
slow, patient creation of a role with the older actors, the new members of the cast were told what Walcott wanted down to the smallest
detail of physical gesture.

As soon as the company returned from Connecticut there were
preparations for an October tour to St Croix and rehearsals for the
November opening of *The Joker of Seville*. Walcott circulated several
letters to the company concerning the new play. In September he
wrote that the TTW would be premièring a work which was likely to
enter the repertoire of the Royal Shakespeare Company. They would
need to work hard on the songs, learning the melodies and the precise
language and rhythm of the script. There could be no improvising.
This play required homework from the actors. While he, Marshall,
and Douglas were in St Croix, Helen Camps would be in charge and
the actors should learn their parts. They should cut down on smoking
and drinking and be a lithe, hard-working company. When he returned on 15 October there would be a run through of Act I.

Walcott hoped to turn what was actually meant to be a St Croix
theatre clinic for the Courtyard Players into a production of *Dream*
and make a profit. Various notes in the University of the West Indies

Walcott Collection at St Augustine show changing plans and hasty calculations. Walcott thought they might workshop two plays in the round, including *One for the Road*, and he could give a poetry reading in place of a seminar. If they could get a week's accommodation during the theatre clinic he could be paid $500 as course director, while Johnson, Marshall, Douglas, and Pilgrim would each earn $250. He hoped afterwards to perform *Dream* for three nights. For *Dream* he would need to pay the cost of accommodation, air fare for some additional Workshop actors, publicity, and the rental of a theatre. At the clinic they had to find some actors, a dancer, and a production crew, and they would require platforms for the orchestra pit, four more African costumes (with beads and bamboo) and a copy of the Semp Studio's tape.[10]

On 6 September 1974 Walcott was sent a letter of agreement from the Courtyard Players that he and 'his associates of the Trinidad Theatre Workshop' provide a Free Theatre Clinic on St Croix from 30 September to 10 October with a minimum of thirty hours of instruction. Walcott should bring with him Astor Johnson, Marshall, Douglas, and 'others'; they would receive $3,000 from the Virgin Islands Council on the Arts. The fee was calculated to cover three seventeen-day excursion fares Trinidad–St Croix–Trinidad, hotel and living expenses for three instructors ($150 each for two weeks), and $700 each for the three instructors for the thirty hours of teaching. Thus $421.77 (tickets), plus $450 (hotels and living costs), plus $2,128.23 (fees for instruction) amounts to $3,000. Walcott was given $100 advance as a binder. Any additional instructors or artists would need to share the fees. The money would be paid to Walcott who was responsible for the artists paying for their meals, transportation, and other bills from the $3,000. The Courtyard Players would spend $150 of its own money on publicity, postage, administrative costs and supplies.[11]

On 9 September Walcott wrote from Trinidad to Ruth Moore informing her that he, Johnson, Marshall, and Douglas would arrive on Sunday, 29 September at 11.30 a.m.; that evening he would like to hold auditions for actors, singers, and dancers for *Dream on Monkey Mountain*. Walcott suggested that to save on expenses the four be invited to stay in people's homes during the first week. Walcott and other tutors would 'invest' part of their fees in a production of *Dream* which he hoped would run for three nights, but which, to play safe, he thought should be advertised as only having two performances. Tony Hall would follow from Canada and Errol Pilgrim would come from Trinidad to lecture on stage management. Jones, Beddeau, and

1a. Albert Laveau and Derek Walcott, 1966, Little Basement Theatre.

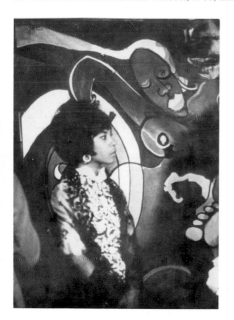

1b. *The Blacks*, Basement Theatre, 1966. Lynette Laveau as Adele Bobo. Set painted by LeRoy Clarke.

1c. *The Sea at Dauphin*, Basement Theatre, 1966. Albert Laveau as Hounakin.

2a. *Dream on Monkey Mountain*. Rehearsal, Basement Theatre, 1967. Errol Jones (right) as Makak, Stanley Marshall as Moustique.

2b. *Dream on Monkey Mountain*. Queen's Hall, 1968. Eunice Alleyne (centre) and Lynette Laveau (right) as Sisters of Revelation.

3a. *Henri Christophe*, 1968. Albert Laveau as Henri Christophe.

3b. *Dream on Monkey Mountain*. From television production, 1969. Errol Jones (left) as Makak, Stanley Marshall as Moustique.

4a. *Ti-Jean and his Brothers*, 1970. Albert Laveau (left) as Planter, Stanley Marshall as Mi-Jean.

4b. *The Charlatan*, 1973. Wilbert Holder (left) as Henderson Josephs, Laurence Goldstraw (seated) as Dr Theodore Holley, Stanley Marshall as Corpie.

5a. *The Joker of Seville*. Little Carib Theatre, 1974. Noble Douglas (left) as dancer, Terry Jones as De Mota, Allison Guerra as dancer. Costumes designed by Walcott.

5b. *The Joker of Seville*. Little Carib Theatre, 1974. Carol La Chapelle as Ana. Costume designed by Walcott.

6a. *O Babylon!* Little Theatre, Kingston, Jamaica, 1976. Sid Skipper (left) as Rufus Johnson, Errol Jones (seated) as Deacon Doxy.

6b. *O Babylon!*, 1976. Back row: Adele Bynoe, Oscila Stewart, Greer Jones. Front row: Jennifer Hobson-Garcia, Wilbert Holder as Samuel Dawson, Corrine Jones as Rudettes.

7a. *Pantomime*. The Boston Playwrights' Theatre, 1993. Nigel Scott (standing) as Trewe and Claude Reid as Jackson.

7b. Albert Laveau and Derek Walcott, backstage at the Boston Playwrights' Theatre, 1993.

8a. *Ti-Jean and His Brothers* from
Nobel Celebration. Rehearsal, Boston,
1993. Stanley Marshall as Mi-Jean.

8b. *Nobel Celebration*, Boston, 1993.
Dancers: Sonja Dumas, Allison
Seepaul, Glenda Thomas, Carol La
Chapelle, Adele Bynoe.

Winston Goddard would arrive later. Walcott hoped that something could be done to avoid a hassle with customs and immigration. Now that the Trinidad Theatre Workshop was rehearsing *Joker* he hoped that they could perform it in St Croix next year on their way to Jamaica.

Two days later Walcott wrote to Tony Hall, in Edmonton, asking him to come to St Croix as an actor and tutor. Could Hall save money by doing part of the trip by train or bus? Hall had earlier left out lines in *Dream* and Walcott warns him to keep up with the text as it keeps changing and will change again in St Croix.[12]

A letter to Ruth Moore, 16 September, enclosed some photographs for publicity and spoke of the hope that Walcott could get for the Clinic prints of the NBC film version of *Dream* along with still photographs from the New York and Los Angeles productions. He would send a tape for radio publicity. Wilbert Holder and the dancer Henry Daniel would probably come at their own expense. Walcott now suggested that it might be fun to workshop *Lysistrata* since many women would probably attend the clinic; they could perform it in contemporary dress in the round at the Courtyard with Virgin Islands' music, masks, phalloi, protest placards, and women's liberation slogans. They would probably need a band and some bawdy calypsos.

Glossy photographs of *Dream* and *Ti-Jean* were being prepared in New York along with a 'presentation' film of *Ti-Jean* being edited by Joan Sandler and others in the hope of support for a film treatment of the play. Walcott's New York contacts had approached the National Endowment for the Arts, a TV channel and other sources including the Smithsonian Institute. In the meantime there was a bill for $94.49 for the cost of the photographs and film. Additional prints of *Dream* cost $45. As the TTW had a credit of $50 paid while in Connecticut, there was still $89 to pay and $3 for each further print that might be needed. Great drama by a great poet-dramatist and a great Caribbean theatre company which he led and directed, perhaps the most significant story of post-colonial theatre, yet so much of the story consists of 'there was still $89 to pay and $3 for each additional print'![13]

In late September Derek Walcott, Marshall, Astor Johnson, Noble Douglas, and Errol Pilgrim flew to St Croix. Over the next two weeks they were joined by Tony Hall, Errol Jones, Andrew Beddeau, and Winston Goddard. Walcott, along with Johnson, Marshall, Douglas, and Pilgrim as tutors, conducted the theatre clinic for the Courtyard Players. *Dream* was performed at the Island Center, St Croix, on 12 and 13 October, with Beddeau as principal drummer and singer, Noble Douglas as principal dancer, Goddard as Tigre, Pilgrim as Souris, Jones as Makak, Hall as Lestrade, Marshall as Moustique, and Johnson as Basil. The other parts were mostly cast from participants in the seminar for the Courtyard Players. During the classes they found Syd Skipper, a black American from Detroit with a beautiful singing voice and emotional problems. He had toured in *Hair*, acted in Chicago, and travelled through Europe with the Chicago Free Street Theatre. He was given a part in *Dream* and during the next two years would be a member of the Trinidad Theatre Workshop.[14]

The programme for *Dream* contained a 'prologue' from Walcott suggesting that West Indian theatre might better develop by an exchange of actors and writers working together than through regional festivals. In presenting *Dream* at the Island Center in St Croix with its original principals along with local actors and production crew, the Courtyard Players and the TTW could work together. The archipelago, despite its many languages and political borders, is a cultural entity.

After returning to Port of Spain Walcott gave a reading from his own works at the Public Library on 17 October, supported by dramatizations from the plays. This was part of an Adult Education Programme at the Library. Two weeks later, in early November, there was a musical evening of 'Songs for Theatre' at the Public Library, showing Walcott's talents as a librettist, using songs from the Theatre Workshop repertoire. MacDermot and Beddeau were featured. Besides songs from *Dream* and *Ti-Jean* there were the new lyrics from the Mark Taper Forum Los Angeles version of *The Charlatan* and a preview of songs from *The Joker of Seville*. In the latter two plays the music was written by Galt MacDermot. MacDermot was in Port of Spain for the rehearsals of *Joker* and led a three-piece orchestra at the library. Others involved were June Nathaniel (a singer and musician who would work with the TTW), Beddeau, Marshall, Parris, and Albert Laveau, who had returned to Trinidad.[15]

Walcott's evenings at the Public Library, besides providing publicity for his forthcoming premiere of *Joker*, introduced MacDermot to Trinidad and allowed people to become accustomed to the notion that a white foreigner could write calypsos and other island music for a Trinidadian theatre company. Walcott also had further ambitions. Broadway musicals now often had many subsidiaries including recordings and Walcott wanted to move into producing records of his plays and their songs.

The most important event of 1974 was the production of *The Joker of Seville*, 28 November–7 December, at the Little Carib Theatre where it was staged arena style with seating in bleachers. This allowed the playing area at various moments to be used as a cock-fight ring, a bullring, and a stick-fight ring. The costumes for this, the first production, were historical and based on Walcott's drawings of sixteenth- and seventeenth-century Spanish clothing. As publicity before the opening Walcott wrote an article in the *Trinidad Guardian* telling how he came to be commissioned to translate a sixteenth-century Spanish play, what attracted him to it, and why the play and its period seemed like Trinidad with its part-Spanish heritage and its parang music. The classics originate in vulgarity. Shakespeare creolized the classic theatre, as much as any Third World writer who 're-invents' these legends, whereas Ben Jonson's classical rule-bound tragedies are dead.[16]

The Joker was a great success; although lasting three and a half hours it sold out for ten nights and a Sunday performance. There were plans to follow with an additional ten nights, but Astor Johnson's Repertory Dance Theatre had already planned a 'season' beginning mid-December. During 1974 and 1975 *The Joker* ran for over thirty performances in Port of Spain, setting a local theatre record at that time. The story of the commissioning of the translation of Tirso de Molina's play by the Royal Shakespeare Company and its subsequent history, including its effect on the Trinidad Theatre Workshop and Walcott, is remarkable, revealing how unlikely are the origins of works of art. Basically, there was talk of the Royal Shakespeare Company perhaps doing *El Burlador de Sevilla* and Ronald Bryden, their literary advisor and himself from the West Indies, was asked by Peter Hall and Terry Hands to find a modern poet with a Shakespearean style to write a verse translation that could be the basis for a script. As no British poet had such a style, Bryden approached Walcott, who as he progressed with his translation kept adapting the original into a new West Indian play. Although Peter Brook had left the RSC he was thought interested in 'primitive' theatre and so Walcott was allowed to develop his script until it became obvious that he had a play ready for production, which the RSC was not ready to produce, especially as Peter Hall was now obsessed by rather different notions of drama. So the TTW was allowed to premiere the play and Terry Hands came to see what Walcott had brought forth.[17]

The Joker of Seville was another fifteenth-anniversary production and had a cast of twenty-three, including a number of dancers who would rapidly join the TTW following Noble Douglas, Carol La Chapelle, and Norline Metivier. The cast included Hamilton Parris, Stanley Marshall, Laurence Goldstraw, Winston Goddard, Nigel Scott, Andrew Beddeau, Adele Bynoe, Errol Jones, Errol Pilgrim, Avis Martin, Helen

Camps, Joy Ryan, Syd Skipper, Anthony Hall and Terry Jones (both returning from Canada), Ivor Picou, Henry Daniel, and Astor Johnson. Albert Laveau shared the role of Don Diego with Johnson and replaced Scott as Juan for one night. Holder on some nights played Don Diego. While Johnson was responsible for the choreography, Carol La Chapelle and Noble Douglas contributed dances.

In keeping with the Christmas season, on Sunday 1 December there was a 'Parang' performance which included the serving of breakfast (shark and 'bake' [hot rolls], souse, coffee, oranges, and sweetbread) and beer along with songs performed by Pat Flores for an hour before the performance. The Flores parang band played at other performances as well. Because of the bleachers the audience was advised to wear casual clothing and many brought cushions with them. The orchestra consisted of a piano, guitar, drums, string bass, quatro, and flute and there were four 'dancers'. The music was supervised by Galt MacDermot as composer, but the actual musical director was June Nathaniel from the piano. John Andrews designed the lighting. The programme also included a somewhat inaccurate basic list of TTW productions and tours over the fifteen years. This list, hastily compiled from programmes and memories, continued for many years to be reprinted at anniversaries and repeated by others. The *Trinidad Guardian* reported that there were sell-out crowds for the 250 seats and people had to be turned away. Afterwards Walcott had his arm 'literally pulled out of its socket' by those offering congratulatory handshakes.[18]

Walcott was perhaps too successful in transforming what began as a translation of an old Spanish play into a West Indian theatrical experience, a local happening. Terry Hands of the Royal Shakespeare Company saw a Sunday performance with the audience eating, drinking, and chatting and said it was the kind of theatre Brecht and Peter Brook wanted to create with actors and audience joined by the 'event'. It was very Trinidadian, so much so that after he left he decided that it could not be duplicated in England. He did not have available such a group of black West Indian actors, singers, and dancers; if he did it was unlikely that there would be a British audience for them or that the audience would understand most of the West Indian cultural allusions. By London standards the production was in places unprofessional and rough, but there was no way the experience of the Little Carib production, with the lively interaction between cast and audience, could be reproduced in a large British theatre, such as the Aldwych where he had thought to produce *Joker*, before a white British audience.

He told members of the RSC that the Little Carib *Joker* was modern theatre history, but had outgrown what they planned and was not for them. In any case new budget cuts made it unlikely that they would have taken on such a large, for them experimental, project at that time. Walcott, impatient with the delays, withdrew his script and began unsuccessfully looking for an American producer.[19]

Walcott had learned much about speed and how to keep a musical in motion during rehearsals of *The Charlatan* at the Mark Taper. Jeremy Taylor, like other reviewers, complained that he wished he had a script to take him through the complicated plot. There was speed, gaiety, wit, and the acting and music were pleasing, but the details kept slipping past and he wanted to stop the show and hear bits again. Although the staging created immediacy, movement, and contact with the audience, the poetic language is so packed with images that Taylor doubted he picked up more than a tenth of what was being implied. Interpreting the play as about the male 'Don Juan complex' and the 'complementary female rape-complex, the fearful longing to be overcome by such as Don Juan', he questioned how seriously Walcott could expect the audience to take Isabella's claim that Don Juan 'made us women'.[20]

Marilyn Jones, however, saw the play as relevant to International Women's Year and as striking a blow for women's liberation. If the males in the play are 'chauvinist pigs' the women are given strong lines and arguments that condemn the narrowness of their society. Walcott examines the aristocratic social structure that determined the way Don Juan assumes his right to abuse women and others. Juan uses his position, but he is also a rebel from his class who recognizes the injustices of his time. Walcott's play is satiric about the role of Christianity in colonization. Jones found everything clear including Walcott's Freudian analysis of Don Juan, whose mother died when he was young. She thought Metivier's performance outstanding and Camps' the most professional and disciplined. Hughes was a born clown, but her voice control was limited. While Skipper's singing brought down the house, he tended to overact. Albert Laveau has tremendous feeling and sympathy in his part of Juan's father. Later interpretations would agree with Jones about Walcott's aims. Calling Isabella 'that fiery feminist', Judy Stone would write that she was best acted 'by the like-minded' Helen Camps.[21]

Therese Mills found the play 'brilliant with the poetry of Walcott's language spiced with dramatic effects and translated into real theatre'. Even Walcott's 'bawdy humour' for once was not out of place. While some of the singing was terrible the dancing and choreography were excellent. The sound system and costumes were poor, the costumes obviously done on the cheap, but the production itself was of high standard. Nigel Scott was strong and kept the focus on himself, which, as Errol Jones was on stage, is an achievement. 'If the original Juan looked, smiled and talked like Scott one does not need to sympathise, but envy the women who were his victims!'[22]

Questel agreed with Taylor that the plot had too many twists and turns. Walcott attempts to capture the illusion of movement by 'capsuling time and arriving at a fierce economy'. He also attempts to capture the rhythms of song, dance, gestures, and words along with the rhythms of life and death, pleasure, pain, self-knowledge, and delusion. Debates about the fall of man, heaven and hell, and nature are woven into the dialogue. Don Juan is 'on the quest for the Holy Grail, a journey which brings him to the New World' where he represents the European male 'who plundered the Americas'. Tisbea represents the people of the New World seduced by Juan. The seduction of Tisbea is the Garden of Eden 'all over again'. Don Juan, as portrayed by Scott, mixes sincerity and mockery. He represents European conquest with smiles and the sword. He is devil and butcher, a joker in the pack of cards where death has the last laugh. He is also a liberator who frees Isabella from innocence and gives her a new knowledge of herself. Hamilton Parris speaks with the slow deliberation of the folk, a manner he has mastered. Walcott sees himself in Rafael who has led a theatre company for fifteen years, while the meeting of Spanish with Trinidadian culture in parang points towards the play itself which like parang paradoxically celebrates death while mocking it. But there are too many incompatible folk elements in the play such as the Baptist revival dance. Syd Skipper's songs are the high point. The play is too long and needs to be cut by forty-five minutes.[23]

Five years later Walcott offered a seminar on *Joker* at the College of the Virgin Islands, St Thomas, in which he said that Juan is given and allows himself no time for reflection; there is no stasis in the play, no examination of conscience, no metaphysical crisis. Juan is anti-establishment, against traditions, someone who challenges God; his concern is how to get around an obstacle, not the deflowering of women. The play consists of a series of ironies or jokes in which the trickery reinforces the flaws of those who are tricked. Much of the trickery involves some exchange of costumes, a Carnivalesque role-playing. Others disguise themselves to get around the rules of conduct, so Juan takes their disguises for himself. At the play's conclusion there is a reversal which leads to Juan's going to hell. There is a kind of morality in the play. De Mota betrays the woman he loves, Juan betrays him by seducing his woman. The Tisbea section is written in prose because prose is rational, which suggests that Old World ways of thinking have been brought to the New World. Tisbea, for all her innocence, is also pretentious; reading has gone to her head. Making a parallel between Juan's shipwreck and Ulysses, she sees herself as Homer's Nausicaä and this makes her vulnerable. Aminta is vulnerable because she has ambitions above her real situation. Another reversal is that Isabella emerges radiant and a full woman after the self-flagellation she puts herself through. Although there is a hint of Juan's sexual ambiguity in a scene where he attracts someone who thinks he is a girl, this is not to suggest that Don Juans are repressed homosexuals unsatisfied with women because they need a male lover. *Joker* is not a play with that kind of simplified psychology which would destroy its argument.

For Walcott a vital interest of *Joker* was to create an equivalent to Tirso's rhymes and rhythm in a modern English verse that can be spoken naturally. The pentameter of the calypso gives him a living oral folk tradition of rhymed, vulgar, contemporary pentameter verse which is not available to poets in the United States (except in the blues) and England. The seeming unfused, disorganized movement of the play is like Carnival in which events do not follow a logical chronology, but in which there is a unity of the disparate. You do not need to understand all the words; as in Shakespeare you can follow what happens through the action. As a West Indian he felt no need to work within traditional notions of Don Juan imported from Europe. The morals do not concern him. What he wants is a similar 'exuberance of performance', especially a vulgarity found in the popular theatre of the past that has been lost and refined away in later theatre. It is a vulgarity found in Shakespeare and Villon but not in Racine.[24]

On 4 December the National Brewery Company (for which Norline Metivier worked as a secretary) offered a $7,000 annual subsidy to the TTW provided that they produce at least two plays a year and two 'free' public performances each season. This was the first time that any business in Trinidad had offered money to support the TTW. Walcott then drew up a proposal for a new, 'semi-professional' phase of the Trinidad Theatre Workshop which would require a grant of $50,000–$60,000. It was based on the assumption that they now had a probable audience of approximately 1,500. He hoped to have regular runs of two weeks as the Little Carib only seated a maximum of 400.

The Workshop needed a secure location so that it could organize a subscription season with seasonal tickets and patrons instead of having to do each play on an ad hoc basis, which had been the situation since eviction from the Basement Theatre. Although the actors were now paid a little, it was minimal because of such overhead expenses as theatre rental, rental of lights and chairs, along with set construction and costumes.[25]

While accepting that local theatre needs to be commercially viable, the TTW needed a grant as security in planning a second phase when it would produce two seasons a year and an annual tour to other islands. Walcott had in a mind a company of twenty-five to thirty actors with a structure of an artistic director, treasurer, secretary, business manager, and tour manager along with committees. There would be a core of six professional actors who would be paid for two seasons including six weeks of rehearsals before the two weeks of actual performance of each play. The figures in Walcott's proposal are difficult to follow, but it seems that the actors would need be paid $4,800 full-time for 12 weeks or $2,400 part-time for 12 weeks. Walcott then began totalling other costs. They now pay $300 a season for lights; so they need a modest light system costing about $3,000–$4,000. Chairs now cost $200 for rental; they should instead own some proper chairs. The actors now pay $2 a month towards 'facilities', but they need to rent a place for costume storage, pay typists, and so on. If they could have two seasons a year and a two-week annual tour, offering three new plays each year and several 'concert' tours, it would be possible to sustain the theatre commercially.

The 10 December *Express* carried a letter to the editor from their drama critic Jeremy Taylor, who had written the one negative review of *Joker*. He saw the play a second time and changed his opinion as 'many things which had puzzled me fell into place'; he now enjoyed 'this vast and complex play better than anything else' he had seen during the past year. Taylor now praises Walcott's abandonment of the naturalistic stage and the freedom gained which allowed conflicts, paradox, and difference to be fused into a coherent experience. He had originally failed to understand that Don Juan was genuinely criticizing the treatment of Isabella and such matters as chivalry and faith, that what 'had first seemed an outrage' was in actuality Isabella's awakening, and that lust for property was no 'purer' than Juan's lust. Such a deep and rich play requires 'continued acquaintance'.[26]

Two days later Walcott replied to Ken Chee, who had informed him of the National Brewery Company subsidy. Walcott could not yet offer a detailed budget for the coming year, but urged that the money be paid in a few large sums so that it can be used properly and not be frittered away on minor expenses. He hoped to revive *Joker* in January and take it on a three-week tour, perhaps with a new Walcott play, to St Croix, Puerto Rico, and Jamaica. He hoped there would be a concert tour of *Songs for the Theatre* to Barbados and St Lucia with June Nathaniel, Patrick Flores, Andrew Beddeau, Syd Skipper, and some other singers and musicians, followed by a concert of André Tanker's music. Later there might be a production of *Threepenny Opera* with a steel band and public workshops.[27]

1974 ended with a video recording of Walcott's *Jourmard* for Trinidad & Tobago Television, directed by Horace James on 15 December and with Astor Johnson's Repertory Dance Theatre (RDT) at the Little Carib, 11–15 December, followed by a performance at the Northeastern College, Sangre Grande, on the 18 December. Adele Bynoe, Astor Johnson, and Noble Douglas went directly from *Joker* into the dance season. Walcott, who was an 'Artistic Adviser', gave the RDT publicity through reviews and articles which suggested that he and Johnson had similar aesthetic aims and programmes.[28]

An unsigned article in *Tapia*, which may have been written by Walcott, or perhaps was closely based on publicity he prepared, points out that this is the 'first theatre season' at the Little Carib for over a decade. It began with *Joker of Seville* in November, followed by the RDT. Although the RDT has been in existence for only two years, it has already presented 'three full seasons of dance', two joint presentations with the Trinidad Theatre Workshop, several experimental projects and has been frequently presented on Trinidad & Tobago Television. The article argues that high standards can only be reached through a definite programme, exercises, and interim performances as part of a repertoire. Local audiences, however, have a Carnival mentality, they always want something new. They do not understand that an artist wants to save what has been created and improve it through revision. Many of the best dances of the past by McBurnie and others have been lost. Audiences must learn to appreciate that 'our arts' are not just entertainments for a season.[29]

If the article is Walcott's then it shows his continuing close support of Johnson, his feeling that dance may be the most important West Indian art, his awareness of being part of an era when West Indians were creating lasting art from their culture despite the 'Carnival' mentality of create, enjoy, destroy, characteristic of Trinidadian society, a destructiveness that Earl Lovelace's *The Dragon Can't Dance* sees as a carry-over from slavery. The article warns that work of value, recent cultural history, already has been lost and is unrecoverable. There is the continuing need for a subsidized theatre with a building of its own, a place to rehearse, a stage of its own, and some paid actors and teachers who can build a tradition of West Indian arts of world standards without the constant hustle to survive from performance to performance. Walcott's dreams were still those with which he returned from New York in 1959 and many of the problems remained the same, but the success of *Joker* showed that by one means or other he had built a national theatre company which would have a place in the history of drama and theatre.

NOTES

1. Walcott's letter to the TTW and his correspondence with Ruth Moore are in the Walcott Collection, University of the West Indies, St Augustine.
2. Henry Goodman, 'Carnival with a Calypso Beat', *The Wall Street Journal* (4 June 1974), 20; repr. as 'Charlatan Scores in Los Angeles', *Sunday Guardian* (16 June 1974), 6.
3. Walcott's notes to Mel Shapiro concerning *The Charlatan* are in the Walcott collection, University of the West Indies, St Augustine.
4. Peter Andrews, 'Introducing Carol La Chapelle', *Sunday Punch* (26 Sept. 1976), 6; interviews in Trinidad (July 1990); programme from Trinidad Theatre Workshop Dance Company (1976).
5. John Falcon, 'The Spiritual Agony of an Old Coal-Burner', *Trinidad Guardian* (5 Aug. 1974), 5.
6. Bruce Paddington, 'Revival of "Monkey Mountain"', *Express* (4 Aug. 1974), 11–12.
7. Victor Questel, ' "Dream on Monkey Mountain" in Perspective', *Tapia* 4/35 (1 Sept. 1974), 2–3 (Independence suppl.); 4/36 (8 Sept. 1974), 6, 7, 10; 4/37 (15 Sept. 1974), 6–7; 4/39 (29 Sept. 1974), 5, 8. In *Dance, Drama, Art, Music*, 1/ 1 (June 1962), 23, Walcott mentions writing a folk epic titled *The Dream of Monkey Mountain*. Campbell, 'The Birth of Professional Theatre in Trinidad', *Sunday Guardian* (22 July 1973), 4; (29 July 1973), 11.
8. 'Walcott's "Dream" Comes to the Carib', *Trinidad Guardian* (22 July 1974), 7; 'White Barn Slates Two Plays by Trinidad Writer', *The Westport News*, sect. 2 (14 Aug. 1974), 10.
9. Aug. 1974, in Walcott Collection, UWI.
10. The various letters, notes and other materials concerning St Croix are in the Walcott Collection, University of the West Indies, St Augustine.
11. Letter of Agreement between the Courtyard Players and Derek Walcott (5 Sept. 1974). Lorraine Joseph, President Courtyard Players and Wyn Heftel, Committee Chairman.
12. Margaret Walcott wrote to BWIA pointing out that as the TTW always

travelled on BWIA she requested a Trinidad–Antigua ticket towards the cost of bringing Tony Hall from Edmonton, Alberta, Canada to St Croix. Margaret Walcott to Tex Hill (18 Sept. 1974).

13. 'Howard', New York, to Derek Walcott (12 Sept. 1974).

14. 'Now St Croix Hails Walcott's "Dream" ', *Trinidad Guardian* (24 Oct. 1974), 4.

15. 'Walcott Reading at Library Tonight', *Express* (17 Oct. 1974), 11; ' "Songs for Theatre" at the Library', *Trinidad Guardian* (5 Nov. 1974), 4.

16. Derek Walcott, 'Soul brother to "The Joker of Seville" ', *Trinidad Guardian* (8 Nov. 1974), 4. Another version of the article was published in the programme of the play and, with further revisions, in the published text of *The Joker of Seville & O Babylon!* (New York: Farrar, Straus and Giroux, 1978), 3–4.

17. Any information about the RSC not in Walcott's letters in the University of the West Indies Walcott Collection is from an interview with Ronald Bryden, Toronto (Nov. 1991).

18. 'Walcott scores with "The Joker" ', *Trinidad Guardian* (30 Nov. 1974), 9. For details of the production see 'Joker of Seville at Little Carib—gayelle style', *Express* (17 Nov. 1974), 7; ' "The Joker of Seville" at the Little Carib', *News*, Showtime sect. (21 Nov. 1974), 4.

19. Correspondence in Walcott Collection, University of the West Indies; interview with Ronald Bryden in Toronto (Nov. 1991).

20. Jeremy Taylor, 'The Joker of Seville—Actors Give Grand Performance', *Express* (4 Dec. 1974), 9, 18.

21. Marylin Jones, 'Striking a Blow for Women's Lib', *Trinidad Guardian* (12 Dec. 1974), 4; Stone, 'Walcott's "Joker" returns', *Trinidad Guardian* (30 Dec. 1987), 10.

22. Therese Mills, 'Sell-out Crowd Enjoys "The Joker" ', *Sunday Guardian* (1 Dec. 1974), 3, 15.

23. Victor Questel, 'Will Walcott Have the Last Laugh on His Joker?', *Trinidad Guardian* (6 Dec. 1974), 4.

24. A partial transcription of the seminar can be found in Derek Walcott, 'Derek Walcott Talks about "The Joker of Seville" ', *Carib*, 4 (1986), 1–15.

25. The correspondence and budget in UWI, Walcott Collection.

26. Jeremy Taylor, 'Praise for Joker of Seville', *Express* (10 Dec. 1974).

27. Derek Walcott to Ken Chee (12 Dec. 1974).

28. Walcott is listed as an 'Artistic Adviser' in the Season Two, 1974 Repertory Dance Theatre Programme and as the 'artistic director' in the eight-page publicity booklet printed for the 'August 1974 Gala Dance Season'. Sometime during 1975 Walcott stopped being artistic director of the RDT, presumably because Johnson's leading dancers were joining the TTW.

29. [Tapia Reporter], 'Something Good is Coming to Dance', *Tapia* (19 Dec. 1974), 10.

The Joker Revised and on Tour

THE JOKER OF SEVILLE had two more runs in Trinidad, was taken on tour to St Lucia and Jamaica and became, along with *Dream* and *Ti-Jean*, one of the legends of West Indian theatre. During 1975 alone there were close to fifty performances. Its record-breaking runs, however, barely made money. There were plans for salvation through sponsorship, state support, and professional tours of England or the United States, but salvation never came. The more artistically successful Walcott and the Theatre Workshop were, the more precarious their continued existence became; time, talent, and money kept being invested in projects that created new cultural areas in the Caribbean, brought fame, but at the end of day left unsolved such basic problems as where the actors could rehearse and perform their next play. The magnificent productions that gained fame abroad were rehearsed in public parks, the zoo, a building owned by a private social work institution, even in pubs. Scenery and props continued to be stored in the garage at Walcott's home.

Besides performing *Joker* the TTW experimented with multimedia theatre, offered a production of Chekhov's *The Seagull*, and workshopped other plays and projects. There were rehearsals for the Walcott version of the Brecht–Weill *Threepenny Opera* and some rehearsals of Philip Sherlock's *Daddy Sharpe* (with music by Olive Lewin apparently intended as a concert), along with plans to produce during the year a revival of *Ti-Jean*, a new Walcott play called *The Isle is Full of Voices* (eventually produced as *The Isle is Full of Noises* in 1982 in the United States), Mustapha Matura's *As Time Goes By* (with Stanley Marshall and Albert Laveau as directors), and a concert series including the painter LeRoy Clarke along with Andrew Beddeau, a concert of André Tanker's music, and a concert with Pat Flores and June Nathaniel. Rehearsals and performance of *As Time Goes By* were tentatively scheduled for August–October and a cast and production staff assigned (Anthony Hall and Errol Jones were the producers), but nothing came of it.[1]

A multimedia concert did take place under Walcott's direction and design at the Little Carib in February featuring LeRoy Clarke's paintings, slides, and poetry, along with dances choreographed by Carol La Chapelle and drumming and folk-singing by Andrew Beddeau. This began with rehearsals earlier in the month as a half-hour programme for television. Clarke, a poet and painter, had in the past designed sets and decor for *The Blacks* and *Moon on a Rainbow Shawl*. The dancers included Noble Douglas, Norline Metivier, Adele Bynoe, and Syd Skipper. There were songs and dances from *Joker*, various slide projections, and choral singing. The production crew included Albert Laveau, Jerline Quamina, and Stanley Marshall. The slide projector was lent by the Canadian High Commission. Walcott's personal notes propose that he, Beddeau, and Clarke would each be paid $100 and La Chapelle $75. Ten per cent would be deducted for the Workshop. A possible salary budget for a concert series is also sketched in with Walcott and La Chapelle to be paid $150, Clarke and Beddeau to be paid a total of $300 for two concerts, and four dancers (Metivier, Douglas, Bynoe, and Chapelle) to be paid $75 each. Victor Questel found unsuccessful the attempt to blend words and images, but praised the dancing and Beddeau's singing and drumming.[2]

There was a meeting at Semp Studios in late January to discuss recording *Joker* on a long-playing recording. The TTW needed to pay $3,000 for a first pressing of 2,000 albums of which only 500 to 1,000 could initially be delivered. 5,000 album jackets were ordered. Galt MacDermot had the music recorded in the United States and the rest was done in Trinidad. The cost was around $10,000 and eventually there was a profit. The LP was officially released on 8 March at a party at the Little Carib Theatre. This was the first LP issued by the TTW and the first of a Trinidadian show. A cassette of the recording is still available, but the master tapes of other recordings made by the Workshop at Semp have disappeared. Besides reel-to-reel taped recordings of music from the shows that were sent ahead for tours, there were plans to issue LPs of *Ti-Jean*, *The Charlatan*, and of Andrew Beddeau singing and drumming. It is not clear what was actually recorded for possible commercial distribution. Nothing else was pressed and the master tapes have a long, confusing history including a probable robbery, someone hiding from creditors, and other unsavoury details. Reel-to-reel tapes in the Walcott Collection at the University of the West Indies, St Augustine, include copies of music from the shows.[3]

During the second run of *Joker* at the Little Carib, 13–23 March, two nights were cancelled because of a transportation strike and lack of electricity and gasoline; two extra nights were added, 25 and 26 March. On the opening day the *Guardian* carried a letter urging that the second run should not have a white leading actor, should not use the word 'nigger', and should stop making fun of being black. Walcott did not delete the vulgarity which obviously pleased the crowd if not everyone, but to make better use of his company over a long run he had Albert Laveau alternate the role of Juan with Nigel Scott. Other alternates were Laveau and Claude Reid as Don Diego, Claude Reid and Errol Pilgrim as Batricio, Joy Ryan and Carol La Chapelle as Ana, and Stephanie King and Brenda Hughes as Tisbea. As La Chapelle was also a dancer she, Laveau, and Reid were scheduled for every performance.[4]

Walcott revised *Joker* for its second run to include more 'vulgar' comedy with prostitutes in the brothel sequence, and the addition of several 'freezes' in the action; songs were moved around, and there were fewer dancers and singers. The effect was less choral and communal, more spare and clean-cut. This resulted in less audience participation. The play continued to pack the house, except for a few nights when political problems brought the country to a standstill.

Walcott's article 'The Joker: Closer to Continuous Theatre' reflected on the way Trinidad might be influenced by two ten-night runs to full houses. Audiences were ready for a permanent repertory company. It was now possible to have continuous theatre in Port of Spain. The three Sunday-morning performances with natural light suggest a possible Trinidadian performance schedule. The local actors usually have to perform at night after a day's work in the office. Maybe there could be short plays offered at lunch time? As some people saw *Joker* three or four times it is difficult to say how much the audience really has been broadened, but it is clearly time for the government to establish a national theatre to train the young. The *Joker* would only break even financially and the actors would need to take reduced salaries as heavy overheads for cost of theatre rental, lights, and seating cut into any profits.[5]

Walcott's 'Open Letter to the Company' mentions that because of the petrol situation they might be playing to small houses for a few nights, but this was not discouraging. They were pioneering continuous runs and it was important to accustom the public to the notion that they could attend a play whenever it is convenient rather than on two or three nights. Ideally there should be a subscription season with advance bookings, but it was at present too difficult to organize. Ten thousand dollars were invested in the revival of *The Joker*, mostly for the rental of the theatre, lights, and better management of the box office. Provided they broke even it would be worth it to continue playing and improve their performances. Walcott had been watching the performances with great joy; regardless of the size of the audiences it was important that the actors concentrate on 'refining' their skills. Ten years ago they felt professional if an actor was paid $10 a week at the Basement Theatre. A few years from now they will feel that pride in a run of twenty nights is equally amusing. Their determination and spirit in educating the public gave him pride and love as their director. As artists they were illuminating life. 'Continue to take joy in that gift.' The real revolution was in their art, not in the strikes and marches outside. 'If I did not believe that, I would not be here and would not have dedicated my life to this work, so press on.'[6]

With the two added performances the revival of *The Joker* had entered its third week. The next week after a sell-out performance at Naparima Bowl, San Fernando, Walcott and two others flew to St Lucia the next day to prepare the St Lucian tour of the play; the rest of the cast arrived on 5 April. There were rehearsals on the 6 April and performances from 7 April until 12 April at the Old Geest Banana Shed, an open-sided structure near the wharves where bananas are collected and sheltered for shipment. It had sometimes been used for boxing matches and Carnival shows. A boxed area was used for the stage. On 13 April there was a performance for hotel guests at Halycon Days, Vieux Fort.

Earlier Walcott had circulated a pre-tour report to the TTW explaining that his hopes for performances in Barbados were unfulfilled. He could not find, as in St Lucia, a committee of people who would actively arrange for a tour. There were no inexpensive accommodations in the tourist season; the dormitories of the Barbados Workers Union College were not available when they would be needed. The Arts Council had not helped. If the TTW were to perform in Barbados they would need to find a well-organized group like the Lions Club to underwrite the tour and arrange accommodations.

Walcott visited St Lucia before Barbados and within three days a committee was formed by Patricia Charles, Dunstan St Omer, Kenneth Monplaisir, Keith Weeks, and others. The Prime Minister was helpful. As usual practical details occupied Walcott's time. They could probably stay at the Morne Training College for $10 a day including meals and linen. This would include breakfast, a sandwich lunch, and a pre-theatre dinner. Otherwise in-season rates could be $40 a person a day as in Barbados. The Morne is on a hill with fantastic views. There is a modern kitchen, but accommodation might be four persons to a room. Transportation within St Lucia would be by a school bus to and from the theatre. Walcott hoped to have rent-free use of the Old Geest Banana shed. He had made notes for wiring and lighting, and discussed the rental of microphones and speakers. They would need to rent spot lights, dimmers, and gels.

There would be a three-feet high platform about 16ft × 24ft which would be used as an open stage. The seating would be full arena style starting 5ft from the platform. A few rows of chairs might be available at no cost. Behind them there would be bleachers. Walcott had left 150 posters behind for publicity and did an interview with Radio St Lucia and a 'radio-ad' which could be used. The government would probably print the tickets for free. As the TTW is a touring company they would need pay a 15 per cent entertainment tax on their gross receipts. The Halycon Hotel was likely to pay $1,500 for a perform-ance. Walcott arranged everything, but the Workshop members would need to discuss the plans and agree at a meeting.[7]

Some idea of the problems Walcott had in moving his large cast and his need to cut costs can be seen from a letter Patricia Charles of the Extra-Mural Department in St Lucia wrote, 12 March, to the permanent secretary of the Ministry of Education and Culture request-ing use of the Iron Barracks on the Morne to house the TTW. She said that the English cricket team would be leaving on the morning of 5 April, when the company arrived, and schools would not resume until 14 April, so the tour had been planned to avoid any conflict. Walcott would pay $10 per day for each person. Walcott had worked hard to cut costs. A six-inch advertisement in The Voice was 'Courtesy of Heinekens'.[8]

As now often happened, Walcott's play, whether intended to do so or not, became part of the ongoing discussion about politics, culture, and race in the West Indies. An editorial in The Voice of St Lucia pro-claimed that Walcott's Joker could offer guidance to those people impatiently searching for identity without the patience to understand the admixtures that have gone into the evolution of the Caribbean people and the nation. 'We cannot be successful in finding the golden egg by tearing the bird apart.'[9]

The 9 April Voice of St Lucia carried a review on the front page saying *The Joker* was up to all the praises it had received in Trinidad. There are so many happenings and so much movement on stage that 'one avoids looking away for fear of missing something'. There were sell-out crowds. After the Workshop returned to Trinidad *The Voice* carried a longer review describing *Joker* as showing the character of the West Indian 'people' and in its plot, language, music, and dance the meeting of cultures. *The Voice* called *Joker* 'a landmark and a standard' for future West Indian plays.[10]

George Odlum, one of the original members of the St Lucia Arts Guild, and one of the group who had performed *Sea at Dauphin* and *Malcochon* in London, had over the years become a leader of the Left opposition in St Lucia. As the editorial in *The Voice* suggests, the island was going through intense political problems at the time and Walcott's *Joker* would be interpreted differently by the various parties. Odlum's *Crusader* of 12 April 1975 had on its masthead two quotations from *Joker* concerning corruption and the dangers of befriending a scorpion, which in the context of the newspaper's two front-page headlines were meant to be applicable to John Compton, head of the government. Inside the paper Odlum reviewed the play as a 'molotov cocktail of enjoyment and revolution'. After finding a political message about social inequality in the New World, Odlum admits that there is a density of texture about *The Joker* which allows many interpretations. Too many lines, however, were gobbled by actors unable to handle Walcott's words and metre. Their diction needs improvement.[11]

The unexpected public success of *The Joker*, along with the way it had expanded the dimensions of West Indian theatre, resulted in critics taking a closer look at what Walcott and the Workshop had been doing over the years, the conditions in which they worked, and why theatre had become significant to local culture. While the TTW was performing in St Lucia, Marylin Jones wrote in the *Trinidad Guardian* deploring the lack of a 'home' for Trinidadian artists. 'A sparsed-leafed tree for cover. For the most part exposed. Exposed, as might be said, "under the pigeon's quick opinion". Or blessings from the sky. It is against this backdrop that the actors of the Trinidad Theatre Workshop performed their latest big success.' Jones describes backstage at the Little Carib as a an overcrowded nightmare in which props are stored against the neighbour's wall, a few small cubicles are used for costume changes and make-up, mirrors are unviewable because of overcrowding, and costumes are hung on hooks unsheltered from the rain.[12]

Apparently those in power claimed that the Greek theatre survived outdoors. Jones says that it is time that either the government or private sector take some responsibility for the arts in Trinidad. If McBurnie had not struggled to create the Little Carib there would be no place for the TTW to perform. The company is beyond teething and needs a home so it can continue to develop. The article ends with a rapid review of the March production comparing it to the December version. In the second run the actors were more confident, but this made the stronger stand out from the weaker actors. The play was revised to build up to several comic peaks, but it seemed to sag towards the end. Was the conclusion cut too much to speed up the play and make it more explicit? The fishing village scene with Tisbea remained her favourite and two songs, 'Big Foot Bertha' and 'The King of Castille Has No Sense of Humour', now appeared hits although she had not liked them at first.

Raoul Pantin contrasted the amazing success of the TTW with the floundering of public institutions in Trinidad. With the San Fernando performance the TTW had performed *Joker* twenty-five times and on many nights crowds were lining up in the streets and had to be turned away. Perhaps 5,000 people had seen the play in Port of Spain alone in comparison with the usual maximum of 500 for four or five nights. Walcott, Errol Jones, and other Workshop members have worked for many years for this success and now Walcott's dreams and hard work have come close to reality. 'Nothing like Derek Walcott's *The Joker of Seville* has ever been in Trinidad! In the world for that matter.' The play replies to Naipaul's 'nothing was ever created in the West Indies'. Walcott has transformed de Molina's play into 'Spanish Trinidad and parang. Calypsonians and stick-fighters. Boot-licking ambassadors. Robber talk. Slave ships. Limbo-dancing Negroes. Sex, scandal and the Roman Catholic Church. Liberated Women.' He has put a large chunk of Trinidad into *Joker* and the achievement is breathtakingly unlike anything seen before. 'When Walcott inserts Trinidad dialect into a play thundering with English couplet precision the effect is shaking.' Jones deserves a Trinidadian equivalent to the Academy Award for his Catalinion; Scott is marvellous as Don Juan. Metivier brings the house down. There is a concerted pooling of talent. The last time West Indies saw extreme political discontent, during the late 1930s and 1940s, it was accompanied by an outburst of creative writing about the colonial and economic situation. Now that 'our politics smell of repression, our artists are restless again. It is significant that our artists, who are but voices of the spirit of our people, are singing about freedom like never before.'[13]

So, paradoxically, Walcott, who has been criticized as apolitical and only concerned with his art, had created a play and theatrical event which in Trinidad, St Lucia, and perhaps elsewhere was viewed as the voice of the people against the repressive regimes that were commonplace in the West Indies during the 1970s. Anyone who reads the West Indian newspapers or Walcott's poems of the period will see that he was outspoken in his opposition to the growing tyranny in Haiti, Trinidad, and throughout the Caribbean. His devotion to his art was part of his belief in the freedom of the individual against repression, whether the oppressor was imperialism, the State, the Church, or intellectuals calling themselves the People. Such a vision animates the plot and themes of *The Joker*. But then a belief in individual expression, free speech, and civil rights is common to most artists, especially in new nations. They would be self-destructive not to be humanists concerned with individuals. It is usually the politician, intellectual, or incompetent artist who disguises the desire for power with claims to speak for the Folk, Worker, People, Race, or Nation.

Patricia Ismond wrote a long, intelligent review in *Tapia* using the theme of women's liberation in *The Joker* as a starting place to survey Walcott's achievement with the TTW. The open, non-naturalistic form of the musical allows Walcott to bring out the universal themes of de Molina's play in modern, West Indian analogies using 'native creole rhythms' from folk culture, dance, and song. The West Indian stick fight corresponds to the Spanish sword fight. The shipwreck which brings Juan to the New World is dramatized as a metaphor for the Middle Passage. The celebration of Tisbea's rape—the Old World's possession of the New—'is patterned on local forms of possession cults'. Don Juan as rebel against the restrictive codes of Spain is the libido or human desire challenging limitations. It is an existential rebellion for freedom since chastity and honour are regarded by their Spanish defenders as God-given. The moral challenge to authority, revealing the hypocrisy of those he seduces and cheats, results in a paradoxical freedom. He can either lose or find himself in freedom. If violation is freedom it brings bitterness and outrage as well as the beneficent and recalls the absurd distance between human aspirations and limitations. While the play counters this absurdity by laughter, Juan cannot find the strength of humility to go beyond rebellion and surrender himself to the creative. He is too proud; in becoming a force of resistance he has lost his humanity, his moral freedom. 'The burden is expressed in the theme song *Sans Humanité*, with which the first production concluded (it is replaced by *Little Red Bird* in the second production to stress the theme of freedom).' Juan the arch-rebel is modern man resisting 'orthodoxies and establishments in order to confront existential contradictions and the imperative of choice'. It is also the choice of the West Indian in the New World.

Ismond sees a clear connection between the existentialist philosophical dimension of the play and its application to West Indian history. Will the region be imprisoned in vengeance because of its past or face the freedom offered by the New World? Juan comes to the New World expecting innocence but finds it already corrupted and contributes to its fall. The Old World repeats itself in seeking vengeance, new laws and uncreative faiths such as Black Power and nostalgia for Africa. These substitute for the former Master's laws. Blackness is artifice rather than 'true consciousness'.

Ismond says that a sign of *The Joker's* popular success is that its music has already become part of 'our everyday experience', the way music from the Carnival does. The play consists of sequences in which the climaxes are unmistakably West Indian in their rhythms, tempo, and sensibility. The Middle Passage 'is mimed in patterned movements which blend elements of the limbo dance with gestures indicating lack of direction and disaster', suggestive both of oppression and shipwreck. The physical style and vigorousness are recognizably black West Indian and will be difficult for directors to replicate elsewhere. There was a communal elation in the audiences of the first run, which was less common in the second. Walcott modulates the high style by contact with the popular which 'remints' it 'into its own coinage' as seen in the bawdy jokes or in the West Indian reductive humour of pun, parody, and calypso which uses verbal extravagance and elaborate metaphors mock-heroically, blending the serious with the ribald. Juan's seduction of Tisbea uses metaphors recalling the garden of Eden and bawdy puns about the physical details. Even the songs have further local resonances. 'Tisbea went and Bathe' recalls the old calypso 'Miss Elsie'.

Hamilton Parris, 'always the most relaxed and unstrenuous of the actors in the Company', who served as the leader of the Chorus, articulated many of the philosophical themes yet retained 'the native inflection throughout'. 'His style shows best of all how intrinsic the basic rhythms of West Indian dialect remain in Walcott's diction.' In Walcott's total theatre the actors must also be able to sing, dance, and mime. Ismond found Metivier hesitant as an actress, and La Chapelle a supple dancer who strains as Ana. Anthony Hall has considerable ability as an actor and in mime; the physical and verbal interact in his portrayal of Don Pedro. The TTW veterans have the versatility Walcott needs. Stanley Marshall can switch from classical acting and the sustained immobility of the statue 'to a remarkable display of body language as stick fighter'. Noble Douglas, 'whose every movement has a special West Indian freedom and eloquence', was outstanding dancing the prostitute.[14]

Walcott had found in the American musical a stylized, nonnaturalistic form, similar to what he had earlier appreciated in Oriental theatre, which could be developed into an authentically West Indian style. Just as American composers and choreographers during the 1940s and 1950s transformed the European operetta into a radically new American musical theatre, using American song and dance, and with its own conventions, so Walcott used calypso, limbo, Baptist spirituals, stick fights, and other elements of West Indian culture to create a new regional form. The *Joker's* plot and basic myth is European, the form he takes over and develops is American; the result is West Indian. Essentially Walcott was taking further the notion of total, non-naturalistic, poetic theatre, but more completely integrating song, dance, mime, verse, and comedy into the play. Many of his early ideas about theatre found new forms of expression. The still points of Japanese theatre were translated by way of Brecht into 'freezes'. As in the Los Angeles *The Charlatan* the story is told as much by song, action, gesture, and movement as by speech. The play operates at various levels of perception. The themes of the verse are counterpointed, supported, treated ironically, or mocked by song, visual symbolism, gesture, or voice. Often the West Indian elements provide both local associations for the larger themes and a more realistic appraisal, or, what West Indian critics call a reductive humour; they are the equivalent of the prose or clown scenes in Shakespearean drama and similar to the Trinidadian fierce verbal satire known as picong.

Song and dance were becoming more and more central to Walcott's dramatic practice. They were no longer just accompaniments; they had become significant parts of the text itself, providing action, symbol, narration, and alternative perspectives. Just as Walcott's verse and plots are filled with echoes of other works, providing a rich intertextuality and suggesting many subtexts and analogies, so the visual setting, the dance, and the music had its metaphoric resonances, recalling artistic movements and periods, drawing on cultural associations ranging from opera to Caribbean Shango and possession cults. Such a form so totally integrated with a regional style meant, however, that Walcott's musicals would be difficult to produce outside the

Caribbean. A director's theatre offering serious musical plays with large casts might be appropriate for a wealthy, state-sponsored theatre company, but Walcott's miracle in taking the TTW so far was really pushing beyond the limits of probability, especially in the West Indies. This might partly account for a surprising new interest in the possibilities of naturalistic theatre, or in the ways the naturalistic and non-naturalistic could be blended, characteristics found in many of Walcott's later plays. The first sign of this interest occurred during the successful runs of *The Joker*. It is as if for a time, having taken verse drama as far as it could go, Walcott suddenly started thinking about the poetic possibilities of prose and realism.

On 6 May Barbara Jenson, the Theatre Workshop's new stage manager, wrote to the Officer of the Commissioner of Police for permission to borrow and use an antique shotgun, serial no. 516S, the property of the Trinidad and Tobago Police Service, for rehearsals and performances of Chekhov's *The Seagull*. Permission was granted on 18 May for such use up to 19 July. Commissioner May informed her that the shotgun would be forwarded to the St Claire Police Station from where it could be collected and '*must*' be returned at the end of each rehearsal and performance.[15]

Even while rehearsing *The Seagull* members of the Workshop were busy trying to scratch a professional career in serious theatre from an impoverished environment. Later in May four TTW actors—Albert Laveau, Hamilton Parris, Stephanie King, and Stanley Marshall—performed in Horace James's Trinidad & Tobago Television's 'Play of the Month', *Meeting* by Lennox Brown. Jeremy Taylor thought it 'a great change' from the usual fare offered by television in Trinidad.[16]

During 10–19 July the TTW performed Chekhov's *The Seagull* for ten nights at the Little Carib with Walcott directing. This was their first big production of a classic of the 'naturalist' or realist European theatre, unlike the avant-garde, non-naturalistic plays of Beckett, Genet, and Ionesco that they had performed during the 1960s. While his recent successes suggested that Walcott now had a cast of actors ready to attempt more difficult roles than in the past (and during the next decade he would be concerned with exploring the uses of a smaller, more realistic theatre), there is reason to think that the choice of the play may have had personal reasons.

Between the first and second run of *Joker* Walcott became Norline Metivier's lover; unlike several other affairs of the heart this one was serious. Metivier, a dancer who became a comic actress in *Joker*, was given, despite her protests, the role of Zaryechnaia in *The Seagull*.

Increasingly Walcott would push her forward into serious acting roles for which she felt unprepared. His friendships now were often with the younger members of the cast, especially the female dancers who had joined during the past year, to whom he would confide his hopes, ambitions, and complaints. Walcott was in his forties, the usual time for a mid-life crisis. His marriage was going through a rough period. He was in contact with the big names of the theatre world of New York and London. *The Seagull* and several of Chekhov's plays might seem appropriate to his own situation.[17]

The cast of *The Seagull* included Helen Camps, Norline Metivier, Carol La Chapelle, Christen Krogh, Errol Jones, Albert Laveau, Claude Reid, Hamilton Parris, and Winston Goddard. Newcomers for the production were Michael De Verteuil, who had acted at university in Canada, and Pat Samuel. Walcott directed and Barbara Jenson was stage manager. Christopher Lynch, who designed the costumes and shared in the set design with Walcott, had designed for London's Royal Court Theatre, the Beatles, Mick Jagger, and Sir Alec Guinness.

Some reasons why Walcott produced *The Seagull* can be found in the 'Homage' he wrote for the programme suggesting that Chekhov is his favourite dramatist and *The Seagull* one the world's most beautiful plays. It presents the truth of the world; its people are mean, selfish, laughable, and egotistical, yet vulnerable. The characters are people not characters; they are in search of self-definition, yet they seek self-definition through others. Groping for greatness they 'embrace inertia'. No sooner do they make vows than they break them and do not realize the damage they do. An actor must 'become a person to play Chekhov'. His characters are filled with contradictions and absurdities, but we do not know them any more than we know any other human being. This requires actors to keep their part 'simple' in contrast to the detail of supposedly naturalistic acting. 'His art is the art of shedding art, of unlearning all.' This is a challenge to ensemble playing; 'an ensemble should only dare Chekhov after years of working together as a company'.

Two articles Walcott wrote at the time mention the attraction of successfully acting such a difficult play. Asking what has made the play a masterpiece, Walcott replies that the hardest task is 'the art of reproducing the banality of life while it illuminates it, the delicacy of its selection of clichés, and its superb economy of action. Lives are revealed in a single gesture, in an unfinished phrase', in the orchestration of pauses. As in music there are melodies, arias, cadenzas, and lyricism. Walcott was aware that this was the première of the play for

Trinidad and after years of creating an audience for his own plays and avant-garde contemporary theatre he was suddenly offering a nineteenth-century naturalistic European classic, the kind of play that was the staple of amateur theatre groups, often poorly acted, and associated with the culturally pretentious. Walcott felt that after '15 years of building up an ensemble' he and the Workshop had earned the right to attempt Chekhov, whose plays require a house style as 'every single character in his plays is different and equally important'; there is a subtle harmony of 'interplaying'. Chekhov's great plays are farces, but farces with compassion and without bitterness. Chekhov does not create plots to illustrate ideas. His characters talk prosaically about money, taxes, possessions, and practical achievements. Wherever there are people they will have similar feelings, ambitions, and losses and will 'probe gently at the use they have made of their lives'. It requires great discipline for an actor to represent such a life.

Walcott then turns to the similarities between Chekhov's plays and the West Indies. 'Like his, the genius of West Indian theatre is also comic.' The West Indian manner is flamboyant, self-dramatizing, close to farce. The West Indies has a similar history of being a province with its landed gentry with their pretensions who mismanage the estate, 'rising bourgeoisie and threatening serf'. Chekhov's characters have rural agricultural beginnings, neglect their homeland and mimic the sophistication and manners of Paris. Chekhov's message is to 'develop and love one's homeland'.[18]

Errol Hill described the Workshop's *Seagull* as a gallant attempt. After discussing Chekhov's interiorization of character, use of atmosphere, actionless plots, and pointillist technique, Hill thought it was courageous to attempt such a complex and difficult play. He had praise for the clarity of speech, movement, and grouping; such matters as decor, lighting, and snatches of Chopin in the background created a tone poem. But only a few of the actors, especially Krogh and Parris, both looked the part and sensitively 'caught the right tone of comic resignation'. They and Marshall were wistfully comic without overdoing their parts. Metivier was misdirected to play Nina in such a melancholic way as if she knew her future misfortunes. She should be exuberant, seeing herself at the start of a glorious career. Hill liked La Chapelle's stage presence and diction, but felt her Masha should be more subdued, less explosive. Albert Laveau looked and acted like Trigorin, but he did not convey ambition and feeling under the technical veneer.[19]

Jeremy Taylor commented that *The Seagull* was the opposite of *The*

Joker, having little movement, scarcely a plot, not much colour, and no local topicality. While Walcott sees the play as comic the production is too heavy. Camps as Arkadina convincingly brings style and vitality to her role, Krogh and Jones are impressive, there is 'a sense of ensemble playing of which the company can be proud', but the comedy and pathos are out of balance. Taylor hoped that *The Seagull* would remain in the Workshop's repertory.[20]

Victor Questel found Walcott's directing conservative but careful in following Chekhov's instructions. The groupings and small talk are done well. Questel would have liked more atmosphere to give a clear insight into motivation, with greater silences. Krogh best sustained the mood and was always in control of his pace and gestures, whereas De Verteuil lost concentration and become wooden as the play progressed. Metivier needed a greater range of tone and feelings. La Chapelle has grown as an actress since *Joker*. Camps was at home playing Arkadina with her large gestures. *The Seagull* brings balance to the Workshop's repertory, but some actors are starting to become stereotyped by a particular kind of role.[21]

After the run of *The Seagull* Astor Johnson's RDT performed in Port of Spain, Tobago, and at Sangre Grande during August. The company included Noble Douglas and Greer Jones, but Carol La Chapelle was out of action due to injury at the time.

On 30 October Stanley Marshall wrote on behalf of the TTW to the Management of Amoco Trinidad Oil seeking assistance. After reviewing the history and achievements of the Workshop, Marshall said they were finding it difficult to maintain and improve their standards because of the poor yet exorbitantly priced facilities in Port of Spain. Queen's Hall is acoustically bad and costs $125 per night. The Little Carib consists only of four walls and a roof, but costs $100 a night. They need to rent chairs, lights, pay for their installation and removal, and somehow dress. There is no place they can store sets, properties, or costumes, which means that materials cannot be reused, adding to the costs of production. The company meets twice a week for workshops and five times a week for rehearsals, but they need to pay $10 a time for using the Little Carib, if it is available. This is a drain on finances. As Amoco has in the past generously assisted the departments of welfare, education, and culture, could it now help the TTW better its facilities?[22]

In October *Joker* returned to the Little Carib for a further ten nights before its Jamaican tour. Contractually *Joker* remained the property of the Royal Shakespeare Company which had permitted the TTW to perform the play in the Caribbean. Lack of Arts Council funding had delayed any possibility of an RSC production in England for another year. Richard Montgomery, who would design sets for the Jamaica production, attended run-throughs in Port of Spain. Besides the principal parts, supporting actors were also alternated for this run. Wilbert Holder and Syd Skipper alternated as Duke Octavio; Helen Camps and Sheila Goldsmith played Isabella; Scott and Laveau took turns as Don Juan. Claude Reid acted Catalinion; La Chapelle was now Ana. La Chapelle also extensively revised the dances; and there were new dancers including Greer Jones, Oscilla Stewart, Jennifer Hobson Garcia, Brian Walker, and Edison Carr. Because of changes in cast many new costumes had to be made. Typical of the improvisation is Barbara Jenson's stage manager's notes for the King of Castille in Scene iii. If Mohammed plays the King he will need a new costume; if Errol Jones is acting he could use his *Seagull* costume 'with epaulettes'.[23]

Mauby described the TTW as the nearest Trinidad has to a national company and commented on the pleasure of being able to follow a production as it matured. *Joker* warranted a completely new review. It is now more taut; the choreography of the stick fighting has been refined and the actors are more skilful in handing the pole, but the death fight between Juan and Don Gonzalo still feels inactive. Claude Reid is more West Indian in his broad laughter at Don Juan's exploits whereas Errol Jones had been restrained as a dignified Moor. Jones had to contain his natural power on stage and aim for an inner steely force, while Reid treats Juan more man to man. Reid's use of slow motion animating his horse is exceptional. Holder as Octavio is more extroverted and emotional than the brooding Skipper. Feroze Mohammed, a last-minute replacement for Laurence Goldstraw, lacks a commanding bearing and looks more like a bellboy than a king. Whereas Stephanie King was femininely provocative as Tisbea, Brenda Hughes is innocent; her sense of timing and intonation get laughs. Beddeau, who was ill at ease as the Ace of Spades in earlier runs, is now relaxed and confident on stage. Metivier remains delightful as Aminta. Anthony Hall remains polished and physically and verbally dexterous as Don Pedro. The play is still too long.[24]

The Jamaica tour of *Joker* involved seventeen performances by thirty members of the TTW between 22 November and 6 December at the University of the West Indies Creative Arts Center. This was the third time Pan-Jamaican Investment Trust brought the Trinidad Theatre Workshop to Jamaica. The Trust covered most of the costs but not salaries; the company stayed at a hotel owned by a member of

Pan-Jamaican. British West Indian Airways donated a large part of the transportation.

A significant difference between the earlier and the Jamaican production was the set by Richard Montgomery and the costumes Richard and Sally Montgomery designed. Whereas Walcott's original costumes were 'period', based on old paintings, the Montgomerys' were impressionistic, using local materials, such as bamboo and raw wood for the set and tie-dyed rags and straws for the costumes. In Montgomery's version the characters would first appear static in Elizabethan poses behind a screen, then move realistically out of the pose and silhouette into the action on stage. This created almost a double vision, which people have called surreal. Photographs show the production reached international professional standards while remaining a theatre of poverty. The effects are somewhat hallucinatory with an almost bare stage, a few props appropriate to a cock-fight ring, the double perspective costumes suggestive of a Spanish Elizabethan period. Masks were constructed by local students. Although Montgomery was Walcott's favourite set designer, there is no consensus about his contribution to *Joker*. Some people prefer the earlier period feel that Walcott created; others speak highly of the professionalism, vibrancy, and immediacy of Montgomery's work. His feeling for matters of texture, sheen, and atmosphere influenced Trinidadian staging of plays. Curiously the two white outsiders made the production even more Caribbean. MacDermot's father's uncle was the well-known Tom Redcam, one of the few significant Jamaican writers earlier in the century. If Walcott wanted to bring the professionalism of Broadway and the Royal Court to the Workshop, he had found people willing to commit themselves to his plays and to the development of West Indian theatre. André Tanker at this time had neither the skills in writing orchestration nor interest in doing the music for *Joker*. The elaborate dance sequences required a written score for support, or at least a predictable regularity, unlike the improvisations of Tanker's musicians. Once again European 'form' was needed for 'Caribbean' content if West Indian art was to move forward.

Montgomery was himself re-examining European culture through his work with Walcott. In *Joker* the high choker of the Queen was made from large leaves. This created the double perspective of 'Elizabethan' and Caribbean and illustrated how the voyages of discovery to the New World had influenced European taste and fashions. Rather than a one-way cultural imperialism, there was a continual, if usually unrecognized, exchange between the New and Old World.

Montgomery's set, costumes, and properties had visual similarities to
Walcott's own vision of the relationship of Caribbean art to Europe.
Accepting Montgomery as a real artist and professional, sharing similar ideas, Walcott trusted him to take an idea and develop it without
supervision or further discussion. Walcott would show Montgomery
his original set and costumes, then Montgomery designed his own set
which the Workshop coming to Jamaica used without any further
consultation.[25]

Joker received considerable publicity, the newspapers carried announcements illustrated with photographs. *The Jamaica Daily News* even
carried a two-page spread of photographs of the scenes from the play.
When Laveau replaced Scott as Don Juan, with Jones replacing Laveau
as Don Diego, even that was reported as a feature of the production
allowing 'audiences to see two different interpretations'.[26]

Jamaica, with its larger population, international businesses, main
campus of the University of the West Indies, a School of Drama, a
Little Theatre, the Barn Theatre, international recording studios, and
government support of the arts, is more interested in the arts than
Trinidad. If it is somewhat more theatrically jaded than Trinidad, its
glorious period of theatre still remains 1950–7 when Walcott and those
associated with him at the University College of the West Indies were
starting modern West Indian drama. Walcott still remained the most
important West Indian dramatist. The week before the TTW came to
Jamaica there had been a production of *Malcochon* and during August
a production of *Dream on Monkey Mountain* was directed by Carroll
Dawes with students from the Jamaica National School of Drama. So
while Jamaica had the facilities and support for serious theatre, Trinidad had Walcott and his theatre company.[27]

The Star headlined its review of *Joker* 'A magnificent play' and described it as 'like a rich Christmas pudding chock full (almost too full)
of every theatrical device one can think of'. There was much to see,
'new surprises popping up here and there along the way', and 'fine
acting'. Montgomery's set is made of bamboo shoots sticking up erect
phallically to match Don Juan's seduction of woman after woman. Syd
Skipper's singing of 'O Pastora Divina' was one of the highlights of the
show. Metivier was lovely, vivacious, and mischievous.[28]

The Jamaica Daily News remarked on the framing device, the meeting on the eve of All Souls of some villagers who honour the dead
great stickman Don Juan, commented briefly on the way freedom was
embodied in the sexual and on Montgomery's phallic symbolism. The
reviewer was especially struck by a noble's fur cape being made from

coconut, crowns jewelled with local spathodia pods, and armour and helmets made from basket weaving. 'There would be no songs, dance, not much pleasure in *Joker* without the fantastic Trinidad Theatre Workshop Group. What a cast.' Their concentration and control is remarkable. Nigel Scott, as Don Juan, must sustain his vigorous character on stage most of the three hours. Syd Skipper's 'La Pastora' is beautiful.[29]

Dennis Scott thought the *Joker's* poetry, music, and acting pure delight, although not flawless. The setting is a stick-fight arena in an old cemetery. The musicians are also costumed like villagers on stage and are part of those honouring the dead. Within this space the TTW demonstrate the value of working together for a long time under Walcott's direction. They are evolving a style of verbal and physical extravagance that makes great demands on the actors. The text becomes a carnival of verse and movement. There are many amusing mimes including the ritual of entering the convent and the 'seduction carried out by a naked hero concealing his rising hope beneath a huge straw basket.' Hamilton Parris admirably controls his body and voice; his restraint aids the other actors. Nigel Scott has boundless energy, is relaxed and charming, but his singing is only adequate. Beddeau, Bynoe, and Jennifer Hobson Garcia act in a disciplined fashion. The music, played by piano, string bass, drums, quatro, flute, and guitar, has an island texture. The production was not successfully transferred from arena to proscenium-arch staging. Actors mask each other, space is often wasted, movements do not always clarify the action. The company has great vigour but lacks precision.[30]

While I sometimes have the impression that Harry Milner was often irritated by Walcott's experimentalism and by non-European aspects of West Indian theatre, he is highly regarded by Jamaicans for his critical standards. He was once more irritated. He missed part of the dialogue. The actors do not project enough, Trinidadians speak faster than Jamaicans and in a slurred manner, the music and 'general business' fights against the verse. Walcott's total theatre is at variance with the subtlety of his words. 'As a small hit musical', however, the play works, although it is far too long and complicated. Milner was often muddled trying to keep straight the various characters; it was too much like following Shakespeare's histories. 'The stage picture, apart from often being exquisite, is always moving and full of visual surprises.' The best part of the acting is visual; the actors have good control of their bodies. Trinidadians are more relaxed, charming, and more based on the curve than straight lines, as in Adele Bynoe's comic dancing of the Queen. There is also excellent miming of a ship and horse-riding. Syd Skipper brings down the house with his singing. Some actors need vocal training.[31]

Before leaving Jamaica Walcott was interviewed by Ulric Mentus of *The Jamaica Daily News* who prefaced the article by mentioning that Walcott is far more popular in the West Indies for his drama than his poetry. The conversation immediately turned to politics and culture. Walcott said that while only socialism is likely to overcome the extreme class divisions in the region, he is against the Stalinist, Castroite socialism that is the basis of many dictatorships in the Caribbean. He sees himself as a protest writer, as any writer who complains about injustice is a protest writer, but such protest is different from those who advocate a cause, party, or ideology and shape their writing towards a specific message. He is an instinctive writer who feels for all his characters and their conflicts; his plays cannot be reduced to a single message. While Caribbeans are predominantly of African descent, West Indian identity must be found within the West Indies, including its mixture of races and cultures, and not in Africa or elsewhere. 'It's getting more and more difficult to tell strains and cross currents, the cross-culturalisations that are happening, especially in a place like Trinidad.' No matter how you came to the West Indies this is your spiritual territory, what you possess and must feel belongs to you. Modern urban art has lost interest in the 'representation of the majesty or degradation of man'. It is only interested in surface textures. The West Indian is a humanist. Instead of providing leadership towards recognition of a West Indian identity, politicians preach micro-nationalism and political causes. They have become tyrannical, preventing the publication of dissenting views and imprisoning dissenters. The theatre, as it reaches the people, is political in opposing the politicians. While in Trinidad, Guyana, Dominica, and Grenada criticism is suppressed, what saves the situation is that the governments are apathetic. 'There is so much censorship of the Press in the Caribbean that one is just waiting for censorship of the theatre.'

Walcott said that none of the West Indian politicians genuinely supports West Indian culture; if they did they would provide scholarships so that artists could study abroad and improve their skills and in other ways help artists to support themselves in the region. Instead they waste large amounts of money on occasional regional festivals in which the artists are supposed to make everyone feel good for a few days, but afterwards artists are neglected until the next festival. The opportunities to make a living in the West Indies as an artist, especially as a dramatist, are very slim. When the TTW began acting at the Basement Theatre actors were excited to earn $7 or $10. If there were sponsorship from business or the government, or if there were proper theatres or film work, younger actors could form a repertory company paying actors $200 or $300 dollars a month.

While Walcott might have left the West Indies for England when he was younger, he now has a theatre company he can work with, writing parts for specific actors, creating a 'theatre that is true to us'. He would like to use other West Indian directors so his actors could have that experience, but the TTW cannot afford it. The Workshop is homeless and hampered by the lack of money. He would like actors and directors going back and forth between the United States and Trinidad, but Equity prevents non-Americans from working in the United States.

Walcott told Mentus that he was writing a play with reggae music concerning the Rastafarian movement. His interest is in the Rastas' serenity, their spiritual peace, not in the drama of returning to Africa. As gangsters and others claim to be Rastas perhaps the spirituality is being lost, but Walcott sees it as similar to the hippie and flower power culture of love and peace. At the core of West Indian societies is 'that revival' spirit, the small churches, the cults. This new play, *O Babylon!*, would become the main achievement of Walcott and the TTW during 1976, as *The Joker* was during 1974–5.[32]

NOTES

1. The script for *Daddy Sharpe* and other documents about plans are in Barbara Jenson's files. As usual I have photocopies of all documents I mention.
2. Victor Questel, 'Our Artists Press on Themselves', *Trinidad Guardian* (21 Feb. 1975), 4. Walcott's notes are in the Walcott Collection, University of the West Indies, St Augustine.
3. 'Rhythms of the "Joker of Seville" on Record', *Trinidad Guardian* (8 Mar. 1975), 5. Plans for the Semp recordings are in the Walcott Collection, University of the West Indies, St Augustine. The cassette produced by Sanch Electronix for Semp Studios (Dec. 1987) in connection with the 1987 Arbee revival of *Joker* is taken from the LP of the 1975 production. Side A begins with 'Sans Humanité'; side B concludes with 'O Little Red Bird'.
4. John H. Irish, 'The Joker of Seville', *Trinidad Guardian* (13 Mar. 1975), 6.
5. Derek Walcott, 'The Joker: Closer to Continuous Theatre', *Trinidad Guardian* (22 Mar. 1975), 8.
6. Derek Walcott, 'Open Letter to the Company', Walcott Collection, University of the West Indies, St Augustine.

7. The various letters and other documents are in the Walcott Collection.
8. Pat Charles to F. G. Louisy, Permanent Secretary, Ministry of Education (12 Mar. 1975). Her reference SL16. Copy to Mrs. C. Lattin, Technical Teachers' College, The Morne. Extra-Mural files St Lucia.
9. 'Editorial—The Joker of Seville', *The Voice of St Lucia* (9 Apr. 1975), 2.
10. Harry Best, 'Character of West Indian People Vivid in Walcott's "The Joker of Seville"', *The Voice of St Lucia* (16 Apr. 1975), 7; Also see Harry Best, ' "Joker of Seville" Worthy of fore-running praises', *The Voice of St Lucia* (9 Apr. 1975), 1.
11. George Odlum, 'The Joker of Seville', *Crusader* (12 Apr. 1975), 2.
12. Marylin Jones, 'A Home for Our Artists Please', *Trinidad Guardian* (9 Apr. 1975), 4. Conditions backstage at the Little Carib are described in Laurence Goldstraw, 'Reminiscences of Derek Walcott and the Trinidad Theatre Workshop', in Hamner (ed.), *Critical Perspectives on Derek Walcott*, 272–81.
13. Raoul Pantin, 'The Amazing "Joker of Seville"', *Express* (6 Apr. 1975), 7, 10.
14. Patricia Ismond, 'Breaking Myths and Maidenheads', *Tapia*, (18 May 1975). 4–5, 9 (1 June 1975), 6–8.
15. C. A. May, Commissioner of Police to Barbara Ann Jenson (28 May 1975). Reference 569. Jenson's files.
16. Jeremy Taylor, 'Play of the Month a Great Change', *Express* (2 June 1975), 8.
17. From interviews with Norline Metivier in Trinidad during June–Aug. 1990 and June 1991.
18. Derek Walcott, 'Why do Chekhov here?', *Sunday Guardian* (29 June 1975), 7; Derek Walcott, 'Story of four loves at the Little Carib: Chekhov's masterpiece in first local premiere', *Trinidad Guardian* (4 July 1975), 4.
19. Errol Hill, 'Gallant Attempt at Chekhov's Complex Classic', *Trinidad Guardian* (14 July 1975), 3.
20. Jeremy Taylor, ' "Seagull" a Brave Attempt at a Beautiful Play', *Express* (15 July 1975), 9.
21. Victor Questel, 'Message is not Fame, but to Endure', *Trinidad Guardian* (17 July 1975), 4. St Marie Therese, 'The Agony of a Seagull', *Catholic News* (20 July 1975), 10 mentions 'There is a lovely lake, the haunt of seagulls—which under the magic of lights, beautifully designed by John Andrews, creates a peaceful and serene atmosphere conducive to romance.'
22. Stanley Marshall to Desmond Ballah, Amoco Trinidad Oil (30 Oct. 1975), Walcott collection.
23. ' "The Joker" Starts Third Run Tonight', *Trinidad Guardian* (15 Oct. 1975), 4. Notes in Barbara Jenson's files.
24. Mauby [Judy Stone], 'Now the Joker's Laugh is Mature and Polished', *Trinidad Guardian* (24 Oct. 1975), 4.
25. Interview with Richard Montgomery, Boston (April 1993); for comparisons between productions of *The Joker* see Mertel E. Thompson, 'Don Juan's "Hilarious Exploits": The Joker of Seville on Stage', *The Literary Half-Yearly*, 26/1 (Jan. 1985), 132–48.
26. 'The Joker of Seville', *The Jamaica Daily News* (30 Nov. 1975), 20–1; 'Actor switches in "Joker"', *The Daily Gleaner* (4 Dec. 1975), 5.
27. For a discussion of the Dawes production of *Dream* which contributes to

understanding of the play's imagery and characters see Slade Hopkinson, 'Good Plays must have a Market', *The Daily Gleaner* (16 Sept. 1975), 4, 19.

28. 'A Magnificent Play', *The Star* (25 Nov. 1975), 4.
29. 'A Play Well Worth Seeing', *The Jamaica Daily News* (27 Nov. 1975), 17, 23.
30. Dennis Scott, 'A Joyful Joker', *The Daily Gleaner* (24 Nov. 1975), 26.
31. Harry Milner, 'Lack of Voice Control', *The Sunday Gleaner* (30 Dec. 1975), 4–5.
32. Ulric Mentus, 'Walcott: Nobody Wants to be a West Indian', *The Jamaica Daily News* (7 Dec. 1975), 5–7.

1976

13

O Babylon!

Carifesta

TTW Dance Company

Walcott's Resignation

SUCCESS brought its own destructive tensions. As the tours and many performances took increasing time from family and jobs, some actors, including Geddes Jennings and Hamilton Parris, left the Workshop. Margaret, who had informally taken on most of the tasks of theatre management, withdrew from Workshop productions after the 1975 runs of *Joker*. Walcott was not an administrator and the Workshop could not afford administrative staff and survived in a haphazard way. There are many stories of Walcott impulsively spending too much for services and of confusing accounts. Some actors questioned Walcott's deciding the fees they should be paid, especially as Walcott, who was the only person working professionally full time for the Workshop, was being paid as artistic director, sometimes as director of plays, and for royalties for the use of his plays. As Walcott kept putting his own money into productions and as Walcott decided acting and other fees, no one was certain what was the financial state of the company. Some of the actors wanted to direct plays and felt that Walcott was hogging the spotlight. Then there was the long-running disagreement between Walcott, who felt that profits from productions should be used to pay those involved in the plays, and others who felt that profits should be put into a fund for the eventual construction of a theatre.

Perhaps more irritating was Walcott's claim that there is no

democracy in theatre; theatre is a dictatorship. Actors would accept
that about his scripts and the productions he directed, but, despite
meetings to agree on decisions, Walcott's command appeared to extend to much else. There were no committees to decide on budgets,
schedules, choice and directors of plays, or how finances should be
allocated. While younger actors felt that Walcott only relied on the
opinion of a small group of older members, the foundation members
were themselves beginning to want a more formal say in decisions.
Recent productions were great artistic successes, but there was little
financial profit and the financial risks were becoming greater. As
Walcott pushed the TTW increasingly towards a full-time national
theatre, often on tour, and increasingly was tempted towards Broadway and a professional career outside the West Indies, his plans and
dreams interfered with jobs, family life, and any activities outside the
Workshop. Walcott wanted to test himself against the world's best,
and it was becoming obvious that he wanted his actors to give up
their jobs, as had Albert Laveau, and follow him to the promised land
of international fame and riches.

Despite meetings to discuss problems, the Workshop had become
Walcott's company. Even outside work on television and radio was
regarded by Walcott as Workshop territory; he felt that he could
negotiate better terms for his performers, but he also wanted 10 per
cent of all earnings for the use of the Workshop. Others now wanted
a legally incorporated company with an administrative structure,
budget, accounts, and long-term plans. In principle Walcott wanted
the same thing; he wanted others to take some of the responsibility.
In practice, however, the legal and administrative structure which
should have freed Walcott to devote himself to the artistic side of the
Workshop shackled his freedom as an artist. There could no longer be
those rapid changes of plans which depended upon opportunities or
how his own writing and hopes of success abroad were progressing.
Walcott's ways were the opposite of those of a committee. An explosion was inevitable. After a board was formed to govern the Workshop, friction rapidly began to develop and Walcott increasingly talked
about leaving Trinidad for greater opportunities abroad.

The friction took fire when Walcott decided to change the Company's publicized season and call rehearsals for his revised version of
The Charlatan for the 1977 Carnival season. Several actors protested
against his decision by not showing up for rehearsals and there were
bitter quarrels. Walcott was irritated by demands for more administrative accountability, but could understand, and himself wanted, the

need for a better organizational structure. To be challenged through indiscipline in what he considered an artistic matter, his directing of a play, was the last straw. André Tanker's not attending a rehearsal for a revival of *Ti-Jean* was the end.[1]

The tensions were made worse by private matters. Walcott had become Norline Metivier's lover. Walcott's openness about his passion was bound to divide a company for whom his wife, Margaret, despite a British university education and her own professional career, had sold tickets at the box office, swept the floor of the theatre, and even cleaned the theatre toilets. Margaret had close friends in the Workshop and was widely respected. Norline Metivier (b. 1951) was young, very pretty, light-skinned, fun, non-intellectual, middle class, a secretary and dance teacher, the dream of a man in his mid-forties. She had danced as a child in Walcott's 1965 carnival show *Batai*, admired him, and was one of Astor Johnson's dancers who had followed Noble Douglas and Carol La Chapelle into the Theatre Workshop for *Joker*. Eventually they became lovers. There was a party for Margaret to which Walcott and Metivier were not invited, as it was felt their presence would be hurtful; Walcott, however, regarded the lack of invitation as insulting. That along with the quarrels over *The Charlatan* brought to a head long-simmering disagreements and Walcott resigned from the Theatre Workshop. Perhaps he would have resigned over some other issue? Several of his friends say that his desire to test himself abroad was in conflict with his feeling of responsibility for the TTW; unable to resolve the conflict within himself he was looking for a quarrel, a reason to resign.

The year, however, had started promisingly. Late January, 1976, the Workshop learned that the National Brewery Company was increasing its grant to $10,000; this allowed the company to schedule the opening of the new Walcott–MacDermot play *O Babylon!* for March. The choreography would be by La Chapelle who was in Baltimore for a Workshop-influenced production of *Dream on Monkey Mountain*.[2]

The Baltimore Central Stage production of *Dream* was directed by Laveau, choreographed by La Chapelle, and Beddeau was musical director and lead drummer. Kenneth Stein, broadcasting for WBJC–FM on National Public Radio, had an inaccurate American tourist-eye view of the West Indies according to which a white colonialist minority still ruled undemocratically over and exploited an impoverished black majority. He thought *Dream* was about white–black conflict, called the play overwritten, but praised the production. As usual a complex Walcott play about a complex society and culture had been interpreted in the United States as social protest overwritten for its audience. R. H. Gardner in *The Sun* was more favourable, both describing the play as a poem and praising the production. La Chapelle's choreography was 'exciting', but the play was long-winded. *The News American* found the play powerful theatre, lyrical, beautiful, and fascinating but puzzling. 'The images of the poet-writer are not those familiar to most of us'; Walcott's experiences are different from those of Americans. La Chapelle's dance patterns are 'exotic and colorful'. As the dancers move across stage, contorted yet graceful, swoop, turn, and explode into fiery turbulence, it is difficult to believe you are sitting in a theatre in Baltimore.[3]

O Babylon! was the third Walcott–MacDermot musical (counting the revised *Charlatan*) and was bound to be controversial. The Rastafarians are a cult specific to Jamaica; they have their own history, social context, rituals, music, beliefs, and version of English. As Jamaican musicians became attracted to the ways the Rastas lived, Rastafarianism became for a time symbolic of a range of attitudes from back-to-Africanism to a black version of 1960s 'flower power'. Through the international popularity of Bob Marley and reggae music, 'Rasta' became trendy. Such 'plastic Rastas', as they adopted the symbolism, jargon, and took to ganga, were often parasitical of and had little relationship to the actual movement. And then there were the middle-class intellectuals determined to show that they could be more Rasta than thou.

Walcott's *O Babylon!* concerns a small Rastafarian community, led by a reformed gangster who has become a wood carver, and therefore a symbol of the artist. They live on land where a big hotel is to be built. While in the conflict between the Rastas and the forces of Babylon the Rastas lose, it is not just Babylon that defeats them; they seem without will and betray each other. Except for the gangster-artist, the characters eventually take what opportunities are offered. The story is told as the memories of a former peanut vendor who observed the situation and who some years later becomes a reggae star and returns to the hotel as a performer. *O Babylon!* includes such Walcott themes as the illusion of the return to Africa, the need for energy to make a place in the world, the temptations of Babylon, and an awareness that celebration of a Caribbean pastoral may be romanticization of poverty, undernourishment, and lack of opportunity.

O Babylon! began in a discussion between Walcott, MacDermot, and Michael Butler, the producer of *Hair*, who invited them to develop a script. Butler first wanted to bring *Joker* to Broadway, but the Royal

Shakespeare Company still had the rights to the play; he thought that a reggae musical might be successful on Broadway. By December 1975 the Workshop was workshopping the idea into a musical which Walcott hoped would be staged in New York, perhaps with TTW actors and dancers. Butler decided not to go ahead with the project; if Walcott, however, could get it off the ground in the West Indies then he might bring it to New York. As so often during the past decade, Walcott had whiffs of the fame and recognition that he felt he deserved, but having raised his hopes the bouquets were always being removed just beyond his reach. Walcott, who had missed out on London and New York productions of *Joker*, now very much wanted a play on Broadway, wanted to show that he could reinvent the Black American musical as a serious West Indian theatre form, and was willing to invest his money in the project.[4]

Trinidad and St Lucia were at the time foreign to Rastafarianism; to Walcott, who was sympathetic to 1960s 'flower power', the Rastas were peaceful black hippies attempting to resist the pressures of Babylon. They also lacked the energy, discipline, and will to confront and remake their world. MacDermot is white. Montgomery, the set and costume designer, is also white. La Chapelle, the choreographer, had been trained in English ballet. Probably the main problem was that Walcott and MacDermot started with the notion of doing a Broadway musical on a subject which at the time in the West Indies was charged with emotion and political attitudes. Everyone in Trinidad would want to prove that they were more Rasta than Walcott–MacDermot. Some bits of theatricality in the play were found offensive or puzzling, such as the ganga dream sequence about returning to Africa on a home-made Rasta reefer rocket ship. This is the kind of production piece and humour expected from a musical, and the kind of amusing parody that a minority might appreciate about itself. The Rastas did recommend use of ganga and the dream of returning to 'Ethiopia' was clearly impractical, except for a few. The Trinidadian critics, however, either found the scene offensive or thought it detracted from the seriousness of the themes. The complexity of the tone, with its unwillingness to take a clear pro-Rasta position, was at the heart of the problem.

O Babylon!, directed by Walcott, opened for a two-week run at the Little Carib on 19 March 1976, and ran for fourteen nights. The strong cast included Wilbert Holder, Anthony Hall, Syd Skipper, Norline Metivier, Ermine Wright, Errol Jones, Brenda Hughes, Winston Goddard, Laurence Goldstraw, Stanley Marshall, and Patrick Flores.

Pan-Jamaican Investments supplied Richard Montgomery as an artistic supervisor. Barbara Jenson was stage manager and also had a small part as a white social worker.

Jeremy Taylor praised *O Babylon!* for its integration of music with action and blend of poetry, dialect, dance, anger, vitality, and laughter. He found more sadness in it than *Joker*, but was puzzled by its tone. Although those associated with Babylon were satirized as corrupt and the Rastafarians treated sympathetically, there was the problem of how much Walcott really believed in Rasta ideas. Was Walcott being ironic in the deification of Salassie? Walcott dislikes bourgeois preju-dice, but is the biblical Rasta symbolism to be understood literally?[5]

Mauby said that while the play is a serious comment on a commu-nity of have-nots struggling to survive against the forces of Babylon, it is less impressive than *The Joker*. It is too static despite the profusion of songs and dances. The choreography is muscular but the music somewhat monotonous; there is too much recitative, rather than aria, and few melodies are memorable. Holder as Rude Bwoy Dawson is a polished performer—loudmouth, lustful, energetic, vulnerable. He and Ermine Wright as Virgie dominate the play. There is a delightful se-quence by Errol Jones in which his eyes become increasingly glazed as he succumbs to marijuana. No one except Holder attempts to speak Jamaican English. *Joker* improved during its runs, so it is likely that *Babylon* will be transformed. The Trinidad Theatre Workshop has a professional pride that makes them perfect and polish their work.[6]

A letter to the editor of the *Trinidad Guardian* suggested that Mauby should go to an eye-and-ear specialist. E. G. Scott enjoyed the show as much as any he had seen on Broadway. It was full of comedy, social comment, and had truly outstanding performances. Holder was superb; his voice was rich. The actors and dancers were excellent in their facial and body movements and voice.[7]

Caribbean Contact carried two contrasting reviews in the same issue. Raoul Pantin noted that in the Rastafarians Walcott saw the West Indian longing to return to Africa. The modern Babylon of Jamaica shows that black men have always sold their brothers into slavery. Walcott rages against the encroachment of Babylon. The most mov-ing moment of the play is Aaron's song about the black horsemen of Bornu. Skipper brilliantly portrayed Aaron, Brenda Hughes's Dolly was luscious, Holder improves with each show and along with Ermine Wright dominates the play. While the TTW is increasingly profes-sional, the music and dance lack the strength of reggae and are too delicate.[8]

In the highly politicized Trinidad of the mid-1970s *O Babylon!* was bound to be politically incorrect to some. Sule Mombara (Horace Campbell) of the Department of Government, University of the West Indies, St Augustine, regarded the play as a typical exploitation of popular culture by the petty bourgeoisie. The presentation of a volatile political theme in a European literary form for the white and black bourgeoisie who attend the Little Carib revealed the contradictions between the light musical and the African-oriented culture of the Rastafarians. The sudden breaking into song was reminiscent of romantic musicals and obscured the content of the play. The scenes ended inconclusively without clear messages. Mombara claims that the part of the white developer 'was hastily included so that the producers would not incur the wrath of the European members' of the Workshop. Jamaican vernacular was used inconsistently. As the language of the Rastafari Brethren purposefully mutilates English so that only other sufferers can understand them, the play should instead have used a Trinidadian accent. The music and dance showed a similar misunderstanding of 'the dominant cultural force in the English Caribbean' and did not reflect the mood of the suffering Rastas. The movements of the dancers were too rapid. 'For dancing to reggae is a reflective and political experience.' Instead of trying to influence the audience *O Babylon!* is 'a cynical castigation of oppressed Jamaicans'. The playwright should 'sink his roots among the people'.[9]

Rawle Gibbons claimed that the TTW had departed from their usual 'standards of artistic excellence' in not being sufficiently committed. Many of the roles were recognizable caricatures. Because Walcott and MacDermot are concerned with individual affirmation, Walcott neglects exploring in depth 'Rastafari meaning and the moods of reggae'. The staging seemed constricted, there was repeated masking, and the action was too horizontal. The theatre symbolism, however, was excellent. 'The dancers' cumberbands unfold to reveal the colours of the Ethiopian flag, duplicated in the rainbow . . . The carving of the Four Horsemen of the Apocalypse is reinforced in dance, song, language, mime.' The choreography seemed rough and some dances uncoordinated. The musical combination of 'light reggae, rock, sentimental' reflects the ideological ambiguities. There should have been drums and other communal rites symbolizing the energy of the Rastafarian community. There is no sense of an apocalyptical end to Babylon, only the dread under which the Rastas live.[10]

The reviews indicate how much the TTW had developed a style of acting that made use of body and facial gestures. Their singing had also improved, but there were still some problems with diction and audibility. While the critics kept saying that characters should be acted with more depth, they usually praised such actors as Wright, Holder, and Jones, who were larger than life and confident. Gibbons finds Hall's acting studied with controlled body work, but complains that it shared in the 'easy' exaggerated tone of the play. Skipper sings very well, but lacks timing and his accent is too American. Metivier has youth, but not the strength of character needed for Priscilla, Aaron's girl friend. Hughes uses her body well, but lacks delicacy. Wright offers a complete performance as a forthright folk-type. Goddard handles language carefully but seemed ineffectual, although that may be how the director wants him to be. Jones offers an accomplished caricature of a corrupt politician. Christopher Pinheiro as Luigi makes good use of his face. Patrick Flores has good ease and posture but is at times inaudible. Holder had clarity and confidence.

Earl Lovelace's thoughtful review is a disagreement with Walcott's art. 'Walcott's Rastafarians are so weak and confused as to be immoral. They have not convinced themselves that they want to battle for the land they live on.' All Walcott's Rastas can do to return to Africa is build a spacecraft powered by ganga. Such lack of power turns the Rastas into 'irretrievable victims' and prevents the play from making a case against the immorality of Babylon. This is not theatre as subversion. If the point is that the Rastas do not want to develop the land and instead return to Africa, why should not the Mafia claim the land? The best that Walcott's Rastas can do is 'elicit pity, a pity that we do not want to feel, since we feel that their real-life counterparts are capable of so much more'. In other words, in pointing to a contradiction within the notion of withdrawal from Babylon—that it leaves Babylon to do as it wants—Walcott failed to portray admirable, victorious revolutionary heroes. Whereas *O Babylon!* shows that you cannot return to Africa and must instead fight for the West Indies and make it your home, Lovelace thinks the affirmation of Africa is a necessary step on the way to such discovery and part of the process of recreating the self.[11]

In April the Trinidad Theatre Workshop decided to incorporate as a legal company, create an organizational structure, and do something concrete towards financing a permanent home. An informal first meeting was followed on 22 April by a meeting to discuss the governing of the TTW. The following were elected as the board:

Chairman	John Andrews
Vice-Chairman	Errol Jones
Executive Secretary	Stanley Marshall
Assistant Secretary	Leonore Bishop
Financial Comptroller	Claude Reid
Business Manager	Nigel Scott
Public Relations Officer	Wilbert Holder
Artistic Director	Derek Walcott
Dance Director	Carol La Chapelle
Drama Director	Albert Laveau
Floor Member	Brenda Hughes

Noble Douglas's name was also added as dance director.

The next week, 29 April, the second general meeting of the board of the TTW was attended by Errol Jones (Vice-Chairman), Stanley Marshall, Claude Reid, Wilbert Holder, Nigel Scott, Anthony Hall, Brenda Hughes, Leonore Bishop (Walcott's secretary), Albert Laveau, and Walcott. John Andrews, the chairman, Noble Douglas, and Carol La Chapelle were absent. Almost immediately Bishop was questioned whether she was actually a member of the Workshop, and whether she could be both Walcott's secretary and fairly perform as recording secretary of the board. As Bishop had often taken time from her secretarial career to provide the company with scripts, handle advertising, and do essential dogsbody work, this was not a good sign. There was a discussion of the duties of the various positions and talk about legal assistance in preparing the aims and objective of the TTW. Then a disciplinary committee was formed to formulate rules to govern the Workshop. Another committee was discussed which would oversee productions and their costs. (As this would be a committee of three persons who would have authority to take decisions concerning productions regardless of financial consequences, it would in actuality be replacing Walcott with a dictatorship of three.) Cheques would need to be signed by two persons from among the chairman, executive secretary and financial comptroller. As there were bound to be bottlenecks there would also be a petty cash fund. Meetings would be held once a month, but further meetings could be called at short notice. Letters would be sent to absent members keeping them informed about the progress of the Workshop; Barclays Bank would be told to change the signatories for cheques for the TTW. The chairman would head a building committee. The financial comptroller would create an accounting system. As Walcott was already planning performances of O Babylon! for Point à Pierre and San Fernando there could be no budget or financial accounts for those shows, for which preparations had already begun before the board was being formed.[12]

Stanley Marshall as executive secretary circulated a letter on 15 June informing members of the Trinidad Theatre Workshop of the new governing board. Membership in the Workshop would be frozen until rules and regulations could be put into operation and new members would know the terms upon which they were joining. While it was assumed that past members would continue within the Workshop, they would need to inform Marshall. The Workshop intended to seek a home and was seeking signed pledges of financial assistance. So far the board as individuals had pledged a total of $6,000. Members were urged to send their signed pledges and attend meetings.

The aim now was to have a paid-up subscription season of plays and other performances. Ever since being evicted from the Basement Theatre the company had not known from year to year where it could perform and when. Now after the success of *Joker* and the National Brewery subsidy (which had been increased to $10,000) the company could afford a season and this in turn meant there would be tickets paid up in advance which along with the subsidy could be used towards acquiring a regular theatre for a home.

The Trinidad Theatre Workshop's first full season was announced. Between mid-July and mid-December they would perform *O Babylon!*, E. M. Roach's *Belle Fanto* (to be co-directed by Albert Laveau and Anthony Hall), Genet's *The Maids*, *Joker of Seville*, and *Ti-Jean*. The TTW Dance Company would offer their first concert and there would be a 'Benefit' to launch the Workshop's Dance and Drama School. Roscoe Lee Browne, the famous black American actor who appeared in *Dream on Monkey Mountain* in New York, would perform at the 'Benefit'. Season tickets would cost $40.

In June a revised *O Babylon!* with new songs and with Galt MacDermot at the piano had two performances at Naparima Bowl, San Fernando. It was supposed to move on to the Little Carib for a second extended run in mid-July. Preparations had begun at the Little Carib when the government suddenly informed the Workshop that *O Babylon!* would be sent to Jamaica to represent Trinidad at Carifesta later in July.[13]

There had been a continuing wave of violent crime connected with political unrest in Jamaica and an island-wide state of emergency was in effect. So the decision to go ahead with Carifesta was unexpected. Jamaica, however, decided that the state of emergency would provide a safer environment than normal (!) and twenty-five countries had about three weeks to plan and send their representations. The *Trinidad Guardian* of 9 July announced that the Cabinet voted $160,000 to send a contingent of eighty persons to represent Trinidad and Tobago at the Caribbean Festival of the Arts in Jamaica from 23 July to 2 August. $100,000 would be used for air fares, accommodation, and fees for performers. Among those Trinidad hoped to send were calypso superstars Mighty Sparrow and Lord Kitchener, the new 1976 calypso star Mighty Chalkdust, the Gay Desperadoes steel band, and the Trinidad Theatre Workshop led by Walcott. Trinidad's contingent eventually grew to 130 and included the story-teller Paul Keens-Douglas, Indian folk dancers, 150 pieces of arts and crafts, and a calypso orchestra. The Dinsley Village Tassa Drummers prepared chicken roti for sale at the Festival, which was a great success.[14]

On 13 July Walcott typed some notes and a possible budget for Stanley Marshall to discuss with the Division of Culture concerning the Workshop's participation in Carifesta and the costs. First there was the problem of the financial commitments already made for re-opening *O Babylon!* on 22 July at the Little Carib as part of the subscription season. The Workshop had already paid for posters, rent, tickets, and rental of lighting, and there would need to be advertising that the opening was postponed. The Workshop had already spent $1,740, including $700 for the Little Carib, which they would lose. Who was going to pay? There would be a cast of thirty-five to send to Jamaica consisting of fifteen actors, nine dancers, four musicians, three singers and four stage crew. Leave arrangements would need be made for those in the public and private sectors and some compensation would need be paid to those in the private sector along with an agreed subsistence in Jamaica ($20 was agreed upon). Then what were the professionals—Walcott and Skipper along with the musicians and singers—to be paid? Walcott suggested that he be paid $1,500 for producing and directing and that $400 be shared with MacDermot for royalties. The musicians would get $700. A singer would be paid $100. That would be $4,440 in professional salaries. Then there were the costs in Jamaica for the set, lighting, costumes and props, sound, transportation, instruments, and accommodation. Would Trinidad pay for packaging and sending props and musical instruments? Who would take care of and pay for such matters as exit taxes, vaccination, and visas?[15]

The day the TTW left for Jamaica Pearl Connor-Mogotsi in the *Trinidad Guardian* discussed the controversy about *O Babylon!*. She claimed that Walcott was giving expression to the actual experience of

Rastafarians, not writing a sociological analysis. While showing their pain and sources of pain and condemning society for mistreating them, he also shows their self-defeating lack of will. They touch our hearts with their alienation and striving for recognition. We see life through their eyes, but among the Rastas there are confused religious beliefs, creeping corruption and depravity. The 'starvation showing on their whitened lips and emaciated bodies does not elevate our spirits'. Hunger makes animals of people and contributes to demoralized confusion.

Errol Jones's Deacon Doxy is 'a recognisable caricature' of some contemporary West Indian politicians. Steve Davis as Edwin the Rastafarian Astronaut stutters, stumbles, and is both pitiable and laughable. Pat Flores sings brilliantly. The music and dance seem insufficiently Jamaican as the dancers are more used to jazz and blues than the movements of the cult, while the Trinidadian musicians are not at home with Jamaican reggae. It must have been difficult to set Walcott's lyrics to reggae and it will not be possible accurately to judge MacDermot's music until it is played by those more familiar with Jamaican rhythms. In a supposedly multiracial society a lot of Trinidadians seem to be against the play because MacDermot is a white writing reggae music. They should remember that the international reggae hit 'Down by the Schoolyard' is by Simon and Garfunkel.[16]

Jamaican reviews were not much interested in the play's authenticity. The general view of *O Babylon!* was that it was a Trinidadian play and should be judged as musical theatre and not for its realism or politics. Most of the nations had sent dance and musical groups, films, and painting. Jamaica put on a pantomime, and offered Dennis Scott's play *Echo in the Bone*; Surinam sent its Folk Theatre. The TTW was among the festival's featured attractions. On the festival calendar *O Babylon!* was scheduled for five performances in three days—24–26 July; only the Danza Nacional de Cuba was scheduled for six performances. That apparently represented the accepted pecking order of Caribbean performing arts groups at the time. The Jamaica *Star* ranked the Cuban National Ballet as 'first prize' followed by the TTW's *O Babylon!*, ahead of the Mexican Ballet Folkloric de la Secretaria de Turismo and other events. *O Babylon!* is too long and complicated but the acting is 'fine'. Skipper, Metivier, Holder, Hughes, Wright, Jones, and Flores are praised as superb. The play is about Jamaica but not Jamaican. Although the Jamaican quality of speech and music is missing, the music is attractive, very good, and excellently sung. Harry Milner thought the first twenty minutes would outlive *Porgy and Bess*, but the play faded afterwards and was far too long. There were too many stereotypical characters and soap opera clichés. It was an old-fashioned sentimental play about the poor in the 'yards'. There was also too much fooling about with a Rastafarian astronaut. The music was excellent in a manner developed from reggae but with lyrics that were much deeper than reggae platitudes. There was a wealth of good songs well sung. *O Babylon!* had a 'good light opera cast'. Because of the length the dancing seemed repetitive and the Trinidadian accent was often difficult to follow. Cut by forty minutes the play could be moved to the West End in London.[17]

The Jamaican government had given a block of seats to the Rastafarians. The final performance of *Babylon* in Jamaica was attended by seventy Rastas, who showed their appreciation of the production by beating their drums. The cast was nervous about the Rastas, fearing that they would interrupt the performance if they disapproved. When drumming started they did not know what was happening, until they were told it was a sign of appreciation. So much for lack of political correctness and inauthentic music! The Jamaica Information Service filmed the production for its archives and a segment was shown on TV. Unfortunately the film has been lost. The songs and music for *O Babylon!* are available on a long-playing recording (Kilmarnock Recording, KIL 72030).[18]

The first night, 30 July, after the Trinidad Theatre Workshop returned from Jamaica, there was a staged reading of scenes from *Dream on Monkey Mountain* at the Little Carib with Roscoe Lee Browne playing Makak, Laveau as Lestrade, Marshall as Moustique, Parris as Souris, Reid as Tiger, and Beddeau drumming and singing along with TTW Dance Company which also provided the chorus. La Chapelle's choreography was used and Andrews was lighting designer. The next night *O Babylon!* reopened at the Little Carib for a two-week run beginning 31 July as part of the new season. Noble Douglas replaced Brenda Hughes as Dolores and was replaced as a Rudette dancer by Corinne Jones.[19]

At the third general meeting of the board, 29 August, now at the Little Carib Theatre, it was announced that the Trinidad Theatre Workshop had become a registered company (Walcott, Laveau, and Scott were listed as partners and Walcott's home address was given as the address) and an account opened at Barclays Bank with the money from the subscription season tickets. As members had objected to the lack of regular meetings, there would be a meeting on the second Monday of each month at the Little Carib. Seven of the eleven members of the board would be required for a quorum. Contracts would be offered to members and non-members of the TTW for productions. Those missing rehearsals would be fined one dollar for each rehearsal missed. Someone, probably Walcott, suggested standardization of salaries for actors ranging from a minimum of $25 per performance for principals to a minimum of $10 for others, along with bonuses. The old arrangement of 10 per cent of salaries to be paid to the Trinidad Theatre Workshop should be reinstituted. There was no agreement on the matter of salaries. It was agreed that a stage manager responsible for such matters as attendance and rehearsal schedules would be appointed for each production and paid the same as a leading actor. Sterling Drugs International would be asked to subsidize the TTW Dance Company. Notes show that some of the matters discussed include how Douglas and La Chapelle could be paid for directing the Dance Company and who would clean up the theatres after performances and rehearsals.[20]

The next day Stanley Marshall wrote on behalf of the Workshop to the Ministry of Agriculture applying to lease the Zoo Pavilion, on the north-west of Queen's Park Savannah, where the Workshop had sometimes rehearsed. The Workshop proposed building a cultural centre with a theatre seating 350. Marshall recapitulated the history and problems of the Workshop, including the need to pay $100 a night for the poorly equipped Little Carib, and described their present season of six productions to be staged between 6 August and mid-December. As the Workshop had been 'fairly successful financially' in recent years, now had a membership subscription, and received an annual grant of $10,000 from the National Brewery Company there should be enough money both for the lease and to improve the company. In the past the TTW had paid up to $11,560 for rental of theatre and rehearsal space.[21]

A note in the University of the West Indies Walcott Collection suggests the kind of financial calculations that were being used. The Workshop had a projected revenue of $20,000—half being the subsidy from National Brewery; $7,500 the expected profits from three productions, and another $2,500 was to be collected from the TTW members as dues and Walcott's proposed 10 per cent levy on all salaries. Renting out the cultural centre for dance and drama and offering classes might earn $65,000. This would make a total proposed income of $85,000 on which the Workshop hoped to secure a capital loan of $135,000 for building the cultural centre. Another note suggests that the Workshop was likely to pay the Little Carib $8,800 during 1976 for rental and rehearsal space to do *O Babylon!*, *Belle Fanto*, *Joker*, and the Dance season.

The September revival of Roach's *Belle Fanto* at the Little Carib was directed by Albert Laveau. Carol La Chapelle acted Belle; Claude Reid performed Frank; Ermine Wright was Tan; Hamilton Parris was Noah; Marshall played Uncle Willie; and Andrew Beddeau was 'Drummer'. Walcott designed and painted the set which was constructed by Laveau. Roach, a well-known Trinidadian poet, had written *Belle Fanto, Calabash of Blood*, and other plays before his death, and *Belle Fanto* had become a 'classic' of the earlier period of drama about the 'yards', in contrast to the sophisticated plays Walcott was now writing.

Walcott's 'Why Belle Fanto Has Survived' recalls Roach attending some rehearsals of the first production of *Belle Fanto* and worrying whether an urban theatre group could portray the 'simplicities' of the folk. Playing peasants risks reducing the 'simple-surface rhythms of rural life' to caricature or melodrama when the actors try to be 'natural'. In a later version Roach revised the play in an attempt to make it more dramatic and interesting and nearly robbed it of its naturalness. It is in places gauche and pompous, but at heart it is about love, admiration, tolerance, and humour. The Workshop has tried to preserve its gossipy simpleness which is its nobility. It is an attempt to see the elementary again.[22]

A review in *Kairi* thought the play no longer interesting, but was enthusiastic about the production which made excellent use of the cramped stage. Laveau had done the impossible by staging the play within the door's mouth of Tan's cottage. The set was fantastic. 'Every detail was there.' Wright is the best actress in the Workshop. The acting of Marshall, La Chapelle, and Parris was praised. The price of tickets at $6 was expensive.[23]

Lee Johnson thought the play about changing values—the white man's Yankee dollars versus village traditions—but felt the archetypical characters lacked depth. Johnson, like the *Kairi* reviewer, praised Parris for convincingly portraying Noah's unyielding defiance of the new values while revealing bewilderment and weakness. Anyone else would have brought laughter, rather than compassion, on himself in the role. Marshall played the Uncle with gusto without overacting and suggested the lost youth behind the bravado. Ermine Wright's face showed the 'mixture of grief, guilt, emptiness and failure' that epitomizes Tan's tragedy. Laveau's directing was tight and restrained. He built the tension towards a climax and avoided the melodramatic. The set created an atmosphere of artistic simplicity and the claustrophobic. From such comments it can be seen that expectations about drama in

Trinidad had moved on from the time when typicality was wanted. The old social realism was no longer real.[24]

Jeremy Taylor also saw the play as about changing values, but felt that Roach had varied the characters so that the positive values were distributed. Where Johnson saw a lack of complexity, Taylor was moved by the integrity, compassion, and humour. Laveau directed a thoughtful, detailed performance from the cast. Wright, Parris, and Marshall gave beautiful performances. Walcott's set convincingly established the atmosphere. The production was fine, but attendance was not good.[25]

Late in September *Joker* was revived for one night at Expo 77, an industrial fair being held on the Savannah. For the occasion a large 72ft × 24ft stage was constructed similar to the kind used for Carnival in which the audience sits on two sides and the actors need to play to two opposite directions. When Andrew Beddeau did not show up, Wilbert Holder, who was in charge of the sound system that evening, took the role of the Ace of Death.[26]

The creation of a TTW Dance Company was rapid but initially unplanned. Douglas and La Chapelle began working with the TTW and brought friends with them. Their friends brought other friends and their students. Soon the Workshop had many of the best dancers in Trinidad. They began their own dance workshops two nights a week as well as the twice weekly actors' workshops. La Chapelle, Douglas, and Metivier were also acting in TTW productions; Walcott hung around with the dancers with whom he shared his dreams of taking them all to Broadway or the West End with a musical. He had fallen in love with Metivier and spent ever more time with the dancers. It was easier to train them to act and sing than to teach the actors to dance well. Besides they were younger than the foundation members of the TTW and shared his excitement about the future.[27]

When the dancers formed themselves into a company with Walcott's encouragement, for Walcott it was like being back in the original Little Carib he knew in the early 1960s when the Theatre Workshop was part of a dance group. It was also like having a national theatre with an acting and dance troupe. It allowed Walcott to move towards a professional, varied, continuous theatre season by his company. Douglas, La Chapelle, Metivier, and some of the other dancers had studied abroad and shared Walcott's desire to fuse the foreign with the local and to achieve international standards. Several Trinidadian dancers had become professionals in the United States, so Walcott's ambitions for Broadway recognition seemed more comprehensible to the younger dancers than to the older actors.

In October and November the new TTW Dance Company performed for seven nights at the Little Carib and then for a night in November at Naparima Bowl, San Fernando. They were immediately recognized as having challenged Astor Johnson's Repertory Dance Company as the leading Trinidadian dance ensemble. They also had the advantages of using the TTW's talents for scenery, lighting and advice. Walcott was Artistic Director, John Andrews did lighting design, Walcott helped supervise costumes, Walcott shared the set design, Laveau built their sets, Stanley Marshall was stage manager. All the reviewers commented on the quality of the production as well as the dancing and choreography.

Pearl Connor-Mogotsi wrote of the TTW Dance Company as representing the rich amalgam of races and cultures in the Caribbean. Besides sensuality, intelligence, discipline, joy, and imagination the Company's dances incorporated the vocabulary of 'African, Spanish, folk, modern and classical themes, with a flavouring of American Soul'. There was skill in the choreography, musicians, designers, and lighting. Connor-Mogotsi especially praised La Chapelle's choreography and dancing of 'Shango' as capturing the Spirituality of the Beyond. Jeremy Taylor praised the fresh handling of folk material in 'Revival', the imaginative choreography, the use of off-stage voices with drumming. The TTWDC is professional in its discipline and intense commitment to its art. It pays attention to the details of costume and design. It is startlingly sensuous, erotic, yet mature and gives respect to women; they dominate the stage. The TTW is now obviously the basis for a national theatre. Raoul Pantin thought the discipline and technique excessive. He was impressed by how the production was strengthened by its use of costume and lighting and by the themes of the dances.[28]

Mauby favourably compared the new dance company with Martha Graham's. She said that while it shows the influence of Graham it has the freedom and vitality that Graham's troupe had lost. Douglas has faultless, coiled, tensile control and is exuberantly physical. There are nuances in her flexing line. 'Even when impassioned, La Chapelle is a grave, almost ethereal dancer measured against Douglas's sensual joy, smacking of forbidden fruit.' The choreography favoured the women dancers. La Chapelle's 'Cages' shows women trapped in female stereotypes. The public grossly underrates local talents. There were some empty seats on opening night, yet the public will pay West End prices to see a touring Russian Music Hall that is not as good. In 'Movements' the stage wings were opened to let the sky appear while the dancers conjured up the movements of Trinidadian birds. In 'Cages', about prostitutes, the sensual pelvic movements were emotive. Douglas's Martha Graham-based style had the audience gasping in excitement with her lifts, spins, swirls, jerks, and distortions.[29]

After seventeen years the Workshop had become the equivalent of a national theatre company with an international reputation. It now had a dance company and a unique repertoire of Walcott plays created with its actors in mind. It was apparently on the verge of acquiring a home that would allow for further developments, such as offering acting and dancing classes to others. Walcott and perhaps Douglas and La Chapelle could live from the theatre. A few others might soon be able to quit their jobs and become full-time professional actors. It was too good to last and did not.

Walcott resigned from the TTW on 15 November, citing the humiliation of being treated by some members, including members of the board, with discourtesy, indiscipline, and contempt. Walcott claimed that if he is treated discourteously, so would be his plays; he was therefore withdrawing them from the Workshop repertory. Marshall, as executive secretary, replied on behalf of the board that as tickets had been sold with Walcott's prior knowledge the TTW would continue to produce *The Joker* and *Ti-Jean*. For Walcott to withdraw his plays would embarrass everyone. The next week, however, Marshall circulated a letter to season subscribers saying that the two Walcott plays had been withdrawn from their repertoire and, along with *The Maids*, two new plays would be produced as part of the season.[30]

A few days later the Ministry of Agriculture replied to Marshall with a long list of qualifications that the TTW would need for a lease on the Zoo Pavilion. The questions ranged from immediate capital available, proof of future income to meet the the $10,000 annual fee, servicing of loans, total outlay for construction, investment in landscaping, building plans, parking facilities, and expertise in the preparation and selling of food. A reply was requested by 25 December, less than two weeks after the next meeting of the general board.[31]

Walcott's resignation had varied causes. One was that he wanted to put on *Charlatan* for the 1977 Carnival season, while others wanted a revival of *The Joker* as was announced for the subscription season. Walcott went as far as handing out scripts for rehearsals of *The Charlatan* but after a heated argument which became personal he took back the scripts. Whereas in the past members of the Workshop sacrificed their private life for productions there were now angry quarrels over Walcott's scheduling of rehearsals and the cast came late or did not show up. Disagreements outside the theatre were common to the Workshop's history, but it was accepted that during a production the Director was a dictator.[32]

The Bomb called Walcott 'The Joker of St. Lucia' in reporting that he had threatened a High Court injunction on the TTW if they performed his plays. According to the article tensions in the Workshop had come to a head after the registration of a company with a board of directors who would have a say in 'the arty business'. The board wanted more say in the selection of plays, especially West Indian plays, and resented Walcott behaving as if 'the Theatre Workshop was exclusively his preserve to do what he liked'. A board member said Walcott was fed up with this 'democratisation shit'.[33]

While Walcott would not discuss the situation with The Bomb, a member of the Workshop said the group would not 'grovel and beg him with our faces in the dust . . . the Workshop is no longer one man'. Later The Sun claimed that the break was over The Charlatan which Walcott wanted to stage instead of the planned programme. The Workshop felt 'that the only reason why the playwright wanted to stage that particular play was because new music had been written for it by American composer Galt MacDermot'. A nasty note in the November Kairi 76 suggested that Laveau's success in directing Belle Fanto caused Walcott to veto Hall's plans to direct The Maids.[34]

Subscribers had paid $40 to see six plays. O Babylon!, Belle Fanto, Revival, The Maids, Ti-Jean and The Joker. Now the Workshop had to replace the two Walcott plays. Trinidad had planned to send The Joker to the Festival of Black and African Arts in Nigeria early in 1977, but that was now impossible.

At the Fifth General Meeting of the board, held at the Little Carib Theatre, 14 December, those present were Andrews, Marshall, Reid, Hall, Jones, Brenda Stillingford (Hughes), and Leonore Bishop. Absent were Holder, Laveau, La Chapelle, Douglas, and Scott. It was agreed to take Walcott's name off the Registration Form and that at the next meeting, 3 January 1977, Anthony Hall 'would say' who would replace Walcott as Artistic Director and the two plays that would be needed to replace Joker and Ti-Jean. They would offer to sell Walcott the 'machinery' (the props) in storage at his home. Andrews and Marshall, along with the architect John Gillespie, would inspect the Zoo Pavilion site before a reply was sent to the Ministry of Agriculture. It is perhaps ironic in view of the large financial sums involved in such a venture that a request by Barbara Jenson to be reimbursed for some expenses connected with the performances of *O Babylon!*, on which a profit was made, at Carifesta, was deferred until money outstanding from the Trinidad and Tobago Government was received. The Financial Comptroller would need to find out the profits on *O Babylon!* to settle claims. Walcott told Marshall that those who held season tickets could use them for his production of *The Charlatan* and wanted to know what the Workshop would contribute towards the production. This would have, in effect, made the company Walcott's without the bother of a committee. Although the board turned down this proposal it decided that as Walcott's suggestion was verbal there would be no written reply.

The TTW formed a governing board in April 1976 and by November, after four board meetings, the seventeen-year-old relationship between the Workshop and Walcott, its founder and leader, ended in bitter acrimony. As West Indian theatre groups have notoriously short life spans and usually depend on the energies of one or two highly profiled, volatile individuals, it was amazing that Walcott had managed to keep a company together so long. The Workshop had undergone various phases of evolution from an actors' studio to becoming an almost full-time acting company specializing in Walcott plays. It was unlikely to develop much further without a better organizational and financial structure, especially as it badly needed a home and that could only be financed through a totally different approach from Walcott's. As the one member of the Workshop who lived from the theatre as a professional, Walcott was naturally interested in what performances would pay, pay him and his actors, and how their productions would further his development and career as a dramatist. Walcott was always testing himself against the best international standards, always wanting to prove that he was the heir to Marlowe and Shakespeare. Each success had to lead to a further challenge. Other members, who had regular jobs, had different goals. Instead of costly, elaborate productions they might have preferred smaller, less demanding efforts and saved the profits towards building a theatre.

Then it seems naive to expect that the Workshop, which had depended all these years so much on Walcott's leadership, contacts, and arrangements, could suddenly turn around and become self-governing with Walcott limiting himself to giving artistic advice. Walcott used workshops to explore and try out his ideas for characters and scenes and used the Workshop to put his plays on stage before they were performed elsewhere. It was also a source of income through royalties and other fees. Even if Walcott had been able overnight to wipe the slate clean, forget his years of leadership, of emotional and financial investment, and accept limitations on his personality and curb his own artistic ambitions, there was a radical misfit between the board's ways and Walcott's. There were already signs that something more than the older relationships was needed to meet the new theatre audience and demand for training actors that Walcott had created. During the year Helen Camps, Tony Hall, and Albert Laveau formed a Theatre Development Centre.

Walcott had always been an extremely hard-working, self-disciplined and productive rebel; incredibly talented, strong willed, obsessed with art, romantic, restless, wildly energetic, ambitious, a visionary, almost cunningly practical, a heavy drinker, Walcott had never been one to take orders, obey rules, or play it safe. He believed that fights cleared the air and made it possible for people to come together on a deeper basis. A well-travelled cosmopolitan, with opportunities apparently awaiting him abroad, he was outgrowing Port of Spain. After the Obie for *Dream*, plans to put on his plays in London and New York, and many international awards for his poetry, he was unlikely to take orders from members of a theatre company he had spent years creating.

The board, however, was led by civil servants; the Chairman, Vice-Chairman, Executive Secretary, and Financial Comptroller had spent their lives as administrators. They were excellent artists as well, but years of committee work, plans, schedules, budgets, rules, and following and giving orders breeds a different approach towards artistic creation from Walcott's blend of total commitment, cliff-hanging survival, improvised solving of problems, and entrepreneurial instincts. Where the board was defining functions, drawing circles around what could be done, wanting to control budgets, stick to rules, Walcott wanted to follow up his ideas without obstructions. Disciplining actors who do not show up for rehearsals would fit in well with Walcott's professionalism, but not allowing him to produce one of his plays that he was revising to include songs by an internationally famous composer would have been a provocation, especially with Walcott's expectations of a successful career abroad. Although Walcott began with the idea of creating a national theatre company it was mainly to perform his plays as he wanted them performed. If the Workshop was not going to do that, then he might as well devote his time and energy to his career.

In principle he wanted some Workshop plays to have other directors than himself; in practice plays that others were rehearsing often were pushed aside for his own plans or their rehearsals were found to be chaotic. Laveau, the only Workshop member who in recent years had directed a large production, was less demanding than Walcott. He lacks a similar vision and drive. It is possible that the lukewarm reviews and poor attendance for *Belle Fanto* made Walcott sceptical of doing plays by other West Indian dramatists. The West Indian plays of the 1950s and 1960s were now outmoded. They referred to a society that had changed. They also belonged to a period when anything written for the stage by a West Indian was welcomed by the small amateur theatre groups of the time. That too had changed. Such plays could not sustain the large audiences needed for the continuous semi-professional theatre that the Workshop was pioneering.

Walcott had resigned from the company before in fits of pique. Would he be willing to return as artistic director or in some other role under the new governing board? His letter of 15 November said that he would not reconsider or discuss his decision with the Workshop. As late as May 1977 members of the Workshop were quoted as saying that they 'loved the man for the genius of his work' and that many people wanted the association to resume; 'one does not give up something that has lasted for 17 years so easily'. Before Christmas 1976 the Trinidad Theatre Workshop Dance Company participated in a programme at the Trinidad & Tobago Sports and Culture Club along with the 'Theatre Workshop Band' which performed, 'with the kind permission of Mr. Derek Walcott', selections from *Joker*. Errol Jones claims that Walcott has difficulty handling love; wanting to leave for the United States, Walcott magnified disagreements and irritations into an excuse to resign from the Trinidad Theatre Workshop. Who, as Walcott wrote about the characters in Chekhov's *The Seagull*, really knows others?[35]

As I listen to my tapes of interviews with Workshop members, compare statements made at various times by the actors, I am struck by how often people contrast the opportunities that were opening to Walcott in the United States and his financial situation in Trinidad at the time. He had stayed in the West Indies to create a great theatre company which would perform his plays and from which he would earn a living. He had created his theatre company and it performed his plays, but he could not live from it. He and Margaret kept investing their own money in productions and in attempts to transfer the productions to Broadway. Everyone agrees that he earned little for what he put into the Workshop. Financial strain appears to have contributed to the crisis in his personal life and his relationship to the core

Workshop members. The West Indies could not support its writers and it certainly could not afford Walcott. Idealism had kept him in the West Indies, but such idealism had required the support of the Rockefeller Foundation, his wife, and a dedicated band of followers. American foundations were no longer interested, his relationship with his wife was in crisis, and the followers were no longer willing to follow on his terms. Fame and money abroad seemed probable. What had formerly been a happy theatre family devoted to shared goals was turning into a free-for-all family quarrel in which everyone was unhappy. It was time to move on.

NOTES

1. Albert Laveau later said the break 'was an accumulation of years of frustration'; Helen Camps said 'it was simply time to move on.' Judy Raymond, 'The Legacy of Derek Walcott', *Sunday Express* (11 Oct. 1992), 2, 3, esp. 18. Information about Tanker and *Ti-Jean* from Errol Jones (July 1990) and others.
2. Information about the National Brewery Company grant is in a press release dated 21 Jan. 1976 in the Walcott Collection, University of the West Indies, St Augustine.
3. Kenneth Stein, 'Dream on Monkey Mountain', WBJC-FM 91.5; R. H. Gardner, 'Center Stage Show is Filled with Poetry, Music and Dance', *The Sun* (19 Feb. 1976), 1, Entertainment sect.; Corinne F. Hammett, ' "Dream": An Exotic Folk Fantasy', *The News American* (18 Feb. 1976), 5D.
4. ' "O Babylon!" opens Friday', *Trinidad Guardian* (14 Mar. 1976), 6. The background for *O Babylon!* is based on interviews with Richard Montgomery and Norline Metivier. Also Keith Smith, 'O Babylon: An Adventure in reggae', *People*, 1/9 (Apr. 1976), 34–9.
5. Jeremy Taylor, 'A Beautifully Simple, Dramatic Idea . . .', *Express* (24 Mar. 1976), 21.
6. Judy Stone [Mauby], 'O Babylon!, do Mafia Play with Beach Balls?', *Trinidad Guardian* (1 Apr. 1976), 4.
7. E. G. Scott, *Trinidad Guardian*, unidentified clipping.
8. Raoul Pantin, 'O Babylon!', *Caribbean Contact*, 4/1 (Apr. 1976), 17.
9. Sule Mombara, ' "O Babylon!"—Where it Went Wrong', *Caribbean Contact*, 4/1 (Apr. 1976), 15.
10. Rawle Gibbons, 'O Babylon!', *Kairi 76* (1976), 12–13.
11. Earl Lovelace, 'Rude Bwoy Walcott', *People* (19 June 1976), 37–9.
12. The various minutes and correspondence concerning the General Meetings and related matters can be found in the Walcott Collection, University of the West Indies, St Augustine.
13. ' "O Babylon!" for Naparima Bowl', *Trinidad Guardian* (14 June 1976), 4.
14. 'An 80-Member T'Dad Team for Carifesta', *Trinidad Guardian* (9 July 1976), 1; 'Dinsley Roti on Sale in Jamaica', *Trinidad Guardian* (29 July 1976), 2. 'Carifesta

on despite Jamaica Emergency', unidentified newspaper clipping, possibly Jamaica *The Daily Gleaner* (June 1976), 1: '. . . the State of Emergency would provide a safer atmosphere for the full development of the Carifesta programme.'

15. Derek Walcott, 'Notes for discussion with division of culture re. Trinidad Theatre Workshop's participation at Carifesta' and 'Trinidad Theatre Workshop–Carifesta–Jamaica 1976' (13 July 1976), Walcott Collection, University of the West Indies, St Augustine.

16. Pearl Connor-Mogotsi, 'Babylon Crushes the Rasta Dream', *Trinidad Guardian* (23 July 1976), 4, 6.

17. 'A Feast of Artistic Goodies', *Star* (27 July 1976), 4; Harry Milner, 'Viable Work . . . with Necessary Changes', *The Daily Gleaner* (27 July 1976), 20.

18. Errol Jones and others in the cast mentioned during interviews their initial puzzlement at the drumming. Franklyn St Juste told me that he had shown a ten-minute segment of *O Babylon!* on his television coverage of the Festival. The unedited film of the complete play was eventually passed on to the Jamaica National Library which has no record of it and could not find it during a search. MacDermot recorded the music in the United States, as he had with *Joker*, and planned to add Workshop voices later. After Walcott's resignation the project was put aside, until later when voices were added in the United States and the recording released in 1980 by Kilmarnock Records (12 Silver Lake Road, Staten Island, NY 10307).

19. 'Roscoe's Makak Hypnotises Little Carib Audience', *Trinidad Guardian* (30 July 1976).

20. The notes and minutes are in the Walcott Collection.

21. Stanley Marshall to Ministry of Agriculture (30 Aug. 1976), Walcott Collection.

22. Derek Walcott, 'Why Belle Fanto Has Survived', *Sunday Guardian* (22 Aug. 1976), 6.

23. 'Notices and Comments', *Kairi 76*, 50.

24. Lee Johnson, 'Roach's Attempt to Pinpoint Changing Values', *Trinidad Guardian* (10 Sept. 1976), 9.

25. Jeremy Taylor, 'Belle Fanto—Beautiful', *Express* (15 Sept. 1976), 12.

26. Interview with George Williams (July 1990).

27. Interviews with La Chapelle and Metivier (1990–91).

28. Pearl Connor-Mogotsi, 'Exuberant Dance Lead into Paradise', *Trinidad Guardian* (4 Nov. 1976), 6; Jeremy Taylor, 'A true revival from Workshop dancers', *Express* (8 Nov. 1976), 19; Raoul Pantin, 'Revival—A Debut of Distinction', *Tapia* (7 Nov. 1976), 4–5.

29. Judy Stone [Mauby], 'Vitality, Freedom beyond Martha', *Trinidad Guardian* (8 Nov. 1976), 15.

30. Derek Walcott to the Chairman (15 Nov. 1976); Stanley Marshall to Derek Walcott (18 Nov. 1976); 'Dear Subscriber' (25 Nov. 1976), Walcott Collection, University of the West Indies, St Augustine.

31. Martin Kernahan to Stanley Marshall (29 Nov. 1976), Walcott Collection, University of the West Indies, St Augustine.

32. Corinne Holder, Barbara Jenson, Metivier, and others told me about the problems with the *Charlatan* rehearsals.

33. 'The Joker of St Lucia', *The Bomb* (20 Dec. 1976), 5.
34. 'Walcott Quits Workshop', *The Sun* (4 May 1977), 2; Christopher Laird, 'The Running of a "Subscription Season"', *Kairi 76*, 3.
35. 'Walcott Quits Workshop', op. cit.; interview with Errol Jones, Boston (Apr. 1993) and Raymond Ramcharitar, 'Baptism of Fire', *Sunday Guardian Magazine* (6 Dec. 1992), 11; Derek Walcott's 'Homage' in the programme for the TTW's 1975 *The Seagull*.

PART III

Separation and Reconciliation

1977–1993

14

The Trinidad Theatre Workshop and Dance Company

THE Trinidad Theatre Workshop had been like a family in which everyone was expected continually to be present and participate during workshops and rehearsals. Walcott was its father-figure and leader, Errol Jones and Stanley Marshall part of its inner core. Claude Reid was one of its foundation members, many others had belonged for over a decade. Those members who had resigned over some disagreement or to pursue a career often felt for years afterwards that a central part of their life was no longer there. Suddenly the family was no more. Walcott and the core members were not even speaking to each other.

With Walcott's resignation the TTW barely existed beyond a title and the continuing interest of a few members. Walcott was founder, leader, producer, theatre director, dramatist, artistic director, scenic designer, fund raiser, manager, publicist, and much else. He scheduled the rehearsals, selected the actors, supplied the scripts, appointed the theatre manager, handled contracts, designed and wrote the programmes, inserted advertisements and announcements in the newspapers, and worked with the musicians and dancers. Few of those remaining with the Workshop had experience in such areas. The cost of advertising and theatre directors proved expensive. The actors were not deeply read in dramatic literature. Walcott's relationship to Norline and his resignation split the company in several directions as many, especially younger members, sided with Derek. For years afterwards former friends would not speak to and would not with work each other. Some drifted away and others decided this was the time to stop fooling around with the stage and instead devote themselves to family and career. Those who participated in Walcott's own productions were likely to be ostracized by those who stood by Margaret. Many of the Workshop's patrons among the professional classes were friends of Derek's. The Workshop was in debt for about $20,000 from *O Babylon!*

The situation was not improved by the reluctance of the small core of early members to entrust leadership to others. The older West Indian male traditionally felt authority should be his. Albert Laveau appeared the heir, but he remained Derek's friend and the time he spent in New York pursuing a career as a professional actor had changed him and his relationship to the Workshop. Although he had joined the Workshop in 1962 he claimed that the Little Carib Theatre Workshop was not really part of the history of the Trinidad Theatre Workshop, which he regarded as beginning with the Basement Theatre in 1966; he was somewhat of an outsider within the inner circle. Wilbert Holder was from Guyana, a comparative newcomer with a sharp tongue and complex personality. Helen Camps was a foreign white woman with radical associations. Brenda Hughes was black, Trinidadian, but younger, a woman, at times abrasive. When Walcott resigned in 1970 he recommended Errol Jones as his successor and Jones had remained his disciple, but now Jones was a leader of the fallen angels. He accepted Walcott's right to artistic leadership, but was less happy working under Walcott's management; for years there had simmered disagreements about such matters as fees for acting on radio and television.

It is difficult to understand the future continuing attempts at reconcilement and wild fights between Walcott and the Workshop without seeing it partly in personal terms as a broken marriage between Walcott and Jones and a few others. There were genuine issues, and during the next fifteen years other issues would arise before Walcott and the Workshop were reconciled, but at the heart of the matter was the nature of Walcott's leadership, with his hopes to make it internationally, and what some of his followers felt they were getting from the relationship. Jones, Marshall, Reid, and Andrews felt they had built the Workshop along with Walcott and it was their possession as much as his. Walcott was unwilling to let the Workshop perform his plays, and there could be no winner, no compromise, unless Jones and others had given up their secure jobs and followed Walcott to New York and professional careers in the theatre. Time would need to change the situation and those involved before there could be a remarriage.

The Workshop reformed around Errol Jones, who in 1977 retired early from his position with the government to devote himself to the theatre, and Stanley Marshall. For many years it would be essentially a production company using the Workshop name to mount or sponsor productions or for publicity when Workshop actors performed with other companies. There were attempts to restart workshops and there were a few spectacular productions, but the continuity, energy, leadership, and larger company were lost. The Workshop struggled on, productions added up, successful productions toured, and those associated with the company were famous in West Indian theatre. It was not until 1990 that the Workshop found a home and could return to the original idea of regularly scheduled productions and training others in the performing arts.

After Walcott's resignation the immediate problems were management of the Workshop and how to finish the 1976–7 season for which tickets had been sold. *Joker* and *Ti-Jean* were originally promised along with Genet's *The Maids* and an evening by the new Trinidad Theatre Workshop Dance Company.

The Maids, the fourth production of the 1976–7 season, took place at the Little Carib 10–20 March 1977 with Anthony Hall's debut as director. Ermine Wright played Solange. Greer Jones, who began as a dancer, had her first principal role as an actress in the part of Madame. *The Maids* was mostly a Helen Camps effort; Camps played Claire, designed and made the costumes, and was producer and in charge of house management. Albert Laveau constructed the set and John Andrews continued to design the lighting.

Judy Stone writing as 'Mauby' was enthusiastic—'an experience no theatre lover should miss'—but had reservations. She commented on Wright's dry detachment and unfussiness in the role of Solange, but felt that Greer Jones exaggerated, and made superficial, the part of Madame, a fault she blamed on Hall whose 'thumbprint is visible on every aspect' of an incisive, tightly controlled production. Hall's production was imaginative and showed sound theatre sense but moved too rapidly without pause and had unnecessary embellishments that smacked of 'drama school'.[1]

While the Theatre Workshop performed nothing else during 1977, the Dance Company, on its own, held a season. Walcott supported strong women who stood up to him and knew what they wanted to do; in Carol La Chapelle the TTWDC had a leader. The TTWDC performed as part of a Christmas programme at Town Hall 10–11 December 1976, and *Season 77* was held at the Little Carib 22 June– 2 July 1977. Later, 23 September 1977, they would perform as part of the programme at the National Agricultural Exhibition in St Augustine.

As the TTW was becalmed by the loss of Walcott's energy, the TTWDC came into its own.

Dance Season 77 lasted two weeks of nightly performances with student matinees on 22 June and 2 July. There was excellent publicity in the newspapers with large attractive photographs of dancers in costumes. Of the eight works performed five were new. The programme consisted of three dances from their repertoire choreographed by La Chapelle—'Revival', 'Movements', and 'Cages'—and five new works— Stefan Bobb's 'Summer Suite', La Chapelle's 'Love Theme', 'Badia' by Trevor Redhead and Noble Douglas; 'Tears of a Woman' by Rosemary Wilkinson-Nellands and Ken McPherson's 'Toute Bagai'. The dancers were Lewt Carrabon, Norline Metivier, Noble Douglas, Carol La Chapelle, Greer Jones, Adele Bynoe, David Byer, Heather Henderson, Stefan Bobb, Sandra Richards, Trevor Redhead, Brenda Baden-Semper, Ancil Bullen, and Corinne Jones. Two members of the company, Oscilla Stewart and Evans Antoine, were currently in New York on scholarships with the Alvin Ailey City Center. Carol La Chapelle was producer and artistic director, with Leonore Bishop her assistant. The set designers were Greer Jones and Lee Johnson. It is impressive how independent the TTWDC had become. Each item in the programme had a different sponsor.[2]

The reviewer for *Express* wrote that the TTWDC is the nation's best dance company. 'It is aiming high, its choreography exploring folk materials with formal dance techniques, obviously pressing for the sort of discipline and technical standards which are still rare on the local stage.' Of the older pieces 'Revival', based on the Caribbean Shango cult, is said to move more smoothly into its final section than previously. Of the new works 'Toute Bagai' is said to be too complex and the reviewer found it difficult to follow even with the aid of the programme note. The reviewer added that the director and choreographer assumed too much sophistication from the audience. Speaking as a 'layman' the reviewer found that the women dancers overshadowed the men ('the company is loaded with sensuous feminine beauty') and that the company seemed to work with real rapport, but there was a problem of communication between the dancers and the audience which did not know what was to be interpreted as narrative.[3]

'Mauby' praised Ken McPherson's 'Toute Bagai' as adding love, death, faith, sex, and life to Carol La Chapelle's 'previously purely ascetic style'. Whereas La Chapelle uses 'the pelvis as a mocking dare; Noble Douglas uses the pelvis as an invitation'. 'Toute Bagai' allowed the men to leap and not just do lifts. In Kenneth McPherson's

'Variations on a theme—LOVE' the 'daydreaming' section with Noble Douglas was in a Martha Graham style, with spins, swirls, jerks, and distortions which made the audience gasp with excitement. Stone found the company remarkably fine and exuberant, but a bit lacking in precision. Adele Bynoe and Metivier in 'Cages' seemed less clear-cut in their roles than previously. In her survey of the arts in Trinidad during 1977 Stone singled out the TTWDC:

The art form in which many of our artists have been able to see the world trends and modern techniques for themselves, thanks to opportunities for overseas training is also, not surprisingly, the form in which the artists have shown themselves most consistently adept—dance. This year the Trinidad Theatre Workshop Dance Company has followed up its stunning first 'Revival' with 'Season 77', a production less remarkable than its predecessor mainly due to deficiencies in production rather than any falling off in the dancers themselves.[4]

The Barbados Writers Workshop performed Anthony Hinkson's *Teacher Teach'er* under Earl Warner's direction at the Little Carib Theatre for a week starting 29 July 1977, with the sponsorship of the Trinidad Theatre Workshop. Subscribers were sent a notice that they could use their subscription to attend *Teacher Teach'er*. So between *The Charlatan* and *Teacher, Teach'er* subscribers were offered two non-Workshop plays to replace *Joker* and *Ti-Jean*. The programme credited the TTW for publicity, Leonore Bishop as House Manager, and Brenda Hughes for co-ordination.

The Barbados Writers Workshop began in 1969 and three years later ventured into theatre by taking a play to Carifesta in Guyana. Although it has a number of writers, Hinkson is the best known and apparently the most prolific, but his plays have not been published. Warner was their Artistic Director and, since 1974, directed most of their productions. 'Mauby' was happy to have a chance to see a Barbadian play and theatre company, found the Bajan accent at times difficult to follow 'but every voice is ringingly audible, a real lesson to some of our own amateur groups'.[5]

During November 1977 Errol Jones and Holder acted in Lennox Brown's *Fog Drifts in the Spring* for Horace James and Trinidad & Tobago Television, but the TTW remained becalmed. There was talk of staging in the Little Carib five productions of serious plays each year, with small casts and simple settings, with the object of grossing ten to twelve thousand dollars, but nothing came of it. Judy Stone, who in 1976 had formed her Touchstone Productions, was to direct

Peter Nichols's *A Day in the Death of Joe Egg* for the TTW, but after rehearsals started the production was cancelled. The next year Helen Camps became director-manager at the Little Carib. Some of the Workshop actors became involved in Banyan Studio's Trinidad Television Workshop which during 1978 produced thirteen half-hour tapes for the Education Department of Trinidad's Family Planning Association. Tony Hall was Drama Director and Errol Jones, Ermine Wright, and Albert Laveau were among the actors.[6]

Earlier when Walcott was dissatisfied with the TTW and feeling that his own development was being held back by their quarrels, he would confide in the dancers and tell them that they would eventually need to go their own way. With the TTW doing little, and unlikely to produce the musicals that would give them an opportunity to perform, the TTWDC in June 1978 became independent under the name of the La Chapelle–Douglas Dance Company. The dancers and dances remained the same but some new male dancers were added.[7]

The *Sunday Guardian* carried an unsigned article, almost certainly by Walcott, 'La Chapelle and Douglas Striving for Cohesion', which concludes with a brief comparison of the problems facing the acceptance of modern dance in the West Indies with the position of Wilson Harris and Naipaul two decades previously. The writer begins by saying that the old controversies resolved elsewhere of classical versus modern dance and folk versus ballet continue in Trinidad. After Ailey, DeMille, Robbins, Graham, and even Balanchine used the jazz idiom to extend classical dance, the American musical has become an art form. While Caribbean dancers and writers have been attempting to create a 'Fusion', Rex Nettleford's Jamaican company still makes the distinction between its varied sources too clear. His folk pieces are more successful than his dances in a more purely modern idiom. The problem is that folk art is stereotyped as ebullient, simple, light-weight, and spontaneous and soon turns to clichés. 'True choreographers do not begin with the idea of tradition. They begin every day with the challenge of the body.' 'What is inherent in the body, organic in its impulses of direction will be brought out, so that a West Indian dancer does not feel pretentious in movement.'

After commenting that Astor Johnson's relentless, honest search is often expressed too diffusely in the work of his company, which may not understand what he is after, the writer turns to the new La Chapelle–Douglas Company. 'Douglas seems to be the choreographer with the most authoritative ideas of what must be done with the West Indian body.' Like all true artists she works from ignorance, 'subjecting her work not to ideas but to the annihilation of ideas'. (This modernist formulation of an aesthetic of discovery recurs in many of Walcott's essays.) La Chapelle is Douglas's opposite, much cooler, more confident, clearer in concept. Such a combination promises to make the new company exciting provided that the conflict of opposites remains. After praising 'Revival' as fresh although indebted to Ailey, the writer finds that the choreographers allow their different styles and kinds of schooling to fuse into one concept. Such dance has developed from Beryl McBurnie's pioneering struggles, although it is not obviously indebted directly to her and might be contrasted to the 'predictable vigorous paralysis' of the Best Village performances with their supposed emphasis on being 'rootsy'. Claiming that the standards of theatre in Trinidad are improving, the writer says of the new dance company, 'In intentions, and in many sections of the programme, its achievements are equal to any good evolving company in New York.' Anyone seeking why Walcott was so interested in dance might want to read this article.[8]

The La Chapelle–Douglas Dance Company presented its *Season '78* at the Little Carib Theatre 1–4 June 1978. La Chapelle remained Artistic Director. Noble Douglas was Rehearsal Director. The company of fifteen included Adele Bynoe, Greer Jones, Norline Metivier, and Heather Henderson. Pat Samuels, John Isaacs, and Brenda Hughes were singers; stage management was shared by John Isaacs and Anthony Gomes. 'Badia', 'Revival', and 'Toute Bagai' were joined by Wendy Joseph's 'Awakening' and Andre Legent's 'Afrique'.

There is a signed, undated, two-page, single-spaced letter in the UWI Walcott Collection, in reply to Jeremy Taylor's review of *Season '78*, which shows how closely Walcott continued emotionally and intellectually to be involved in development of dance in Trinidad, and why. The abstraction and physicality of dance exemplified the problems raised by modern art in relation to meaning, humanism, and West Indian art. Walcott objects that Jeremy Taylor's dismissal of the performance while pretending to be ignorant is professionally irresponsible for a critic, especially as the review could create economic problems for the development of dance in Trinidad by discouraging people from attending. Taylor was bewildered about the meaning of the dances, unable to follow story lines, and dismissed the evening as meaningless obscurity and gymnastics. Walcott says it is the responsibility of the critic to look for meaning. In the arts meaning can be reduced to materials. A painting is paint, a dance is gymnastics. Modern art has tried to make art on such premises as a painting consists of the surface, texture, and whatever else is applied to the canvas. Modern art cannot be dismissed just because it has explored first principles. In any case there is always meaning. All activity is meaningful. Not even God can create chaos. Any act of creation is an attempt at meaning. The critic's job is to search for that meaning.

Walcott says that the meaning of art changes with each generation; while we never completely understand, it is possible to 'enjoy' art without understanding. He praises Douglas's 'Untitled' as the 'most intelligent and exciting' local dance he has seen for years. He compares it to an abstract painting in which the painter has carefully thought where to place each supposedly meaningless stroke of the brush. But as Douglas is a West Indian artist she is an 'inescapable humanist'; there is warmth in her use of the body in contrast to the abstractionist's attempt to annihilate. As dance is the least abstract of the arts a critic must not expect programme notes to explain what can only be understood by following the gestures of the dancers.[9]

The La Chapelle–Douglas remained active and performed *Encore* for two nights in November 1978, at the Little Carib. The programme included La Chapelle's 'Trindolesence', La Chapelle's 'US & Moore', Wendy Joseph's 'Awakening', Douglas's 'Untitled' and the Douglas–La Chapelle 'Revival'.

It was not until September 1978 that the TTW showed some life again. There was a reading at the Desperadoes Panyard in Laventille of excerpts from Earl Lovelace's forthcoming novel *The Dragon Can't Dance* (published 1979), collectively directed by the actors and Lovelace. It included such regulars as Errol Jones, Eunice Alleyne, Ermine Wright, Stanley Marshall, Brenda Hughes, Fred Hope, and Claude Reid, with music by André Tanker. There was a close, immediate response between the Laventville audience and the players and for the original performance Eunice Alleyne led the performers, including the Dragon, into the streets to dance Carnival. As the novel concerns the poor living in the hills of Port of Spain and their culture of the steelbands and Carnival, the setting was ideal. The audience was seeing a play about themselves and their conflict with dominant elements of society. There were readings in several venues including San Fernando until Ermine Wright died in October. Later Earl Lovelace was to make his own dramatic adaptation which after being workshopped at the Eugene O'Neill Foundation (1984) opened at Queen's Hall (1986) and eventually was taken to London. There were readings of *Dragon* by some TTW members in New York (1980) and at the 1981 Carifesta in Barbados.

The Dragon Can't Dance was immediately placed on the school and university syllabus and Lovelace joined Samuel Selvon, V. S. Naipaul, Shiva Naipaul, Wayne Brown, St Lucian Derek Walcott, and later Neil Bissoondath as Trinidad's surprisingly large contribution to contemporary literature. As Lovelace's novel shows, many non-white Trinidadians had become wealthy, middle class or had risen beyond the poverty of the 1930s and 1940s. Because it is set in Port of Spain and concerns the social, economic, and cultural protests, transformations, evolution, and conflicting ideals of the post-emancipation black through the transitional 1950s and political independence to the futile Black Power rebellion of the 1970s, *The Dragon Can't Dance* has a classic status in Trinidad. It is black national history as seen from the perspective of the poor and a criticism of continuing self-destructive violence and wasteful protest in a society which has become self-governing, wealthier, and now more threatened by American consumerism as a way of life than by the racial injustices of the past. The novel—complexly written with elaborate patterns of imagery and symbolism—is both a celebration of the culture of resistance in the past and an attempt by celebrating it to transform it into a more vitally productive community culture.

The reading of *Dragon* at the Desperadoes Panyard was proclaimed a 'triumph' by Raoul Pantin. When the reading had to be cut because of other events on the programme, the audience groaned its disapproval. While praising Jones, Ermine Wright, Alleyne, and especially Claude Reid (someone in the audience shouted 'But he is a real starboy in truth!'), Pantin gave most attention to the actor and playwright Ralph Maraj who came from San Fernando for the part of Pariag. 'In a few moving scenes, Maraj absolutely captures the pain of the Indian living in urbanized African society. So true was his performance that more than one member of the audience was visibly moved to tears.' Jeremy Taylor reviewing the production after it transferred to the Little Carib noted that audience reaction was 'warm, appreciative' but found the production casual, almost like a rehearsal. Lovelace and Jones 'perched high on the Little Carib balcony' shared the narration while behind them Tanker's musicians played delicately. Below them the actors half dramatized, half read, with the script in hand.[10]

During 18–28 January 1979, at the Little Carib, the TTW came together again for their Twentieth Anniversary Production, *Departure in the Dark* by the Jamaican Sam Hillary. The director was the Trinidadian George McKenzie with Errol Jones the producer. The cast included Eunice Alleyne, Avis Martin, Sheila Watson, Ellsworth Primus,

Stanley Marshall, Claude Reid, Brenda Hughes, and Jerline Quamina. As it was the Twentieth Anniversary the TTW printed a larger than usual programme listing previous productions. *Departure in the Dark* was one of those early plays first published by the UWI Extra-Mural Department in duplicated typewritten form. Its subject, the poverty and indignities of life in the barrack-yards, was common to many West Indian plays in the 1950s. Jeremy Taylor found the production well paced and carefully interpreted, but remarked that it was time West Indian drama caught up with the world of taxi-drivers, union bosses, and steel company executives. It was a sad rambling play of little interest. Eunice Alleyne was excellent in creating the faded elegance and proud voice and movements of Aunt Lil or Mrs Martin. 'The little jaw daintily gobbling breakfast toast could place the character by itself.'[11]

As often happened, a post-Walcott TTW production lost money. The total receipts from ticket and programme sales were $5,223. The total costs of production were $18,753, resulting in a loss of $13,530. One-third of the expenses, $6,200, were for the author's royalties and payment to nine actors, the director, and stage manager; $800 were for costumes; $2,000 went into the set; and $600 was paid to the make-up artist ($50 a night). Lighting cost $2,000 and sound, including the operator, $1,000. Advertising and photography cost around $1,500. The rental of rehearsal space, the theatre for performances, and chairs cost $2,480. Then there was the cost of printing tickets, handbills, programmes, paying sales persons to sell the tickets, and such incidentals as transportation and paying cleaners. (Many of these tasks had been done by the Walcotts and their friends.) As it was impossible to raise ticket prices much higher, the TTW decided to look for subsidies from local businesses.[12]

In May 1979 there was a three-day conference at the Hotel Normandie hosted by the US International Communications Agency to create exchange of personnel, skills, and information between the United States and the West Indies. There were workshops concerning script development, theatre management, media, arts in education, training, and information sources. Those attending included Helen Camps, Errol Jones, James Lee Wah, Derek Walcott, Alwin Bully from Dominica, Ken Corsbie and Earl Warner from Barbados, Richard Montgomery, Dennis Scott, and Noel Vaz from Jamaica, and others from Guyana and the United States including George White of the O'Neill Foundation. Alwin Bully was awarded a grant of TT$7,000 and the United States Embassy along with the Trinidad Theatre

Workshop held a reception in honour of George White and members of the Caribbean–US Theatre Workshop Planning Committee.[13]

During the weekends from 1–13 June 1979, Trevor Rhone's *Old Story Time* was presented at Arthur Bentley's new Hotel Normandie Dinner Theatre 'in association with the TTW'. Trevor Rhone directed his play; the cast of six included Errol Jones, Stanley Marshall, Jerline Quamina, and Nigel Scott. This was the first TTW production of a Trevor Rhone play; increasingly Rhone's dramas would become their standard fare. Rhone's plays with their small casts and proven popular success were suited for the present limited means of the Workshop. Rhone (who was born in Jamaica in 1940, studied at the Rose Bruford College of Speech and Drama in Kent, England, and is co-founder of the Barn Theatre in Jamaica) had become the next important West Indian dramatist after Walcott. His plays were more realistic, less 'élite' literature, less ambitious, more an amusing but sympathetic portrayal of the contemporary lives of the upper-working- and lower-middle-class black West Indian. Usually set in Jamaica after independence, Rhone's plays show a demoralized, corrupt, often violent society, with rapidly dropping educational standards, inefficiency on jobs, living off tourism, continuing social prejudices (including reverse discrimination), and bad relationships between men and women. Rhone, who has a Trinidadian wife, was thinking of moving to Port of Spain because of the increasing violence and deteriorating political situation in Jamaica.[14]

Judy Stone found Rhone's characters and plot, despite its twists, simplified to the point of caricature, but commented that this might be appropriate for an Old Time Story. Rhone directed the play in the broad old time style with lots of mugging. Jones, who has an extremely changeable face on stage, delighted the audience. Nigel Scott's heart did not seem to be in his role as villain. As in many reviews of the TTW, Stanley Marshall is praised for his comic acting. He is perhaps the most undervalued of the Workshop actors.[15]

In the *Sunday Guardian* Independence Supplement, Judy Stone surveyed theatre in Trinidad during recent decades. She was excited that Helen Camps had formed All Theatre Productions and was managing the Little Carib Theatre. Besides hiring actors for Little Carib productions the ATP would act as an agent for other companies. Although the Little Carib was closed for renovations as the government had given Beryl McBurnie $70,000 towards lighting equipment, the ATP was involved with Arthur Bentley's Dinner Theatre at the Hotel Normandie. The TTW was slowly recovering from the crisis caused by Walcott's resignation. Stone hoped that the May CARIBUSTE conference would lead to a more professional theatre in Trinidad and that George White would show the artists how to raise funds. The lack of theatres remains a problem for Trinidadian performers. Even the Naparima Bowl in San Fernando has not been rebuilt after a 1977 fire. The Little Carib is often closed or not available to drama groups. The 120 ft-wide stage at Queen's Hall 'swallows small productions'.[16]

An attempt during 1980 by Errol Jones and Stanley Marshall to hold weekly theatre workshops for young actors did not last long. Helen Camps appeared to have the energy that they lacked. She produced *Mas in Yuh Mas* by poet-performer Paul Keens-Douglas and musician Felix Edinborough. Ken Corsbie said that in its use of such old time carnival characters as jab jabs, king sailors, bats, dragons, Pierrot Grenade and Dame Lorraine, this was the first time in the Caribbean that popular folk festival and street theatre was transferred to the legitimate stage. Camps would follow this with such colourful musicals as *Cinderama, King Jab Jab, Snokone and the Seven Dwarfs* and *J'Ouvert* (which included Paul Keens-Douglas, several calypsonians, choreographer Astor Johnson and an Indian Trinidadian steel band).[17]

During April 1980 at the Little Carib, Camps's Trinidad All Theatre Productions produced Athol Fugard's *Sizwe Bansi is Dead* with Errol Jones and Holder, which she directed and took to Barbados in June. It was highly praised by Jeremy Taylor and Victor Questel. Walcott wrote a letter to the *Express* saying the Little Carib production was 'one of the finest' he had seen in years. 'I see a fair amount of theatre in New York. This production is at least equal to the best.'[18]

This production toured the islands. In 1981 it was revived at the Little Carib, taken to Tobago, Carifesta in Barbados, and Surinam. Reviewing the past year in Barbadian theatre John Wickham said that *Sizwe* was the best theatre he had seen in a long time as Holder and Jones gave virtuosi displays of brilliant sustained acting. As Jones and Holder toured without Camps as director, the origin and legal ownership of the production became unclear as did the status of other productions in which the Theatre Workshop actors appeared. *The Nation Carifesta Bulletin* said that the Trinidad and Tobago Theatre Company incorporates the Trinidad Theatre Workshop. In 1982 *Sizwe Bansi* was in St Thomas and by August the production was no longer Camps's for its ten performances in Nassau, where Lyn Sweeting described it as 'West Indian theatre at its best' and recommended every Bahamian to see it. Jeanne Thompson in the *Nassau Guardian* wrote that the high standard of the performance 'rivals any which can be seen on the stages in London and New York'. *Sizwe Bansi* had become an official

TTW production by 27 September 1984 when it was again performed in Trinidad by Jones and Holder. As late as January 1987 Holder and Jones were performing *Sizwe Bansi* in St Vincent where Holder also conducted workshops in voice and movement.[19]

Victor Questel's review of Camps's original Little Carib production captures some of the power that Jones and Holder had developed by this time in their careers as actors. When Jones enters the play it is stunning. 'What a sad, shuffling bundle of humility and humiliation.' 'Using every muscle, every tissue of his theatre experience, Jones enters the bodies of two victims of apartheid.' 'Wilbert Holder switches smoothly from one persona to the next. He changes from one mask to the other and thus effortlessly informs us of his capacity to fantasize, to survive by becoming other people, and so entertain himself.' 'If Errol worked Sizwe from the inside, Wilbert worked Styles from the outside. His almost constant movement defines him. Styles is here, there and everywhere. He is everybody . . . the whole city of Port Elizabeth comes alive through the quick portraits conjured by the mercurial magic energy of Holder.' As a director Camps got Jones and Holder 'to explore the total emotional score of the script. Working with the raw fibres of their nerve ends, Errol and Wilbert are able to create a textured pattern of emotions that criss cross through the territories of comedy and pathos.'[20]

Helen Camps could be said to have carried on and extended some of Walcott's roles. Her Trinidad All Theatre Productions was used by Walcott to premiere his *Pantomime* at the Little Carib, April 1978, with Albert Laveau as director, and she directed the play in December at the Little Carib. Her company also sponsored the Walcott-directed *Remembrance* at Bentley's Hotel Normandie Dinner Theatre, July 1979, and for six weeks in 1982 she toured England and Europe with *J'Ouvert*. Such an international tour had always been a dream of Walcott for the TTW. Camps's use of folk and carnival characters and masks brought together the two approaches to West Indian theatre that Walcott and Errol Hill had argued about in the early 1960s; to this she added an interest in psychology, myth, and took further the kind of experimental theatre that Walcott explored during the 1960s. She had created an avant-garde Alternative Theatre. Her strong personality and convictions, which made her a leader and achiever and one of the few members of the TTW who could stand up to Walcott, also made her, especially as a foreign, Irish, white woman, unacceptable to many Trinidadians. In February 1982, Beryl McBurnie accused Camps of 'taking over' the Little Carib and Camps resigned as director-manager.

Many felt that the Little Carib had had an unusually active period and what followed there was less impressive.[21]

By September 1982 Camps had organized the Trinidad Tent Theatre to provide theatre workshops and build a repertory. Working with actors in their teens and twenties, and the composer Roger Israel, she rapidly developed four plays making use of Carnival characters, pop music, and such themes as materialism and nuclear war, and for two months brought in Henk Tjon, the well-known artistic director of Surinam's Doe Theatre to produce a season called 'Statements'. Trinidad Tent Theatre's answer to the problem of lack of performance space was to use a tent for productions, which also had the symbolic advantage of being closer to Trinidadian folk traditions. Camps also began training twenty-five young people as performers and technicians, beginning with a year's apprenticeship in formal courses. Many of these, such as Raymond Choo Kong, were to be the next generation of Trinidad's actors and actresses. There was also an Outreach Children's Programme on Saturdays involving story-telling, folk-singing and role-playing.[22]

The TTW had settled into an annual production. There was *Dragon* (1978), *Departure in the Dark* (1979) and during 30 April–24 May 1981 occurred a 'brief reunion with our respected founder' when the TTW presented the world premiere of Walcott's Trinidadian comedy *Beef, No Chicken* at the Little Carib with Cecil Gray directing. *Beef, No Chicken* was part of Walcott's then current concern with preserving the past, the West Indies he had known, as opposed to its recent pseudo-Americanization; this concern with the past was set against the need of individuals to progress and fulfil themselves, a need made difficult in the limited material conditions of the past, limitations suggested comically by the play's title. It is also a play which touches on corruption in Trinidad. The cast included Errol Jones, Claude Reid, Brenda Hughes, Charles Applewhaite, Jerline Quamina, and Stanley Marshall, with John Andrews in charge of lighting; there was also Sonya Moze, a white Trinidadian actress who had first appeared in Walcott's 1980 production of *Marie Laveau*. Cecil Gray, a poet, anthologist, and school teacher, had a long history in Trinidadian theatre. He was a leading actor in Mr Roberts's Nelson Street Boys' RC School and one of the original members of the Whitehall Players in the 1940s. He had since taught in Jamaica for many years and recently returned to Trinidad.[23]

Mark Lyndersay said that *Beef, No Chicken* was about 'progress' and the fight to resist it, but found the play 'a bit of a sitcom, with lots of jokes and witticisms, but no direction and purpose at the core'. While finding it funny he did not like the play and complained that actions dangle and nothing seems to happen. Later, surveying Trinidadian theatre during 1981, Lyndersay felt that Gray's direction was responsible for Walcott's 'sly pokes and slicing commentary' being lost in the buffoonery and free-for-all on stage. Lyndersay praised Helen Camps and Judy Stone for their dedication in keeping theatre alive in Trinidad. Besides twelve productions at the Little Carib under Camps's management her Trinidad All Theatre Production was directly responsible for *Sizwe Bansi is Dead*, *King Jab Jab* and two other plays. Stone's Touchstone productions had produced six shows (most of them foreign comedies). Lyndersay noted the increasing importance of Ralph Maraj's plays with the San Fernando Drama Guild. For the present, original West Indian drama in Trinidad seemed to consist of Walcott's plays, Maraj's plays, and Camps's creations.[24]

When the Theatre Workshop eventually mounted a major production it was a financial disaster from which they still have not recovered. *A 'Nancy Story* by Elliot Bastien was a large and important production directed at the Little Carib by former Beryl McBurnie dancer Jeff Henry (who had moved to Toronto where he teaches at York University). This was a Carnival folk-musical, for the Carnival season, which cost TT$200,000 to mount and ran for twenty-two performances, 22 January–11 February 1982. Money had to be raised and the Trinidad & Tobago Telephone Company alone gave $15,000 to be listed as a sponsor. It had a large cast including Stanley Marshall (as Anancy the story teller), Errol Jones, Helen Camps, Albert Laveau, Claude Reid, Adele Bynoe, Joy Ryan, Eunice Alleyne, Carol La Chapelle, Wilbert Holder, and music by André Tanker. Costumes were elaborate, in the Carnival tradition. The advertising focused on its 'over 20 original song hits' and claimed that this is the 'roots' story of the Caribbean which many, especially the young, have forgotten.[25]

Raoul Pantin thought it a good idea to bring the traditional Trinidadian folklore of loup garou, papa bois, and soucoyant alive again for a younger generation steeped in imported culture, but he was disappointed with the production which was too rapidly paced. The singing was poor, the dancing barely competent. Veteran TTW actors seemed to wither away tackling such lightweight material. They were being wasted. Even the political allegory seemed confused between a supposed cultural assertion and implied warnings about scaring away foreign investment. Mark Lyndersay found the production shaky despite its rumoured $250,000 cost. There was not much story and the characters emerged from the play mysteriously and without explanation. He praised André Tanker's music and Gillian Bishop's costumes.[26]

Christopher Pinheiro also argues with the claim in the programme that 'A Nancy Story' is the 'Roots' Caribbean story and calls it 'candied ginger' rather than cassava. While enjoying André Tanker's music and Gillian Bishop's art direction, Pinheiro said that compromise had replaced authenticity. The play started slowly and had a 'fluffy' ending. Its lack of a unified dramatic and philosophical vision was reflected in its form. 'In the light of our cultural complexity, simplistic solutions are no longer satisfactory.' Art cannot exist without integrity. If the only reason for A 'Nancy Story is sentimental—to keep the folk-story alive—it is better to let it die peacefully. After being four years in the writing and six months of pre-production, it was mechanically assembled. A director was flown in, someone was flown to New York to purchase sound equipment, and instead of less-is-more the production seemed to be based on the-more-the-merrier, mixing Shango with a wake, Papa Bois with reggae.[27]

This was the kind of large-scale costly musical that Walcott had inaugurated in Trinidad. Such a production could be a success and still lose large sums of money. This one was not a success artistically or financially, although Tanker's music and the costumes are still remembered. Lacking Walcott's ability to draw upon the resources of others, but following on with his notion that Trinidadian theatre should be professional, that actors and directors should be paid, the Workshop ran up large debts of around $100,000 which hampered its redevelopment. While A 'Nancy Story had temporarily brought together many of the core of the TTW, the majority of plays it performed would be less ambitious, with smaller casts. For over three weeks during July 1982 Trevor Rhone directed his Smile Orange for the TTW at the Little Carib Theatre with Holder, Brenda Hughes, Marshall, Reid, and set construction by Albert Laveau.[28]

October 1983 the TTW put on Like Them That Dream by Edgar White, directed by Earl Warner. Warner had been touring with a production he made by joining two of Victor Questel's plays, when he was asked by Jones to direct for the Workshop. Edgar White, originally from Montserrat, had lived in Jamaica, the United States, and Europe. Like Them That Dream had been performed in London by White's Lumumba Theatre Group. One of White's plays, The Defense, had been performed at the Creative Arts Centre, in Jamaica, earlier in 1983 with Warner as director. Warner felt that White wrote for the theatre in compressed, although naturalistic language, which because of its economy was lyrical, poetical, and expressionistic. The central concern of *Like Them That Dream* is people 'being contained and limited by social taboos, by religion . . . and attempting to break through . . . into freer space'. The characters are displaced whether Irish, South African, or black American. Warner was happy to be working with the experienced actors of the TTW. 'In the Caribbean when you direct a play half of the task is trying to make the play in the first place. You don't ever get into a sense of really getting into that freer ground where creation is a sense of enjoyment and not simply a task of working at trying to make a play happen.' The cast included Helen Camps ('courtesy Trinidad Tent Theatre'), Patrick Cambridge ('courtesy Caribbean Theatre Guild'), Laurence Goldstraw and Sheila Harikirtan ('who has worked Off-Broadway'); the props were by Claude Reid; Earl Warner did the lighting design and set design. While two of the actors had been TTW members during Walcott's days, this was largely a production drawing upon the talents of others.[29]

In losing the use of Walcott's plays the TTW had started producing a wider variety of West Indian dramatists—Rhone, Hillary, White—thus coming closer to fulfilling one of its original Walcottian aims, an aim that had been lost sight of as the Workshop had become a vehicle for performing Walcott's own plays and as others associated with the Workshop, such as Slade Hopkinson, had failed to produce a body of their own work. But the TTW was unadventuresome in its plays. With Walcott they often premièred new work by the most famous and adventurous West Indian dramatist. While producing a play by White was adventurous—it appears not to have been done in the Caribbean before—in the case of Hillary and Rhone they were doing plays that had been successful elsewhere and which were becoming part of the new West Indian repertoire as Jamaica, Barbados, Montserrat, and other islands developed their own theatres. During the 1960s and part of the 1970s the TTW under Walcott had been at the forefront of what was happening in West Indian theatre; as it pulled itself together after his departure it continued to be hampered by the lack of an exciting playwright or director of its own or of anyone with Walcott's wide intellectual interests who read widely and found new plays. It had become some actors in search of an author and director.

Individually, however, members of the Workshop were far from inactive and many of their triumphs resulted from their association with Walcott, who continued to promote his former actors in the

United States. Michael Andrew Minor, director of the Actors Theatre in St Paul, Minnesota, had come to know Walcott through the annual CARIBUSTE conferences, decided to produce *Pantomime* and brought Wilbert Holder to Minnesota as he and Walcott felt it was necessary to use a West Indian actor. 'A black [American] would kill the white master on the spot for the things he says . . . but we're more comfortable . . . Our country is 90 per cent black . . . We have two cultures, but they're not divided by race.' Holder added that when he is asked how he feels as a black actor: 'The question threw me at first. I don't have to make these decisions: that doesn't come across my sphere.'[30]

NOTES

1. Judy Stone [Mauby], 'The Maids': Message with Entertainment', *Trinidad Guardian* (18 Mar. 1977), 8. Another favourable review was Jeremy Taylor, 'Workshop Helps Us Understand The Maids', *Express* (13 Mar. 1977), 9.
2. Each of the eight dance pieces has a 'patron'. 'Toute Bagai' (Trinidad & Tobago Air Services); 'Cages' (Workers Bank); 'Love Theme' (Gillette Hardware & Lumber); 'Tears of a Woman' (Y. de Lima); etc.
3. 'Theatre Workshop Doing Things', *Express* (30 June 1977), 12.
4. Judy Stone [Mauby], 'Love, Death, Faith, Sex, Life—Toute Bagai!', *Trinidad Guardian* (28 June 1977), 7; Judy Stone, 'National Theatre Wanted', *Trinidad & Tobago Review* (Dec. 1977), 9.
5. Judy Stone [Mauby], 'Young Bajan Actors Star at Little Carib', *Trinidad Guardian* (5 Aug. 1977), 4.
6. Willian Doyle-Marshall, 'Albert Le Veau', 49–51; Judy Stone, 'Top Actors Join Banyan in Family Planning Series', *Trinidad Guardian* (6 Jan. 1978).
7. 'Get Ready for Third Season of Dance', *Express* (22 May 1978), 18.
8. [Derek Walcott, unsigned], 'La Chapelle and Douglas Striving for Cohesion', *Sunday Guardian* (26 May 1978), 5. A single-spaced, two-page typescript of the article is in the UWI Walcott collection; the typescript is marked 'Derek Walcott' in ink.
9. 'Derek Walcott: Letter to Jeremy Taylor'. Two pages, single-spaced, signed by Walcott, undated, probably June 1978, Walcott Collection, University of the West Indies, St Augustine.
10. Raoul Pantin, 'Raoul Pantin reviews The Dragon Can't Dance', *Sun* (11 Sept. 1978), 1, 8–9; Jeremy Taylor, 'Dragon Can't Dance', *Express* (10 Oct. 1978), 17.
11. Jeremy Taylor, ' "Departure"—Sad and Rambling', *Express* (27 Jan. 1979), 15, 22.
12. Undated, unsigned, letter to 'Dear Member' concerning *Departure in the Dark*, sent from Errol Jones's address.
13. 'Caribbean—US artists in exciting link-up', unidentified newspaper clipping (May 1979). Reception invitation.

14. Interview with Trevor Rhone, Jamaica (Aug. 1991). Bruce King, 'Trevor Rhone', in D. L. Kirkpatrick (ed.) *Contemporary Dramatists* (Chicago: St James Press, 1989), 449.

15. Judy Stone, 'Sell-out Start for Dinner Theatre', *Trinidad Guardian* (7 June 1979), 4, 13.

16. Judy Stone, 'Caribuste: Promises Bright Era for the Theatre', *Sunday Guardian* (9 June 1979), 36–8, 40–4.

17. Angela Martin, 'Stanley gives all for art', *Express* (3 May 1980), 10–11; Ken Corsbie, 'A long history of struggle', *Express* (18 May 1982), 16–17; Ken Corsbie, 'A legend of "love"', *Nation* [Barbados] (17 May 1982), 8; Mark Lyndersay ''81 in the Arts', *Trinidad and Tobago Review* ('New Year's', 1982), 22–3.

18. Jeremy Taylor, 'Sizwe Bansi really first rate', *Express* (22 Apr. 1980), 10; Derek Walcott, 'Sizwe Bansi Excellent', *Express* (8 May 1980).

19. John Wickham, 'Nothing Much New', *Sunday Sun* (4 Jan. 1981), 27; Jacqui Jones, 'The Dragon Can't Dance', *The Nation, Carifesta Bulletin* (4 Aug. 1981), 2–3; Lyn Sweeting, 'Standing ovation for "Sizwe Bansi"', *The Tribune* (8 June 1982); Jeanne Thompson, '"Sizwe Bansi is Dead"—Superb Theatre!', *Nassau Guardian* (9 Aug. 1982), 3B.

20. Victor Questel, 'Apartheid in Action', *The Sun* (15 May 1980), 4, 8; Victor Questel, 'Sizwe Bansi: A Moving Experience', *Trinidad and Tobago Review* ('Governor Plum', 1980), 4, 25.

21. Corsbie, 'A long history', op. cit.; 'A legend', op. cit.

22. Helen Camps, 'A Season of Statements: Opening Statement'. Programme for Trinidad Tent Theatre's *Statements* by Athol Fugard; Judy Stone, 'Group that's Trying to get Back to the Basics', *Trinidad Guardian* (28 June 1983), 12, 20. Also see Corsbie's articles above (n. 17).

23. Programme for TTW's *Beef No Chicken* (30 Apr.–24 May 1981).

24. Mark Lyndersay, 'You Want Jokes? I'll Give You Jokes', *Trinidad Guardian* (12 May 1981), 15; Lyndersay, ''81 in the Arts', *Trinidad & Tobago Review* (New Year's 1982), 22, 23.

25. Shirley McIntosh, Asst. General Manager, Trinidad and Tobago Telephone Company, to Ann Marie Stewart, Production Manager, *A 'Nancy Story* (27 Jan. 1982). Vashty Maharaj, 'Vital Themes Woven into "A Nancy Story"', *Trinidad Guardian* (2 Jan. 1982), 18.

26. Raoul Pantin, '"A Nancy Story": A Tale of Yore', *Express* (27 Jan. 1982), 12; Mark Lyndersay, 'Theatre of Mas', *Trinidad and Tobago Review* ('Kaiso', 1982), 22–3.

27. Christopher Pinheiro, '"A Nancy Story": An Elegant Best Village', *Sunday Guardian* (24 Jan. 1982), 9, 17.

28. 'These Nights at the Little Carib', *Sunday Express* (28 July 1982), 44; 'Going Places', *Sunday Express* (25 July 1982), 19.

29. Judy Stone, 'New Realisations the Essence of "Like Them That Dream"', *Trinidad Guardian* (11 Oct. 1983), 19.

30. Peter Vaughan, 'Holder Brings a Tropical Coolness to "Pantomime" Role', *Minneapolis Star and Tribune* (25 Mar. 1983), 2C; Carla Waldermar, 'Cultural Exchanging', *Sunday Magazine* (8 May 1983), 3. Judy Stone, 'Derek Pushing our Actors for more Recognition Abroad', *Trinidad Guardian* (10 Dec. 1985), 17.

Walcott 1977–1981

Pantomime
Remembrance
Marie Laveau

15

WALCOTT'S resignation from the Theatre Workshop was a turning-point in his life. He had come to Trinidad at the time of the Federation, found a hospitable environment in which to work, became a leader of the island's cultural life, and had a supporting network of friends in the professions and the arts. His Theatre Workshop was a means to produce his plays throughout the region; it was the best theatre company in the West Indies with many of the best actors and dancers. Their workshops enabled him to try out and change his plays. He had actors for whom he wrote parts and whose stage presence was a source of characterization. He had observed and become part of a community rich in talent, eccentricities, history, ethnicities, and religions. While he was at odds with Eric Williams over the ruling party's cultural policy, corruption and repressiveness, Walcott was still closer to those in power and to those likely to hold future power than writers are in England and the United States. Outside the West Indies he was a prize-winning poet still unread by most professors of English literature, in Trinidad he was a public figure who dominated its cultural and intellectual life. His second wife, Margaret, was very supportive of his work. With her salary, his foreign grants, the royalties from his writing, and his salary as Artistic Director of the Workshop, he no longer had to support himself through journalism and he had money to put into productions of his plays. TTW performances of his plays earned him money, regional fame, and were becoming try-outs of his scripts for possible production abroad.

With the increasing seriousness of his affair with Norline Metivier and in resigning from the Workshop he risked destroying what had taken him two decades to accomplish. He would need once more to construct a life. Walcott's finances had always been precarious. He had always lived with a certain stylishness, always using taxis rather than walking or using public transport. He would carefully budget for a play and then wildly overspend by trusting workmen and suppliers without first getting written estimates. He had tried to live from the theatre, but he and Margaret had probably put more money into the TTW than he had received. He had no steady income and was still dependent upon royalties, grants, and what he could earn as a teacher. Despite his highly favourable reputation among certain literary critics and theatre directors, Walcott was not an overnight star in America. Americans regarded him primarily as a poet and secondarily as a playwright. In the United States his years as director of the TTW counted for little. Universities offered him employment, but at first as a temporary visiting professor or to teach part-time. He was an outsider having to make his way in a highly competitive society. In 1980 he told a friend that here he was fifty years old and flat broke. It was not until the MacArthur award that Walcott's life and finances began to become stable.

Although there were times when he was somewhat free from immediate financial worries, as when he was awarded a Guggenheim Fellowship for 1977–8, there was a five-year period when his life was in flux, moving from island to island, living in hotels and borrowed apartments, often hastily mounting productions of his plays with improvised groups of actors. After becoming lovers, Walcott and Norline left Trinidad when Walcott was offered a teaching position at Yale University. They lived together in New York at the Chelsea Hotel or with friends, such as in the apartment of Joseph Brodsky, while Walcott commuted between New Haven and New York, where he was also teaching from time to time at New York University and Columbia University. After Margaret obtained a divorce, Derek married Norline 28 May 1982. In 1981 he joined Boston University and Boston became his base when not in the West Indies. His daughters came from Trinidad to attend Boston University and his son Peter often lived with him. After Norline returned to Trinidad, he re-established a close working relationship with Margaret.[1]

He still needed the West Indies to feel 'at home'; home remained his subject-matter and offered him his poetic language and themes, and he remained a West Indian dramatist. American audiences did not understand the complexities and assumptions of his plays. American actors lacked West Indian body movements, speech cadences, and understanding of the society that Walcott portrayed. He needed West Indian audiences to appreciate what he was writing, he even needed West Indian theatre critics. His plays needed to be performed in the West Indies either in productions he mounted himself or by others working in a tradition he established.

St Croix, in the American Virgin Islands, provided him with a temporary base from time to time. Barbados, which was economically flourishing and had started to develop a lively theatre scene although lacking an outstanding local dramatist, would often have productions of his plays. Ken Corsbie, Earl Warner, and Michael Gilkes were three excellent, serious directors who worked in Barbados. Cynthia Wilson, who had an important role in establishing Bajan modern dance and theatre, was a friend from the University College of the West Indies. Walcott often returned to St Lucia, spending every Christmas holiday and most of his summers there and in Trinidad. He long put off becoming a permanent resident of the United States as to obtain a 'green card' he had to remain for eighteen months without leaving. From the time that St Lucia was a British colony he travelled on a British passport, preferring his freedom to return to the West Indies to the greater economic advantages and security possible at American universities which would only give him a tenured distinguished professorship if he took American citizenship.[2]

After Walcott resigned from the TTW he decided to produce his own plays in Trinidad and began rehearsing *The Charlatan*. The *Trinidad Guardian*, 23 December 1976, carried an announcement that a completely revised version of the play, with music by Galt MacDermot, would open at the Little Carib for a run of ten nights in January. 'The new book has been adapted to the design of a musical comedy, and the play itself one of the first productions of the Trinidad Theatre Workshop, has been through several changes.' *The Charlatan* had changed from three to two acts, had less text and more new songs. As the central characters are calypsonians it was thought appropriate for the Carnival season. The 'production is designed and directed by the author'. There were also plans for a performance in San Fernando. A longer, also unsigned article in *Express* mentions Walcott's break with the TTW, that the play will be produced by him, and that in future he will produce his own plays in Trinidad using some TTW actors and actors not associated with the Workshop. As often with newspaper articles based on Walcott's press releases there is an interpretation of the play. Charlatanism is endemic to mankind and creative. ' "Divided by class, united by bacchanal" is a familiar Carnival theme.'³

Rehearsals of *The Charlatan* began in November 1976, but there were a number of changes in cast before it was produced. Barbara Jenson's list, as stage manager, of those who attended rehearsals is confusing and suggestive of a rushed, underrehearsed production. The cast continually changes, actors do not show up for rehearsals, even the musicians change. Four days before the opening Syd Skipper, who had come to Trinidad less than three years before and long suffered from emotional problems, retreated to a monastery and was replaced by Wilbert Holder as Mighty Cobo. Holder, whom Walcott had first asked to play the part instead of Skipper, was Mighty Cobo in 1973 at Town Hall and on the Jamaican tour; he now became the star of the show in a role which made full use of his hip-driven body movements. The opening night cast included Laurence Goldstraw repeating his role as Dr Theodore Holley, Belinda Barnes, Winston Goddard, Norline Metivier, Helen Ross, Robert Mayers, and Michael de Verteuil. None of the foundation members of the TTW participated. Music was provided by the Flamingos with the soon internationally famous Boogsie Sharpe and Vonrick Maynard. Walcott and Lee Johnson designed the set which tried to catch the feeling of a calypso tent to give a theatrical expression of the Carnival in Port of Spain at the time. To avoid ill will over the withdrawal of his two plays from the TTW season, Walcott accepted Theatre Workshop subscriptions. A second run, 27–29 January, was cancelled because of a fire.⁴

Judy Stone as Mauby found the new version 'much improved', praising its tautness, MacDermot's music, and the increased probability of its otherwise improbable story. 'The combination of MacDermot's faithful calypso compositions . . . and Holder's neatly observant, loud kaisonian can evoke the authentic atmosphere of the Carnival Tents— and many a tent-bound tourist might find easier listening at the Little Carib.' Holder 'gives a brilliant interpretation' with fire and panache, Belinda Barnes has 'a joyous impetuosity that is delightful' but her mannered style jarred with the rest of the cast. Stone praised Norline Metivier, who was to become one of Trinidad's better comic actresses. 'Norline Metivier . . . has revamped gawky little Heloise Upshot into one of the funniest characters in the comedy.' Several actors seemed staid; she found missing in the production 'the comprehensive technique of the Theatre Workshop', but thought that Trinidad would benefit from having two quality theatrical groups.⁵

Jeremy Taylor felt that Holder and Goddard carried a production that otherwise suffered from 'low blood pressure'. The play's themes are the universality of charlatanism, individualism, and eccentricity, and suggest that the courage of one's delusions is both creative and necessary to the enjoyment of life. The play, however, was disappointing in 1973 and not much better now; it is still disunified and lifeless. Structurally the first half is focused on the calypsonians, the second half concerning the romantic relationship between Clarissa and Dr Holley is uninteresting. MacDermot's music lacks the warmth of real calypso performances. Ross made what she could of the improbable character of Clarissa. Later in the magazine *Kairi 78* a critic complained that *The Charlatan* had become weaker; while the staging was more like that of a calypso tent the music was less so. Walcott is accused of staging 'Shango as if it were a joke, something to be mocked so as to gain the approval of a very insensitive middle class'. An end-of-the-year review of the arts in Trinidad for 1977, 'National Theatre Wanted' commented that *The Charlatan* met such a lukewarm response that Walcott 'tucked his new script under his arm and walked', staging the première of *Remembrance* in St Croix.[6]

The Charlatan is set in Belmont, an area of Port of Spain, where Walcott and the Workshop actors often went to drink after rehearsals. It is both a rough area, famous for its fights, and long settled with a respectable older, now lower-middle class. There are streets just 'over the bridge' which can be dangerous even during daylight, there is a steel band, a public library, and lovely houses and gardens. Walcott used Belmont as a setting in *Remembrance*, a new play which had its world première at the Dorsch Centre in Frederiksted, St Croix, 23 April–1 May 1977. He wrote *Remembrance* on a commission for the first 'season' of the Courtyard Players. Writing for the Courtyard Players meant a change from the large musicals he had been previously developing. The Courtyard Players wanted a play with a small cast to be done in the round. This was the first time in years Walcott had premièred a play outside Trinidad and was the first of a number of plays he would write for small casts. Besides the availability of an existing theatre company with which he had worked in the past and a good theatre for performances, there was also financial support from the Virgin Islands Council of the Arts. St Croix offered Walcott a company responsible for the production, allowing him to concentrate on directing his play. While the Courtyard Players could not offer him the long friendships, well-trained actors, and closeness to the community of the TTW, it had other advantages. St Croix has a large St Lucian community; Walcott could work in American conditions with

West Indian actors in a Caribbean environment. He could, once more, build where there was little previously.[7]

He took Wilbert Holder with him, this time to play the leading character, Albert Perez Jordan, an old-fashioned elderly assistant head-master who remembers a failed love affair with a white English woman when he was young and who objects to his son's relationship with a white American hippie woman. These two relationships with foreign white women are part of the play's symbolism in which, as in *Dream on Monkey Mountain*, the white woman is the muse, an apparition of a foreign culture. Here, however, there are real women, with wills and lives of their own, rather than just cultural illusions. There is an ironic counterpoint between what they are and what they at first appear. Social and political history is true and untrue. People live in societies, but they are also individuals with desires who make choices. As in many of Walcott's plays (and as in his own life and his life in the theatre), energy, individual will, and passion, the pushing beyond nor-mal social limits, are regarded as the basis of a full life and creativity. In such assumptions Walcott remains the heir of the Romantics, Van Gogh, and such modernists as Yeats and Joyce.

Remembrance, however, is also a play of reconciliation of genera-tions. Thomas Gray's 'Elegy written in a Country Churchyard' is also true. The unheroic provincial can also be the subject of literature, a literature of commemoration and celebration and not just of Flaubertian irony. The unsung colonial school teachers gave their students the discipline needed to conquer the world, taught them the values and ideals that are at the basis of postcolonial rebellion and equality. *Re-membrance* is Chekhovian in its distillation of the poetic into prose symbols and in its story of a failure of courage and energy, but it is West Indian in recognizing how far its non-white middle class had to travel, and against what obstacles, to accomplish what they did, and how they made possible the future. What may now seem colonial acceptance and failure of nerve is in fact a powerful drama worthy of being commemorated. Those who do not understand and remember this past will have no true knowledge of their own past and some of the most significant influences on West Indian culture.

Besides inaugurating a new period of Walcott's playwriting charac-terized by smaller casts, with an emphasis on the complexity of indi-vidual psychology, a more introspective mood and subject matter, the commission to write *Remembrance* involved Walcott with deep per-sonal concerns. The published play is dedicated to Ruth and Joe Moore and Alix Walcott. Ruth Moore, American, was the energy behind the

Courtyard Players at the time and the person with whom Walcott usually negotiated. Alix Walcott is his mother, the headmistress of the Methodist school in Castries. The play can be seen memorializing the older generation of highly educated, disciplinarian West Indian colonial school teachers who, in love with English language and culture, faced discrimination and insecurity and lived divided between their actual West Indian lives and their dreams of being loved by the English. Even when faced by the possibility of being accepted they lacked the courage for 'marriage', symbolic of the creative coming together of the two social groups. By contrast the son in the play criticizes the Americans who buy his art and is not afraid of marrying a white American. This could be seen as expressive of Walcott's own relationship to America. The play contains other contrasting themes that have preoccupied Walcott. There is a dead son whom the school teacher rejected. The dead son belongs to the less cultured, less disciplined, Americanized Black Power generation that Walcott had criticized and here, as in The Last Carnival, there is a concluding symbolic acceptance of the ways of a younger generation along with the past.[8]

Walcott still wanted to stage his plays throughout the West Indies. He returned to Trinidad and by early December 1977 was holding readings for a production of Remembrance. Preliminary plans had Albert Laveau directing with Norline Metivier his assistant, Barbara Jenson stage manager and Leonore Bishop as assistant to the house manager. Walcott had thought of casting Holder, Ermine Wright, Laurence Goldstraw, and Winston Goddard. There was a problem finding an available performance space. The Hilton Hotel, Holiday Inn, Town Hall, Bishop Anstey High School, and the Tapia court yard were considered, but by the middle of the month the production was abandoned.[9]

Helen Camps, who had worked closely with Walcott in the TTW, formed All Theatre Productions and in 1978 became the director and manager of the Little Carib. She formed All Theatre Productions to hire actors for her productions and as an agent for other companies. She began by presenting between April and May 1978 the new Walcott play, Pantomime, Brian Friel's Freedom of the City and Genet's The Maids. Although Camps used some actors associated with Walcott and the TTW, she cast her net more widely, especially using new younger talents such as Maurice Brash, who had previously been in school plays and the Trinidad Light Operatic Society, or John Isaacs, another singer, who had mostly appeared in school plays, musicals, and on a television Teen Talent show.

Walcott and All Theatre Productions premièred *Pantomime*, with Albert Laveau directing, at the Little Carib, 12–22 April. The cast consisted of two actors, Holder as Jackson and Maurice Brash as Mr Trewe. During August Horace James, using a revised script that Walcott prepared, shot in Tobago a performance of Holder and Brash for Trinidad & Tobago Television, but because TTT did not at the time have proper equipment for recording in the open the video tape (available through Banyan Studios) is visually poor.

Pantomime was written while Walcott was staying at a hotel in Tobago managed by Arthur Bentley, a former British actor who after the breakdown of his marriage moved to Trinidad. Bentley suggested that Walcott write something to provide an evening's entertainment for the hotel's guests. As Walcott listened to the banter between Bentley and one of his employees the idea for the play came to him. Although the situation involved a white English hotel manager and a local black employee, there was an equality in the exchange of repartee that dissolved the racial, class, and economic differences. This was Walcott's idea of the Caribbean.[10]

This 'history' shows what is lacking in productions dominated by black anger and white racial guilt. Holder, an extremely strong actor who had a personality that was always testing people and seeing how far he could push them, would physically and emotionally dominate white actors playing Trewe unless the white man fought back and also had a strong stage personality. Walcott has spoken of the difficulties of casting the play in the United States where racial relationships are different from those in the West Indies; black American actors turn Jackson into an angry victim accusing a guilty white man.[11]

Walcott said that the play emerged whole as he heard two characters arguing in his head. They dictated the play to him and he wrote it in three nights and tried it out at the hotel before it moved to Port of Spain for its official opening. He offered three interpretations. *Pantomime* 'is about the two actors, and their different racial and cultural origins, creating whatever conflicts exist from their different approach to the theatre, its ritual, its meaning, its style'. It may also show that 'the self-torturing schizophrenia that precedes the resolution of an identity can achieve that resolution with dignity. It may also be a political play, with its subject independence; but that process first has to be human before it can become political.'[12]

According to Anne Hilton, Wilbert Holder dominated the small stage of the Little Carib with his voice, eyes, and body language. The audience saw the play in racial terms as 'stabs at past white supremacy and present degeneracy', raucously laughing, even, at one point, breaking into 'something closely resembling an impromptu war dance'. Hilton interpreted the play as showing the pain of white and black learning to live together, unable to see the other's point of view, and sharing a failure to build a better world. Mark Lyndersay contrasted the image-laden lines of Walcott's earlier plays with the fast-paced narrative of *Pantomime* in which a sophisticated master and slave fight an intellectual battle; Walcott carefully reworked the popular West Indian carefree, frivolous play into something more serious, using crisp vicious wit to probe black–white roles, racialism, equality, friendship, loneliness, and reality. The outcome of the confrontation is open-ended. As Trewe, a modern Crusoe, is forced to make adjustments and tries to act the part of Friday he begins to regret his willingness to change roles, but Jackson, now Crusoe, is also unhappy. 'Social adjustments, particularly enforced ones, are just not that easy to put right.'[13]

Pantomime remained popular and controversial. Although it has not received the same attention from literary critics as such earlier works as *Ti-Jean* and *Dream on Monkey Mountain*, it may well be the most performed Walcott play. There always seem to be productions of it. I believe that along with *Dream* and *The Joker of Seville* it will be regarded as a modern classic of the theatre. Christopher Gunness interviewing Walcott remarked that what appears a theatrical allegory about colonialism and the social, political, and cultural interactions between white and black leaves out the more significant human interactions between two humans. Walcott replied,

There is that stolid facade, that mask of the Englishman, that wall behind which there is much horror and fear and trembling. The cracks appear and it is where these cracks appear that Jackson darts in and widens. The play is about Jackson besieging and darting in and out until the whole thing crumbles, the wall is broken down and we look into his room and see Trewe naked and exposed. This is how confessional psychodrama works.

Jackson represents Creole energies, coarse and unsophisticated, but necessary for healing as he forces Trewe into recognizing his own problems. Gunness claimed that Walcott was dissatisfied with the ending which does not show clearly what came out of the conflict.[14]

There was an instructive restaging of *Pantomime* by Helen Camps at the Little Carib during the 1978 Christmas season with Horace James playing Jackson and Maurice Brash again as Trewe. Helen Camps's programme note mentions that while Trewe is neocolonial, someone who is not serious about reversing roles by learning the other person's manner, language, religion, and customs, Jackson brings out the West Indian audience's schizophrenia, laughing at Trewe's English accent while wanting to 'talk better'. James, one of the original Trinidadian black actors of the 1940s, was trained at RADA, worked on the British stage, has been in films, and has a successful career on television. He is a good comic actor with a presence on stage. But to 'RAP', either because James played Jackson as mostly comic or because Helen Camps tried to shift the balance from Holder's racial attacks in the earlier production, the new version seemed miscast or misdirected, a series of jokes. Most actors I have spoken with who saw the production felt that the balance was more what Walcott intended, especially since Brash as Trewe had become stronger and more believable, but James lacked the necessary seriousness as an actor. He forgot lines, improvised jokes, and as a result there was a loss of significance.[15]

Ken Corsbie, now working freelance, directed *Pantomime* for Stage One in Barbados during May 1980, with Clairmonte Taitt and Patrick Foster, and later, during October, directed *Pantomime* at the Little Carib with Holder and the British actor Robin Kealy. Corsbie treated the text freely, constructed a set that sprawled over the entire stage and up into the balcony, used voice overdubs and dramatic lighting. In his review, Mark Lyndersay understood Jackson as a catalyst who changes the relationship between the two men, leading to mutual respect and the expunging of Trewe's hidden demons. The pace was more measured than in the Holder–Brasch version, which resulted in some of the wit sounding like pronouncements. While Kealy did not seem up to the kind of virtuoso performance the part of Trewe demanded, Holder flexed his artistic muscles. When Trewe confesses to his failures as a classical and creole actor, Holder 'laughs derisively, swaggers about like every eleven year old to come out of the Roxy Cinema after seeing "Shane", drops into a crouch and whips out his hammer: BOW! BOW! PEEEMGGG! "Hah," he laughs, "a western kinda creole acting?"'[16]

The headline and subhead of Judy Stone's 'What Corsbie did to Walcott's *Pantomime* proves that is he is perhaps the most gifted director in the Caribbean theatre today' introduced a comparison between the three Port of Spain productions. In the first production Albert Laveau's direction was static and Brash unsuccessfully tried to be what he is not, a middle-aged Englishman. Holder was too successful in being a brilliant performer at the expense of the character. In Camps's in-the-round production Brash was more accomplished as James did not constantly upstage him and the director had a clearer insight into the character of Trewe. The play, however, lost its bite and became jokey, and the essential human conflict between Jackson and Trewe lost its danger as James transformed Jackson into a 'kindly nurse-companion Friday humoring a senile Crusoe'. Walcott was incensed at James's lack of respect for the text. While Corsbie is usually no re-specter of texts, Holder and Kealy were. In this production the audience were conscious of many lines which they failed to appreciate previously. 'Corsbie is a director of action' with an instinct for moves that physically bring out the meaning of lines and their irony such as 'Jackson at exactly the right moment wiping his hands on Trewe's towel'. This was the first production in which the nervous tension of the relationship between the two men was brought out and heightened by the physical danger of the cliff top setting. There was 'an abrupt black precipice of a rock wall falling away into the sea'. Both Jackson and Trewe at various times were seen teetering or stumbling near the wall. Under Corsbie's direction Holder reined himself in and found the character of Jackson. While Kealy was more physically a match for Holder than Brash, he lacked the flair and subtlety of technique for Holder to play against.[17]

Watching rehearsals for the April 1993 Boston TTW production that Walcott directed with Nigel Scott and Claude Reid, I was struck by the way Walcott continually shifted exchanges between comedy and threat, between text and subtext. Within seconds the play could move from vaudeville farce to near violence, from tragedy to froth. Reid acted Jackson in a generally more subdued manner than I had seen in American productions, far less aggressively than had Holder; even the threats of violence and racial anger seemed quiet, while the farce and bragging was larger than life, a sophisticated self-aware performance. He was more a confidant, someone who had closely watched and had a better understanding of his employer than Trewe had of himself, but Jackson was also someone who knew he could break rules with impunity, had a cool violence under his surface, and was very self-assured and true to himself. Reid's Jackson was no laughing nigger, no minstrel man, no servant in revolt; he had his own past and private life, did his job, found his space impinged upon by Trewe's wish to use him in a play, and despite the employer–employee relationship was the stronger of the two. Nigel Scott's Trewe began with an almost manic British sprightly cheerful mateyness, like an over-wound spring, but he was quick to sense Jackson's stepping across class, across personal and emotional barriers; old wounds and failure had clearly brought him to the West Indies and left him touchy, on the edge of disintegration. I had previously wondered how American actors could perform Jackson; I now wondered how any actor could bring out the knife-sharp complexity of Trewe. As lines and episodes were tried in different tones of voice, with different gestures, and different distances between the actors, it seemed that the published text was like a musical score awaiting its realization in a sophisticated, complex interpretation more like dance than the crudities of literary interpretation. Walcott shaped each phrase of each speech like a painter aware that every brush stroke contributes to the rich fullness of a scene. I could see why in 'What the Twilight Says' he wrote of his Workshop actors as extensions of his limbs and sensibility. The analogy was not a metaphor, it expressed the kind of detailed control he had over the acting of his plays by the TTW.[18]

Remembrance was not seen in Trinidad until July 1979, when Walcott directed and designed it for Trinidad All Theatre Productions at the Dinner Theatre at the Hotel Normandie. Peter Walcott did the set. The cast included Wilbert Holder, Joy Ryan, Errol Roberts, Fred Hope, Laurence Goldstraw, and John Isaacs. None of the actors were core Workshop members. In the programme for the Dinner Theatre production Walcott wrote that there was a generation of West Indian teachers who laid the foundations for those who went to colleges and universities. *Remembrance* 'is a sincere and painful tribute to such a teacher. If this play appears to praise convention it may be more radical than it seems, in a time when nothing is more conventional now than revolution.' The play was written to honour the great teachers Walcott had known when a boy and through whose encouragement it is now possible for him, a generation later, 'to write a play for them'.

Victor Questel described *Remembrance* as an 'excellent lesson in playwriting and stage craft, and in the tradition of all great works of art, it inspires you'. It is a dramatic seamless web in which the stage is very economically used. 'As Walcott begins to trust his ear for the language more and more, and tones down the poetry in his plays, the narrative lines are getting clearer—the tension sharper, since the actors get to use the language more easily, without falling over the metaphors.' The set is economical, but Walcott's directing is somewhat literal although the pace is excellent. The play treats the problem of how the artist deals with the possibly corrupting influence of sponsorship, especially from American sources, and the temptation to compromise. Holder as Jordan is a model of the art of acting in his timing, pace, range, and concentration. His quick changes of mood in bringing out

Jordan's complexity seemed natural and unforced. Joy Ryan was tremendous in her sensitive expressions of pain and determination while being brisk and vigorous. Carol Watling as Miss Hope marvellously used her mouth and eyes in a close-up manner suitable for the smallness of the Normandie Theatre. John Isaacs has potential but acts supercool to the point of flippancy.[19]

Judy Stone in a *Trinidad Guardian* review headlined 'At Last, Masterpiece on the Middle Class' described *Remembrance* as memorable, mature, and better crafted than some Walcott plays, very nearly a perfect piece of writing by any standard. The characters are richly drawn, the language sparse and muscular. The form is based on the rhythmic recurrence of the Remembrance motif through echoed lines, movements, and characters. The theme is loyalty and changing values. The play is a vehicle for the actor playing Albert Perez Jordan; Holder finds new depths of interpretation as he switches back and forth between the youthful and aged Albert Jordan. 'Normally a wholly extroverted performer, as Jordan Holder is superbly controlled. He is most forceful in his silences.' *Remembrance* also has the most fully rounded part Walcott has written for a woman; Joy Ryan is magnificent as Mabel Jordan. Unfortunately the second half dragged in pace and the resolution is too drawn out.[20]

Walcott's fiftieth birthday, on 23 January 1980, was marked by celebrations throughout the West Indies. The University of the West Indies, Barbados, performed *Dream on Monkey Mountain* with four of the male parts played by women to show that the problems and themes were 'universal'; Ken Corsbie directed *Pantomime* for Stage One, Barbados, and then took the production to St Lucia. In Trinidad there was a birthday party and reading by Walcott, Joseph Brodsky, and the Canadian-born American poet Mark Strand at the newly renovated Little Carib. Each of the three poets was an 'exile' of some sort. In London, where *Pantomime* was currently playing at the Keskidee Theatre, at a meeting of Caribbean artists the Guyanan director Francis Farrier praised Walcott's role in raising the status and professionalism of West Indian drama.[21]

In *Caribbean Contact* Jeremy Taylor briefly surveyed Walcott's achievement as a dramatist since 1973 when he first saw *Franklin* in Port of Spain. According to Taylor, Walcott begins, unlike many West Indian intellectuals, by rejecting the burden of history. To retrieve the past, with its brutality and degradation, is to perpetuate it. Revolutionary literature is dependent on the very object it attacks. If guilt and revenge are useless to the artist, the truly tough New World aesthetic neither explains nor forgives history. The New World artist is an Adam inventing by naming his world. The conflict between cultures is present but must be resolved on the human before the political level. *Franklin* offers a recurring Walcott figure, the expatriate wandering Englishman trying to work off his sense of guilt and alienation by putting down roots in a black world. This half of the Caribbean psyche reappeared in the comic Dr Holley of *The Charlatan*. While *Joker* may turn out to be Walcott's masterpiece, *O Babylon!* is Walcott's most explicit commitment to West Indian society and politics. 'Through the Rasta mythology, even more than through the Don Juan legend, Walcott was able to evoke some of the deepest fears and aspirations in Caribbean, indeed human, consciousness.'[22]

Walcott was writer in residence for the Fall semester, 1979, at the College of the Virgin Islands, St Thomas. While there he offered a seminar on *Joker* and directed *Pantomime* at the Dorsch Center, St Croix. On St Thomas during 1979, Walcott directed his new musical *Marie Laveau* with an American cast. Walcott wrote the lyrics and Galt MacDermot wrote the music. Although it was his first play with an American setting, Marie Laveau's black French-Creole world of New Orleans, a Caribbean seaport of mixed races, could be seen as taking further north the vision of the New World Walcott had formed in St Lucia. A video tape of the St Croix production, which appears rather stiff and stilted, is held by Banyan. Excerpts from the play were published in the Christmas issue of *Trinidad & Tobago Review* as publicity for his forthcoming Port of Spain production.[23]

Walcott directed, partly cast, and designed the set for a restaged production of *Marie Laveau* at the Little Carib, 29 May–8 June 1980. This was very much a Walcott production with the energies, finances, and responsibilities depending upon Walcott, his family, and patrons. Walcott and Clara Rosa de Lima, who directs the Art Creators Limited gallery in Port of Spain where he exhibits his paintings, were producers. If any money were lost in productions she backed, De Lima, who is also a poet and novelist, would be repaid by Walcott's paintings. Stella Beaubrun was executive producer. She co-directs the gallery and is the wife of Norman Beaubrun, an old friend of Walcott's from the University of West Indies in Jamaica. (Norman Beaubrun is a Professor of Psychiatric Medicine whom Walcott has consulted during times of personal crisis.) Peter Walcott was in charge of set decoration. Norline Metivier was choreographer.

Eunice Alleyne played Marie Laveau, along with such Walcott regulars as Joan Belfon, Heather Henderson, Errol Roberts, Brenda Hughes and Adele Bynoe. The British actor Robin Kealy played Blondin. There were also a number of new or recent faces to the Trinidadian theatre scene, such as Sonya Moze, Raymond Choo Kong, and John Isaacs. There were also some Americans whom Walcott brought with him from the St Croix production, who arrived without passports, could not get work permits, and left. An argument about using American actors and dancers erupted in the local press.

With the American subject-matter, the few American actors, Walcott's divorce from Margaret, the new importance of Norline, and Walcott's top-down manner towards casting, the production of *Marie Laveau* opened in Port of Spain with hostility in the air, which may have influenced the lack of enthusiasm in the reviews. Jeremy Taylor sarcastically mentions that Walcott is hoping to take the play to Broadway. 'You can just see the precision-drilled chorus line and 150 strings in the pit swing into action with "You've Got to be True to Yourself," the big number that ends Act One.' He argues that Walcott had written an American play with 'Caribbean exoticism to tickle the New York fancy'. It is closer to a genuine musical, not a play with songs like *Joker*. The opening night was very rough, 'scarcely off the ground'. Taylor questioned why Walcott had brought some principal actors with him, only liking Donald Jones as Charlie Dupray.[24]

Debra John commented, 'It beats me how an experienced man like Derek Walcott could surround himself with a cast so full of paradoxes'. His actors cannot sing, his singers cannot act, his dancers cannot sing or act. 'And would you believe there are even three individuals (thank God not part of the local cast) who can't act or sing'. She sympathized with local members of the play who had to struggle through the entire night speaking like Americans. There were, however, some professional touches. Donald Jones 'is totally professional although it is hard to catch some of his lines'. Sonya Moze offers 'one of the few consistent performances in the production'. Eunice Alleyne, however, could not sing or hold to an American accent.[25]

Mark Lyndersay also mentioned that *Marie Laveau* was intended for Broadway. While the plot is flimsy and Walcott's lyrics are stilted, the imagery is 'limpid'. But as a musical it is a triumph. 'In paring down his lyrics to the necessary, he has given Galt MacDermot room to use the vibrant rhythms of New Orleans jazz to define the mood and flavour of the production.' Lyndersay praises Donald Jones; 'Sonya Moze is in fine, bouncy form' and 'by far the finest of the supporting cast'. This is Eunice Alleyne's first singing role and she seems a little quiet and humble. 'She doesn't come across as being particularly evil or venomous' as Marie Laveau. The poet-painter LeRoy Clarke was sufficiently vicious that a reader wrote a long letter to the editor complaining of Clarke's regular attacks on West Indian artists and his 'Mr. "We Who Know"' attitude. Clarke, who had returned from New York where he exhibits and who can sound militantly 'Black', accused Walcott of selling out and plundering his people's 'origins'. *Marie Laveau* is 'sheer decor', 'Shim-sham con and popular gloss'. The music lacked conviction and 'congo blood'.[26]

Victor Questel found the production disappointingly uneven. Sonya Moze and Lawrence Scott were charming and humorous; Norline Metivier's choreography was excellent, Eunice Alleyne, however, lacked electricity in more than one sense; she had weak lines and songs and was 'defeated by the inadequate lighting at the Carib'. She was at times almost invisible. Questel understood that the use of Americans was intended to help heal the fracture of Federation and as a response to the region's isolation. The need to replace the passportless American West Indians resulted in signs of haste.

Questel regarded *Marie Laveau* as a change in direction by Walcott, who formerly used the creative tensions of unresolved conflicts, but now aims at psychic harmony, wholeness. From a religious-philosophical point of view, instead of blaspheming his 'lost' European and African gods, as in *Dream*, Walcott accepts their synthesis in a Caribbean syncretism. Questel discusses how *Marie Laveau* may be read allegorically both in terms of its plot and its symbols to show the mulatto resurrecting the gods of Africa. Marie is a mulatto of three cultures. The weak songs that other critics mentioned are seen by Questel as indicating her whiteness in contrast to the black music sung by the chorus.

New Orleans in the early nineteenth century is the setting as that was the time and place where assimilation and acculturation were happening, with voodoo, for example, becoming infused with Christian influences. The symbolism is introduced through the narrator who is 'really the houngan'; the opening scene is the circle in Congo Square. Charlie Dupray's way of walking shows the origins of West Indian movements and body language. Marie's dead husband is symbolic of the Yoruba god Ogun, the god of war. (Whether or not Questel is correct about Walcott's symbolism, and he usually is, Ogun is to the Yorubas much more than a god of war, which was only a small part of his life.) Marie's medium 'was Damballa'. Walcott uses such voodoo symbols as the sword, and the voodoo colours black, red, blue and white. 'Adele Bynoe mounting the back of a slave was on one level . . . a "mount", a possession, a horseman of the voodoo gods.'

Questel says, Walcott had always aimed at self-knowledge in the quest for wholeness, but here the resolution comes too easy in terms of the play's drama. 'Walcott is saying home is where our loa are at. He is saying home is where Christ circles with Damballa and Erzulie turns with Mary.'[27]

Walcott's interviews of this period reveal an awareness of a psychiatric perspective. Even if he had not years before read Fanon on the psychological problems of the colonized cultural mulatto, Walcott's resignation from the Trinidad Theatre Workshop, his attraction towards success abroad, the breakup of his second marriage, and his increasingly homeless wandering as he attempted to go beyond the limitations of Port of Spain were likely to have resulted in a need for help to see clearly where he was heading and why. This might 'explain' the new mood apparent in *Remembrance* and later in *The Last Carnival* where the younger, more Black-Powerish generation, at the conclusion of the plays, are conceded their right to approach white–black relations in their own way.

During January 1981 Questel video-taped a long, important, interview with Walcott at the Banyan Studio in Port of Spain where it can be consulted. Later an edited version appeared in *Trinidad and Tobago Review*. The published interview begins with Walcott saying that an advantage of being a playwright in a poor country is that your language has do the work that elsewhere might be left to changes of scenery and the set. Whenever the set has been least important, drama has been most powerful. Lately Walcott has been learning to be more concentrated, to crystallize into the minimum amount of words what the scene is about, what is going on at the moment. It is not a matter of writing shorter speeches but of intensifying and reducing the experience more to what an actor feels. Soyinka's *The Road*, for example, is not overtly in verse, the power is in the diction and rhetoric. When he read the play he had not realized how much its strength depended on all the African religion behind it. The concentrated space of the Basement Theatre did not allow the visual presentation of the contrasting spaces of the church, the Professor's hut, and the junk yard, so it missed out on the symbolism of the Professor being between two religions. It is Soyinka's masterpiece but has never really been done in America, except by the Workshop and a college production.

The level of the acting by certain members of the Trinidad Theatre Workshop was as good as the best in New York and drove Walcott to trying to create plays that challenged the actors. There was a mutual drive between him, as director and playwright, and the actors to reach a high pitch of performance. The ensemble style of the Workshop was already there in Caribbean actors. As the TTW actors improved and became confident, they realized that there was nothing artificial about working at their professional best. If you compare Theatre Workshop actors with the best American actors they are somewhat less technical, but Errol Jones and Stanley Marshall have the advantage of people working in their own language and playing their own material. American actors have the advantage of being auditioned daily; it's a profession and you cannot assume that you will get a part.

In the United States Walcott developed a renewed awareness of the actor as the core of theatre. After seeing the complexity, pain, intensity, mental stress of the best actors, he was angry with the way Trinidadian actors were wasting themselves in superficialities and depending on their personalities. 'The more genius an actor has the harder he works.' Actors need material that terrifies them. Walcott would have liked to take another direction with the TTW for five years to do hard roles. Give the best actors one role to prepare for the year—Richard III, King Lear, Oedipus. He had started to work with one actor on Richard III and was prepared to work individually with others in a studio. To support himself he would have needed to charge a fee; no one wanted to pay. The problem is that actors are easily satisfied. They think if they did do a great role no one would see it. He had shown that he could take his plays overseas; Trinidad's actors should have similar ambitions. Actors in Trinidad are too good to stop with Walcott plays. 'You are not finally a great actor until you have done the great parts.'

When Questel asked about the use of echoes of or allusions to paintings in Walcott's scenes, Walcott replied that all directors are like scenic artists in having an image of human beings and a backdrop. Although he is a painter, all directors are really painters. Sometimes Walcott deliberately chooses a painting to imitate; in Drums and Colour he used 'The Boyhood of Raleigh'; in Marie Laveau he wanted something impressionistic and used Manet's 'Déjeuner sur l'herbe'. In such cases he wants the audience to catch the imitation. Walcott often paints a scene with characters before he writes it. Even the dialogue may come out of his paintings as he envisions characters in attitudes in a scene. He knew someone who was the basis of Makak, but at the time was copying and learning from Japanese paintings. He does not paint to create scenes for his plays, or force his plays to look like his paintings, but what he has painted causes him see drama pictorially rather than linguistically.

Language often overburdens his plays and he has trouble with plots; 'I am not a plotter.' There is also the problem that when his plays are done in America the audience and actors only see blacks and whites on stage. In America or England the play is 'pre-set' in the minds of people as soon as it involves whites and blacks on stage. 'We don't look at a white actress here and say she is a white actress or this guy is a black actor. This is a great liberating thing for the writer.' The West Indies can produce a theatre in which 'a white guy can play a black part, a white part is being played by black man'. In the United States a black writer is expected to write a certain kind of play, take on certain questions; black actors may even be hostile to white actors with whom they are playing. The West Indies, however, has not produced many dramatists because of the lack of places to perform. The most prolific playwrights have a company with which to work, like Roderick Walcott.

Walcott tried to avoid writing a simple reversal of white–black or class relations in *Pantomime*; it is mainly about two 'guys feinting and exploring and throwing punches and ducking'. It is more boxing than symbolism. It becomes serious the way a joke goes on too long and stops being a joke and you enter another dimension. You begin with two clichés which are worked against each other until hostilities begin that dissolve the clichés; intimacy is reached through conflict. There are also two contrasting styles. European acting teaches that exuberance is bad, you do not overact; you achieve passion through control. Jackson is a healing angel. He invades Trewe's privacy and breaks him down which is therapeutic. It does not matter if at the end of the play things are materially the same. The issues are at a different level than the sociological. Jackson and Trewe have confronted each other man to man. When he wrote *Pantomime* he had no particular stage in mind. He wanted to write a play that could be done anywhere—'all you need is a hat; you can always get a table'. 'That whole idea of reduction' is there.

Remembrance was a tribute to Walcott's mother. 'My mother brought us up and was a teacher and endured a lot and had certain values . . . also the people around her, the teachers I knew, but it was really a dedication to the spirit of someone who was very sacrificial.' 'A lot of it had to do with the possibility . . . that my father could have been a writer or a painter, professionally, in another country . . . prior to our own . . . generation.'

What counts is that you feel you have written something that for the best intelligence is not insulting or pretentious. West Indian critics can be more succinctly critical than New York critics. Writers are provincials who go towards the metropolis. They have the astonishment of those who are not metropolitans. 'Shakespeare came in as a hick.' 'The freshness is there because of the exploration.' There is a West Indian kind of humour, found in Samuel Selvon and V. S. Naipaul, that contains sorrow and pathos. It is courage and the ability to endure.

When Questel asked whether he was writing musicals to make use of the West Indian actors' ability to draw upon the local dance tradition, Walcott replied that while the dances were powerful they had become habitual. There was a need for choreographers to develop narrative and dramatic power, a need to make dance more mimetic and heraldic. There is the need to avoid the black American situation of having powerful dances that are only used in musicals as entertainments. While the costs make it unlikely that black Americans will get a chance to do serious musicals, it would be a challenge to try it in the West Indies where the cost would be less. The form of the musical is difficult, but you could work to make it into serious theatre. Walcott thought Yeats' *Purgatory* 'the greatest piece of modern poetic theatre', but he was drawn to the vulgarity of James Joyce and the broadness of Shakespeare. He had no reputation as a director in the United States and had only twice directed plays there. Americans do not think writers should direct their own plays, although theatre history is filled with writers who were directors. They do not take seriously his directing experience in the West Indies.[28]

Walcott's methods as a director continued to be controversial. Although many praise his directing for the way plays appear an ever changing series of visually strong pictures, others have expressed reservations. Judy Stone felt it is better to employ a separate director as Walcott's directing is influenced by his 'other selves, the poet and the painter'. He is a painter-director who in *Dream*, *In A Fine Castle* and *Marie Laveau* visualizes 'tableaux' at the risk of losing the pace of the drama. His respect for words can work against his text; lovely, sonorous sentences may cause the audience to lose the thread of the argument.[29]

Walcott returned to Trinidad in May 1981 for three days of reading and talks at schools. His topic was 'The Relevance of West Indian Poetry to the Young'. His plays *Malcochon*, *Henri Christophe* and *Dream on Monkey Mountain* were set books on the schools CXC examinations for the year and the TTW was currently acting his *Beef, No Chicken* at the Little Carib.[30]

NOTES

1. Information from interviews with Leonore Bishop, Albert Laveau, and Charles Applewhaite (July 1990) and from interviews with and letters from Norline Metivier.
2. Interviews with Metivier and Walcott.
3. 'Charlatan Returns More Musically', Trinidad Guardian (23 Dec. 1976), 6; ' "Charlatan" Just Right for the Carnival Season', Express (13 Jan. 1977), 11.
4. Barbara Jenson's files. Interviews with Jenson, Judy Stone, and Corinne Jones Holder during 1990–1.
5. Judy Stone [Mauby], 'Charlatan? Yes, Walcott is Still With Us', Trinidad Guardian (20 Jan. 1977), 4.
6. Jeremy Taylor, 'Perhaps "The Charlatan" is a Little Overworked?', Express (19 Jan. 1977), 22; 'Notices and Comments', Kairi 78, 67; Stone, 'National Theatre Wanted', Trinidad & Tobago Review (Dec. 1977), 9.
7. Raoul Pantin [RAP], 'I've Written a New Play: It's on in St Croix and it's Getting Good Reviews', Tapia 7/19 (8 May 1977), 9.
8. Derek Walcott, Remembrance & Pantomime (New York: Farrar, Straus and Giroux, 1980).
9. Information in Barbara Jenson files and Walcott Collection, University of the West Indies, St Augustine.
10. Interview with Arthur Bentley, Port of Spain (6 July 1990). The story has been confirmed by Walcott in various interviews and articles.
11. During several conversations with Walcott (1989–93), and in a 'discussion' with students at the University of Valparaiso (Nov. 1993).
12. Programme for Pantomime, directed by Ken Corsbie, at Little Carib Theatre (10 Oct. 1980).
13. Anne Hilton, 'Pantomime', Express (23 Apr. 1978), 14–15; Mark Lyndersay, '. . . and the Audience Make Three', Catholic News (30 Apr. 1978), 5.
14. Christopher Gunness, 'White Man, Black Man', People (June 1978), 14, 51–2.
15. Raoul Pantin [RAP], ' "Pantomime" It was a Frivolous Show', The Sun (2 Dec. 1978).
16. Mark Lyndersay, 'Pantomime is Still a Joy', Express (14 Oct. 1980), 11.
17. Judy Stone, 'What Corsbie Did to Walcott's "Pantomime" ', Trinidad Guardian (5 Feb. 1981), 13.
18. Due to the haste with which it was assembled the TTW April 1993 Pantomime was disappointing. During rehearsals Errol Jones told me that from 1959 onwards Walcott had directed in such a manner, trying out each phrase with different interpretations. See Walcott, 'What the Twilight Says', in Dream on Monkey Mountain, 24: 'they have become limbs, extensions of your sensibility'.
19. Victor Questel, 'Remembrance: An inspiring Elegy for the Afro-Saxon', Trinidad Guardian (3 July 1979), 7; ' "Remembrance" next on the Dinner Theatre stage', Express (24 June 1979), 10.
20. Judy Stone, 'At Last, Masterpiece on the Middle Class', Trinidad Guardian (13 July 1979), 4. Also Jeremy Taylor, ' "Remembrance"—A Moving Tender Play', Express (6 July 1979), 13.
21. 'Derek Walcott Hailed', Trinidad Guardian (25 Jan. 1980), 8; 'Russian Sounds

Fill Little Carib', *Express* (25 Jan. 1980); Victor Questel, 'Poets get Standing Ovation', *Sunday Guardian* (27 Jan. 1980), 6.

22. Jeremy Taylor, 'Walcott—at 50', *Caribbean Contact* (March 1980), 14.

23. The seminar is published as 'Derek Walcott Talks About "The Joker of Seville"' *Carib*, 4 (1986), 1–15; 'Marie La Veau', *Trinidad and Tobago Review*, 3/6 (Dec. 1979); Walcott had problems with the singing of *Marie La Veau* in St Croix and there were last-minute cast changes (according to Gilbert Sprauve).

24. Jeremy Taylor, 'Walcott Nudging up to Broadway', *Express* (2 June 1980), 14–15.

25. Debra John, 'Marie La Veau, and the people who really had my sympathy', *The Sun* (6 June 1980), 6.

26. Mark Lyndersay, The Week at a Glance, NBS Radio 610 (8 June 1980); and 'Under the Spell of Marie La Veau',*Catholic News* (15 June 1980), 13; LeRoy Clarke, 'Marie La Veau—An Artificial Resurrection', *Express* (18 June 1980), 24–5; Roland Graham, 'An Art of Wind Upon Water of Wave Upon Shore', *Express*, unidentified clipping (June 1980).

27. Victor Questel, 'Marie Laveau—Disappointing, Uneven', *Trinidad & Tobago Review*, 3/10 ('Governor Plum', 1980), 8, 18, 21, 22, 23.

28. Victor Questel, 'I Have Moved Away from the Big Speech', *Trinidad and Tobago Review*, 5/1 ('Peewah', 1981), 11–14; Victor Questel, 'The Black American Not Given a Chance', *Trinidad and Tobago Review*, 5/3 ('Parang', 1981), 11–14.

29. Stone, 'What Corsbie Did to "Pantomime"', op. cit. Barbara Jenson, who studied theatre, felt that Walcott's continually dissolving pictures were unlike anything she has seen on stage and felt that others are unable to duplicate such effects.

30. 'Derek Walcott Goes Back to School to Read Poetry', *Express* (4 May 1981), 23.

Walcott 1982–1983   *16*

The Last Carnival

A Branch of the Blue Nile

WALCOTT was re-examining the nature of theatre. He had always been restless, learning quickly, picking up and adapting various methods, conventions, and styles. He began as a poet-dramatist in the rhetorical mode of the Elizabethan and Jacobean stage, was influenced by the Abbey Irish theatre, learned about Method acting, Oriental stage conventions, Brecht, the theatre of the absurd, and the American musical; as can be seen by *Pantomime* and *The Charlatan* he was conscious of the various conventions and styles of the theatre including British musical hall and Trinidadian calypso tent performances. He knew that circumstances made West Indian theatre a theatre of poverty, a poor theatre without much in the way of properties, scenery, and costumes, but it could be a total theatre of acting, mime, dance, and music. He wanted a director's theatre in which the actor was an extension of himself, like his fingers writing, but he also thought of the theatre as a collaboration between actors and the dramatist as they tried out lines and scenes in workshops. The creative tensions between such contrasts and contradictions and different methods gave his plays and staging their vitality, their feeling of new worlds being conquered, but Walcott needed further worlds to conquer, was challenged by the lack of a theatre company, and was aware that the greatest plays often had a depth of characterization that his own usually lacked. He was aware that acting itself was a great art, not just a means to perform good plays. He had written parts using local character types and found actors that looked the type and then continued, as most obviously with Errol Jones and Stanley Marshall, to write further parts of that kind for the actor. The actor's stage personality

had been his model. Now Walcott wanted to go in the opposite direction. The art of acting was as important as, perhaps greater than, the
text. Actors had to be challenged with roles that were unlike themselves.

Henri Christophe, Dream, even *Joker,* were plays in which ideas and
poetry were foregrounded. From *Dream on Monkey Mountain* and the
revised *Ti-Jean* to *Joker, O Babylon!,* and the revised *Charlatan,* Walcott
had worked towards total theatre with the story increasingly told
through gesture; this became an attempt to turn the American musical
into a vehicle for serious drama. *Joker* and *Babylon* showed the improb-
ability of mounting such plays outside the West Indies. The integration of ballet and serious music had sometimes been attempted in the
white musical, but such plays about blacks and using their cultural
traditions were unlikely to be produced: the cost of production was
too expensive in relation to the probable audience. While not abandoning hopes of writing and producing musicals, Walcott began re-
exploring the possibilities of a 'poor' theatre requiring few props with
greater focus on character psychology. The lessons of the avant-garde
would be applied to more conventional settings in which shifts of
time, actors doubling parts, or deep emotional changes within a character would take place through memories, parallels, and verbal battles. Instead of exteriorizing psychology through action there would
be increased interiorization. The centrality of character, psychology,
and the inward turmoil of change found in Oedipus, Othello, Samson,
and Albee's *Who's Afraid of Virginia Woolf* replaces character types in
Pantomime, Remembrance, and *A Branch of the Blue Nile.*

Along with such a different approach towards the theatre and character there was an increased interest in time, the past, how the West
Indies had changed, and the various strands that were parts of its
culture. The increasing Americanization of the young and the middle
class, their limited sense of the complexities of history, and perhaps
the increasing amount of time he was spending outside the West Indies
made Walcott nostalgic and analytically conscious of how much European cultural and political traditions had contributed to the West Indies
and how much of what he had known might soon be lost with the
passing of generations and Americanized progress.

Walcott needed West Indian actors for his new plays, and he needed
actors who could handle complex, conflicting emotions without stere-
otyping them; he needed actors who could play several roles in a play
or interpret a character at various times in his or her life. His greater
maturity as an artist and understanding of the possibilities of the

theatre, perhaps quickened by regularly teaching in the United States and the opportunity to see more plays, brought him back to the West Indies. In 1981 he was awarded by the MacArthur Foundation $50,000 a year for five years, one of the so-called genius grants. The MacArthur award allowed Walcott to purchase an apartment in Boston; he planned to use half the money to start a second phase with the TTW.

Walcott approached the TTW about leading them again, this time into a 'second period' when he would train actors to do the great classical roles of dramatic literature and produce two of his plays each summer, beginning with a revival of Joker during the summer of 1982. Rather than a reconciliation the negotiations resulted in a tempestuous argument and a nasty series of events. Relations between Walcott and the TTW would remain stormy for a few years. What happened is controversial.[1]

Walcott said he booked the Little Carib for The Last Carnival and a revival of The Joker of Seville, but when he arrived he found the booking cancelled in favour of a TTW production of a Trevor Rhone play. Immediately a dispute erupted concerning Walcott's use of Americans in West Indian theatre. Walcott had raised US $22,000 for his plays that summer and claimed that he offered to give the TTW US $100,000 for five Trinidadians to have scholarships to study theatre abroad. Instead he was told he had overbudgeted and the TTW would not accept a foreign choreographer for Joker. 'The dance company had no objection to a foreigner, why the Workshop?' Instead Walcott gave the $100,000 to the O'Neill Foundation for scholarships. 'What shocked me was to have the company I founded telling me that they preferred to sacrifice $100,000 that would assist young Trinidadians to study.' He said that local actors had become self-satisfied and were now paid better than off-Broadway Americans. Local actors had settled into mannerisms and routines; they needed a challenge to bring out their best. Both the Americans and Trinidadians would learn from each other. Trinidadian dancers are first class and 'moving up and out at a fast pace'. 'The dancers are subjecting themselves to challenges where they have to be good. The actors are not.'[2]

Relations between Walcott and the TTW soon reached the lowest point since the conflicts that led to his resignation in 1976. Walcott was thinking internationally, wanting Trinidadian theatre to reach the standards of New York and London. His view was that of a committed artist testing himself against the best anywhere regardless of the cost. He felt that he could show others where they should be going. The foundation Workshop members, however, had become the leading actors of Trinidad and wanted to enjoy their success. They no longer saw themselves as Walcott's company. They were putting on plays, acting on television, sometimes working abroad, and trying to repay debts; they would have liked to continue working with Walcott, but on their terms, not his. There was now good commercial work for a few actors in Trinidad, whereas Walcott's terms meant accepting what he could pay and often paying him in various ways. It also meant accepting his leadership and vision.

The TTW replied to Walcott's criticism by offering its own perspective on the events that had happened and by questioning some of the supposed facts. The Workshop argued that it worked with Walcott on *Marie Laveau* and *Beef, No Chicken* and had not objected to foreign actors in the first productions of *Joker* or *Marie Laveau*. They claimed to have bought the rights for a 1982 production of *Joker* and to have brought Walcott from Boston to Trinidad in March for a poetry reading to raise funds and to hold auditions. He said he was not satisfied with the available talent for Don Juan and Isabella and wanted to bring two Americans for the roles. They had vaguely talked of doing *The Last Carnival*, but only as a workshop with a director from Chicago. As the United States International Communications Agency was to sponsor the workshop and drama classes, the USICA booked the Little Carib for a month and the TTW had paid for it. (Both Walcott and the TTW claimed to have receipts.) Walcott also agreed to donate $30,000 from his MacArthur grant for scholarships.

Then Mr Gilman Thomas-Hessen of the International Trust Limited entered into negotiations with the idea of raising one million dollars for Haitian refugees by selling tickets for at least $1,000 each for two gala performances at the Globe Cinema. There would be three further nights with proceeds to go to the TTW after which the production would move to the Little Carib with ITL underwriting the costs of the production. International Trust Limited was 'a little diffident' about importing foreigners but agreed to the two actors along with Galt MacDermot and the Montgomerys. After Walcott returned to the United States he telephoned to say that an American choreographer was necessary. This was the last straw for ITL which called off the project. When Walcott insisted on an American choreographer the TTW refused to co-operate further. Walcott then told them they could not produce *Joker* although they had bought performing rights; he withdrew his offer to donate $30,000. As a result the feud restarted and Walcott came to Trinidad with *The Last Carnival* and his Warwick Productions.[3]

The Last Carnival was a revision of *In A Fine Castle*. Walcott had revised *Castle, Charlatan,* and *Franklin* after a publisher expressed interest in bringing out the three unpublished plays together in a book. (So far only *The Last Carnival* has been published.)[4]

The Last Carnival, produced and directed by Walcott at the Government Training College, 1–17 July 1982, now conflicted with the TTW's production of *Smile Orange,* directed by Trevor Rhone, at the Little Carib, 8–31 July. Walcott brought with him two foreign artists, Fran McDormand and Cotter Smith, to play leading roles. While this was part of his long-time ambition to have a programme of cultural exchanges, it was seen by local actors as imported competition. Although the issue was more symbolic than practical, since McDormand and Smith were both whites playing parts that required whites, none of the main TTW actors were involved in the production. Walcott directed and the cast included, along with McDormand and Smith, Maurice Brash, Fred Hope, Mavis Lee Wah, Charles Applewhaite and Errol Roberts. *The Last Carnival* was poorly attended. While the programme promised that Warwick Productions would next offer a revival of *Joker* with new songs by Galt MacDermot that did not take place.

The Last Carnival continued to stir controversy. *Express* carried three reviews and various other articles about it. Although the reviewers agreed that the play was disappointing, their reviews disagreed about the reasons and there was an unusual emphasis on arguing with the plot which concerned the history of a French-Creole family. Jeremy Taylor thought the production meandering and without emotional coherence. What was the character Brown doing in the script? Fran McDormand was convincing but the Americans simply were not Creoles and their accents kept reminding you that they were Americans playing Trinidadians. Why is Walcott still going on about the collisions between white–black, creole–classic, old–new world? The play seemed like 'another of Walcott's try-outs', far from its final form and, like *The Charlatan,* destined to years of rewriting.[5]

Earl Lovelace's review was concerned with Walcott's treatment of the story. Although *The Last Carnival* is a strong play about people and the French Creoles which cuts through the hypocrisy of 'All ah we is One', it has not reached its potential. Walcott offers too many easy sentiments. That Clodia leaves Trinidad saying 'I love this island' ignores the stronger truth that she, unlike the older generation, belongs to Trinidad by birth and culture; France, the land of her forefathers, is not her home. Walcott should have pressed on such truths which are within the fabric of the play. Brown, who should have much potential, is limp. Brown could have offered Clodia hope, but is gutless and indecisive. He should have provided an alternative to the unfocused rage that Walcott imposes on Sidney, the Black Power radical. Still, Brown's inadequacies are cautionary and should be heeded. Lovelace objects that using foreign actors does not allow the local French Creoles to deal 'with their own important story'.[6]

'RAP' found *The Last Carnival* long, wordy, tedious, but 'saved' by Walcott's directing and fine language. McDormand and Cotter were 'very credible', but the parts played by the other actors were thinly sketched. Again the critic, but in less sophisticated ways than Lovelace, argues with the plot. Was the two-hundred-year-old French Trinidadian family 'weighty enough to fill out the Trinidad landscape'? The play is not concerned with why black people revolted in 1970. A Trinidadian French-Creole family is of insufficient interest for an entire play. The social and economic history is incorrect. The whites still have the privileges; the blacks are still enraged.[7]

Judy Stone did not see *The Last Carnival* until the end of the second week. She went without enthusiasm as she had not sympathized with it when she acted in the 1971 version of *In A Fine Castle*. She was stunned by the way Walcott had 'unthreaded the characters and themes of one play, and rewoven them into a wonderfully different, richer, far more effective dramatic tapestry'. It was a new work. She was saddened that a production of such quality was forced to camp like a refugee in the unlovely tent of the Government Training College. Not one production she had seen over the past year came close to achieving the 'transcendence' of *The Last Carnival*. Stone regarded the play as a study of 'Trinidad's dodos, the French-creole plantocracy'. Questions are raised whether Trinidad will be deprived or improved by the death of the dodos and whether dodo culture should be preserved. Visually, white and black perspectives are balanced by shifts between the La Fontaine castle and the Black Power gathering. The reporter Brown bridges the gulf. The racial conflict is really about social conditions. There are three black positions represented by: Brown—the rationalist; butler George—the conservative; and Sidney—the rebel. The earlier version of the play covered one Carnival day; the revised version spans two generations tracing the roots of the revolution. The opening is marvellous. The dialogue in the second half is less taut, the acting and direction less sure, although Walcott's direction remains visually stimulating. It is marvellous to watch Fran McDormand's face. Cotter Smith gives a subtle, underplayed interpretation which builds.

The characterization is thorough. Yes, the accents of the Americans are a hindrance.[8]

Fran McDormand, who was then a young actress (before she won an Oscar), fresh from graduate school, was interviewed by Anthony Milne. Although she was used to working with an English accent she had to be coached by Norline Walcott on sounding Trinidadian by adding French, Spanish, and 'African' dialects. When asked whether she felt the play was less relevant by being about the white minority, she interestingly replied: 'I don't think the play was about the plight of French Creoles particularly, but just about somebody, a minority group, being wiped out. I can't claim to know all the history behind what this society is now, but I have felt, since I have been here, that I was at a disadvantage here because I am a white woman.'[9]

The controversy continued with William Gordon rekindling smouldering issues. Finding it 'almost unthinkable' that the 'degrading low-level humour' of *Smile Orange* replaced *The Last Carnival* at the Little Carib, Gordon claimed that 'the Workshop got things laid out too damn easy for them'. 'The real scenario in Derek Walcott's life is trying to uplift the consciousness of his own people, and compared to that his plays are just so many fascinating pieces.' *The Last Carnival* has the kind of power that only comes from a mature talent after years of experience and is loaded with 'our typical attitudes and glimpses of ourselves at more characteristic and revealing moments'; it 'put you through the embarrassment of self recognition'. That is the job of theatre, although Walcott sometimes sacrifices it to his quest for identity and habits of irony and confrontation. 'The whole thing was such a harrowing put-through that maybe this is the real reason that Derek's company can't stand putting on his plays—or why this extraordinary experience was so sparsely attended.' The level of acting was tremendous. Cotter Smith was amazing in managing to sound passably Trinidadian in only five weeks. Gordon agreed with Walcott that the Workshop members seemed uninterested in passing on their knowledge as actors to the younger generation.[10]

After *The Last Carnival* Walcott remained active in Trinidad with *The Rig*, a film for television that he wrote and directed for Banyan (which has a copy in its archives). It included Nigel Scott, Joy Ryan, John Isaacs, Maurice Brash, Carol La Chapelle, and Adele Bynoe. Set in rural Mayaro the film shows the effects of off-shore oil drilling on the community and has some similarities to *Beef, No Chicken* in examining the effect of 'progress' on rural Trinidad. It treats such themes as the artist's commitment to Trinidad and the temptation to seek glory abroad. There is a girl who is part of a folk-dance group but who finds from working in a disco that she might have a brilliant career abroad. The budget for the film was $100,000, which was highly unlikely to be recuperated through bookings on Caribbean television stations, so the project itself was a quixotic commitment to Trinidadian art by Banyan Studio.[11]

If Walcott's relations with the TTW remained tempestuous and his inability to produce his plays in a satisfactory environment in Trinidad continued to be a problem, elsewhere in the West Indies he had become the region's foremost dramatist, someone with classical status. This was especially true in Barbados where earlier, at the time of nationalism and cultural affirmation, the English plantocracy retained power and the Green Room, the equivalent of the new theatre groups in the other islands, was begun by and long remained white and 'near white'. Later, when non-white theatre companies began, Walcott's plays had a predominant place. Black Power movements also came late to Barbados, a country with far fewer black 'folk' traditions or African survivals than Trinidad or St Lucia, so Walcott's concern about the relationship of the New World black to European culture was unchallenged by strong radical voices. In Barbados, Stage One Productions, a non-profit theatre company, was formed in 1978, 'to advance cultural development'. Stage One's leadership is multiracial, and while mostly producing West Indian plays, Stage One has also performed Molière, Strindberg, and Shakespeare. Two of its first four productions were Walcott's Ti-Jean during 1979 and Pantomime in 1981. Walcott was also fortunate that in Barbados a founder of Stage One, Michael Gilkes, is a playwright, actor, and a notable literary critic. The directors Earl Warner and Ken Corsbie (from Guyana) are among the new breed of West Indian professionals who went from island to island and to North America directing plays. Barbados has a pool of talented actors and directors needing significant plays.

After Walcott returned to Boston, where he now taught creative writing and playwriting, at Boston University, there was an important Stage One production of Remembrance in Barbados late September 1982, directed by Earl Warner. The reception was rather different from the polarized controversies that seemed to plague productions of Walcott's plays in Trinidad. The critic for the Advocate-News said that the script was substantial and solid and the evening memorable. 'The story itself . . . strikes chords throughout the entire West Indian archipelago.' It portrays the 'dilemma of a split social history, the obsession with education, speaking good English, the struggle towards unity in the "mind without a country", the indelible gouges of a colonialist past, Black Power and nationalism, independence, revolutionary thought, dead memories and hymn-singing mothers'. It would have been possible to have become lost in the various time shifts but Earl Warner, as director, 'focused our attention' through the classical spider-in-his-web image. The image was on stage as a backdrop emerging from the belly of a grandfather clock 'whose frame provided the open space of a doorway' through which the actors moved into the past and present time. The school teacher was like a fly trapped in a web, trapped in the past, unfit for the future. Jordan changed on stage from a coat rack (which the reviewer thought Brechtian). Michael Gilkes's Jordan revealed the character's vulnerability without being sentimental. The performance aimed at neither pity nor contempt. The play became a collaborative effort as the audience and actors were 'probing, darting in and out of the past and sifting choices made'. This was truly West Indian theatre as celebration, rite, 'probes through history', remembrance of things past, clearing away whispering ghosts, and 'forging on through'. The images were drawn from 'our own national vocabulary'.[12]

The challenge that Walcott had made to the TTW was being, in a more restricted way, taken up in Barbados when doing his plays. John Wickham, the editor of *Bim*, called the Stage One production of *Remembrance* one of the three greatest stage performances he had seen in the Caribbean. One of the other two was Slade Hopkinson's Lestrade in *Dream*. Wickham raved about Michael Gilkes's Jordan as a tour de force, the '"image of epic grandeur" which is Walcott's gift to West Indians'. It is about the origins of 'our deepest wells of experience'. Jordan is a familiar figure in every West Indian community, the school teacher whose accent and bearing proclaim his attachment to the standards of the foreign mother country and whose failure to reach his aspirations results in beating of and affection for his students. It would be easy to caricature him, but Walcott celebrates a human personality.[13]

The emphasis in reviews of these later plays on the audience's experience shows that Walcott was touching on what the audiences felt were central to their lives and that he was now writing plays for actors in which the words did not get in the way of dramatic realization. Mark McWatt also felt that *Remembrance* was a rare, fortunate theatre event in which words and plot came to life and were part of the audience's experience. McWatt felt that Walcott was now at the peak of his powers of stagecraft and theatrical invention. Jordan is someone 'whose conflict of values many of us still carry around inside, with varying degrees of reluctance'. McWatt discusses Jordan's two short stories as representative of the conflict. The complex layers of time and memory in the play are demanding, but Gilkes moves easily between them with the authority and wit that the role requires. McWatt was impressed by the set, especially the use of the grandfather clock and the spider web. 'It is difficult to imagine the Steel Shed used more effectively as a theatre space.' McWatt, like the other critics, praised the actors as working as an ensemble in bringing out the delicate balance of values that is part of being West Indian.[14]

The Stage One production of *Remembrance* made an impression. In the past Walcott and the TTW were invited to Jamaica to put on Walcott's plays; now Earl Warner and Michael Gilkes were invited by the Creative Arts Centre to recreate their Stage One version at UWI, Mona, in April 1983.

Walcott had in 1982, according to one Workshop member, dropped on Port of Spain like a cat among pigeons. The pigeons fought back in their own way and he lost $30,000 on *The Last Carnival*. The wound remained open. He returned to Trinidad during the summer of 1983 where he conducted acting workshops and was writing a film script around Nigel Scott, the white actor in the TTW who had continued to work with both him and the TTW. He pointed out that all the talent in his first film, *The Rig*, had worked for nothing; this was 'restorative' for him. It was the good side of Trinidad, 'not the nasty thing you find when people are paid in excess of their talent and want to think of themselves as personalities'. He mentioned that he earned money from royalties of the many productions of his plays in regional theatres in the United States 'without having to lift a finger' but he wanted to see his plays done by West Indian actors, and that he hoped that those participating in his TV films would not become 'swell-headed' or consider themselves 'over-night stars'.[15]

When his new play, *A Branch of the Blue Nile* premièred in Barbados, using many of those who had been involved in the Stage One *Remembrance*, reviewers wrote that they were seeing a classic play by a great author at the height of his powers given a great performance, and all remarked how thankful they were for Walcott opening his play in Barbados. How different from Walcott's recent Trinidadian reviews! The planning for the play was, however, marked by another rumpus between Walcott and a Trinidadian in which Walcott was at least partly in the wrong. It was a dispute over the employment of an actress: Sonya Moze was cast for a part by the director, but Walcott demanded the part for his wife Norline.

According to Judy Stone, Earl Warner, who was then in Trinidad to direct *Like Them That Dream* for the TTW, told her that *A Branch of the Blue Nile* was an important play, Walcott's 'definitive statement on theatre in the Caribbean', tracing the conflict in the region between the classical and the folk. Can a Caribbean actress play Cleopatra? To what extent can she really be like Cleopatra in contrast to a West Indian actor's close identification with the people and situations in a West Indian play like *Malcochon*? The play concerns the private lives of the actors in relation to the parts they improvise in workshop and has resemblances to the TTW. The improvisations are part of trying to develop two plays, *Antony and Cleopatra* and a folk play. The play itself concerns an author writing about a group improvising two plays and the experiences behind them. The new play would be staged first in Barbados—partly because it was less expensive to produce there, partly because Walcott had lost money on his last play in Trinidad, and probably because of his recent fight with the TTW.

Stage One had bought from Walcott world rights for a year and a half and planned a gala champagne opening with special invitees and $40 tickets. Stage One asked Sonya Moze to be one of the actresses and she rehearsed in Barbados for two weeks. Then when Walcott saw the cast list he, according to Stone, demanded that Moze be replaced by his wife Norline or he would cancel the production, buy back the rights, and refund Stage One for what they had spent. Stone mused, 'Perhaps Derek assumed that by selling the play to Barbados, he had put it out of reach of Trinidad actors.' Stone thought the incident was caused by Walcott's feeling of betrayal by the TTW and concluded that while she still loved the man and honoured his genius she did not always admire his conduct. A charismatic leader could become a wilful tyrant. There are, of course, other ways of looking at the situation, such as what the French consider the moral right of an artist to what is done to his or her property, or Walcott's love of his wife and desire that she be given a chance to develop as an artist. Still, regardless of Walcott's rights, it was not a pretty deed.[16]

A Branch of the Blue Nile, presented by Stage One and produced by Cynthia Wilson, premièred on 25 November 1983, before invited guests, including several government ministers, bank governors, the Commissioner of the Police, and Derek's sister Pamela Walcott St Hill and her husband Leonard St Hill, both original members of Walcott's St Lucia Arts Guild. Directed by Earl Warner the cast included Norline Walcott, Michael Gilkes, Patrick Foster, and Elizabeth Clarke. The *Barbados Advocate* called it delightful, a triumph, and thought it

captured the feelings of frustration, struggle, envy, bitchiness, tenderness, love, courage, hope, fear, and despair that characterize West
Indian theatre.[17]

The Nation reviewer felt it inconceivable that A Branch of the Blue Nile
should be played to other than West Indian audiences by other than
West Indian actors. 'Its authority and its integrity spring from its being
at home', an authority and integrity reflected in a performance that
might not have been possible with a play from someone else. For the
first time the actors had material which was not only appropriate but
provided them with 'keys to enter the kingdom'. Several of the actors
have never been better or achieved such significance and presence in
their roles. Warner's direction contributed to the interpretation of
Walcott's dense poetic language. It is a lesson in theatre and worthy
of the award that it was given. Norline Walcott had a brilliantly intuitive understanding of her part.[18]

According to The Weekend Nation in just over two hours Walcott,
by the magic that only an artist in lucky moments can call up, 'un-
earths the roots of Caribbean man and holds them up before the eyes
of a pleased and participating audience'. While some myopic observers
are prepared only to acknowledge the African roots of the region,
Walcott also examines the English and American influences. He im-
aginatively links the English and African roots through the jointure of
Shakespeare's Antony and Cleopatra, the Serpent of Old Nile. Walcott
began by wanting to be an Elizabethan and his language is wittier and
sparkles more than earlier in his career, while moving like a clear and
'ardent' stream. It is filled with puns which reveal the anger, jealousy,
frustration, and despair that come from the conflict of cultural roots.
There are many occasions in the play when the audience are as involved as the players and the room seems to vibrate. The play is
fortunate in its casting. The players move easily through a number of
national accents. Gilkes has presence, plays with intense feelings masked
by casualness and an air of cynicism, and can easily slip from English
to Trinidadian dialect. He makes 'one's ears wiggle with joy'. Some
patrons objected to the obscene words, but that is part of Walcott's
Elizabethanism. A Branch of the Blue Nile is bound to be a classic. We
should be grateful to Walcott and Warner.[19]

Earl Warner's use of the possibilities of the theatre originally had
been prompted by Walcott's Ti-Jean and his Brothers. Walcott's 'whole
use of animalisation, the whole use of a Caribbean form in terms of
the narrator', led Warner to explore the use of sound, space, and body
in the Caribbean theatre—he ran an experimental Caribbean Lab for

a few years at the Jamaica School of Drama. He decided that the Caribbean mind 'does not operate in a linear progression in terms of naturalism' and that he wanted to weave a balance between expressionism and naturalism into the productions he directed. When directing Walcott's *Remembrance*, instead of giving emphasis to a realistic setting he tried to show Jordan 'weaving remembrances'. 'I captured Jordan in a large clock web, to do with Time, and the weaving of things, and allowing the characters to unfold ... through that space into another space.'[20]

NOTES

1. 'What Ever Happened to Walcott's Second Phase?' *Sunday Express* (25 July 1982), 24–5.
2. 'Walcott tells of Local Amateur Actors in Disguise', *Sunday Guardian* (11 July 1982), 5, 10.
3. 'What Ever Happened to Walcott's Second Phase?', op. cit.
4. Derek Walcott, *Three Plays: The Last Carnival, Beef, No Chicken, and A Branch of the Blue Nile* (New York: Farrar, Straus & Giroux, 1986).
5. Jeremy Taylor, ' "The Last Carnival" ', *Express* (6 July 1982), 24.
6. Earl Lovelace, 'The Last Carnival', *Express* (25 July 1982), 15, 18.
7. Raoul Pantin [RAP], 'Disappointing', *Express* (6 July 1982), 16.
8. Judy Stone, 'Death of our Dodos in "The Last Carnival" ', *Trinidad Guardian* (15 July 1982), 18–19.
9. Anthony Milne, 'Fran McDormand's Trinidad Adventure', *Express* (25 July 1982).
10. William Gordon, 'Rich Drama of Walcott's "Last Carnival" ', *Trinidad Guardian* (2 Aug. 1982), 19.
11. Jeremy Taylor, 'Bunyan and Walcott Team up on "The Rig" ', *Express* [25 July 1982]; 'Shooting begins on Walcott movie' [n.d.].
12. B. Elizabeth Clarke, ' "Remembrance" Proved to be Fulfilling', *Advocate-News* (11 Oct. 1982), 6. Desmond Bourne, who played Mr Barrley, was originally from Trinidad and an early member of the LCTW. 'Bourne has Long Link with Theatre', *Advocate-News* (25 Sept. 1982), 7.
13. John Wickham, 'Much More than Acting', *The Nation* (5 Oct. 1982), 9.
14. Mark McWatt, 'Remembrance', *Caribbean Contact*, 10/8 (Dec. 1982), 11.
15. Kathlyn Russell, 'Give me Film, says Derek Walcott', *Sunday Express* (4 Sept. 1983), 31; Diane Chun, 'Raw Talent and Vibrant Personalities Fuel Trinidad Drama', *Gainesville Sun* (5 Sept. 1982), 1E, 11E.
16. Judy Stone, 'I may Lose Derek's Friendship', *Trinidad Guardian* (15 Nov. 1983), 17.
17. Ulric Rice, 'An Outstanding Play', *Advocate* (27 Nov. 1983), 6.
18. 'Play which Deserves the Award', *The Nation* (29 Nov. 1983), 10.

19. Gladstone Holder, 'A Branch of the Blue Nile', *The Weekend Nation* (2 Dec. 1983), 6.

20. Judy Stone, 'Earl Warner Shares his Thoughts', *Trinidad Guardian* (22 Nov. 1983), 19; Judy Stone, 'Exploring Sound, Body and Use of Space', *Trinidad Guardian* (29 Nov. 1983), 23.

Walcott 1984–1990 **17**

Haytian Earth
Another New *Dream*
Another *Branch*
Another *Franklin*

WITH Walcott teaching at Boston University and his plays increasingly performed in the United States and England, he began premiering his new works outside the West Indies. There was, however, one more big Caribbean production, the world premiere of *The Haytian Earth* in St Lucia, 1–5 August 1984, and several important productions with which Walcott was associated before the renewal of his relationship with the Trinidad Theatre Workshop in 1992. Four productions between 1984 and 1990 are of especial interest for what they show about the varying contexts in which Walcott's plays are performed and reviewed.

The Haytian Earth was produced by the St Lucian Ministry of Education and Culture, performed at the Morne Fortune Theatre, directed by Derek Walcott with sets and costume design by Richard and Sally Montgomery. Anthony Gomes, who now often worked with Walcott, came from Trinidad as stage manager, but otherwise this was a local production using many actors from the St Lucia Arts Guild. *The Haytian Earth* was written on commission from the government of St Lucia to celebrate 150 years of emancipation from slavery. An open-air theatre on the Morne was specially created for the occasion. Originally the government asked Walcott to revive his early *Henri Christophe*, which was concerned with political events that followed the rebellion of the Haitian slaves and Haitian independence. Walcott instead proposed revising a film script about Haiti he had written seven years earlier.[1]

The St Lucian government approved a budget of $70,000 to cover the cost of creating an outdoor theatre, costumes for a cast of about fifty, sets for changes of scene, and transportation to and housing in St Lucia for Walcott and the Montgomerys. The government and local artists hoped that the production would give a boost to St Lucian drama both in having Derek Walcott back and in bringing together younger actors (trained in Jamaica) with older members of the Arts Guild. This was the first time in over twenty years that Walcott had worked on a production in St Lucia and there was talk of having him return every summer. A few weeks before *The Haytian Earth* a new theatre, the Lighthouse Theatre, opened with plays by Lennox Brown and Fernando Arrabal. Its director, the poet Kendel Hippolyte, who was Assistant Director of Culture, was one of those who had originally proposed to Walcott a revival of *Henri Christophe*. Dunstan St Omer, the painter who was an early member of the Arts Guild and whose friendship with Walcott and their role in creating an authentic local modern culture are recounted in *Another Life*, also initiated the project.[2]

The Haitian slave rebellion, leading to the first black independent nation in the New World, had been part of Walcott's subject matter in *Henri Christophe* and *Drums and Colours*. In *Haytian Earth* Walcott wanted to go beyond the usual textbook history of great men, whether white or black, to show that the peasantry were the real heroes of the revolution, while examining the nature of revolutions and revolutionaries.[3]

The Trinidadian *Express*, which had been a vehicle for attacks on Walcott during the 1982 controversy, ruefully noted this was the first summer for many years that Walcott had not been involved in a theatre production in Port of Spain and it was the first time in years that he was producing a major play in St Lucia. 'Theatre in either place may never be the same again.' *The Haytian Earth* was performed in 'a picture-perfect setting', the historic military barracks on the Morne, the hill towering over Castries which provides a magnificent panoramic view of the harbour and city. The open-air theatre could seat 300. A courtyard was the playing area backed by wings originally constructed by the French and English armies. There are beautiful Roman arches. Across the street there is a row of ruined guardrooms used for the rear wall of the amphitheatre. The audience sat on folding chairs.[4]

The setting for the theatre, chosen by Walcott and the Montgomerys, was fully utilized for the production to create many pageant-like effects. A model globe filled with flames moved across the upper stage to 'symbolise the physical and psychological destruction brought about by both the slave owners and slaves as master'. Dessalines and Christophe were crowned king by an enormous crown of woven palm leaves decorated with blue and pink paper flowers, which was moved by pulleys and ropes across the upper balconies. The sailing of the French fleet was symbolized by a huge mast sliding on stage and the unfurling of a large triangular sail. Unfortunately no roof was erected over the seating area and when severe showers occurred during the first night many people fled and the dialogue was at times inaudible.

Clara Rosa de Lima, one of the Trinidadians who travelled to St Lucia for the opening, felt that the setting was acoustically ideal and provided a feeling of being in the past. She was especially impressed by the arches of one of the old barracks. She thought that Arthur Jacobs, who had not acted for many years, was ideal as Toussaint; 'without any added make up, he grew old before my eyes'. Norline Metivier blended high drama with humour, childishness with seriousness. De Lima observed that Walcott brought out such paradoxes as a freed black man having the right to vote, but not 'the man of colour' who was born of a slave and plantation owner. 'Men of colour' sent to Paris for education were thought unacceptable when they returned to Haiti. The lighting gave a feeling of plantations being burnt.[5]

One critic felt The Haytian Earth lacked clear plot development, climax, and denouement. It was, however, the most ambitious production staged in St Lucia since Joker nine years earlier. The location, lighting, set, costuming, and use of the stage were impressive and effective, although there were too many changes of scene and too many characters, which disjointed the action. Toussaint and Christophe remained too flat. Pompey was the personification of the psychological trauma of Haiti, the peasant, the black man as survivor, driven by love of the land and 'the typical uncluttered rural perspective so often found in Walcott's writing'. But Walcott leaves Pompey in limbo, a comic tragic hero, with a fatal flaw, his love for the mulatto whore, Yette. She is the enigma that is Haiti, caught between the attractions of the land and fleeting sensations of the city. 'The main theme of fervent nationalist-turned-despot united the roles of Toussaint, Dessalines and Christophe, who followed the same path of self-destruction.' The examination of Absolute Power remains relevant, especially 'in the light of St Lucia's recent political history and other power struggles in the region'. The reviewer objected that the play was too much like a pageant, lacked psychological depth and should have made its politics more explicit with clear heroes and villains.[6]

George Odlum, a member of the St Lucia Arts Guild, a leading intellectual, and a central figure in the failed attempt to create a St Lucian Cuba, commented in his *Crusader* that it was ironic for the government to spend $70,000 to celebrate the emancipation of the slaves and then charge a $30 entrance fee, 'which is half of a week's salary of a Pompey-type agricultural labourer today'. Otherwise Odlum praised the production and Walcott's play. It was historically appropriate to use the military barracks, a place of bloody battles, treachery, exploitation, and the clash of races. Walcott had progressed from the stylized poetic drama of his youth to a racy earthiness. There is a 'honed-down economy of style language which brings realism and dramatic point'. The characters are down-to-earth rather than literary. Christophe, Toussaint, Dessalines in *Haytian Earth*, unlike in *Henri Christophe*, are 'ordinary men nursing ordinary dreams and ambitions' caught in the web of history, revolution, and change. Walcott's poetry now has the speech rhythms of ordinary men. *Haytian Earth* tells black history in a way that the common man can understand and appreciate. 'Walcott has virtually swallowed his craft of words to allow this unvarnished tale to unfold' and is more sure-footed in the maze of racial tensions than in his earlier poetry where he was haunted by his 'divided skin'. While both the whites and blacks are trapped in the circumstances of history and revolution, the truth is in his handling of Pompey and Yette.[7]

Odlum sees a Hegelian structure within the play. The Haitian revolution is the Thesis. The Anti-Thesis is the treachery of the black generals and the French counter-revolution. The Synthesis is the evolution of the landless slave and agricultural worker Pompey and mulatto Yette as 'the central figures in the struggle for emancipation'. There is maturity and depth of feeling in the performance of Norline Walcott as Yette, which ranges from virginal whore to cocky mulatto. There are beautiful lines in the Pompey–Yette dialogue recalling the lyricism of Walcott's early poetry. 'In the flowering of this beautiful relationship between mulatto-whore and nigger-peasant Walcott makes his crucial statement.' Love is what counts in life. After all the bloodshed, suffering and racial conflict, 'the love of Yette and Pompey comes laughing down the corridors of power, laughing across the barriers of race, mocking the tyrants, tittering at the revolutionaries'. Walcott is cynical of power, politicians, colour, and the church. Though objecting to priests he sees superstition and religion as part of the slave life, part of the history of the people.

While praising the acting talent available for the production, Odlum felt that there was amateurism and failures to bring out full characterization. The show was insufficiently rehearsed, with badly placed props and actors, although the Arts Guild 'troupers' came through the opening night mishaps with 'unruffled competence'. Later performances were more smooth. A weakness of the Arts Guild veterans is to offer the same personalities regardless of the role. Arthur Jacobs, however, acted Toussaint with control and discipline; his movements and speech varied from held pauses to crisp alacrity to sluggish inertia. Jacobs' portrait of imprisoned Toussaint as crumbled resignation was mature acting.

A second review of *Haytian Earth* in *The Weekend Voice* notes the revisionary history. Whereas Haiti had been seen as a story of black heroes, Walcott recognizes 'betrayers, abusers and oppressors of the simple Haitian people'. After the overthrow of the whites, the black rulers had had high hopes but instead left a 'legacy of bloodshed, death and destruction'. Walcott's multiple themes are both universal and relevant to the post-colonial world. He knows our politicians are the pigs of *Animal Farm*. The Haitian revolutionary heroes were the start of 'power-hungry maniacs in government, too ignorant to rule a country, too weak to face their own weaknesses and too inexperienced in power to use it wisely. They are non-whites driven and blinded by egoism and ambition at the expense of the people.' The people were better off as slaves than with Christophe emperor. Revolutionary ideals turn corrupt with power; the leaders think they are indispensable. Walcott's heroes are the common man, the peasant.[8]

Kennedy Samuel continues by examining some of Walcott's symbolism. The country as woman, wife, and whore is expressed in Yette, the whore paid for and abused by a white man, loved by Pompey, raped by Dessalines and hanged by Christophe. The leaders are associated with pig imagery. Christophe is crowned 'Wa Kochon', King Pig. The play is filled with puns, alliterations, and a variety of registers of language. Norline Walcott revealed the restless, frustrated, sensitive woman within the crude, obscene, brash whore. 'The deadly smile she gave to Christophe before her death should haunt all politicians.' Many of the veteran actors lacked competence and were unable to bring out depth of character. Walcott's directing abilities were shown by the integration of the stage crew into the performance, the handling of such a large cast and the visual success of many scenes.

Samuel asks why does the government only find money for the arts when Derek and Roderick Walcott are around? Money should be spent on cultural centres and performance spaces. Why was it possible to build a theatre for Walcott in days when one could not be built before? The cost of the tickets meant that whites and browns were celebrating the emancipation of blacks in a black country. Is Walcott the possession of a certain class of St Lucians? What has really changed since 1834? Are the descendants of the slaves really in control?

Walcott returned to Port of Spain during the New Year holidays and said that he was thinking of staging *Branch of the Blue Nile* in Trinidad, depending on the costs. He asked whether local actors were still getting 'unrealistically high salaries'. ($250 a performance appears to have been the top asking price at the time.) When asked why he did not produce *Joker* again he replied that it would cost 'a half-million dollars in Trinidad today'. The Trinidad Theatre Workshop was talking about reviving *Dream on Monkey Mountain* and asking people to read for parts.[9]

Having in effect deserted Trinidad for several years after his new quarrel with the Trinidad Theatre Workshop and the problems with *The Last Carnival*, Walcott was again available. Brenda Hughes persuaded Walcott to let her Arbee Productions put on *Dream of Monkey Mountain* at the Astor Cinema, with Albert Laveau directing, for two weeks in March 1985. Although some reviewers mentioned that Laveau and Hughes were members of the Workshop, this was not a Trinidad Theatre Workshop production and most of the cast and production team came from outside. Errol Jones, Marshall, and Reid were not involved. Only Hughes, Laveau, and Eunice Alleyne had been in Walcott's own productions of *Dream*. Walcott suggested that the St Lucian actor Arthur Jacobs be brought in to play Makak, the role Jones created during the early workshops. Jacobs had played Toussaint in *Haytian Earth* and had performed in *Hart Crane*, a video film Walcott made, with Nigel Scott, for a proposed American Public Radio series on American poets. Jacobs, who is a wood carver and sculptor, joined the St Lucia Arts Guild under Roderick Walcott in 1959 and attended the first University of West Indies Extra-Mural Department summer school in Drama in 1965. A consistent winner of acting awards in St Lucia, Jacobs, with his beard, looks the part Errol Jones had created. He has a strong presence.[10]

Dream on Monkey Mountain had not been performed in Trinidad for fourteen years and many of the younger generation had not seen it. In the publicity before the opening of its revival it was described as about 'the most devastating type of colonialism—that of the mind and the confusion that results therefrom'. The literary critic and UWI lecturer Patricia Ismond called *Dream* Walcott's most important play and his 'fullest statement on the question of Caribbean freedom and identity'. She interprets Makak as pursuing a dream of African greatness only to learn that the true value is inner freedom. Ismond suggests a parallel political and psychological development in Makak from lowly peasant, through militant overthrowing the white man to independence. Makak is tested by Lestrade's mulatto cynicism, his own egomaniac delusions, and Moustique's exploitation of blackness.[11]

There was a division of opinion about the production, reviewers differing even about the effectiveness of the set, and how well the play had worn. The opening night audience was sparse and hardly responded. The *Express* reviewer felt that it was a good production and praised both Jacobs and Noel Blandin, but thought many of the actors were too conscious of playing roles and the singing was not good. The music was too slow and the rhythms too steady. Patricia Ismond thought that the production's unevenness was the result of having to co-ordinate a play of such scope and such a wide-ranging cast. Albert Laveau, however, had responded to the poetic vision and put together a stylized, total theatre of shadows, light, gloom, and glow, 'through which the waking spirit struggles' to come alive. There was much humour and energy. Jacobs played a 'bemused', 'more sedated' Makak than an ardent hallucinated revolutionary. If he lacked Errol Jones's dominating figure he brought a sense of the rustic setting to the part. Blandin's Moustique had too much comic energy and came close to being a cartoon. Errol Roberts had studied his part of Lestrade, holding back from dominating in the first half, and letting himself go in the second half.[12]

Judy Stone said she had never before heard such a range of conflicting opinions about any one production. At first everyone found it disappointing, then in the second week of the run everyone praised it highly. It had been called lightweight; others found its impact stunning. Some said the pace was monotonous; one 'theatre person' said it was superior to Walcott's 1974 production. One reason for such difference of opinion was that this was an ambitious production organized in a short time and it took a week for the production to come together. Stone agreed that the 'balletic interpretation' of the Apparition did not work (in the execution scene the accused should face the accuser), but she felt that it was a coherent production although lacking in dramatic pointing. The simple set with the help of lighting effects remarkably changed the mood to fit the action.[13]

Stone's comments are significant. She felt *Dream* needed powerful actors and that Jacobs lacked the power of Jones in previous productions; several actors did not have the contrasting builds and personalities for the roles. In other words Stone was seeing the play in terms of Walcott's character types. Also she

missed Derek's eye for tableau, his ability to design the tilt of each actor's head, the height of his hand, his shoulder, his knee, so that each moving tableau had the rhythmic lines of an Old Master; there were tableaux in this production, but with little art in them, and so uncontrolled that actors masked each other and sometimes even a principal speaker.

Wayne Brown, a very good Trinidadian poet and commentator on Walcott, saw a cultural significance in the production and the way it had been approached by the actors. The back to Africa and Black Power 1960s had proved illusions, false dreams; West Indians now placed their faith elsewhere. Yet their psyche still shared in the emotions and earlier history that had created such dreams. Brown wrote that 'at the surface level' Walcott's play had dated, although its depths 'rang true'. The depths called without an echo from the surface and therefore the production risked falling into pure poetry. So much had happened since Walcott wrote *Dream*—the death of Martin Luther King, the unmasking of Trinidadian Michael X as 'a mere murderer', the death of Haile Selassie, the Marxist regime in Ethiopia, the Haitian boat people, the rise of black politicians in the United States, and the famine in Africa—that 'who would be King of Africa now?' Not only had the dream of Africa (and black Haiti) lost its glamour, the Caribbean people had turned Westward, become consumers, living high on oil money or desiring to do so. The mystical glories and glooms of Blackness had faded. Revolutionary fervour had abated, so the surface of the play had dated, thus Jacobs played Makak with bemusement. This left Blandin's Moustique no tragic echo to bounce against comically. If the play lacked tension it is probably because 'it is too late to suspend disbelief in Makak's dreams—and too early by far to disown them'.[14]

Helen Camps's Trinidad Tent Theatre on the Savannah in Port of Spain was thriving with eight productions planned in late 1985. The season began when Walcott's own Warwick Productions presented his *A Branch of the Blue Nile* at the Tent Theatre, with Earl Warner directing, in August 1985. The opening night was preceded by the usual barrage of newspaper articles that Walcott generated as advance publicity. There was publicity parading as articles by 'Theatre Writer' and others during August about some of the actors, Joy Ryan and

Norline Walcott, as well as a careful interpretation of the play which is described as a clever blend of themes from American and British theatre of the 1980s in Caribbean material. Because of leap-frogging backwards and forwards in time, and the play within the play, *Branch* will require attention from the audience. The plot concerns talented Trinidadian actors frustrated by the lack of an established theatre. They are limited to money-making dialect farces produced by a local entrepreneur. Then an English director decides to develop their talent by rehearsing *Antony and Cleopatra*. As they experience the emotional range of their roles, they begin personally to develop through identification with the characters and one actress drops out and joins a religious sect after starting a love affair with a married local producer. While exploring the relationships between the characters during rehearsals, the play shows that the frustrations of life in Trinidad often cause actors to fail to make it abroad in 'white' countries. Those intending to go to the theatre are warned that the dialogue is filled with 'totally relevant undeleted expletives'.[15]

Although Warner had directed the Stage One production of *Branch* in Barbados, this was essentially a Trinidadian company with Norline Metivier the only actor in both productions. The cast was excellent with Joy Ryan, Errol Sitahal, Maurice Brash, Wilbert Holder, Errol Roberts, Devindra Dookie, Noel Blandin, and Sandra Bushell. No foundation Trinidad Theatre Workshop actors were involved, although it could be said that the play was about them in the sense of reflecting arguments that were going on during the Walcott–Trinidad Theatre Workshop era. Ryan and Holder continued to perform both with the Trinidad Theatre Workshop and Walcott. They were highly individualistic, not really part of any group. Sitahal, Blandin, and Dookie were among the better younger actors who had developed outside Trinidad Theatre Workshop circles since 1976. The production team included Brenda Hughes as associate producer, Albert Laveau for set construction, Anthony Gomes as stage manager, and Greer Jones (now Woodham), originally a Trinidad Theatre Workshop dancer, then actress, now costume designer and, along with Walcott and Warner, partly responsible for set design.[16]

Since 1977 Walcott had been on an ad hoc basis assembling a team to replace the Trinidad Theatre Workshop. It included some friends from the Trinidad Theatre Workshop, such as Laveau, some of those who had joined the Trinidad Theatre Workshop in its Dance Workshop expansion, and a number of younger actors and technicians who were coming into the Trinidad theatre world from such new sources as Camps's Tent Theatre and even the government's Best Village shows, which had started to reach a higher standard than previously. Walcott's continuing personal ability to tap sources of support can be seen from the 'Acknowledgments' in the *Branch* programme which include several banks, the National Brewing Company, Angostura Ltd, several trading companies, Amoco Oil, Kentucky Fried Chicken, and Mario's Pizza.

Earl Warner's 'Director's Note' prefacing the programme speaks of *Branch* as envisioning theatre as 'a means towards cultural integrity and self-definition' concerning 'our private attitudes to ourselves'. Warner calls it Walcott's most innovative play, mirroring within its reflections the play within the play and speaks of its Shakespearean compression of the classical and the folk. 'It is rare to have such a powerful company of players.'

Raoul Pantin (RAP), who at times seemed aggressively critical of Walcott's plays and productions, wrote favourably in *Express* of *A Branch of the Blue Nile*. Noting its appreciative audience he said that they would grow larger as word of 'Walcott's tour de force spreads'. Although the play is wordy it 'strikes at truth like an anvil'. Theatre had been Walcott's life for over two decades and it is put under a microscope reasserting his dislike of the philistine world. The production tended to drag but its 'sheer weight of psychic energy' left the audience drained. Pantin found Norline Walcott impressive and was impressed by Dookie. Sitahal played Chris in a matter-of-fact manner between high camp and dreary cynicism. Holder was 'his usual boisterous self'.[17]

Another writer commented that *A Branch of the Blue Nile* was about the Tent Theatre, the Basement Theatre, the Trinidad Theatre Workshop, in being about 'the struggle to reach through the accumulated cultural and social garbage we all have been programmed with to get to something resembling honesty, and about the battle back from that self to express that honestly on stage. It's about the terrifying responsibility of being truly talented.' There is the camaraderie and battles that create a group, and the wound that occurs when the bright and talented leave to gain outside recognition, and the courage of those who remain at home. The play expresses Walcott's affair with the theatre, an affair that includes passion, anger, bitterness, self-laceration, gentleness, fun, and resignation. Walcott has a poet's ear for the rhythms and nuances of Trinidadian speech and has raised dialect from caricature to literature, giving it a legitimacy. Holder combined gentleness with Trinidadian clowning. Norline Walcott's expressively mobile face contributes to her comic abilities. Errol Sitahal did not make a false move, tone, or gesture. He was seemingly effortlessly 'untheatrical'. Devindra Dookie as Phil was the gem of the evening. 'Even his voice cracked in the right places.'[18]

Although Walcott drew on his own experiences in writing *Branch*, which clearly mirrors controversies that occurred in Walcott's relationship to members of the Trinidad Theatre Workshop and the Trinidad Theatre Workshop Dance Workshop, especially controversies about the relationship of classical to folk art and the artist's need to develop his or her talent by leaving home for greater opportunities abroad, the themes, as Pantin observes, grow out of those which have occupied Walcott from early in his life as a writer. The arguments with Slade Hopkinson, Albert Laveau's attempt to make a career as an actor in the United States, the controversy about a Caribbean–American theatre exchange, Walcott's feeling that both Freddie Kissoon and Best Village theatre were misdirecting local talents away from their full potential, were some of the many emotions that went into his play. Perhaps the best tribute to the effectiveness of *Branch* is that many Trinidadians, in recognizing similarities to local theatre history, sought for exact parallels. I have been told by many actors who have been in Walcott's productions that he or she is the basis of a character in the play. Perhaps, but as others make the same claim for the same character it might be better to regard the characters as composites of people Walcott knew over the years, although at times certain speeches and situations might indeed be based on individuals.

Syl Lowhar seemed unable to keep the plot of *A Branch of the Blue Nile* separate from the history of the Trinidad Theatre Workshop and the lives of the actors and the playwright. In his review the play appears like one of those novels based on a real people who can be identified by someone in the know. 'Derek Walcott came alive on stage in the person of Chris.' Sheila, lead actress and folk dancer, represents the Trinidad Theatre Workshop and the Little Carib. Marilyn (Norline Walcott) is the less talented dancer who gets the best parts. 'Walcott is claiming that the theatre which he founded flows like the Blue Nile from the heartland of Africa into Egypt which stood at the crossroads of so many influences . . . He has learnt from Shakespeare, Racine, Chekhov, but has had to develop his own style and medium that has more relevance and meaning to the indigenous folk'. 'Caroni cannot be the Blue Nile' means that Best Village performances must be elevated; the pure water comes from the mountain, not the muddy plain. As in *Dream* it is necessary to kill the alien spirit to become free. The play is frank. 'Here was Walcott's acid commentary on the break-up of the Little Carib Theatre which evolved from the banana background of the folk.' Harvey Le Just, the white man who teaches classical drama, might be Slade Hopkinson or the Company of Players 'playing Shakespeare in Barataria'. This is a decayed colonialism. The first split in the Trinidad Theatre Workshop occurred when Harvey collapses after a disagreement with Chris and receives so much sympathy from the group, 'which fell out of love with Walcott'. There are those actors who went abroad and returned with an accent but could always be relied upon. The confusion in Lowhar's review between the plot of the play and real life shows how closely the audience identified the characters and action with actual people and historical events. As Wayne Brown's review of *Dream* suggested, Walcott's plays have both an actual historical context (although not such a precise correspondence to specific facts as Lowhar feels) and a deeper core of continuing concerns and obsessions.[19]

Later Judy Stone surveyed the local theatre scene and called *Branch* magnificent. Whereas a decade ago Walcott was often too lyrical and long-winded for the stage he is now fully into his stride as a craftsman although still reluctant to bring his plays to a precise conclusion. Many people felt annoyed and baffled by the content in *Branch*, especially the play within the play, as they felt it insulted Caribbean theatre in suggesting its limitations in contrast to the classical. For Stone, however, the main significance was Walcott's love of the theatre.[20]

Walcott returned to Trinidad later in the year to participate in a symposium at the Hilton Hotel, sponsored by the Beryl McBurnie Foundation, on the role of the critic. Other speakers included the Nigerian novelist Chinua Achebe, the London *Times* drama critic Irving Wardle, and Professor Kenneth Ramchand from the University of the West Indies, St Augustine. Whereas Wardle saw metropolitan criticism as advising people where they can get best value for their money, West Indian critics saw themselves more as teachers explaining to the public what the artist intended and the problems involved. The metropolitan critic reviewing a play that is likely to have a run of a month or more advises people what to see; the Caribbean critic whose review is likely to appear after the end of a three-night run of a production is more concerned with the relationship of the arts to a developing society. The symposium suddenly erupted into a controversy which shows just how relevant the issues raised by *A Branch of the Blue Nile* remained in Trinidad and indeed for most of the post-colonial world. When someone in the audience objected that Wardle had no special knowledge of West Indian drama (to which he readily admitted as he is a critic of London theatre) and that only a West Indian could understand West Indian art, Walcott replied that theatre is the art form that is most successful in communicating between cultures. Trinidad, he said, was in a unique position to draw on a multitude of cultures including Africa, England, China, and the Middle East.[21]

The controversy about the relationship of Caribbean theatre to that in Europe and the United States continued. Besides the cultural politics there was a more practical problem that American Equity and many governments raised impossible hurdles to Trinidadian artists who wanted to work abroad. Pat Flores, who had sung in Walcott's plays, was attempting to have a career in European opera and was having visa problems. As a result the Ministry of External Affairs hoped that the government would start lobbying abroad for visas for Trinidadian artists. Walcott continued with his efforts to bring Trinidadian actors to the United States. He had earlier persuaded Joseph Papp to audition Holder and Albert Laveau for a black Shakespearean production, but their West Indian style did not mesh with the black Americans. He had persuaded Papp to audition Errol Sitahal and Devindra Dookie for a leading part that required an Indian actor, but Equity objected and the play had to be cancelled as there was no suitable American Asian Indian actor for the role. Even the invitation of Holder to play the part of Jackson in the St Paul production of *Pantomime* involved a fight with Equity by the Actors Theatre. Walcott continued to feel that Trinidadian actors were extremely talented; he made a videotape of Holder, Sitahal, Dookie, Laveau, Brenda Hughes, Sonya Moze, Nigel Scott, and others to show to American producers.[22]

If Walcott's immediate quarrel was with some of his former associates in the Trinidad Theatre Workshop, especially Errol Jones and Stanley Marshall, there was a longer, more important argument with the politicians who had run Trinidad since independence. He felt that the politicians had not supported the arts. There was no lasting evidence of the impact of his work with the Trinidad Theatre Workshop or the work of Astor Johnson; no theatre had been built, no performance space or attempt to provide continuity. Such a lack of support was a cultural crime as, especially for dance, there would only be ephemeral memories.[23]

During September 1986 Walcott was again in Trinidad, this time to look for possible locations for a filmed version of his *To Die for Grenada*, a new play that would soon open in Cleveland. The New York producer Lawrence Pitkethly, of the Center for Visual History, was with him. While in Trinidad Walcott exhibited his water colours at the Art Creators Limited gallery.[24]

While Walcott often returned to Trinidad to work on his own scripts, give readings of his poems, and sometimes discuss possible reunions with the Trinidad Theatre Workshop there were no more theatre productions by Walcott in Trinidad until the award of the Nobel Prize in Literature brought him and the Trinidad Theatre Workshop together again. While there were revivals in Trinidad of his *Joker*, *Ti-Jean*, *Remembrance*, *Pantomime*, and *Beef, No Chicken*, produced and directed by others, none of his new plays premièred in the West Indies, with one qualified exception in Barbados. Michael Gilkes, who had acted in *Franklin* in Guyana, always felt it was an interesting, neglected work and decided to produce it. For the occasion Walcott provided a revised script and came to the rehearsals. After Barbados, where it played for several weeks during January and February 1990, this production was then taken in March to the Little Carib to celebrate Walcott's sixtieth birthday.[25]

The new *Franklin* was a WWB production directed by Michael Gilkes with Cynthia Wilson as producer. WWB Productions is a Barbadian company formed by Earl Warner, Cynthia Wilson, and Dorsie Boyse, which sometimes offers workshops and uses profits for a theatre arts training programme. The cast included Patrick Foster, who had played in *Pantomime* and *A Branch of the Blue Nile*, Clairmonte Taitt, who had performed in *Beef, No Chicken* as well as the two Walcott plays with Foster, Errol Jones from the Trinidad Theatre Workshop, the Trinidadian Errol Sitahal, and Natasha Seepersadsingh, a Trinidadian who was then a student in Barbados. Jones had played Charbon in Walcott's Trinidad Theatre Workshop productions of *Franklin*. The set was adapted from Richard Montgomery's design. The Trinidadian tour was produced by the Barbados High Commission and the National Drama Association of Trinidad and Tobago. Gilkes' 'Director's Note' in the programme says *Franklin* is 'about the rites/rights of possession and belonging'. What makes someone Caribbean? Both the native and expatriate are strangers. Possession can only result from love, not from narrow patriotism or political or cultural ideologies. 'There is also the question of the growing East Indian community . . . marginalised in most of our societies, seen mainly as business people, traders or agricultural workers.' Although in the majority in Guyana and Trinidad, they have little political power.

Walcott's play suggests that 'a whole, authentic Caribbean society can emerge only if it takes into full account *all* of its parts, especially its three main surviving cultures: Europe, Africa and Asia'.

These views are similar to remarks made by Walcott and Gilkes during the rehearsals. Michael Gilkes points out that besides questioning facile politics, *Franklin* offers rich opportunities for actors and directors.

In almost every character there is a contradictory quality, so you don't go as it were to a superficial character portrayal. Every character, and there are no small or weak characters at all in the play, each character has a complicated response to the Caribbean and to each other. And it is played out on the stage of the great house of the Caribbean which is our set.

During the *Together* interview Andy Taitt questions how Gilkes can say 'we in Barbados' when Gilkes was from Guyana. And, of course, such petty, legalistic distinctions are just what Walcott's play is against. Gilkes replied 'I *am* a Barbadian. I am a citizen of Barbados, unless you are subscribing to this nationalistic, I think rather superficial view that you have to be born in a country to be of it . . . So I see myself as a Barbadian'.[26]

The complexity of the characters is shown by two different reviews of *Franklin* in the Barbados *Daily Nation*. Where one critic thought the play was about St Lucia and the Englishman Pritchett was 'a gin-soaked idiot', a subsequent reviewer said 'the play is about the plight of our Caribbean today, while thinking leadership strives to make it a unified nation'. Pritchett typifies the English who come to the Caribbean hoping to help the unprivileged, only to find that 'his efforts to identify . . . are unsuccessful'. Cursed by the other whites, unable to identify with the underprivileged, isolated, cut off from home, he takes 'some comfort in liquor' but avoids 'the last phase, the "Queen Victoria Club"'. Charbon's problem is that he is the black overseer turned seer. A black ousted from ownership by a white and lacking means of a livelihood he is 'on the way to becoming a dangerous demagogue' in showing '"black people could lead too"'.[27]

The immediate relevance of Walcott's play can be seen from this exchange. The first reviewer felt that unsympathetic portrayal of whites was racism on the part of black intellectuals and advised Barbadians to avoid the play. The second reviewer called such attitudes 'that offensive kind of Britishity which we want most to forget'. It is necessary to learn to swim 'as a team in the world's tempestuous sea', otherwise 'immature nationalism' can create the tidal wave of 'intransigent racism' that has half-drowned Guyana, which threatens Trinidad and which is likely to hit Barbados. From this review we can see reasons why Gilkes, an Indian from Guyana, would find *Franklin* attractive beyond the virtues of the play as theatre. Barbados, often seen as a politically calm 'Little England', has in recent years experienced an increase in violence, racial incidents, and talk of Black Power, and has begun to show signs of a consequent racial polarization. The *Barbados Advocate* headlined its review '*Franklin* shows the Caribbean as a quilt'.[28]

NOTES

1. Kathlyn Russell, 'Walcott's "Haytian Earth" Sets Pace for Arts Revival', *Express* (14 Aug. 1984), 13.
2. Interviews with Dunstan St Omer and Kendel Hippolyte, St Lucia (July 1991). Several people mentioned to me that instructors at School of Drama in Jamaica were unfamiliar with the folk culture of St Lucia and treated it as inauthentic to the region.
3. 'Haytian Earth', *The Weekend Voice* (28 July 1984), 12.
4. Kathlyn Russell, 'The Saint Lucian Theatre Proved a Natural for the Magic of Walcott', *Express* (10 Aug. 1984), 14.
5. Clara Rosa de Lima, 'Walcott's Drama in the Rain Something to Remember', *Sunday Express* (12 Aug. 1984), 14.
6. Adrian Augier, 'The Haytian Earth', *The Weekend Voice* (11 Aug. 1984), 14.
7. George Odlum, '"The Haytian Earth" An Efflorescence of Talent/Walcott Triumphs!', *Crusader*, 14/29 (11 Aug. 1984), 1, 6–7.
8. Kennedy Samuel, 'The Vision & The Reality', *The Weekend Voice* (18 Aug. 1984), 12.
9. 'Buff', 'Good News for Theatre Lovers', *Express* (7 Jan. 1985), 10.
10. Interview with Brenda Hughes, Port of Spain, 1990. Interview with Arthur Jacobs, St Lucia (Aug. 1990).
11. 'La Veau to Direct Walcott's "Dream"', *Sunday Express* (10 Feb. 1985), 39; Patricia Ismond, '"Dream" A Story of Struggle', *Sunday Express* (3 Mar. 1985).
12. Kathlyn Russell, 'Walcott's Monkey Mountain deserves warmer responses', *Express* (12 Mar. 1985), 23; Patricia Ismond, '"Dream" Comes True under La Veau', *Sunday Express* (17 Mar. 1985).
13. Judy Stone, 'Walcott's Dream Wakes Up to New Life', *Trinidad Guardian* (25 Mar. 1985), 21.
14. Wayne Brown, 'Chow Time, King Kong', *Express* (21 Mar. 1985), 10.
15. K. R. [Kathlyn Russell], 'Walcott's Blue Nile is a Drama about Theatre', *Express* (13 Aug. 1985), 23.
16. Anthony Hall, 'Nobody who Knows Greer is Surprised at her Success', *Southern Star* (16 Oct. 1977), 15, 19.
17. RAP [Raoul Pantin], '"Blue Nile" Speaks the Truth', *Express* (1985).
18. 'Walcott's "Blue Nile" at Home in Tent Theatre', *Express* (18 Aug. 1985), 8.
19. Syl Lowhar, '"Blue Nile" a Play for the Young', *People Magazine* (1 Sept. 1985), 16.

20. Judy Stone, 'Superb Surrealism in "Nightmare" ', *Trinidad Guardian* (12 Nov. 1985), 21.
21. Judy Stone, 'We can Gain from Outside Experience', *Trinidad Guardian* (3 Dec. 1985), 17.
22. Stone, 'Derek Pushing our Actors', *Trinidad Guardian* (10 Dec. 1985), 17.
23. William Doyle-Marshall, 'No Real Poet is Ever Proud of his Poems', *Trinidad Guardian* (30 July 1986), 34.
24. Kathy Ann Waterman, 'Walcott play to be filmed here', *Sunday Express* (21 Sept. 1986), 12.
25. ' "Franklin" to be staged in T&T', *W Magazine*, sect. B (17 Mar. 1990).
26. Andy Taitt, 'Powerful Play Speaks of WI Situation', *Together Magazine* (26 Jan. 1990), 4; 'Andy Taitt Interviews Michael Gilkes', *Together Magazine* (26 Jan. 1990), 5.
27. Rothwell, 'Focus', *Daily Nation* (2 Feb. 1990), 25; Richard Allsopp, 'Franklin a Play to See', *Daily Nation* (7 Feb. 1990), 9.
28. Ulric Rice, ' "Franklin Shows the Caribbean as a Quilt', *Barbados Advocate* (21 Feb. 1990), 22.

18

The Trinidad Theatre Workshop
'Let Resurrection Come!'

OVER the decades modern West Indian theatre had developed beyond the small groups that had started in St Lucia, Jamaica and Trinidad during the 1950s and 1960s. The Barn Theatre in Jamaica showed it was possible to have a professional small theatre and the success of Trevor Rhone's plays mapped a new area of subject matter between the high cultural themes of Walcott and the lives of the poor that had formed the subject matter of the plays of the 1940s. Alwin Bully in Dominica, Henk Tjon in Surinam, and Helen Camps developed a new experimental theatre. Roderick Walcott had a body of plays produced in St Lucia. The semi-professionalization of West Indian theatre, one of Walcott's goals, was slowly becoming possible with the development of a local upper-middle-class audience, work on television, and theatre productions which used actors and directors from throughout the region. Walcott's Twilight of the Empire was passing. The New Day had produced a non-white bourgeoisie. The inter-island tours by Errol Jones and Holder were a sign of how far West Indian theatre had come since the time, only a decade earlier, when the Walcott-led Theatre Workshop depended on hospitality to perform outside Trinidad. Now salaries were paid, hotel rooms booked, and it was possible for Errol Jones to be a professional actor. Holder worked on television and the stage. Other actors began as television personalities and moved to the stage. An audience had been created for West Indian plays and theatre performed by West Indians. There was, however, no active theatre company of the same international standard as the Workshop had achieved under Walcott's leadership; there were no regional tours of West Indian plays with immense casts like *Joker* or *O Babylon!*. Rex Nettleford's Jamaican dance company had replaced McBurnie's Little Carib and Walcott's Theatre Workshop as the international attraction.[1]

Earl Warner, who directed *Like Them That Dream* and who was to direct other plays for the Workshop, illustrates the change in West Indian theatre economics. A Barbadian who currently lives in Jamaica, he is probably the first professional West Indian director, travelling between the islands and North America. He has also probably directed more Walcott plays than anyone except Walcott. The Guyanan Ken Corsbie, who lives in Barbados, has, along with Michael Gilkes, developed a reputation throughout the West Indies as a director. In 1980 Corsbie directed Walcott's *Pantomime* at the Little Carib for Helen Camps.

The Workshop without Walcott struggled along at times as an umbrella for Errol Jones's acting, at other times erupting into activity. Walcott had been criticized for not developing other West Indian dramatists, but the Workshop now depended on plays successful elsewhere. A decade earlier the Workshop was the leader in the creation of a West Indian theatre culture, now the leadership had passed to Camps, Bully, Rhone, Gilkes, and Warner. Stage One in Barbados offered productions the Workshop should have had. Camps, Gilkes, Corsbie, and Warner saw themselves as working within Walcott's tradition. The Workshop had the actors, but the lack of a suitable artistic director, regular theatre director, and dramatist working with the company meant that there was no energizing force planning ahead, no one to move the actors in new directions. The Workshop slowly built up a credible record of productions, some of which were outstanding, but the Workshop as an ensemble hardly existed except when some project brought the actors together.

Warner returned to Port of Spain in 1984 to direct the South African play *Woza Albert!* as part of the TTW's Twenty-Fifth Anniversary Celebrations at the Little Carib. This included Wilbert Holder, Noel Blandin, music by André Tanker, lighting design by John Andrews, and set construction by Albert Laveau. The choreography was by Alyson Browne and the mime by Lynette Laveau. The South African subject-matter, the story of Nobel Peace Prize winner Albert Luthuli, was of interest to the West Indies, and the use of elements of commedia dell'arte, mime, and circus added to the interest. That the play had already been a success in New York and London made it a likely hit, as did the presence of Holder, who had become a star of West Indian drama. Blandin had developed from Camps's Trinidad Tent Theatre.

Kathlyn Russell thought the production was carefully crafted and sensitively acted. There was no set, limited props—red clown noses to indicate whites; 'Warner who uses body language as a principal tool of the trade, and whose timing is as precise as a stop watch, has the actors switch persona literally every few seconds, sing, dance and leap about on cue.' The pace of the performance was energetic. Tanker and a percussionist provided music as did the two actors who sang. After a limited run during April the production was taken on tour to Barbados, and reopened in October at the Astor Cinema in Port of Spain.[2]

Sizwe Bansi was revived for a single performance by Holder and Errol Jones at the Amoco Sports and Cultural Club, Mayaro, Trinidad, in September, then for its Twenty-Fifth Anniversary production the Theatre Workshop offered at the Astor Theatre *We Can't Pay, We Won't Pay!* by the Italian Dario Fo. An attractive large programme, '1959–1984 25th Anniversary Trinidad Theatre Workshop', was printed with photographs of many past productions. The director of *We Can't Pay* was Anthony Hall and set construction was by Albert Laveau. The cast included Errol Jones, Brenda Hughes, Stanley Marshall, Sonya Moze, and Errol Sitahal, an extremely good Indian actor, the first Indian to have a principal part in a TTW play for some years. The Astor Theatre is a former movie hall which holds a large audience. *We Can't Pay* ran 16–21 October 1984, and reopened 7–11 November with Syd Skipper replacing Stanley Marshall.

During October the Foyer Gallery of the Astor was used for an exhibition, organized by Judy Stone, celebrating the Workshop's Twenty-Fifth Anniversary. Local newspapers carried articles listing Theatre Workshop productions. In the eight years since Walcott resigned the Workshop had produced an average of more than one play each year—*The Maids, The Dragon Can't Dance, Departure in the Dark, Beef, No Chicken, A 'Nancy Story, Like Them That Dream, Woza Albert!, We Can't Pay, Old Story Time, Smile Orange,* and various productions with which it was associated, such as Helen Camps's *Sizwe Bansi.* Seven of the plays were West Indian.[3]

The Theatre Workshop co-operated with the Caribbean Theatre Guild on restaging Errol John's *Moon on a Rainbow Shawl* for the sixth Trinidad and Tobago Drama Festival. The director was Errol Sitahal; Errol Jones was the only Workshop actor in the cast. Judy Stone remarked that despite the advertising of a joint production this was a CTG show with a guest. The previous year Errol Jones had been 'honoured' by the Festival; this year Slade Hopkinson was brought from Canada to be 'honoured'. This was the fifteenth anniversary of the Caribbean Theatre Guild which Hopkinson founded after he broke with Walcott in 1970. The *Sunday Express* carried in large italic headlines Hopkinson's earlier remark: 'Until there is a theatre based on a drama rooted in Trinidad, the theatre and drama in Trinidad will remain essentially artificial, colonial things, interesting chiefly as symptoms of the psychological sickness of a fragmented, confused people.' Hopkinson, however, had since changed, and moreover was ill and living in Canada. In an interview in the same issue he spoke of the need for West Indian actors to 'handle Shakespeare', praised the greatness of Strindberg, and admitted that he was no longer obsessed by being black and was more concerned with humanness. 'I think we have to stop being neurotic about being black.' 'Was the violence of Idi Amin against Ugandans of an inferior moral grade than the violence of the South African Government? I say not.'[4]

Errol Jones appeared in May 1985 in the Stage One production in Barbados of Walcott's *Beef, No Chicken*, directed by Earl Warner. Judy Stone found this Barbadian production superior to the 1981 TTW premiere. Where Cecil Gray's directing had been pedestrian, the acting lifeless, and the play itself meandering, Walcott had now rewritten part of the script and Warner edited it to make it sharper, more amusing, yet dotted with small personal tragedies. Warner kept the tragic element in sight whereas Gray stressed the comedy. The actresses projected less personality, however, than the quartet of women in the TTW production.[5]

The next Workshop production, September 1985, was Marsha Norman's *Night, Mother*, directed at the Little Carib by Earl Warner, with Eunice Alleyne and Sonya Moze. Stanley Marshall was in charge of the sound. Publicity was better than usual, with articles about the play and production appearing in the local press. This was Earl Warner's fourth play with the TTW. The advance publicity described him as 'The Caribbean's Most Imaginative Director'. Although it included two of the best local women actors, a Pulitzer Prize-winning play and an excellent director, the production was not successful. Anthony Gomes questioned the partial adaptation of an American play to Trinidadian speech. It would be better to keep to the original rather than use an incomplete, uneven adaptation. While Eunice Alleyne's mannerisms portrayed the churning bitterness of a woman groping for self-gratification, Warner shrouded the set with mosquito net and cobwebs, a symbolic metaphor that contrasted to the meaning of the play and the character of the two women. Warner's direction was too heavy in its use of ritual. Judy Stone also objected to Warner's cobweb symbolism, anti-realism, and ritualistic staging. He should have resisted the urge to be a creative director.[6]

The next year, 1986, many from the TTW were involved in the Twenty-Fifth Anniversary programme at the University of West Indies, St Augustine, when Derek Walcott was the recipient of the first honorary degree conferred at the campus. The programme, *Let Resurrection Come!* (the title of a song from *The Joker of Seville*), included excerpts from *Dream*, *Ti-Jean*, *A Branch of the Blue Nile*, *Pantomime*, and *The Joker of Seville*. Those performing included Albert Laveau, Wilbert Holder, Stanley Marshall, Eunice Alleyne, Noel Blandin, Brenda Hughes, and Nigel Scott. The director was Albert Laveau, Brenda Hughes was producer, and André Tanker performed with Michael Boothman's band. The TTW also sponsored a touring visit from the Barbadian Stage One of *Lights Two*, a series of sketches about women, directed by Earl Warner.[7]

For its twenty-seventh anniversary the TTW returned to the Little Carib in late July; Rawle Gibbons directed Athol Fugard's *Boesman and Lena* with Holder, Alleyne, and Errol Jones. Stanley Marshall was producer and in charge of property. Andrews did the lighting. Gibbons, who had been active in theatre since his undergraduate days at UWI, Mona, and who was a tutor in Directing at the Jamaica School of Drama, had recently returned to Trinidad; he suggested *Boesman and Lena* to the TTW. Judy Stone thought it one of the best productions of the TTW since the Walcott era, certainly the best since *Woza Albert!*. 'Eunice Alleyne, as Lena, gives a performance that touches greatness. Bewildered, angry, tender, defiant, she doesn't act Lena, she is Lena.' If this was the outstanding interpretation in Eunice's career 'she has never before had the opportunity of a comparable role nor . . . a director who suited her so well'. The production was taken to St Lucia in January 1987 under the sponsorship of the St Lucian Lighthouse Theatre Company and the Department of Culture.[8]

The continuing usefulness of the TTW's name and its former relationship with Derek Walcott can be seen from the St Lucia *Weekend Voice*, where the headline of a publicity article read 'WALCOTT'S THEATRE WORKSHOP COMING'. The opening paragraph is 'The Trinidad Theatre Workshop, a group formed by world renowned St Lucian poet and playwright, Derek Walcott, arrives here later this month to stage a number of shows based on the South African play *Boesman and Lena*.' The Lighthouse Theatre Company's programme for the production said:

The Workshop has maintained throughout its history a commitment to highly professional standards, to developing a Caribbean style of theatre and to exploring the issues and styles of theatrical traditions throughout the world. The group is in many ways a model of what a Caribbean theatre group should be—rooted in its own environment remaining open to influences from outside. . . . We, of the Lighthouse Theatre and Cultural Department, are honoured to be able to bring this highly acclaimed group to you.

Earlier in January Holder and Jones performed *Sizwe Bansi* in St Vincent.[9]

Plays by West Indian, South African, American, and Italian dramatists, inter-island tours, and guest performances by actors with other theatre companies formed a credible record for those who had kept the Theatre Workshop going, but the Workshop still had no theatre of its own, offered no training to actors, and there was no season of plays, no new plays or dramatists. The Workshop was now essentially a production company drawing from a pool of actors for one or two productions a year. The Workshop reassembled in various forms as needed, usually around Jones, Marshall, Alleyne, Holder, and Scott. New faces who had appeared since 1976, such as Sonya Moze, Patrick Cambridge, and, backstage, Anthony Gomes, were part of the pool upon which it relied. The Theatre Workshop had made West Indian theatre history and could claim to be the senior serious West Indian theatre company that was still active, as well as having many of the best West Indian actors, but in other ways it had been overtaken. Helen Camps had for a time provided more exciting theatre; the young actors she had trained were forming their own theatre companies that managed to make money on productions while the TTW often lost money even on good runs.[10]

Brenda Hughes kept in contact with Walcott and attempted to bridge the differences between him and the others. Having first become aware of the theatre in her teens, when Walcott's TTW productions were the year's main cultural and social happenings, a year without a Walcott play in Port of Spain seems unnatural to her. Where was the excitement of *Joker* and *O Babylon!?* Her Arbee company produced *Dream on Monkey Mountain* in 1985, under Albert Laveau's direction; she was also associate producer of Walcott's own Warwick Productions' *A Branch of the Blue Nile* that year. She produced *Let Resurrection Come!* for the Twenty-Fifth Anniversary of the University of West Indies, St Augustine.

Hughes gained Walcott's agreement for the TTW to perform his comedy *Beef, No Chicken* at the Little Carib during the summer of

1987, although in effect she was producer. Wilbert Holder began as the director but died before the play opened and was replaced by Tony Hall. The cast included such Workshop regulars as Jones, Marshall, Reid, Sonya Moze, and Hughes along with Theresa Awai, Finbar Ryan, Christine Johnson, and Raymond Choo Kong. The TTW was beginning to draw upon the talents of another, younger generation. Lighting remained the responsibility of John Andrews, set design was by Charles Applewhaite, and construction by Laveau. As in other recent production Joy Sitahal was responsible for the costumes.

Holder had hoped to take *Beef* to the next year Carifesta in Jamaica and was holding rehearsals for four hours a night, from 7.30 p.m. until 11.30 p.m. before his death on 14 July. The production of *Beef, No Chicken* ran from a 30 July preview benefit for Holder, until 8 August. The payment for the actors, directors, and stage crew of the production (according to notes on a copy of the programme) was $9,700. Most of the actors received $500 each with minor parts earning $350 to $450. The director was paid $1,500, the stage manager $500, the assistant stage manager $250, while the lighting designer earned $300 and the person in charge of sound was paid $400. This would not have included the costs of renting the Little Carib, author's royalties, cost of costumes and set materials, or publicity. Judy Stone in the *Trinidad Guardian* thought this livelier and funnier than the previous TTW production of the play, but it lacked the energy of the Stage One production Earl Warner had directed in Barbados. The experienced members of the TTW 'seem to be coasting along on their roles, taking the easiest and most accustomed approaches to characterisation'. Although Walcott's revisions made the play much tighter, the role of Mitzi Almondoz, which stole the show in the original production, has been practically 'obliterated'.[11]

During August Ronald John wrote that the TTW had lost its 'magic'. 'Some would even agree that the wit and panache of this well known ensemble disappeared when Derek Walcott ceased being its resident playwright/director. . . . during the '70s a visiting American writer told me, "the standard of theatre here is like off-Broadway back home."' Since Walcott left the TTW had presented some 'flawless' plays but 'the old magic was missing. The ensemble was no more.' Two post-Walcott productions stood out in his mind, *Sizwe Bansi* and *Woza Albert!*, both vehicles for Wilbert Holder.[12]

Wilbert Holder (1935–87) was raised in British Guyana. Like many West Indians he spent his teens playing sports. Unlike most who had their youth in the 'yards' Holder's circle of friends took ballet lessons and became involved with the arts. The yard was owned by Dorothy and Dr Jabez Taitt who loved music. Dorothy was in a choir. Her son Clairmonte Taitt played violin and is an actor with Stage One in Barbados. Ken Corsbie was part of the group as was Michael Gilkes. Holder used to sing in National Festivals where he and Clairmonte Taitt sang duets from Gilbert and Sullivan. He also played pan in the yard steelband. He attended Queens College where he acted and danced in school productions. Corsbie introduced Holder into the Guyana Theatre Guild and he became one of its founding members; he acted in such plays as *Dial M for Murder, Julius Caesar,* and *Summer and Smoke.* The worsening conditions in Guyana drove Holder, and many of his friends, abroad. After emigrating to Trinidad in 1962 he acted in a Company of Players production of Douglas Archibald's *The Rose Slip.* Perhaps because he was an expatriate he joined the Trinidad Dramatic Club. He did not join the TTW until 1968, but became one of its main actors. He often argued with Walcott but remained loyal to him and thought of himself as a Walcottian actor. He had the ability to play or combine Shakespeare and folk. He had extremely good diction and could use dialect. He also had that exuberance and larger-than-life personality on and off stage that characterizes Walcott and those who worked with him. With a quick mind, a memory for scripts, and a talent for mimicry he would take over roles in emergencies. Walcott insisted that he play in the Hippodrome Theatre, Gainesville, Florida production of *Pantomime* (1981) directed by Ken Corsbie.

A videotape of this performance is held at Banyan and shows Holder's tremendous power, sense of timing, and complexity as an actor, especially in his use of voice and body and facial motions. He can play comedy and clown about without losing dignity; indeed he even gains dignity from his sense of irony and subtexts. There is tension and strength under the apparently relaxed surface. He has, however, a tendency to telegraph his responses as if he were preparing for the delivery; this gives him control of the rhythm of repartee but can seem a bit slow.

Holder was a local television personality, a 'household name', hosting a popular morning talk show, acting in films and plays, and directing plays for radio and television. Among his awards were one from the Trinidad government for his role in *Sizwe Bansi,* one from the Caribbean US Theatre Exchange and, posthumously, the Hummingbird award by the Trinidad government for his services to drama. All the newspapers carried appreciations of his work, including a long piece by Judy Stone.[13]

Holder's death, like that of Ermine Wright, deprived the TTW of one of its outstanding actors. Over the years there was an attrition of its stars. Hopkinson resigned. Laveau was concentrating on his carpentry shop and set designs while waiting for the TTW to find a home and begin workshops for which he planned to teach. Hamilton Parris gave up the theatre for family reasons. Nigel Scott was still involved in TTW finances and management but was concentrating on his business. John Andrews and Eunice Alleyne, while available, were increasingly important in the government. Although Jones, Reid, Marshall, Laveau, and Scott had become the core of the company, productions often depended on the energies of younger female associates who had worked with Walcott and who felt unwelcomed by some of the older generation.

The West Indies, and especially Trinidad, remained enamoured of Walcott's plays even if relations with the man were at times difficult. His plays were set texts for the schools and university courses and had begun to attract the attention of literary critics throughout the world. A special Derek Walcott issue of *The Literary Half-Yearly*, published during 1985 in Mysore, India, consisted mostly of articles and research about his plays from scholars in Nigeria, the United States, India, and the West Indies. No one else was the West Indian Shakespeare. Towards the end of November 1987 Rawle Gibbons directed for the Creative Arts Centre at UWI, St Augustine, a student production of *Ti-Jean*, Noble Douglas's Lilliput Children's Theatre performed *Ti-Jean* under Tony Hall's direction, and a major revival of *Joker* was being put together.[14]

Hughes's Arbee productions and the TTW co-operated in a new production of *The Joker of Seville*, directed by Albert Laveau, which played at the Central Bank Auditorium from 26 December 1987 until 9 January 1988. There was a benefit performance for Errol Jones and Beryl McBurnie on 2 January. John Andrews did the lighting and Richard and Sally Montgomery (who designed the set for the Jamaican tour), along with their twelve-year-old daughter, came to Trinidad to do the set and costume design and the masks. The production was originally budgeted by Hughes at $92,000: rental of rehearsal space ($1,500), rental of the Central Bank Auditorium for rehearsals and performances ($8,100), costume design fees ($1,500), costume material and labour ($3,600), director ($3,000), musical director ($1,500), 2 stage managers ($1,500 each), choreographer ($1,300), six musicians ($7,200), 3 principal actors (total $3,900), 11 minor leads ($11,000), 12 supporting actors ($7,800), combined author's and composer's royalties (US

$700; TT $2,500) advertising ($18,000); scripts ($1,200); secretarial services ($1,500), set design and construction ($18,000), design and printing of posters, programmes, flyers ($5,500), stationery and postage ($800).

An idea of the costs can be seen by Barbara Jenson now being paid $1,300 as stage manager and Adele Bynoe $650 for her role. One of the musicians was paid $1,200. Brenda Hughes on Arbee stationery signed the letters of contract on behalf of Arbee Productions and the TTW. It is of interest that of the $92,000 budget about $23,000 was paid to the actors and $2,500 (US $700) was shared by Walcott and MacDermot as author and composer. More than two-thirds of the budget went into the costs of the production. Hughes would later, 26 December 1991–25 January 1992, produce and direct *Pantomime* with Walcott in the audience.[15]

The new Central Bank auditorium was now the preferred place for productions with long runs. Although rental initially cost more than three times the Little Carib and a large deposit was required against damages, the Central Bank Auditorium has computerized lighting and a good sound system (but no real backstage), whereas the Little Carib's costs added up, with nightly performance charges plus a weekly charge and a percentage of the gate. At the Little Carib the lights and sound were bad which meant bringing in your own lights and sound. As the rental of the Central Bank Auditorium drops greatly after the first week, the venue is best for farces, musicals, and other plays likely to have long runs.

The idea of reviving *Joker* was raised by Adele Bynoe at the funeral of Wilbert Holder, when many of the former members of the cast were together for the first time in years. From the original 1974 production Adele Bynoe would once more play the Queen of Hearts, Nigel Scott was Don Juan the Joker, and Stanley Marshall was Don Gonzalo. Claude Reid had played Catalinion in 1975. Others from the original cast and the 1975 revival were taking on new roles. Errol Jones was now Don Diego rather than Catalinion. Brenda Hughes had become Isabella. Carol La Chapelle now assisted with the choreography. Many of the old TTW regulars were involved, including Eunice Alleyne and Charles Applewhaite, but many in the cast were younger actors. There was a new song for Isabella by Galt MacDermot. The production was video-taped by both Brenda Hughes and Richard Montgomery, and a recording of the music from the original production was issued for sale to the public. There were also T-shirts for sale.[16]

Judy Stone found the new *Joker* memorable for the visual beauty of the costumes, the tableaux, the lighting, the set, and the movement. There was a beauty in the texture and tones of the costumes with their pastels, natural straw and 'grimy white'. The tying and draping contributed to an awareness of lines. Clara Rosa de Lima also praised the way Richard Montgomery used basket weaving for the costumes, especially in the collars and hats. Stone said that the dances were lively, witty, dramatic. The large cast 'flows picturesquely in and out and about the stage'. Nigel Scott as Don Juan was now more a world-weary, more comprehensible Don Juan and depended less on ingenuous charm. Instead of Laurence Goldstraw's dignified King of Castille, Raymond Choo Kong offered a possible alternative interpretation in 'camping up' the role. The silhouetted seduction of Isabella (Brenda Hughes) was not credible. The script had been interpreted poorly by many actors, especially by the newer members, who missed the 'inner meaning' of lines.[17]

Ken Jaikeransingh wrote that the theme of *Joker* was freedom, especially the challenge to repressive other-worldliness, and saw in it the discovery of new worlds, especially the freedom of the Caribbean. Don Juan was Caribbean man. In the new revival the score had been slowed down to enable a greater focus on the poetry. Whereas the arena staging in the Little Carib Theatre allowed for an immediacy between actors and audiences, the proscenium stage at the Central Bank prevented such a relationship. The musicians were obscured from view, but the entrances and exits of the actors through the audience attempted to recreate some of the original immediacy. Claude Reid as Catalinion could have been more laconic, more of a Sancho Panza. Charles Applewhaite as Rafael lacked the authority and cynicism of the character. Although the spirit of *The Joker* was still alive, this production missed the mark. Another critic appreciated Sonja Dumas's carefully rehearsed Tisbea, which draw laughter from the audience as she brought out the sexual implications of Walcott's metaphors, but complained that the second half of the production felt long-winded. Jan Murray, a Canadian dance critic and arts journalist who was in Trinidad, called the production leaden, unpoetic, and lacking pace; most of the cast could not sing or speak the complex lines with clarity or understanding. Murray only had praise for Sonja Dumas as Tisbea.[18]

The TTW finished the 1988 season with a production of Dario Fo's farce *Accidental Death of an Anarchist*. This was advertised as the Twenty-Ninth Anniversary production and ran for two weeks in August at the Little Carib. Rawle Gibbons directed and Marshall was producer. The actors included Jones, Errol Fabien, and Patrick Cambridge. Joy Sitahal was in charge of make-up and costumes; Laveau constructed the set. During the year Errol Jones, Stanley Marshall, and Claude Reid continued to act in the productions of others, including the Malick Folk Performers and a stage version of Lovelace's novel *The Wine of Astonishment*.

For the thirtieth anniversary of the TTW there were elaborate negotiations with Walcott concerning a possible reunion. Walcott was excited by the prospect and talked about inviting Wole Soyinka, Joseph Brodsky, and other international literary stars, but both sides had different perspectives which represented points of view formed years ago. If anything the two sides had grown further apart. Walcott wanted several American actors. The costs would have been enormous for the Workshop which once more objected to importing foreign actors. There was talk of doing Shakespeare's *Othello*, but whereas Walcott wanted a white Desdemona, the Workshop wanted an Indian as the white–black conflict of the past had been superseded by tensions between Trinidadian Asian Indians and those of African descent. If he could not import an American, Walcott wanted to cast one of the white women who had played in his past productions. Those days, however, were now long over. Helen Camps was seldom in Trinidad, had developed other interests beyond the theatre and would soon begin working towards a university degree in Ireland. Judy Stone was now a mother trying to make a living as a freelance journalist. In the meantime the best theatre space for such a production, the Central Bank Auditorium, had been booked by others.[19]

Brenda Hughes was asked about producing a play at the Irvine Bay Hotel in Tobago for a few nights in August. She turned the request over to the TTW which staged Rhone's *Smile Orange* with Laveau directing. Marshall, Hughes, Errol Fabien, Learie Joseph, and Peter Kelly were the actors. The production then moved in late September 1989 to the Little Carib for two weeks and returned to Tobago in November for two nights. The TTW had produced *Smile Orange* in 1982 and Rhone's *Old Story Time* in 1979. While theatre economics make Rhone's plays attractive and they are likely to be successful, they are not ambitious. During 1989 there were at least two productions of Walcott's plays in Trinidad by other companies, *Malcochon* by Theatre Studio and *Remembrance* by Bagasse Company at the Central Bank Auditorium. The TTW appeared directionless, bogged down in old disputes, and unable to move beyond occasional, if excellent, productions.[20]

Appearances were deceiving; during August 1989 the Trinidad

Theatre Workshop found a home. Eric Williams had refused to put money into a national theatre and élite arts; he found it politically more expedient to promote a folk culture and theatre based on the villages. After Williams lost power the situation loosened up slightly and through friends in the government the TTW rented the 94-year-old Old Fire Brigade Station on Hart Street for a five-year lease.[21]

The TTW began immediately with the help of architects to plan the conversion of the Old Fire Station into a theatre, with a formal auditorium, gallery, sound and light equipment, rehearsal space, and rooms to hold acting classes and workshops. Outside, using bleachers left from the Tent Theatre, they hoped to have an amphitheatre. The TTW was incorporated as a non-profit company and a board of directors formed, which included Nigel Scott. The management committee was Brenda Hughes, Eunice Alleyne, Stanley Marshall, and Errol Jones. Albert Laveau spent most of his time on the conversion, informal classes were being held, and plans were under way to inaugurate the new theatre with Rhone's *Two Can Play*, when an attempted Black Muslim (the Jamaat-al-Muslimeen) *coup d'état* on 27 July 1990 threw Trinidad into chaos for many months. The Red House, the parliamentary building across from the Old Fire Station, was in the hands of the revolutionaries who held most of the government officials hostage, wiring some of them with explosives. Government troops regained the Old Fire Station and used it as a base of operations. Shots were exchanged and a rocket hit the Old Fire Station.[22]

After life returned to near normal the Old Fire Station needed further repairs. *Two Can Play* opened instead at the Little Carib where it ran for twenty-two performances between 18 October–11 November 1990. The director was from the younger generation, John Isaacs. The actors were Brenda Hughes and Peter Kelly. The opening night was attended by the Prime Minister and the Culture Minister, accompanied by armed soldiers. The original script was revised so that instead of being set in Kingston during the political violence of the late 1970s the play now took place in Port of Spain with mortar and rocket explosions replacing the original gunshots. The play only took two hours so that people could return home well before the 11 p.m. curfew each night.[23]

This was a young production, old wounds were ignored. Brenda Hughes was in charge of production management, marketing, and promotion. Norline Metivier, whose relationship with Walcott had been a cause of the events that led to his resignation, was assistant to the production manager and assistant to the stage manager, John Isaacs;

Albert Laveau shared responsibility for the set. In the programme the board now included Barbara Jenson as Business Manager along with Jones, Marshall, Scott, Laveau and six others, mostly from the business community. The aim of the new School for the Arts was: a Resident Theatre Company, a Resident Dance Company, a Theatre Arts Training Programme, a Children's Theatre, a Playwright's Workshop, and an Audio-Visual Programme. As in Walcott's days, the TTW was attempting on its own to do the job that should have been done by a government-sponsored National Theatre or Performing Arts Centre, or by a university faculty of Performing Arts. Plans were for at least two productions a year.

The 1991 Cacique Awards, a new event to celebrate the best Trinidadian theatrical achievements of the past year, went to John Isaacs for *Two Can Play* and the best actress award was shared between Brenda Hughes and Carol La Chapelle (who had returned recently to acting). In late January the TTW circulated a request to organizations and institutions for twenty thousand dollars for security gates, repairs, lighting, and plumbing. It had already repaired the roof and sanded the floor (to be used by 'the dance department'). The object was to establish a School of Arts. Later in 1991, from July until September, the TTW—under the management of Jones, Marshall, and Scott and with Laveau as Artistic Director—started giving its first classes in acting, directing, voice, speech, playwriting, and other theatrical arts at the Old Fire Station.

For those who want an American or British happy ending the story of the TTW between 1977 and 1991 must seem puzzling; it is a Caribbean equivalent of a success story, like the conclusion of V. S. Naipaul's *A House for Mr Biswas* where the triumph may seem small by North American standards unless one considers how far one had to travel, and in what difficult circumstances, to have made such progress. The Old Fire Station was the first home that TTW had had since they were evicted from the Basement Theatre in 1968 and it is the first potentially important new centre for the performing arts in Port of Spain since the founding of the Little Carib in 1948. That the Trinidad Theatre Workshop remained active since it was founded in 1959 is remarkable, especially in the West Indies. It survived without Walcott since 1977. It has continued annually, and sometimes more often, to perform West Indian plays and serious drama when other theatre groups have survived on foreign comedy and farce. It provided the region with some of its best actors. By way of Helen Camps it gave birth to a new generation of actors and theatre companies. One need only see productions by other theatre groups on other West Indian islands to realize just how much the region gains by having a core of experienced serious actors who regard themselves as professionals, and work to achieve professional standards. Four of the first six persons to receive the Award of Merit of the National Drama Association of Trinidad and Tobago were from the TTW—Errol Jones, Slade Hopkinson, Wilbert Holder, and Stanley Marshall. When the history of post-colonial culture is written a central story should be that of Walcott's life in West Indian theatre, the years he devoted to the Trinidad Theatre Workshop, and the way Walcott, Jones, Laveau, and others created a West Indian theatre culture of international standards. Like many West Indian stories, it is a frustrating tale of only a partial success, but, I think, one of the more significant stories of our time.

Resurrection is one of the recurring themes of Walcott's plays, where it is, surprisingly, less a miracle or regeneration through the young than the effect of hard work, struggle, and conflict. Walcott often writes of 'faith', but he has a particularly Protestant notion, shaped by his Methodist heritage, of 'faith' in the God within each individual; faith is the courage to strive to fulfil one's talents regardless of the circumstances. An example occurs in *Pantomime* where Jackson comically uses a folding chair to demonstrate how a West Indian Robinson Crusoe would not give up when faced by a hostile environment, but having seen a goat would fight it, man to man, and would build his own world and empire from his victory, finding food, clothing, housing, and symbols of authority in what Trewe considers a life of defeat and an environment alien to his British notions of civilization. The Theatre Workshop's struggle with its goat began when it started in 1959, and for a time it was in a crisis after Walcott resigned in 1976; then slowly faith returned. But it was not until 1990, with the rental of the Old Fire Station, that reconversion of its goat became a serious objective rather than a dream. At first slowly, then as a consequence of Walcott's Nobel award rapidly, the Workshop experienced renewal. Teaching of the performing arts started, and a theatre, called the Wilbert Holder Theatre, was built with the capacity for about 190 in the audience. During December 1992 there was a *Celebration* of scenes from Walcott's plays at the Old Fire House, performances in St Lucia, and productions of *Henry V* and Wole Soyinka's *Swamp Dwellers* for a new Theatre in Education project. In 1993 *Celebration II* was performed, and then staged under Walcott's direction in Boston on 26 April, after which the Workshop's *Pantomime* (directed by Walcott with Nigel

Scott and Claude Reid) opened Walcott's *Boston Playwrights' Theatre*, 28 April–1 May; then *Celebration II* toured the West Indies.[24]

By 1993 resurrection had come. Walcott rejoined the Workshop to begin rehearsals of a dramatized reading at the Old Fire House of his *The Odyssey*, scheduled for 5–8 August, and directed and designed by Gregory Doran of the Royal Shakespeare Company, who commissioned Walcott's adaptation of Homer's epic and directed the play in Stratford and at the Barbican Arts Centre in London. Actually there was a preview on 4 August, a gala the next night, 5 August, but because of the threat of tropical storm Brett the performance of 6 August was cancelled. Because of demand, however, the run extended from 7 August to 11 August. Further performances could not be held as rehearsals had to begin for a revival of *Dream on Monkey Mountain*. These may seem petty details, but to understand how working conditions differ in the Caribbean from, say, New York, it is necessary to be aware of how a tropical storm, attempted revolution, or the opportunity for an overseas tour may affect the run of a scheduled theatre production. That is part of the context in which West Indian culture is created. The Workshop published with the programme for *The Odyssey* a revised, updated, and still incorrect chronology of productions.[25]

The Odyssey requires a large cast and the Workshop reassembled with Jones, Scott, Joy Ryan Gomez, Eunice Alleyne, Belinda Barnes, Albert Laveau (who was now acting as well as teaching), Stanley Marshall, Charles Applewhaite, Brenda Hughes, Laurence Goldstraw, and Carol La Chapelle. Carol La Chapelle was in charge of the choreography and Greer Jones Woodham was responsible for costuming. With John Andrews busy in government affairs, lighting became Ronald Rudder's responsibility. Reviewers and Doran were impressed by the way the younger generation—John Isaacs, Leah Gordon and Cecilia Salazar (a member of the Bagasse Company and Peter Minshall's Callaloo Company)—fitted into the company and were themselves rapidly becoming disciplined, vigorous actors. Parts of Walcott's play began to take on a new light in Trinidad. Doran mentioned that the Shango ceremony, before Odysseus descends to the Underworld, had a fiery rhythmic life in the TTW production that it lacked in England. Raymond Ramcharitar's review was headlined 'Odyssey—Best Production to Hit TT Theatre in Years'. Eunice Alleyne, Cecilia Salazar, and Walcott (as Menelaus) participated in a reading of *Odyssey* in New York on 20 September; 21–22 September the TTW performed *Dream on Monkey Mountain*, and 23–24 September *Celebration II*, at the Afro-Caribe Festival in Rotterdam, Holland.

The casts included Errol Jones, Stanley Marshall, Albert Laveau, Nigel Scott, Claude Reid, Adele Bynoe, Carol La Chapelle, Charles Applewhaite, and a recent discovery, Glenda Thomas. Albert Laveau was now TTW Artistic Director and Carol La Chapelle Choreographer. Although there were a few new faces, such as Wendell Manwarren, the continuity of the Workshop was remarkable. Allison Guerra, one of the dancers of the mid-1970s in *Joker*, who had since then worked as a dancer and choreographer in Europe, returned to Trinidad, and married, was again with the company as Allison Seepaul, a dancer in *Celebration* and the Apparition in *Dream*. Even the same problems continued. She was now a school teacher who had to return directly to her classes from tours abroad, teaching the day after she returned. *Dream* was performed in Port of Spain and tours during 1994 to St Lucia, St Croix, St Thomas, Boston, and Singapore were being planned. *Celebration*, *The Joker of Seville*, *Pantomime*, *Dream on Monkey Mountain*, and *The Odyssey* were currently available for performances.

The Workshop was not only fully active but Walcott demanded the same energy as in the past when he would expect actors to begin rehearsals immediately after arriving in a foreign land, construct a set late at night after rehearsals, rehearse the next morning and afternoon, and perform that night. Some of the foundation members were now in their sixties and seventies, yet they kept up with the younger ones in their twenties! During the April 1993 Boston tour I, and others who were following the events, had often gone to bed before the actors were finished rehearsing, yet they were rehearsing in the morning before we arrived.[26]

When, in 1990, I began my research about Derek Walcott and the Trinidad Theatre Workshop, I thought I was writing about theatre history, something in the past. Very little had appeared about the Workshop in academic publications and this seemed almost totally unmapped territory. As I began reading West Indian reviews of productions, West Indian interviews with Walcott and his actors, and articles in West Indian magazines by Victor Questel, Patricia Ismond, and others, I saw that there was indeed much written about my topic, but it had somehow fallen outside the usual boundaries of academic scholarship. Who was interested in a West Indian theatre company? As I put dates, productions, tours, and cast lists together into a chronology, I realized that what I had assumed to be a minor amateur local acting company was in fact a remarkable story about Walcott, and about West Indian and post-colonial theatre and culture, a view that was supported by American and British theatre directors who had seen the TTW and thought it one of the best ensembles in the world, although working in the worst imaginable conditions. Surprisingly the story of the TTW kept intersecting with the recognized history of modern theatre: the Actors Studio, the O'Neill Foundation, the Royal Shakespeare Company, the Negro Ensemble Company, the Rockefeller Foundation, Roscoe Lee Browne, André Gregory, Joseph Papp, and Galt MacDermot, all came into the story.

I had come to the story at either the worst or best time. The Workshop's plans for a thirtieth anniversary reunion with Walcott floundered on the same disagreements that had kept them apart for years and the two sides now seemed to live in different worlds. Walcott now had and expected American money; his plays had not made Broadway, but their American productions were reviewed in *Time* and *Newsweek*. *O Babylon!* had even been staged in London. The Workshop was seemingly bogged down on its own, without much money or even a secure lease, in reconverting an old abandoned fire station into the national centre for the arts, a dream that had been the theme of endless newspaper articles by Walcott and others since the late 1950s. These may be great actors (I had not yet seen any of them perform) but they appeared inept at raising and keeping money. Lumber for the rebuilding was stolen and even a small barbecue I attended lost money. This was a great love story which after the divorce had left both sides still desiring the other, yet it seemed that after 1976 the TTW and Walcott had become two separate identities which were unlikely to come together again.[27]

I had not then understood that the longings which prompted Walcott to suggest that I should write a history of the TTW were not nostalgia for the past, but were part of a continuing vision that he had formed in the late 1950s and which he shared with Errol Jones, Stanley Marshall, Albert Laveau, and others. Not being West Indian I also did not understand how much it meant to them, nor did I have the same long-range vision in which men in their sixties could still be struggling towards goals they had set in their twenties. I should have known. Walcott's plays and poems concern the need to be a new Adam, a Crusoe, the need for dedication, struggle, and conflict to build a new 'home' in the West Indies. Walcott was always on the telephone to Trinidad, and he spent part of each year there. Slowly, patiently, with many setbacks, the Fire Station was being converted. Walcott's plays were once more getting attention abroad. Besides American productions and the commission to write *The Odyssey* for the Royal Shakespeare Company, he directed *The Last Carnival* at the Theatre Royale in Stockholm. He kept complaining that he needed his West Indian actors.

The Nobel award was the catalyst needed to bring the TTW and Walcott together again. Rapidly what had seemed almost dormant became alive and I was no longer writing about theatre history, but about living contemporary theatre. Each attempt to write concluding paragraphs had to be abandoned as I learned of new plans, new performances, and new details. I had long been troubled by the problem of shaping what seemed two overlapping topics—a history of the Trinidad Theatre Workshop and a biography of Derek Walcott's life in West Indian theatre—into one book. Now there was still another book to be written concerning the resurrection of the Trinidad Theatre Workshop under Walcott's leadership and it would somehow need to be squeezed into my manuscript.

I had come across, and had not understood, the story of Walcott and the TTW when I began reading West Indian literature during the 1970s. I was puzzled by 'What the Twilight Says', Walcott's 'Overture' to *Dream on Monkey Mountain and Other Plays*, with its allusions to rehearsals, fights, performances on various islands, actors who were an extension of himself, and 'the last one among us who knows of the melodies of the old songs fakes his African'. As co-editor of a series of books on Modern Dramatists I tried, without success, to find someone to write about Walcott's plays in performance. Even now the story is not over. Walcott's earliest articles for the *Trinidad Guardian* were about the need for a national theatre; over thirty years later at a celebration at the Old Fire Station he said 'I prefer the building to the Nobel Prize' and the Workshop members were still raising money for the building and fighting the new government's plans to evict them as part of a scheme to redevelop downtown Port of Spain. While the University of the West Indies was bragging that it would become an international centre for research on Walcott and was talking of creating a Derek Walcott Professorship of Creative Writing, the politicians had decided that the Old Fire Station could not become a Walcott Centre for the Performing Arts, but had to be torn down to make way for a future National Library; there were vague promises of building in the future a national centre for the arts which the Workshop might use. Walcott said that he would donate part of his Nobel Prize money to the Workshop and would spend part of each year directing and teaching theatre in Trinidad if the Workshop was allowed to keep the Old Fire Station. Little had changed since the 1950s and 1960s when Eric Williams made promises of building a national cultural centre and

Walcott was writing newspaper articles about the actors' immediate need for a Little Theatre and scholarships for training rather than unsuitable grandiose schemes for the future. There was even the same vague talk about linking the future arts centre and the TTW to the university and Walcott was once more angrily protesting the government's mistreatment of its artists. However, books must conclude and this one might as well end here.[28]

The first book I wrote was a study of John Dryden's plays which in passing asked how Dryden's plays and Restoration drama were performed. I had found some evidence that what we now read as straight-faced heroics was then acted with ironic awareness and to gain a 'laugh of approbation'. Later research suggested that there had been a long tradition of such acting until the late seventeenth century. To understand drama we need to know how plays were acted, especially by those who worked with the dramatist or who understood the performance conventions. Except for still photographs and a badly shot shortened version of *Dream on Monkey Mountain*, there is no visual record of the Trinidad Theatre Workshop as directed by Walcott. Proper equipment was not available in the West Indies, the cost was too much, and what was filmed has disappeared. If I and others are right in thinking that Walcott is a major dramatist and the Trinidad Theatre Workshop the company that can best perform his plays, then it is necessary, if only as a historical record, to film productions of Walcott's plays with him directing his company while it is still possible. It is a debt we owe to the future. Is Walcott the Shakespeare of our time? Is he perhaps only the Webster or Marston of our time? I doubt that such comparative evaluations matter. Think, however, if we had a visual record of performances of the plays by the actors of their time who knew what the dramatists wanted.[29]

NOTES

1. Ken Corsbie, *Theatre in the Caribbean* (London: Hodder and Stoughton, 1984).
2. Kathlyn Russell, '"Woza Albert" Scores a Hit', *Express* (14 Apr. 1984); '"Woza Albert" Story of Luthuli', *Trinidad Guardian* (13 Apr. 1984), 20; 'Woza (Rise up) Albert!', *Sunday Express* (8 Apr. 1984), 45–6; 'Wilbert Holder Back at Little Carib Theatre', *Sunday Guardian* (8 Apr. 1984), 19.
3. 'Astor Foyer Exhibition No. 2, 9th October–3rd November 1984, Twenty-Five Years of the Trinidad Theatre Workshop' (Judy Stone's files); 'Theatre Workshop—The First 25 Years', *Sunday Express* (8 Apr. 1984), 46.
4. Judy Stone, 'Savage Lives in West Indian Backyard', *Trinidad Guardian* (10 June 1985), 25; Kathy Waterman, 'A Man Called Slade', *Sunday Express* (9 June 1985), 29.

5. Judy Stone, 'Warner's *Beef No Chicken* an Inspired Production', *Caribbean Contact*, 13/1 (June 1985), 14.
6. Antony Gomes, 'An Evening of Choices Facing Contemporary Women', *Trinidad Guardian* (20 Sept. 1985), 16; Stone, 'Superb surrealism', *Trinidad Guardian* (12 Nov. 1985), 21.
7. Judy Stone, 'Crowds Enjoy Slices of Derek Walcott Plays', *Trinidad Guardian* (24 Apr. 1986), 21. The programme for *Let Resurrection Come!* credits Brenda Hughes as 'Producer—on behalf of The University of the West Indies (St Augustine)'. The selections from *Dream, Ti-Jean, Pantomime* and *Joker* look forward to excerpts in the 1992–93 *Celebration II*.
8. Judy Stone, 'Eunice Alleyne does not Act Lena, She Is Lena', *Trinidad Guardian* (13 Aug. 1986), 24; Judy Stone, 'Rawle Gibbons Makes Time to Direct', *Trinidad Guardian* (22 July 1986), 17; Kamla Rampersad, 'A Look into the Souls of Racism', *Express* (3 Aug. 1986).
9. 'Walcott's Theatre Workshop Coming', *The Weekend Voice* (24 Jan. 1987), 13.
10. Judy Stone, 'Theatre Life: Camps Taught . . .', *Trinidad Guardian* (2 Oct. 1987), 16.
11. Judy Stone, 'Wilbert would have been Proud of "Beef" performance', *Trinidad Guardian* (11 Aug. 1987).
12. Ronald John, 'Trinidad Theatre Workshop Magic is Gone', *Trinidad Guardian* (16 Aug. 1987), 18.
13. Judy Stone, 'Brotherhood of the Yard', *Sunday Guardian* (16 Aug. 1987), 18, 19, 25. Raoul Pantin, 'A Life Devoted to Life', *Express* (20 July 1987), 9. 'The Final Farewell to Wilbert Holder', *Sunday Express* (19 July 1987); Judy Stone, 'Wilbert Holder Left a Vacuum in Trinidad Theatre', *Trinidad Guardian* (13 May 1988), 14.
14. *The Literary Half-Yearly*, 'Derek Walcott Number', 26/1 (Jan. 1985).
15. Arbee Productions, *The Joker of Seville* budget, dated 30 Sept. 1987. Various letters during November from 'Brenda Hughes for Arbee Productions', offering terms of employment. The apparent haste with which the production was assembled is suggested by an undated Arbee Productions 'Press Release' saying *Joker* 'is being directed by Rawle Gibbons'.
16. Stone, 'Walcott's "Joker" returns' (30 Dec. 1987).
17. Judy Stone, 'Magnificent Directing by Laveau', *Trinidad Guardian* (7 Jan. 1988), 9; Clara Rosa de Lima 'Walcott's "Joker" most impressive', *Trinidad Guardian* (14 Jan. 1988), 8.
18. Ken Jaikeransingh, 'This "Joker" missed the mark', *Express* (5 Jan. 1988), 16; ' "Joker of Seville" is in town', *Express* (1 Jan. 1988), 25; Jan Murray, 'The Joke was on the Joker', *Sunday Express*, sect. 2 (10 Jan. 1988), 8, 13.
19. During late June 1990 I attended a Workshop meeting at which Walcott's plans for *Othello* were discussed.
20. During July 1990 Brenda Hughes told me that she had passed on to the Workshop the request that she produce *Smile Orange*.
21. 'Drama gets home at Old Fire Headquarters', *Trinidad Guardian* (3 Aug. 1989), 3.
22. Terry Joseph [T. R. J.], ' "Two Can Play" Plays Little Carib Oct. 18', *Trinidad Guardian* (5 Oct. 1990), 22; Terry Joseph, 'The Arts', *Sunday Guardian* (28 Oct. 1990), 5.

23. Terry Joseph, 'Peter Kelly Finally Takes the "Award"', *Trinidad Guardian* (25 Oct. 1990), 16.
24. Walcott, *Remembrance & Pantomime* (1980), 121, 146–8.
25. Information about performances of *The Odyssey* from a letter Brenda Hughes to Bruce King (Oct. 1993) and Simon Lee, 'Sailing to Ithaca', *Sunday Guardian* (22 Aug. 1993), 3–4. The new incorrect 'official' chronology fails to distinguish between shows the TTW produced and those it sponsored and claims credit for productions by others such as the West Indian Arts Festival, the 1965 Carnival show, Arbee Productions, Walcott's own post-TTW productions, *Haytian Earth*, etc.
26. Raymond Ramcharitar, 'Walcott's *Odyssey* won't be Easy to Direct', *Trinidad Guardian* (27 July 1993), 17; 'Stratford Director Meets Calypso Lingo', *Sunday Express* (1 Aug. 1993), 4, 8; Raymond Ramcharitar, 'Odyssey—Best Production to Hit TT Theatre in Years', *Trinidad Guardian* (10 Aug. 1993), 13; Judy Raymond, 'Fascinating First Glimpse of Walcott's Latest', *Sunday Express* (8 Aug. 1993).
27. For the Riverside Theatre production, see Edward Pearce, 'Oh, Babylon', *Encounter*, 70/5 (May 1988), 76.
28. Walcott, 'What the Twilight Says', in *Dream on Monkey Mountain* (1970), 3–27. Kevin Baldeosingh, 'Walcott Seeks Home for Theatre Workshop', *Express* (17 Nov. 1992); Anthony Milne, 'I Prefer the Building to the Nobel Prize', *Express* (20 Nov. 1992), 33; Judy Raymond, 'Future Site of Walcott School for Arts?', *Sunday Express* (22 Nov. 1992), 2; Wayne Brown, 'A Home for Mr Walcott', *Sunday Guardian* (22 Nov, 1992); Yuille-William, 'Statement by the Hon. Minister of Community Development, Culture and Women's Affairs in Respect of the use of The Old Fire Brigade Station Currently Occupied by the Trinidad Theatre Workshop' (12 Jan. 1993); 'A Home now for Mr Walcott', *Sunday Express* (14 Jan. 1993), 8; Judy Raymond, 'Enter a New Set of Strolling Players', *Sunday Express* (17 Jan. 1993); Kay Baldeosingh, 'Walcott: Immoral to Move Workshop', *Daily Express* (5 July 1993), 1, 4.
29. Bruce King, *Dryden's Major Plays* (Edinburgh: Oliver & Boyd, 1966).

Theatre Calendar

THE Theatre Calendar covers the work of the Trinidad Theatre Workshop, and also some other non-TTW productions, which are marked (*). Unless otherwise listed the productions are in Port of Spain.

1958

* 25, 27, 28–30 April and 1 May World Premiere of *Drums and Colours*, by Derek Walcott, dir. by Noel Vaz, with Mrs Dagmar Butt and Errol Hill as 'guest producers'. West Indies Festival of the Arts. Royal Botanical Gardens.

* 27–9 June *Ti-Jean and his Brothers*, by Derek Walcott, and prod. and dir. by Walcott. Little Carib Theatre.

* 2 July *Ti-Jean*. San Fernando.

1959

11 December (before private audience). *Showcase 1*, six scenes from four plays and an adaptation of 'Basement Lullaby' by Sam Selvon. Plays: Errol John's *Moon on a Rainbow Shawl*, Tennessee Williams's *This Property is Condemned*, Shaw's *Saint Joan*, and Arthur Miller's *The Crucible*. Dir. by Walcott and others. Little Carib Theatre.

1960

1961

1962

11–13 May Double bill. *Krapp's Last Tape*, by Samuel Beckett; dir. by Walcott. *The Caged*, by Dennis Scott; dir. by Slade Hopkinson. Little Carib Theatre.

7–10 December *The Charlatan*, by Derek Walcott, dir. by Walcott and Slade Hopkinson, with lyrics also by Walcott. Little Carib Theatre.

1963

1964

22–4 January Double bill. *The Lesson*, by Ionesco. *Malcochon*, by Derek Walcott. Both dir. by Walcott. Little Carib Theatre.

[n.d.] *The Lesson* and *Malcochon*. Guild Hall, University of the West Indies, St Augustine, and Naparima Bowl, San Fernando.

1965

* *28 February*   *Batai*, by Derek Walcott, and dir. by 'Derek Walcott of Theatre Workshop'. Carnival Development Committee. Savanah.

1966

7–12 January   Double bill. *Sea at Dauphin*, by Derek Walcott, and dir. by Walcott. *Zoo Story*, by Edward Albee, dir. by Walcott. Basement Theatre, Bretton Hall Hotel.

24–5 March   Readings: E. M. Roach, Derek Walcott, Lionel Kearns. Basement Theatre, Bretton Hall Hotel.

14–27 April   *Belle Fanto*, by Eric Roach; dir. by Walcott. Basement Theatre, Bretton Hall Hotel.

1 May   Readings: 'Voices' group (little magazine edited by Clifford Sealy). Basement Theatre, Bretton Hall Hotel.

[2–3] June   Readings: John Hearne, George Lamming. Basement Theatre, Bretton Hall Hotel.

[n.d.]   Exhibition of painting by Naomi Mendel (Israeli). Basement Theatre, Bretton Hall Hotel.

15 October–5 November   First season: *The Blacks*, by Jean Genet (6–15 Oct.); *Belle Fanto*, by E. M. Roach (20–22 Oct.); *The Road*, by Wole Soyinka (26 Oct.–5 Nov.). Dir. by Walcott. Basement Theatre, Bretton Hall Hotel.

1967

14–19 April   *Moon on a Rainbow Shawl*, by Errol John; dir. by Walcott. Queen's Hall.

[n.d.]   *Moon on a Rainbow Shawl*. San Fernando.

21 June   *Zoo Story* by Edward Albee and *Jourmard* by Walcott. Guild Hall, University of the West Indies, St Augustine.

30 June–2 July   Barbados tour: *Zoo Story* and *Jourmard* (30 June and 2 July); *Belle Fanto*, by E. M. Roach, setting by Derek Walcott, LeRoy Clarke (1–2 July). Dir. by Walcott. St Winifred's School, Barbados.

14–16 July   Double bill. *Zoo Story* and *Jourmard*, dir. by Walcott. Basement Theatre, Bretton Hall Hotel.

23 July   *Belle Fanto*. Bishop High School, Scarborough, Tobago.

28 July   *Belle Fanto*. Naparima Bowl, San Fernando.

5–13 August   Caribana Festival, Toronto, Canada: *Belle Fanto*, *Jourmard* and *Zoo Story*, at Centre Island (5–7 Aug.); world premiere of *Dream on Monkey Mountain*, by Derek Walcott, and dir. by Walcott (12 Aug.) *Zoo Story* and *Jourmard*, at Central Library Theatre (13 Aug.).

5–14 August   Lennox Brown, *Fog Drifts in the Spring* and Wilson Harris, *Crew from Sorrow Hill* (adapted from *Palace of the Peacock*). Recording for CBC.

17–26 August   Guyana tour: *Zoo Story* and *Jourmard* (17–19 Aug.); *Belle Fanto* (21–23 Aug.); *Dream on Monkey Mountain* (24–26 Aug.); Dir. by Walcott. Theatre Guild Playhouse, Kingston, Guyana.

1968

26–30 January   *Dream on Monkey Mountain*, dir. by Walcott. Queen's Hall.

26–28 April   *Henri Christophe*, by Derek Walcott, and dir. by Walcott. Queen's Hall.

11 May   *Henri Christophe*. Naparima Bowl, San Fernando.

20–2 June   *Under Milkwood*, by Dylan Thomas. Brian Barnes' One Man Theatre. Trinidad Workshop Production. Basement Theatre, Bretton Hall Hotel.

10–27 October   Five-island tour. Grenada: *Belle Fanto* (Oct. 10), Government House, Grenada; *Dream* (Oct. 11) and *Belle Fanto* (Oct. 12), Grenada Boys' Secondary School. St Lucia: *Belle Fanto* (Oct. 15–16), and *Dream* (Oct. 17), Town Hall, Castries. Barbados: *Dream* (Oct. 18–19), Combermere HS. Antigua: *Belle Fanto* (Oct. 22–23). St Vincent: *Belle Fanto* (Oct. 25–26), Memorial Hall. Dir. by Derek Walcott.

9 December   *Dream on Monkey Mountain*. Queen's Hall.

1969

6–7 March   *The World of Sam Selvon*, designed and dir. by Walcott. Naparima Bowl, San Fernando.

15 March   *The World of Sam Selvon*. Town Hall.

30 April   *Selvon's England*, adaptation of *The World of Sam Selvon* (30 minutes). Trinidad and Tobago Television production. Dir. by Walcott.

13–15 June   Double bill. *Stepchild*, *Stepchild*, by Oliver Jackman and *The Lover*, by Harold Pinter. Designed and dir. by Walcott. Town Hall.

1–9 August   *Dream on Monkey Mountain*, prod. by George C. White, dir. by Walcott, choreog. by Percival Borde. Eugene O'Neill Memorial Theatre, Waterford, Conn., USA.

10 November–14 December   *Dream on Monkey Mountain*, prod. Bruce Bassett, dir. by Hugh Robertson. NBC Experiment in Television, filmed in Trinidad.

1970

February   *Ti-Jean and his Brothers*, by Derek Walcott, prod. Peter Donkin. CBC Radio, 50 minutes, recorded in Trinidad.

13 March   *The Pickwickians at Manor Farm*, by Charles Dickens, pres. by Brian Barnes. Trinidad Workshop Production. Town Hall.

25–27, 29–30 June   *Ti-Jean and his Brothers*, by Derek Walcott, music by André Tanker, designed and dir. by Walcott. Première of new musical version. Town Hall.

3–20 July Tour of *Ti-Jean*. Grenada (July 3–5): Government House and Grenada Boys' Secondary School. St Lucia (July 8–11): Town Hall. Barbados (July 16–18): Combermere School Hall. Designed and dir. by Walcott.

July Video recording of *Ti-Jean and his Brothers*, adapted by Helen Camps with Trinidad Theatre Workshop. Caribbean Broadcasting Corporation, Barbados.

6 August *Ti-Jean*. Naparima Bowl, San Fernando.

15 August *Ti-Jean*. Bishop Anstey High School, Tobago.

* *27 August–October* *Dream on Monkey Mountain*, dir. by Michael Schultz, with the Negro Ensemble Company. Eight weeks. Mark Taper Forum, Los Angeles.

18–19 September *Ti-Jean and his Brothers*. Town Hall.

* *[29–] October* Première of *In A Fine Castle*, by Derek Walcott. Dir. by Walcott, with Jamaican actors; designed by Richard Montgomery; costumes by Sally Thompson. Creative Arts Centre, UWI, Jamaica.

1971

* *14 March–18 April* *Dream on Monkey Mountain*, dir. by Michael Schultz, with the Negro Ensemble Company. St Mark's Playhouse, New York. Wins Obie for 'Distinguished Foreign Play' for 1970–1. Taken by Negro Ensemble to Munich as one of America's presentations for Olympics 1972.

16 April–1 May Jamaica tour: *Ti-Jean and his Brothers* (Apr. 16–25); *Dream on Monkey Mountain* (Apr. 26–1 May). Designed and dir. by Walcott. Creative Arts Center, UWI, Jamaica.

[27–] May Wilson Harris, *The Crew from Sorrow Hill*; Lennox Brown, *The Throne in an Autumn Room*. CBC. Recording began 27 May; prod. by Peter Donkin.

8 August–10 October Radio series, with plays every Sunday. 610 Radio–Trinidad Workshop Production. Theatre Ten. Recorded: *Anne Marie*, by Douglas Archibald. Dir. by Stanley Marshall, in two half-hour segments; *Belle Fanto*, by Eric Roach, in two half-hour segments; *The Harrowing of Benjy*, by Roderick Walcott, dir. by Helen Camps; *Henri Christophe*, by Derek Walcott, and dir. by Walcott, in two 45-minute segments; *Fog Drifts in the Spring*, by Lennox Brown, dir. by Walcott; *Odale's Choice*, by E. Brathwaite, dir. by Ken Corsbie; *Sea at Dauphin*, by Derek Walcott.

13 October *Ti-Jean and his Brothers*. Town Hall.

23–4 October *Ti-Jean and his Brothers*. Queen's Hall.

28–30 October *In A Fine Castle*, by Derek Walcott, designed and dir. by Walcott. Queen's Hall.

28–29 November, 2 December *In A Fine Castle*. Town Hall.

1972

Spring *The Throne in an Autumn Room*, by Lennox Brown, prod. by Peter Donkin for CBC. Radio Canada International. Cast 'courtesy' of the Trinidad Theatre Workshop.

* *13–30 July* *Ti-Jean and his Brothers*, prod. by Joseph Papp and dir. by Walcott, with the New York Shakespeare Festival Company. Albert Laveau—Devil, Papa Bois, Planter; Hamilton Parris—Frog. Delacorte Theatre, Central Park.

* *2–30 August* *Ti-Jean*. Mobile Theatre, tour of boroughs.

July – Theatre Fifteen. 610 Radio–Trinidad Workshop Production. *Jourmard*, by Derek Walcott and dir. by Walcott; *As Time Goes By*, by Mustapha Matura, dir. by Stanley Marshall, in two half-hour segments; *B. Wordsworth*, by V. S. Naipaul, dir: Ken Corsbie; *Calabash of Blood*, by Eric Roach, dir. by Claude Reid, in two half-hour segments; *My Brother's Keeper*, by Carmen Manley, dir. by Judy Stone; *The Rape of Fair Helen*, by Stanley French, dir. by Judy Stone; *Taxi Mister*, by Daniel Joseph Samaroo, dir. by Wilbert Holder; double bill with *Basement Lullaby*, by Samuel Selvon, dir. by W. Holder; *Wine in Winter*, by Lennox Brown, dir. by Stanley Marshall; *Henri Christophe*, by Derek Walcott, and dir. by Walcott.

8–9 December *Pieces One—Presenting the Repertory Dance Theatre*: 'Fusion', 'Victim', 'House of the Lord', 'For Better or For Worse' (Astor Johnson); *One for the Road* by Neville de La Bastide; two short sketches by TTW. Trinidad Workshop Production. Production supervised and dir. by Walcott, choreog. by Astor Johnson. Bishop Anstey Auditorium.

12 December *Malcochon*, by Derek Walcott; adapted by Walcott, and dir. by Ossie Maingot. Trinidad and Tobago Television. 40 minutes.

1973

March *In a Fine Castle*, by Derek Walcott, with casting and production by Peter Donkin. CBC Radio. Two-hour production.

14–21 April *Franklin, a tale from the islands*, by Derek Walcott, and designed and dir. by Walcott. Bishop Anstey Auditorium.

25–29 April *Pieces Two*: a Trinidad Workshop production. First Part: Repertory Dance Theatre. Second Part: 'Wings of a Dove', from *Rights of Passage*, by Edward Brathwaite, dir. by Malcolm Jones, with design by Walcott, Malcolm Jones, and Astor Johnson. Bishop Anstey Auditorium.

29 June–3 July *The Charlatan*, by Derek Walcott, with costumes, backdrop and dir. by Walcott. Revised with new songs. Town Hall.

11–21 July Jamaica tour: *Franklin* (11–15 July); *The Charlatan* (16–21 July). Dir. by Walcott, with sets by Richard Montgomery. Little Theatre, Crossroads, Kingston.

14–19 November Scenes from *Dream on Monkey Mountain*, *The Charlatan* and *Franklin*, with a cast of seven. St Croix University and The College of the Virgin Islands, St Thomas.

30 November–1 December *Dem Two*: Ken Corsbie and Mark Matthews. Readings, dramatizations and songs by West Indian poets. Bishop Anstey Auditorium.

1974

* *31 March–6 April Ti-Jean.* Dir. by Walcott, with the Courtyard Players. Frederiksted, St Croix. Dorsch Center.

* *21 April– Ti-Jean,* prod. by Courtyard Players, dir. by Walcott. St Croix. Dorsch Center.

* *23 May–7 July The Charlatan,* by Derek Walcott, dir. by Mel Shapiro, and with music by Galt MacDermot. Mark Taper Forum, Los Angeles.

30–1 May Readings: Carolyn Reid-Wallace (African–American Poetry). Little Carib Theatre.

June Sea at Dauphin, by Derek Walcott, dir. by Horace James. Trinidad and Tobago Television.

1–6 August Dream on Monkey Mountain, designed and dir. by Walcott, with choreog. by Astor Johnson. Little Carib Theatre.

15–27 August Dream on Monkey Mountain and *Ti-Jean and his Brothers,* designed and dir. by Walcott. White Barn Festival, Conn., USA.

12–14 October Dream on Monkey Mountain, designed and dir. by Walcott, with choreog. by Astor Johnson. (Some actors cast from seminar for Courtyard Players.) Island Center, St Croix.

17 October Walcott reading from his work, 'supported by dramatisations of his plays'. Public Library, Port of Spain.

8 November Songs from *Ti-Jean and his Brothers, The Charlatan* and *The Joker of Seville,* featuring Galt MacDermot and Andrew Beddeau. Public Library.

28 November–8 December Premiere of *The Joker of Seville,* by Derek Walcott, and designed and dir. by Walcott, with music by Galt MacDermot, choreog. by Carol La Chapelle, and costumes designed by Walcott and Helen Camps. Little Carib Theatre.

15 December Jourmard recorded for TTT; adapted by Walcott. 27 minutes.

1975

14–15 February Concert with LeRoy Clarke and Andrew Beddeau. Designed and dir. by Walcott, with choreog. by Carol La Chapelle. (Multimedia event.) Little Carib Theatre.

8 March LP of *Joker of Seville* released. Music recorded in New York.

13–23 March The Joker of Seville. Little Carib Theatre.

2 April Joker of Seville. Naparima Bowl, San Fernando.

7–12 April Joker of Seville. Geest's Old Banana Shed, Castries, St Lucia.

13 April The Joker of Seville, Piton Room, Halycon Days Hotel, Vieux Fort, St Lucia.

10–19 July The Seagull, by Chekhov, dir. by Walcott, with the set designed by Walcott and Christopher Lynch. Little Carib Theatre.

15–27 October The Joker of Seville, dir. by Walcott, with choreog. by La Chapelle. Little Carib Theatre.

22 November–6 December The Joker of Seville, dir. by Walcott, with costumes and set by Richard Montgomery, choreog. by Carol La Chapelle, and music supervised by Galt MacDermot. Creative Arts Centre, Jamaica.

1976

19 March–2 April Première of O Babylon!, by Derek Walcott, and dir. by Walcott, with music by Galt MacDermot, choreog. by Carol La Chapelle, and artistic supervision by Richard Montgomery. Little Carib Theatre.

14–15 June O Babylon!, revised by Walcott and with new songs by MacDermot, who played piano. Naparima Bowl, San Fernando.

24–6 July O Babylon!, dir. by Walcott, with choreog. by La Chapelle. Carifesta 76, Jamaica. Little Theatre, Kingston.

30 July Stage reading of Dream on Monkey Mountain, with Roscoe Lee Browne. Dir. by Walcott, with the Theatre Workshop Dance Company and Chorus. Little Carib Theatre.

31 July 31–[14] August O Babylon!. Little Carib Theatre.

2–11 September Belle Fanto, by E. M. Roach, dir. by Albert Laveau, with set design and backdrop by Walcott. Little Carib Theatre.

24 September Joker of Seville. Expo 77 (industrial fair) in the Savannah, on 72ft. by 24ft. stage.

28–31 October, 1, 6–7 November Revival, with the Trinidad Theatre Workshop Dance Company. Artistic Director: Walcott; Dance Director: Carol La Chapelle; costume supervision by Seitu and Walcott; set design by Lee Johnson and Walcott. Little Carib Theatre.

28 November Revival. Naparima Bowl, San Fernando.

10–11 December Trinidad & Tobago Telephone Sports and Culture Club, Christmas programme. Programme included Theatre Workshop Dance Company and selections from Joker with Theatre Workshop Band. Queen's Hall (10 Dec.); Town Hall (11 Dec.).

1977

* *13–23 January* The Charlatan, by Derek Walcott, and dir. by Walcott, with music by Galt MacDermot, and the set designed by Walcott and Lee Johnson. (Two-act version; music written for Los Angeles '74 production, added to original score.) Little Carib Theatre.

10–20 March The Maids, by Jean Genet, designed and dir. by Anthony Hall, and production and house management by Helen Camps. Little Carib Theatre.

* *22– April* Remembrance, by Derek Walcott, premiered by the Courtyard Players, and dir. by Walcott. Dorsch Center, St Croix.

* *27– April* Remembrance, by Derek Walcott, with the Courtyard Players, and dir. by Walcott. College of the Virgin Islands, Little Theatre, St Thomas.

22 June–2 July Season 77, with the Trinidad Theatre Workshop Dance Company. Producer and Artistic Director: La Chapelle. Little Carib Theatre.

29 July–6 August   Teacher Teach'er, by Anthony Hinkson, dir. by Earl Warner. Trinidad Theatre Workshop presents the Barbados Writers' Workshop. Little Carib Theatre.

* *20 November   Fog Drifts in the Spring*, by Lennox Brown. TTT (for Horace James).

1978

* *12–22 April*   Premiere of *Pantomime*, by Derek Walcott, dir. by Albert Laveau. All Theatre Productions. Little Carib Theatre.

8 September   Readings from *The Dragon Can't Dance*, by Earl Lovelace; collective direction with Earl Lovelace. Composer and Musical Director: André Tanker. Desperadoes' Panyard, Laventille. (Performed at other venues including San Fernando and Little Carib until Ermine Wright's death in October.)

* *14–16 December   Pantomime*, dir. by Helen Camps. All Theatre Productions. Little Carib Theatre.

1979

18–28 January   Departure in the Dark, by Sam Hillary, dir. by George McKenzie, and prod by Errol Jones. Little Carib Theatre.

1–3, 8–10, 11–13 June   Old Story Time, by Trevor Rhone. Trevor Rhone in association with the Trinidad Theatre Workshop. Hotel Normandie.

* *5–7 July   Remembrance*, designed and dir. by Walcott. All Theatre Productions. Dinner Theatre, Hotel Normandie.

* *9–14 November*   Premiere of *Marie Laveau*, by Derek Walcott, dir. by Walcott, and prod. by Dennis Parker. Lyrics by Walcott, with music by Galt MacDermot, and choreog. by Norline Metivier. Production: College of the Virgin Islands, St Thomas, US Virgin Islands. American cast.

* [n.d.]   *Pantomime*, dir. by Walcott, with the Courtyard Players. Dorsch Center, St Croix.

1980

* *22–6 April   Sizwe Bansi is Dead*, by Athol Fugard, John Kani, and Winston Ntshona, and Prod. and dir. by Helen Camps. All Theatre Productions. Little Carib Theatre.

* *29 May–8 June   Marie Laveau*, by Derek Walcott, dir. by Walcott, and prod. by Walcott and Clara Rosa de Lima. Composer Galt MacDermot, choreog. by Norline Metivier, and set design by Walcott. Little Carib Theatre.

* *June   Sizwe Bansi is Dead*, dir by Helen Camps. Queen's Park, Barbados.

* *10–18 October   Pantomime*, dir. by Ken Corsbie, and prod. by Helen Camps. All Theatre Productions Little Carib Theatre.

1981

30 April–24 May   World premiere of *Beef, No Chicken*, by Derek Walcott, dir. by Cecil Gray. Little Carib Theatre.

* *3–6 June   Sizwe Bansi is Dead*, dir. by Helen Camps. All Theatre Productions. Little Carib Theatre.

* *13 June   Sizwe Bansi is Dead*. (Helen Camps's 1980 production.) Tobago.

30 July   Carifesta, Bridgetown, Barbados: *The Dragon Can't Dance*, by Earl Lovelace. with music by André Tanker. Dramatic reading. Trinidad and Tobago Theatre Company; *Sizwe Bansi is Dead*, performed at Black Rock Cultural Centre. 'The Trinidad and Tobago Theatre Company incorporates the Trinidad Theatre Workshop.'

1982

[n.d.]   *Sizwe Bansi is Dead* (now TTW Production) tours Reichold Centre in St Thomas and Thalia Theatre in Surinam.

22 January–11 February   A 'Nancy Story, by Elliot Bastien, dir. by Jeff Henry, with music. by André Tanker. Little Carib Theatre.

* *1–17 July*   World premiere of *The Last Carnival*, by Derek Walcott, and designed and dir. by Walcott. Warwick Productions. Government Training College.

8–31 July   Smile Orange, by Trevor Rhone, dir. by Trevor Rhone. Little Carib Theatre.

5–15 August   Sizwe Banzi is Dead. Dundas Centre for the Performing Arts, Nassau, Bahamas.

* *29 September–[ ] October   Remembrance*, dir. by Earl Warner. Stage One Production. Queen's Park, Bridgetown, Barbados.

1–2 October   Trinidad Theatre Workshop presents *The Actor and His Art*, devised and dir. by Henk Tjon. Little Carib Theatre.

1983

6–16 October   Like Them That Dream, by Edgar White, dir. by Earl Warner. Little Carib Theatre.

* *25 November–4 December*   Premiere of *A Branch of the Blue Nile*, by Derek Walcott, dir. by Earl Warner. Stage One and The Nation Publishing Company. Barbados.

1984

11–15 April   Woza Albert!, by Mbongeni Ngema, Percy Mtwa and Barney Simon, dir. by Earl Warner. Little Carib Theatre.

June   Woza Albert! in Barbados.

* *1–5 August*   World premiere of *The Haytian Earth*, by Derek Walcott, and dir. by Walcott. Presented by the Ministry of Education and Culture, and designed by Richard and Sally Montgomery. Morne Fortune Theatre, Castries, St Lucia.

27 September   Sizwe Bansi is Dead. Amoco Club House, Beaumont Estate, Mayaro.

9–13 October   Woza Albert!. Astor Theatre.

16, 17–21 October; 7–11 November   We Can't Pay, We Won't Pay!, by Dario Fo, dir. by Anthony Hall and actors. Little Carib Theatre.

1985

* *6–16 March   Dream on Monkey Mountain*, dir. by Albert Laveau. Arbee Productions. Astor Theatre.

* *17–28 April   Beef, No Chicken*, dir. Earl Warner. Stage One Production. Queen's Park, Barbados.

31 May–1 June   Moon on a Rainbow Shawl, by Errol John. Caribbean Theatre Guild/Trinidad Theatre Workshop. Little Carib Theatre.

* *14–18, 21–24 August   A Branch of the Blue Nile*, by Derek Walcott, dir. by Earl Warner, and prod. by Walcott, with set design. by Earl Warner, Walcott, Greer Jones Woodham. Warwick Productions. Tent Theatre, Savannah.

12–22 September   Night, Mother, by Marsha Norman, dir. by Earl Warner. Little Carib Theatre.

1986

* *21–22 March   Let Resurrection Come*. (Excerpts from Walcott's plays.) University of the West Indies, St Augustine.

July   Lights 2, dir. by Earl Warner, prod. by Trinidad Theatre Workshop, and performed by Stage One Theatre of Barbados. Little Carib Theatre.

24 July–3 August   Boesman and Lena, by Athol Fugard, dir. by Rawle Gibbons. Little Carib Theatre.

1987

January   Sizwe Bansi. St Vincent.

30 January–1 February   Boesman and Lena. Castries Comprehensive Auditorium, St Lucia.

31 July–8 August   Beef, No Chicken, dir. by Anthony Hall and Wilbert Holder. Trinidad Theatre Workshop and the Theatre Company (Brenda Hughes). (Preview benefit performance on 30 July for Wilbert Holder, who died on 14 July.) Little Carib Theatre.

26 December 1987–9 January 1988   Joker of Seville, dir. by Albert Laveau. Arbee Productions and Trinidad Theatre Workshop. Central Bank Auditorium.

1988

4–17 August   Accidental Death of an Anarchist, by Dario Fo, dir. by Rawle Gibbons. Little Carib Theatre.

1989

11–13 August   Smile Orange, by Trevor Rhone, dir. by Albert Laveau. Irvine Bay Hotel, Tobago.

26 September–8 October   *Smile Orange.* Little Carib Theatre.

17–18 November   *Smile Orange.* Bishop Anstey High School, Tobago.

1990

* *25 January–11 February*   *Franklin,* by Derek Walcott, dir. by Michael Gilkes. WWB Production. Queen's Park, Barbados.

* *22–7 March*   *Franklin.* WWB Production. Little Carib Theatre.

18 October–11 November   *Two Can Play,* by Trevor Rhone, dir. by John Isaacs. Little Carib Theatre.

1991

1992

28 December   *Celebration* (dramatized poems, plays and songs from Walcott's works), Old Fire Station.

1993

January   *Celebration* in St Lucia.

February   *Celebration* in Trinidad.

25 April   *Nobel Celebration.* Selections from *Dream on Monkey Mountain, Pantomime, Ti-Jean and His Brothers, The Joker of Seville.* Artistic Director: Albert Laveau. Charles Playhouse, Boston.

29 April–2 May   *Pantomime.* Boston Playwrights' Theatre, Boston University.

5–8 August   *The Odyssey,* a dramatized reading, by Derek Walcott, dir. by Gregory Doran. Wilbert Holder Theatre, Old Fire Station.

September   Fifth Afro Caribe Festival, Schouwburg, Rotterdam, The Netherlands: *Dream on Monkey Mountain* (21–22 Sept.); *Celebration* (23–24 Sept.) Artistic Director: Albert Laveau.

20–24 October   *Dream on Monkey Mountain.* Little Carib Theatre.

Select Bibliography

Bibliographies of Derek Walcott can be found under Goldstraw and Hamner. Goldstraw includes details of earlier versions of some Walcott plays later revised for wider publication. For other dramatists and their plays see Stone's book on West Indian theatre and editions of *Contemporary Dramatists*, London: St James Press.

I. Signed Publications

[A Correspondent], 'When Belle Says "No!"', *Sunday Mirror* (3 Apr. 1966), 7.

Ackrill, Lesley, 'Because of his Good Looks and Acting Skill', *People* (Apr. 1980), 41–2.

——, 'Her Writing is Mostly a Labour of Love', *People* (Apr. 1980), 42–3.

——, 'For Eunice Alleyne's . . .', *People* (Sept. 1980), 41–2.

Ahye, Molly, *Cradle of Caribbean Dance: Beryl McBurnie and the Little Carib Theatre* (Trinidad: Heritage Cultures, 1983).

Allan, George, 'Dream on Monkey Mountain', *Trinidad Guardian* (20 Feb. 1970), 8.

Allsopp, Richard, 'Franklin a Play to See', *Daily Nation* (7 Feb. 1990), 9.

Andrews, Peter, 'Introducing Carol La Chapelle', *Sunday Punch* (26 Sept. 1976), 6.

Anthony, Michael, 'Conversation with Slade Hopkinson', *Sunday Guardian* (8 Sept. 1970).

Asein, Samuel O., 'Walcott's Jamaica Years', *The Literary Half-Yearly*, 21/2 (July 1980), 23–41.

——, 'Walcott and the Great Tradition', *The Literary Criterion*, 16/2 (1981), 18–30.

——, 'Drama, The Church and The Nation in the Caribbean', *The Literary Half-Yearly*, 26/1 (Jan. 1985), 149–62.

——, (guest ed.), *The Literary Half-Yearly*, 26/1 (Jan. 1985), 'Derek Walcott Number'.

[A. Seeker], 'The Offending Poem', *The Voice of St Lucia* (9 Aug. 1944), 3.

Augier, Adrian, 'The Haytian Earth', *The Weekend Voice* (11 Aug. 1984), 14.

Augustus, Earl, 'In A Fine Castle', *Express* (7 Nov. 1971), 17, 30.

BALDEOSINGH, KAY, 'Walcott: Immoral to Move Workshop', Daily Express (5 July 1993), 1, 4.

BALDEOSINGH, KEVIN, 'Walcott Seeks Home for Theatre Workshop', Express (17 Nov. 1992).

BARKER, J. S., 'Not the Stuff for a West Indian Theatre', Trinidad Guardian (15 Aug. 1954), 4.

BARNES, CLIVE, 'Walcott's "Ti-Jean" Opens in Park', The New York Times (28 July 1972), 20.

BAUGH, EDWARD, Derek Walcott: Memory as Vision: Another Life (London: Longman, 1978).

BEAUFORT, JOHN, ' "Ti-Jean" as Told by Frog; Trinidad Play in Central Park', The Christian Science Monitor (31 July 1972), 7.

BENJAMIN, JOEL, 'The Early Theatre in Guyana', Kyk-over-al, 37 (Dec. 1987), 24–44.

BEST, HARRY, ' "Joker of Seville" Worthy of Fore-running Praises', The Voice of St Lucia (9 Apr. 1975), 1.

——, 'Character of West Indian People Vivid in Walcott's "The Joker of Seville"', The Voice of St Lucia (16 Apr. 1975), 7.

BORDNER, RAYMOND K., 'Allegorical Folk Play Produced in Waterford', The Day [New London, Conn.] (2 Aug. 1969), 15.

BROWN, STEWART (ed.), The Art of Derek Walcott (Wales: Sren Books, 1991).

BROWN, WAYNE, 'Chow Time, King Kong', Express (21 Mar. 1985), 10.

——, 'A Home for Mr Walcott', Sunday Guardian (22 Nov. 1992).

'BUFF', 'Good news for theatre lovers', Express (7 Jan. 1985).

C., L., 'Actors Score with Comedy and Drama', Trinidad Guardian (24 Jan. 1964), 7.

——, 'Basement Develops Sure Touch!', Trinidad Guardian (22 Oct. 1966), 5.

CAMPBELL, RALPH, 'To whom can the playwright turn?', Trinidad Guardian (5 July 1973).

——, 'The Birth of Professional Theatre in Trinidad', Sunday Guardian (22 July 1973), 4; (29 July 1973), 11.

CAMPS, HELEN, 'A Season of Statements: Opening Statement', programme for Trinidad Tent Theatre's Statements.

CARIB, JOHN, 'From All Quarters', Sunday Guardian (7 May 1967).

CHUN, DIANE, 'Raw Talent and Vibrant Personalities Fuel Trinidad Drama', Gainesville Sun (5 Sept. 1982), 1E, 11E.

CLARKE, B. ELIZABETH, ' "Remembrance" Proved to be Fulfilling', Advocate-News (11 Oct. 1982), 6.

CLARKE, LeROY, 'Marie La Veau—An Artificial Resurrection', Express (18 June 1980), 24–5.

COBHAM SANDER, RHONDA, 'The Background', in Bruce King (ed.), West Indian Literature (London: Macmillan, 1979), 9–29.

COKE, LLOYD, 'Walcott's Mad Innocents', Savacou, 5 (June 1971), 121–4.

CONNOR-MOGOTSI, PEARL, 'Babylon Crushes the Rasta Dream', Trinidad Guardian (23 July 1976), 4, 6.

CONNOR-MOGOTSI, PEARL, 'Exuberant Dance Lead into Paradise', *Trinidad Guardian* (4 Nov. 1976), 6.

CORSBIE, KEN, 'A Legend of "Love"', *Nation* (17 May 1982), 8.

——, 'A Long History of Struggle', *Express* (18 May 1982), 16.

——, *Theatre in the Caribbean* (London: Hodder & Stoughton, 1984).

DE LIMA, CLARA ROSA, 'Walcott's Drama in the Rain Something to Remember', *Sunday Express* (12 Aug. 1984), 14.

——, 'Walcott's "Joker" Most Impressive', *Trinidad Guardian* (14 Jan. 1988), 8.

——, 'Walcott: Painting and the Shadow of Van Gogh', in Stewart Brown (ed.), *The Art of Derek Walcott* (Wales: Sren Books, 1991), 171–92.

DOCKRAY, BRIAN, 'A Most Significant Musical Contribution', *Trinidad Guardian* (27 June 1970), 4.

DOUGLAS, KARL, 'Requiem on Tape for a Lost Soul', *Trinidad Guardian* (13 May 1962), 13.

——, '"Charlatan" Scores—Comedy Wise', *Trinidad Guardian* (10 Dec. 1962), 5.

DOYLE-MARSHALL, WILLIAM, 'Bouquets Thrown in the US at the Theatre Workshop', *Express* (22 Sept. 1969), 4.

——, 'Albert Le Veau Still Dreams of Pro Theatre', *People* (Oct. 1978), 49–51.

——, 'No Real Poet is Ever Proud of his Poems', *Trinidad Guardian* (30 July 1986), 34.

DRAYTON, KATHLEEN, 'A Dream to Change the World', *Caribbean Contact*, 7/11 (Mar. 1980), 15.

ESPINET, ADRIAN, '"Drums and Colours" Seeks to Trace Evolution of West Indian Consciousness', *Sunday Guardian* (27 Apr. 1958), 7.

——, 'Undistinguished—That's The Word for "Ti-Jean"', *Trinidad Guardian* (1 July 1958), 4.

EUBA, AKIN, *Essays on Music in Africa 2: Intercultural Perspectives*, Bayreuth African Studies, 16 (1989).

——, *Yoruba Drumming: The Dundun Tradition*, Bayreuth African Studies, 21/22 (1990).

FALCON, JOHN, 'The Spiritual Agony of an Old Coal-Burner', *Trinidad Guardian* (5 Aug. 1974), 5.

FIELDS, SIDNEY, 'A Gift for Words', *Daily News* [New York] (20 June 1972), 68; repub. as '"Another Life" Coming', *Express* (22 Aug. 1972), 24.

FIGUEROA, JOHN, '"Ione": A Stimulating Play', *Public Opinion* (23 Mar. 1957), 6.

GARDNER, R. H., 'Center Stage Show is Filled with Poetry, Music and Dance', *The Sun* [Baltimore] (19 Feb. 1976), Entertainment Sect., 1.

GIBBONS, RAWLE, 'O Babylon!', *Kairi 76* (1976), 12–13.

GOLDSTRAW, IRMA, *Derek Walcott: An Annotated Bibliography of His Works* (New York: Garland, 1984).

GOLDSTRAW, LAURENCE, 'Reminiscences of Derek Walcott and the Trinidad Theatre Workshop', in Robert Hamner (ed.), *Critical Perspectives on Derek Walcott* (Washington, DC: Three Continents Press, 1993), 272–81.

GOMES, ANTONY, 'An Evening of Choices Facing Contemporary Women', *Trinidad Guardian* (20 Sept. 1985), 16.

GONZALEZ, ANSON, 'In A Fine Castle', *Embryo*, 4/4 (1971), 2–3.

GOODMAN, HARRY, 'Carnival with a Calypso Beat', *The Wall Street Journal* (4 June 1974), 20; repr. as 'Charlatan Scores in Los Angeles', *Sunday Guardian* (16 June 1974), 6.

GORDON, WILLIAM, 'Rich Drama of Walcott's "Last Carnival"', *Trinidad Guardian* (2 Aug. 1982), 19.

GRAHAM, ROLAND, 'An Art of Wind upon Water of Wave upon Shore', *Express*, unidentified clipping (June 1980).

GRIMES, JOHN, ' "Company of Players" Win Praise for "Ione" ', *Trinidad Guardian* (9 Nov. 1957), 5.

GUILBAUT, JOCELYNE, *Zouk: World Music in the West Indies* (Chicago: University of Chicago Press, 1993).

GUNNESS, CHRISTOPHER, 'White Man, Black Man', *People* (June 1978), 14, 51–2.

HALL, ANTHONY, 'Nobody Who Knows Greer is Surprised at Her Success', *Southern Star* (16 Oct. 1977), 15, 19.

HAMMETT, CORINNE F., ' "Dream": An Exotic Folk Fantasy', *The News American* (18 Feb. 1976), 5D.

HAMNER, ROBERT D., *Derek Walcott* (New York: Twayne, 1993).

—— (ed.), *Critical Perspectives on Derek Walcott* (Washington, DC: Three Continents Press, 1993).

——, 'Bibliography', in Robert Hamner (ed.), *Critical Perspectives on Derek Walcott* (Washington, DC: Three Continents Press, 1993), 410–30.

HILL, ERROL, 'The West Indian Theatre (1–4)', *Public Opinion* (31 May 1958), 9; (7 June 1958), 7; (14 June 1958), 7; (21 June 1958), 9.

——, 'No Tears for Narcissus', *Sunday Guardian* (7 Mar. 1965), 7.

——, 'The Emergence of a National Drama in the West Indies', *Caribbean Quarterly*, 18/4 (December 1972), 9–40.

——, *The Trinidad Carnival, Mandate for a National Theatre* (Austin: University of Texas Press, 1972).

——, 'Gallant Attempt at Chekhov's Complex Classic', *Trinidad Guardian* (14 July 1975), 3.

——, *The Jamaican Stage 1655–1900: Profile of a Colonial Theatre* (Amherst: University of Massachusetts Press, 1992).

HILTON, ANNE, 'Pantomime', *Express* (23 Apr. 1978), 14–15.

HIRSCH, SAMUEL, 'Ensemble of Extraordinary Power', *Sunday Herald Tribune*, S Travel sect., Show Guide (10 Aug. 1969), 1, 9.

HOLDER, GLADSTONE, 'A Branch of the Blue Nile', *The Weekend Nation* (2 Dec. 1983), 6.

HOPE, FRED AND HOPKINSON, SLADE, 'The Changing Needs of our Theatre', *Sunday Guardian* (4 July 1971), 5.

HOPKINSON, SLADE, 'So the Sun Went Down', *The Daily Gleaner* (15 Apr. 1956), 17.

HOPKINSON, SLADE, 'Poor Response to Quality WI Plays', *Sunday Graphic* [Guyana] (10 Sept. 1967).

——, 'Good Plays must have a Market', *The Daily Gleaner* (16 Sept. 1975), 4, 19.

——, 'Dream on Monkey Mountain and the Popular Response', *Arts Review*, Jamaican Creative Arts Centre, 1/1 (Jan. 1976), 3–7; repub. in *Caribbean Quarterly* 23/2–3 (June–Sept., 1977), 77–9.

HOSEIN, CLYDE, 'See Walcott's "Dream" on Television Tonight', *Trinidad Guardian* (14 Feb. 1970), 2.

——, 'Focus on the Arts: No Beating About the Bush', *Trinidad Guardian* (4 Mar. 1970), 4.

——, 'Stormy Applause Well Deserved', *Trinidad Guardian* (27 June 1970), 4.

——, 'The Creative Man's Two Worlds', *Trinidad Guardian* (21 Apr. 1971), 6.

——, 'Actors Define Theatre Problems', *Trinidad Guardian* (9 June 1971), 6.

——, 'Lack of Appreciation Drives One to Madness', *Trinidad Guardian* (10 June 1971), 6.

——, 'Stepping-up the Creative Drive', *Trinidad Guardian* (23 June 1971), 6, 8.

'HUMMINGBIRD', 'Talk of Trinidad', *Trinidad Guardian* (17 Sept. 1970), 5.

HUNTLEY, EARL, 'Dr Figueroa So Right', *The Voice of St Lucia* (11 July 1970), 10.

IRISH, JOHN H., 'The Joker of Seville', *Trinidad Guardian* (13 Mar. 1975), 6.

ISMOND, PATRICIA, 'Breaking Myths and Maidenheads', *Tapia* (18 May 1975), 4–5, 9; (1 June 1975), 6–8.

——, '"Dream" a Story of Struggle', *Sunday Express* (3 Mar. 1985).

——, '"Dream" comes true under La Veau', *Sunday Express* (17 Mar. 1985).

JAIKERANSINGH, KEN, 'This "Joker" missed the mark', *Express* (5 Jan. 1988), 16.

JAMES, DALTON, 'Ti-Jean and his Brothers: A Brilliant Effort—But Why was Queen's Hall Half-filled?', *Express* (7 Nov. 1971), 16.

JENKIN, VERONICA, 'Drums and Colours', *Bim*, 7/27 (July–Dec. 1958), 183–4.

JESSE, C., FMI., 'Reflections on Reading the Poem "1944"', *The Voice of St Lucia* (5 Aug. 1944), 4.

——, 'Arts Guild Play Objectionable', *The Voice of St Lucia* (7 Mar. 1959), 8.

JOHN, DEBRA, 'Marie La Veau, and the People Who Really had My Sympathy', *The Sun* (6 June 1980), 6.

JOHN, RONALD, 'Errol Jones Remembers', *Trinidad Guardian* (29 July 1987), 28.

——, 'Trinidad Theatre Workshop Magic is Gone', *Trinidad Guardian* (12 Aug. 1987), 18.

JOHNSON, ASTOR, 'Two Years of Steady Progress', *The Repertory Dance Theatre*, 8-page programme, August 1974 season, p. 7.

JOHNSON, LEE, 'Roach's Attempt to Pinpoint Changing Values', *Trinidad Guardian* (10 Sept. 1976).

JONES, BRUNELL, 'Walcott's Play—A Success at Festival', *Evening News* (3 May 1968).

JONES, JACQUI, 'The Dragon Can't Dance', *The Nation, Carifesta Bulletin* (4 Aug. 1981), 2–3.

JONES, MARYLIN, 'Striking a Blow for Women's Lib', *Trinidad Guardian* (12 Dec. 1974), 4.

——, 'A Home for Our Artists Please', *Trinidad Guardian* (9 Apr. 1975), 4.

JOSEPH, TERRY [T. R. J.], '"Two Can Play" Plays Little Carib Oct. 18', *Trinidad Guardian* (5 Oct. 1990), 22.

——, 'Peter Kelly Finally Takes the "Award"', *Trinidad Guardian* (25 Oct. 1990), 16.

——, 'The Arts', *Sunday Guardian* (28 Oct. 1990), 5.

——, 'Derek's Forgotten Friends', *Sunday Mirror* (18 Oct. 1992), 30.

KING, BRUCE, *Dryden's Major Plays* (Edinburgh: Oliver & Boyd, 1966).

——, (ed.), *West Indian Literature* (London: Macmillan, 1979).

——, *New English Literatures: Cultural Nationalism in a Changing World* (London: Macmillan, 1980).

——, *Modern Indian Poetry in English* (Delhi: Oxford University Press, 1987, rev. 1989, 1992, 1994).

——, 'Trevor Rhone', in D. L. Kirkpatrick (ed.), *Contemporary Dramatists* (Chicago: St James Press, 1989), 449.

——, (ed.), *Post-Colonial English Drama: Commonwealth Drama since 1960* (London: Macmillan, 1992).

——, 'West Indian Drama and the Rockefeller Foundation, 1957–1970', *Research Reports from the Rockefeller Archive Center* [spring, 1994], 1–4.

——, 'Caribbean Conundrum', *Transition: An International Review*, 62 [spring, 1994], 140–57.

KISSOON, FREDDIE, 'Playwright: Let Me Do My Thing', *Trinidad Guardian* (29 May 1969), 40.

LAIRD, CHRISTOPHER, 'The Running of a "Subscription Season"', *Kairi* 76 (1976), 3.

LAIRD, COLIN, 'The Arts in the West Indies', *Shell Trinidad* (Sept. 1958), 8.

LEE, SIMON, 'Sailing to Ithaca', *Sunday Guardian* (22 Aug. 1993), 3–4.

LINDO, ARCHIE, 'Two Plays—Both Interesting', *The Star* [Jamaica] (19 July 1973), 18.

LOVELACE, EARL, ' "Dream" Exposes Truths we Try to Suppress', *Sunday Express* (1968).

——, 'Christophe—Image Packed Essay Mouthed by Actors', *Express* (30 Apr. 1968), 12.

——, 'Derek's "Stepchild" was Nothing but a Big Disappointment', *Express* (16 June 1969), 9,15.

——, 'Rude Bwoy Walcott', *People* (19 June 1976), 37–9.

——, 'The Last Carnival', *Express* (25 July 1982), 15, 18.

LOWHAR, SYL, 'Ti-Jean—A Mom and Son's Battle for a Better Life', *Express*, (14 July 1970), 13.

——, 'A Struggle for Freedom', *Tapia*, 8 (9 Aug. 1970), 6.

——, 'Another Station of the Cross', *Tapia*, 23 (26 Dec. 1971), 19.

——, 'Drums and Colours', *Tapia*, 3/18 (6 May 1973), 9–10.

——, '"Blue Nile" a Play for the Young', *People Magazine* (1 Sept. 1985), 16.

LOWRIE, JEAN, 'Tears, Laughter in Walcott Play', *Jamaica Daily News* (13 July 1973), 18.

——, 'Carnival Comes to Little Theatre', *Jamaica Daily News* (18 July 1973), 20.

LYNDERSAY, MARK, '. . . and the Audience Make Three', *Catholic News* (30 Apr. 1978), 5.

——, 'Under the Spell of Marie La Veau', *Catholic News* (15 June 1980), 13.

——, 'Pantomime is Still a Joy', *Express* (14 Oct. 1980), 11.

——, 'You Want Jokes? I'll Give You Jokes', *Trinidad Guardian* (12 May 1981), 15.

——, "81 in the Arts', *Trinidad and Tobago Review* (New Year 1982), 22–3.

——, 'Theatre of Mas', *Trinidad and Tobago Review* ('Kaiso' 1982), 22–3.

McWATT, MARK, 'Remembrance', *Caribbean Contact*, 10/8 (Dec. 1982), 11.

MAHARAJ, VASHTY, 'Vital Themes Woven into "A Nancy Story"', *Trinidad Guardian* (2 Jan. 1982), 18.

MANLEY, MICHAEL, 'Root of the Matter', *Public Opinion* (23 Mar. 1957), 4.

MARSHALL, FAITH, 'Such Brilliance Seldom Seen on Barbadian Stage', *Advocate News* (22 Oct. 1968), 4.

MARTIN, ANGELA, 'Stanley Gives All for Art', *Express* (3 May 1980), 10–11.

MAXWELL, MARINA, 'Towards a Revolution in the Arts', *Savacou*, 2 (Sept. 1970), 19–32.

MELSER, JOHN, 'Landmark for Local Drama and Triumph for Workshop', *Trinidad Guardian* (29 Jan. 1968), 11.

——, 'Basement Proves a Genius for Comedy', *Trinidad Guardian* (21 Mar. 1969), 6.

MENTUS, ULRIC, 'The Little Workshop's Mammoth Task of 5 Plays a Year', *Sunday Mirror* (8 May 1966), 19.

——, 'Reading', *Daily Mirror* (7 June 1966), 9.

——, 'Warhead in "Dream" Has Not Yet Exploded', *Evening News* (31 Jan. 1968), 5.

——, '10 Years Old—But Still Going Strong', *Evening News* [1969].

——, 'Walcott: Nobody Wants to be a West Indian', *The Jamaica Daily News* (7 Dec. 1975), 5–7.

MILLS, THERESE, 'The Theatre Workshop', *Sunday Guardian* (23 Apr. 1967), 1.

——, 'No "Stardust," Just the Polish of Hard Work', *Sunday Guardian* (23 July 1967), 5.

——, 'All the Time I am Bursting to be On Stage', *Sunday Guardian* (1968).

——, 'A Taste of Honey on the Campus' *Sunday Guardian* (Aug. 1968).

——, 'Conversation with Derek Walcott', *Sunday Guardian* (20 June 1971), 10, 17.

——, 'This Is an Experiment in Courage', *Sunday Guardian* (15 Apr. 1973), 8.

——, 'Don Juan was a Stickman!', *Sunday Guardian* (18 Nov. 1973), 5.

——, 'Sell-out Crowd Enjoys "The Joker"', *Sunday Guardian* (1 Dec. 1974), 3, 15.

MILNE, ANTHONY, 'Fran McDormand's Trinidad Adventure', *Express* (25 July 1982).

——, 'I Prefer the Building to the Nobel Prize', *Express* (20 Nov. 1992), 33.

MILNER, HARRY, 'The Beauty of Decadence', *The Sunday Gleaner* (1 Nov. 1970), 5, 9.

——, 'Masterly Work', *The Daily Gleaner* (2 Apr. 1971), 6.

——, 'Two Theatrical Treats', *The Sunday Gleaner* (25 Apr. 1971), 5, 8.

——, 'Makak's Nightmare', *The Sunday Gleaner* (2 May 1971), 4.

——, 'Courage of the Classical', *The Sunday Gleaner* (22 July 1973), 14.

——, 'Lack of Voice Control', *The Sunday Gleaner* (30 Dec. 1975), 4–5.

——, 'Viable Work . . . with Necessary Changes', *The Daily Gleaner* (27 July 1976), 20.

MOMBARA, SULE, '"O Babylon!"—Where it Went Wrong', *Caribbean Contact*, 4/1 (April 1976), 15.

MORGAN, MARY E., 'Trinidad Theatre Workshop in St Vincent', *The Vincentian* (9 Nov. 1968), 6, 12.

MORRIS, MERVYN, 'Folk Theatre as Fine Art', *The Daily Gleaner* (20 Apr. 1971), 24.

——, 'A Vision Betrayed', *The Daily Gleaner* (28 Apr. 1971), 22.

MURRAY, JAN, 'The Joke was on the Joker', *Sunday Express*, sect. 2 (10 Jan. 1988), 8, 13.

NUNES, MARY, 'The Wandering T'dad Theatre', [Guyana, unidentified newspaper review] (1967).

ODLUM, GEORGE, 'Rave Notices For Theatre Workshop', *Voice of St Lucia* (12 Oct. 1968), 3.

——, 'The Joker of Seville', *Crusader* (12 Apr. 1975), 2.

——, '"The Haytian Earth" An Efflorescence of Talent/Walcott Triumphs!', *Crusader*, 14/29 (11 Aug. 1984), 1, 6–7.

OXAAL, IVAR, *Race and Revolutionary Consciousness: A Documentary Interpretation of the 1970 Black Power Revolt in Trinidad* (Cambridge, Mass.: Schenkman, 1971).

PADDINGTON, BRUCE, 'Revival of "Monkey Mountain"', *Express* (4 Aug. 1974), 11–12.

PANTIN, RAOUL, [interview with Derek Walcott], 'We are Still Being Betrayed', *Caribbean Contact*, 1/7 (July 1973), 14–16.

——, [interview with Derek Walcott], 'Any Revolution Based on Race is Suicidal', *Caribbean Contact*, 1/8 (Aug. 1973), 14–16.

——, 'The Amazing "Joker of Seville"', *Express* (6 Apr. 1975), 7, 10.

——, 'O Babylon!', *Caribbean Contact*, 14/1 (Apr. 1976), 17.

——, 'Revival—A Debut of Distinction', *Tapia* (7 Nov. 1976), 4–5.

——, [RAP], 'I've Written a New Play: It's on in St Croix and it's Getting Good Reviews', *Tapia*, 7/19 (8 May 1977), 9.

——, 'Raoul Pantin Reviews The Dragon Can't Dance', *The Sun* (11 Sept. 1978), 1, 8–9.

—— [RAP], '"Pantomime" It was a Frivolous Show', *The Sun* (2 Dec. 1978), 16.

——, '"A Nancy Story": A Tale of Yore', *Express* (27 Jan. 1982), 12.

—— [RAP], 'Disappointing', *Express* (6 July 1982), 16.

—— [RAP], '"Blue Nile" Speaks the Truth', *Express* (1985).

——, 'A Life Devoted to Life', *Express* (20 July 1987), 9.

PEARCE, EDWARD, 'O, Babylon!', *Encounter*, 70/5 (May 1988), 76.

PHELPS, KAREN, 'Where Actors and Audience Share Same Level', *Trinidad Guardian* (12 Jan. 1966), 3.

——, '"Belle Fanto" Much Too Confined', *Sunday Guardian* (17 Apr. 1966), 6.

PINHEIRO, CHRISTOPHER, '"A Nancy Story": An Elegant Best Village', *Sunday Guardian* (24 Jan. 1982), 9, 17.

POYNTING, JEREMY, 'At Homes, Tagore and Jive', *Kyk-over-al*, 37 (Dec. 1987), 45–8.

QUESTEL, VICTOR D., 'The Horns of Derek's Dilemma', *Tapia*, 3/12 (25 Mar. 1973), 4–5.

——, 'From the horses mouth', *Tapia*, 3/31 (5 Aug. 1973).

——, '"Dream on Monkey Mountain" in Perspective', *Tapia*, 4/35 (1 Sept. 1974), 2–3 (Independence suppl.); 4/36 (8 Sept. 1974), 6, 7, 10; 4/37 (15 Sept. 1974), 6–7; 4/39 (29 Sept. 1974), 5, 8.

——, 'Will Walcott Have the Last Laugh on His Joker?', *Trinidad Guardian* (6 Dec. 1974), 4.

——, 'Our Artists Press on Themselves', *Trinidad Guardian* (21 Feb. 1975), 4.

——, 'Message is not Fame, but to Endure', *Trinidad Guardian* (17 July 1975), 4.

——, 'Trinidad Theatre Workshop: A Bibliography', *Kairi* 76 (1976), 53–59.

——, 'The Little Carib Theatre (1948–1976)', *Caribbean Contact*, 4 (Dec. 1976), 22.

——, 'The Trinidad Theatre Workshop 1959–76', in 'Derek Walcott: Contradiction and Resolution', app. III, Ph.D. thesis (University of the West Indies, St Augustine, 1979), 559–625.

——, 'Remembrance: An Inspiring Elegy for the Afro-Saxon', *Trinidad Guardian* (3 July 1979), 7.

——, 'Poets get Standing Ovation', *Sunday Guardian* (27 Jan. 1980), 6.

——, 'Apartheid in Action', *The Sun* (15 May 1980), 4, 8.

——, 'Sizwe Bansi: A Moving Experience', *Trinidad and Tobago Review*, 3/10 ('Governor Plum', 1980), 4, 25.

——, 'Marie Laveau—Disappointing, Uneven', *Trinidad & Tobago Review*, 3/10 ('Governor Plum', 1980), 8, 18, 21, 22, 23.

——, 'I Have Moved Away from the Big Speech', *Trinidad and Tobago Review*, 5/1 ('Peewah', 1981), 11–14.

——, 'The Black American Not Given a Chance', *Trinidad and Tobago Review*, 5/3 ('Parang', 1981), 11–14.

——, 'The Trinidad Theatre Workshop 1966–1967', *The Literary Half-Yearly*, 26/1 (Jan. 1985), 163–79.

R. R., 'Merry-Go-Round', *The Daily Gleaner* (27 Apr. 1971).

RAE, NORMAN, '"Ione" Colourful but Academic', *The Daily Gleaner* (18 Mar. 1957), 18–19.

——, 'Fine Productions—But Where were the Audiences?', *The Daily Gleaner* (20 Dec. 1957), 28.

RAIDY, WILLIAM A., 'Exhilarating and Free!', *Long Island Press* (27 July 1972), 16.

RAMCHARITAR, RAYMOND, 'Baptism of Fire', *Sunday Guardian Magazine* (6 Dec. 1992), 11.

——, 'Walcott's "Odyssey" won't be Easy to Direct', *Trinidad Guardian* (27 July 1993), 17.

——, 'Odyssey—Best Production to Hit TT Theatre in Years', *Trinidad Guardian* (10 Aug. 1993), 13.

RAMPERSAD, KAMLA, 'A Look into the Souls of Racism', *Express* (3 Aug. 1986).

RAYMOND, JUDY, 'The Legacy of Derek Walcott', *Sunday Express* (11 Oct. 1992), 2, 3, 18.

——, 'Future Site of Walcott School for Arts?', *Sunday Express* (22 Nov. 1992), 2.

——, 'Enter a New Set of Strolling Players', *Sunday Express* (17 Jan. 1993).

——, 'Fascinating First Glimpse of Walcott's Latest', *Sunday Express* (8 Aug. 1993).

REID, STANLEY, 'St Omer Has Made Several Mistakes', *The Voice of St Lucia* (9 Nov. 1968), 6.

——, 'Ti Jean And His Brothers', *The Voice of St Lucia* (11 July 1970), 9.

——, 'A Moving Interpretation of Local Tradition', *Advocate-News* (20 Aug. 1970), 1.

RICE, ULRIC, 'An Outstanding Play', *Advocate* (27 Nov. 1983), 6.

——, '"Franklin" Shows the Caribbean as a Quilt', *Barbados Advocate* (21 Feb. 1990), 22.

ROACH, ERIC, 'It must Be an Agonising Place to Act', *Evening News* (17 Jan. 1966).

——, 'This Fierce Satire is Wildly Amusing', *Sunday Guardian* (6 Oct. 1966).

——, 'Mrs Adams—The Heroine', *Trinidad Guardian* (19 Apr. 1967), 7.

——, 'Theatre Workshop Season Off to Breezy Start / Return to Sanity', *Trinidad Guardian* (1969).

——, 'Double-Bill of Mere Frustrations', *Trinidad Guardian* (17 June 1969), 7.

——, 'This Musical Fuses Both Traditions of Folk Legend', *Sunday Guardian* (28 June 1970), 11.

——, 'Walcott Makes Fine Castle of Hate, Fear', *Trinidad Guardian* (1 Nov. 1971), 6.

——, '. . . of Creole T'dad's Dance and Drama', *Trinidad Guardian* (12 Dec. 1972), 3.

——, 'Experiment in Establishing the West Indian Theatre', *Trinidad Guardian* (18 Apr. 1973).

——, '"Pieces Two" Is an Experiment in Progress', *Trinidad Guardian* (28 Apr. 1973).

ROBINSON, RON, 'Guyanese Professional Theatre', *Kyk-over-al*, 37 (Dec. 1987), 55–8.

ROTHWELL, 'Focus', *Daily Nation* (2 Feb. 1990), 25.

RUSSELL, KATHLYN, 'Give Me film, Says Derek Walcott', *Sunday Express* (4 Sept. 1983), 31.

384   Select Bibliography

RUSSELL, KATHLYN, '"Woza Albert" Scores a Hit', *Express* (14 Apr. 1984).

——, 'The Saint Lucian Theatre Proved a Natural for the Magic of Walcott', *Express* (10 Aug. 1984), 14.

——, 'Walcott's "Haytian Earth" sets pace for arts revival', *Express* (14 Aug. 1984), 13.

——, 'Walcott's Monkey Mountain Deserves Warmer Responses', *Express* (12 Mar. 1985), 23.

—— [K. R.], 'Walcott's Blue Nile is a Drama about Theatre', *Express* (13 Aug. 1985), 23.

ST HILL, C. A. P., 'Errol Jones—T'dad's No. 1 Actor Soon to Appear Here', *The Voice of St Lucia* (9 Oct. 1968), 3.

——, 'The Belle of 'Belle Fanto', *The Voice of St Lucia* (16 Oct. 1968).

——, '"Psyche derek" [sic] Folk Opera', *The Crusader* (12 July 1970), 11–12.

ST OMER, GARTH, 'Dream, But Not Please, on Monkey Mountain', *The Voice of St Lucia* (2 Nov. 1968), 3, 6.

SAMUEL, KENNEDY, 'The Vision & The Reality', *The Weekend Voice* (18 Aug. 1984), 12.

SANDER, REINHARD, *The Trinidad Awakening: West Indian Literature of the Nineteen-Thirties* (New York: Greenwood Press, 1988).

SCOTT, DENNIS, 'Walcott on Walcott', *Caribbean Quarterly*, 14/1–2 (Mar./June 1968), 77–82, 120–6.

——, 'The Man Who Belonged', *The Daily Gleaner* (13 July 1973), 30.

——, 'An Ending in Carnival', *The Daily Gleaner* (18 Sept. 1973), 27.

——, 'A Joyful Joker', *The Daily Gleaner* (24 Nov. 1975), 26.

SCOTT, E. G. *Trinidad Guardian*, undated clipping.

SHAWN, WALLACE AND ANDRÉ GREGORY, *My Dinner with André* (New York: Grove Press, 1981).

SIMON, JOHN, 'Theatre: Debilitated Debbil', *New York Magazine* (14 Aug. 1972), 69.

SMART, WINSTON, 'There Were More Faults than Virtues', *Trinidad Guardian* (14 May 1968).

SMITH, KEITH, 'O Babylon!: An Adventure in Reggae', *People*, 1/9 (April 1976), 34–9.

SOLOMON, DENIS, 'Ape and Essence', *Tapia*, 7 (19 Apr. 1970), 6.

——, 'Can Walcott Deal with the Poor of our Society?', *Express* (4 Jan. 1972), 9, 12 (5 Jan. 1972), 9.

——, 'Beginning or End?' *Tapia*, 3/16 (22 Apr. 1973), 2–3.

——, 'Divided by Class, United by Bacchanal', *Tapia*, 3/27 (8 July 1973), 6.

[SPECIAL CORRESPONDENT], 'Derek Walcott's Basement Theatre', *Trinidad Guardian* (4 Nov. 1966), 12.

STELLA, 'Partyline', *The Star* [Jamaica] (24 Apr. 1971), 10.

STONE, IRVING AND JEAN (eds.), *Dear Theo: The Autobiography of Vincent Van Gogh* (Garden City, NY: Doubleday, 1937).

STONE, JUDY [MAUBY], 'Now the Joker's Laugh is Mature and Polished', *Trinidad Guardian* (24 Oct. 1975), 4.

—— [MAUBY], 'O Babylon!, Do Mafia Play with Beach Balls?', *Trinidad Guardian* (1 Apr. 1976), 4.

—— [MAUBY], 'Vitality, Freedom Beyond Martha', *Trinidad Guardian* (8 Nov. 1976), 15.

—— [MAUBY], 'Charlatan? Yes, Walcott is Still With Us', *Trinidad Guardian* (20 Jan. 1977), 4.

—— [MAUBY], 'The Maids': Message with Entertainment', *Trinidad Guardian* (28 Mar. 1977), 8.

—— [MAUBY], 'Love, Death, Faith, Sex, Life—Toute Bagai!', *Trinidad Guardian* (28 June 1977), 7.

—— [MAUBY], 'Young Bajan Actors Star at Little Carib', *Trinidad Guardian* (5 Aug. 1977), 4.

——, 'National Theatre Wanted', *Trinidad and Tobago Review* (December 1977), 9.

——, 'Top Actors Join Banyan in Family Planning Series', *Trinidad Guardian* (6 Jan. 1978).

——, 'Sell-out Start for Dinner Theatre', *Trinidad Guardian* (7 June 1979), 4, 13.

——, 'Caribuste: Promises Bright Era for the Theatre', *Sunday Guardian* (9 June 1979), 36–8, 40–4.

——, 'At Last, Masterpiece on the Middle Class', *Trinidad Guardian* (13 July 1979), 4.

——, 'What Corsbie Did to Walcott's "Pantomime"', *Trinidad Guardian* (5 Feb. 1981), 13.

——, 'Death of our Dodos in "The Last Carnival"', *Trinidad Guardian* (15 July 1982), 18–19.

——, 'Group that's Trying to get Back to the Basics', *Trinidad Guardian* (28 June 1983), 21.

——, 'Highway Drama of Cops and Naked Actors', *Trinidad Guardian* (26 July 1983), 12, 20.

——, 'New Realisations the Essence of "Like Them That Dream"', *Trinidad Guardian* (11 Oct. 1983), 19.

——, 'I May Lose Derek's Friendship', *Trinidad Guardian* (15 Nov. 1983), 17.

——, 'Earl Warner Shares his Thoughts', *Trinidad Guardian* (22 Nov. 1983), 19.

——, 'Exploring Sound, Body and Use of Space', *Trinidad Guardian* (29 Nov. 1983), 23.

——, 'Street Theatre could be Winner', *Trinidad Guardian* (19 Feb. 1985), 6.

——, 'Walcott's Dream Wakes up to New Life', *Trinidad Guardian* (25 Mar. 1985), 21.

——, 'Warner's "Beef No Chicken" an Inspired Production', *Caribbean Contact*, 13/1 (June 1985), 14.

——, 'Savage Lives in West Indian Backyard', *Trinidad Guardian* (10 June 1985), 25.

——, 'Superb Surrealism in "Nightmare"', *Trinidad Guardian* (12 Nov. 1985), 21.

386   Select Bibliography

STONE, JUDY, 'We Can Gain from Outside Experience', *Trinidad Guardian* (3 Dec. 1985), 17.

——, 'Derek Pushing our Actors for More Recognition Abroad', *Trinidad Guardian* (10 Dec. 1985), 17.

——, 'Crowds Enjoy Slices of Derek Walcott Plays', *Trinidad Guardian* (24 Apr. 1986), 21.

——, 'Eunice Alleyne does not Act Lena, She Is Lena', *Trinidad Guardian* (13 Aug. 1986), 24.

——, 'Rawle Gibbons Makes Time to Direct', *Trinidad Guardian* (22 July 1986).

——, 'Wilbert would have been Proud of "Beef" Performance', *Trinidad Guardian* (11 Aug. 1987).

——, 'Brotherhood of the Yard', *Sunday Guardian* (16 Aug. 1987), 18, 19, 25.

——, 'Theatre Life: Camps Taught . . .', *Trinidad Guardian* (2 Oct. 1987).

——, 'Walcott's "Joker" returns after 12 years', *Trinidad Guardian* (30 Dec. 1987), 10.

——, 'Magnificent Directing by Laveau', *Trinidad Guardian* (7 Jan. 1988), 9.

——, 'Just Who is this Richard Montgomery?', *Trinidad Guardian* (8 Jan. 1988), 5.

——, 'Wilbert Holder Left a Vacuum in Trinidad Theatre', *Trinidad Guardian* (13 May 1988), 14.

——, 'Albert Laveau: One of the Finest TT Actors', *Trinidad Guardian* (1 May 1989), 11.

——, *Studies in West Indian Literature: Theatre* (London: Macmillan Caribbean, 1994).

SWANN, TONY, 'Drums and Colours—Guts at Least', *Public Opinion* (10 May 1958), 7.

SWEETING, LYN, 'Standing Ovation for "Sizwe Bansi"', *The Tribune* (8 June 1982).

SYDNEY-SMITH, AGNES, '"Henri Christophe" Poet Walcott's First Major Play on Haitian Revolution', *Evening News* (21 Apr. 1968).

TAITT, ANDY, 'Powerful Play Speaks of WI Situation', *Together Magazine* (26 Jan. 1990), 4.

——, 'Andy Taitt Interviews Michael Gilkes', *Together Magazine* (26 Jan. 1990), 5.

[TAPIA REPORTER], 'Something Good is Coming to Dance', *Tapia* (19 Dec. 1974), 10.

TAYLOR, JEREMY, 'Perfect Blend of Music and Dance', *Express* (16 Dec. 1972), 9, 10.

——, 'The Joker of Seville—Actors Give Grand Performance', *Express* (4 Dec. 1974) 9, 18.

——, 'Praise for Joker of Seville', *Express* (10 Dec. 1974).

——, 'Play of the Month a Great Change', *Express* (2 June 1975), 8.

——, '"Seagull" a Brave Attempt at a Beautiful Play', *Express* (15 July 1975), 9.

——, 'A Beautifully Simple, Dramatic Idea . . .', *Express* (24 Mar. 1976), 21.

——, 'Belle Fanto—Beautiful', *Express* (15 Sept. 1976), 12.

——, 'Perhaps "The Charlatan" is a Little Overworked?', *Express* (19 Jan. 1977), 22.

——, 'Workshop Helps Us Understand The Maids', *Express* (13 Mar. 1977), 9.

——, 'Dragon Can't Dance', *Express* (10 Oct. 1978), 17.

——, ' "Departure"—Sad and Rambling', *Express* (27 Jan. 1979), 15, 22.

——, ' "Remembrance"—A Moving Tender Play', *Express* (6 July 1979), 13.

——, 'A True Revival from Workshop Dancers', *Express* (8 Nov. 1976), 19.

——, 'Walcott—at 50', *Caribbean Contact* (March 1980), 14.

——, 'Sizwe Bansi Really First Rate', *Express* (22 Apr. 1980), 10.

——, 'Walcott Nudging up to Broadway', *Express* (2 June 1980), 14–15.

——, ' "The Last Carnival" ', *Express* (6 July 1982), 24.

——, 'Bunyan and Walcott Team up on "The Rig" ', *Express* [25 July 1982].

THERESE, SR MARIE 'The Agony of a Seagull', *Catholic News* (20 July 1975), 10.

THOMASSON, FRANK, 'Down Memor [sic] Lane', *Kyk-over-al*, 37 (Dec. 1987), 49–54.

THOMPSON, JEANNE, ' "Sizwe Bansi is Dead"—Superb Theatre!', *Nassau Guardian* (9 Aug. 1982), 3B.

THOMPSON, MERTEL E., 'Don Juan's "Hilarious Exploits": The Joker of Seville on Stage', *The Literary Half-Yearly*, 26/1 (January 1985), 132–48.

TRETICK, JOYCE, 'Dream on Monkey Mountain', *Show Business* (5 Aug. 1969), 13, 17.

VAUGHAN, PETER, 'Holder Brings a Tropical Coolness to "Pantomime" Role', *Minneapolis Star and Tribune* (25 Mar. 1983), 2C.

WAGGONER, JEAN, 'Independence Dance and Drama', *DJ Weekly Magazine* (July/Aug. 1966), 3, 6.

WALCOTT, DEREK, '1944', *The Voice of St Lucia* (2 Aug. 1944), 3.

——, *Henri Christophe: A Chronicle in Seven Scenes* (Barbados: Advocate, 1950).

——, *Ione*, Extra-Mural Department, University of the West Indies, 1957. (Caribbean Plays, 8)

——, 'A Modern Theatre', *The Daily Gleaner* (25 Mar. 1957).

——, 'Drums and Colours', *West Indies Festival of Arts Trinidad April 1958*, 8–9.

——, *Journard or A Comedy Till the Last Minute*, Extra-Mural Department, University of the West Indies, cyclostyled: (n. d.; 1959 or after.), 14 pages. (Caribbean Plays)

——, 'Need for a Little Theatre in POS', *Sunday Guardian* (10 July 1960), 22.

——, *Drums and Colours*, *Caribbean Quarterly*, 7/1–2 (Mar.–June, 1961); repub. *Caribbean Quarterly*, 30/4 (Dec. 1992), 22–135.

——, 'Unique Lighting Equipment Offered New Little Carib', *Sunday Guardian* (20 Aug. 1961), 7.

——, 'US Stage Director Takes A Look At Queen's Hall', *Trinidad Guardian* (30 Aug. 1961), 5.

388   Select Bibliography

WALCOTT, DEREK, 'US Stage Director on Observation Trip', *Trinidad Guardian* (4 Mar. 1962), 5.

——, 'Public Debut for Theatre Workshop', *Sunday Guardian* (25 Mar. 1962), 7.

——, *The Charlatan*, mimeo., Extra-Mural Department, University of the West Indies, [1962]. (Caribbean Plays)

——, 'West Indian Dance, Dancers', *Sunday Guardian* (28 July 1963), 14.

——, 'Derek Walcott Looks At Off-Broadway Theatre', *Trinidad Guardian* (20 Oct. 1963), 15.

——, 'A Need for Supporters', *Trinidad Guardian* (25 Dec. 1963), 5.

——, 'National Theatre is the Answer', *Trinidad Guardian* (12 Aug. 1964), 5.

——, 'Leaving School', *London Magazine*, 5/6 (1965), 1–14.

——, 'The Theatre of Abuse', *Sunday Guardian* (3 Jan. 1965), 4.

——, 'S. Grande Tonight; Broadway Next', *Trinidad Guardian* (27 Jan. 1965), 5.

——, 'Energetic Guild Comes to Town', *Trinidad Guardian* (19 May 1965), 5.

——, 'Actor Slade Hopkinson Gives a Farewell Interview', *Trinidad Guardian* (14 July 1965), 6.

——, 'Interview with an Actor', *Trinidad Guardian* (13 Oct. 1965), 5.

——, 'Writing for Children Pt. III'. *Sunday Guardian* (13 Feb. 1966), 3.

——, 'The Prospects of a National Theatre', *Sunday Guardian* (6 Mar. 1966).

——, 'West Indian Art Today', *Sunday Guardian* (8 May 1966), 8.

——, 'Writer's Cramp on a Stage', *Trinidad Guardian* (8 June 1966), 5.

——, 'Trinidad's 1st Repertory Season Opens Next Month', *Sunday Guardian* (11 Sept. 1966), 6.

——, 'The Great Irony', *Sunday Guardian* (25 Sept. 1966), 6.

——, 'Opening the Road', *Sunday Guardian* (25 Sept. 1966), 6.

——, 'Beyond the Backyard' , *Sunday Guardian* (11 Dec. 1966), 10, 27.

——, 'Fellowships', *Sunday Guardian* (15 Jan. 1967), 8.

——, 'On the Theatre', *Trinidad Guardian* (30 Jan. 1967), 8.

——, 'Othello Off and On', *Sunday Guardian* (7 May 1967), 6.

——, 'Bajans Are Still Very Insular and Prejudiced', *Sunday Guardian* (23 July 1967), 5.

——, 'The Theatre Workshop at the Crossroads', *Sunday Guardian* (29 Sept. 1968), 4, 11.

——, 'What the Twilight Says: An Overture', in *Dream on Monkey Mountain and Other Plays* (New York: Farrar, Straus & Giroux, 1970), 3–40.

——, *Dream on Monkey Mountain and Other Plays* (New York: Farrar, Straus & Giroux, 1970).

——, 'Derek's Most West Indian Play', *Sunday Guardian Magazine* (21 June 1970), 7.

——, 'Meanings', *Savacou*, 2 (Sept. 1970), 45–51.

——, 'Superfluous Defence of a Revolutionary', *Express* (20 Aug. 1971), 4.

——, 'Conscience of a Revolutionary', *Express* (24 Oct. 1971), 22–4.

——, 'Mixing the Dance and Drama', *Trinidad Guardian* (6 Dec. 1972), 4.

WALCOTT, DEREK, *Another Life* (New York: Farrar, Straus & Giroux, 1973).
——, 'Why This Astigmatism toward the Workshop's White Actors?', *Trinidad Guardian* (19 Apr. 1973), 5.
——, ' "Rights of Passage" Drama in Itself', *Trinidad Guardian* (25 Apr. 1973), 5.
——, 'Walcott on the Theatre in Trinidad and Jamaica', *The Sunday Gleaner* (15 July 1973), 5.
——, 'The Caribbean: Culture or Mimicry?', *Journal of Interamerican Studies and World Affairs*, 16/1 (Feb. 1974), 3–13.
——, 'Soul Brother to "The Joker of Seville" ', *Trinidad Guardian* (8 Nov. 1974), 4.
——, 'On Choosing Port of Spain', in *David Frost Introduces Trinidad and Tobago* (London: André Deutsch, 1975), 14–23.
——, 'The Joker: Closer to Continuous Theatre', *Trinidad Guardian* (22 Mar. 1975), 8.
——, 'Why do Chekhov here?', *Sunday Guardian* (29 June 1975), 7.
——, 'Story of Four Loves at the Little Carib: Chekhov's Masterpiece in First Local Premiere', *Trinidad Guardian* (4 July 1975), 4.
——, 'Why Belle Fanto Has Survived', *Sunday Guardian* (22 Aug. 1976), 6.
——, *The Joker of Seville & O Babylon!* (New York: Farrar, Straus & Giroux, 1978).
—— [?], 'La Chapelle and Douglas Striving for Cohesion', *Sunday Guardian* (26 May 1978), 5.
——, *Remembrance & Pantomime* (New York: Farrar, Straus & Giroux, 1980).
——, 'Sizwe Bansi Excellent', *Express* (8 May 1980).
——, *Three Plays: The Last Carnival, Beef, No Chicken, and A Branch of the Blue Nile* (New York: Farrar, Straus & Giroux, 1986).
——, 'Derek Walcott Talks About "The Joker of Seville" ', *Carib*, 4 (1986), 1–15.
——, 'The Poet in the Theatre', *Poetry Review*, 80/4 (winter 1990–91), 4–8.
——, *The Odyssey: A Stage Version* (New York: Farrar, Straus & Giroux, 1993).
WALDERMAR, CARLA, 'Cultural Exchanging', *Sunday Magazine* (8 May 1983), 3.
WATERMAN, KATHY, 'A Man Called Slade', *Sunday Express* (9 June 1985), 29.
——, 'Walcott Play to be Filmed Here', *Sunday Express* (21 Sept. 1986), 12.
WATT, DOUGLAS, ' "Ti-Jean & Brothers" Comes to Central Park', *Daily News* (28 July 1972), 57.
WICKHAM, JOHN, 'Theatre: "Dream on Monkey Mountain" ', *Bim* 12/48 (Jan.– June 1969), 267–8.
——, 'A Tale of Two Dreams', *Sunday Sun* (3 Feb. 1980), 27.
——, 'Nothing Much New', *Sunday Sun* (4 Jan. 1981), 27.
——, 'Much More than Acting', *The Nation* (5 Oct. 1982), 9.
WIGHT, BENEDICT, 'The Success of Derek Walcott', *Express* (16 Feb. 1970), 9.
YUILLE-WILLIAM, 'Statement by the Hon. Minister of Community Development, Culture and Women's Affairs in Respect of the use of The Old Fire Brigade Station Currently Occupied by the Trinidad Theatre Workshop' (12 Jan. 1993).

II. Unsigned Articles, in Chronological Order

'Next Production', *The Pelican*, 3/4 (Jan. 1956), 9.

'West Indian Plays', *The Pelican*, 3/5 (Feb. 1956), 6.

'Drama Festival Awards', *Public Opinion* (28 July 1956), 7.

' "Wine of the Country" Walcott's new play at UCWI Friday', *The Daily Gleaner* (14 Aug. 1956), 14.

'Violent Walcott Verse Play', *Public Opinion* (18 Aug. 1956), 8.

' "Wine of the Country" Stark, Bold and Ruthless', *The Daily Gleaner* (20 Aug. 1956), 16–17.

'Strong Cast for "Ione" ', *The Daily Gleaner* (14 Mar. 1957), 18.

' "Ione" Opens New Era in Jamaican Theatre', *Sunday Gleaner* (10 May 1957), 12.

'Company of Players Try A Walcott Opus', *Sunday Guardian* (13 Oct. 1957). 7.

'Trinidad to See A Walcott Play Again', *Trinidad Guardian* (30 Oct. 1957).

'Place of Drama in the New West Indian World', *Sunday Guardian* (1 Dec. 1957), 8.

'Top Actors for Roles in "Ti-Jean" ', *Trinidad Guardian* (June 1958), 5.

'Poor audience saw "Ti-Jean" ', *Chronicle* ([June] 1958).

'The Little Carib Theatre Workshop', *Opus*, 1/1 (Feb. 1960), 31–2.

'Workshop Makes Debut', *Trinidad Guardian* (1 May 1962).

'Little Carib Turns Now to Drama', *Trinidad Guardian* (6 May 1962), 6.

'Caribbean Writers—The Walcotts of St Lucia', *Drama Dance Art Music* [Jamaica], 1 (June 1962), 22–3.

'P. O. S. to See "Charlatan" ', *Trinidad Guardian* (4 Dec. 1962), 6.

' "The Charlatan" Gets 5 Calls', *Evening News* (11 Dec. 1962).

'Batai—Battle of the Cannes Brules', *Daily Mirror* (23 Jan. 1965).

'Two Plays that Lifted the Basement Theatre', *Trinidad Guardian* (11 Jan. 1966), 5.

'Mr Priestly Sees for Himself', *Daily Mirror* (12 Jan. 1966), 14.

'Kicking Off with The Blacks', *Trinidad Guardian* (6 Oct. 1966), 10.

' "The Road" Starts Scheduled Run Tonight', *Trinidad Guardian* (26 Oct. 1966), 5.

'Walcott Loads his Tiny Basement Bus', *Trinidad Guardian* (1 Nov. 1966), 16.

'Errol John's Prized Play at Queen's Hall', *Trinidad Guardian* (17 Apr. 1967), 4.

'Double Bill at UWI', *Trinidad Guardian* (21 June 1967), 5.

'From All Quarters', *Sunday Guardian* (2 July 1967), 6.

'Players Return to Base', *Trinidad Guardian* (11 July 1967), 5.

'Theatre Group for Canada', *Express* (15 July 1967), 9.

' "Belle Fanto" goes to its "birthplace" ', *Trinidad Guardian* (27 July 1967), 4.

'Caribana '67', *Toronto Daily Star* (5 Aug. 1967), 32.

'Drama in the Idiom at Guild', *Guyana Graphic* (17 Aug. 1967), 6, 7.

'Small Audiences at T.G.', *Guyana Graphic* (25 Aug. 1967).

' "Belle Fanto"—A Review', unidentified newspaper review, Guyana (1967).

'Theatre Guild', unidentified newspaper review, Guyana (1967).

'What We Think', unidentified newspaper editorial, Guyana (1967).
'Dream on Monkey Mountain Called the Best in W. I.', *Sunday Guardian* (14 Jan. 1968), 6.
'Two Expo Dancers Added to Cast of "Monkey Mountain"', *Trinidad Guardian* (25 Jan. 1968), 5.
'Tonight: Walcott's "Henri Christophe"', *Trinidad Guardian* (26 Apr. 1968), 6.
'The Lights in the Basement Dim Out', *Sunday Express* (6 Oct. 1968), 5.
'Walcott and Group Arrive on Monday', *Voice of St Lucia* (12 Oct. 1968), 2.
'Five-Island Tour', *Sunday Guardian* (3 Nov. 1968), 11.
'"The World of Selvon"—That's the Workshop's Big Anniversary Opener', *Express* (25 Feb. 1969), 10.
'"Workshop" Starts Anniversary with Readings by Selvon', *Trinidad Guardian* (26 Feb. 1969), 5.
'"Selvon's England" for TTT', *Trinidad Guardian* (29 Apr. 1969), 4.
'Televiewing with Argus/ "Selvon's England"—a nice surprise', *Evening News*, (1969).
'Double-Bill by Theatre Workshop Next Month', *Sunday Guardian* (25 May 1969).
'The Nervous Strain of an Inter-Racial Marriage', *Express* (25 May 1969), 15.
'Theatre Workshop to Perform in the US', *Trinidad Guardian* (10 June 1969), 7.
'Trinidad's Foremost Dramatic Group's Visit Sponsored by Eugene O'Neil [sic] Memorial Theatre Foundation', *Trinidad Guardian* (10 June 1969), 7.
'Theatre Workshop to Perform WI Plays in US Next Month', *Express* (10 June 1969), 13.
'The Company', *The Scene*, special edn. [Waterford, Conn.], 'Theatre Workshop of Trinidad', 1/10 (29 July 1969).
'Trinidad Group Does Folk Play At O'Neill Meet', *Variety* (13 Aug. 1969).
'Walcott Plans "Instant Theatre!"' *Trinidad Guardian* (20 Aug. 1969), 8.
'NBC Crew Due Next Week to Film Play by Derek Walcott', *Evening News* (24 Oct. 1969).
'Theatre Workshop gets $10,000', *Trinidad Guardian* (Dec. 1969), 1.
'$10,000 Grant from NBC for Workshop', unidentified press clipping (Dec. 1969).
'Walcott's 'Dream on TTT', *Trinidad Guardian* (12 Feb. 1970), 4.
'Workshop Looking for a New Home', *Evening News* (20 Mar. 1970).
'Has Anyone A Suitable Site for the Theatre?', *Express* (24 Mar. 1970), 12.
'Theatre Workshop Revives a Musical', *Express* (11 June 1970), 2.
'Theatre Workshop to Tour Caribbean Islands', *Trinidad Guardian* (13 June 1970).
'Walcott Records Success in Jamaica and New York', *Trinidad Guardian* (29 Apr. 1971), 7.
'Theatre Workshop Leaves', *The Daily Gleaner* (3 May 1971), 22.
'Behind-the-Bridge Play to Get World Audience', *Trinidad Guardian* (26 May 1971).
'Dream Gets Top U.S. Award', *Trinidad Guardian* (29 May 1971), 9.

' "Dream" at Tapia House Moonlight Theatre', *Tapia*, 17 (27 June 1971).

'Caribbean Works for Radio Series', *Trinidad Guardian* (31 July 1971), 9.

'The Plays and the Playwrights', *The Texaco Star* (13 Aug. 1971), 1.

'Texaco Sponsors Radio Theatre', *The Texaco Star* (13 Aug. 1971), 1.

'Hit Play Comes to Queen's Hall', *Express* (13 Oct. 1971), 13.

'Weekend Billing Start of New Lease for "Ti-Jean" ', *Trinidad Guardian* (21 Oct. 1971), 7.

' "In A Fine Castle" may be in for it', *Express* (30 Oct. 1971).

'Future Fan?', *The New York Times* (27 Feb. 1972), D17.

'Local Writers Featured on the Air', *Express* (27 July 1972), 12.

'Workshop to Present Theatre 15', *Trinidad Guardian* (1 Aug. 1972), 4.

'Picking Up Where "Pieces" Left Off', *Express* (20 Mar. 1973), 7.

'Second Season Ends with Dance, Drama', *Trinidad Guardian* (25 Apr. 1973), 5.

'Mimic Men? Absurd', *Sunday Guardian* (29 Apr. 1973), 1.

'Walcott's "Dream" Comes to the Carib', *Trinidad Guardian* (22 July 1974), 7.

'White Barn Slates Two Plays by Trinidad Writer', *The Westport News* sect. 2 (14 Aug. 1974), 10.

'Walcott Reading at Library Tonight', *Express* (17 Oct. 1974), 11.

'Now St Croix Hails Walcott's "Dream" ', *Trinidad Guardian* (23 Oct. 1974), 4.

' "Songs for Theatre" at the Library', *Trinidad Guardian* (5 Nov. 1974), 4.

'Joker of Seville at Little Carib—Gayelle Style', *Express* (17 Nov. 1974), 7.

' "The Joker of Seville" at the Little Carib', *News*, Showtime sect. (21 Nov. 1974), 4.

'Walcott Scores with "The Joker" ', *Trinidad Guardian* (30 Nov. 1974), 9.

'Rhythms of the "Joker of Seville" on Record', *Trinidad Guardian* (8 Mar. 1975), 5.

'Editorial—The Joker of Seville', *The Voice of St Lucia* (9 Apr. 1975), 2.

' "The Joker" starts third run tonight', *Trinidad Guardian* (15 Oct. 1975), 4.

'A Magnificent Play', *The Star* (25 Nov. 1975), 4.

'A Play Well Worth Seeing', *The Jamaica Daily News* (27 Nov. 1975), 17, 23.

'The Joker of Seville', *The Jamaica Daily News* (30 Nov. 1975), 20–1.

'Actor switches in "Joker" ', *The Daily Gleaner* (4 Dec. 1975), 5.

' "O Babylon" Opens Friday', *Trinidad Guardian* (14 Mar. 1976), 6.

' "O Babylon!" for Naparima Bowl', *Trinidad Guardian* (14 June 1976), 4.

'Carifesta on Despite Jamaica Emergency', unidentified newspaper clipping, possibly Jamaica *The Daily Gleaner* (June 1976), 1.

'An 80-Member T'Dad Team for Carifesta', *Trinidad Guardian* (9 July 1976), 1.

'A Feast of Artistic Goodies', *The Star* (27 July 1976), 4.

'Dinsley Roti on Sale in Jamaica', *Trinidad Guardian* (29 July 1976), 2.

'Roscoe's Makak Hypnotises Little Carib Audience', *Trinidad Guardian* (30 July 1976).

'The Joker of St Lucia', *The Bomb* (20 Dec. 1976), 5.

'Charlatan Returns More Musically', *Trinidad Guardian* (23 Dec. 1976), 6.

'Notices Comments', *Kairi 76*, 50.

'"Charlatan" Just Right for the Carnival Season', *Express* (13 Jan. 1977), 11.
'Walcott Quits Workshop', *The Sun* (4 May 1977), 2.
'Theatre Workshop Doing Things', *Express* (30 June 1977), 12.
'Get Ready for Third Season of Dance', *Express* (22 May 1978), 18.
'Notices and Comments', *Kairi 78*, 67.
'Caribbean—US Artists in Exciting Link-up', unidentified newspaper clipping (May 1979).
'"Remembrance" Next on the Dinner Theatre Stage', *Express* (24 June 1979), 10.
'Marie La Veau', *Trinidad and Tobago Review*, 3/6 (Dec. 1979).
'Derek Walcott Hailed', *Trinidad Guardian* (25 Jan. 1980), 8.
'Russian Sounds Fill Little Carib', *Express* (25 Jan. 1980).
'Derek Walcott Goes Back to School to Read Poetry', *Express* (4 May 1981), 23.
'Walcott Tells of Local Amateur Actors in Disguise', *Sunday Guardian* (11 July 1982), 5, 10.
'What Ever Happened to Walcott's Second Phase?', *Sunday Express* (25 July 1982), 24–5.
'Going Places', *Sunday Express* (25 July 1982), 19.
'These Nights at the Little Carib', *Sunday Express* (28 July 1982), 44.
'Bourne has Long Link with Theatre', *Advocate-News* (25 Sept. 1982), 7.
'Play which Deserves the Award', *The Nation* (29 Nov. 1983), 10.
'Theatre Workshop—The First 25 Years', *Sunday Express* (8 Apr. 1984), 46.
'Woza (Rise up) Albert!', *Sunday Express* (8 Apr. 1984), 45–6.
'Wilbert Holder Back at Little Carib Theatre', *Sunday Guardian* (8 Apr. 1984), 19.
'"Woza Albert" story of Luthuli', *Trinidad Guardian* (13 Apr. 1984), 20.
'Haytian Earth', *The Weekend Voice* (28 July 1984), 12.
'La Veau to Direct Walcott's "Dream"', *Sunday Express* (10 Feb. 1985), 39.
'Walcott's "Blue Nile" at Home in Tent Theatre', *Express* (18 Aug. 1985), 8.
'WALCOTT'S THEATRE WORKSHOP COMING', *The Weekend Voice* (24 Jan. 1987), 13.
'The Final Farewell to Wilbert Holder', *Sunday Express* (19 July 1987).
'"Joker of Seville" is in Town', *Express* (1 Jan. 1988), 25.
'Drama Gets Home at Old Fire Headquarters', *Trinidad Guardian* (3 Aug. 1989), 3.
'"Franklin" to be staged in T&T', *W Magazine*, sect. B (17 Mar. 1990).
'Tiny School Produces Two Nobel Winners', *Trinidad Guardian* (9 Oct. 1992), 6.
'A Home now for Mr Walcott', *Sunday Express* (14 Jan. 1993), 8.
'Stratford Director Meets Calypso Lingo', *Sunday Express* (1 Aug. 1993), 4, 8.

III. Recordings

The Throne in an Autumn Room, by Lennox Brown, for Radio Canada International, Montreal, with TTW actors (E–1024) (1972).

The Joker of Seville, Semp, with voices of original cast (1975); reissued on cassette for Semp Studios (Dec. 1987).

O Babylon!, Kilmarnock Records, Staten Island, NY; voices non-TTW and featuring Carl Hall (KIL 72030) [1980].

IV.   Towards a Filmography

Copies of the NBC 1969 film of *Dream on Monkey Mountain* are held by the Library of Congress and some university media centres. Most video films of the Trinidad Theatre Workshop on wide tape appear to have been lost, erased, or destroyed, but some copies of Trinidad Tobago Televison productions are housed at Banyan Studios, Port of Spain.

Banyan Ltd, 15 Cipriani Boulevard, Newtown, Port of Spain, Trinidad, has video tapes of the St Thomas production of *Marie Laveau*, *Last Carnival*, rehearsals of the Trinidad Theatre Workshop production of *Beef, No Chicken*, the TTT production of *Pantomime*, Victor Questel's 1980 interview with Walcott, *The Rig*, and some other materials including excerpts from later TTW productions and TTW actors in other productions of Walcott plays.

Index

....

Abbey Theatre 9, 17, 25, 310
Achebe, Chinua 12, 335
Actors' Studio (USA) 30, 40
Actors Theatre (St Paul) 286
Adult Drama Festival 11, 14, 43
Albee, Edward 59; Zoo Story 57, 58, 79,
  82, 83, 84
Aldwych Theatre 183, 194, 212
All Theatre Productions, see Camps, Helen
Alleyne, Eunice 5, 18, 22, 79, 147, 167,
  190, 345, 349; acting style 48, 153; and
  TTW management 94, 131, 353; in Ione
  (1957) 18–19, 48; in Drums and Colours
  (1958) 22, 48; in Malcochon (1964) 47; in
  Belle Fanto (1966) 60, 68; in Belle Fanto
  (1967) 84; in Dream (1967) 83; in Dream
  (1968) 88, 90; five island tour (1968)
  100, 101, 102; in Dream (1969) 114; in
  Dragon (1978) 276, 277; in Departure
  (1979) 278; in Marie Laveau (1980)
  301–3; in A 'Nancy Story (1982) 283; in
  Dream (1985) 329; in Night, Mother
  (1985) 344; in Boesman and Lena (1986)
  345; in Let Resurrection Come! (1986)
  345; in Joker (1987) 350; in The Odyssey
  (1993) 5, 356
Alleyne, Ken 89
Allsop, Constance 57, 60, 65, 77, 78, 84
Alswang, Ralph 206
American Dance Festival 111
Amoco Oil 233, 333
Andrews, John 32, 65, 77, 89, 108, 112,
  114, 117, 121, 132, 138, 147, 185, 186,
  190, 201, 271, 282, 342, 345, 349, 356;
  lighting design 65, 108, 212, 232, 254,
  258, 347; TTW management 94, 131,
  250
Anthony, Michael 125
Antigua 100, 103

Antoine, Evans 272
Applewhaite, Charles 141, 147, 156, 186,
  314, 347; Jamaica tour (1971) 149, 171;
  in Beef (1981) 282; as Raphael in 1987
  Joker 350, 351; in The Odyssey (1993) 356;
  in tour to the Netherlands (1993) 357
Arbee Productions, see Hughes, Brenda
Archibald, Douglas 36, 61, 109, 123, 135,
  159, 190; Anne-Marie 36, 155; Junction
  Village 36; The Rose Slip 109, 135, 348
Archibald, William 36
'Argus' 109
Artaud, Antonin 56
Art Creators Limited Gallery 301, 337
Arts Guild, The (St Lucia) 10, 11, 12, 14,
  17, 21, 24–5, 39, 42, 47, 100, 143, 320,
  324, 325, 327, 328
Assoon, Barbara 77
Astor Cinema 81, 329, 343
Atherly, Shirley 88
audience 57, 59, 61, 76, 77, 84–5, 97, 100,
  103–4, 123, 126, 191, 196, 217, 226, 290,
  306, 341
Augier, Roy 12
Augustus, Earl 157, 158
Awai, Theresa 347

Baden-Semper, Brenda 272
Bagasse Company 352, 356
Bahamas 280
Bailey, Esther 65, 88, 98, 100, 108, 118
Banyan Studios 295, 301, 304, 316, 348;
  Trinidad Television Workshop 274
Baptiste, Lucita 57, 60
Barb, The 12
Barbados 81, 100, 102, 103, 104, 130, 131,
  132, 140, 141, 280, 290, 297, 317–19,
  337–9, 342; problems of taking Joker to
  223

Barbados Arts Council 79, 85, 92, 223
Barbados Writers Workshop 273
Barclays Bank 99, 250
Barker, John S. 36
Barn Theatre (Jamaica) 236, 341
Barnes, Belinda 131, 138, 140, 291
Barnes, Brian 94, 98, 122
Barnes, Clive 164
Basement Theatre, The 50, 55–98, 99,
    304, 333; as Arts Centre 61; dimensions
    56, 97; eviction from 98; intimacy 56,
    70; lighting 57
Bastien, Eliot: A 'Nancy Story 283–4
Baxter, Ivy 26
BBC 10, 12
Beaubrun, Norman 301
Beaubrun, Stella 301
Beaufort, John 165
Beckett, Samuel 99; Krapp's Last Tape 42;
    Waiting for Godot 62, 63, 71, 92, 125
Beddeau, Andrew 66, 88, 114, 115, 118, 147,
    210, 220, 221, 234, 237, 244, 254, 256;
    Shango priest 69, 88, 119; in Dream (1968)
    88; in Dream (1974) 202, 205; in St
    Croix Dream 208, 209; in Joker (1974) 211
Belfon, Joan 301
Belmont 35, 69, 292
Benedict, Stephen 117
Bentley, Arthur 279, 295
Berghoff, Herbert 40
Bernhardt, Melvin 111
Berrigan, Daniel 178, 184, 194
Best, Sydney 60, 65, 69, 77, 83, 88, 90, 147
Bishop Anstey High School (Tobago) 82
Bishop Anstey High School (Trinidad) 98,
    131, 173, 174, 179, 194
Bishop, Gillian 284
Bishop, Leonore 250, 272, 273
Black, Joseph 70–1, 76
Black Power 126–8, 131, 141, 143, 155,
    317, 339
Blackman, Hurley 89
Blandin, Noel 342–3, 345; as Moustique
    (1985) 330, 331; in Branch (1985) 332
Bobb, Stefan 272
Bonaparte, Wayne 207
Boothman, Michael 187, 193, 203, 345
Borde, Percival 17, 114, 118
Borges, Jorge Luis 62
Boston 3, 4, 289, 312, 317
Boston Playwrights' Theatre 356
Boston University 289, 317, 324
Boyse, Dorsie 337
Bradford, Noreen 147, 148, 149, 156, 168,
    181, 184, 188, 193

Brash, Maurice 294, 295, 296, 297, 314,
    316, 332
Brathwaite, Edward Kamau 13, 104;
    Odale's Choice 155, 168, 178, 179, 182,
    183; Rights of Passage 182, 183
Brathwaite, Mary 13, 14
Brecht, Bertold 27, 56, 126, 139, 204, 205,
    212, 229, 310, 318; Berlin Ensemble and
    TTW compared 96; Three Penny Opera
    99, 107, 126, 217, 220
Bretton Hall Hotel 50, 55, 98
Briggs, Asa 78
British Council 10, 11, 30, 44, 48, 58, 85
British West Indian Airlines 235
Brodsky, Joseph 289, 300, 352
Brook, Peter 211, 212
Brown, Lennox 169–70, 171, 175, 190,
    325; Fog Drifts in the Spring 84, 155, 273;
    Meeting 230; Song of a Spear 170, 180;
    The Throne in an Autumn Room 152, 167;
    Wine in Winter 168
Brown, Tom 20
Brown, Wayne 331, 335
Browne, Alyson 242
Browne, Roscoe Lee 148, 251, 254
Bruce, Peter 57, 58, 60
Bruno, Eunice, see Alleyne, Eunice
Bryden, Ronald 183, 184, 192–3, 194, 211
Bullen, Ancil 272
Bully, Alwyn 278, 341
Bushell, Sandra 332
Butler, Michael 245–6
Butler, Uriah 140
Byer, David 272
Bynoe, Adele 3, 100, 147, 156, 221, 237,
    272, 273, 275, 283, 316; in Ti-Jean (1971)
    149, 150; in Astor Johnson's RDT 173,
    217; in Dream (1974) 203; Cricket in
    Ti-Jean (1974) 207; in Joker (1974) 211;
    in Marie Laveau (1980) 302, 303; in Joker
    (1987) 350; in tour to the Netherlands
    (1993) 357
Bynoe, Hilda 100, 140

Cacique Awards 354
calypso 31, 46, 155, 201, 215, 290, 310;
    influence on acting 184, 200–1
Cambridge, Patrick 285, 346, 352
Cameron, Norman 6
Campbell, Leone 47, 48, 57, 65, 77, 78, 88
Campbell, Ralph 43, 47, 48, 50, 57, 65, 69,
    77, 79, 94, 95, 114, 147, 206; as Lestrade
    in Dream 83, 88, 90, 91; interviewed 91,
    192
Campbell, Roy 184

Camps, Helen 108, 112, 147, 155, 156, 160, 168, 184, 207, 262, 270, 278, 285, 341, 352, 354; All Theatre Productions 279, 280–1, 284, 285, 295, 299; costumes 138; as director 280–1; director-manager of Little Carib 274, 279, 281–2, 283; production of J'Ouvert 280, 281; production of King Jab Jab 280, 283; production of Pantomime 295–6, 297, 342; production of Sizwe Bansi 280–1, 283; TV adaptation of Ti-Jean 140–1; Trinidad Tent Theatre 282, 331–3, 342; in Dream (1968) 88, 89; in Ti-Jean and Dream (1971) 149; in The Charlatan (1973) 185, 190; in Joker (1974) 211–12, 213; in The Seagull (1975) 231, 233; and Sheila Goldsmith alternate Isabella (Joker, 1975) 234; in The Maids (1977) 271

Camus, Albert (Caligula) 125

Canada 78, 170, 190, 344; Stratford Shakespeare Festival 16, 17, 20, 37

Canada Council 37

Canadian Broadcasting Company 84, 122, 138, 152, 180

Capek, Karel (The Insects) 40

Caribana Festival (Toronto) 82–3

Caribbean Plays (series) 13, 65, 135, 278

Caribbean Theatre Guild 135, 285, 343

Caribuste Conference 286

Carifesta 21, 41, 170, 273, 280; Trinidad's representation in Jamaica (1976) 251–3

Carmichael, Stokely 127

Carnegie Players 18, 60, 166

Carnival 46, 158, 193, 198, 215, 217, 243, 283, 290; Carnival Dimanche Gras show 46, 48; Carnival in Port of Spain 41, 127; characters and masks 280, 281, 282

Carr, Edison 234

Carrabon, Lewt 272

Carriacou 26

Carribeat 79

Castro, Fidel 179

Catholic Youth League 98

Cayonne, Johnny 43, 47, 48

Celebration 3, 141

Central Bank Auditorium 349, 350, 351, 352

Chandler, Malcolm 138

Chandler, Terry 89, 100, 114, 116

Chang, Carlisle 12, 22, 61

Charles, Patricia 223, 224

Chee, Ken 216–17

Chekhov, Anton 10, 99, 334; Marriage Proposal 44; The Seagull 220, 230–3

Chelsea Hotel 289

Chong, Hollister 147

Circle in the Square 24

Clark, J. P. 12, 71, 85, 107

Clarke, Elizabeth 320

Clarke, LeRoy 65, 77, 84, 147, 220, 303; multimedia concert 221

Clarke, Marilyn 23, 65, 88

Coke, Lloyd 151–2

Commonwealth Arts Festival (1965) 40

Company of Five, The 18, 77

Company of Players, The 18–19, 40, 41, 166, 335, 348

conferences 278, 335

Connecticut College for Women 114

Connor-Mogotsi, Pearl 252–3, 258

Corbie, George 88–9

Corsbie, Ken 155, 168, 190, 194, 278, 290, 317, 342, 348; and Pantomime 297–8, 300

Coryat, Michael 147

Courtyard Players, The 197–8, 207–10, 292, 294

Creative Arts Centre (UWI) 42, 92, 143, 149, 187, 234, 284, 319

Creteau, Claire 22

Daniel, Henry 212

Daniel, John 89

Davidson, Gordon 125

Davis, Steve 117, 253

Dawes, Carol 190, 236

Day, The 115

De Laurentiis, Dino 172

De Lima, Clara Rosa 301, 326, 351

De Verteuil, Michael 231, 233, 291

Dean, Roger 77

Dem Two 194

Desperadoes Panyard 277

Dockray, Brian 139

Dominica 341

Don Quixote 92

Donkin, Peter 122, 138, 152, 180

Dookie, Devindra 332, 334, 336

Doran, Gregory 356

Douglas, Karl 43

Douglas, Noble 173, 175, 201, 203, 207, 208, 212, 217, 221, 229, 233, 254, 255, 257, 272–3, 349; returns to Trinidad 198; Douglas and La Chapelle contrasted 202, 258, 272, 275; Bolom in Ti-Jean (1974) 207; in St Croix Dream (1974) 208, 209; in Joker (1974) 211; Walcott about ('Untitled') 276

Drama Guild (San Fernando) 18, 44

Drayton, Kathleen 103
Dumas, Sonja, as Tisbea in *Joker* (1987)
    351
Dunham, Katherine 26, 172
Dunn, Winnifred 40

Edinborough, Felix 280
Edinborough, Walter 89
Elder, J. D. 18, 19, 26
Eliot, T. S. 22, 193, 198; *Murder in the
    Cathedral* 35, 92
Ellington, Duke 16
Extra Mural Department (UWI) 11, 16,
    60, 79, 108, 109, 224

Fabien, Errol 352
Falcon, John 203–4
Fanon, Frantz 204
Farrier, Francis 300
Federal Theatre Company 14
Figueroa, John 92
Flores, Pat 212, 220, 246, 249, 253, 336
Fo, Dario: *Accidental Death of an Anarchist*
    351–2; *We Can't Pay, We Won't Pay* 343
Folk Singers of Trinidad 19
Foster, Patrick 297, 320, 337
Franco, Pamela 88, 98, 100, 108, 114, 131,
    138
Frankel, Gene 40
Frazer, Mae 47
French, Stanley (*The Rape of Fair Helen*)
    168
Freund, Gerald 39, 40, 97, 117; and
    Walcott 59, 78, 85, 98, 110, 111, 116
Friedman, Gary 184, 193
Friel, Brian 294
Frisch, Max 147
Fry, Christopher 10, 22
Fugard, Athol: *Boesman and Lena* 349–50;
    Sizwe Bansi is Dead 343

Garcia, Jennifer Hobson 234, 237
Gardner, R. H. 245
Garrison Theatre (Barbados) 5
Geest Banana Shed (St Lucia) 223, 224
Genet, Jean: *The Balcony* 126, 128; *The
    Blacks* 57, 64–5, 66, 67–8, 70, 81, 92, 99,
    107, 110, 152; *The Maids* 251, 259, 271,
    294
Gibbons, Rawle 41, 248, 349, 351
Gilder, Vanessa 156
Gilkes, Michael 290, 317, 318, 319, 320,
    342, 348; directs revised *Franklin* 337–9
Gillen, Leon 114
Gillespie, John 59, 260

Giuseppi, Ewart 89, 108
Goddard, Winston 185, 200, 207, 291; in
    Joker (1974) 211; in *The Seagull* (1975)
    231; in *O Babylon!* (1976) 246, 249
Goldsmith, Sheila 234
Goldstraw, Irma 'Billie' 19
Goldstraw, Laurence 19, 181, 184, 285,
    299, 351; in *The Charlatan* (1973) 185,
    186, 189; in *Franklin* (1973) 181, 188; in
    Joker (1974) 211; in *O Babylon!* (1976)
    246; in *The Charlatan* (1977) 291; in *The
    Odyssey* (1993) 356
Gomes, Albert 158
Gomes, Anthony 275, 324, 332, 344, 346
Gomez, Joy, *see* Ryan, Joy
Gonzalez, Anson 157–8
Goodman, Henry 198, 199
Gordon, Leah 356
Gordon, William 316
Government Training College 50, 91, 314,
    315
Graham, Martha 26, 198
Graves, George 81
Gray, Cecil 65, 282, 283, 344
Gray, Thomas 293
Green Room, The (Barbados) 81, 317
Greenidge, Avis 88
Gregory, André 85, 94, 110, 111, 117; *My
    Dinner with André* 94; report to
    Rockefeller Foundation 95–7
Grenada 11, 26, 42, 100, 104, 132, 140
Grey, Lennox 65
Grinnell College 41, 116, 117
Grotowski, Jerzy 56, 139
Guardian Players 63
Guerra, Allison 357
guerrillas (1973) 179
Guggenheim Fellowship 77, 108
Gunness, Christopher 296
Guthrie, Tyrone 16, 17
Guyana 21, 84–5, 170, 337–9, 347–8;
    Theatre Guild 348

Hahn, Stuart 89
Hall, Anthony 228–9, 234, 260, 262, 274,
    349; Lestrade in 1974 *Dream* 202;
    compared to Hopkinson's Lestrade
    205–6; Mi-Jean in 1974 *Ti-Jean* 207;
    Lestrade in St Croix *Dream* (1974) 210
    in *Joker* (1974) 212; in *O Babylon!* (1976)
    246, 249; directs *The Maids* (1977) 271;
    directs *We Can't Pay* (1984) 343;
    replaces Holder as director of *Beef*
    (1987) 347
Hall, Peter 211

Hands, Terry 4, 183, 193, 211, 212
Harikirtan, Sheila 285
Harris, Wilson: *Crew from Sorrow Hill*
   (*Palace of the Peacock*) 84, 152
Harrison, John P. 16, 17, 24, 34, 37, 38,
   39; Harrison-Walcott letters 38, 39
Hearne, John 6, 15, 19, 61–2, 85, 98
Henderson, Heather 272, 275, 301
Henderson, John 23, 121
Henry, Bertrand 23
Henry, Jeff 23, 25, 37, 46, 134, 283
Herbert, Jean 19, 23
Hiland Park Entertainers 88, 89
Hill, Errol 10, 11, 12, 13, 14, 16, 17, 18,
   22, 36, 44, 46, 62, 72, 77, 109, 135, 159,
   190; edits *Caribbean Plays* 13; Extra-
   Mural tutor 11, 16; reviews TTW 232;
   Man Better Man 36, 40; *Square Peg* 63
Hill, Jean, *see* Herbert, Jean
Hill, Lima 43, 47
Hill, Sydney 11, 18, 23, 44
Hillary, Samuel 190; *Departure in the Dark*
   277–8
Hilton, Anne 89, 295
Hilton, John 131
Hinkson, Anthony (*Teacher Teach'er*) 273
Hippolyte, Kendel 325
Hirsch, Samuel 115
Holder, Bosco 17
Holder, Corinne, *see* Jones, Corinne
Holder, Wilbert 124, 156, 167, 168, 183,
   184, 190, 193, 194, 201, 257, 270, 273,
   336, 341, 342, 343, 345; acting style 249,
   281, 297, 299–300, 348; biography
   347–8, honours 348, 355, and TTW
   management 131, 250; and Walcott
   348; in *Henri Christophe* 94–5; Basil in
   Dream (1969) 114; in *The Charlatan*
   (1973) 189; in St Croix *Ti-Jean* (1974)
   196; in *Joker* (1974) 212; alternates Duke
   Octavio with Syd Skipper, *Joker* (1975)
   234; in *O Babylon!* (1976) 246, 247, 253;
   in *The Charlatan* (1977) 291; in
   Remembrance (1977) 293; in première of
   Pantomime (1978) 295, 297; as Jordan in
   Remembrance (1979) 299–300; in Corsbie's
   Pantomime (1980) 297–8; in *Sizwe Bansi*
   (1980) 280, 281, 346; in Gainesville,
   Florida *Pantomime* (1981) 348; in *A
   'Nancy Story* (1982) 283; in *Smile Orange*
   (1982) 284; interviewed in USA
   (1983) 286; in *Branch* (1985) 332, 333
Hope, Fred 43, 47, 48, 50, 276, 299, 314
Hopkinson, Slade 12, 13, 14, 25, 43, 46,
   47, 48, 72, 85, 88, 112, 114, 117, 118,

119, 122, 123, 159, 334, 335; accuses
   Walcott 129, 135; acting style 43, 115;
   and black nationalism 128, 130, 344;
   forms Caribbean Theatre Guild 135; *Fall
   of a Chief* 50; five-island tour 100–4;
   honoured 343–4, 355; as King Lear 43;
   as Lestrade 101, 102, 103, 114, 115, 318;
   in NBC *Dream* 206; in *The Charlatan*
   (1962) 43
Hosein, Clyde 122, 139, 153
Hotel Normandie Dinner Theatre 279,
   281, 299
Hughes, Brenda 63, 77, 79, 155, 270, 273,
   277, 278, 336, 343, 345, 346, 352; and
   TTW management 250, 353; in *Dream*
   and *Belle Fanto* (1967) 83, 84; in *Joker*
   (1974) 213; shares Tisbea with
   Stephanie King in 1975 *Joker* 222; as
   Tisbea in 1975 *Joker* 234; in *O Babylon!*
   (1976) 246, 247, 249, 253; in *Marie
   Laveau* (1980) 301; in *Beef* (1981) 282; in
   Smile Orange (1982) 284; Arbee
   Productions *Dream* (1985) 329–31;
   Arbee-TTW Productions *Joker* (1987)
   349–51; Isabella in 1987 *Joker* 350, 351;
   in *Two Can Play* (1990) 353, 354; Arbee
   Productions *Pantomime* (1991) 350; in
   The Odyssey (1993) 356
Hummingbird Medal 41, 123

Ibsen, Henrik (*An Enemy of the People*) 40
India Overseas 81
International Trust Limited 313
Ionesco, Eugène (*The Lesson*) 46–7
Isaacs, John 275, 294, 299, 302, 316;
   directs *Two Can Play* (1990) 353, 354; in
   The Odyssey (1993) 356
Islander Hotel 140
Ismond, Patricia 330, 357; reviews *Joker of
   Seville* 227–9
Israel, Roger 282
Izenour, George 37

Jackman, Oliver 112; *Stepchild, Stepchild*
   107, 112
Jacobs, Arthur: in *The Haytian Earth* (1984)
   326, 328; as Makak in *Dream* (1985) 329,
   330, 331
Jaikeransingh, Ken 351
Jamaica 93, 143, 186, 245, 251, 322;
   support of arts 42, 188; drama in 12,
   236
James, C. L. R. 5–6, 62
James, Elena 64, 65, 77, 78, 79, 83–4, 89,
   100, 114

James, Horace 11, 18, 22, 23, 44, 190, 194,
    217, 230, 273; and Pantomime
    (1978) 295, 296–8
Jenkin, Veronica 19, 22, 23, 34
Jennings, Geddes 43, 47, 48, 57, 60, 65, 94,
    100, 108, 242
Jenson, Barbara 230, 231, 234, 247, 261,
    291, 350, 353
John, Debra 302
John, Errol 12, 17, 38, 77, 109, 124, 159,
    190, 273; Moon on a Rainbow Shawl 34,
    35, 36, 41, 63, 99, 114, 343, Moon (1967)
    76–8, CTG production of Moon 135;
    The Tout 36
John, Ronald 347
Johnson, Astor 172–5, 180, 183, 194, 201,
    202, 203, 211, 217, 233, 244, 274, 280;
    original Basil in Dream 172; Basil in
    1974 Dream 202; in St Croix Dream
    (1974) 208, 210; in Joker (1974) 212
Johnson, Christine 347
Johnson, Lee 256–7, 272
Jones, Brunell 95
Jones, Corinne 272
Jones, Donald 302
Jones, Errol 3, 34, 40–1, 43, 45, 48, 50, 57,
    59, 65, 79, 196, 112, 113, 116, 117, 125,
    131, 147, 153, 155, 156, 166, 167, 168,
    169, 171, 178, 181, 190, 221, 226, 234,
    274, 276, 277, 278, 280, 305, 310, 341,
    343, 352, 355; acting style 40, 58, 249;
    honours 41; as Makak 56, 82, 89, 92,
    102, 103, 115, 118, 151, 152, 205;
    producer 277; retires from government
    270; Rockefeller Fellowship 40; shared
    vision of TTW 358; and Trinidad
    Dramatic Club 18, 40; and TTW
    management 94, 250, 353, 354; and
    Walcott 47, 132, 133, 270; about
    Walcott's resignation 263; in Sea at
    Dauphin (1954) 13; in Henri Christophe
    (1954) 13; in Drums and Colours (1958)
    22; in Showcase (1959) 34; in Ti-Jean
    (1958) 23; in Malcochon (1964) 47; in
    Dream (1967) 83–4; in Dream (1968) 88;
    five-island tour (1968) 100, 101, 102,
    103; in Henri Christophe (1968) 94; in
    Dream (1969) 114, 115; in Franklin
    (1973) 188, 189; Jamaica tour (1973)
    manager 186; in Dream (1974) 202, 205;
    in Joker (1974) 211, 214; in St Croix
    (1974) 209–10; as Catalinion in Joker
    (1975) 226, 234; in The Seagull (1975)
    231, 233; in O Babylon! (1976) 246, 247,
    253; in Old Story Time (1979) 279; in

Sizwe Banzi (1980) 280, 281, 346; in Beef
    (1981) 282; in Stage One Beef (1985)
    344; in Boesman and Lena (1986) 345; in
    Joker (1987) 349; in Franklin (1990) 337;
    in Celebration (1993) 3; in tour to the
    Netherlands (1993) 357; in The Odyssey
    (1993) 356
Jones, Greer 233, 234, 272, 275, 356; in
    The Maids (1977) 271; costume and set
    designer for Branch (1985) 327
Jones, Malcolm 183
Jones, Marilyn 213, 225–6
Jones, Terry, in Joker (1974) 212
Jonson, Ben 211
Jordan, Christopher 88
Jordan, Glenn 111
Joseph, Learie 352
Joseph, Terrence 77, 84, 88
Joseph, Wendy 275, 276
Joyce, James 307
Judson Theatre 47, 78, 137

Kairi 256, 260, 292
Kealy, Robin 297–8, 302
Kearns, Lionel 60, 61
Keens-Douglas, Paul 252, 280
Kelly, Peter 352, 353
Keskidee Theatre (London) 300
King, Stephanie 203, 207, 222, 230
Kissoon, Freddie 11, 22, 23, 35, 44, 60, 72,
    109, 190, 334
Klein, Howard 117
Kong, Raymond Choo 282, 302, 347, 351
Krogh, Christen 181, 182, 186, 231, 232,
    233
Kurosawa, Akira 24

La Bastide, Neville de 131; One for the
    Road 173, 174, 206
La Chapelle, Carol 3, 172, 175, 198, 201–2,
    212, 221, 228, 254, 255, 257, 271, 283,
    350, 354; choreographer 244, 245, 357;
    and TTW management 250; similar
    views to Walcott 202; in Joker (1974)
    211; shares Ana with Joy Ryan in Joker
    (1975) 222; Ana in October 1975
    Joker (1975) 231,
    232, 233; in Belle Fanto (1976) 256;
    choreographer for O Babylon!
    (1976) 244, 246; in Celebration (1993) 3;
    in The Odyssey (1993) 356
La Chapelle–Douglas Dance Company
    274–6
Laird, Colin 19, 21, 22, 23, 36, 37, 77
Lam, Wilfredo 62

La Mama 116, 206
Lamming, George 12, 61–2
Lashley, Felice 89
Laveau, Albert 3, 21, 45, 47, 48, 50, 57,
    65, 77, 79, 103, 112, 118, 119, 124, 125,
    131, 140, 147, 153, 155, 158, 159, 164,
    165–7, 169, 190, 202, 220, 221, 230, 243,
    254, 258, 262, 271, 274, 332, 336, 342,
    343, 349; acting style 152, 166; and
    conversion of Old Fire Station 353;
    director 166, 167, 168, 244, 251, 256,
    263, 352; in Negro Ensemble Company
    tour 198; as professional actor 163, 165;
    returns to Trinidad 167, 210; and TTW
    management 94, 250; Basil in Dream
    (1967) 83, 172; Basil in Dream
    (1968) 88, 90; in Henri Christophe (1968)
    94; in Ti-Jean (1970) 138, 139, 141;
    Lestrade in Dream (1971) 149; in Ti-Jean
    (1971) 150; in In a Fine Castle (1971)
    156; in Ti-Jean (1972, New York) 160,
    163, 164, 165; in Joker (1974) 212, 213;
    alternates Juan and Don Diego in Joker
    (1975) 222; alternates Juan with Nigel
    Scott in Joker (1975) 234, 236; in The
    Seagull (1975) 231, 232; directs première
    of Pantomime (1978) 281, 295, 297; in A
    'Nancy Story (1982) 283; directs Dream
    (1985) 329, 330; directs Let Resurrection
    Come! (1986) 345; directs Joker (1987)
    34; in Celebration (1993) 3; in The
    Odyssey (1993) 357
Laveau, Lynette 60, 65, 77, 79, 84, 88,
    147, 166, 342
Laventille 276
Legent, Andre 275
Let Resurrection Come! 345, 346
Lewin, Olive 220
Lewis, Arthur 8
Light House Theatre (St Lucia) 325, 345, 346
lighting 32, 37, 41–2, 80, 99, 185, 216, 224,
    303, 350
Lights Two 345
Lindo, Archie 188
Literary Half-Yearly, The 349
Little Carib, The 15, 17, 18, 23, 25, 26, 93,
    98, 201, 210, 217, 230, 233, 246, 247,
    254, 258, 270, 273, 277, 282, 283, 284,
    290, 303, 312, 335, 337, 344, 345;
    backstage 225; Little Carib Theatre
    Workshop 30–50, 77, 166, 257;
    renovated 300; rental 233, 255, 350,
    351, 353; seating 212, 215
Little Theatre, The (Jamaica) 15, 183,
    186, 187

Llanos, Ronnie 14, 18, 43
Lloyd, Norman 112
London School of Contemporary Dance
    198
Lorca, Federico Garcia 139
Lovelace, Earl 90–1, 95, 109, 113, 249,
    314–15, 352; The Dragon Can't Dance
    217–18, 276–7
Lowell, Robert 63
Lowhar, Syl 140, 154, 183, 334–5
Lowrie, Jean 189
Lynch, Christopher 231
Lyndersay, Mark 282, 283, 284, 296
Lysistrata 99, 209

McBurnie, Beryl 17, 21, 22, 25, 26, 30, 38,
    50, 88, 89, 98, 134, 172, 173, 174, 175,
    201, 217, 275, 349; and Helen Camps
    281; and Walcott 25, 43, 49–50, 134
McBurnie Foundation 335
MacDermot, Galt 143, 196, 199–200, 235,
    246, 313, 350; Two Gentlemen of Verona
    200; The Charlatan (Los Angeles) 200,
    210; 'Songs for Theatre' (1974) 210;
    Joker 200, 210, 212, 221; O Babylon!
    (1976) 200, 245, 246, 248, 251, 252, 253;
    The Charlatan (1977) 290, 291, 292;
    Marie Laveau 200, 301, 302; Haytian
    Earth 200
McDormand, Fran 314, 315, 316
McDougall, Alexander 98
Machiz, Herbert 38–9
McKenna, Siobhán 17
McKenzie, George 277
McPherson, Ken 272
McTair, Roger 84
McWatt, Mark 318–19
Maillard, Margaret, see Walcott, Margaret
Mais, Roger 6, 15
Malick Folk Performers 352
Mandel, Naomi 62
Manet, Edouard 184, 305
Manley, Carmen 14; My Brother's Keeper
    168
Manley, Michael 149, 152
Manwarren, Wendell 357
Maraj, Ralph 190, 277, 283
Mark, Gloria 88
Mark Taper Forum 116, 117, 125, 130,
    137, 156, 198
Marlowe, Christopher 10, 125–6
Marshall, Faith 101
Marshall, Stanley 3, 21, 43–4, 45, 47, 65,
    69, 77, 79, 82, 83, 108, 112, 118, 131,
    132, 133, 147, 152, 153, 155, 156, 158,

Marshall, Stanley (cont.): 168, 169, 171, 181, 184, 193, 201, 207, 208, 210, 220, 221, 254, 258, 277, 280, 305, 310, 343, 344, 345, 351, 352, 355; acting style 44, 229; filming of Dream 119; and Ministry of Agriculture 255, 259; requests sponsorship from Amoco 233; TTW management 138, 250, 251, 252, 353, 354; in The Charlatan (1962) 43; in Belle Fanto (1966) 60; in Dream and Belle Fanto (1967) 83, 84; in Dream (1968) 88, 90; in Henri Christophe (1968) 94–5; five-island tour (1968) 100, 102; in Dream (1969) 114; in Ti-Jean (1970) 138; in Joker (1970); Jamaica tour (1971) 151; in Franklin (1973) 185, 186; Jamaica tour (1973) manager 186; in The Charlatan (1973) 189; in Dream (1974) 202, 205; Devil in Ti-Jean (1974) 207; in Joker (1974) 211; in The Seagull (1975) 230, 232; in O Babylon! (1976) 246; in Belle Fanto (1976) 256, 257; in Departure (1979) 278; in Old Story Time (1979) 279; in Beef (1981) 282; in A 'Nancy Story (1982) 283; in Smile Orange (1982) 284; in Beef (1987) 347; as Don Gonzalo in Joker (1987) 350; in The Odyssey (1993) 356; in tour to the Netherlands (1993) 357
Martin, Avis 147, 156, 203, 211, 277
Mason, Maurice 10, 12
Matthews, Mark 194
Matura, Mustapha 3, 190; As Time Goes By 168, 220, 221
Mauby, see Stone, Judy
Maxwell, Marina 61, 93; Play Mas 93
Mayers, Robert 291
Maynard, Vonrick 291
Melser, John 89–90, 94, 108, 112, 113
Mentus, Ulric 62, 78, 90, 238–9
method acting 27, 31, 56, 92
Metivier, Norline 215, 221, 226, 227, 234, 244, 257, 272, 273, 275, 289, 316, 319, 320, 321, 326, 328, 353; choreographer 301, 303; in Joker (1974) 211, 213; in The Seagull (1975) 230–1, 232; in O Babylon! (1976) 246, 249, 253; in The Charlatan (1977) 291; in Branch (1985) 332, 333, 334
micro-nationalism 42, 60, 80, 238
Mighty Sparrow 124, 252
Miles, Judy 43
Millais, Sir John Everett 19
Miller, Arthur 34, 99; The Crucible 81
Mills, Therese 77, 82, 91, 153–4, 180, 194, 213–14

Milne, Anthony 316
Milner, Harry 144, 150, 151, 188, 237–8, 253–4
Minor, Michael A. 286
Minshall, Peter 22, 43, 187, 356
Mohammed, Feroze 234
Molière 125, 317
Molina, Tirso de 178, 193, 211, 226, 227
Mombara, Sule (Horace Campbell) 248
Monplaisir, Kenneth 12, 223
Montgomery, Richard 187, 246, 278, 313, 337; similar vision to Walcott 236; In a Fine Castle (1970) 143–4; In a Fine Castle (1971) 156; Franklin and The Charlatan (1973) 186, 190; comes to Port of Spain for Joker 234; sets for Joker in Jamaica 235–7; O Babylon! (1976) 247; Haytian Earth (1984) 324, 325–6; 1987 Joker 349, 350, costumes 351
Montgomery, Sally Thompson 143–4, 235, 324, 325
Moore, Bernardine 47
Moore, Ruth 187, 208–9, 293–4
Morgan, Mary E. 102
Morne, The (St Lucia) 224, 324, 325
Morris, Ken 65, 138, 203
Morris, Mervyn 149–50, 151
Moyston, Faye 15
Moze, Sonya 63, 282, 302, 303, 319, 320, 336, 343, 344, 346, 348
Murray, Jan 351

Naipaul, V. S. 6, 12, 18, 57, 62, 307; B. Wordsworth 36, 62, 63, 168; Flag on the Island 82, 171; Guerrillas 179; A House for Mr Biswas 354; The Suffrage of Elvira 66
Naparima Bowl 43, 47, 82, 94, 108, 223, 251, 258, 280
Nassau 280
Nathaniel, June 210, 212, 220
National Brewery Company 215, 216–17, 244, 333
National Broadcasting Company (NBC) 116, 118, 122, 126, 163
National Drama Association of Trinidad and Tobago 337, 355
National Education Television 152
national theatre 24, 39, 42, 50, 80, 111, 162, 218, 243, 257, 259, 262, 354, 359
Negro Ensemble Company 4, 111, 148, 163, 166, 198
Neruda, Pablo 62
Nettleford, Rex 13, 14, 26, 155–6, 274, 342
New Company, The 18

New York Times, The 151
New York University Drama School 160, 163
Nigeria 12
Norman, Marsha (Night, Mother) 344–5
Nunez, Suzanne 114, 118

O'Casey, Sean 135; Juno and the Paycock 40
Odlum, George 225, 327–8
Off-Broadway 32, 148
O'Hara, Frank 99
Old Fire Station 98, 353, 356
O'Neill Memorial Theatre 108–9, 111, 114, 116, 117, 125, 163, 203, 312
Orwell, George 10

Paddington, Bruce 204
Pan-Jamaican Investment Trust 148, 186, 234, 247
Pantin, Raoul (RAP) 190, 191–2, 226, 247, 258, 277, 283, 297, 315, 333, 334
Papp, Joseph 4, 160, 163–4, 166, 167, 197, 200, 336
parang 23, 193, 194, 211, 212
Parker, Desmond 131
Parris, Hamilton 65–6, 77, 79, 100, 108, 109, 114, 115, 118, 119, 124, 131, 138, 141, 147, 152, 155, 156, 171, 178, 181, 184, 210, 230, 242, 254; acting style 66, 150, 214, 228, 237; in Dream (1967) 83; in Dream (1968) 88, 90; in Ti-Jean (1971) 150; in Ti-Jean (1972, New York) 160, 163, 164, 165; in Joker (1974) 211, 214; in The Seagull (1975) 231, 232; in Belle Fanto (1976) 256, 257
Patterson, Thomas 16, 37, 190
Pelican, The 12, 14
pelvic movement 31, 202, 272
Phelps, Karen 58, 61
Phoenix Theatre 24
Picasso, Pablo 184
Pickwickians at Manor Farm 122
Picou, Ivor 190, 202, 205, 207, 212
Pieces One 173–5
Pieces Two 180, 182–3
Pilgrim, Billie, see Goldstraw, Irma 122
Pilgrim, Errol 89, 100, 114, 155, 184, 187, 203; and TTW management 94; Souris in Dream (1974) 202; Frog in Ti-Jean (1974) 207; Souris in St Croix Dream 208, 209; in Joker (1974) 211; in Joker (1975) 222
Pilgrim, Frank 12
Pinheiro, Christopher 156, 249, 284

Pinter, Harold (The Lover) 85, 107, 112
Pitkethly, Lawrence 337
Point à Pierre 181, 250
Polakov, Lester 24
possession 69, 227, 229, 303
Priestly, J. B. 58; An Inspector Calls 60
Primus, Ellsworth 147, 156; as Ti-Jean 138, 139, 141, 152; Jamaica tour (1971) 149, 150; in Departure (1979) 277
Procope, Bruce 19, 35, 37, 38
Public Library 41, 210
Public Opinion 13

Quamina, Jerline 169, 203, 221, 278, 279, 282
Queen's Hall 36–7, 57, 76, 88, 94, 99, 103, 126, 152, 155, 156, 174; rental 233; size of stage 280
Questel, Victor 109, 179, 192, 214, 221, 233, 281, 284, 299–300, 303–4, 357; review of 1974 Dream 204–6; 1981 interview of Walcott 304–7
Quintero, Jose 24

Radio 610: 44
Radio Canada International 167
Raidy, William 165
Rambert, Vicki 35
Ramchand, Kenneth 335
Ramcharitar, Raymond 356
Rampersad, Arnold 40, 43, 44, 168, 169
Ranelli, Jay 117, 125, 126, 128
Rappaport, Roslyn 207
Rastafarians 245, 247, 248, 254; at O Babylon! 254
Reckord, Barry 190
Reckord, Lloyd 141, 190
Reckord, Michael 93
Redhead, Trevor 272
Redhead, Wilfred 11, 48; Goose and Gander 48
Regis, Gregory 141
Reid, Claude 3, 34, 43, 45, 47, 57, 79, 84, 108, 114, 115, 118, 124, 131, 147, 156, 168, 169, 178, 181, 190, 254, 285, 352; in Malcochon (1964) 47; in Belle Fanto (1966) 60; in Dream (1967) 83; in Dream (1968) 88, 90, 91; in Henri Christophe (1968) 94; five-island tour (1968) 100; in Ti-Jean (1970) 138; Jamaica tour (1971) 149; in Ti-Jean (1971) 150; in Franklin (1973) 186; alternates Don Diego and Batricio in 1975 Joker 222; in The Seagull (1975) 231; Catalinion in Oct. 1975 Joker 234; in Belle Fanto (1976) 256; in Dragon

Reid, Claude (*cont.*): (1978) 276, 277; in
  Departure (1978) 278; in *Beef* (1981) 282;
  in *A 'Nancy Story* (1982) 289; in *Smile
  Orange* (1982) 284; in *Beef* (1987) 347;
  Catalinion in 1987 *Joker* 350, 351; in
  Pantomime (1993) 356; rehearsing
  Pantomime (1993) 298–9; in *Celebration*
  (1993) 3; in tour to the Netherlands
  (1993) 357
Reid, Stanley 101, 141
Reid-Wallace, Carolyn 201
Reinhart, Charles 111
Repertory Dance Theatre, *see* Johnson,
  Astor
Reynolds, Susan 112
Rhone, Trevor 190, 279, 341; *Old Story
  Time* 279; *Smile Orange* 188, 284, 314,
  316, 352; *Two Can Play* 353, 354
Richards, Lloyd 110, 163
Richards, Sandra 272
River Niger 166, 198
Roach, Eric 61, 109, 158, 180; *Belle Fanto*
  80, 82, 99, 155, 1966 production 60–1,
  65, 68, 70, 1967 production 80, 83, 84,
  1968 production 100–3, 1976 production
  251, 256–7, 263; *Calabash of Blood* 168;
  theatre reviewer 68, 78, 108, 113–14,
  139–40, 157, 174, 181–2, 183
Roberts, Errol 301, 330, 332
Robertson, Hugh 118–19, 122, 124, 141
Robinson, A. N. R. 12, 122, 153
Rockefeller Foundation 15, 16, 17, 20, 21,
  24, 59, 60, 77, 88, 97–8, 104, 110, 111,
  125, 264; and Little Carib 37–8;
  fellowships 24, 37, 40, 41, 72; and
  regional theatre 19, 24; 1967–70
  Walcott grant 63, 70–3; inability to aid
  TTW 78, 112, 114; sends André
  Gregory 94
Ross, Helen 156, 291, 292
Rothwell, Bernard 156
Royal Court Theatre 47
Royal Shakespeare Company 111, 184,
  192–3, 207, 211, 213, 233–4, 356, 358
Rudder, Ronald 356
Rufino, Leo 43, 47, 77
Russell, Kathlyn 343
Ryan, Finbar 347
Ryan, Joy 47, 283, 316; in *Joker*
  (1974) 212; shares Ana in 1975
  Joker 222; in *Remembrance* (1979) 299,
  300; in *Branch* (1985) 331; in *The
  Odyssey* (1993) 356

St Augustine Players 18, 82

St Croix and St Thomas 193, 197, 206,
  207–10, 214–15, 290, 292, 301, 357
St Helene, Joel 35, 65, 83
St Hill, C. A. P. 141
St Hill, Leonard 320
St Hill, Pamela Walcott 320
St Juste, Franklyn 143
St Lucia 7–8, 139, 140, 141, 290, 345–6;
  African culture in St Lucia 7–8; *Dream
  on Monkey Mountain* in St Lucia 100,
  104; French in St Lucia 7–8; and
  Haytian Earth 324–5, 329; history 7;
  Methodists 8; St Mary's College 9, 10
St Mary's College (Toronto) 83
St Omer, Dunstan 9, 101, 223, 325
St Omer, Garth 101
St Vincent 100, 103, 104, 281, 346
Salazar, Cecilia 356
Samaroo, Daniel; *Taxi Mister* 168
Samuel, Kennedy 328–9
Samuels, Pat 231, 275
San Fernando 18, 21, 23, 30, 40, 43, 66,
  77, 141, 172, 185, 226, 250, 276
San Fernando Carnegie Players 18, 60,
  166, 187
Sandhurst Guest House 149, 186
Sandler, Joan 209
Schultz, Michael 111, 117
Scott, Dennis 92, 189, 190, 237, 253, 278;
  The Caged 42; interviews Walcott 93
Scott, E. G. 247
Scott, Lawrence 303
Scott, Nigel 3, 112–13, 147, 148, 149, 155,
  156, 158, 160, 167, 168, 169, 170, 182,
  184, 193, 316, 319, 336, 345, 349; TTW
  management 250, 353; in *Joker* (1974)
  211, 214; as Don Juan 226, 234, 237; in
  Old Story Time (1979) 279; Don Juan in
  Joker (1987) 350, 351; in *Pantomime*
  (1993) 356; rehearsing *Pantomime* (1993)
  298–9; in *Celebration* (1993) 3; in tour to
  the Netherlands (1993) 357
Scott, Rowena 147
Seaga, Edward 149
Sealy, Clifford 61
Seepaul, Allison, *see* Guerra, Allison
Seepersadsingh, Natasha 337
Selman, Anthony 34
Selvon, Samuel 6, 34, 170, 307; *Basement
  Lullabies* 63, 168; *The World of Sam
  Selvon* 107–9
Semp Studios 208, 221
Shakespeare, William 10, 26, 192, 211,
  215, 229, 307, 317, 334, 344; *Antony and
  Cleopatra* 320, 321, 332; *Henry V* 355;

King Lear 43; Macbeth 125, 126, 143, 147, 148; Othello 40, 76, 112–13, 352; Richard II 10; Romeo and Juliet 41; Twelfth Night 35
Shango 69, 136, 272, 284, 356
Shapiro, Mel 198, 199, 200
Sharpe, Boogsie 291
Shaw, George Bernard 12, 159; Saint Joan 12, 34
Sherlock, Philip 16, 37, 38; Daddy Sharpe 220
Shim, Peter 147
Showcase 34–5, 44
Simmons, Harold 9, 26
Simon, John 164
Sitahal, Errol 332, 333, 336, 337, 343
Sitahal, Joy 347, 352
Skipper, Syd 221, 343; in St Croix Dream (1974) 210; in Joker (1974) 212, 213, 214; in Jamaica Joker (1975) 234, 235, 236, 238; in O Babylon! (1976) 247, 249, 252, 253; is replaced in The Charlatan (1977) 291
Slaney, Marcia 84
Smart, Winston 95
Smith, Cotter 314, 315, 316
Solomon, Denis 35, 123–4, 158–9, 182, 184, 185
Solomon, Patrick 17, 35
Soyinka, Wole 12, 26, 352, 355; Lion and the Jewel 135; The Road 57, 64, 65, 68–70, 92
Stage One (Barbados) 297, 300, 317, 318, 319, 344, 345
Stanley, Janet 57
Stein, Kenneth 244
Steinberg, Robert 117
Stewart, Oscilla 234
Stillingford, Brenda, see Hughes, Brenda
Stone, Irving 9
Stone, Judy 63, 112–13, 125, 147, 155, 156, 160, 167, 168, 169, 170, 175, 180, 184, 190, 320, 343, 348, 352; resigns from TTW 185, 186; reviews 213, 234, 247, 258–9, 271, 272–3, 279–80, 291, 297–8, 300, 307, 315–16, 330, 335, 344, 345, 347, 350–1; Touchstone Productions 273, 283; and TTW management 131; in In a Fine Castle (1971) 315; in The Charlatan (1973) 185
Strand, Mark 300
Strindberg, August 151, 204, 317, 344
Strolling Players 72
Surinam 253, 280, 282, 341
Sweeting, Lyn 280
Synge, J. B. 9, 22, 26, 44, 135

Taitt, Andy 338
Taitt, Clairmonte 297, 337, 348
Tanker, André 3, 132, 139, 140, 147, 160, 194, 201, 220, 235, 244, 342, 343, 345; music for Ti-Jean 138, 139; Ti-Jean in New York 163, 165; music for Dragon 276; music for A 'Nancy Story 283–4; in Celebration 3
Tapia House 153
Taylor, Jeremy 174, 213, 214, 216, 230, 232–3, 247, 257, 258, 277, 278, 291–2, 300–1, 302, 314
Theatre Fifteen 168–9, 171
Theatre Guild (Guyana) 11, 84
Theatre Ten 155
Thomas, Dylan 25, 26
Thomas, Fred 59
Thomas, Glenda 357
Thompson, Jeanne 280
Thompson, Ralph 148, 183, 186
Tjon, Henk 282, 341
Town Hall 36–7, 108, 112, 122, 138, 156, 185
Tretick, Joyce 115
Trinidad and the arts 42, 188, 191–2, 359 60
Trinidad, attempted coup in (1990) 353
Trinidad and Tobago Television 108, 171, 194, 201, 217, 230, 273, 295
Trinidad Dramatic Club 18, 30, 76, 93, 112, 113, 348
Trinidad, Hindu-Black tensions 18, 337, 352
Trinidad Light Operatic Society 18, 284
Trinidad Tent Theatre, see Camps, Helen
Trinidad-Tesoro 168
Trinidad Theatre Workshop Dance Company 175, 197, 251, 254, 255, 257–9, 263, 312; Season 77: 271–3; origins 257; sponsors 272
Trinidad Theatre Workshop 278–9; actors' fees 59, 99, 129, 133, 169, 194, 221, 239, 255, 347, 349–50; actors' social background 31, 35, 40, 41–2, 43–4, 44–7, 47–8, 65–6, 112–13, 114, 165–7, 203; as agent 152, 194, 221, 243, 255; becomes Basement Theatre 50, 55; board of directors 250, 262, 353, 354; changing membership 128; conference plans 190, 201; debts 270, 278, 284; donations to 59, 71, 81, 119, 215; dues 30, 71; ensemble style 55 237, 249, 305; exercises 31, 33, 82; failed reconciliations with Walcott 312–13, 352; finances 71, 76, 77, 78, 81, 85,

Trinidad Theatre Workshop (*cont.*): 128–9, 243; foundation members 45, 133, 166, 243, 312–13; general meetings 129, 132, 249, 250, 254, 260; Hughes attempts reconciliation 346, 349; Indian actors 47, 64, 181, 343; legal status 107, 128, 133, 243, 249, 254; loss of actors 349; management committee 93–4, 131, 243; members in 1971 147; Old Fire Station 353, 354, 355, 358, 359; origins 257; plans for redevelopment 354; principal tours: Barbados (1967) 79–80, 81; Toronto and Guyana (1967) 82–5, Five-Island tour (1968) 100–4, Waterford, Connecticut (1969) 114–17, *Ti-Jean* tour to Grenada, St Lucia, Barbados (1970) 130, 131, 132, 133, 140–1, *Dream* and *Ti-Jean* tour to Jamaica (1971) 148–52, *Franklin* and *Charlatan* tour to Jamaica (1973) 186–90, St Croix (1973) 193, Connecticut (1974) 206–7, St Croix (1974) 207–10, *Joker* in St Lucia (1975) 223–5, *Joker* in Jamaica (1975) 234–8, *O Babylon!* in Jamaica (1976) 252, 253–4, Boston, West Indies and the Netherlands (1993) 3, 5, 355–6, 357; problems replacing Walcott 269–70; problems touring 80, 83, 186, 223–4, 252; radio work 152, 155, 168–9, 180; rebuilds around Jones and Marshall 270–1, 342, 346; and Trevor Rhone 179, 184, 314; a source of *Branch of the Blue Nile* 333–4; sponsors 94, 188, 234–5, 244, 283; subscription season 216, 251, 254, 259–60, 273; tour schedules 148–9, 186–7; television work 194, 274; Walcott's return to in 1970 141; Walcott withdraws plays from 259–60; white actors 19, 47, 112, 143, 159–60, 170, 176; Wilbert Holder Theatre 355; women in 47, 57–8
Tutuola, Amos 123

University of Ibadan 12, 16
University of the West Indies (Barbados) 300
University of the West Indies (Jamaica) 10, 11, 12, 21, 236
University of the West Indies summer school 22, 25, 38, 41, 64, 98, 108, 329
University of the West Indies (Trinidad) 37, 345, 359
US Information Services 122
Ustinov, Peter; *The Different Shepherd* 40

Van Gogh, Vincent 9
Variety 115
Vaughan, Stuart 24
Vaz, Noel 11, 12, 16, 17, 187, 190, 278
Verity, Robert 16
Vincent, Inniss 57
Virgin Islands Council on the Arts 208
Voices 61

Waggoner, Jean 66
Wah, James Lee 13, 21, 35, 43, 61, 190, 278
Wah, Mavis Lee 21, 43, 61, 186, 190, 314
Walcott, Alix 8, 9, 293–4, 306

Walcott, Derek:
and acting style for TTW 25–6, 151
Adam symbolism 142–3, 204, 301, 358
and Africa 69, 127, 143, 154, 204, 205, 227, 245, 303
and African-Americans 24, 75, 137
and American actors in Trinidad 302–3, 312–13, 314, 316, 334
after Nobel Prize 3, 4, 337, 355, 359
aims and origins of Trinidad Theatre Workshop 3, 25–7, 99–100, 119, 128, 218
Aquarius Productions 130–1, 132, 133
use of artistic forms 24, 229, 246
avant garde and theatre of the absurd 27, 42–3, 67, 310
and Black Power 128, 154, 160, 190, 191, 227, 294, 315
body language and gesture 20, 31, 33, 200, 201, 303
and Boston Playwrights' Theatre 356
and Carnival 22, 49, 198–9, 291, 315
Cholmondeley Award 110
commission to write *Drums and Colours* 16
and Commonwealth writers 69
Crusoe symbolism 142, 181, 296, 355, 358
and Cuba 75, 238
and dance 25, 30–1, 119, 136, 172–5, 229, 274–7, 307, 336
and decolonization 26, 154
and dialect 25, 26, 33, 119, 138, 226, 227
different views from Errol Hill 49, 199
director 12, 14, 18, 23, 43, 46, 60, 65, 77, 89, 108, 138, 140, 148, 155, 160, 171, 173, 199, 230, 233, 242, 290, 299, 304, 328, 331
director as painter 305, 307

director of *Dream* (1968) 90
director's theatre 25, 27, 199, 230
drawings for scripts 108, 138, 211
drumming 12
early productions of his plays 9, 12–14
early publications 9–10
education 9, 12, 13
and epic 20, 21, 205
existentialism 23, 184, 205, 227–8
faith and God 15, 205, 355
family 8, 45, 294
and Fanon and psychology 91–2, 304
and Farfield Foundation 59–60
and films 82, 130, 143–4, 171–2,
    316–17, 319, 325, 329, 336
fiftieth birthday celebrations 300
finances 35, 71, 110, 263, 288–9
and relationship of folk culture to high
    art 49, 155, 320, 334
and Genet 67
Guggenheim Award 289
and Haitian revolution 19, 20, 22, 75,
    94–5, 324–8
and history 20, 22, 75, 143, 205, 227,
    300
honours 179, 345
and humanism 62, 238, 276
individual freedom 227
influences on verse 22
Ingram Merrill Award 38
interviews 81, 93, 153–5, 171, 187,
    190–2, 193–4, 238–9, 296, 304–7
Japanese influence (Hokusai, Kabuki
    and Noh) 24, 26, 27, 93, 136, 139,
    142, 205, 305, 310
recognition of Astor Johnson 172–3
journalism 13, 35, 46, 71, 359
lectures 14, 92, 183, 307
Leeds University invitation 78–9, 111,
    117, 122
letter to Group III/IV 130–1
letter about *Sizwe Bansi* 280
letter to Jeremy Taylor 275–6
letters to Theatre Workshop 132–3,
    148, 185–6, 197, 206, 207, 222–3, 223
and lighting 32, 42
and Little Carib 38
and lyrics 200, 201, 210
MacArthur Award 289, 312, 313
meets Beryl McBurnie 22, 25
marriages 15, 35, 289
Methodism 8, 9, 294, 355
metre and metrics 136, 138, 215
and modern arts 10, 81, 181, 238
move to Trinidad 18

and musicals 196–7, 198, 229, 274, 290,
    307, 310
nationalism 21, 26, 174–5
hopes of New York productions 196
and V. S. Naipaul 183, 191, 197
in *The Odyssey* 356
painter 9, 12, 25, 337
patois 58, 93, 101
and patronage 46, 264
new period of plays 293, 305, 310–11
plans for thirtieth anniversary of TTW
    352
poetry readings 61, 100, 110, 114, 210,
    300, 307
politics 42, 95, 154, 224, 227, 238, 301,
    338
and post-impressionism 93
producer 100, 104, 129, 170, 198, 208,
    252, 290
promoting actors abroad 285–6, 336
and Rastafarians 239, 246
reputation 12, 14, 317, 349
resignation from TTW (1970) 129, 131,
    137
resignation from TTW (1976) 244, 259
Rockefeller fellowship 24, 26, 119, 137
Rockefeller grant (1967–70) 59, 76,
    128–9
royalties 21, 194, 242, 252, 349–50
and 'Second Period' 305, 312–13
seminar on *Joker* 215
set painter 61
use of songs 151, 190, 200, 201, 227–8,
    229
and Stratford, Ontario 17, 20
symbolism of plays 20, 82, 119, 142,
    205, 293, 303–4, 328
tableaux, use of 20, 305, 307, 331
as teacher 10, 12, 13, 38, 55–6, 64, 72,
    88, 192, 209, 289, 294, 311–12, 359
testing people 63
theatre as cultural revolution 128, 154,
    190, 191, 223
theatre of poverty 20, 139, 304, 310,
    311
theatre as profession 25, 49, 111, 120,
    171, 239, 242, 259, 261, 305
thoughts of emigrating 15, 17, 239
total theatre 56, 89, 196, 228, 229, 311
and *Trinidad Guardian* 35, 59
and Trinidad pronunciation 31
and TTW actors 185, 207, 304–5
TTW as history 203
unsigned reviews and publicity 58, 61,
    68, 69, 70, 217, 290–1, 331

Walcott, Derek (cont.):
    and USA 136, 137, 162–3, 197, 243, 246,
    258, 263, 289, 295
    verse in drama 20, 31, 310
    vision 5, 25, 26–7, 136–7, 138, 218, 263,
    313, 358
    visual imagination 56, 229
    Warwick Productions 313–14, 331
    and West Indian theatre 36, 46, 300,
    320
    workshop methods 30, 32–3, 82, 96, 185

    WRITINGS
    FILMS:
        Hart Crane 329; The Rig 316–17, 319
    PLAYS:
        Another World for the Lost 10
        Batai 48–9, 244
        Beef, No Chicken 282–3, 307, 316;
            Barbados production (1985) 344;
            TTW production (1987) 346–7
        A Branch of the Blue Nile 64, 311, 325;
            Barbados production (1983)
            319–21; Trinidad production (1985)
            331–5
        Celebration (selections) 3, 4, 5, 201,
            355, 356, 357
        The Charlatan 14, 160, 167, 171, 176,
            178, 179, 180, 192, 213, 301, 311,
            314; Carnival and Calypso
            influences 184–5; Productions: San
            Fernando/ Port of Spain (1962) 43,
            Trinidad and Jamaica (1973) 55,
            184–6, 189–90, Mark Taper (1974)
            196, 198–201, Walcott's notes on
            Mark Taper production 199–201,
            Trinidad (1977) 243, 259, 261, 273,
            290–2
        The Countess of Quinine 14
        Cross Roads 14
        Dream on Monkey Mountain 77, 78,
            109, 110, 127, 130, 147, 153, 159,
            163, 175, 186, 236, 254, 300, 307,
            311, 329, 357; film version 4,
            118–19, 122–4, 209, 360; writing to
            Gordon Davidson about Dream
            136–7; and Negro Ensemble
            Company 4; and Obie 4, 148, 164;
            and St Lucia 91; to Michael
            Schultz 142–3; Productions:
            Canada and Guyana (1967) 82–4,
            Queen's Hall and five-island tour
            (1968) 88–92, 100–4, at O'Neill
            (1969) 111, 114–17, and Mark
            Taper (1970) 135–6, 142–3, Jamaica

    (1971) 149, 1974 revival, Trinidad
        and Connecticut 202–6, 207, St
        Croix (1974) 207–10, Baltimore
        production (1976) 244–5, Astor
        (Arbee, 1985) 329–31, Trinidad and
        Netherlands (1993) 5, 356, 357
    Drums and Colours 19–20, 21–3, 48,
        305, 325
    Franklin 91–2, 125, 159, 160, 171,
        176, 178, 179, 192, 301, 314; 1973
        production 55, 180–2, 185–6;
        Barbados (1990) 337–9
    Harry Dernier 10, 12, 26
    The Haytian Earth 22, 324–9
    Henri Christophe 10, 26, 85, 112, 155,
        158, 168, 307, 311, 324, 325;
        London 12–13; Jamaica 13;
        Trinidad 13, 40; Trinidad
        (1968) 94–5
    In A Fine Castle 70, 124, 130, 150,
        160, 162, 171, 180, 182, 192, 307,
        314; Jamaica (1970) 140–1;
        Trinidad (1971) 156–60; condensed
        version 156
    Ione 14, 18, 47
    The Isle is Full of Noises 220
    The Joker of Seville 111, 149, 183,
        192–3, 196, 197, 201, 207, 217, 218,
        221, 301, 302, 311, 312–14, 342,
        357; early version 184; historical
        costumes (1974) 211; Joker, long-
        playing recording, 221; Joker, 1974
        and 'Parang' performance, 212;
        Joker revised (1975) 222, 226; Joker
        and RSC 4, 245–6; and West
        Indian politics 224–5; and women's
        lib 213, 227; Productions: March
        1975 production 222, October
        1975 production 223–34, Expo 77:
        257; Arbee–TTW production
        (1987) 349–51
    Journard 24, 63, 79, 82, 83, 84, 168,
        217
    The Last Carnival 304, 312, 313–17,
        358–9
    Malcochon 14, 24, 26, 46–7, 93, 137,
        171, 236, 307, 352
    Marie Laveau 301–4, 307
    O Babylon! 196, 239, 244, 245–9, 251,
        261, 301, 311, 342, 358
    The Odyssey 5, 356, 357, 358
    Pantomime 22, 281, 286, 300, 301,
        306, 310, 311, 317, 336, 355, 357;
        origins 295; Walcott's
        interpretations 295–6, 306; Walcott

rehearsing 299; Productions: première (1978) 294–6, with Horace James (1978) 296–7, Barbados (1980) 297–8, Trinidad (Hughes, 1991) 350, Boston (1993) 298–9, 355–6

Paolo and Francesca 10

Remembrance 281, 304, 306, 311, 352; Productions: St Croix (1977) 292–4, Trinidad (1979) 299–300, Barbados (1982) 317–19, 322

The Sea at Dauphin 10, 12, 15, 155, 175, 194, 201; Productions: Trinidad (1954) 13, St Lucia (1954) 14, Jamaica (1956) 14, Trinidad (1966) 57–8

Senza Alcun Sospetto 10

'Songs for Theatre' 210, 217

Three Assassins 10

Ti-Jean and his Brothers 10, 17, 26, 82, 130, 131, 147, 152–3, 156, 159, 160, 163, 175, 181, 206, 209, 220, 251, 311, 317, 321, 349; St Lucia production (1957) 17; Little Carib (1958) 23–4, 50; with music by Tanker (1970) 122, 126, 138–41; Walcott's rehearsal notes (1971) 148; Jamaica (1971) 149–51; New York production (1972) 4, 160, 163–5; St Croix and Connecticut (1974) 198, 207

To Die for Grenada 336

The Wine of the Country 14, 70

POETRY:

Another Life 9, 325

'Let Resurrection Come!' 345

PROSE:

'Author's Note' (to *In a Fine Castle*) 143–4

'Beyond the Backyard' 72

'Caribbean: Culture or Mimicry' 183

'Derek's Most West Indian Play' 138–9

'Drums and Colours' 19–20

'Fellowships' 75–6

'Great irony' 67

'Homage' (*The Seagull*) 231–2

'The Joker: closer to continuous theatre' 222

'La Chapelle and Douglas Striving for cohesion' 274–5

'Lengthened shadow of a man' 181

'Mixing the Dance and Drama' 173–4

'Modern Theatre' 14–15

'Need for Little Theatre in POS' 36

'Need for Supporters' 46

'Note to Audience' (*Showcase*) 34

'Opening *The Road*' 69

'Overture' 180

'Personal note' to 1974 *Dream* 203

'Prologue to *Ti-Jean*' (1970) 139

'"Rights of Passage" drama in itself' 182

'Story of four loves at the Little Carib' 231–2

'Soul Brother to "The Joker of Seville"' 211

'Superfluous Defence of a Revolutionary' 155–6

'The Theatre of Abuse' 67

'Theatre Workshop at the Crossroads' 99–100

'West Indian Art Today' 62

'What the Twilight Says' 98, 193, 299, 359

'Why Belle Fanto Has Survived' 256

'Why do Chekhov here?' 231–2

'Why this astigmatism . . .?' 182

'Writers Cramp on Stage' 63–4

Walcott, Margaret Maillard 22, 35, 59, 61, 94, 242, 244, 263, 264, 289

Walcott, Norline, *see* Metivier, Norline

Walcott, Peter 15, 289, 299, 301

Walcott, Roderick 8, 10, 11, 13, 17, 21, 25, 94, 190, 306, 329, 341; *Banjo Man* 21; *Flight of Sparrows* 14, 63; *Harrowing of Benjy* 10, 11, 155; *One Eye is King* 10; *Shrove Tuesday March* 10

Walcott, Warwick 8, 9

Walke, Grace 57

Walker, Brian 234

Ward Theatre 14

Wardle, Irving 335–6

Warner, Earl 273, 278, 284–5, 290, 317, 319, 320, 321–2, 344–5; influenced by Walcott 321, 342; directs *Woza Albert!* (1984) 342–3; 'Director's Note' to *Branch* (1985) 333; directs *Beef* (1985) 344

Warwick Productions 346

Wasserman, Dale 114

Watling, Carol 300

Watson, Sheila 277

Watt, Douglas 165

Watteau, Antoine 144

Webster, John 26, 31

Weeks, Keith 223

West Indian acting comparisons 31, 55

West Indian Federation 7, 16, 42, 50, 80, 162

West Indies Festival of the Arts 16, 17, 19–20, 21, 41, 190

White Barn (Connecticut) 206

White, Edgar (*Like Them That Dream*) 284–5, 320

White, George 109–10, 111, 116, 118, 278–9, 280

Whitehall Players 10, 18, 40, 41, 77, 282

Wickham, John 102, 103, 280, 318

Wight, Benedict 123

Wilkinson-Nellands, Rosemary 272

Williams, Eric 35, 42, 127, 154, 156, 288, 353, 359–60; prologue to *Henri Christophe* 13

Williams, George 22, 32, 40, 41–2, 47, 65

Williams, Ronald 23

Williams, Tennessee 10, 117, 143; *Camino Real* 107, 117, 125, 143; *I Rise in Flames* 10; *This Property Condemned* 34

Wilson, Avis 100, 108

Wilson, Cynthia 290, 320, 337

Wilson, Lynette 88

Winston, Russell 35

Wood, Audrey 116, 117

Woodham, Greer, *see* Jones, Greer

Wooding, H. O. B. 38

Wooding, Selby 59

Woza Albert! 342–3

Wright, Ermine 108, 131, 152, 155, 156, 168, 169, 181, 184, 193, 194, 249, 274; mother in *Ti-Jean* 138, 141, 207; in *Franklin* (1973) 188; in *The Charlatan* (1973) 190; in *Dream* (1974) 202; in *O Babylon!* (1976) 246, 247, 253; in *Belle Fanto* (1976) 256, 257; in *The Maids* (1976) 271; death 276, 277

WWB Productions 337

Yale University 37, 40, 41, 72, 289

Yeats, William Butler 9, 17, 25, 135, 307

Yoruba mythology 68, 303

Zoo Pavilion 98, 107, 111, 126, 255, 259, 260